SATHER CLASSICAL LECTURES

Volume 76

The Greeks and the Rational

The Joan Palevsky   Imprint in Classical Literature

In honor of beloved Virgil—

"O degli altri poeti onore e lume . . ."

—Dante, *Inferno*

The publisher and the University of California Press Foundation gratefully acknowledge the generous support of the Joan Palevsky Imprint in Classical Literature.

The Greeks and the Rational

The Greeks and the Rational

The Discovery of Practical Reason

Josiah Ober

UNIVERSITY OF CALIFORNIA PRESS

University of California Press
Oakland, California

Library of Congress Cataloging-in-Publication Data

Names: Ober, Josiah, author.
Title: The Greeks and the rational : the discovery of
    practical reason / Josiah Ober.
Other titles: Sather classical lectures ; 76.
Description: Oakland, California : University of
    California Press, [2022] | Series: Sather classical
    lectures ; 76 | Includes bibliographical references
    and index.
Identifiers: LCCN 2022008892 (print) | LCCN 2022008893
    (ebook) | ISBN 9780520380165 (hardback) | ISBN
    9780520380172 (ebook)
Subjects: LCSH: Practical reason—History. | Practical
    reason—Moral and ethical aspects. | Democracy—
    Greece—Athens—History. | Athens (Greece—
    Civilization.
Classification: LCC BC177 .O24 2022 (print) | LCC BC177
    (ebook) | DDC 171/.2—dc23/eng20220528
LC record available at https://lccn.loc.gov/2022008892
LC ebook record available at https://lccn.loc
    .gov/2022008893

28 27 26 25 24 23 22
10 9 8 7 6 5 4 3 2 1

For Barry Weingast
Friend, colleague, teacher, Magister ludi

Contents

Illustrations

TABLES

Preface

This book addresses a problem of deep and abiding concern to humanists and social scientists, legislators, and citizens: Cooperation is a choice, not a given. It is a choice that must be made time and again if people are to live well, together. The problem arises because what is believed by rationally self-interested individuals, or by like-minded groups, to be best for themselves may not be good for others. Under the right conditions, enlightened self-interest can foster mutually beneficial forms of cooperation. But the selfish pursuit of individual and factional interests can also be detrimental to the welfare of others, even a threat to the survival of the community.

My hypothesis is that ancient Greek theorists and lawmakers recognized the question of why and how people choose to cooperate as basic. They saw that it must be answered at the level of the individual's motives for action, because individuals are the "atoms"—the irreducible, fundamental parts—of social order. Inquiries by Greek thinkers into the rationality of choice-making led to new theories of motivation, action, and ethics, to new approaches to teaching and learning, and to the design of new institutions by political entrepreneurs. In brief, Greeks discovered practical reason and the discovery was quickly put to practical use.

Similar intuitions lie at the heart of contemporary formal theories concerned with the "microfoundations" of social order. Those theories have been prominent in the social sciences ever since the publication of John von Neumann and Oskar Morgenstern's landmark *Theory of Games and*

Economic Behavior in 1944. Over the course of the next several decades, a body of work on rational choice-making posed a range of questions about cooperation and proposed mathematical methods for answering them. Strategic reason—the logic of decisions made by rational agents seeking their desired ends under conditions of uncertainty—became central to the field of economics. Following the development in the early 1980s of new techniques for illustrating games in extensive form, rational choice theory was integrated into political science.

The ideas of modern theorists on strategic reasoning are much in evidence in this book, although the math is not. I postulate that Greek writers anticipated some of the ideas about motivation and expectation that underpin modern choice theory and employed them in building theories and applying theory to practice. If that is correct, critics of rational choice should be wary of discounting it as a contingent artifact of neoclassical economics or military strategy in a nuclear age. Moreover, I contend that applying certain of the characteristic tools of modern choice theory to ancient texts aids in excavating a lost foundation-stone in the grand edifice of premodern social thought and practice. That foundation could be repurposed for modern political theory. If those assertions are correct, humanists who reject rational choice as foreign to humanistic inquiry risk impoverishing their own fields—as do choice theorists who slight literature, history, and moral philosophy.

The book claims to offer something of value to classicists, historians, and philosophers, to political theorists, economists, and empirical political scientists. I seek to validate that claim, first, by demonstrating the payoffs for students of history, philosophy, and literature: By establishing the unexpectedly close relationship between Socratic and sophistic theories of motivation and action, and between specific passages in historical, philosophical, and poetic texts; by offering new insights into Greek ideas about kingship, constitutional development, and state performance; by demonstrating the role of rational acquiescence to domination and its limits in interstate relations; by recovering the firm philosophical grasp of rational economic behavior and the connection between expected utility and human flourishing. Next, I attempt to show social scientists that the study of literary texts complements formal approaches to rationality, offering deeper insight into the role of rationality in complex choice situations. Finally, I seek to demonstrate that the Greek engagement with instrumental and ethical rationality provides a model for conjoining normative and positive political theory.

At this point readers are entitled to pose two questions along the following lines: "Suppose we grant, for the sake of the argument, that there is benefit to humanists and social scientists of reading ancient texts in a framework set by modern choice theory. The Greek texts have been around for a very long time, and the basic insights of formal theory have been available for two generations. So, is there really anything new and true left to say? And if there *are* still benefits to be gained, why is that?" In the introduction, I offer a survey of scholarship that applies game theory and related approaches to classical texts. The brevity of that survey answers the first question: Yes, there is indeed much to say. Yet it also sharpens the second question: Why is that so? My answer, sketched below, is that three separate trends have conspired to impede interdisciplinary work along the lines I am proposing here. In brief: In the mid-twentieth century, while the groundwork was being laid for the rational choice revolution in social science, the study of ancient Greek thought and practice was likewise revolutionized. But the revolutionaries in the two fields were headed in opposite directions.

The first trend: In 1951 E. R. Dodds, Regius Professor of Greek at the University of Oxford, published *The Greeks and the Irrational*. The book was based on his Sather Classical Lectures, delivered at the University of California at Berkeley in the autumn of 1949. That was just seventy years before my own Sather Lectures, on which this book is based. I first read Dodds' seminal study of irrationality as a student, about a quarter-century after its first publication; my advisor, Chester G. Starr, listed it among the most important contributions to Greek history of the twentieth century. And indeed, forty-five years later, Dodds' work is still in print and has proved enduringly popular and influential. Although, as Robert Parker (2020) has noted, Dodds' book is no longer often cited by professional classicists as an authoritative source, it played a leading role in reorienting classical history towards the study of phenomena that fall outside the ambit of "the rational."

Dodds' goal was to draw attention to "irrational" aspects of Greek culture—magic, superstition, shamanism, and ecstatic experience in religious rituals. These "Dionysian" parts of the ancient Greek experience, he argued, had been devalued and understudied by classicists, who tended to emphasize rational, "Apollonian" features of ancient Greek life. Of course, the contrast between the Dionysian and Apollonian had long been familiar within classical studies. It was popularized by Friedrich Nietzsche in *The Birth of Tragedy*, originally published in 1872. Then, at the turn of the twentieth century, the "Cambridge Ritualists"—

spearheaded by James G. Frazer's publication of *The Golden Bough* (1890) and including Francis Cornford (1907), Jane Harrison (1912), and Gilbert Murray (1925)—emphasized nonrational elements of Greek religious practices and beliefs. By the mid-twentieth century, however, Nietzsche and the Cambridge Ritualists had fallen out of favor with mainstream classicists. Dodds' breakthrough was to resituate work on the irrational in respectable, contemporary social science: in psychology and, especially, in the new cultural anthropology being developed by Ruth Benedict (1946).

Dodds' project was likewise innovative in that he self-consciously wrote for a readership that extended far beyond professional classicists. In the preface to *The Greeks and Irrational,* Dodds notes that the audience for his Sather Lectures "included many anthropologists and other scholars who had no specialist knowledge of ancient Greece." Because he expected scholars outside the field of classics to read his book, Dodds translated Greek quotations and transliterated Greek terms lacking obvious English equivalents. Moreover, he purposefully abstained from "encumbering the text with controversial arguments on points of detail . . . and from complicating my main theme by pursuing the numerous side-issues which tempt the professional [classical] scholar" (Dodds 1951: preface, pages unnumbered).

I believe that Dodds' innovations can be adapted to the study of strategic rationality. By borrowing Dodds' title (less two letters) for my Sather Lectures and this book, I signal my ambition of following his example in three ways. First is his goal of including both social scientists and humanists in the audience of his lectures and book. I define Greek and social scientific terms at first use and I have relegated technical matters to notes, along with scholarly controversies and side-issues. Next, like Dodds, I am motivated by the belief that an important aspect of ancient Greek experience has been largely overlooked. That neglect can be attributed in part to the attention paid by classicists, inspired or provoked by Dodds' book, to nonrational aspects of Greek experience. The sustained interest in what Dodds called "the irrational" has expanded and improved our understanding of Greek history, but Dodds never intended it to crowd out attention to rationality. Finally, like Dodds, I believe that classicists and social scientists ought to be in dialogue as they explore a neglected topic, because each side has much to learn from the other. It is not just a matter of classicists adopting techniques of social scientists. Attention to how Greek texts probed the potential and limits of strategic rationality offers formal theorists a pathway into salient aspects of strategic behavior that are not readily captured by mathematical models.

The second trend: In 1951, the same year that Dodds published *The Greeks and the Irrational,* Moses I. Finley, who became the most influential Anglophone ancient historian of the twentieth century, published his first book. Finley's *Studies in Land and Credit in Ancient Athens, 500–200 B.C.,* an analysis of how real estate was used as collateral for monetary loans, inaugurated an approach to Greek culture that was different from Dodds' but complementary to it. Finley, like Dodds, believed that classicists were overconcerned with rational aspects of Greek experience. The rationality that Finley sought to transcend was the economic rationality assumed by market capitalism and just then being formalized in new theories of choice.

Like Dodds, Finley was influenced by social science, most notably the sociology of Karl Polanyi and Max Weber. And, like Dodds, Finley emphasized how different the world of Greek antiquity was from modernity. Finley staunchly opposed the notion, at that time widely held by ancient historians, that the Greek economy was driven by market-oriented behavior. He rejected the idea that the ancients were motivated in much the way investors in modern developed countries are, by the expectation of monetary profit from capital investment. He deemphasized self-interested individual choices aimed at utility maximization in favor of the structural role of norms centered on social status. We will consider Finley's position in more detail in chapter 7. Here the important point is that Finley's influential dismissal of the historical value of "modernizing" economic concepts discouraged the incorporation of modern choice theory in the study of ancient Greek economic and political history.

The third trend that has served to deflect classical scholarship on Greek texts from an engagement with economic approaches to rationality is the tendency of classical philosophers to identify "rationality" with an ethicized approach to the role of human reason in motivating choice and action. That approach was inaugurated by Socrates and pursued in a systematic and immensely influential way by Plato and Aristotle. The reduction of rationality to its Socratic ideal type is exemplified in contemporary philosophy by Michael Frede's introduction to an important collection of essays on *Rationality in Greek Thought* (Frede and Striker 2002).

Frede specifically equates rationality as such with the philosophical approach to ethical reason that begins with Socrates. Acknowledging that "it is not entirely clear what is to count as a notion of reason," he concludes, "on balance I think that the answer is that the notion of reason originally was a philosophical construct, rather than part of the framework in terms of which Greeks had always thought about things" (p. 3). Moreover, "it is clear that we only get a fully developed notion of reason which is conceived of in such a way as to account for our cognitive abilities and their exercise, but also for the role thought plays in action, when we come to Socrates" (p. 5). Frede goes on to explain the key Socratic idea that high-end desires, for example, to know truth or to obtain what is thought to be good, "are desires of reason itself, rather than desires reason merely endorses . . . so that it becomes part of what it is to be endowed with reason to have certain preferences"—that is, the preferences of reason itself (p. 6). "So it would seem that historically the decisive step was taken by Socrates in conceiving of a human being as being run by a mind or reason . . . and that it was this entity that is the ancestor of our reason" (p. 19).

Frede's approach is cogent and convincing, as far as it goes, and it certainly accords with the mainstream of analytic classical philosophy. But by the same token, by embracing the Socratic conception of rationality as an ethicized, cognitive capacity, as reason that has its own desires for truly choice-worthy ends, Frede's definition excludes from the realm of rationality any process in which preferences arise from a source that is external to reason itself. The excluded alternative is the situation assumed in contemporary choice theory. It is also, as I will hope to show, the assumption of much systematic Greek thought about motivation, choice, and action. In this alternative conception of rationality, strategic reason comes into play in identifying and going for the available option that self-interested agents expect will be best for themselves. If we take "best" as "has most utility," we have arrived at expected utility maximization—the basic premise of contemporary choice theory.

I conclude these prefatory remarks with four caveats: First, the aim of this book is not to displace work on nonrational aspects of Greek historical experience. Nor it is meant to suggest that classical philosophers' focus on what I am calling ethicized Socratic rationality is misplaced. I hope to augment, rather than transcend, those large and important bodies of scholarship. Second, the work attempted here is only a beginning, a "proof of concept" rather than a comprehensive survey of Greek thought on instrumental rationality. Much more could be said about rationality in each of the Greek texts I address. Many texts relevant to the study of rationality are not even mentioned in this book. Third, rationality is only one aspect of the texts that I discuss. Identifying a concern for strategic reasoning in a given text falls far short of explaining the text's full meaning or significance.

Fourth and finally, the *identification* of strategic reason as an important discovery of Greek thought must not be confused with *celebration*. While I suppose that theorizing rationality offered social benefits, in antiquity as in modernity, it also imposed substantial costs. Attention to harm as well as utility, to the danger of liberating choice and action from traditional constraints while operationalizing reason as a tool and a weapon, is in the forefront of Greek thought on instrumental rationality. Here, as elsewhere, we moderns could learn from the ancients. In the epilogue, I discuss how ancient reflections on cooperation problems bear on our contemporary situation.

This book is meant to offer humanists new insight into ancient texts and institutions, while showing social scientists how much the study of classical literature, history, and philosophy has to offer. I hope it will also exemplify the promise of a field of inquiry that might productively be worked in common by historians, philosophers, literary scholars, and by theoretical and empirical social scientists—and through collaborations among them. If their results supersede mine, just as research on Greek religion, magic, and the self eventually superseded Dodds', I will judge the book to have been a success.

Acknowledgments

The original inspiration for this book came in 1987. An anonymous reader of the manuscript later published as *Mass and Elite in Democratic Athens* noted that a puzzle I posed about Athenian political sociology could be characterized as a Prisoner's Dilemma. That reader turned out to be the wise and stunningly well-read classicist Daniel Tompkins. At the time, I found his suggestion unsettling, intriguing, and (given my limited grasp of game theory) untimely, so I put it aside for later. It was not until 2015, when I was invited to give the Sather Classical Lectures at the University of California, Berkeley, that the time to pursue Dan's insight seemed right. My deep thanks to the Sather Committee and the entire Berkeley Faculty of Classics for naming me Visiting Sather Professor for Autumn 2019 and for marvelous collegiality and stimulating discussions, most often over justly famous Berkeley cuisine. The students in my Sather seminar were inspiring and bravely willing to work on an unfamiliar topic—to the extent of meeting *al fresco* when a power outage closed campus buildings. The Berkeley audiences for the six lectures included both humanists and social scientists who were more loyal and enthusiastic than I ever could have hoped.

While preparing the lectures and working on the book I was invited to give workshops and seminars for classicists, historians, political theorists, and philosophers at Australian National University, Brown University, the University of Chicago, Canberra University, Cordoba National University, Jyväskla University, King's College London, Louisiana State

University, McGill University, Münster University, Oxford University, Princeton University, Stanford University, St. Mary's College (California), Sun Yat Sen University, University of Tennessee, Texas Tech University, the Universities of California at Berkeley, Los Angeles, San Diego, and Santa Barbara, Uppsala University, Yale University, and the University of Zurich. Under auspices of the Hellenic Australian Lawyers Association, I lectured to marvelously responsive audiences of lawyers and jurists in Darwin, Melbourne, Sydney, Hobart, and Brisbane. The discussions at each of those venues proved invaluable in the development of the arguments presented here. Students in my Stanford seminars on Greek Rationality and High Stakes Politics (cotaught with Chris Bobonich and Barry Weingast) were a constant source of new ideas.

I have incurred profound debts of gratitude from a stellar array of classicists, economists, historians, game theorists, philosophers, and political scientists, who read drafts of chapters (in many cases embarrassingly preliminary), shared unpublished work, and offered advice and comments (formal and informal). They saved me from a frighteningly long list of mistakes and infelicities. My thanks to Jacob Abolafia, Avi Acharya, Sonja Amadae, Jacqueline Basu, Jenna Bednar, Chris Bobonich, Geoffrey Brennan, Lara Buchak, Mirko Canevaro, Federica Carugati, Hun Chung, Manuela dal Borgo, Carol Dougherty, Matthew Draper, Ned Dobos, Cynthia Farrar, Sylvia Fedi, John Ferejohn, Rob Fleck, Emily Fletcher, Sara Forsdyke, Laurent Gauthier, Robert Goodin, Deborah Gordon, Bruce Hitchner, Kinch Hoekstra, Phillip Horky, Sean Ingham, Monte Johnson, James Kierstead, Jacob Levy, John Ma, Chrystotomos Mantzavinos, Brook Manville, Richard Martin, John McCormick, Robert Morstein-Marx, Reviel Netz, Ümit Öztürk, Elodie Paillard, John Padgett, Philip Petrov, Steve Pincus, Stephen Sawyer, Thomas Slabon, Nicholas Southwood, Sam Stevens, Peter Stone, Benjamin Straumann, Ana Tanasoca, Oliver Taplin, David Teegarden, Dan Tompkins, Oda Tvedt, Paul Vădan, Barry Weingast, David Wiens, and Sam Zeitlin.

Special thanks are due to Ümit Öztürk and Avshalom Schwartz, who helped me assemble a catalog of passages relevant to rationality from an array of Greek texts. Only a few of those passages are analyzed here, but I hope the catalog will be the basis for future work. Nick Gardner, Sara Forsdyke, Emily Mackil, and Avshalom Schwartz read near-complete drafts, making detailed and hugely helpful comments throughout. Jonathan Bendor commented on each chapter of a late draft with an eye to the game-theoretic arguments, resulting in substantial revisions. Two other anonymous readers from the University of California Press carefully combed through the entire manuscript and offered insightful and invariably helpful suggestions for revision. James Macksoud, as reference-checker, and Ben Alexander, as copyeditor, saved me from numerous errors in the final draft. The staff of the press, notably my editor Eric Schmidt and his able assistant LeKeisha Hughes, were professional, helpful, and supportive throughout.

Barry Weingast, to whom this book is dedicated, is a cherished friend and colleague. It was during many long and happy conversations with Barry (often while bicycling or walking), through teaching courses with him, and by coauthoring a series of papers (with many others sketched, but as yet unwritten), that I became convinced that formal theory would open a new window onto classical Greek social thought. Along with my other wonderful colleagues in Stanford's Departments of Political Science, Classics, and Philosophy, Barry offered me the invaluable gift of an expansive new intellectual horizon, and patient, friendly, and knowledgeable guidance as I set about exploring it.

Adrienne Mayor, who read the manuscript more than once and discussed every idea in it, is my best reader, my boon companion, the light and love of my life.

Abbreviations and Classical References

Ath. Pol.	Pseudo-Aristototle, *Athēnaiōn Politeia* (Constitution of Athens)
EE	Aristotle, *Eudemian Ethics*
F	Fragment (a quotation of an otherwise lost text)
LM	André Laks and Glenn W. Most, eds. 2016. *Early Greek Philosophy VIII and IX: The Sophists.* 2 vols. Cambridge, MA: Harvard University Press.
LSJ	Henry George Liddell, Robert Scott, and Henry Stuart Jones. 1968. *A Greek-English Lexicon.* Oxford: Clarendon Press.
NE	Aristotle, *Nicomachean Ethics*
PD	Prisoner's Dilemma
Plut.	Plutarch

Classical Greek and Latin texts are cited according to the usual conventions of the field, by book, section, and subsection (e.g., for Herodotus, Thucydides); by Stephanus page number and line (for Plato and Aristotle); by book (where relevant) and line (for poetic texts).

Translations, unless otherwise specified, are adapted from the Loeb Classical Library.

Three-figure dates and corresponding centuries (e.g., 404, fifth century) are BCE.

Greek words and technical terms are usually defined at first use; in the index, a term's definition is indicated by page number in boldface.

Introduction

Discovering Practical Reason

O.I THEORIZING RATIONALITY

This book is about an intellectual discovery, a theory of practical reasoning. The theory defined rationality as the self-conscious, deliberative use of reason as an instrument for the strategic pursuit of goals. It explained human motivation and action by reference to basic mental processes of desire and belief. It offered solutions to problems in ethics and politics. The theory, first developed in the fifth and fourth centuries BCE, was influential for the rest of classical antiquity—and long after. It remains consequential today and could provide a platform for reconnecting the study of politics and political economy with history, ethics, and literature.

To speak of practical reasoning as a "discovery" invites comparison to Molière's disingenuous M. Jourdain, who, under the tutelage of a "master of philosophy," discovered to his amazement that he had been speaking prose for his entire life.[1] Molière's send-up of seventeenth-century intellectuals reminds us that ancient Greeks (and others) were

---

1. *Le bougeois gentilhomme* (1670: act 2, scene 6. Greek philosophers (e.g. Aristotle, *Metaphysics* 981b14–24) were very concerned with the process of discovery (*heuresis*); ancient writers of what historians of science call heurematography sought to identify the "original discoverer" (*protos heuretēs*) of various phenomena (Zhmud 2006: chap. 1). For reasons outlined below, no first discoverer of practical reason was named, but see chapter 8.3 for a mythic account.

I

quite capable of employing reason in pursuit of their goals long before rationality became a subject of theoretical inquiry. They were also capable of theorizing practical reason well before Aristotle addressed it in his ethical treatises. Aristotle identified practical reason as the intellectual counterpart to virtuous character, thereby establishing a standard interpretation for two millennia.[2] As I hope to show in the rest of this book, the original, pre-Aristotelian theorization of practical, means-to-ends reasoning was indeed a discovery, a big idea with real-world impact, whose salience was quickly recognized by poets, historians, and philosophers—including Aristotle. It is an overlooked chapter in the history of classical thought, with a long afterlife. It offers new insight into ancient history, Greek literature, and classical philosophy. And it provides methodological resources for contemporary political and ethical theorists.[3]

Practical reasoning is only one part of the wider domain of human reason. Unlike, for example, scientific reasoning, practical reason always concerns motivations for action. I will argue that, for the Greeks, practical reason invariably included, but was not always reduced to, instrumental (means to ends) rationality. Aristotle's "reinvention" of practical reason, as a central component of his ethics (chapter 8.6), subordinated instrumentalism to the exercise of complete virtue—while acknowledging the role of instrumental rationality in the achievement of virtuous ends. As we will see, in the ethical and political thought of the Socratic philosophers, rationality included the choice of worthy ends, as well as the means for achieving them. Because the rationality

---

2. The key text is Aristotle, *Nicomachean Ethics*, book 6. Aristotle's account of practical reason (*phronēsis*) was dominant until the seventeenth and eighteenth centuries, and it remains a major topic in ethical philosophy today. See further, chapter 8.5–7.

3. Instrumental rationality, as well as its relationship to practical reasoning, is a significant topic in contemporary ethics and moral philosophy. See, for example, Williams 1985; Broome and Piller 2001; Broome 2002, 2021; Fernandez 2016. As Kolodny and Brunero (2018) explain: "Someone displays instrumental rationality insofar as she adopts suitable means to her ends. Instrumental rationality, by virtually any reckoning, is an important, and presumably indispensable, part of practical rationality. However, philosophers have been interested in it for further reasons . . . it has been argued that instrumental rationality is not only a part, but a special part, or even the whole, of practical rationality. This thesis appears to threaten the 'rational authority' of morality. It seems possible that acting morally on some occasion might not be a suitable means to an agent's ends. If so, then according to this thesis, it would not be irrational for her to refuse to act morally on such an occasion." As we will see, a related concern motivated ancient Greek work on ethics. I do not, here, distinguish instrumentalism (sometimes defined as acting to satisfy *immediately present* desires) from prudentialism (sometimes defined as acting to satisfy desires *over time*, which may involve foregoing immediate satisfaction), although the distinction between short- and long-term advantage was, as we will see, a live one in Greek thought.

with which I am primarily concerned in this book is instrumental, however, when I use the term *rationality* without a modifier, it refers to the use of reason to choose the best means to a desired end.

The theorization of practical reason had specifiable effects when it was mixed into Greek social thought and when it was deployed in political and economic practice. Those effects were especially evident in democratic Athens. The theory features prominently in texts that became canonical in the Western tradition. The long-run survival and impact of those texts meant that instrumental rationality was poured into the foundations of Western civilization. It remains a feature—and perhaps also a bug—of our locally conflicted and increasingly globalized world.

In the following pages I address three questions: First, just what was discovered? Next, how did the discovery bear on Greek literature, ethics, and politics? And finally, why does it matter for contemporary historians of thought, students of literature, and political and ethical theorists? The short answer is that *instrumental rationality was identified as a core human capacity, capable of being refined as a powerful and versatile tool for making strategic choices among feasible options under conditions of social constraint and uncertainty.* The expert use of that tool was promoted as a specialized skill by the so-called Sophists and is manifest in Greek political institutions, international relations, and economic behavior. Its misuse was characterized as a social, political, and ethical problem by, among others, historians and philosophers. And, finally, because instrumentalism features prominently in Greek texts, and because it was integrated into the moral philosophy of Plato, Aristotle, and their successors, Greek ideas about practical reasoning crystallized into a persistently influential tradition of thought.

I make no claim here for the *uniqueness, priority,* or *superiority* of the Greek discovery. Roughly contemporary and highly sophisticated traditions of reasoning from means to ends arose, for example, in China and India.[4] While I am confident that a thorough, cross-cultural, comparative

---

4. China: Moody 2008, on the *Han Feizi*, a third-century BCE text in the Legalist tradition, which "shares the same individualistic and instrumental assumptions about human behavior and political action as contemporary rational choice theory" (p. 96), while also insisting that rationality be understood within its "conditions" (*shi*), including institutional structure and cultural setting. India: Trautmann 2012, on the *Arthashastra* of Kautilya (fourth century BCE or first/second century CE), a work of political economy that addresses scaling up household-level provisioning of goods, but also "values cool analysis of comparative benefits and choice-making among them, which corresponds to the notion of economizing behavior and the rational calculation of benefits and costs" (p.8). Examples could surely be multiplied.

study of premodern practical reasoning would be illuminating, I lack the skills necessary to undertake it. In any event, leaving aside the currently unanswerable question of whether an exhaustive comparative survey of global intellectual history might grant some premodern tradition of reasoning a position of uniqueness, priority, or superiority (however measured), the answer to the question of why the Greek discovery matters draws on other considerations.

Greeks writing in a range of genres addressed intellectually challenging issues related to the practice of reasoning from means to ends: *self-interest* and its limits; the psychological sources of motivating *desires;* the calculation of *risk, feasibility,* and the *strategic behavior* of others when deciding among options; and the possibility of coherent and effective *collective action.* A similar set of issues lies at the heart of contemporary formal choice theory. When applied to economics, and politics, formal approaches are practiced under the rubrics of rational choice and positive political theory.[5]

I contend that Greek thinkers and lawmakers anticipated the central assumptions about *desire, belief,* and *expectation* that underpin contemporary choice theory.[6] The ancient Greek approach to practical reason conjoins elements of three modern fields: a formal approach to rationality that assumes ideal-type agents with unlimited cognitive capacity, an experimental approach to behavior that studies the decisions of real people under controlled conditions, and an empirical approach to performance that analyzes the achievement of experts with high, but never final, mastery of specialized domains.[7] Ancient Greek writers and institutional designers, like contemporary behavioral game

---

5. Decision theory, game theory, and social choice theory are prominent methodological variants, discussed below. Each variant depends on the basic premises of rational choice and each is employed by economists and political scientists. As exemplified by the works cited in n. 3, above, contemporary analytic moral philosophers, while concerned with some of the same issues, have often approached the question of instrumental rationality in quite different ways than do formal choice theorists. My focus is on the latter, because it is the use of rationality as a tool (or a weapon) that most interested and worried classical thinkers.

6. For a clear and concise sketch of preferences, beliefs, expectations, and actions in contemporary rational choice theory, see Ferejohn 2009.

7. Formal theory and behavioral experiments: see below. Expertise and how it is acquired: Ericsson 2006; expertise in decision-making: Yates and Tschirhart 2006. On the different reference points assumed in each approach, see Bendor 2021, discussing the seminal work of Herbert Simon. In contemporary choice literature the conjunction of ideal-type theorizing and empirical applications is manifest in popular-audience books, such as Dixit and Nalebuff 2008.

theorists, recognized that there are limits to human reason and expertise.[8] They knew that real choice-makers cannot be reduced to mechanistic, ideal calculators of optimal outcomes. Yet they typically saw these limits as adjustments to or deviations from a fundamentally rational approach to decision-making under conditions of uncertainty, rather than as a nonrational alternative.[9] Although the Greeks did not analyze decision-making in mathematical terms, their rich literary exploration of instrumental reasoning complements modern theory and offers valuable resources for contemporary choice theorists—just as formal theory and empirical social science offer resources for humanists. That line of thought, if it is on the right track, has significant consequences for how we might think about ancient Greek civilization and the modern scientific study of rationality.[10]

In sum, the Greek approach to practical reason is valuable because it can be studied as a distinctive, well-documented, influential, and at least potentially enlightening contribution to deep and enduring questions of human *motivation, decision,* and *action.* It refutes the notion that the intuitions underpinning contemporary choice theory are nothing more than a by-product of unique conditions of modernity. I hope that juxtaposing ancient and modern theories of choice will encourage formal theorists to appreciate the value of complex literary narratives for expanding the "library of mechanisms" (Gailmard 2021) available to

8. Behavioral game theory seeks to address the gap between analytic choice theory and actual human practices. See, for example, Camerer 2003: 3: "Behavioral game theory is about what players *actually* do. It expands analytic theory by adding emotion, mistakes, limited foresight, doubts about how smart others are, and learning to analytical game theory . . . Behavioral game theory is one branch of behavioral economics, an approach to economics which uses psychological regularity to suggest ways to weaken rationality assumptions and extend theory."

9. Compare Schelling (1960) 1980: 16–17: "Furthermore, theory that is based on the assumption that the participants coolly and 'rationally' calculate their advantages according to a consistent value system forces us to think more thoroughly about the meaning of 'irrationality' . . . departures from complete rationality may be in many different directions . . . It may not be an exaggeration to say that our sophistication sometimes suppresses sound intuitions, and one of the effects of an explicit theory [of rationality] may be to restore some intuitive notions that were only superficially 'irrational.'"

10. Compare Brams 1994: 52: "What makes a literary creation is not just its overall structure but its details, including the emotional lives of its characters. Game theorists need to ponder these and adapt their theory accordingly, just as literary scholars need to appreciate that game theory has its own richness that goes beyond mathematical symbols and abstract forms." Gailmard (2021: 79–81) argues that the virtues of rational choice theory for the study of history include intelligibility (making past behavior more intelligible to us) and epistemic humility (the premise that decision makers in the past understood their problems as well as do contemporary analysts).

rational decision-makers. It may help humanists and citizens to make better use of some techniques drawn from contemporary decision and game theory. If the argument of this book goes through, those techniques can be redeployed as analytic tools for exploring the ancient history of certain ideas often thought to be uniquely modern. The same tools might also be adapted for practicing an approach to citizenship often thought to be uniquely ancient.

0.2 SOCRATES ON CHOICE AND ACTION

The approach to practical reason with which this book is primarily concerned is succinctly captured in a line attributed to Socrates by the Athenian polymath Xenophon. Asked if persons who know what they should do and yet do the opposite are "wise and yet intemperate," Socrates responds that they are unwise:[11]

> For I think that all persons deliberately choose, out of what is available to them, what they think is most advantageous to themselves, and they do this. (*Memorabilia* 3.9.4 = LM 33.D48)[12]

Xenophon's Socrates offers a concise, quasi-algorithmic description of choice-making, aimed at specifiable goals and resulting in purposeful activity.[13] While he does not, here, employ the philosophical vocabulary associated with reason (*logos*) or calculation (*logismos*), Socrates models the agent as a coherent persona, a self that employs integrated cognitive faculties to decide among ranked options, with the intent of securing the best among them.[14]

---

11. Some manuscripts read "wise and temperate" (*sophous te kai egkrateis*), which makes little sense. Likewise, depending on the manuscript, Socrates' immediate rejoinder is either that they are unwise and intemperate (*asophous te kai akrateis*) or unwise and ignorant (*amatheis*); the latter reading accords with Plato, *Protagoras* 358b–60d.

12. Trans. Laks and Most (2016), adapted. Greek: πάντας γὰρ οἶμαι προαιρουμένους ἐκ τῶν ἐνδεχομένων ἃ οἴονται συμφορώτατα αὑτοῖς εἶναι, ταῦτα πράττειν. Socrates concludes that "those who act incorrectly [*mē orthōs prattontes*] are neither wise nor moderate [*sōphronas*]." Their error is presumably in *thinking* something is in their best interests when, according to Socrates, it is not.

13. Cf. Carugati and Levi 2021: 53–54: "Algorithms are, essentially, rule-based structures for making decisions . . . Algorithms follow logical rules to optimize for a given outcome."

14. *Logos*, when used in philosophical contexts, is traditionally translated as "reason." Moss (2014) surveys Plato's and Aristotle's use of the term, emphasizing the range of meanings of *logos* and the difficulties involved in simply equating *logos* with reason but, as Moss (2017: n. 3) elsewhere suggests, in sketching Aristotle's ethical psychology, "there is no harm for our purposes, however, in sticking with the traditional translation."

Socrates' account of choice-making is *universalizing* in its claim that a standard approach to reasoning about advantage is available to everyone ("all persons"). That approach is *deliberative*, in that it is a process of *advance* reasoning leading to a *choice* ("deliberately choose": *proairoumenous*). The process of deliberately choosing employs the agents' relevant *beliefs* ("they think") and it is carried out under contingent conditions of *feasibility* ("out of what is available to them"). The goal of the agents is *maximization of utility* ("most advantageous": *sumphorōtata*) *to the agents* ("to themselves"). The process ends in *action* ("they do this").[15]

Xenophon's Socrates need not be read as claiming that a process of clear-headed, comparative evaluation of options and outcomes is the approach to choice-making uniquely employed by all persons in all circumstances of willed action. Actions may be unwise, based on momentary impulse. Beliefs about what is most advantageous may arise from emotion or illusion rather than knowledge. People may vainly strive for an infeasible ideal outcome (Bendor in progress). The point, then, is not that Socrates has given us the germ of an account aimed at explaining an instrumentally rational mental process underpinning all human behavior. But he has given us an account of practical reasoning as a coherent, comparative method of making choices among options— motivated by desire, engaged with beliefs about the world, and ending in action in pursuit of the best available end. The process is not limited to philosophers. It is common enough to bear on the important ethical question of whether anyone knowingly goes for an inferior option.

Xenophon's quote assimilates what, in Plato's dialogues, we learn is Socrates' own highly distinctive approach to choosing among possible courses of action to the process employed by ordinary people. Plato's reader learns that Socrates' understanding of what it takes for a person to make a *truly*—or, in the terminology I adopt here, "ethically"— rational choice is very demanding. It requires objective knowledge of value, not just subjective preference and opinion. Ordinary persons may

15. The adjective *sumpheron/sumphoron/xumpheron* may be translated as advantageous, useful profitable, or expedient: LSJ s.v. The general sense is of "utility" to an agent; the superlative *sumphorōtata* alludes to maximum utility. Depending on how we read the force of *pro-* in the participle *proairoumenous,* it may be that Socrates means that if and when people engage in a process of deliberating in advance on how they ought to choose, and when they base their deliberations on an assessment of what is available to them, then (and perhaps only then), they make their choice based on what they think is most advantageous to themselves, and act accordingly. My thanks to Terence Irwin for discussion of this point.

be instrumentally rational, in the sense of being able to calculate costs and benefits in weighing options. But, under ordinary conditions (lacking the guidance of enlightened rulers) they are often incapable of acting virtuously, because their souls are not properly ordered. The ethically rational person's soul is ruled by reason. Her preferences are for objectively good ends identified and desired by reason (not by mere appetite or emotion). Thus, only the ethically rational choice-maker is capable of choosing that which is actually "most advantageous."[16]

In the passage cited above, Xenophon's Socrates must include himself in the universe of "all persons" whose deliberate choices purposefully aim at goals and result in action. The rare and special kind of reasoning that, at least in Plato's view, enables a true philosopher to identify and then pursue the objectively best end is, therefore, an extension and refinement of, rather than an alternative to, a much more common kind of practical reasoning: an instrumental process of choice-making based on comparing ranked options.[17] This suggests that, while Socratic moral

16. In treating the agent as a persona, the Xenophon passage does not invoke Plato's distinctive moral psychology. Nor will I be much concerned in this book with the details of Plato's complicated and controversial ideas about the partitioning of the soul, ideas that were, in part, taken over by Aristotle. Briefly, Plato conceived of the human soul as having three ranked parts: reason, spirit, and appetite. Each part has its own desires. Reason: for knowledge and to rule; spirit for honor and esteem; appetite for (at least) bodily gratification. Each is involved in motivating action (Cooper 1999: chap. 4). Contemporary classical philosophers differ on whether each part has beliefs and the capacity to reason in the sense of calculating costs and benefits, if not in identifying and aiming at objectively good ends. Lorenz (2006), arguing for strict partitioning between the parts of the soul, denies that the two lower parts employ even instrumental reason. However, Bobonich (2002, 2010), rightly in my view, argues that each part has "contentful beliefs and desires and this content is, at least partly, conceptual" (2010: 149). Citing *Republic* 580e–81a on appetite's desire for money as an effective means to gratification of various other desires, Bobonich concludes, "Even the Appetitive part is capable, according to Plato, of means-end reasoning" (2002: 244). Bobonich (2002) shows that Plato revised his psychology in later works, but the core idea relevant to instrumental reason, that nonrational motivations involve beliefs or concepts, is retained. See also Annas 1981: 129–30; Irwin 1977: 327, 1995: 207–17.

17. Cooper (1999: 124–25 n. 9) proposes two possible models for Plato's idea of what it is for reason to rule in one's soul. On the weaker view, reason works out the means to an overall scheme of life, by calculating the relative weights of things desired, taking into account the intensity of wants and tradeoffs among them. On the stronger view, reason's work and its desires are more fundamental. Here reason determines what is good and how good, with other desires being subsidiary. In the *Republic*, the Form of the Good provides the relevant knowledge of goodness. Likewise, Lorenz (2006: 44 n. 9) suggests, "One strategy [for separating means-end reasoning from "Platonic reasoning"] might be to distinguish between (say) 'purely instrumental reasoning' (or calculation) and 'reasoning about the good'—about, that is, how it is good (or best) to act, in the circumstances—

philosophy strictly subordinated instrumental reasoning about means to ethical reasoning about ends, its practitioners remained deeply concerned with nonideal motivations for action. The Socratics carefully analyzed practical reason as a worldly phenomenon, grounded in self-interest and feasibility. They deployed it in elaborate thought experiments, as a dangerous, essential tool. But it was not discovered by them.[18]

A Folk Theory of Instrumental Rationality

Socrates is often thought to have broken with the background intellectual culture of his age, and most decisively with the thought of the loose collection of Greek intellectuals and teachers known collectively as Sophists (below, section 0.4). And in many ways, he certainly did. Yet the passage cited above is included in a recent, authoritative edition of the surviving fragments of texts written by the Greek Sophists. The editors, André Laks and Glenn Most, posit that, based on his interests and argumentative methods, Socrates can be seen as "an idiosyncratic Athenian 'sophist.'"[19]

I propose that Xenophon has put in Socrates' mouth a concise statement of a "folk theory of practical reasoning." By folk theory, I do *not*

and then to suggest that Plato reserves the vocabulary of reason for the latter." Although Lorenz rejects this suggestion, it seems to me roughly right. Lorenz's objections are defused if we recognize that the distinction is between subjective, fallible instrumental reasoning and reasoning *correctly* about the *actual* good.

18. Xenophon's Socrates is, in various ways, different from Plato's character of that name. For example, Xenophon's Socrates is more concerned on practical matters of household and polis management (see chapter 7.5). As Irwin (1974: 412) notes, relative to Plato and Aristotle's "queer and philosophically provocative" claims about virtue and motivation, those of Xenophon's Socrates are "bland, familiar, and unexciting." And yet, the statement attributed to Socrates by Xenophon is well aligned with Plato's Socrates. While never mentioning Xenophon, Bobonich (2011) shows that the Socrates of the early dialogues accepts a descriptive "Principle of Psychological Eudaimonism" (see below, n. 34) that employs each element of the Xenophon passage: a universal practice of practical deliberation predicated on beliefs, leading to a choice among limited options, aimed at maximizing or optimizing the happiness (good, advantage) of the agent himself, and resulting in action. Vivienne Gray (1998: chap. 1) reviews the generally deflationary views of an earlier generation of scholarship on Xenophon's *Memorabilia* and offers a sympathetic reading of the *Memorabilia* in the context of classical era wisdom literature and rhetoric. Pangle (2018) updates the esoteric reading of Leo Strauss and offers a comprehensive bibliography. Christ (2020: chap. 2) reads *Memorabilia* as teaching Athenian elites how to be worthy of leadership in the new political context of the post–Peloponnesian War era.

19. Laks and Most 2016: 2.4–5, quote: 293. On the relationship of Socrates' thought and methods to those of the Sophists, see Woodruff 2006, 2010.

mean a naïve belief held only by the ignorant. Rather, it is a theory common to, and debated among, the diverse members of an intellectual community.[20] That theory was strongly associated with Sophists, but it was hardly unique to them. It had no identifiable author (hence "folk"), but it emerged as a shared feature of social thought at a specifiable time: the mid-fifth century BCE, and in a particular place: Athens. If that is right, Xenophon's Socrates was not offering an original observation. While giving it a distinctively paradoxical spin, he was in agreement with an account of how people choose to act that was (1) the discovery of a broad-based social network of intellectuals, centered in Athens, (2) sufficiently coherent and analytic to count as a theory, (3) widely known and discussed by classical-era Greek thinkers and writers, and (4) put into practice by sociopolitical entrepreneurs.[21]

The folk theory accounts for behavior by reference to two distinct mental states: desire and belief. It holds that a rational person will go for whatever she believes is best for herself, in terms of desire satisfaction, among the options she supposes are open to her. It is a *theory* insofar as it is an axiomatic, internally coherent account of human motivation, deliberation, choice, and action. In Plato's philosophically sophisticated restatement, considered below (especially chapters 1, 2), the theory is evaluatively *normative*, in the narrow (nonmoralized) sense of specifying the conditions necessary for an agent to be correctly judged to be in a positively evaluated state.[22] That is, it specifies how, to count as fully rational, an agent ought

---

20. In contrast to some other Greek intellectual "discoveries" (e.g., LM 37.R4: disputes over whether Antiphon or someone else discovered rhetoric; 35.D10, D11), the folk theory has no acknowledged author. It is not the modern "Folk Theorem" of repeated Prisoner's Dilemma games, discussed by Binmore (2007: 75–76), but my use of the term "folk theory" is inspired by that rubric.

21. This hypothesis would help explain why, as Vivienne Gray (1998: 1) reports, Olof Gigon (1979: 3–5) could have supposed that Xenophon's *Memorabilia* consisted of excerpts from the Sophists. Kamtekar (2018: 44–45) argues that "the many" in classical Athens assumed that anger or laziness led agents to choose worse options, citing examples from Euripidean tragedy.

22. Wedgwood (2017b) offers a detailed defense of the normativity of the concept of rationality, summarizing as follows: "To think rationally is to think *properly*, or to think as one *should* think . . . Rationality is a kind of *virtue* displayed in some of the mental states (like the beliefs and intentions) that agents have, and in the ways in which agents form and revise those mental states in response to reflection and experience" (p. 1, emphasis in original). In introducing their "prospect theory" critique (see chapter 6), Kahneman and Tversky (1979: 263) write: "Expected utility theory has dominated the analysis of decision making under risk. It has been generally accepted as a normative model of rational choice, and widely applied as a descriptive model of economic behavior, e.g.

to act. It is also *analytical,* in that it proposes causes and deductively yields explanations for behavior. Those explanations were tested against observations, hypotheticals, and counterfactual cases. Finally, it is *prescriptive* in that it purports to offer guidance for the conduct of personal affairs, social policy, and institutional design. As I will show in this book, the folk theory was pervasive in classical and postclassical traditions of social thought and assumed by Greek designers of formal institutions.

The philosophical works of Xenophon, Plato, and Aristotle feature prominently in the following chapters. I refer to them generically as "classical Socratics" in light of their common intellectual heritage, while fully recognizing substantive differences in their philosophical positions.[23] Plato and the other Socratics developed specialized vocabularies and methods for investigating and analyzing practical reason. We cannot inquire of ordinary Greeks, living in the classical period, whether they had any sort of theory of motivation and action. But we do have many ancient Greek texts in multiple genres beyond philosophy— including histories, biographies, forensic speeches, tragedies and comedies, political essays, and technical manuals. They shed light on background assumptions concerning reasoning about choices, assumptions that informed and were challenged by Socratic texts.

Passages from Plato's *Republic* frame each of the following chapters. While that was not my original plan, it soon became apparent that among that dialogue's less-often-recognized features is a profound and sustained interrogation of strategic reasoning and its limits. Given its status as, by some accounts, the greatest ancient work of political philosophy, and consequently its familiarity to a modern readership, the *Republic* provides continuity for an argument that ranges widely across historical eras and literary genres. Moreover, given Plato's ambition to specify the conditions for an ideal state, the *Republic* provides a test case for the depth and breadth of the folk theory's uptake by Greek intellectuals. Unlike modern ideal political theory, which "idealizes away the

---

Thus, it is assumed that all reasonable people would wish to obey the axioms of the theory, and that most people actually do, most of the time." What I am calling the *narrowly normative* account of rationality, adopted by contemporary choice theorists, does concern evaluation based on specifiable criteria, but does not require that the agent's motivations for action arise from reasons that are objectively (or even widely agreed to be) good or right, as does the broader sense of normativity common to ancient and modern discussions of ethics and morality. See discussion in Broome and Piller 2001; Broome 2002, 2021; Abizadeh 2018.

23. In using this nomenclature, I follow ancient precedents: Compare LM 33.D62 (= Cicero, *On the Orator* 3.16.61–17.62), D63, D64.

possibility of law-breaking, either by individuals (crime) or societies (aggressive war)," Plato confronts cooperation dilemmas head-on.[24]

In the course of developing a bold new approach to metaphysics and epistemology, the *Republic* analyzes the self-interested motives and lawless choices of a hypothetical unconstrained rational individual (chapter 1), self-interested behavior as both an impediment to and prerequisite for the emergence of social order (chapter 2), the dangers of instrumentalism when rulers have a monopoly on violence (chapter 3), the relationship between the rational individual and the rational state (chapter 4), probability estimation as an essential aspect of choice-making in the high-stakes context of war (chapter 5), preference diversity as a problem for democratic rationality (chapter 6), the rationality of wealth accumulation and its pitfalls (chapter 7), and how the conscious and strategic pursuit of self-interest relates to human flourishing (chapter 8).

Texts discussed below were written over a millennium, from the eighth century BCE (Homer) to the second century CE (Plutarch). The primary focus is, however, on the classical era of the fifth and fourth centuries. I suggest that the folk theory crystallized at a certain time and place: in mid-fifth-century Athens. But I do not, here, offer a detailed explanation for *why* just there and then.[25] I seek to restore a missing part of the intellectual context by showing that classical-era historians and Socratic philosophers responded in detail to earlier sophistic claims about the role of self-interest in human affairs, as well as to one another. But I do not explore in detail the relationship between texts written by elites and the attitudes of ordinary citizens.[26] Chapters 4–6 are framed by the history of Athenian political development from the early sixth to the later fourth century BCE. But I forgo the strictly historicist approach to the history of

24. Quote: Wenar 2021a: sec. 2.3, with reference to the political philosophy of John Rawls. On ideal and nonideal theory, see further, chapter 8.7, with literature cited in n. 49.

25. The answer to that question must be sought in the broader context of the development of Greek culture, politics, and economics. As Solmsen (1975) and Netz (2019) (among others) have shown, Athens was the intellectual center of classical-era Greece and the site of dramatic advances in a wide range of fields. Mantzavinos (2014) shows that textual interpretation of the sort attempted here—aimed at answering questions of the type "what is (or was) the case?"—can be scientific in the sense of formulating conjectures and testing them by with the aid of empirical evidence.

26. Contrast Ober (1989, 1996, 2005), where a primary focus is on the attitudes of ordinary Athenians. I hope that the topic of instrumental rationality in popular Greek thought and culture, along with popular concerns about its dangers, will be explored in future scholarship. A catalog-in-progress of passages in (among other sources) Greek rhetoric, comedy, and epigraphy, being assembled by myself and some of my students, suggests that the evidence for such a study is rich and varied.

thought and practice that treats each historical period as an entity unto itself and regards each era's questions and concepts as distinctly its own.[27]

To illustrate the prevalence and persistence of themes and concepts, I move back and forth in time and across genres, juxtaposing passages drawn from Hellenistic and Roman historiography with archaic poetry and classical philosophy. In so doing, I slight what are, for intellectual historians and literary scholars, centrally important issues of context, influence, and intertextuality. That sacrifice is in aid of two goals: First, establishing that there was a coherent ancient Greek tradition of thinking and writing about strategic reason. Next, showing that the Greek tradition, taken as a whole, shared core intuitions with contemporary choice theory. And therefore that ancient ideas about rationality illuminate and are illuminated by modern theory. If this book clears the high bar of achieving those goals, others may choose to go further, by developing the fine-grained, deeply contextualized intellectual history that is forgone here.

0.3 RATIONALITY ANCIENT AND MODERN

The bar is high in part because of a tendency to emphasize how fundamentally *different* ancient Greek culture, thought, and social practices were from the forms of rationality characteristic of modernity. That tendency has been marked in the last two generations of classical scholarship.[28] In ethical and political philosophy it dates back to the seventeenth century and remains a common trope in contemporary ethics and political theory.[29] Meanwhile, for their part, formal choice theorists

27. For the historicist/contextualist approach associated with Quentin Skinner and the "Cambridge school of intellectual history," see the essays collected in Brett and Tully 2007 and discussion in Ober 1998a: 8, 31–32, 36–38, with works cited.

28. Greg Anderson (2018) makes a particularly strong statement of the "unlikeness" thesis in classical scholarship, concluding that the ancient Greeks were "ontologically" different from us and, as such, unknowable by ordinary methods of historical inquiry. For critical discussion see Ober 2020. For other examples see the preface and chapter 7 of the present volume.

29. For example: Thomas Hobbes's ([1651] 1996) stark rejection of Aristotle's theory of natural sociability, Benjamin Constant's 1819 essay "The Liberty of Ancients Compared with That of Moderns," and more recently in the work of both conservatives, notably Leo Strauss and Alasdair MacIntyre, who lament modernity's loss of ancient wisdom and virtue, and liberals, for example Isaiah Berlin (1969), who reject classical eudaimonism, civic republicanism, and an emphasis on virtues of character as inimical to ideals of autonomy, moral duty, and freedom as noninterference: See discussion in Berkowitz 1999: 7–21; Kalyvas and Katznelson 2008; Annas 2017.

tend to trace the origins of their fields only as far back as the philosophical and mathematical thought of the eighteenth century—for example, to Hume, Rousseau, and Condorcet (Binmore 2007; R. Hardin 2007; Sen 2017).

The question then arises: Does the "rationality of choice" capture a deep (if necessarily partial) truth about cognition and human behavior generally? Or is it only (if at all) a contingent feature of some people, inhabiting certain roles in certain modern societies? Of persons who think and act as they do only because they have been subjected to a culture of science and to economic conditions that are unique to modernity? Insofar as we, today, are instrumentally rational, is it because we are human? Or because we are modern?[30] Even if one accepts, as I do, that modernity has put its stamp on expressions of humanity, these questions may seem important. This book is addressed to those who think that they are.

Comparing Contemporary and Ancient Theories of Choice

It is, I suppose, uncontroversial to say that reasoning about how individuals and groups make choices provided part of the intellectual infrastructure for Greek writers, including Plato, Aristotle, Herodotus, Thucydides, Xenophon, Polybius, Plutarch, and the dramatists. They aimed, in the first instance, at contributing to (or revolutionizing) existing bodies of work in the domains of history, moral and political philosophy, comedy, tragedy, and so on. There was no ancient Greek literary genre that corresponds to the modern fields of decision and game theory, or to the modern disciplines of economics and political science. But the central claims of this book are, first, that ancient Greek writers knew, developed, and criticized ideas about rationality, choice, and action in ways that were sophisticated, systematic, and well worth closer investigation. And, next, that those ideas were operationalized in individual behavior and in formal rules. Incidents described in Greek literature and various Greek political institutions are best understood as the result of rational choices and bargains. As such, they can readily be modeled by simple strategic games. In brief, ancient Greek thinkers may, in some

---

30. See discussion in Amadae 2003 (with critical response by Stone 2004) and 2016. Instrumental reason was described as a distinctive, and troubling, feature of modernity by the critical theorists of the "Frankfurt School" and, more recently, by Habermas (1996). Leese (2021: 6–10, 223–28), surveys recent historical work that rejects the possibility of premodern economic rationality.

ways at least, be more "like us" than is allowed by recent classical scholarship or by a long tradition of political and ethical theory.

To investigate Greek thought on the rationality of choice, I offer a series of close readings of Greek texts, employing the conventional methods of history, philosophy, and philology. I analyze the vocabulary of, for example, calculation, measurement, choice, constraint, utility, advantage, profit, risk, and likelihood.[31] Although I introduce some Greek terms and some of the specialized terminology employed by positive political theorists, I do not assume that the reader has prior knowledge of either classical Greek or game theory. I draw attention to metaphors (e.g., path or road) and allegorical tales (e.g., about Gyges the Lydian) that Greek writers employed to illustrate the relationship between individual decisions and social behavior. I also seek to show, by reference to decision trees and strategic games, illustrated in normal (box matrix) or extensive (branching) form, that the authors of the relevant Greek texts and institutional arrangements posed and answered questions like those raised by contemporary choice theorists. Schematic illustrations are simplifications that can clarify connections and contrasts among ideas, situations, and texts.

Humanists may worry that the approach I employ here is reductive. Indeed, turning passages of artful and subtle writing into games *is* reductive—it strips away much that every reader of Greek texts (including myself) cares about. But that need not be a cause for worry. I claim that, in the examples featured in this book, employing analytic tools that are self-consciously, scientifically reductive foregrounds otherwise obscure aspects of ancient rules, practices, and texts. The goal of reducing complexity is to increase analytic clarity (Gailmard 2021: 79–80). Gaining greater clarity can in turn help us to better understand the complex original—whether it is a normative claim, a phenomenon of social interaction, an institution, or a passage of Greek prose. It can help us to be better readers, better historians, and better students of human behavior. But formal analysis cannot and is never intended to replace the text or its context, which is *always* "more complicated than that." Formality may enable us to see new facets of the meaning of a complex text, but never exhausts it.

The concern of formal theorists is likely to be the opposite: that the Greek approach to rationality is too informal, not reductive enough.

---

31. Respectively: *logismos, metron, hairesis (and prohairesis), anangkē, chrēsis, sumpheron, lusiteleia, kindunos, eikos.* See index for these and other Greek terms.

Greek writers and legislators concerned with the rationality of choice lacked the advanced mathematical tools, algebraic expression, and quantitative precision that exemplifies contemporary formal theories of decision and games. As we will see, Greek writers on practical reason worked out the implications of the folk theory primarily through narratives: some blatantly fictitious, others historical or quasi-historical. Even when we restrict ourselves to disciplinary domains centered on ethics, politics, and social organization (leaving aside mathematics and statistics), the mathematical formalization of choice theory has obvious benefits: It is a uniquely powerful and rigorous kind of abstraction and systematization. As such, formal theory makes it possible to treat hard problems that lack intuitive solutions, to compare seemingly dissimilar cases by using standard methods, and to incorporate precisely quantified estimates of probability.

I do not pretend that the Greeks anticipated those vital features and cardinal virtues of contemporary formal theory. But, so I will argue, the ideas underpinning the ancient and modern theories are relevantly similar, as are the habits of illustrating the theory with fanciful stories and historical anecdotes, and testing it against the observed behavior of individuals, groups, and states. As introductory texts by prominent game theorists demonstrate, the basic premises of formal theories of choice can be explained in ordinary language and simple illustrations, without algebra.[32] It is therefore quite possible that intuitions about motivation, rationality, and social behavior on which formal theory is predicated would be accessible to a culture lacking the mathematical methods that constitute contemporary formal theory's defining feature. And, taking the next step, such a culture might conjoin informal understandings of how the various intuitions cohere into a theoretical paradigm useful for explaining (and perhaps even predicting) phenomena that otherwise remained opaque. And, finally, that culture might develop ways of thinking about practical reason, applying abstract theory to real-world choice situations, that are sophisticated, powerful, and yet not readily captured by mathematical methods. This book con-

---

32. Textbooks on game theory: Davis 1983; Dixit and Skeath 1999; Camerer 2003; Binmore 2007. Camerer (2003: 3) notes, "The spread of game theory outside of economics has suffered, I believe, from the misconception that you need to know a lot of fancy math to apply it, and from the fact that most predictions of analytical game theory are not well grounded in observation." Cf. Myerson 2009 on the way in which analytic but informal work on conflict by Thomas Schelling ([1960] 1980) both anticipated and stimulated the development of formal game theory.

tends that the ancient Greeks did just that and that their results merit the attention of anyone concerned with rationality and cooperation.

Desire, Belief, Expectation

The "family" to which modern rational choice theory belongs is the moral psychology associated, in the history of philosophy, with David Hume ([1739] 1978). Theories in this family understand choice as a psychological process conjoining desire and belief. For Hume, the agent's motivating desires or preferences (conative states) were taken as being prior to, distinct from, and not, themselves, derived from or motivated by the agent's beliefs about the world (cognitive states). Once a preference has been formed, belief informs deliberation aimed at calculating the feasibility of options and the likelihood of outcomes. The agent chooses accordingly, going for the most desired option among those believed to be available. While ancient theories did not strictly insulate belief from desire, they were similarly concerned with explaining how desire and belief relate to deliberation and choice, and thereby motivate purposeful actions.[33]

In common with modern choice theory, the ancient Greek folk theory, as it was reformulated by Plato in the *Republic,* abstracted from ordinary human choice-makers. It imagined in their stead hypothetical agents freed from certain of the cognitive limitations and social constraints that affect the choices of ordinary persons. Like modern choice theory, the ancient folk theory was, therefore, normative in that it specified how a fully rational agent ought to act. Yet it was also analytically descriptive and explanatory in that it inferred the causes of actions that people are observed to undertake.[34]

---

33. Hume's theory of motivation: R. Hardin 2007; Sinhababu 2017. Irwin (1977: 80) claims that the Socrates of Plato's early dialogues "agrees entirely with Hume that reasoning moves us only because it depends on some previous desire for an end, and disagrees with Hume only in rejecting desires independent of the final good." Hume's psychological theory contrasted to that of Plato: Lorenz 2006: 32–33; to that of Aristotle: Anscombe 1977: 69; A. Price 2011.

34. Bobonich (2011) defends the consensus view among classical philosophers that in the early (pre-*Republic*) dialogues Plato's Socrates already accepts both (1) a normative "Principle of Rational Eudaimonism: It is rationally required that, for each person, his own (greatest) happiness is the decisive consideration for all his actions," and (2) a descriptive "Principle of Psychological Eudaimonism: Each person pursues (and tries to act upon) his own (greatest) happiness as the decisive consideration for all his actions" (quotation: p. 296). On the essential role of causal explanation in Aristotle's account of the deliberative reasoning that results in action, and its relationship to Aristotelian eudaimonism, see Moss 2014, 2017.

Like modern choice theory, the folk theory was predicated on the assumption that a rational agent will act according to well-ordered desires and beliefs. That is to say that the agent (1) has ranked preferences over outcomes;[35] (2) has coherent (not internally contradictory) beliefs about the relevant state of the world; (3) chooses the best available option; and (4) acts accordingly. The agent's choices and actions are determined by the anticipation of preference satisfaction. That anticipation is predicated on beliefs about the world: the perceived likelihood of certain things coming to pass. Agents, as we will see, may be either individuals or groups capable of modeling the choice processes employed by a rational individual. Specifying the conditions under which a group could be rational became a major concern of Greek theories of practical reason.

In the ancient and modern theories alike, the rational agent forms a *judgment* about possible outcomes. She does so through *deliberation*—getting clear about her preferences and beliefs relevant to a given situation. Deliberation involves thinking matters through and/or discussing the situation with others. She chooses the course of action that, having done the necessary calculations, she *expects* will lead to the best available outcome—that is, per Xenophon's Socrates (above), the *feasible* option she thinks is *most* advantageous (profitable, beneficial, satisfactory) *to herself.*[36] Thus, we may say that if *subjective value* (understood as an agent's satisfaction with outcomes) is conditioned by her *expectations* regarding preference satisfaction (the likelihood, desirability, and feasibility of alternative outcomes), rational action can be defined as behavior that *maximizes expected subjective value.*

---

35. Ideal-type ordered preferences are complete (covering all feasible outcomes), hierarchically ranked, and transitive, meaning that if there are three feasible outcomes (X,Y,Z), then in pairwise choices, X is preferred to Y, Y to Z , and X to Z. See further, chapter 1.3.

36. While reformulating the folk theory in terms of his own psychology and epistemology, in the early dialogues Plato's Socrates employs the ordinary assumptions of the folk theory as a sort of intuition pump for his interlocutors. See, for example, Plato, *Protagoras* 358c–d: Socrates claims that no one goes willingly (*hēkon*) toward evils (*kaka*), or what he considers evil, nor is it within human nature (*anthropou phusis*) to wish to go towards what one thinks to be evil rather than good. "And when one is forced to choose between two evils, no one will choose the greater [evil] if the lesser [evil] is available." For Plato's Socrates' association of "goods and evils" with "pleasures and pains," see Plato, *Protagoras* 357d–e: People make mistakes with regard to the choice of pleasures and pains (*ton hēdonon . . . kai lupon*)—that is (*tauta de esti*), with regard to *agatha* and *kaka*—and make these mistakes out of lack of knowledge. On the question of Socrates' hedonism in *Protagoras*, see below, n. 43.

Self-Interest, Utility Maximization, Measurement

Such behavior may be roughly described as egoistic, as *self-interested*. Even when the agent's highest-ranked preference includes, or just is, the good of others, getting that outcome is to her own advantage in the sense of desire satisfaction. Her rationality is *instrumental* insofar as the end is chosen because it is thought to be the most advantageous available outcome, in the sense of best satisfying a desire of the agent.[37] It need not, therefore, be chosen specifically for its own sake, as something that is choice-worthy as a good in itself, or as a moral duty owed to others, irrespective of its expected value for the choosing agent.[38] The definition of the "self" whose advantage is sought by a rational agent is not determined by the Greek folk theory. While pure, impartial, and disinterested other-regarding altruism is not accommodated by the theory, the self whose interests are served need not be, and often was not, limited to an individual. The extension beyond the individual of the self whose interests might be sought by a rational agent became a matter of intense interest for Greek theorists.[39]

In the quote attributed to him by Xenophon, Socrates described the process of choice as aimed at maximization of utility, based on the agent's beliefs. One method used by modern choice theorists for determining *intrapersonal* preference strength (that is, cardinal weighting rather than just ordinal ranking: see chapter 1.3, 1.8) is by comparing lotteries.[40] Treating each outcome as a lottery enables sums of utility

37. As we will see in chapter 1.6–7, the available outcomes may be very far from what the agent most desires; a rational agent's choice may reduce to the "least bad" among a limited set of bad options.

38. The instrumentally rational agent might choose an option that is regarded by the agent as a good in itself. That is, instrumental rationality does not preclude the belief that some things—e.g. justice, virtue—are intrinsically valuable. But it is the expected advantage to the agent, not the inherent goodness of the option, that is the reason for the agent's choice. See further, chapter 8.

39. Christ (2006: chap. 1) reviews the evidence for "self-interested citizens" in classical Athens, demonstrating the prevalence of the assumption that individuals were fundamentally self-interested. Balot (2001) focuses on Greek literature that concerns the devolution of self-interest into vicious greed: excessive desire to get more for oneself without regard for the claims of others.

40. The expected utility to a risk-neutral (neither risk-averse nor risk-preferring) rational agent of a given outcome is deduced by assuming that the agent is indifferent between a "sure thing" payoff (e.g., a 100% chance at $1 vs. 0% at nothing) and a fair chance (expressed as a probability distribution) for a higher payoff (e.g., a 10% chance at $10 vs. 90% at nothing). On the standard theory of expected utility maximization, and its limitations, see Buchak 2013. On maximization in Greek economic theory and practice, see Leese 2021.

associated with more and less likely outcomes, measured in an actual or pseudo-currency (e.g., dollars or "utils"), to be directly compared. The point at which the agent is indifferent between lotteries specifies the relative strength of the agent's subjective preferences.[41] Her "utility function," that is, her preference for one bundle of goods over another, is operationalized in her choice of the lottery offering the highest expected yield.[42] As we will see, some ancient narratives centering on consequential choices are readily redescribed as choices among lotteries, with payoffs to available outcomes imaged as measurable in a real or pseudo currency; I offer examples in the following chapters.

Ancient choice theorists concerned themselves with standards for measurement and comparison of desire satisfaction across available outcomes. The probability of a given outcome was not quantified as a frequency distribution. But the questions of how to gauge the likelihood of possible outcomes and how to measure the value of outcomes in a standard currency were hotly debated by Greek ethical philosophers. In Plato's *Republic,* for example, oligarchs measure the comparative value of possible outcomes by a straightforward monetary standard. In Plato's *Protagoras* (356a–57b) Socrates emphasizes the great value of an "art of measurement" that allows for choice and action to be predicated on the precise calculation of the size and number of current and anticipated pleasures and pains.[43]

The Socratics diverged from the background Greek "folk theory" and from modern choice theorists in their concern with the objectivity of value and the rationality of desires. For each of the Socratics, happi-

41. For example: Lottery x = sure thing of outcome X (0% chance of getting nothing); lottery y = 50% chance of outcome Y (and 50% chance of nothing); lottery z = 10% chance of outcome Z (and 90% chance of nothing). The agent who is indifferent among these lotteries ($x = y = z$) has expressed a preference-strength ranking (cardinal subjective valuation of X,Y,Z) in the ratio X:1, Y:2, Z:10. For discussion see Diaconis and Skyrms 2017.

42. Hun Chung (per litt. December 2019) suggests a slightly more formal account: "What modern expected utility theory simply assumes is that agents have preferences over available actions (seen as lotteries, i.e. probability distributions over sure outcomes) and whenever these preferences satisfy a number of formal consistency conditions (e.g. continuity, independence, etc.), then we are able to find a real-valued utility function representing the agent's preferences that has (what people call) the 'expected utility property'—viz. the utility of an action (seen as a lottery) is equal to its expected utility, and, hence, the agent strictly prefers option x to option y if and only if the expected utility of option x is greater than the expected utility of option y."

43. Whether the Socrates of the *Protagoras* advocates an explicitly hedonistic standard for happiness (explicitly rejected elsewhere in Plato's Socratic dialogues) is debated: See Irwin 1977: chap. 4, 1995: 85–92; Weiss 1989; Bobonich 2011; Kamtekar 2018: chap. 3.

ness, understood as complete human flourishing (*eudaimonia*), was the highest, best, end of human life: the goal pursued by an ethically rational person.[44] Unlike Greek Sophists and modern choice theorists, Socratic philosophers sought to establish an objective basis for measuring happiness in comparative, *interpersonal* terms. Abstracting from the subjective preferences of any specifiable individual, Plato's Socrates at one point (*Republic* 9.587b–e) calculates that "the philosopher" is precisely 729 times happier than "the tyrant." Yet each of the Socratics also recognized that instrumental rationality, determining the best means to desired ends, was necessary for attaining that highest end, and all the subsidiary goals leading to it. And they saw that instrumental rationality was employed by those who aimed at what they regarded as bad ends. The potential value for *us,* today, of comparing ancient with modern accounts of value, choice, and reason is the primary justification for this book.

In the next chapters, I attempt to demonstrate that there was an influential "ancient Greek folk theory" of practical reasoning that centered on instrumental rationality and its limits. That is to say, the internally coherent set of assumptions about motivation and action sketched above was widely known in Greek antiquity and was operationalized in actual choice-making. Moreover, that set of assumptions was adopted as a *point d'appui* by Greek writers who concerned themselves with ethics, politics, and history—even when it was *not* considered a complete account of observed behavior or an adequate basis for morally choice-worthy action. Greek writers employed the folk theory as a foundation for more elaborate arguments aimed at causally explaining and normatively evaluating human behavior and social development.

The folk theory was adapted and refined over time. None of the thinkers with whom we will be concerned supposed that it accounted for all relevant human behavior or all aspects of development. It failed, for example, to explain human aspirations to identify objectively correct ends; to act well, finely, and justly; to "do the right thing, in the right way, for the right reasons." Understanding why people, individually and

---

44. I am ignoring, here, salient differences between Aristotle and Plato, and between Plato's earlier and later dialogues, in the definition of happiness, its relationship to virtue, and concerning who is, or could possibly be, either completely or adequately happy; see discussion in Bobonich 2017, concluding (p. 298): "Being happy is, very roughly and with the caveat that different philosophers have distinctive conceptions of happiness, the attainment and correct use of the human goods or living the best possible (or at any rate, the superlatively choiceworthy) life for you."

in groups, act as they do in different contexts required substantial adjustments to the folk theory's premises. But the base-line theory to which the adjustments were made was taken as an indispensable starting point by Greek thinkers. The folk theory sets the frame for the study of Greek thought about the rationality of choice, by individuals, social groups, and states; about behavior that conforms to predictions arising from the theory; and about behavior that deviates from those predictions.

0.4 FOLK THEORY VARIATIONS

In the following chapters I trace some influential strands of the ancient Greek folk theory of practical reasoning. The theory was manifest in literary works and in the institutions of Greek city-states. I have kept the primary focus on well-known Greek states (especially Athens) and a handful of texts, mostly by philosophers and historians. Along with the Socratics, these include Herodotus, Thucydides, Polybius, and Plutarch. While I will touch on a much wider range of authors, genres, and texts, a full-scale intellectual history of ancient Greek ideas about practical reason, and how those ideas were manifest in public and private practices, would run to multiple volumes. Writing that detailed history exceeds my ambitions as a political theorist and historian. Here, I trace certain threads through what I imagine as a large, rich tapestry. That tapestry—of thought, writing, cultural practices, social institutions, and individual behavior—is the context in which the threads I trace were spun and into which they were woven. It is the set of ideas, questions, and problems by which the authors of the texts and designers of institutions I focus on were inspired, and to which they sought to respond.

Preclassical Intuitions

While the folk theory crystallized at a certain time and place—in mid-fifth- through late-fourth-century-BCE Athens—it had a long "prehistory" in earlier Greek thought and social practice. An intuitive understanding of motivated action as "going for what is regarded by an agent as being in his own best interest" is already present in our earliest Greek texts: Homer, Hesiod, and lyric poetry. I will touch on certain passages in early texts in subsequent chapters. The elements of desire and belief are already in play, along with a grasp of strategic behavior, a conception of likelihood, and the use of proof techniques, including counterfactuals. Some passages in early Greek texts, including Hesiod's

Works and Days (e.g. 270–273) and nuggets of proverbial wisdom dating back to Homer (Lardinois 1997, 2000), imply a recognition of two facts: First, strategic, self-interested behavior is foundational—an irreducible psychological aspect of social life. And, next, when taken to extremes, such behavior is subversive of public order—a threat to norms of cooperative behavior essential to the survival of human communities.

Certain figures depicted in early texts (for example, Homeric elders: chapter 7.3) are portrayed as having a deserved reputation for a kind of practical wisdom. They are regarded as especially skilled in defining options and advocating for the choice that is most likely to have a good outcome. In some cases (for example, Solon of Athens: chapter 4.2) an individual, regarded as practically wise, took a leading role in the design and implementation of new political institutions. A grasp of the need to align incentives of office-holders with those of the wider community, through publicly announced sanctions for violations, informs some of the earliest examples of Greek written law—notably, the Great Code of Gortyn on Crete.[45]

Looking back to these earlier texts and documents, from the perspective of a Greek intellectual in the classical period, what would appear to be lacking is an explicit theorization of rationality, as a process by which correct choices were made and as the distinguishing characteristic of practical wisdom.[46] In the absence of a theory, there was no systematic account of the elements involved in practical reasoning, no readily transferable decision-making expertise, no general doctrine or set of techniques that could be taught or applied to particular cases. It was the distinctive political and economic conditions of the classical age that set the stage for the emergence and refinement of a theory of reason that could be taught, mastered, and operationalized in private and public practices.

Classical Era Context

By the fifth century BCE, the Greek world was characterized by consolidated city-states (*poleis*), differing in size and public rules, but sharing a

---

45. Early Greek law: Gagarin 1986, 2005; Abgrall 2019.

46. A tendency to theorization was, however, imputed to authors of early texts, for example by Plato's Protagoras (Plato, *Protagoras* 316d), who claims Homer, Hesiod, and Simonides as early (albeit cryptic) Sophists.

number of cultural features (Hansen 2006; Hansen and Nielsen 2004). Forms of social order in which ruling was monopolized by an individual or family were well known to the Greeks and remained common outside the world of the Greek poleis (chapter 3). But by the fifth century monarchic poleis were the exception, at least outside the western-Greek regions of Sicily and southern Italy. Among the salient features of the Greek polis was self-government by citizens. In some poleis, notably Athens, the regime was democratic, according to ancient Greek standards, in that the citizen body was roughly coextensive with the adult, native, male population (chapter 4). In other poleis the regime was oligarchic, in that participatory citizenship was restricted to owners of substantial property or to those whose wealth was acquired in specified ways.

Meanwhile, although interpolis warfare was frequent and consequential, individuals and goods moved freely across the Greek world, their mobility facilitated by geography (ready access to low-cost transport by sea), a shared language, and a common background culture. The most prosperous of the mid-fifth-century poleis was Athens, at that time the hegemon of an extensive Aegean empire (chapter 5). Athens lost its empire at the end of the fifth century, but its democratic political and legal system survived and matured in the fourth century, when the philosophical schools of Plato and Aristotle were founded (chapter 6). Specialized production and exchange of goods and services led over time to increased consumption: Many classical-era Greek poleis, and notably Athens, were prosperous by ancient standards (chapter 7). Both during and after its imperial era, Athens was the center of a thriving market of goods, services, and ideas. As such, Athens attracted inquisitive, talented, and entrepreneurial individuals from across the Greek world.

Sophists, Conventional, and Thrasymachean

Among the specialized services that were being marketed by mobile entrepreneurs in mid-fifth-century Athens was training in the expert management of the household (*oikos*) and the state (*polis*)—that is, roughly, private and public affairs. Those offering such training were dubbed Sophists. As we will see (chapter 2), various of the Sophists were known for their mastery of clever arguments and persuasive rhetoric. Only fragments now survive (collected in Laks and Most 2016 = LM) of what was once a rich body of sophistic texts. As a consequence, we lack anything like a full account, by a practicing Sophist, of the substantive content of sophistic teaching. Presumably the specifics of the training offered by individual Sophists varied considerably: They competed for students based on salient distinctions. But, going by the fragments and the (albeit largely hostile) portrayal of Sophists in the works of the classical Socratics, it appears that the shared intellectual underpinning of the expertise they purported to be able to teach, for suitable fees, was what I have called the Greek folk theory of instrumental rationality.[47] It therefore seems likely that it is the members of this loose network of entrepreneurial intellectuals, hailing from various parts of the Greek world, who, collectively, should be credited with the original Greek discovery of practical reason. That is to say, they were the first to devise and promulgate a coherent theory to explain the wellsprings of choice and willed action and to specify the processes of reasoning characteristic of a rational agent.[48]

Among the organizing tropes of sophistic thought was the distinction between law or custom (*nomos,* plural *nomoi*) and nature (*phusis*).[49] Two main variants of the folk theory, called here Conventionalist and Thrasymachean (after the Sophist who figures prominently in Plato, *Republic* book 1; see chapter 1.1), can be schematically distinguished, based on differences in their views of the relationship between *nomos* and *phusis.* Insofar as instrumentalist reasoning is understood as a universal human capacity (per Xenophon's Socrates, above), it appears to

---

47. The fragments collected in LM allow the following composite sketch of sophistic thought: Humans are concerned with their own good (LM 33.D48; 37.D38). Value is subjective (31.D9, D38, R4–29; 32.R26; 41.1). It is determined by what appears pleasurable or painful (33.D49; 34.D22e; 37.D38a), profitable or unprofitable (32.D25.19), "good for" or "bad for" the agent (32.D25.18; 33.D45). The rational agent chooses by comparing available options, preferring (between any two) and going for the one that calculation reveals to be the "greater good" or "lesser evil" (32.D25.14; 33.D26, D44, D53a, D54b). Option sets are constrained by others' preferences and artificial social rules (38.D3). If rules conflict with natural preferences, the rational, unobserved agent may violate rules (32.D25.12–13; 37.D38a). Money facilitates measurement of value and obtaining preferred ends (32.D40, 37.D83). Power is the capacity to widen one's feasible option set, often by constraining the options available to others (32.D24.12). Sophistic education/training (42.R9–11) promotes expertise in instrumentally rational choice-making, calculation of costs and benefits, counterfactual reasoning (32.D25.7–12), and estimation of risk (32.D25.13). It discourages socially inculcated notions of goodness as a fixed standard, and increases the agent's power through expertise in persuasive speech (31.D37; 32.D24.12, D49–51; 42.R14). Bonazzi (2020: 23) neatly sums it up by describing the Sophists as "masters of usefulness."

48. On the Sophists and sophistic thought, see Kerferd 1981; de Romilly 1992; Poulakos 1995; Dillon 2003; Tindale 2010; Bonazzi 2020, with extensive bibliography.

49. See Guthrie 1962: vol. 3, chap. 4; McKirahan 1994: chap. 19; C.C.W. Taylor 2007; Bonazzi 2020: chap. 4, esp. p. 66: "The relationship between *nomos* and *physis* is probably the topic most fiercely debated by fifth-century authors."

be an aspect of human nature: *phusis*. Like other human capacities (say, physical strength or memory), the natural human capacity for practical reasoning could be refined by teaching and practice.

The *nomos/phusis* question that is relevant to a folk theory typology is whether ideal-type instrumentally rational agents, or those whose capacity to choose beneficial options was highly developed by expert training, ordinarily see their self-interest, and thus their utility-maximizing strategic choices, as likely to be aligned with or against the existing *nomoi*—the customary norms and formal rules of the polis. The alignment of *nomos* and *phusis* leads to a cooperative model of human society, one in which individuals regard their self-interest as consistent with the interest of others, thus allowing for reciprocity and at least local altruism. Competition is, in this case, subordinated to and supportive of the common good as mutual advantage. Nonalignment leads to a noncooperative model. Laws (other than those devised by the agent himself, as ruler) and social norms are regarded as "unnatural" constraints on freedom, while maximizing self-interest involves exploitation of others within the community. Competition for utility is zero-sum and winners dominate losers.[50]

The Conventionalist variant of the folk theory saw *nomos* as consistent with *phusis*—and therefore obedience to the rules of the local community as characteristic of the rational agent. The Thrasymachean variant saw *nomos* and *phusis* as aligned only when the desiring agent is an unconstrained ruler, able to make and enforce rules in furtherance of his goals without external interference. The Thrasymachaean rational agent follows the rules only when it is to his advantage to do so; he will devise means to circumvent the rules whenever they interfere with his desires. A third, Socratic, variant is distinguished by its emphasis on rationality as "reason's desire"—in that reason must determine the objective value of ends sought in order for an agent's process of choice and action to count as rational. The Thrasymachean and Socratic variants of the folk theory will be discussed in more detail in the following chapters. The Conventionalist version of the theory deserves a somewhat fuller introduction here. Although, like the Thrasymachean version, the Conven-

---

50. The *nomos/phusis* contrast, including its relationship to costs and benefits, the conception of laws as constraints (*desmoi*), and cooperation in punishment as a cost, is very prominent in a long fragment of the Sophist Antiphon's text "On Truth": LM 37.D38, with discussion in Bonazzi 2020. Note that the categorization into Conventionalist and Thrasymachean variants is schematic, and it elides salient differences between exemplars in each category.

tionalist variant was a critical target of Socratic thought, it is for the most part relegated to the background in Plato's *Republic*.

The Conventionalist variant of the folk theory held that ideal-type instrumental rationality is ordinarily compatible with the rules of the polis and with some concern for the welfare of others. The Conventionalist agent recognizes the power of the rulers (in a democracy: the demos) to establish rules as legitimate authority, on the assumption that a rule-bound social order is in the common interest of those subject to it. The rulers monitor social behavior and demand the obedience of individuals subject to the rules. The ruled ought, rationally, to obey, given that it is in their interest and in accord with their nature to do so. But when they do not, the rulers can and will punish violations by even the most prominent and powerful individuals. All of this is consistent with the nature of humans as at once self-conscious, substantially (if not narrowly) self-interested individuals and interdependent social beings, whose individual security and well-being require close and continuing association with others.

The Conventionalist variant was a theorization of what we can guess was the general attitude of law-abiding Athenians and, mutatis mutandis, of Spartans and citizens of other nontyrannical Greek states. As theorized accounts of human behavior percolated into elite Greek discourse, and then into the wider population through the deliberative processes of democratic states (chapter 6), the Conventionalist variant was, over time, built into the institutions and the normative political culture of Athens and other Greek poleis. In practice, when enough citizens came to accept those institutions and norms as legitimately authoritative (that is, worthy of being obeyed even in the absence of coercive threats), and when they were willing to join in mutual monitoring and enforcement, the costs of violation (punishment) typically exceeded its benefits. At that point, obedience to the rules was a rational choice of the utility-maximizing individual agent assumed in all versions of the folk theory, in that the expected net sum of utility was positive. And so, the Conventionalist variant of the theory could claim some degree of observational validation.

We will consider several expressions of the Conventionalist variant in later chapters, including speeches by Thucydides' Pericles and the text of Pseudo-Xenophon (the "Old Oligarch"). Other examples include the Sophist Lycophron (LM 38), the orators Demosthenes and Aeschines, and various characters in tragedy and comedy. A particularly clear statement of the Conventionalist variant is preserved in three anonymous fragments (numbers 6, 7, 8) inserted into the corpus of works by the Neoplatonist philosopher Iamblichus. The "Anonymous Iamblichi" (LM 40), dated to the classical period (probably ca. 400 BCE), offered a theoretical justification for rationally cooperative and prosocial behavior.[51] I take it as exemplary of the sort of justification that had emerged by the time Socrates was engaged in his philosophical investigations and that formed an important part of the argumentative context in which Thrasymachean instrumentalists and the classical Socratics wrote their texts.

A Conventionalist Thought Experiment

In fragment 6, the author of the Anonymous Iamblichi argues against unnamed opponents (here called "Thrasymacheans") who claim that greed (*pleonexia*) is both worthy of aspiration and the foundation of power (*kratos*), whereas obedience to the rules (*nomoi*) is a product of cowardice.[52] The author asserts that this set of claims is both ignoble and harmful. His argument against his Thrasymachean opponents turns on an assumption of natural interdependence: Humans cannot long survive as solitary beings. By necessity they join in associations with one another, and they thereby discovered the means and mechanisms (*technēmata*: presumably both technological and institutional; see chapter 2.5–6) necessary for survival. Moreover, if people did attempt to associate with one another, but in a state of lawlessness (*anomia*), the losses suffered by each would be even greater than those borne by someone living alone. It is because of these necessities that law (*nomos*) and justice (*to dikaion*) are strongly bound in us by nature (*phusis*).

To prove his point, the author offers a thought experiment based on the fiction of a superman: Suppose that someone were born who was invulnerable in his flesh, immune to disease, possessing supernatural strength and an adamantine body. Even such a being would obey and actively support the laws and justice. He would do so because only thus

---

51. Horky (2020) offers a detailed and helpful discussion of the text and its democratic context.

52. Balot (2001: 28–33) argues that the Greek term *pleonexia* (as well as its periphrastic variants) operates between the semantic fields of fairness and unfairness, moderation and excess. It is more than mere "acquisitiveness" or "wanting more than one's share." The ethical concern it raises exceeds the threat to distributive justice. Used pejoratively, *pleonexia* refers to an excessive desire to have more and more, conjoined with a willful disregard of the claims of others.

could he ensure his safety. The superman's choice is determined by a counterfactual: Were he to act according to excessive self-aggrandizing greed (*pleonexia*), all other people (i.e., all those in his community) would resolve to oppose him. They would do so because of their commitment to the law—which, per above, is what ensures their own survival. In such circumstances, the author asserts, the multitude (*plēthos*) would overcome the superman, either through skill (*technē*) or might (*dunamis*). So, to avoid that predictable and undesirable outcome, the superman must support the laws and justice. Thus, our author concludes, it is evident that true power (*auto to kratos*) is preserved by law and justice. Contrary to the Thrasymacheans, who took *kratos* as power to dominate and exploit others, the Anonymous Iamblichi asserts, with Greek democrats, that "true *kratos*" is the capacity of a demos to achieve collective goals.[53]

Throughout, the Anonymous Iamblichi freely interweaves moral (nobility, justice) and prudential (survival, safety) arguments for the naturalness of social cooperation and law-abidingness. But the "adamantine superman" thought experiment is designed to show that the basis of obedience to the law rests solidly on a self-interested concern for one's own physical safety. Personal security cannot be preserved, even by a supernaturally powerful being, in the face of the self-interested opposition of "the multitude" of the lawful. Thus, someone who, by dint of great strength, might otherwise be led to believe that lawless behavior better served his own interests would rationally obey the law.

Notably, the superman thought experiment models classical-era Athenian democratic institutions—the people's courts and ostracism, through which "the multitude" of citizens credibly threatened to punish even the most powerful individuals, if and when they were perceived to have deviated from public norms (chapter 6.6). That thought experiment is backed up in the author's cost-benefit analysis of interdependence and lawfulness. The text establishes a hierarchy of payoffs, and thus a ranked order among imaginable states of existence. The ranking is based on the assumed desirability of safety and survival: Best is living safely in a human association according to the law. Next (and much worse) is living alone with no hope of long-term survival. Worst of all, perhaps because constant fear of vicious others will attend the

---

53. The fragment is evidence of the classical-era struggle over the true meaning of *kratos*—Cf. Ober 2017: chap. 2 (pace Cammack 2019) on the democratic definition of *kratos* as capacity rather than domination.

presumably brief duration of life, is an association without law. The conclusion that obedience to the law is both rational and in accord with nature follows directly from that ranking of available options.

Thrasymachean and Socratic Variants

The author of the Anonymous Iamblichi wrote in an intellectual context defined by an active debate between what I am calling the Conventionalist and Thrasymachean variants of the folk theory of practical reason. We will consider various exemplars of the Thrasymachean variant, and Plato's refinement of it in book 2 of the *Republic,* in greater detail in chapters 1 and 2. Various classical-era examples of Thrasymachean attitudes could be cited, including fragments of other sophistic works and a range of characters from tragedy and comedy. Here it suffices to contrast the argument of the Anonymous Iamblichi in favor of the law with Plato's Callicles in the dialogue *Gorgias.* Callicles, a politically ambitious Athenian student of the prominent Sophist Gorgias (LM 32), is portrayed as an advocate of the position that greed is natural and good and that law-abiding behavior is unnatural and harmful to the strong. Callicles opines that the people who institute laws in poleis are "the weak and the many." Those persons establish law, and praise lawfulness, "with themselves and their own advantage in mind." They fear the powerful among them, who are "capable of having a greater share" (*dunatoi pleon echein*). And so, they deploy moralizing language, calling getting more than one's share shameful (*aischron*) and unjust (*adikon*). The weak do this, Callicles concludes, so that the strong will not have a greater share than themselves (Plato, *Gorgias* 483b4–c5; see further chapter 2.3).

Both the Anonymous Iamblichi and Plato's Callicles agree on the motivating role of self-interest in the rational behavior of both especially powerful individuals and the relatively weaker individuals constituting the multitude. What separates them is the question of whether the many are naturally capable of sustaining their own self-interested position (sustaining the laws, thereby getting their share) in the face of a willful strongman. The Anonymous Iamblichi foresaw the many cooperating in overcoming the (counterfactual) deviant strongman by skill or force. For Callicles, the unnatural condition in which the strong are constrained by the weak is sustained only by the persuasive power of vacuous moralizing. As such, the constraints imposed by the many can and will be undone just as soon as a person of "sufficient nature" sees through the fog of ideology and breaks the feeble bonds of moral mystification. Then, with the true order of nature restored, the strong will do as they please. The constraining rules will be overthrown—or remade to fit the preferences of the strongman, now in his natural political role as ruler. In sharp contrast to the prodemocratic conclusion of the argument offered by the Anonymous Iamblichi, Callicles' argument from nature ends in tyranny.

As we will see, the classical Socratics and other Greek writers, including Herodotus and Thucydides, both criticize and draw from each of these approaches to instrumental rationality. Plato, for example, sought to show that, contrary to the contrast between democracy and tyranny sketched above, self-interested choices, in the absence of rulers with knowledge of objectively valuable ends, will lead democracy naturally to devolve into tyranny (chapter 6.1–2). In common with the Conventionalists, one goal of the ethical and political philosophy of the classical Socratics was refuting the most philosophically refined version of the Thrasymachean claim that the strong would not rationally obey established laws. The Socratic answer incorporated fundamental assumptions about human interdependence prominent in the Conventionalist variant of the folk theory. Grafted on to that set of assumptions was, however, a new norm of rationality that required reason's own desire for objectively valuable ends.

I conclude this section with a caveat: While the typology of Conventionalist, Thrasymachean, and Socratic variants of the folk theory of practical reason will prove analytically useful in the rest of this book, the typology is schematic and artificial. It is "etic" rather than "emic," insofar as it is a modern imposition of a certain kind of analytic order, rather than a native artifact of ancient culture. There are substantial differences among those I assign to each category (e.g., between Plato and Aristotle, Callicles and Thrasymachus). Greek texts, including some that feature prominently in this book, draw on variants from more than one category. Thucydides is a prime example of an author who is deeply concerned with practical reasoning, but who does not fit neatly into any one of the categories sketched above.

0.5 LITERATURE REVIEW: RATIONAL AND IRRATIONAL GREEKS

Rationality in its various aspects—ethical, political, scientific, aesthetic—has been regarded as a constitutive feature of classical Greek thought and culture since the Hellenistic era. The "intellectual experiments of the Greek Enlightenment" (Solmsen 1975) have often been taken as ancestors of ways of thinking about humanity, reason, and nature that characterize the Italian and Northern Renaissances, the Scientific Revolution of the seventeenth century, and the eighteenth-century European Enlightenment. Those ways of thinking centered on a humanistic conception of individuals as self-consciously aware of themselves as coherent selves, as capable of forming judgments about value and the interests of self and others. By extension, human communities are conceived as aggregates of individuals, persons who choose to join together with others in recognition of their need for one another, and the potential for beneficial alignments of individual, group, and common concerns. But the centrality of rationality as a constitutive feature of Greek culture has not gone unchallenged.

Primitivism, Holism, and Theories of Psychological Development

In the nineteenth century scholars in France, Germany, and Britain began exploring alternative approaches to Greek civilization. They aimed to take proper account of nonrational elements inherited from preclassical times and still visible in classical art, literature, and ritual practices. Most important for the question of instrumental rationality, they challenged the notion of the self-conscious individual as the primary locus of choice and action. Fustel de Coulanges' *The Ancient Greek City* (1874, original French edition 1864) emphasized kinship and the family, rather than the individual, as the center of ancient identity. He posited religion as the factor bonding families with states, and thus as the primary driver of the cultural evolution of Greek and Roman societies. For Fustel, it was the decline of religious belief during the Roman imperial era, and the consequent liberation of the individual from the grip of a holistic tribalism that ultimately doomed the ancient Greek city and, with it, ancient civilization. Fustel's emphasis on religion, holism over individualism, and his rejection of utilitarianism resonated with the later, and highly influential, sociology of Emile Durkheim (Prendergast 1983).

Friederich Nietzsche's *Birth of Tragedy* (2000, original German edition 1872) attacked the traditional emphasis on Greek rationalism from another direction, emphasizing dark, passionate, emotive "Dionysian" aspects of Greek culture. Those aspects had been largely suppressed by classical scholarship centered on enlightened "Apollonian" reason.

Nietzsche's work provoked a sharply critical response by the German classical establishment, leading him to leave the field of classics and turn to the philosophical projects for which he became famous. But his surfacing of the nonrational elements of Greek culture remained influential.

In the United Kingdom the so-called "Cambridge Ritualists," inspired by James G. Frazer's massive collection of ritual practices from around the world, *The Golden Bough* (expanded 12-vol. 3rd ed. 1911–15; first edition 1890), emphasized primitivism and an eclectic, comparativist, archetype-based anthropology to explain Greek religious ritual. Like Fustel, the Cambridge Ritualists saw religion as the primary feature of Greek culture, and like Nietzsche, they emphasized nonrational aspects of Greek culture. Frazer himself was trained as a classicist; between the two editions of the *Golden Bough,* he published an edition, with learned commentary, on the Greek travel writer Pausanias. Works by his Cambridge classical colleagues included Jane Harrison's *Prolegomena to the Study of Greek Religion* (1903) and *Themis: Social Origins of Greek Religion* (1912); Frances M. Cornford's *Thucydides Mythhistoricus* (1907); and Gilbert Murray's *Four,* then *Five Stages of Greek Religion* (1925, original publication 1912).

While Nietzsche's and the Cambridge Ritualists' ideas about Greek culture have remained influential outside classical studies, their specific arguments had been largely marginalized within mainstream classical scholarship by the 1930s. That was due to the conservatism of a field devoted to the philological study of literary classics and, in the case of the Cambridge Ritualists, to the limitations inherent in an anthropology predicated on explaining ritual behavior by reference to a set of presumptively universal primitive archetypes. Yet meanwhile, in a series of articles culminating in his book *The Discovery of the Mind: The Greek Origins of European Thought* (1953, original German edition 1948), the German classical philologist, Bruno Snell, introduced a new theory of human consciousness. Snell held that the emergence of the self-conscious individual was a historical development that postdated the Homeric era. For Snell, early Greeks were not integrated, self-conscious selves. They therefore lacked coherent preferences and were incapable of self-interest or decision-making as it is now understood. Consciousness of the self was, Snell argued, a revolutionary discovery, albeit one that emerged only slowly, with the development of post-Homeric Greek civilization:

> The rise of thinking among the Greeks was nothing less than a revolution. They did not, by means of a mental equipment already at their disposal, merely map out new subjects for discussion, such as the sciences and

philosophy. They discovered the human mind. This drama, man's gradual understanding of himself, is revealed to us in the career of Greek poetry and philosophy. The stages of the journey which saw a rational view of the nature of man establish itself are to be traced in the creations of epic and lyric poetry, and in the plays. (Snell [1948] 1953: v)

Snell's work was a major influence on E. R. Dodds's seminal *The Greeks and the Irrational* (1951—see preface), which in turn set the study of nonrational elements of Greek culture on a new footing. Dodds's work was predicated on a fascination with the paranormal, Freudian psychology and the new scientific anthropology being practiced by, among others, Ruth Benedict (*The Chrysanthemum and the Sword:* 1946). Dodds accepted Snell's developmental schema but emphasized the role of democratic Athens in the breakthrough, declaring that the emergence of the self-conscious individual was "one of the major achievements of Greek rationalism, and one for which the credit must go to Athenian democracy" (Dodds 1951: 34).

To Snell's theory of the emergence of self-consciousness, Dodds added a second developmental notion, borrowed from Ruth Benedict's anthropology: Greek culture, from Homer to the classical era, was characterized by an (incomplete) shift from a shame-centered moral psychology to one that was guilt-centered. Shame is characterized by a deep concern for public censure, reputation, and honor; wrong is in the eyes and attitudes of others. Shame, for the Greeks, was associated with a sense of human helplessness in the face of divine powers. Those powers were in turn characterized by divine jealousy (*phthonos*)—which might be moralized as retribution (*nemesis*). The transition from shame to guilt was, Dodds argued, characterized by the internalization of the sense of wrong. It is accompanied by a growing fear of ritual pollution (*miasma*) and a consequent longing for purification (*katharsis*). Notably, Dodds supposed that the earlier shame-based conception lingered on beyond the era of "democratic rationalization." Throughout, Dodds emphasized religion, ritual, and nonrational "Dionysian" elements of Greek culture.

Snell's developmental scheme and Dodds' idea of the move from shame to guilt were borrowed, adapted, and popularized by the American sociologist Alvin Gouldner in *Enter Plato: Classical Greece and the Origins of Social Theory* (1965). Gouldner offered a new developmental history of Greek society and culture, with the key revolution in social thought coming only with Plato. Gouldner's aim was to redescribe Athenian society, applying perspectives employed by modern sociologists to the Hellenic world, in order to understand how this civilization gave rise to and shaped Plato's social theory (Gouldner 1965: 4). Like Dodds, Gouldner was concerned with two sorts of rationality: psychological (ethical) and institutional (political). Gouldner saw evidence of institutional rationality in the bold new constitutions of early Greek colonies, in the way tribal structures were deliberately manipulated by Greek lawmakers, and in Solon's masterful approach to mending the Athenian class system. In terms of moral psychology and behavior, Gouldner embraced the idea that a "shame culture" was necessarily characterized by bitter, zero-sum games:

> Certain peculiarities of the [Greek] contest system deserve to be stressed. For one it approximates a zero-sum game in that someone can win only if someone else loses. This, of course, is manifest in the case of victory won by "wars" and "threats"; but it seems to be the case in "competitions," especially by the standards of a "shame culture." . . . [S]omeone is the loser. (Gouldner 1965: 49)

For Gouldner, the Greek solution to the social problems arising from zero-sum competitions was an acute moral stress on moderation: "nothing in excess" (Gouldner 1965: 51).

Developmental Theories Refuted and Questions of Motivation

The "discovery of the mind" thesis, combined with the "shame culture to guilt culture" thesis, would seem to imply that what I have been calling "the discovery of practical reason" was not, in and of itself, a distinctive intellectual advance, but rather a part of a much more profound transformation that had occurred sometime between the Homeric era and the floruit of Athenian democracy in the fourth century BCE. Moreover, the intense emphasis on social holism and the centrality of communal rituals is antithetical to motivation predicated on expected utility maximization. The developmental story embraced by Snell, Dodds, and Gouldner (among others) has been overthrown in more recent scholarship.[54] But the emphasis on Durkheimian sociological holism over economic models of behavior favoring individual choices based on expected utility (Barry 1978) remains a feature of mainstream classical studies. M. I. Finley, the influential ancient historian whose work on "the ancient economy" helped define classical scholarship on social and

---

54. For cogent discussion and critique of Snell's developmental thesis, see, for example, Sharples 1983; Gaskin 1998. On Dodds, see Williams 1993; Parker 2019.

economic aspects of Greek and Roman history (see preface and chapter 7.4), rejected Durkheim's sociology in favor of that of Max Weber. But he remained committed to the essential "foreignness" of classical Greek civilization and dismissive of the idea that "modernizing" economic concepts could help explain individual motivation or social behavior in antiquity.

In his 1990 essay "Cities of Reason," the Oxford classical historian Oswyn Murray addressed Greek rationality through a critical comparison of Emile Durkheim's and Max Weber's schools of sociology. Murray rejected Durkheim's (and Fustel's) emphasis on religious holism and related notions of Greek tribalism and primitivism, in favor of Weber's approach centered on institutional rationality. Murray argued that Greek culture was rational from the time of Homer onwards, pointing out that development took the form, not of the discovery of consciousness, but of self-conscious reforms in the direction of greater effectiveness of political institutions. Sparta exhibited archaic rationality; Athens showed the rationality of self-conscious institutional design—and in both cases there was a hierarchy of politics over religion and kinship, rather than vice versa. Murray retained Durkheim's notion of collective consciousness, but saw that consciousness as political, not religious. Thus, for Murray, the ancient Greeks remained fundamentally different from the moderns, concerning themselves not with negotiated compromises among interest groups, but with the society as a unitary association (*koinōnia*). The self-seeking individual, for example one involved in economic competition, was thus regarded as deviant and wicked rather than normative.

In *Shame and Necessity* (1993), the philosopher Bernard Williams challenged the very idea of moral-psychological "progressivism"—and with it the strong distinction between ancient and modern motivation that had been the premise of much of the anthropological and sociological work in classical studies since Fustel. Like Murray, Williams rejected the vision of Homeric "primitivism" that was the common feature of much of the nineteenth- and early- to mid-twentieth-century work discussed above, and on which the progressivists, notably Snell and Dodds, had grounded their arguments. But in contrast to Murray, Williams argued, persuasively, that from the perspective of modernity there was nothing especially foreign about the moral psychology of Homeric or tragic heroes, nor did a putative "shame culture" call out a unique psychology that is unknown, or even rare, in modernity. Williams pointed out that what the progressivists saw as lacking in the Greeks was the moralization of motives:

The strangeness, to some people, of the Homeric notions of action lies ultimately just in this, that they did *not* revolve round a distinction between moral and nonmoral motivations. . . . Duty in some abstract modern sense is largely unknown to the Greeks, in particular to archaic Greeks, and this is of course one of their characteristics noted by the progressivists. (Williams 1993: 41)

Williams notes that the moralization of motives, and thus the linkage of rationality to morality, was an original feature of Plato's thought—a feature which (for Williams, regretably) was then never completely lost in later European (and especially Kantian) philosophical thinking about motives and action. This helps explain, for example, the argument of the classical philosopher Michael Frede (1996) that Greek rationality begins with the Socratic claims that reason must have its own desires and that the rational agent is the one in which reason's desires provide the motives for action. Williams' liberation of the ancient Greeks from the shackles of both primitivism and the necessity of moralized motivation for rational choice and action opens the way to seeing "the discovery of practical reason" as a genuine intellectual breakthrough, worth studying on its own terms. Williams' work does not address the question of whether Greek individuals were understood by classical Greek theorists to be motivated by the considerations of preference and belief similar to those on which modern rational choice theory is based. But it leaves open the possibility that they could have been.

Turning from theory to practice, Paul Christesen (2003) asked in what sense the economic behavior of Athenians of the fourth century BCE was rational. Borrowing the typology of Shaun Hargreaves Heap (1989), Christensen divided economic rationality into instrumental (preference-driven, per the "folk theory"), procedural (rule-following and status-driven), and expressive (agents are reflexively self-conscious about preferences but also respond to norms—roughly, the position of many experimental behavioralists). He then demonstrated the prevalence of instrumental rationality in Athenian economic activity, notably contracting for mine leases and investment choices predicated on balancing expected returns against risk. Christesen rejected the commonly held belief that Greek economic rationality was primarily procedural, concluding that the "mixed form" of expressive rationality best captures economic practice in the age of Plato and Aristotle. We return to Greek theories of economic behavior in chapter 7. For now, the important point is that the social context of fourth-century Greek theory featured observable behavior that was readily explained by what I have been calling the "Greek folk theory of instrumental rationality."

Game Theory and the Greeks

The systematic use of formal theory in humanistic disciplines is still relatively uncommon, but far from unknown. Game-theoretic analysis of early modern political thought is an established genre: For example, the arguments of Thomas Hobbes have been analyzed in formal terms by (among others) David Gauthier (1969), Jean Hampton (1988), Peter Stone (2015), and Hun Chung (2015); those of David Hume by Russell Hardin (2007); Jean-Jacques Rousseau's Stag Hunt thought experiment is analyzed in game-theoretic terms by Brian Skyrms (2001, 2004).

Game theory has been applied to historical events and literary texts since the early days of formal theory, although "game theory and literature have their own coordination problem, with game theorists and literary analysts not often benefiting from each others' insights" (Brams 1994, quote p. 52). The work of the game theorist Steven Brams on biblical narrative (Brams [1980] 2003), and on topics in fiction, theology, history, philosophy, and law (Brams 2011), is especially prominent. Robert Bates et al., in *Analytic Narratives* (1998), extended the formal analysis of historical cases. In *Rational Ritual: Culture, Coordination, and Common Knowledge* (Chwe 2001), Michael Chwe analyzes a range of collective behavior in various cultures, showing that what might appear to be "irrational" rituals are in fact explicable in cost-benefit terms, once one accounts for the value of common knowledge in facilitating incentive-compatible social coordination. Chwe (2013) also argues that the novelist Jane Austen had a full (albeit nonmathematical) appreciation for the intuitions about preferences, beliefs, and strategic behavior that underpin contemporary game theory. Chwe suggests that Austen has things to teach game theorists, notably in accounting for agents who appear extremely bad at strategic reasoning, the phenomenon that Chwe (borrowing a term from the popular 1995 Amy Heckerling film) calls "cluelessness." Bannerjee (2018) extends Chwe's game-theoretic analysis of Austen.

The literature exploring analogies to formal theory in ancient Greek literature is relatively small. The closest thing to a survey is an essay by William Charron, "Greeks and Games: Forerunners of Modern Game Theory" (2000). Charron discussed three examples of Greek thinkers anticipating modern game theory: Aristotle's concern for rationality as consistency of beliefs, Plato's and Epicurus' interest in measuring attitudinal states, and Thucydides' understanding of the logic of individual rational choices in strategic situations. Paralleling game-theoretic approaches to early modern political philosophers, there has been some interest in analyzing the "Ring of Gyges" thought experiment in Plato, *Republic* book 2 (chapter 1.2), in game-theoretic terms. David Gauthier (1986) suggests that the Ring of Gyges fable offers a challenge to contractarian theories of morality, through its suggestion that the reality of exploitation lurks in any understanding of human motivation modeled on "economic man." Brian Barry (1989: 6–7, following Rawls 1958: 174–75 with n. 9) makes the association with game theory explicit, suggesting that Plato's Ring of Gyges is the first literary expression of a theory that is worked out in more detail in works by Hobbes, Hume, and modern decision and game theorists. More recently, Hun Chung (2016) has offered a game-theoretic analysis of the inconsistency between Thrasymachus' and Glaucon's accounts of instrumental rationality in *Republic* books 1 and 2, with specific reference to the Prisoner's Dilemma game, and Halkos, Kyriazis, and Economou (2021) model a passage in *Republic* book 2 as a repeated Prisoner's Dilemma (see further, chapter 2). Benjamin Straumann (2020) analyzes a passage in Polybius' history as an assurance game, suggesting that Polybius' "naturalistic, proto–game-theoretical views show similarities with Hume, Smith and especially Hobbes' doctrine of sovereignty by acquisition" (see chapter 3.7–8). And in *Thucydides, Father of Game Theory* (in progress), a revised version of her 2015 PhD thesis, Manuela dal Borgo develops a full-scale narratological analysis of Thucydides' history of the Peloponnesian War, with detailed recourse to game-theoretic arguments.

Turning to institutional and social practice, there is a growing literature by economists analyzing a range of ancient Greek (and especially Athenian) fiscal, political, and legal institutions in game-theoretic terms, in some cases with mathematical models.[55] Within the field of Greek history, James Quillin (2002) and Gabriel Herman (2006: chap. 10) pioneered the use of game-theoretic reasoning to explain the relative lack of "eye for an eye" retaliatory norms and behavior in democratic Athens. Other historians, inspired by the scholarship and courses of my Stanford University colleague Barry Weingast, incorporate rational choice analysis in book-length treatments of Greek institutions: David Teegarden (2014) shows that Greek laws on tyrant killing were designed

---

55. See, for example, Lyttkens 1997, 2006, 2012; Kyriazis and Zouboulakis 2004; Fleck and Hanssen 2006, 2009, 2012, 2019; Kaiser 2007; Kyriazis 2007, 2009; Tangian 2008; Guha 2011; Kyriazis and Economou 2013; McCannon 2010a, 2010b, 2011, 2012; Tridimas 2011, 2012, 2013, 2015, 2016, 2017; Arvanitidis and Kyriazis 2013; Lyttkens, Tridimas, and Lindgren 2018.

to create incentives for first-movers to resist tyrants by violence, thus deterring would-be revolutionaries from challenging democratic regimes. Matthew Simonton (2017) analyzes the strategic design of oligarchic institutions as systematically obstructing the emergence of common knowledge among prodemocracy sectors of the population, thus forestalling effective collective action. Federica Carugati (2019) offers a full-scale cost-benefit analysis of Athenian elite and mass choices in the aftermath of the Peloponnesian War and, in a series of articles, employs formal games to explain otherwise puzzling features of Athenian legal institutions.[56] My own recent work, some of it coauthored with Barry Weingast, has employed extensive-form games to illustrate problems in Greek institutional history.[57]

0.6 OUTLINE OF THE BOOK

The narrative arc of the remaining chapters starts with the motives for action of the rational individual, then moves to the problem of the emergence of social order and sustained social cooperation among many self-interested persons. We next turn to the question of political authority, looking first at monarchy, then at the constitutional bargaining that led to Athens' citizen-centered regime. After considering the issue of rationality in interstate relations, we turn to the puzzle of democratic state performance. With individual psychology and political rationality thus established, we circle back to the economic choices made by individuals in the context of developed states. The book's conclusion concerns the role of utility in ancient Greek and contemporary theories of human flourishing, and the relationship between instrumental and ethical approaches to rationality.

Chapter 1 describes how, in book 1 of Plato's *Republic,* the Sophist Thrasymachus offers a narrowly egoistic version of the Greek folk theory, premised on the choices that would be made by an unerring craftsman of self-interest. Thrasymachus' approach is refined in a thought experiment in book 2 of the *Republic*. Plato's story of "Gyges and the ring of invisibility" was based on an anecdote in Herodotus' *Histories,* describing how Gyges became king of Lydia. In Herodotus' story, Gyges' options are constrained by other characters, introducing the problem of strategic reason. Because, in Plato's version of the story,

---

56. See further, Carugati and Weingast 2018; Carugati, Calvert, and Weingast 2021.
57. For example: Ober 2012, 2013, 2017a; Ober and Weingast 2018.

invisible Gyges did just as he pleased, ideal-type individual preferences are revealed by the socially unconstrained choices of an infallibly self-interested agent.

Chapter 2 turns to social dilemmas, especially the problem of how a beneficial social order could emerge and persist in a population of self-interested persons. The Greek tradition of political thought understood that cooperation was an imperative for human survival, but cooperation was a problem in light of self-interest and strategic reasoning: Inferior outcomes (payoffs for all agents are lower than in feasible alternatives) can arise from individually rational choices. Moreover, an inferior outcome can take the form of a stable equilibrium. Greek theorists proposed thought-experimental solutions to the game of cooperation by focusing on coordinated responses to existential threats, revising the assumed motivations of self-interested players to include the interests of others, and postulating repeated play with communication and learning.

Chapter 3 moves from social order to the constitutional question of political rule and governance, which becomes pressing in the context of large and complex states. The Greeks supposed that monarchy was the original form of political authority. Herodotus offers two case studies of the establishment of monarchy in western Asia. First is the story of how Deioces, an expert at legal arbitration, was chosen as king of the Medes. Next is the story of how a small group of Persian nobles first decided that Persia should remain a monarchy, rather than an oligarchy or a democracy, and then chose one of their number as king. In each story, Herodotus emphasizes that reason-giving in open deliberations preceded a vote and shows how procedures of public choice are vulnerable to strategic manipulation. Polybius offers a conjectural history of the emergence of primitive monarchy. He shows how, through the evolution of shared social norms, despotism, as the rule of the strongest, transitions to a constitutional kingship in which the rational ruler's position is stabilized by the active support of his rational subjects.

Chapter 4 turns to the question of rule by citizens. The citizen-centered legislative program attributed by the Greek tradition, as exemplified by Aristotle and Plutarch, to the early-sixth-century Athenian lawgiver Solon offers a bargaining solution to the problem of order in a society polarized by inequality and threatened by strife. Democracy was established in the late sixth century by a revolution, narrated by Herodotus. The revolution succeeded because both the demos of Athens and leaders of factions proved capable of acting as rational agents and committing to future cooperation in the face of uncertainty. Thucydides proposed rational leadership, manifest in expert risk assessment and rhetorical skill, and aimed at the provision of public goods, as the explanation for Athens' postrevolutionary, early- to mid-fifth-century rise to greatness.

Chapter 5 concerns rationality in relations between states, exploring both zero-sum conflicts and positive-sum bargains. Plato's *Republic* addresses war and interstate bargaining in the idealized state of Callipolis, foregrounding the measurement of risk for effective military policy. Thucydides' history is an extended treatment of both interstate conflict and bargaining. He offers the fifth-century Athenian empire as a case study in rational cooperation among unequal states, predicated on calculated costs and benefits. Athens' imperial policy rested on the rationality of fear and self-interest. Because Athens could credibly commit to moderate taxes in exchange for high levels of cooperation, rational subjects had no reason to defect from the coalition. But defect they did. Thucydides' narrative of the revolt of Mytilene explores the motives of the defectors and the implications for Athenian imperial policy. The limits of ideal-type rationality are foregrounded in Thucydides' account of the events leading to the destruction of the small island state of Melos, centered on the failed bargain chronicled in the Melian Dialogue.

Chapter 6 juxtaposes political theory with historical practice. In *Republic* book 8, Plato depicts democracy as fatally beset by unstable preference-ranking among available options, arising from democratic commitments to both freedom and equality. Yet Plato elsewhere acknowledged the capacity for the Athenian demos to identify and follow the lead of trustworthy experts in various domains relevant to material well-being. Recent historical reconstructions of the operation of innovative Athenian legislative, judicial, and executive institutions help to explain how a diverse body of citizens consistently converged on a best-available option. As a result, fourth-century-BCE Athens provides a model of an instrumentally rational state with self-enforcing, yet revisable and adaptive, rules. The rationality of the Athenian state enabled individuals and groups to pursue their goals while sustaining the public goods of security and welfare.

Chapter 7 returns to economic relations among individuals. Homer's *Iliad* offers a paradigm case of archaic cooperative failure and costly conflicts over distribution of goods taken by force by the strong. The alternative was mutually beneficial exchange. Modern neoclassical economists sometimes claim that open markets themselves produce efficient exchanges among individuals. But the Greek tradition recognized that sustained, efficient cooperation demands self-enforcing rules. What was gained was efficiency in production and exchange of goods and services, leading to growing public and private wealth, increased state capacity, and private opportunity for free males. But, in the view of Socratic philosophy, much had been lost. Economic rationality risked corrupting interpersonal relations by reducing utility to material gain and decoupling willful action from virtue.

Chapter 8 summarizes the results of previous chapters and then returns to the original, mid-fifth-century discovery of practical reason through a reading of Aeschylus' tragedy *Eumenides*. The play presents instrumental rationality as both a solution to cooperation problems and a problem for just relations among gods and mortals. The classical Socratics emphasized threats to ethical reason posed by instrumentalism, notably in the domain of friendship. But they also recognized that the rational pursuit of self-interest was an ineliminable aspect of practical reason and therefore an essential foundation for human flourishing. The chapter concludes with an assessment of the role of instrumental rationality in contemporary political and ethical theory. The Greek tradition shows that rationality can provide the foundation for normatively demanding and robustly sustainable systems of social cooperation. Viewing instrumental rationality as a fundamental human capacity is, moreover, consistent with the recognition that there are irreducible limits to human reason and that theorizing strategic behavior has costs as well as benefits.

CHAPTER I

Gyges' Choice

Rationality and Visibility

How can we know what other people really want? The Greek folk theory of practical reasoning sketched in the introduction held that a rationally self-interested agent will go for the feasible option that best accords with her desires and beliefs. In the terminology of contemporary choice theory, this is the one that maximizes her expected utility. The set of feasible options available to the agent is, however, typically constrained by choices of others. Options are, furthermore, limited by choices made in the past and canonized as laws, norms, and action-guiding beliefs about justice and morality. These social constraints are strengthened by habitual behavior. While, as we saw, the Conventionalist variant of the folk theory asserted the naturalness of rational obedience to the rules, the Thrasymachean variant saw obedience to socially imposed constraints on self-aggrandizement as contrary to nature. In any event, the ubiquity and complexity of constraints serving to limit any given individual's option set make it difficult for an observer to infer an agent's highest-ranked preferences by observing her actions.

Capturing the underpinnings of individual motivation "in the wild" required stripping away those constraints. That is the imaginative task that Socrates' interlocutors undertake in the second book of Plato's *Republic*. In the fanciful story of Gyges of Lydia and his ring of invisibility, Plato presents Gyges as an ideal-type, socially unconstrained, rationally self-interested agent. Comparing Plato's tale of "Gyges and the ring" with an earlier story of Gyges, narrated by the historian

Herodotus, differentiates unconstrained decisions from strategic choices, and therefore contemporary decision theory from game theory. By adding a magic ring to Herodotus' story of lust, betrayal, murder, and usurpation, Plato reduced a complex narrative of strategic choice-making under conditions of uncertainty, in which individuals were forced to take account of others' preferences and beliefs, to an analysis of individual motivation and willed action. He did so to further his philosophical project: setting up the challenge to Socrates of proving that justice is, in and of itself, preferable to injustice.

1.1 THE CHOSEN PATH: GLAUCON'S THOUGHT EXPERIMENT

By the end of the first book of Plato's *Republic,* a conversation on the topic of justice has reached the dead-end characteristic of Plato's earlier Socratic dialogues. The first book concludes with Socrates' refutation of the Sophist Thrasymachus, who had argued for one version of what we are calling the folk theory of practical reasoning.[1] Thrasymachus rejected the usual form of arguments made by Conventionalist proponents of the folk theory, who sought to show that it was actually in the best interest of every individual to act justly, that is, giving and taking according to established norms, and to obey the laws (introduction, section 0.4).

Thrasymachus asserted that justice was nothing other than the advantage of the stronger (*Republic* 338c). The strong take what they want from the weak, just as shepherds do with their sheep (343a–b). In political terms, this meant that rulers—whether they happen to be a majority in a democracy, or a few oligarchs, or a monarch—will use political power to establish rules maximizing their own advantages at the expense of subjects (338d, 343b–c). Justice, as the advantage of the strong, is, from the viewpoint of the weak, the good of another: The weak subject promotes the good of the strong ruler at his own expense, by obeying the rules and thereby harming himself (343c). A ruler who seeks the good of his subjects likewise harms himself. He shows himself to be, in fact, weak and is therefore miserable. Injustice, by contrast, is one's own good, gained at others' expense. The tyrant, as absolute ruler,

---

1. I refer to the character "Thrasymachus" in the *Republic;* the surviving fragments of works by the Sophist Thrasymachus (LM 35) do not focus on narrow egoism. Thrasymachus' argument in *Republic* book I is discussed in Kerferd 1947; Hourani 1962; Irwin 1977: 30 with n. 24; Everson 1998; Barney 2006, 2017; Wedgwood 2017a.

has the fullest opportunity to satisfy his preferences by exploitation of his subjects. So, a rational person concerned with his own advantage and profit will seek tyranny, as "complete injustice." Should he achieve it, he can expect to be called happy and blessed (343c–44c).

Socrates' questioning yielded the important point, asserted by Thrasymachus and not contested by Socrates, that the true "craftsman" (*dēmiourgos*) of self-interest never errs in his assessment of how best to pursue his own interest: "A ruler, insofar as he is a ruler, never makes errors and unerringly decrees [*tithesthai*] what is best for himself" (340e–41a).[2] There is an ambiguity here, deftly exploited by Socrates, between "decreeing what is best for himself" as "achieving what the agent wants" (the perfection is in the means he employs to gain his subjectively valued ends) and "what is objectively best for him" (the perfection is in the ends he chooses). Taken in the first way (perfect means), Thrasymachus' ideal craftsman of self-interest resembles the choice theorist's idealized rational agent, who employs complete information and unlimited cognitive capacity when calculating how his highest-ranked preferences may best be satisfied, given the available options.

Socrates ultimately leads a blushing Thrasymachus to concede, grudgingly, that justice, properly so understood, is virtue and wisdom (350d) and that injustice is never more profitable (*lusitelesteron*) than justice (354a).[3] But Thrasymachus clearly remains unconvinced by the propositions to which he has been led to accede, and Plato's readers are still in the dark about why justice is desirable as an end if it fails to produce the goods that most people seem to want most. In the second book of the dialogue, two of Socrates' interlocutors, Plato's brothers Glaucon and Adeimantus, propose a new beginning for the inquiry. Claiming (358b) that Thrasymachus was charmed by Socrates, "too soon, like a snake," Glaucon proposes to revive Thrasymachus' argument, predicating it directly on the beliefs of ordinary people about how choices are made.[4]

---

2. On Thrasymachus' unerring craftsman as an ideal type and Socrates' acceptance of the ideal type, see Nawar 2018. On the conception of a complete "art" that must account for the possibility of failure that is implied in this passage, see J. Allen 1994: 87–89: the true craftsman may fail in his results, but he never fails as a craftsman, qua craftsman, or at his craft. As Allen points out, this places the full onus on the performance of the craftsman; other ancient conceptions of failure appeal to external circumstances or luck.

3. Socrates' refutation of Thrasymachus is detailed in Irwin 1995: 174–80.

4. Ferrari (2003) cogently analyzes Plato's characterization of the two brothers in the dialogue, and their role in advancing its argument.

Glaucon announces his program: He will first state what kind of thing "people say justice is and where it comes from" (see chapter 2.1). Then he will show that those who practice justice do so unwillingly (*akontes*), as if under constraint (*hōs anangkaion*), in order to avoid the worst outcome. They do not act justly because they think it a positive good, for the life of an unjust person is much better than that of a just one, "as they say." This is not, he hastens to add, his own opinion, but an argument he has heard from Thrasymachus "and a myriad of others" (358b–c). In brief, the two brothers plan to produce a philosophically rigorous version of the Thrasymachean variant of the folk theory of practical reasoning. They evidently believe that the standard Conventionalist arguments for the rationality of legal obedience and acting in accordance with justice are actually Thrasymachean arguments in disguise. Thus, if justice, as something other than the advantage of the strong, is to be defended, it must be on a new and firmer foundation.

The brothers' explicit goal is to prepare the ground so that Socrates can proceed to demonstrate the true relationship between justice and happiness (*eudaimonia*): why justice is a choice-worthy end in itself, even after it has been divorced from extraneous instrumental considerations, and why the just person will invariably be happier than the unjust. In order to embark on that enterprise (which requires the construction of a theory of moral psychology and an ideal state, and which will not be completed until the last book of the long dialogue), Plato's readers must have a prior understanding of what most Greeks believed about human motivation. We need to grasp what lies behind an ostensibly rational, but nonphilosophical, individual's choice to act in some specific way, when he or she is seeking to achieve some desired goal. Before coming to terms with the rationality of ends, a theme that Socrates will develop in the course of the dialogue, readers must be reintroduced to an ordinary, but heretofore inadequately theorized, sort of practical reasoning. This is the rationality of means: the process of choice-making that, according to modern theories of rational choice, underpins goal-oriented human behavior in the phenomenal world.[5]

5. On the challenge offered by Glaucon and Adeimantus and the philosophical purposes to which the story of Gyges is put by Plato, see Kirwan 1965; Gauthier 1986; Barry 1989: 6–7; Irwin 1995: chap. 12, 1999; Shields 2006; Williams 2006: chap. 6; Weiss 2007; C. C. W. Taylor 2007: 13–19; Reeve 2008. Annas (1981: 64–71) argues that "we live in a world where we have to take account of the natural and artificial consequences of injustice, and it is merely silly to ask what we would do if we escaped these by having magic rings" (p. 69). She concludes that by the inclusion of the Gyges story, Plato shows

Like Socrates, Glaucon and Adeimantus believe that ordinary people are *not* ethically rational. That is, they do not consistently want what is truly best for themselves. Nor do they consistently go for what is best by employing true beliefs about the world. The brothers want Socrates to demonstrate to them, in a form that will survive attacks by critics, that, despite appearances to the contrary, justice (being a just person and always acting accordingly) is more desirable than the goals sought by ordinary people. They want Socrates to show that justice is not reducible to an instrument aimed at any goal other than ultimate and genuinely highest ends. They want Socrates to refute the argument that an ethically rational person would ever employ practical reasoning to gain an unjust outcome (say, being a tyrant). Glaucon and Adeimantus accordingly devise a philosophical challenge that is designed to be as demanding as possible, so that Socrates' final demonstration can be defended against the objection that the relationship of justice to happiness was not tested against the hardest imaginable case (Irwin 1995: 188–89).

The challenge takes the form of an extended thought experiment. Glaucon first establishes that, according to a commonly held view ("they say . . ."), people originally established and now obey law only because no one is in a position to do injustice (seek only his own advantage) with impunity in the face of similarly self-interested others. We will consider that argument in detail in chapter 2. He then sets out the counterfactual condition to which Socrates' defense of the inherent value of justice must be a refutation:

> We can see most clearly that those who practice [justice] do it unwillingly and because they lack the power to do injustice, if we construct something like this in thought [*dianoia*]: we grant to an [ostensibly] "just" and an [explicitly] unjust person the freedom [*exousia*] to do whatever they like. Then we may follow along, seeing where desire [*epithumia*] leads each one of them. We should then catch the just man, self-revealed, going along to the same destination as the unjust man, because of the striving to gain more and more [*pleonexia*] that every creature by its nature pursues as a good. (Plato, *Republic* 359b–c)

The image that Plato invites his readers to form in their minds is one of following and observing someone as he travels on a chosen path,

---

that his theory of justice is not meant to be realistic. While the *Republic* is certainly not meant to be merely realistic, I think Annas misses the point of the Gyges story as a thought experiment aimed at separating what she describes as "natural and artificial consequences." The applicability of the Gyges story to real-world social conditions is defended in Irwin 1995: 186–87, 1999.

aiming to get to his desired destination. The translation of G.M.A. Grube (revised by C.D.C. Reeve: Hackett edition, 1997) makes this explicit: "We'll catch the just person red-handed travelling the same road as the unjust."[6] Glaucon explains that the reason that both persons will, if free to do so, follow the same path is the universal and natural drive of *pleonexia:* striving to get more and more.[7] Fulfilling that general preference to get more of whatever one happens to desire, to maximize advantage (here defined, with Thrasymachus, narrowly egoistically—as advantage *only* to oneself), he concludes, is what any individual would naturally choose as good for himself in a condition of pristine freedom in which his highest-order desires align neatly with his expectations.

A Conventionalist theorist might point to the observed norm-obedient behavior of most people to buttress an argument that obedience is natural. But natural, socially unconstrained choice-making is, Glaucon claims, not often in evidence in the phenomenal world because top-ranked outcomes are absent from the feasible option set whenever people are forced by social convention (*nomos*) to respect issues of equity (*ton ison:* 359c). The difference between the apparently just and the explicitly unjust man, Glaucon suggests, has nothing to do with their preferences over outcomes. It is entirely a matter of the reputation each happens to have. The "just man" is not truly just, in that he acts out of moral principles different from those of the unjust man. He is only apparently just: He has a reputation for being just that he does not deserve. Either he has not been caught breaking rules or he is too afraid of the likely consequences to take the chance of doing so. The "unjust man" acts in accordance with his preferences and is unlucky enough to have been discovered doing so. He thereby gained a bad reputation for breaking the same rules that the "just" man would break if he could do so with impunity. Glaucon here asserts that the ultimate driver of human action, the motivation of all freely chosen behavior, is the attempt to satisfy personal, subjective preferences.

The deeper truth about human motivation is assumed, in Glaucon's challenge, to be obscured by the noise or, adopting Grube's road meta-

---

6. Compare Davis 1983: 61: "The game theorist, to paraphrase Lewis Carroll, must pick the proper road after being told the player's destination; and players don't need to know anything about game theory, but they have to know what they like." On the road as a metaphor for the kind of life one leads in Plato and elsewhere in Greek literature, see Laird 2001: 16–17; Bakewell 2020.

7. On the meaning of the Greek term *pleonexia* as the desire to have more and more, without regard for the claims of others, see introduction, n. 52.

phor, the "heavy traffic" of *ordinary human behavior*. That is: behavior under conditions in which each individual's options are constrained by considerations arising from the expected responses of others to his or her choices. Responses may be by individuals pursuing their own interests (the members of the punishing multitude in the thought experiment proposed by the Anonymous Iamblichi: see introduction). Or, at the societal level, through the coercive force of laws and through cultural norms bearing on reputation and threatening divine sanction (the mystifying ideology described by Plato's Callicles: chapter 2.3). The basic idea is that, because the road to our most-preferred outcome is so often blocked by social traffic, we must ordinarily take less-desirable paths and end up at less-preferred destinations.

But, the challenge asserts, freed from these constraints, absent any concern for the social consequences of acting according to our actual preferences, each individual would ignore the interests of others and inconvenient rules, and would always travel the road that leads directly to the expectation of having more and more of whatever is most desired. The need to clear the road of the traffic of ordinary behavior, in order to test intuitions about justice and choice, is the context in which Glaucon narrates how a shepherd became a king—the first extended tale in a dialogue famous for its memorable images, allegories, and stories.

1.2 THE STORY OF GYGES' RING

Glaucon's story concerns "an ancestor of Gyges the Lydian." Following a convention long-standing among commentators on this passage, I will simply call him Gyges.[8] At the beginning of the story, Gyges is a shepherd in the king's service—and so, presumably the reader is to imagine (based on Greek social conventions: Roy 2012) that he is poor, lacks a social network that includes influential persons, and spends much of his time alone with his flock. One day a thunderstorm and earthquake opens a chasm at the place where Gyges is tending his sheep. Gyges descends and sees many wonders. The only wonder that is described is

8. Plato's Gyges story and its origins: Laird 2001; Danzig 2008; see further, below, 1.6. Many commentators have taken the protagonist of the book 2 narrative to be named Gyges on the basis of *Republic* 10 (612b): Socrates refers to "the ring of Gyges" (*ton Gugou daktulion*). See, however, Adam and Rees (1963: 126–27 = book 2 appendix 1) for the difficulty and various possible solutions. See further, Laird 2001: 14–15. I will suggest, below (section 1.9), a reason that Plato might have chosen to speak of an "ancestor of Gyges" in book 2.

a hollow bronze horse. It has windows in its sides, through which Gyges spots an oversized corpse wearing only a gold ring. From this point in the story to its end, Gyges acts completely selfishly and systematically in gaining his desired ends. Violating the norm forbidding grave-robbing, Gyges takes the ring and soon discovers that it has the power to render him invisible. Gyges then arranges—how, we are not told—to become "one of the messengers sent to report to the King." After arriving at the palace, he "seduced the King's wife, attacked the King with her help, and took over the kingdom" (359c–60c). So, the story ends with Gyges, having ascended from the bottom to the peak of Lydian society, apparently amply rewarded for acting entirely in his own self-interest.

Having completed his tale, Glaucon stipulates that the two hypothetical persons, one thought to be just and the other unjust, are provided with invisibility rings.[9] He specifies that the unjust man, for his part, will do what he pleases in complete secrecy. Moreover, taking over a key concept from Socrates' earlier conversation with Thrasymachus, Glaucon specifies that he will be a perfect craftsman of self-interest (360e–61a). Either he makes no errors (that is, he will always make choices that fulfill his preferences for having more and more) or, failing that, he will always be able to correct his errors. Glaucon proposes that under these conditions, the perfectly unjust and the ostensibly just man, as noted above, would behave in an identical self-serving way: He lists as the predicted behaviors stealing goods from the market with impunity, entering other men's homes to have sex with whomever he pleases, and doing all the other things that would make him equal to a god among humans.[10] Both men would, he concludes, proceed to precisely the same place (360c).

Unsurprisingly, these predicated behaviors track the actions of Thrasymachus' tyrant-craftsman of self-interest (344a–b) and of Gyges. Plato's Gyges story begins with the theft of the ring under presumed conditions of secrecy: Gyges is evidently alone when he enters the chasm, and even if someone happens upon the chasm later, no one need know that the corpse was wearing a ring or that Gyges was ever there.

---

9. Note that Plato first offers an accessible narrative, followed by abstraction: the compelling narrative about a person with a background story (Gyges the Lydian shepherd), immediately followed by a discussion of abstract agents (the "two men"). The reader is thereby dissuaded from reading anything into Gyges' background by, for example, imagining that his motivation is specific to someone in a certain social role. My thanks for Demetra Kasimis for pressing me on this point.

10. Note that being *isotheos* "equal to a god" is comparable to being *eudaimōn*, literally "well-godded." Here the reference is clearly to subjective preference satisfaction.

Gyges then uses the ring to enter the palace, have sex with the queen, and, having killed the king with her help, gain political power—the control of the famously wealthy kingdom.[11] Thus, we are to suppose that the package of goods that would be maximized by any person unconstrained by social rules reduces to wealth, sex, and power.

The value of the ring of invisibility to the thought experiment is underlined when Glaucon specifies that the rule-breaking of the unjust man will *never* be found out—so, not only will there be no punishment, but there will be no reputation cost, now or ever, for doing exactly as he pleases (361a). Moreover, Adeimantus adds a lengthy addendum to the thought experiment, specifying that there will be no divine retribution for rule breaking (362d–66b). Despite all his misdeeds, the perfectly unjust man will be loved, not hated, by the gods, because with his stolen wealth he will be able to perform all requisite sacrifices and other god-pleasing rituals. So, the unjust individual is unconstrained by "third party" divine authority or concerns about punishment for wrongdoing in some putative afterlife. Gyges, we may suppose, really will live happily ever after—at least according to the egoistical standard of having more and more.

Finally, neither in the Gyges story nor in the follow-up account of the two ("just" and unjust) men is there any meaningful element of chance (at least after the ring has been found and its powers discovered). Gyges and the "two men" in Glaucon's thought experiment act as if they were certain of the outcomes of their choices and actions. The absence of uncertainty in the experiment is underlined by Adeimantus' addendum stipulating the permanence of good reputation and the benevolent attitude of the gods.

1.3 PLATO ON RATIONALITY OF MEANS AND ENDS

The conclusion of the thought experiment, then, is that every individual, when completely free from extraneous social considerations, will seek to satisfy his own preferences, pursuing his own self-interest in a

---

11. If we assume, as I think we should, that Gyges exemplifies an individual ruled by appetite (per the *Republic*'s later explication of the tripartite soul), the passage suggests that appetite is indeed capable of instrumental reasoning (cf. introduction n. 16): Gyges advances toward his apparent final goal (kingship) by sequential, evidently planned, steps: messenger, seduction, murder. Why the queen, having been somehow seduced by an invisible man, then helped him to kill her husband, and how Gyges then gained the kingship remain opaque in Plato's story. Contrast Herodotus' story of Gyges, below, in which the queen's motivation is made clear and Gyges must overcome opposition to gain the kingship.

purposeful manner, and that he will identify his own self-interest as gaining possession of desired goods. A person who achieves that position will be "equal to a god." The goods in question are summed up, in the Gyges story and in Glaucon's subsequent argument, as consumer goods (the things that can be bought or stolen in the market), access to sex, and power over others.

Because the socially unconstrained individual expects that such things will make him maximally happy (i.e., godlike), we may call this the premise of maximization of expected subjective value: happiness as utility or advantage. Thus:

> *Maximization.* Expected value is maximized when an agent makes choices that result in satisfying his preferences.

A second, implicit, premise of ranking complements the first.

> *Ranking.* The agent's preferences over outcomes are hierarchically rank-ordered.

In Glaucon's story the relevant ranking for an unconstrained agent is (1) having wealth/sex/power; (2) living according to the norms of justice/law; (3) being punished for lawbreaking.

While we do not know how Gyges or the unjust man ranks wealth against sex or power, Gyges demonstrates unambiguously by his actions upon the opening of the chasm, and then upon learning the power of the ring, that he prefers the package of wealth, sex, and power to acting according to a conventional conception of justice and not having those goods. After all, he could have chosen to leave the ring on the finger of the corpse, could have left the king's wife alone and not attacked the king's person. But clearly, he expected to gain greater advantage by stealing, seducing, attacking, and ruling.

Likewise, Gyges' rule-abiding life before gaining the ring (Glaucon calls him a shepherd and servant, not an outlaw) shows that he preferred *not* to suffer the consequences of being caught breaking the established rules. In conformity with Glaucon's description of the everyday behavior of most people, before the chasm opened Gyges acted "justly"—that is, he obeyed the established rules forbidding theft, etc. But he did so only because he expected bad consequences to himself were he to break them.

In more formal terms, we may say that if X is having the preference-satisfying goods, Y is living an ordinary rule-obedient existence, and Z is paying the penalty for being caught breaking the rules, Gyges' preferences are ranked in the order X > Y > Z. The ranking of these ordinal preferences is *transitive:* that is to say, he never prefers Z to X; if he did, his decision process would be incoherent.[12] The coherence of Gyges' decision process is demonstrated by the sequence of choices that ended in the goal state (ruling) that was, according to Thrasymachus, the acme of narrowly self-interested behavior. If we suppose, furthermore, that {X, Y, Z} is the full set of feasible options, then his preference ranking is also *complete.* With complete and transitive ranking of feasible options we have fulfilled the standard preconditions for a formally rational choice.

Gyges' choice of which option to pursue in action will be determined by his beliefs about the likelihood of each outcome. Since invisibility renders his action undetectable by others, it eliminates uncertainty: He is (per the logic of the story) certain to gain whatever end he pursues. He is at no risk of failure or of being punished. Thus, in predicting his behavior, there is no need to weigh the cardinal strength of his preferences (how *much* he prefers X to Y to Z). With risk of failure and punishment eliminated, his ordinal ranking is all that matters.[13]

Plato makes a point of emphasizing that behavior that accords with *Maximization* and *Ranking* is, in the view of most people, *rational* behavior: Glaucon states that, for someone who (like Gyges with the ring) *does* have the power to satisfy his preferences just as he pleases, to accept any limits on that power by making a binding agreement with someone else to abstain from doing injustice would be seen as irrational in multiple senses. He would be regarded as "insane" (*mainesthai:* 359b). Moreover, such a person would be thought of as "completely wretched and utterly senseless" by any honest observer of his situation (i.e., anyone not constrained to say otherwise by worries about social rules: 360d). Plato links the conception of rationality as correctly calculating the means to one's most desired ends with an assumption that those ends will be egoistically self-interested. He does this, as we have seen, by having Glaucon borrow Thrasymachus' stipulation that the unjust man must be a true craftsman (*dēmiourgos*) of self-interest,

---

12. If transitivity is violated, so that Z > X, then a cycle ensues, and so no option is consistently top-ranked, thereby inducing formal irrationality. See further, chapter 3.5. Note that > is, in practice, ≥.

13. The fundamental unreality of decision-making in the absence of uncertainty and the vacuity for real-world choices of hypotheticals that assume epistemic certainty over outcomes are emphasized by Fried (2018, 2020). Plato concedes the point by predicating his hypothetical explicitly on the conceit of an invisibility ring.

unerring in his calculations of what is best for himself. The perfectly unjust man will be able to correct any mistakes he makes in regard to what is obtainable and what is not (360e–61b).

The premises of *Maximization* and *Ranking* roughly track the definition of rationality in contemporary choice theory.[14] For Glaucon's instrumentally rational exemplar, expected subjective value stands in for what classical philosophers, including Plato, took as the correct standard—*eudaimonia*—as the condition that is desired by the rational individual. This matters, for our purposes, insofar as *eudaimonia* was understood by the classical Socratics to concern *true* human interests. For Plato (along with Aristotle and other ancient moral philosophers) *eudaimonia* was an objective state. The theory of rationality that Socrates will develop in the course of the *Republic* is normative in a moralized sense that theories of instrumental rationality, ancient and modern, are not. I will suggest, below, that Plato's Socrates accepts *Maximization* and *Ranking* but adds a further stipulation: Preferences must be *right* preferences (that is, desire only for ends that are *genuine* goods), and beliefs must be *true*—knowledge (not just opinion) about the value of outcomes as well as about how desired outcomes are best obtained.

In order to realize (moralized, objective) *eudaimonia,* the choice-maker's actions must follow from the expectations that emerge when both preferences and beliefs are morally, objectively correct. Since (per Plato's metaphysics) seeming and being are radically disjoint realms, quotidian preferences and beliefs typically come apart from right preferences and true beliefs. They are only securely and consistently conjoined under the very special conditions pertaining, for example, in the *Republic*'s ideal state of Callipolis. There, a fully informed rule-breaking Gyges would in fact prefer Z (punishment) to X (unjustly taking sex, wealth, power) because he will realize that, given that he has done wrong, punishment (in the form of correction of his mistake in pursuing an end that is not objectively valuable) is in his true interest: It will maximize his true advantage.

We will return to *eudaimonia* in chapter 8. For our present purposes, the important point is that in book 2, Plato has designed a thought experiment aimed at clarifying how most people in his original Greek audience would make choices and act in regard to others if two condi-

---

14. E.g., Dixit and Skeath 1999: 27: "rationality has two essential ingredients: complete knowledge of one's own interests, and flawless calculation of what action will best serve those interests."

tions held: First, if they could ignore the preferences of others and thus be free of social "traffic." And, next, if they could be certain that a choice among options would result in a specified outcome—if chance were eliminated from the equation. Glaucon's thought experiment clearly establishes the grounding of rationality in preferences and beliefs. It draws a causal arrow pointing from the expectations associated with sets of preferences and beliefs to the choices and actions made by individuals and, as we will see, rational collectivities.

The story of Gyges' ring advances the instrumental rationality thought experiment by, in contemporary parlance, backing away from the complexities of a game with multiple players, to a decision that centers on the psychological processes involved with individual choice. Moreover, as we have seen, it eliminates uncertainty. The introduction of the conceit of the ring of invisibility allows Gyges to satisfy his top-ranked preference without social constraint or doubt about results, to behave in unproblematically (within the realm of subjective preferences and beliefs) advantage-maximizing ways, with complete confidence that the outcome will follow from his choices. Because his road is traffic-free, he can expect that his preferences will be consistently achieved through his actions; his choices will result in his most-favored outcomes. Thus, ironically (in that it is achieved via invisibility), Gyges' behavior *reveals* his preferences. The relationship between Gyges' observable (to the reader of the story, although not to the other characters in the story) choices and his private preferences over outcomes is disambiguated. No consideration for social rules impedes his choice. No other person acts in ways that would require rational Gyges to detour from his most-desired path. Nor need he compare options based on their likelihood of being realized.[15]

Here we can see the potential utility of Plato's Gyges story for an ideal-type theory that abstracts from ordinary practical reasoning: It solves the problem, which is basic to rational-choice economic theory, of how to determine a given choice-maker's preferences. A standard modern approach to the revelation of preferences, as we have seen (introduction), is based on treating actions as choices between lotteries over outcomes: Relative preference strength is established by determining the point at which the risk-neutral agent is indifferent between more

---

15. Per n. 11, above, the motivation of the queen in becoming his collaborator in killing the king is unspecified in Plato's story and does not affect Gyges' freedom. Her role is very different in Herodotus' story of Gyges; see below.

and less likely outcomes.[16] This approach, which assumes that outcomes are uncertain but that uncertainty can be converted to calculable risk rather than mere chance, does something that Glaucon's experiment does not: It allows for the determination of relative preference intensity. But it is necessarily contextual: The agent's choice must account for the contingencies of the choice situation. It does not reveal how the agent will act in a different context.[17]

Glaucon's thought experiment aims at revealing the "primitive" (in the sense of basic rather than vulgar) preferences that, he posits, lurk behind the readily observable, via agents' choices, constrained preferences of everyday life. He suggests, at a minimum, that every rational person seeks to maximize his own expected advantage, and maximizing advantage means that X: having more of a set of subjectively valued goods, will be consistently chosen over Y: not having or having less of those goods. Y will in turn be chosen if there is a high enough risk of Z: suffering the consequences of being detected in violating social rules and punished accordingly.[18]

But Plato's Glaucon is even more ambitious: He suggests not only that Gyges' ranked preferences are complete, transitive, and stable over time, but also that (unless and until Socrates can demonstrate the value of justice as an end inherently choice-worthy in itself), *all* individuals would make similar choices under similarly "traffic-free" conditions. Everyone (at least every adult male, "real man": 359b) is assumed to have similarly ranked primitive preferences over outcomes, reducible to a general preference simultaneously to have superabundant wealth, sex, and power (359c; 360b–c). This last generalization seems precarious, at best, insofar as it does not accurately describe Socrates' preferences, nor (so he claims) those of Glaucon himself. But even if Glaucon's posited set of egoistic primitive preferences cannot be universalized,

16. Revealed preferences: Binmore 2007: 6–7. Buchak (2013) emphasizes that people are not typically risk-neutral, and develops a more realistic alternative to the standard approach.

17. Say that on an ordinary day, J will choose to purchase whiskey rather than flowers: His revealed preference is whiskey. But suppose we observe J on the day of his wedding anniversary: He chooses flowers over whiskey because he dreads facing the disappointment of his spouse or the disdain of society. Under the circumstances, he ranks relationship and reputation over whiskey and chooses flowers accordingly. But were it not his anniversary, he would buy the whiskey. My thanks to Avidit Acharya for help with this hypothetical.

18. This problem of the risk associated with the likelihood (or probability) of an outcome will be treated in more detail below. Suffice it to say here that what seems excessively risky to one choice-maker might not seem so to another.

it may nonetheless be the case that many people are motivated by them.[19]

In the Greek political tradition and as Plato's Thrasymachus pointed out (344a–d), these wants are strongly associated with the figure of the tyrant. Gyges suggests, therefore, that an "ordinary man"—even a poor shepherd—would act as a tyrant if he were free from social constraints. It is essential to note, however, that the basic "folk theoretic" logic of rational choice, as sketched by Xenophon's Socrates in the *Memorabilia* passage (based on preferences and beliefs), need *not* imply that interests (outcomes sought) are viciously egoistic (self-interested in the narrow sense of discounting the interests of all others). Nor need it imply that interests can be reduced to the primitive triad advanced by Glaucon in *Republic* book 2.

The distinction between the general logic of rational choice and the particular ends that might be pursued by a given rational agent (say, Gyges) is highly significant. It means that the "folk theoretic" framework of instrumental rationality remains available to Plato (and other moral eudaimonists), once it has been separated from "Thrasymachean" assumptions about desired ends. But the seriousness with which Socrates takes Glaucon's carefully constructed challenge demonstrates the importance Plato attached to addressing the Thrasymachean variant of the folk theory: It is a matter of coming to grips with the underlying motivations of ordinary people, not just the behavior of actual tyrants.

In books 8 and 9 of Plato's *Republic* the political implications of instrumental rationality, uncoupled from the right preferences and true beliefs that have been specified in the intervening books, are made manifest: The collapse of harmonious Callipolis is followed by a degenerative cycle of regimes that leads to the anarchic diversity of individual desires, absence of legal constraint, and dangerous individual freedom of choice that Plato associates with democracy (see chapter 6.1). With the ultimate degeneration of democracy into the rule of the tyrant, political order is reduced to the expression of the primitive preferences specified by Glaucon. Plato's Socrates' point here (*Republic* book 9) is to reveal the profound personal unhappiness that attends that

19. In the psychology developed in the *Republic*, Gyges' actions appear to be motivated by the appetitive part of this soul; see above, n. 11. This was a common, but not universal psychological profile; the timocrats of *Republic* book 8 and the warrior-guardians and philosopher-rulers of Callipolis are otherwise motivated. Tvedt (2021), with literature cited) argues that Glaucon, as the exemplar of the honor-lover whose desires have been shaped by a democratic society, is insincere in his "Socratic" disavowal of Gyges-type preferences.

expression. While seemingly rational according to the Thrasymachean variant of the folk theory, the tyrant's choices lead him to the depths of misery. As will be evident in the following chapters, exploration of the implications of equating unconstrained egoistical self-interest with tyrannical desires and behavior is not unique to Plato's dialogues. Distinguishing behavior that was instrumentally rational from that which was viciously egoistic was a central theme in Greek ethics.

A primary conclusion of Plato's *Republic,* in books 9 and 10, is that the tyrant is utterly miserable. His apparent freedom from constraint in fact renders him an abject "slave of slaves."[20] And so, a rational eudaimonist—one who consistently chooses objectively valuable ends, not merely the best means to subjectively valued ends—would never take the path leading to that destination. But, meanwhile, back in book 2, Glaucon has established the preconditions of a theory of practical reasoning that is free from the complicating factor of primitive preference diversity. It is therefore a fitting alternative to the theory of objective value and ethically rational choice that Socrates will develop in the course of the dialogue. By the same token, it begs the question of the normative status of a thoroughly subjective theory of preference and choice, and it leaves us with the problem of distinguishing ordinal preference rank from cardinal preference intensity.

Glaucon's approach here might be likened to a "vulgar economist" approach to choice, one that assumes that all preferences are reducible to material welfare.[21] Contemporary choice theory typically assumes, on the contrary, that different people want quite different things. Rationality is not predicated on *what* people prefer (rationality over ends), but, per above on the completeness of the option set, transitive ranking of options, the coherence of their beliefs about the state of the world, and the alignment of their actions with the resulting expectations. Thus, when a choice theorist represents the value of an option to an agent by a quantity, it represents what is assumed to matter (based on revealed preferences) to that agent, not to everyone.[22] As we will see

20. *Republic* 577d–79e. See further, chapters 5.2 and 8.4.

21. Gauthier (1986) employs Plato's Gyges as a stand-in for "economic man"—the rational individual who lacks concern for others and is motivated only by material self-interest.

22. The quantity is referred to in choice theory as a "utility function": it is a reductive measure of utility the agent expects from the satisfaction of preferences. Diversity of preferences in game theory: Davis 1983: 61: "In fact, we cannot make any general assumption about people's wants, because different people want different things." P. 62: "A utility function is simply a 'quantification' of a person's preferences with respect to certain objects."

in the coming chapters, the Greek tradition of thinking about the rationality of choice offered some thoughtful alternatives to Glaucon's reductionism concerning choice-worthy ends.

1.4 GYGES' RING DECISION TREE

We are now in a position to illustrate Plato's Gyges story, employing the "tree form" used in contemporary decision theory (see figure 1). The illustration allows a more formal comparison of Plato's story to that of Herodotus, discussed below. The illustration presents a simplified visual expression of Plato's story, by employing the image, evoked by Glaucon in the opening quotation, of the choices made by a rational person traveling a chosen path. The main road (the path that the rational choice-maker is predicted to take) is indicated by the long dark line. Potential alternatives to the main road are indicated by lighter, shorter lines. At each intersection, or "node," a choice is made by a decision-maker. Here, the decision tree illustrates a parametric choice (i.e., an environment in which the relevant parameters, the determinants of choice, are fixed) rather than a nonparametric strategic game. This is because the only "player," other than Gyges (G) himself, is "Nature" (N), here meant only to stand in for contingency.[23] Unlike the decision-maker, Nature has no preferences over outcomes.

The value for the decision-maker of each outcome, labeled α to ζ, is indicated at the end of each path. The value is specified by a payoff quantity, in this case set at 0–4 and meant only to capture Gyges' ordinal ranking of preferences over outcomes (lowest to highest), rather than the cardinal value of each outcome (how much weight he attaches to each outcome relative to each other outcome). Listing payoff quantities allows us to indicate the ranking of the preferences over outcomes

23. On the difference between parametric choice situations and strategic games, see Bermudez 2015: 792–93): "In parametric choice situations agents make their choices with the background fixed. The only dimension of variation is the agent's own choice. The classically rational decision-maker therefore seeks to maximize expected utility relative to parameters that are set by the environment, and her choice depends only on her preferences and probability assignments. . . . As Jon Elster puts it, 'In the strategic or game-theoretic mode of interaction, each actor has to take account of the expectations of all other actors, including the fact that their actions are based upon their expectations concerning his own' (Elster 1979, p.18). But when the outcome can be identified by specifying one's own choice, no such taking account of the expectations of other participants is required. The other participants are simply pieces of the environment, and so these situations are better viewed as instances of parametric choice."

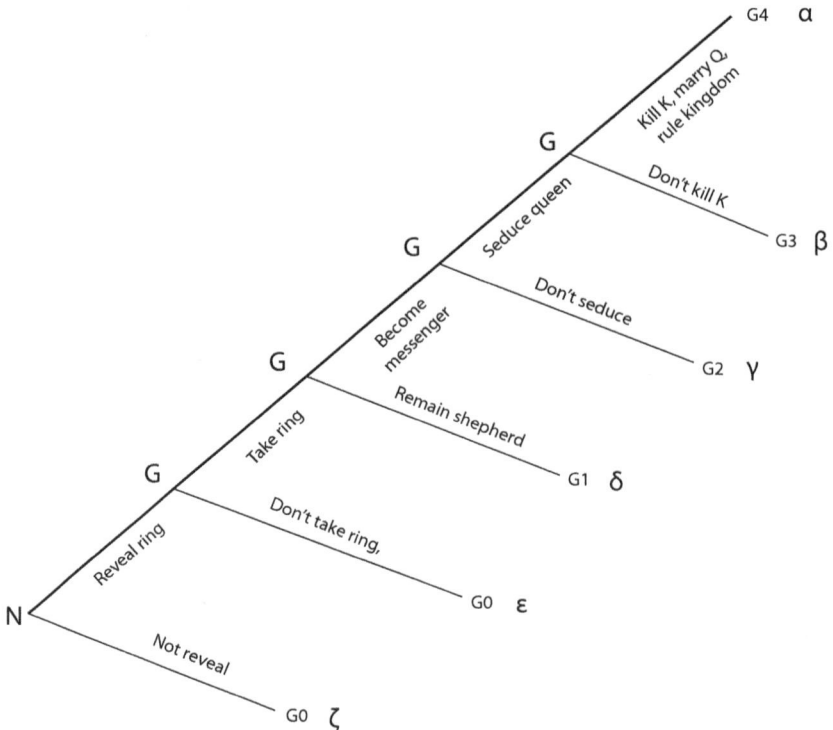

FIGURE 1. Gyges and the Ring Decision Tree.
NOTE: N = Nature; G = Gyges. Ordinal payoffs, 4 = high; 0 = low.

of the decision-maker, who, per above, is assumed to be a rational expected advantage maximizer, with complete, transitively ordered preferences. When it comes to a choice between two or more outcomes, the decision-maker will always choose the available outcome with the highest payoff.

In the "Gyges decision tree" (figure 1) we begin, as usual, at the "root" of the tree; in this illustration the root is in the lower-left corner of the figure. "Nature" (N) moves first, either revealing or not revealing the ring to Gyges. N is added to this game to indicate that there is an element of chance involved. Since Plato does not suggest that the ring was revealed through the will of some purposeful divine authority, we can suppose that the chasm opened by accident. It might not have opened when and where it did, and so Gyges might have lived out his life as a shepherd. If the ring were never revealed, then we would end up at outcome ζ; Gyges would get a payoff of o and the process would end there.

But, as we know from the story, N did reveal the ring; since we suppose that N has no actual volition, it just so happens that the ring is revealed. Since it is revealed, we proceed to the second node (fork) on the path; here Gyges (G) moves, choosing either to ignore the ring and remain a shepherd, or to take the ring. At the third node he chooses whether or not to become a messenger. At the fourth node he chooses whether or not to seduce the queen. At the fifth and final node he chooses between killing the king, marrying the queen, and ruling the kingdom and not doing these things.

We can determine the normative (ideally rational) decision-maker's choices by the standard choice-theoretic method of backwards induction—even if we cannot say for sure whether this analytic method was used by the ancient Greeks.[24] By beginning at the most-preferred available outcome and working back through a sequence of choices that lead to that outcome, backwards induction explains why the rational agent acts as he does. In this case, after N has revealed the ring, Gyges is the only choice-maker in this decision matrix, meaning that Gyges does not need to consider the choices of any other actors. But, as in the strategic game to be considered below, we will assume that the normative choice-maker has complete information (he is a "perfect craftsman," per above): That is, Gyges can

---

24. That the method of backwards induction was available to Greek thinkers concerned with normative rationality is suggested by Plato's *Gorgias* 467c–68c (the rational agent aims at some good and chooses a series of intermediate steps with the expectation of gaining it) and by Aristotle's teleological approach to choice-making, see *NE* 1112b15–24 and discussion in chapter 8.6. Briefly, Aristotle supposed that for a rational agent there was a "final end" of a chain of actions, each being chosen "for the sake of" the next. Choice-making for Aristotle was truly rational when the final end, towards which all previous actions in the chain were ultimately aimed, was a deliberately chosen way of life. In the best case this is the happy life (*eudaimonia*) that realized the human good for the completely virtuous person (Anscombe 1977). So, beginning at the end, it is in principle possible for the agent to work backwards down the chain, link by link, to his current position and thereby make the appropriate choice among currently available options. This general approach of reasoning back from the ultimately desired end, through a series of deliberately chosen actions, to an appropriate present choice is not unique to Plato and Aristotle: see for example chapter 3.2 for Herodotus' earlier narrative of Deioces the Mede, who, from the beginning, passionately desired tyranny as an end and planned a series of actions, from beginning to end, to achieve that goal. Chapter 7.3 suggests that the core intuition about reasoning backwards from desired ends to choice of actions was already present in Homer's *Iliad*. Backwards induction quickly becomes implausible as a *practical* approach to reasoning as the chain becomes longer and as the number of players increases.

look ahead (up the decision tree) to the decision nodes and he knows the payoff for each outcome. We begin the process of backwards induction at the last (fifth) node, in the upper-right-hand corner of the figure. Gyges chooses α (payoff 4: wealth, sex, and political power) over β (payoff 3: having seduced the queen he has got some wealth and sex). So, thinking of the diagram as a tree, we can cut off the β branch (not killing the king), since it will never be chosen.

Next, backing up to the fourth node, Gyges now chooses between the surviving outcome α and γ, which has a payoff of 2 (becoming a messenger is more lucrative than not doing so). Since 4 > 2 Gyges chooses to seduce the queen, and we cut off branch γ (not seduce). At the third and second nodes, Gyges chooses between α and δ (payoff 1: he has the gold ring), then between α and ε (payoff 0: he has not improved his situation in any way). In each case, the payoff for α (4) is better than the alternative outcomes (1,0), so δ and ε are cut off. With all the branches (alternate paths and outcomes) now cut from Gyges' decision tree, his path forward from the second node (his first choice) to the outcome α is obvious: He will take the ring, become a messenger, seduce the queen, kill the king, marry the queen, and rule the kingdom.

Once again, my assumption is that it is Plato's intended reader, concerned with ideal-type instrumental rationality, rather than any real decision-maker, who is expected to work all this out. Plato's illustration of normative rationality encourages a careful reader to think more deeply about practical reasoning in the real world but ought not to be conflated with it.

1.5 THE ILLUSTRATIVE VALUE OF SIMPLIFICATION

Obviously, Plato did not include an illustration of a decision tree in his original written text of the *Republic*. But Glaucon's reference to following the choices made by a rational person traveling on an imagined path to a chosen destination suggests that Plato meant the reader to visualize something like an extensive form decision tree when considering Gyges' choices and their implications for human motivation under ideal-type socially unconstrained conditions. Mutatis mutandis, the extensive form decision tree looks somewhat like, and has much the same function as, standard illustrations of the Line (*Republic* 509d–11e), which modern editors of Plato's *Republic* produce to clarify the complex metaphysical-epistemological argument of book 6 (e.g., Hackett edition 1997, p. 1130). Moreover, in his discussion of the Line, Plato himself calls attention to his contemporaries' practice of drawing figures to illustrate concepts in "geometry, calculation, and the like" (510c–e). It does not, therefore, seem too much of a stretch to say that, in *Republic* book 2, Plato has sketched a theory of instrumental rationality and that he (and his intended readers) would quickly grasp the pedagogic value of decision trees and other illustrations.

Moreover, while Plato did not employ shorthand notation, in the form of letters to indicate conditions, or the methods of formal logic, when discussing preferences and how they are rationally ordered, Plato's student, Aristotle, certainly did. In a passage of one of his fundamental works on deductive reasoning, the *Prior Analytics* (2.68a), Aristotle discusses preference ranking in a way that is strikingly reminiscent of contemporary decision theory: "When, of two opposite alternatives A and B, A is preferable [*haireteron*] to B, and similarly D is preferable to C, if A and C together are preferable to B and D together, A is preferable to D." Aristotle goes on to clear up any confusion about the ranking, by describing A and B, D and C as respective polar opposites, and by specifying that A and D are goods to be pursued, while C and B are evils to be avoided. So, we might illustrate the argument in one dimension, on the models of Plato's allusion to illustrations in geometry and calculation, and contemporary illustrations of Plato's analogy of the Line, as in figure 2.

If we take *haireteron* to be equivalent to "greater than" (more highly ranked in a preference ordering), Aristotle's description of the preference ordering may be written as $A > B$, $D > C$, $(A + C) > (B + D) \to A > D$, $C > B$.[25]

Aristotle's example of preference ranking concerns the attitude of a lover towards the relations he may have with his beloved:

> If then every lover under the influence of his love would prefer his beloved to be disposed to gratify him (A) without actually doing so (C), rather than actually gratifying him (D) without being inclined to do so (B), clearly A—that the beloved should be so inclined—is preferable to the act of gratification. Therefore, in love to have one's affection returned is preferable to having sex with the beloved. Therefore, love aims at affection [*philia*] rather than at having

25. We could (as Aristotle did not) assign quantities to each condition according to Aristotle's specifications: $A = 4$, $D = 3$, $C = 2$, $B = 1$. Per the formula above: $4 > 1$, $3 > 2$, $(4+2) > (1+3) \to 4 > 3$, $2 > 1$. Note, however, that there are other cases in which the conditions are satisfied but A is not preferable to (greater than) D. For example, $A = 5$, $B = 1$, $C = 4$, and $D = 6$. So, in this latter case, having sex (D) would be preferred to affection (A), falsifying Aristotle's conclusion. So, either Aristotle did not think of this problem in terms of quantities (thus *haireteron* is not to be thought of as "greater than in a generally quantifiable sense"), or he has offered a false result. My thanks to Peter Stone for pointing this out.

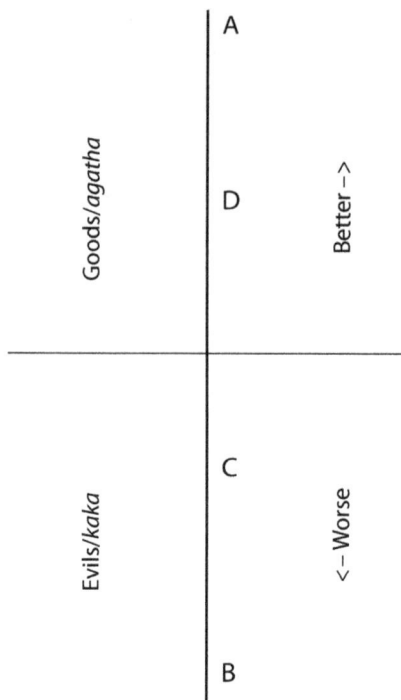

FIGURE 2. Aristotelian Preference Ranking

NOTE: A preferred to B; D preferred to C; (A+C) preferred to (B+D).

sex; and if affection is the principle aim of love, it is also the end [*telos*] of love. Therefore, having sex is either not an end at all, or only with a view to receiving affection.

Aristotle thus suggests that "every lover" will have a complete and transitive preference ordering, ranked as follows:

A. Affection, having the beloved's love and "disposition to gratify" (even without sex);

D. Having consensual sex with the beloved;

C. Not having consensual sex with the beloved;

B. No affection, not having the beloved's love and "desire to please" (even with sex).[26]

26. Note that there seems to be a missing term E: that is, having the love of the beloved and having sex with the willing beloved. It seems on the face of it that Aristotle thinks E would be better than A (since D > C) but E is not interesting in regard to getting the ranking of *philia* and *sunousia* right, so E is left out of the ranking. On the passage and its place in Aristotle's account of eros, see A. Price 1989: 239.

He concludes this passage by asserting the generality of the result: "The same principle, indeed governs all other desires [*epithumiai*] and crafts [*technai*]." The key point, for our purposes, is that Aristotle's approach to establishing a complete ordinal ranking of preferences as the basis for assessing the choices that a rational individual will make appears rather similar to the approach used in contemporary theoretic approaches to rational choice- and decision-making. While Aristotle's work on formal logic was ground-breaking, there is no reason to think that Plato, or other Greek writers concerned with problems of choice, would have had any difficulty in following the argument, or (leaving aside the specific example of love and sex—which obviously contradicts Glaucon's specification of primitive human preferences) any objection to the general applicability of his method.

I show in this book that reading ancient Greek texts and institutions through the lens of elementary (mostly nonalgebraic) contemporary decision and game theory, and the toy models and illustrations that contemporary theorists employ, sheds light on the meaning of otherwise obscure passages and seemingly peculiar rules. It can illuminate relationships between disparate texts. And it can clarify some of the working assumptions shared by the ancients who wrote the texts, by those who first read them, and by those who later critically discussed and built upon them. But even for those who accept that the approach sketched here is a useful addition to the humanist's interpretive toolbox, it is in no sense a panacea. Studying an editor's illustration of Plato's Line may help readers to follow the complex argument, but it does not replace a close reading of *Republic* book 6.

Moreover, we need not suppose that instrumental rationality was the sum total, or even the primary concern, of Greek writers concerned with the choices and actions of individuals and groups. As we will see, it was often the *limits* upon and *violations* of the sort of rationality exemplified by Plato's thought experiments in *Republic* book 2 that most interested Greek writers. They recorded and commented on the mistakes made by choice-makers who imagined themselves as rational actors. And they were deeply interested in the behavior of those who understood their own motivations as something other than calculating narrow self-interest.

Nevertheless, as I will try to show, Greek writers were concerned with the premises of the folk theory. It was against the background of assumptions about instrumental rationality that irrational behavior became an object of analytic attention. Strategic choice-making is the point of departure for the large body of contemporary empirical scholarship in behavioral economics and behavioral psychology. Empirical studies in those fields demonstrate that theories assuming perfectly rational choice-making fail to predict actual human behavior in real-world situations. But the object of such study is not to show that human behavior is simply irrational. Rather, it is to explore how, under what conditions, and with what regularity real-world human choice-makers diverge from the predictions arising from choice theory. The situation is in some ways similar, or so I will argue, in Greek political thought.[27]

1.6 HERODOTUS' GYGES NARRATIVE

If a theory of choice were limited to explaining the decisions made by a socially unconstrained individual, as illustrated by the Gyges Decision Tree, its application to human society would be limited. But decision theory can incorporate attention to the likelihood of outcomes (see chapter 6.1 and appendix), and the strategic game theory to which we now turn concerns two or more choice-making players. When we add uncertainty and multiple choice-makers to the decision problem, we move from purely hypothetical thought experiments to the kinds of situations that were and are encountered in literature, history, and daily life. And so, choice theory becomes useful for humanists concerned with understanding cultural representations of the phenomenal world. And, by the same token, it is useful for analyzing the social, political, and economic problems of interpersonal cooperation and competition addressed by empirical social science.

The complete freedom always to choose the outcome that most fully satisfies personal preferences, as enjoyed by Plato's invisible Gyges, is unavailable to most actual persons—and likewise unavailable to players in strategic games. Uncertainty and social constraint in the form of the choices of other agents, the "traffic" that Plato stripped away with Glaucon's thought experiment, are precisely what strategic game theory is meant to address. The point of the exercise is to determine the choices that each advantage-maximizing player will make when the desires and beliefs of other players frustrate each player's aim of achieving her

---

27. Camerer (2003) discusses the relationship between analytic choice theory and behavior as revealed in experimental settings. Behavioral economics followed soon upon the original program of rational choice and game theory: Simon 1955. Behavioral psychology: Kahneman 2011.

highest-ranked outcome. In some two-player games, the frustration is mutual in that *neither* player will get a high-ranked outcome. Under these conditions, to be considered in more detail in chapter 2, the players are confronted with a dilemma: When each narrowly pursues his own self-interest, both the individual and the aggregate social utility available to them (as imaginatively measured in some pseudo-currency) is lower than the value that they could enjoy if they could somehow find a rational way to cooperate.

The historian Herodotus' earlier story of Gyges' ascent to power in Lydia, the likely original from which Plato's tale was adapted, is readily modeled as a strategic game.[28] Considering the relationship between the Gyges stories related in Plato's *Republic* and Herodotus' *Histories* (1.8–14) strengthens the presumption that Plato self-consciously constructed, in words, a one-actor parametric decision tree by eliminating the other choice-making agents who take key roles in Herodotus' account. Herodotus' Gyges story, like Plato's, explicitly concerns choices—the Greek vocabulary of choice (*hairesis*) is prominently featured. But, in contrast to Plato's story, Herodotus' narrative emphasizes the limits imposed on Gyges as a choice-maker; his options are reduced to "live or die." Herodotus signals the limited choice set through the Greek vocabulary of forcible constraint (*anangkē*).[29]

In Herodotus' story, there is no ring of invisibility and Gyges' motives, other than his desire to stay alive, remain obscure. They are obscure because, in contrast to Plato's Gyges, the options available to Herodotus' Gyges are fixed by the preferences of others. Herodotus' Gyges is the bodyguard and confidant of Kandaules, king of Sardis (capital city of Lydia). Herodotus informs us that, madly in love with his (nameless in this story) wife and concerned that his bodyguard did not believe his description of her unmatched beauty, Kandaules ordered

28. Herodotus' Gyges story, with literature review: Asheri et al. 2007: 81–83.

29. Gyges' choices exemplify what Aristotle (*NE* 3.1) describes as a "mixed" (voluntary yet compelled) action, chosen relative to the circumstances, for fear of a worse alternative. Among Aristotle's examples is performing a shameful act at a tyrant's command, in order to save one's family. Gyges, of course, acts to save his own life. Cf. Laird 2001: 19: "The kind of crises of moral choice which involve Candaules, his wife and Gyges in Herodotus are, in Glaucon's story, more instructively centred on one person." This accurately captures the difference between the one-player and multi-player version of the story, but it puts too much emphasis on morality. Danzig (2008: 174) correctly notes that "the term *hairesis* (choice), which appears [in Herodotus' story] twice as a noun and once as a verb (1.11.2,3,4), does not signify a specifically moral choice for which Gyges is to be called to account but a practical choice between two alternatives."

Gyges to hide behind the door of the royal bedroom and to observe the queen as she undressed for bed. Gyges objected to the plan, calling it "lawless" (anomon). Herodotus specifies, however, that Gyges protested because he feared that the plan would lead to a bad outcome for himself (1.9.1). We are given no reason to think that Gyges regards the badness of the outcome as the wrong inherent in violating a norm. Rather, per the king's assurances (below), Gyges seems to worry that the queen might spot him and, were she offended and vengeful, punish him.

Kandaules is adamant, however, and Gyges, as a servant of the king, is unable to avoid the choice of either obeying the order to spy on the queen or suffering some (unspecified, but presumably capital) punishment (1.10.1). Kandaules assures Gyges that he, the king, has managed things (mēchanēsomai) so that the queen will remain ignorant of the fact that Gyges has seen her undressed (1.9.1). But he does acknowledge that there would be risk of discovery if Gyges were clumsy, since he urges Gyges to exercise care in exiting the bedroom (1.9.3).

In the event, the queen does spot Gyges. Depicted as a knowledgeable and rational agent, she grasps what her husband has done. Herodotus emphasizes the modesty of Lydian women; the queen is shamed by the violation and predictably so. But she controls any emotional response she might have had upon seeing Gyges leaving the room. Herodotus specifies that she did not cry out or otherwise reveal that she had noticed Gyges. Her goal, as we soon learn by her subsequent actions, is now revenge upon the king. Gyges will be the means she employs to that end. He is the right choice of means, since, by agreeing to spy, he has revealed his preference for his life over the expected bad consequences of disobeying the king. He will perform a "lawless" act in order to preserve his life.

The queen gathers trusted guards, summons Gyges, and presents him with a choice between "two roads" (1.11.2). If Gyges takes the first road, he will agree to kill the king according to the queen's instructions. At the end of this road, she says, is marriage to herself and rulership over the Lydians. On the second road, Gyges refuses to commit to killing Kandaules. At the end of this short road Gyges is immediately executed by the queen's guards. As he had when Kandaules first ordered him to spy on the queen, Gyges seeks to avoid the binary choice forced upon him by another player capable of taking his life: "He begged her not to force [anangkaiēi] him to make such a choice" (hairesis: 1.11.3).

We are not told why Gyges begs to be offered a third option (neither killing nor being killed), or whether he is sincere in requesting it. Herodotus' language does not point to moral qualms: He does not say that

Gyges objected that killing Kandaules would be *wrong*. By analogy with Gyges' reported worries about his own safety when ordered by Kandaules to spy, we may suppose that high among his reasons for preferring a third way is rational fear of the risk to himself: The murder plot might go wrong; the queen might have him executed after he kills the king. In these readily imagined scenarios, the payoff at the end of the first road is bad for Gyges. But, like Kandaules, the queen is adamant and the threat of immediate execution is credible (her guards are right there). Gyges "saw that constraint [*anangkē*] was truly set before him," and "chose [*haireetai*] to go on living" (1.11.4). The constraint that is "set before him" by the queen's threat is the reduction of the set of options from which he must choose to "live or die."

At this point in the story, Gyges has, in effect, been given a choice between two lottery tickets: Ticket 1, refusing to kill the king, brings a sure thing of immediate death. Ticket 2, agreeing to kill the king, means living for the time being, with some chance of marrying the queen and becoming king and some chance of being killed in the attempt or after the murder. Gyges, by his choice, shows that he prefers the second ticket.[30] As it turns out, the murder plot succeeds: Gyges stabs the king to death in his sleep. The queen fulfills her part of the arrangement; Gyges marries her and becomes king of Lydia. Whatever Herodotus' Gyges' original preferences (beyond simply staying alive), he has achieved the payoffs of sex, wealth, and power. That is, he has gained what Plato's narrowly selfish, socially unconstrained Gyges had achieved by ruthlessly pursuing his own preferred ends.

Even in the absence of the ring, the similarity of Herodotus' story to Plato's is obvious: In each tale Gyges (or his ancestor), a servant of the king, colludes with the queen, murders the king, and comes to rule the kingdom. Some classical scholars have suggested that both stories derive from some now-lost and more detailed third source that, hypothetically, combines the key features of Plato's and Herodotus's Gyges stories. While certainty in such matters is impossible, Andrew Laird (2001) has made a strong case that there is no third source, and that Plato deliberately adopted and imaginatively reworked Herodotus' original tale for his own philosophical purposes.

---

30. Ticket 1, immediate death, can be assigned a payoff of 0; Ticket 2 is the value of living for the time being plus p(king)—that is, the value of marrying the queen and becoming king, multiplied by the probability (p) of becoming king. So long as living on for the time being (having betrayed the king) has positive value, even were the values of p and (king) both 0 (which is counterfactual), Gyges' choice is rational.

I have argued that one of Plato's goals in book 2 of the *Republic* is to specify the underlying motivations of ordinary persons, and thereby clarify the premises of the folk theory of practical reasoning. He does so by eliminating uncertainty and the "traffic" of ordinary, rule-following social behavior. Plato's Glaucon implies that "every Gyges," every rational individual from servant to monarch, has similar, narrowly self-interested ends in view. Laird's thesis, that Plato took the story directly from Herodotus and reworked it for his own purposes, gains further plausibility when we reduce Herodotus' story to an extensive game form and compare it to the decision tree illustrated above.[31]

1.7 GYGES, THE QUEEN, AND KANDAULES, TWO- AND THREE-PLAYER GAMES

We are, I suggest, encouraged to think of Herodotus' story as something like a sequential, extensive-form game (figures 3 and 4) by attending to the queen's reference to Gyges' necessity of choosing between "two roads." The allusion to a choice-maker at a fork in the road anticipates a decision node of just the sort that is illustrated by the extensive game form. The queen's metaphor of two roads recalls Glaucon's image of the single path that would be followed by both an ostensibly just and an explicitly unjust possessor of an invisibility ring, suggesting that, at least in their Gyges tales, Plato and Herodotus were working with similar choice-theoretic toolkits. The key difference, of course, is that in Herodotus' story Gyges' preference ranking, other than preferring life to death, is not revealed by his behavior. Because the queen is a player and may, depending on Gyges' choice, choose to execute him on the spot, we can only guess whether he prefers "kill the king with some chance (depending on the credibility of the queen's promise) of marrying the queen and becoming king" or the excluded option of "neither kill nor be killed."

We know from Gyges' actual choice that he prefers to kill (and take his chances) than be killed. This is reflected in the limited range of Gyges' payoffs (0–1) in the games illustrated below. But we remain in the dark as to whether his request for a third way was (1) motivated by a preference not to kill the king, or (2) reflects his belief that the queen was unlikely to fulfill her promise, or (3) was a tactic for gaining more

---

31. Other literature on the relationship between the two stories and their Nachleben: K. Smith 1920; Laird 2001: 29 with n. 59.

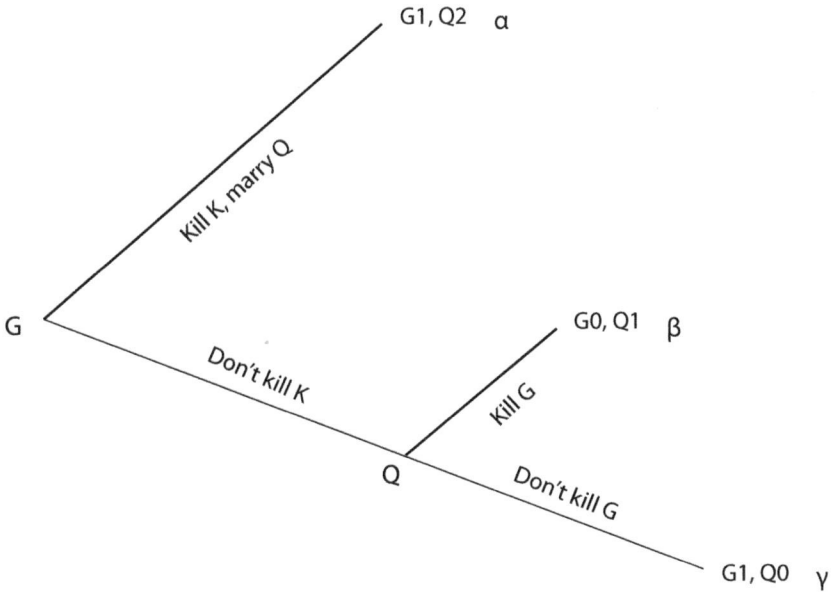

FIGURE 3. Gyges and Queen Subgame
NOTE: G = Gyges; Q = Queen. Ordinal payoffs, 2 = high; 0 = low.

information about her intentions. Plato's story, by revealing Gyges' complete and transitive preferences through his unconstrained choices, eliminates the guesswork.

The fork described by the queen is illustrated by the simple game tree in figure 3. As in the Gyges' ring decision tree, rank-ordered payoffs are assigned to outcomes for each player (Queen: 0–2, Gyges: 0–1). As in the Gyges decision tree (figure 1), the payoff quantities are, initially, meant to capture ordinal rankings of preferences over outcomes of each player. We will need to consider the king's cardinal (preference strength) orderings, below.

Gyges (G) moves first, choosing to kill the king with outcome α, or not. If he chooses not to kill the king, then the queen (Q) moves, choosing to kill Gyges with outcome β or not to kill him with outcome γ. The queen is credibly committed to killing Gyges if he refuses her offer. Her commitment is underwritten by comparing her bad payoff of 0 at γ (Q suffers the humiliation of having been spied upon, and the added burden of being disobeyed without consequences) to her relatively good payoff at β (1: she punishes the instrument of her humiliation). So, we cut off the branch leading to outcome γ. Gyges must, therefore, choose between β and α—as the queen succinctly points out, given her resolve, the road before Gyges has only two forks. Because Gyges' payoff for α (1: living for the time being) is better than for β (0: he is killed), he chooses to accept the queen's proposal. The predicted outcome of the game is therefore α: Gyges kills the king, expecting to live for the time being and (with better than zero likelihood) to marry the queen and become king.

The fork in the road alluded to by the queen is the last node in a more complicated game played by Gyges, the queen, and King Kandaules; the simple game illustrated in figure 3 can be thought of as a subgame of a complex three-player sequential game. The extensive game form for Herodotus' tale of Gyges is more elaborate than that of Plato's story because there are three, rather than just one, choice-making players, each with his or her own payoffs for possible outcomes, and because uncertainty (N in the game form) is a factor in players' choices. The complete game is much too complex to be a mental construct of any of the characters in the story. As with Plato's Gyges story, it is the *reader* who is provided with all the information necessary for constructing the form of the game and working out its implications.

The full game is illustrated as a tree in figure 4. As in the other games considered in this chapter, payoffs for each player indicate ordinal preference rankings for each player (King: 0–4, Gyges: 0–1, Queen: 0–3), from lowest to highest. Note that a given player's preference ranking may be the same for different outcomes. When this is the case, the player is assumed (for the purposes of the game) to be indifferent between outcomes (i.e., is willing to have the choice between them made by a coin flip).[32] Indifference between outcomes does not affect the result of this game, but it becomes relevant in other games; see section 1.8, below, and chapter 2.2.

In this game, King Kandaules (K) moves first, choosing to order Gyges to spy on his wife or not to give that order. If he does not order Gyges to spy, the game ends at θ with payoff to the king of 2 (he is denied the pleasure of knowing that Gyges has seen his wife naked). If K orders Gyges to spy, Gyges (G) chooses to obey or disobey. If he disobeys, K chooses whether to forgive or to kill him for disobedience. If G obeys, then Nature (N) determines with some probability whether or not the queen (Q) spots Gyges spying on her. Because K cannot be sure that Gyges will exit the bedroom without been seen, there is a level of uncer-

---

32. King is indifferent between γ and ε: 4, β, δ, and ζ: 3. Gyges is indifferent between α and ε, and η: 1; β, δ, and ζ: 0.

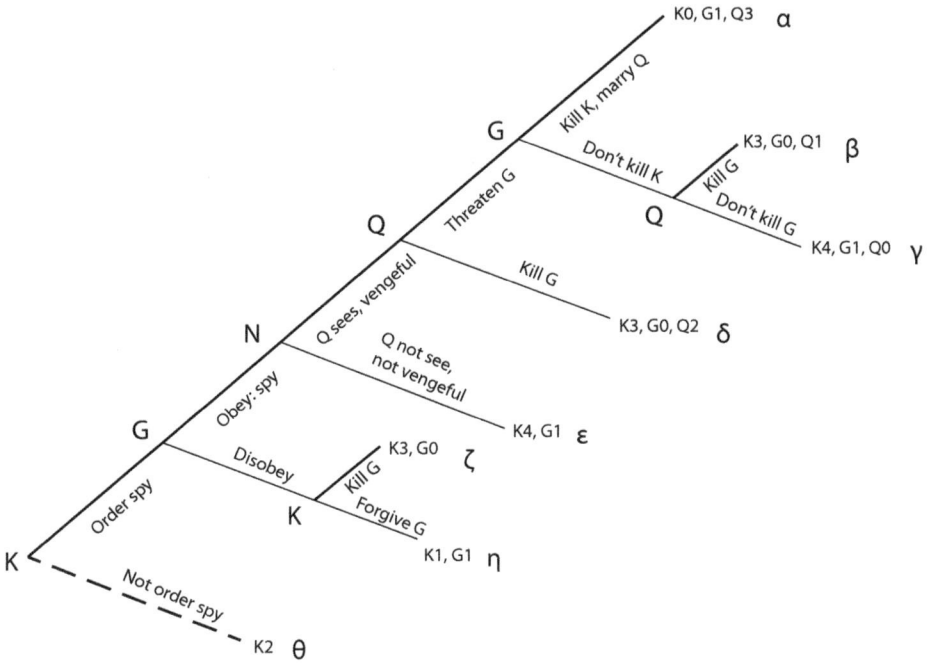

FIGURE 4. King, Gyges, and Queen Game

NOTE: K = King Kandaules; G = Gyges; N = Nature; Q = Queen. Ordinal payoffs, 4 = high; o = low.

tainty in this game. If the queen happened not to spot Gyges, the game would end at ε, and there would be no bad consequences for Gyges or the king. If N determines that Q sees Gyges, Q chooses whether to kill Gyges outright, or to threaten Gyges with death if he does not agree to kill the king. If Q threatens, we end up at the subgame illustrated in figure 3.

As we already know from the backward induction that cut off outcomes β and γ, at the last node G will choose α. One node back, Q chooses between α (3: she gets revenge on Kandaules, the source of her humiliation) and δ (2: she punishes the instrument of her humiliation but fails to punish the principal). Thus, we cut off δ. As we have seen, N fails to determine outcome ε. Thus, one node back, G chooses between α (1, per above) and ζ (o: he is killed by the king as punishment for disobedience). His choice is limited to α or ζ because outcome η (1: G is forgiven by the king) is cut off by K's choice. Confronted with a disobedient Gyges, K will choose ζ (3: K has the satisfaction of punishing disobedience) over η (1: K's direct order is disobeyed, and disobedience goes unpunished, making future disobedience more likely). Preferring life to death, G chooses α. The equilibrium path of the game is for G obediently to spy, then when (as it happened) N determines that Q spots G, for Q to threaten, and for G to agree to kill K, which results in his marrying the queen and ruling the kingdom.

1.8 KANDAULES' CHOICE: PREFERENCE STRENGTH AND LIKELY OUTCOMES

Thus far in our backwards induction of this extensive form game, each player has chosen rationally, according to the ranked preference orderings listed in figure 3. But at the very first (root) decision node, we encounter an apparent anomaly: With outcomes β through η cut from the decision tree, K chooses between α (0: K is murdered by Gyges) and θ (2: not giving the order to spy, he is denied some measure of pleasure, as above). As we know from the story, K rejects θ. Since 0 < 2, the king seems to have acted irrationally. Why? Whether or not Greek readers used something like backwards induction in analyzing this kind of situation, the question of why Kandaules started down the path that ended in his death is a question raised by Herodotus' story.

Assume, for the moment, that K is a rational decision-maker. Have we listed K's preference ranking incorrectly? In Herodotus' story, Kandaules strongly desires the outcome "Gyges spies on his wife." But Herodotus does not depict Kandaules as preferring his spying plan to life itself. Perhaps, then, he has a false belief about some relevant state of the world: that the queen is immodest (uncaring about her own exposure) or incapable of planning revenge, or that Gyges is so loyal that he would choose death over killing his king. But this would require the king to be ignorant of the famous modesty of Lydian women (a point emphasized by Herodotus) or willfully ignorant of his wife's cognitive abilities. And Gyges has already revealed his preference for life over adherence to rules.

I suggested, above, that Plato borrowed from Herodotus a story about rational choice-making. We may explain Kandaules' choice as formally rational by moving beyond simple ordinal ranking of his preferences to a cardinal ordering of relative preference strength and by attending to uncertainty. Contingency is a major factor in many strategic games. Skilled players may accurately estimate relative likelihoods, but an outcome judged unlikely may nevertheless come about. Kandaules may have been rational, and perhaps even skillful, yet unlucky. Below, we will consider Herodotus' suggestion that Kandaules' bad end was fated. But Kandaules did not know that when he ordered Gyges to spy; a fated outcome and instrumentally rational choice-making are not incompatible.

Herodotus' story hinges on a question (the "Nature" node in figure 4) whose answer is not known to the players with certainty: Will the queen see Gyges? Kandaules makes light of this possibility: When encouraging Gyges to do his bidding, he expresses full confidence in his own machinations. He assures Gyges that no harm will come to him from the queen (1.9.1). If the likelihood that the queen will spot Gyges were reduced to zero, we could imagine the situation as that of Plato's Gyges with the ring: The king remains, in effect, invisible if his servant is never seen. The queen is eliminated as a choice-making player; she is reduced to an object of Kandaules' preference satisfaction. Gyges himself is reduced to an animate tool whose proper functioning (spying) achieves the tool-user's end. In that counterfactual case, the Queen-Gyges subgame never takes place. With reference to figure 4, the game ends at outcome ε and the king gains his most-preferred outcome with certainty. But Herodotus' Kandaules himself raises the possibility that Gyges *might* be spotted, when he urges his servant to be careful in exiting the bedroom. That possibility brings us back to the three-player strategic game.

Greek writers on the rationality of choice were, as we will see (chapters 5, 7, and appendix), very concerned with risk (*kindunos*) and likelihood (*eikos*). Plato confidently asserted that it was possible for experts to correctly measure the probability of feasible outcomes (*Republic* 467c–d; see discussion in chapter 5.1). Herodotus did not express likelihood in quantitative terms, as a frequency distribution; nor did other Greek writers. Yet Herodotus' readers could surely have made sense of this game without resort to precisely quantified probabilities.

Herodotus' narrative allows us to think of Kandaules as choosing between two lottery tickets: Ticket 1 is 100 percent certainty of living on without Gyges viewing the queen naked against zero chance of imminent death. Ticket 2 is a gamble: the chance that Gyges will view the queen without consequences against the chance that the queen will see Gyges. If the queen sees Gyges, ticket 2 leads, via the expected choices of the queen and Gyges (per above), to the king's death. The questions that faced a (completely informed, risk-neutral) Kandaules when deciding between the two tickets were: (1) What value (denominated in some imagined currency) does he put on his life itself and on Gyges' spying? (2) What is the likelihood that Gyges will be spotted, inaugurating a sequence leading to the king's death? By comparing payoffs in the imagined currency, rational

Kandaules can decide which lottery ticket to choose.[33] The king chose ticket 2. So, assuming he valued his own life highly, we must also assume (with support from Herodotus' text) that the intensity of his desire for Gyges to see the queen naked was high, and his belief that the likelihood of Gyges being spotted was low (being sure of his machinations and Gyges' dexterity). In the event, Kandaules was unlucky; he gambled and lost.

I suppose that some of Herodotus' Greek readers would conclude that Kandaules was not only unlucky, but also inexpert. Either his calculation of risk or his evaluation of others' motives and capacities was somehow flawed. Adding inexpert to unlucky invites speculation on Kandaules' deliberative processes: Perhaps he had an excessive tolerance for risk. Perhaps his judgment about the likelihood of Gyges being spotted was compromised by an unruly passion for his wife. Perhaps his royal position led him to overestimate his own cleverness. Perhaps he foolishly discounted the queen as a self-interested, strategic agent in her own right. Perhaps he simply did not think ahead and was oblivious to the high stakes of the game. Herodotus' text (1.8.1, 1.9.1) offers support for each of those possibilities.

I suggest that Herodotus meant the reader to realize that it is not possible to come to a final decision about which was the decisive factor. If that is correct, we may say that Herodotus leads the reader to think about strategic choices in the face of uncertainty, and in a way that resists the notion that historically salient outcomes (like the death of a king) will be readily forecast by, or prevented through, the exercise of practical reason. The reader who compares the Gyges narrative in Herodotus' *Histories* with that of Plato's *Republic* is confronted both with the role of practical reason in choice-making and with its limits as a predictive science. The Greek folk theory, in common with contemporary game theory, may in the end prove to be more valuable for analysis of complex choice situations than it is for the prediction of results. We will return to prediction and its limits in ancient and modern theories of rationality in chapter 5.

---

33. If, counterfactually, Herodotus had assigned a percentage to Kandaules' assessment of the probability of the sequence, "Gyges discovered, the rational choices of the queen and Gyges lead to the king's death," we would be able to assign cardinal values (in imagined currency) to Kandaules' preferences for spying and living. Suppose Kandaules believed that there was a 1 in 1000 chance of that sequence. If he is risk-neutral and indifferent between the lotteries (orders Gyges to spy or not by flipping a coin), 1:1000 is the unit ratio between his preferences.

1.9 ORACULAR INFORMATION AND CHOICE

As noted above, Herodotus adds another variable into his Lydian narrative. Kandaules was certain to come to a bad end (*chrēn . . . genesthai kakōs*: 1.8.2). It seems, then, that the plans of even a craftsman of self-interest might be upset by fate. Must we then conclude that Herodotus' Greek readers concluded that there is no value to practical reasoning?[34] The conclusion that "what is certain" and "how rational agents choose" are mutually exclusive explanations for the course of human affairs is, however, too hasty. We need not suppose that certainty implies "divinely contrived" in the sense that an extrahuman agency directed Kandaules' mental processes. Perhaps Kandaules was certain to come to a bad end *because* of some combination of his unruly passion and his royal arrogance. Perhaps, even if fated, his bad end might have been forestalled (even if it could not be prevented) by utilizing the best available sources of information.

Herodotus in propria persona, like many of the characters in his *Histories,* was famously interested in oracles and he supposed that certain oracles, notably including the oracle at Delphi, could in fact reveal salient information relevant to human choices. So, the possibility arises that a true craftsman of rational self-interest would not make a highly consequential choice without gaining the information available from an oracle. The uncertainty represented by the N node might, if all went well, be reduced by consulting an oracle. Of course, that requires, first, that the oracle be real (capable of providing relevant information) and, next, that the oracle's answer be either unambiguous or correctly interpreted by the player.

As every reader of Herodotus soon learns, those very demanding conditions often go unmet.[35] But oracles, at least the sort of oracles described and accepted as valid by Herodotus and his characters in the *Histories,* make sense *only* in a world in which choice-makers assume that much human behavior can be understood as rational, in the "folk

34. The stark contrast between ancient practices of oracular divination and modern assessments of risk is, for example, the theme of Bernstein 1996. See, however, the appendix to the present volume.

35. On the basis of inscriptions and Athenian law court speeches, Bowden (2005: 22–24) argues that, at least in the case of the Delphi, oracular ambiguity of the kind that figures so prominently in Herodotus' *Histories* was atypical: "The most common form of question was: 'would it be more profitable and better for us to . . .'? This would normally lead to a response of either 'it would be more profitable and better . . .' or 'it would not be more profitable and better'."

theory" sense sketched above. Herodotus introduces the story of Gyges by reference to his famous descendant and the last of his line, King Croesus (1.6). Croesus was interested in oracles specifically as instruments for gaining valuable information that could (he supposed) allow him to eliminate uncertainty when faced with a momentous decision. Herodotus' Croesus is in certain ways a model of the instrumentally rational (although not mistake-free) oracle-user, first subjecting the oracle to what amounts to a blind test of its veracity, and then using its answers as inputs when making salient choices about foreign policy.[36]

Plato's Glaucon ended the story of Gyges' murder of the king with marriage to the queen, and the hypothesis (eventually to be disproved by Socrates) of his blissfully happy subsequent life and afterlife. But Herodotus offers a coda to the story: Gyges took the kingship and ruled only after a conflict arbitrated by the Delphic oracle (1.13.1). The oracle was instrumental in consolidating Gyges' authority because it ended a civil war that broke out after Kandaules' fate was learned, between armed Lydian partisans of the family of Kandaules and the faction of Gyges. Both sides eventually agreed (*sunebēsan*) that if the oracle at Delphi decreed that Gyges was to rule, he would do so by common agreement of the Lydians. If the oracle decided against him, he would return the throne to Kandaules' relatives. The oracle decided in favor of Gyges (1.13.2), who then sent many offerings to Delphi in thanks for the happy outcome of the arbitration. These were the first such offerings from an Asian ruler; the gifts were consequential enough to be later called "the Gygian [treasure]" (1.14).

In this case, the oracle seems not to have supplied information relevant to assessing the likelihood of a given outcome. Rather, the two disputing parties agreed to designate the oracle as an arbitrator. It was accepted by both sides because of its assumed impartiality and empowered by them to make a choice between two alternatives that would be binding on the contestants. Arbitration and the importance of impartiality to the arbitrator's success in solving bargaining problems will be a recurring theme in later chapters.

Although Herodotus provides no details, coming to an agreement to accept arbitration is necessarily a difficult process (see further, chapters

---

36. This in some ways anticipates the use of the concept of the "oracle" in computer science, as "a succinct, precise and unambiguous device to provide information or knowledge that was not available or discoverable . . . using normal procedures" and "a trusted source whose 'authority' draws from the consensus around its correctness" (Poblet et al. 2020: 3).

3.4 and 4.3), raising questions of how it was that the many members of the pro-Kandaules faction agreed among themselves to abide by the oracle's decision and why each party regarded as credible the commitment of the other side to abide by the outcome. What is tolerably clear is that the resort to an arbitrator, because it was successful, avoided what might have been a debilitating conflict, ultimately destructive to both sides. And it is significant that the oracle was handsomely rewarded for its service: Herodotus' concern with the "arbitrator's payoff" (Karachalios 2013) in the process of state formation will figure prominently in chapter 3.

Plato alludes to the original emergence of structured social order in the passage from book 2 of the *Republic* with which we began. There, Glaucon claims that social constraints on the pristine freedom of each individual to act so as to gain "more and more" were established by an agreement (*sunthēkai*) among mutually fearful persons. The question we are faced with, as in the story of the Delphic solution to the Lydian civil war, is how people can come to that sort of agreement, given the conditions of rationality that emerge from the story of Gyges. That is the subject of the next chapter.

But before leaving the paired tales of Gyges the Lydian, there is a final puzzle that we might hope to solve: Why, assuming that Plato adapted his version of the story from that of Herodotus, did he move the story of seduction and usurpation back one or more generations, from "Gyges" to "an ancestor of Gyges"? Herodotus' tale of Gyges concludes (1.13.2) with the comment that, after the Delphic oracle had awarded the throne to Gyges, it warned that the relatives of Kandaules would have vengeance on Gyges' descendants "in the fifth generation." Herodotus notes that the Lydians and their kings paid no attention to this (that is, they discounted future costs relative to current gains). But, he continues, the oracle was fulfilled with the defeat of Gyges' great-great-grandson, Croesus, by Cyrus of Persia. Herodotus' story of Gyges is framed, beginning and end, by the shadow of divine retribution.

As we have seen, in Plato's version of the story, Adeimantus pointedly insists that the opportunity for preference satisfaction of the unconstrained rational man, modeled by the holder of a ring of invisibility, must not be compromised by any concern for divine retribution. By pushing the responsibility for the lawless act of regicide that founded a new dynasty back to "an ancestor of Gyges," who could not, therefore, have known the "fifth-generation" oracle delivered to Herodotus' Gyges, the donor of Delphi's "Gygian treasure," Plato confounded the "fifth-generation" oracle. Thus he dispelled whatever shadow a divinely ordained future might have cast on the payoffs to the anonymous, fully informed, fully rational, egoistically self-interested subject of his carefully plotted tale.

In his story of Gyges, Herodotus offered an account of seemingly rational actors with ranked (if not fully revealed) preferences and coherent (if not always accurate) beliefs. Herodotus' Gyges made his life-or-death choices based on the choices he had reason to believe would be made by other agents, each seeking his or her own goals.[37] Herodotus' readers thus confront a situation that is readily illustrated as a strategic game. Plato, writing a generation after Herodotus, adapted the now-familiar Gyges story to his own purposes. He transformed it, by the device of the magic ring, into a simple parametric decision problem. He was able to do so because, even with its allusions to the constraints on Gyges' options and the certainty of Kandaules' bad end, Herodotus' story about Gyges was already framed around the choices of instrumentally, but not ethically, rational actors.

Both Herodotus and Plato assumed readers who were familiar with what I have been calling the Greek folk theory of practical reasoning. As we will see in the following chapters, Herodotus and Plato were not exceptional within their intellectual milieu in presenting situations of choice in narratives that can be analyzed and compared by decision trees and strategic games. Nor were they exceptional in offering their readers models of human rationality that can be tested against the observed behavior of choice-making agents in the real world.

37. Dewald (2003: 41–42, 49) generalizes the point: "What the self-contained Herodotean *logos* focuses on is the immediate context, an individual's goals, and his or her consequent actions within that *logos*. Whether the individual depicted is a poor herdsman, someone's wife or mother, royal courtier, Greek citizen, prostitute, eastern potentate, or Sicilian adventurer, his or her actions in the Herodotean narrative are first defined by the constraints of external circumstances. Within those constraints, he or she is shown acting out of a desire to obtain some particular objective through whatever means are realistically available . . . Each man or woman in Herodotus wants as much scope for following his or her personal objectives as he or she can get. Each one, however, is ultimately held in check by the existence of all the others and their competing and contradictory desires."

CHAPTER 2

Glaucon's Dilemma

The Origins of Social Order

How and why do self-interested individuals cooperate with others when costs must be paid before benefits are gained? Glaucon's thought experiment in book 2 of Plato's *Republic* posited that ordinary persons are motivated by narrow self-interest. His story of Gyges and the ring of invisibility illustrated a pure form of rationally self-interested behavior through revealing the preferences of a choice-maker freed from the social constraints imposed by laws, norms, and others' preferences. Glaucon proposed that Gyges' revealed preferences for material goods, access to sex, and power over others are universally top ranked. So, absent the fear of punishment, all "real men" are presumed to be willing to steal, seduce, and kill to achieve their highest-ranked preferences. Punishment for rule-breaking assumes some kind of social order, with enforceable rules. But how did social order arise in the first place? That is the problem we take up on this chapter.

2.1 SOCIAL ORDER AS A PROBLEM

An ancient Greek reader of *Republic* book 2, willing to be convinced that humans are motivated in the ways that emerged from Glaucon's thought experiment, confronted a puzzle: How could many persons, each with a primary goal of maximizing his or her share of a limited pool of material goods, sexual access, and power, ever have come to cooperate with one another? How did self-interested free agents become rule-following residents of a sustainable community? This chapter discusses the answers that Plato, and others in the classical Greek tradition of social and political thought, offered to that puzzle. They did so in narratives that are, like Herodotus' tale of Gyges discussed in chapter 1, illuminated by, and seem to anticipate, some of the standard devices of strategic game theory.[1]

For a polis-dwelling Greek in the age of Plato, as for us today, it was self-evident that most people do live in rule-bounded communities of one sort or another. For the Greeks these communities prominently included states in the form of *poleis* and rules in the form of *nomoi*: formal laws, social norms, and established customs. Those states had regularized systems of political authority, such that the question of how, and by whom, rules are interpreted and enforced had been at least provisionally answered. Social order meant that people could expect most other people to obey most of the rules most of the time.

But where did the rules—and the authority to make, interpret, and enforce them—come from? What is the origin of law, political legitimacy, and the enforceable duty to obey? How did those in authority come to wield power? In communities ruled by kings or tyrants, power might give persons in authority the opportunity to behave more or less like Gyges with the magic ring—taking other people's possessions at will, having superior access to sex, and dominating subjects (see chapter 3). Alternatively, in a civic community power was distributed among citizens—so that no one enjoyed a Gyges-type freedom of choice and action (see chapters 4 and 6). But why would rational and self-interested individuals ever choose to place themselves in a position of having to take orders from someone (or everyone) else? Why would I willingly agree to obey your orders, if I expect those orders to obstruct the course of action that leads to my most preferred outcome? How could I commit to a future course of action, such that you would find my commitment credible and feel secure in acting accordingly? The ordinary, constraining social conditions that Glaucon's narrative thought experiment was designed to strip away may begin to seem strange, once the thought experiment has been performed.

1. Elizabeth Anderson (2000) is critical of all rational-choice-based attempts to explain cooperative behavior, on the grounds that they fail to explain the actual scope of observed cooperation and norm-following. As we will see, the Greek tradition is attentive to the incompleteness of rational explanations for social behavior. Greek thinkers, like contemporary choice theorists, recognized instrumental rationality as an essential foundation on which to build richer and more descriptively satisfactory accounts of behavior under constraint.

The notion that, for humans (unlike other animals), nature does not simply determine social order, that *nomos* (law, norm, or custom) is both different from and at least potentially in conflict with *phusis* (human nature), was, as we have seen (introduction, section 0.4), one of the defining ideas of classical Greek political thought. That distinction and the role it played in Greek culture have been the subjects of much scholarly attention. Yet there is, I think, more to say about the implications of the *nomos/phusis* disjunction for Greek explanations of the origins of human social order in the face of instrumental rationality.

Plato's Glaucon introduced his thought experiment by claiming that it is commonly supposed that social order, understood as a voluntary agreement on rules by persons seeking to constrain egregious behavior, along with the positive evaluation of justice, arose as a compromise. Each party to that compromise would have preferred to act unjustly in accordance with egoistic self-interest, but each recognized the costs to himself of others doing so:

> By nature, they [other people] say, to commit injustice is [for each individual] a good and to suffer it is an evil, but that the excess of evil in suffering injustice is greater than the excess of good in doing injustice. So that, when men do injustice and suffer it from one another and have experienced both, for those who lack the power at once to avoid the one and choose [*hairein*] the other, it seems profitable [*lusitelein*] to make a compact with one another [*sunthesthai allēlois*] neither to commit nor to suffer injustice; and [they say] that this is the beginning of the establishment of laws [*nomoi*] and covenants [*sunthēkai*] between men and that they name the command of the law "the lawful" and "the just" and [they say] that this is the genesis and essential nature of justice—in between the best, which is to do wrong with impunity, and the worst, which is to be wronged and be impotent to get one's revenge. (Plato, *Republic* 358e–59a)

In this passage, Glaucon sketches a folk theory ("they say") of the origins of social order.[2] It is a companion-idea and logical consequence

---

2. I follow Williams (2006: 39, 99, 119, 165) and others who have seen this passage as an early example of contract theory and thus concerned with the origins of social order. The passage is cited by Barry (1989: 6) as an example of a theory of a contractual theory of justice that "continues to be a live option and is one of the two theories around which" his own book is constructed. Per the introduction, Barry (following Rawls 1958: 174–75 with n. 9) sees the theory sketched by Glaucon as an early version of the line of thought later developed by Hobbes, Hume, and contemporary game theory. Reeve (2008: 128) contends, to the contrary, that it is an account of democratic order, and assumes the prior existence of a nondemocratic order that will be overthrown by the newly agreed-upon rules. But I see no textual or philosophically compelling reason to limit Glaucon's account of what "they say" to arguments offered by Greek democrats. For the intellectual context, see Horky (2021), who identifies "them" as both Sophists and other Socratics.

of the folk theory of instrumental rationality discussed in the introduction and chapter 1. In essence, Glaucon's "they" embrace the Conventionalist's conclusion (obedience to the law is rational) via initially Thrasymachean arguments (the law is contrary to the natural preferences of each person). Neither Glaucon nor Socrates endorses what "they say" about the origins of order, but the passage quoted above is framed by Thrasymachus' (340e–41a) and Glaucon's (360e–61a) specification that, when seeking to understand rationality and self-interest, one must identify the choices of hypothetical perfect craftsmen (*dēmiourgoi*) of self-interest: human agents who unerringly (or, having erred, correct the error) choose the course of action that most benefits themselves. The hypothetical "craftsman," a device unchallenged by Plato's Socrates, is relevantly similar to the hypothetical fully rational, completely informed, and cognitively capable agent assumed in contemporary choice theory.

The passage quoted above is immediately followed by the extended thought experiment that includes the Gyges story. As we saw in chapter 1, Glaucon's thought experiment imaginatively places two persons on the same path. One is reputed to be just and the other unjust. But Glaucon predicts that were we to follow the two men, "We should then catch the just man going along to the same destination as the unjust man, because of the striving to gain more and more [*pleonexia*] which every creature by its nature pursues as a good" (359c).

Glaucon's thought experiment continues by freeing the two men from all social constraints by giving them Gyges-type rings (359c, 360b). Glaucon asserts that under conditions of pristine freedom (as it is elucidated in the Gyges story) each person indeed arrives at the same destination, which is now glossed (360b–c) as acting at others' expense so as to maximize his own access to the goods of material possessions, sex, and rule.[3] By having his "just" and unjust man travel the same path and arrive at the same destination, Glaucon has, at least implicitly, placed his two craftsmen of self-interest in a situation of strategic interaction and choice. The issue of the origins of social cooperation that he raised in the passage quoted above might, therefore, be addressed, in a radically simplified form, by imagining what course of action each of those hypothetical individuals would choose in consideration of the choice likely to be made by the other. In brief, we can transform the parametric Gyges' ring choice situation into a strategic game, by attending to the

---

3. On the road/path metaphor in Plato and Herodotus and in game theory, see chapter 1, n. 6; chapter 7, n. 7.

thought experiment's extension from a single choice-maker to two choice-makers. In so doing, Plato raises problems for what "they," the Conventionalists, were saying about the rational basis of social order.[4]

2.2 STRATEGIC GAMES

We are, I suggest, entitled to think of Glaucon's two self-interested, instrumentally rational individuals as the players in a strategic game: that is, a game in which each player (an ideal-type rational agent, per above) chooses her move in light of the move she believes will be made by the other. The game may be illustrated in "normal form" as a two-by-two matrix, as in figure 5.[5] Each player (1, 2) has two possible choices (a, b), meaning that there are four possible choice pairs (1:a, 2:a; 1:a, 2:b; 1:b, 2:a; 1:b, 2:b). Each of the four boxes in the matrix represents a choice pair (for example a, a) as a possible outcome and lists a quantity as the payoff for each player (for example 3,3) in case that choice pair is played. The payoff for player 1 (row player) is listed in the lower-left corner of each box; the payoff for player 2 (column player) is in the upper-right corner. Payoffs are descriptively listed in the order: row player, column player. Each player seeks to maximize her payoff by choosing the box with the highest available payoff to herself, taking into account the best move available to the other player. Each expects the other player to do likewise. Each has complete information; that is, the available strategies, payoffs, and each player's "type" (psychological profile) are common knowledge. In sum, players choose based on their ordered preferences (highest payoff = most preferred) and what they have good reason to believe the other player will do.

Players choose simultaneously; that is, each one lacks advance knowledge of the other player's move. They may communicate with each other,

4. Chung (2016) seeks to square Thrasymachus' and Glaucon's accounts of justice as the good of others or oneself, the weak or the strong, with reference to simple games, focusing, as I do below, on the Prisoner's Dilemma. He argues that there are two solutions to resolving inconsistencies: a democracy in which the many weak are the rulers (thus by definition strong), and a dictatorship in which the strong appropriate all social surplus, leaving the weak with only protection as an improvement in their prepolitical, "state of nature" condition. Chung does not draw attention to the co-presence of the "two men" at the end of the path of injustice or to the abstraction of "perfect craftsmen" of self-interest.

5. While employed for different purposes, Plato, *Meno* 84b–d shows that Greek thinkers were familiar with four-box matrix illustrations. Two-person games of this sort may also be played with sequential moves, and visualized with simple "extensive form" game trees; see for example chapter 3, figure 16.

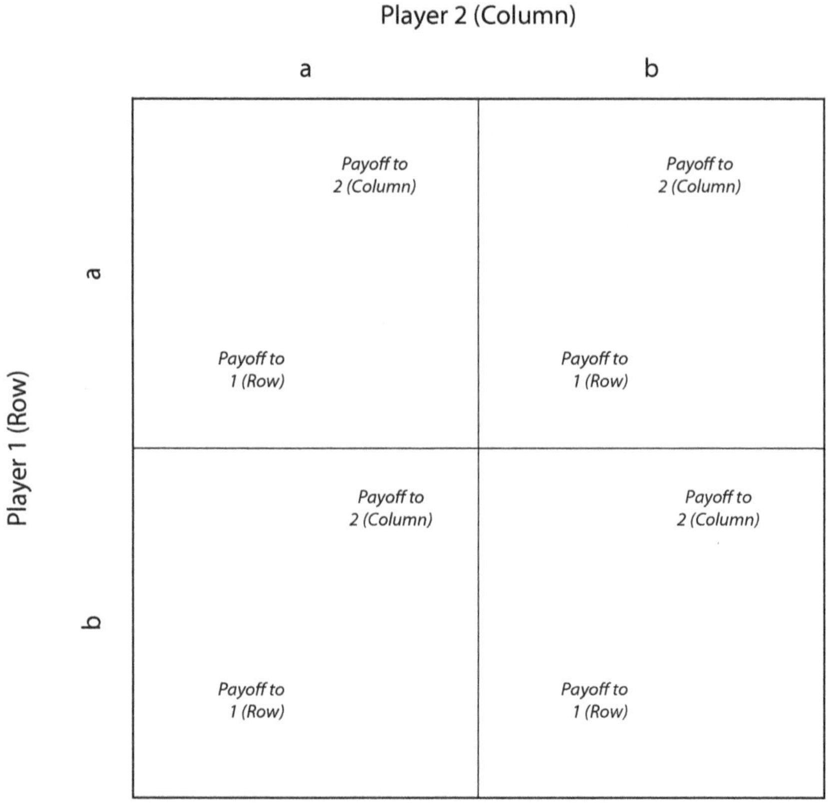

Player 2 (Column)

	a	b

(Figure: four-box normal form game)

Player 1 (Row)

a

Payoff to 2 (Column)   Payoff to 2 (Column)

Payoff to 1 (Row)   Payoff to 1 (Row)

b

Payoff to 2 (Column)   Payoff to 2 (Column)

Payoff to 1 (Row)   Payoff to 1 (Row)

FIGURE 5. Four-Box Normal Form Game: Basic Setup

NOTE: Payoff to Player 1 (row) in this and subsequent 4-box games is in the lower left of each box; payoff to Player 2 (column) is in the upper right of each box.

but a commitment (a promise to make a certain move) made by one player is credible to the other only if it leads to the promise-maker's best available payoff. After each player has chosen, they receive the payoffs in the relevant box. As in chapter 1, we are initially concerned with the basic intuitions behind each game. Thus, we begin with payoffs that indicate only ordinal ranking of preferences, rather than the relative (cardinal) weights of each player's preferences over outcomes. Preference weighting will, however, prove to be an essential part of the story, when (beginning with figure 10) we introduce the issue of aggregated social value—the collective advantage each outcome offers the players understood as a community.

If we assume (*ex hypothesi*) that in *Republic* book 2 Plato has set up something like a strategic two-player strategic game for modeling a

Greek folk theory of the origins of social order, the question we must ask is, "what sort of game is it?" Here we consider four possibilities: Harmony, Negotiation, Chicken, and Prisoner's Dilemma. In the first of these, cooperation between the players is easy; with each subsequent game cooperation becomes more difficult. Only the last game, in which cooperation is most difficult, will prove a tolerably good fit for the passages in *Republic* book 2 that we have been considering. But the other games will be useful for thinking about other passages in Greek texts.

Harmony

In the first game, if player 1 gets her most preferred outcome, so too does player 2. Their interests do not conflict; each is best off by cooperating with the other. We assume that both players are seeking similar goals—say (recalling Gyges) arriving at the destination of one of two equally nice kingdoms that lie at the opposite ends of a single road. The players are on the road, heading in opposite directions. The goals in this case are nonrival, that is, there is no competition between the players. The right strategy for each player in this game is to coordinate her actions with those of the other player so as to avoid unnecessary interference in getting to her destination. Suppose that the players must pass each other, and that the road is wide enough for them to pass without interference. All that is necessary for each to get to her destination without trouble is that each stay either to (her own) right or left as they pass.

As illustrated in figure 6, two outcomes (1:Right, 2:Right and 1:Left, 2:Left) are equally good (payoff 1 to each player). The other two (1:Right, 2:Left and 1:Left, 2:Right) result in a crash, and so are equally bad (payoff 0 to each). Both players prefer passing to crashing; neither has a preference for Right or Left. So, in this game there are two equilibria—that is, the condition in which neither player has a better move given the best move of the other player. It is just a question of which will be chosen. Assuming that there is some norm about passing (around here, when driving, we stay to the right . . . or left), the problem is solved. Absent a norm, if the players communicate, one can propose that each play Right (or Left) and the other will rationally agree. These commitments are mutually credible because they are backed by an expectation of best payoffs. So, with either a norm or communication, each player can expect to receive her full-value best outcome. With no norm or communication, the players would have an equal chance of

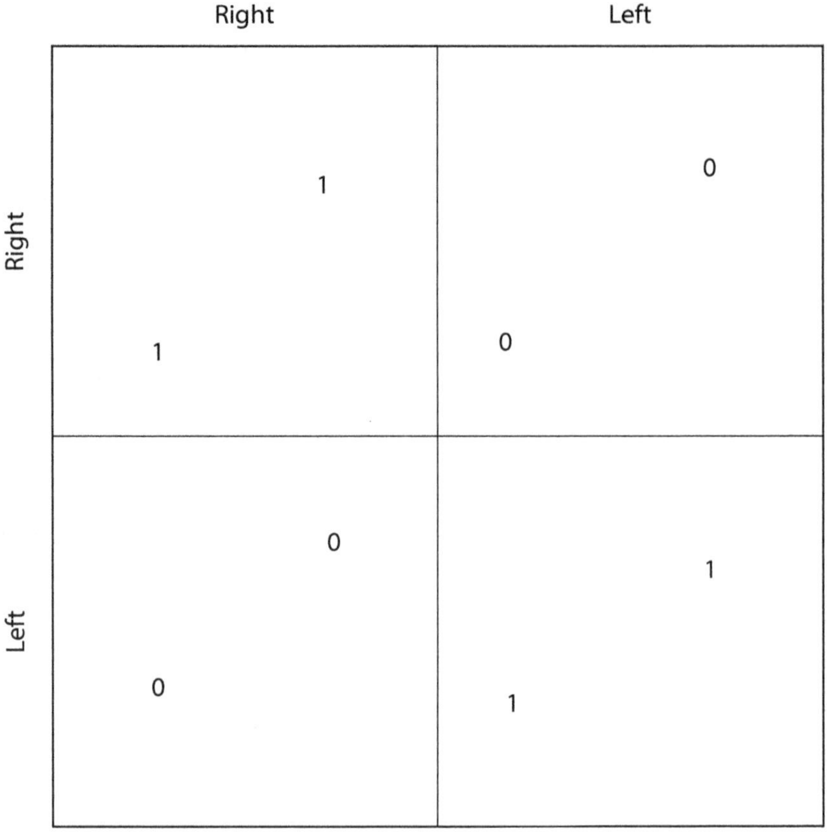

Right · Left

FIGURE 6. Harmony
NOTE: 1 is good, 0 is bad.

passing or crashing, so the expectation for each would be receiving only half of full value.[6]

Negotiation

In the second game, if player 1 gets her first-ranked, most preferred, outcome, player 2 gets only his second-best outcome. Their interests are partially, but not fully, aligned. We assume that the players are headed for some mutually desired destination (say a nice kingdom), which they

6. Coordination in game theory: R. Hardin 1991, 1995; Calvert 1995; Camerer 2003: chap. 7.

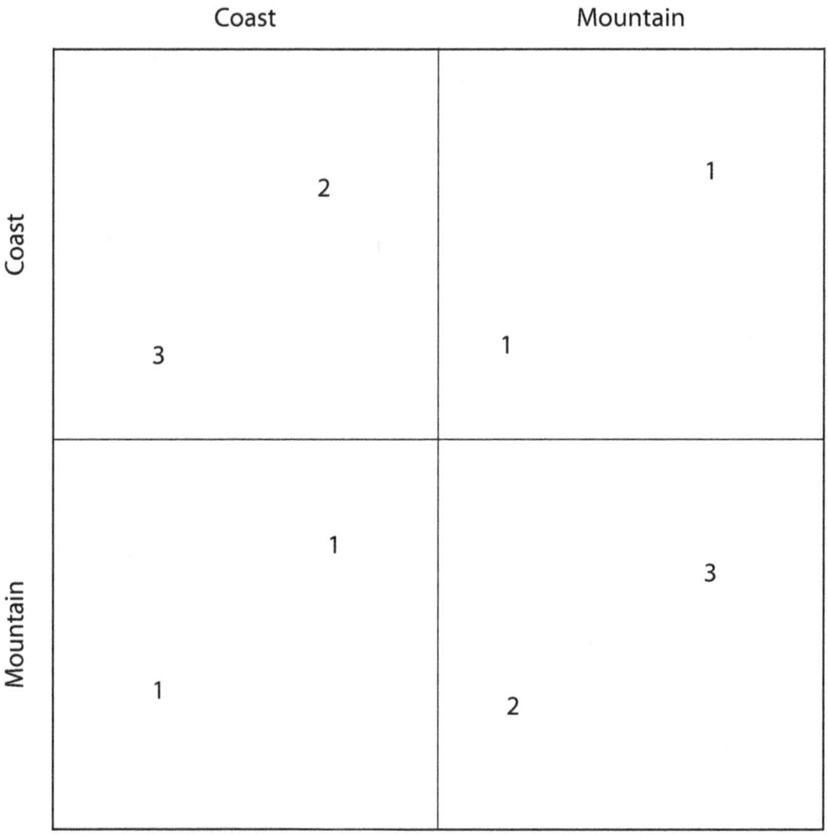

	Coast	Mountain
Coast	2 3	1 1
Mountain	1 1	3 2

FIGURE 7. Negotiation

NOTE: 3 is best payoff, 1 is worst.

will gain if and only if they cohabit (one as king, the other as queen). Otherwise (if they do not cohabit) each gets a low payoff (each lives as a commoner). Player 1 prefers that the capital, the city they will live in if they cohabit, be located on the coast (but rather likes mountains); player 2 prefers the mountains (but rather likes the coast). In this game, coordinated play will result in one player coming out ahead with a great payoff; the other will get a good payoff. The alternative to coordinating their choices (1:Coast, 2:Coast or 1:Mountain, 2:Mountain) is that both get a low payoff. The situation is illustrated in figure 7. Because they both prefer a good payoff to a low payoff, they will prefer coordination to noncoordination. Since each player does better, by avoiding the risk of the two low-payoff outcomes, by coming to an agreement with the other, communication can lead to some fair way (say flipping an honest coin) to decide between living together on the coast or the mountains, and thus who gets the great payoff and who must settle for the good payoff. To cement the cooperative agreement, the winner might offer the loser a side payment of some sort (say the right to decorate the palace to his or her taste). In any event, because of the uncertainty regarding the outcome, the *ex ante* expectation of each player in this game is gaining a part (but not all) of a full-value best outcome.[7]

Chicken

In the third game, if player 1 gets his top-ranked outcome, player 2 must settle for his third-best outcome. Conflict of interest is substantial. We assume that the situation is like Harmony, in that the players are traveling in opposite directions on the same road, each headed for a nice kingdom, and must pass each other. But now suppose that the road is so narrow that they cannot pass unless one player pulls off the road and is therefore delayed. Assume further that if one arrives at his kingdom before the other, he gets an extra payoff, becoming king (a queen has promised to marry the one who arrives at a kingdom first) while the loser's reputation suffers, so he lives as a commoner. The options for each player are Swerve (chicken out by pulling over) or Straight (aggressively continue down the road). If 1 plays straight and 2 swerves, 1 gets a great payoff and 2 gets a low payoff; and vice versa if 2 plays straight and 1 swerves. If both play straight (neither chickens out), both players crash, in which case each gets nothing. If both swerve they both survive, but are equally delayed; each gets a payoff that is good (arrives at kingdom with no loss of reputation) but not great (the queen tires of waiting on them and marries someone else). The situation is illustrated in figure 8. In this case communication can take the form of a threat: Either can assert that he will play straight no matter what. If the threat

---

7. This game is typically called "Battle of the Sexes" in standard game theory texts. See Camerer 2003: 27–29, 353–67. As an anonymous reader suggested, we could suppose payoffs are in money terms, and the Coast payoffs are increased to 3 1/2 and 2 1/2. If Player 1 wins the toss, the choice will be Coast. If Player 2 (who still prefers the mountains) wins the toss, both players will have the incentive to negotiate a side payment: Player 1 pays Player 2 some amount above 1/2 but below 1 1/2, and then they locate on the Coast. In this case, the question of who wins the coin flip affects only how the maximized sum of payoffs gets shared, not the choice of location. The upshot is that net gains are increased, in a way that was famously described by the Coase Theorem.

	Straight	Swerve
Straight	0 0	1 3
Swerve	3 1	2 2

FIGURE 8. Chicken

NOTE: 3 is best payoff, 0 is worst.

is credible (say the driver has visibly thrown away his steering wheel), the other player's best move is then to swerve. If both simultaneously credibly threaten, they crash. If neither credibly threatens, and both are risk-neutral, the outcome is mixed (each might privately flip a coin to decide whether to drive straight or swerve). Like Negotiation, the expectation in this game is for each to gain a part of their full-value best outcome.[8]

8. Chicken game in theory and experiments: Rapoport and Chammah 1966, with helpful summary at https://en.wikipedia.org/wiki/Chicken_(game). A vivid ancient example is the chariot race in Homer, *Iliad* book 23.

Prisoner's Dilemma

In the fourth game, if player 1 gets her most-preferred outcome, player 2 is left with his fourth-best, that is, worst outcome. Their interests are, it seems, bluntly opposed. Each player may choose to play Cooperate, that is, seek a cooperative (in the language of *Republic* book 2: "just") outcome, potentially sacrificing some immediate personal advantage in favor of a longer-term individual *and* social advantage. Or he may defect from any cooperative scheme by playing Defect whenever it furthers his immediate interests, acting, per Glaucon's specification of self-interested rationality as "injustice," to maximize his payoff without concern for the well-being of the other player.

The usual story of the Prisoner's Dilemma game (hereafter: PD) is that each of two criminals, caught by the police, is offered a choice: rat out his partner, defecting from whatever agreement he had made with her (play Defect), or clam up, cooperatively stick by that agreement (play Cooperate). If one rats out (defects) and the other clams up (cooperates), the rat is let out free (payoff 3) and the clam serves a very long sentence (payoff 0). If each rats the other out (both defect), they each get a moderately long sentence (payoff 1,1). If both clam up (both cooperate), they are convicted on some lesser charge and each serves a short sentence (payoff 2,2). The situation is illustrated in figure 9. Other stories can be told about this game. For example, for modeling social order, suppose that, if one player defects and the other cooperates, the defector becomes an absolute monarch: Per Thrasymachus' ideal-type "completely unjust" tyrant, she seizes the goods of the cooperator and enslaves him. If both defect they each live in isolation and poverty. If they both cooperate they live relatively well, sharing returns to social cooperation, as fellow citizens. Whatever the background story, each individual's highest payoff is gained by defecting while the other cooperates. Each individual's second-best payoff comes with mutual cooperation. Third-best is mutual defection. Worst is the "sucker's payoff" of cooperating when the other player defects. Defect is therefore a dominant strategy for both players. The equilibrium solution to the game is the lower-right box, with each player getting his second-to-worst payoff. It is an equilibrium solution because it represents each player's best choice (Defect), in light of the predicted choice (Defect) that will be made by the other player. In this and subsequent games in this chapter, equilibrium solutions are indicated by circled payoffs.[9]

---

9. Figures 10, 11, 12, 13, 14. For a detailed, and critical, account of the Prisoner's Dilemma game, and its role in contemporary social theory, see Amadae 2016.

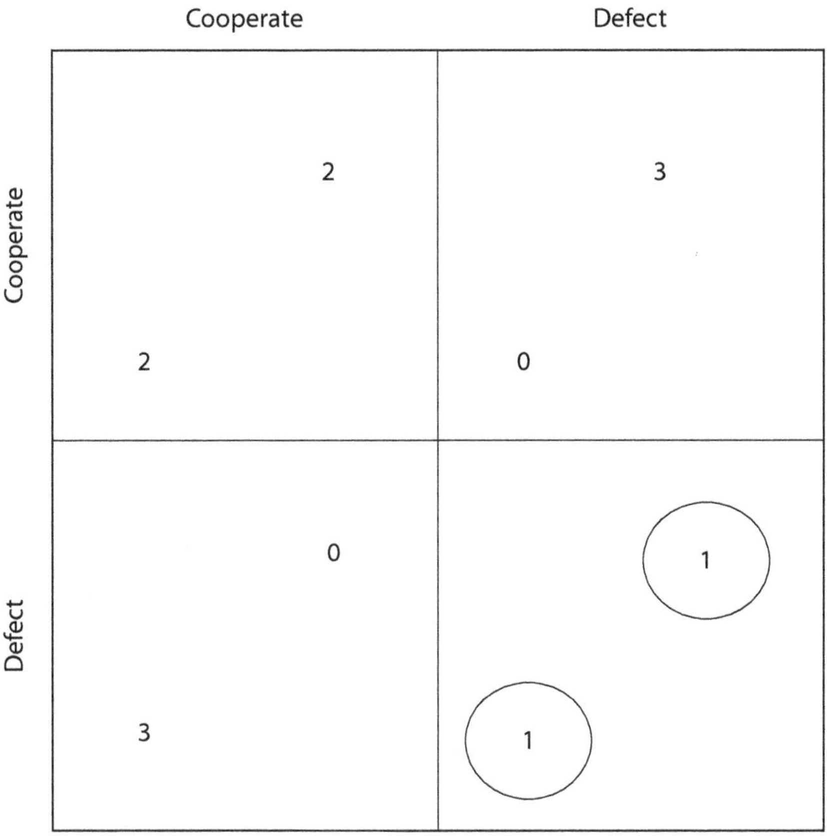

	Cooperate	Defect
Cooperate	2 2	3 0
Defect	0 3	1 1

FIGURE 9. Prisoner's Dilemma (ordinal preference ranking)

NOTE: 3 is best payoff, 0 is worst.

One other feature of this game emerges if we move from simple ordinal ranking of preferences to weighted preferences: that is, the quantities indicate the preference *strength* of each player for each outcome, not merely preference *order*. So, in figure 10, a payoff of 4 is regarded by each player as four times as good as a payoff of 1 and a payoff of -5 is not just least-good, but extremely bad. In this case, we can employ a pseudo-currency (call it "utils") to compare payoffs and also to measure the aggregated social value of the pair of payoffs in each box: We assume that adding the payoffs in each box determines the social value of the outcome. The hypothetical community (modeled by the two players) does relatively better (gets a better aggregate payoff) if both cooperate (3+3 = 6) than when both defect (1+1 = 2). So, the PD is a "dilemma" for two reasons: The equilibrium solution is suboptimal for each player *and* for the imagined community the players collectively model.

The social aggregates would, of course, change if the preference weighting were different. The essential point is that the social aggregate of the cooperative community is higher than that of the defecting community. Mutual cooperation is "Pareto optimal" in that it is the highest aggregate that is achievable without lowering the payoff to anyone.[10] But how ought we to set the relative weights for the remaining two boxes, for the choice-pairs Defect, Cooperate and Cooperate, Defect? Glaucon's specifies in the "origins of social order" passage that "the excess of evil in suffering injustice is greater than the excess of good in doing injustice" (cited above: *Republic* 358e). Thus, the loss from a "sucker's payoff," incurred from cooperating when the other defects, is greater than the gain for defecting when the other cooperates. To capture that asymmetry, along with the high cost of naïve cooperation, we may set the loss at -5 and the gain at 4. The revised PD with weighted payoffs is illustrated in figure 10.

If we try to imagine Glaucon's craftsmen of self-interest as players in one of the games sketched above, we can quickly dispense with Harmony and Negotiation. Plato's Gyges story is certainly not about coordinating in order to secure mutually advantageous access to nonrivalrous goods: There is only one queen and one kingdom; Gyges kills the former king to get them. Moreover, when provided with magic rings, each of the "two men" takes goods from others, so goods are regarded as scarce rather than nonrivalrous.[11] Finally, in the "origins of order" passage quoted above, Glaucon specifies that the players fear suffering injustice, but in coordination games there is no injustice. We can assume, then, that the game played by Glaucon's craftsmen of self-interest is competitive. Does either Chicken or PD fit Glaucon's specifications?

To decide that question, we can return to Glaucon's description of the folk theory of social cooperation: the hypothesized origins of the contractual agreement that results, "they say," in social order. Glaucon claims that, lacking the advantages that come with being uniquely empowered (as a Gygean ring-holder), each individual is in a compromised position. Her preferences are ranked in the order: (1) "act unjustly

---

10. Pareto optimality: Hausman 2018: sec. 6.2.

11. Likewise, Thrasymachus' account of the behavior of the craftsman of self-interest emphasizes the goods that he seizes, through stealth or force, at the expense of others: 343c–44c.

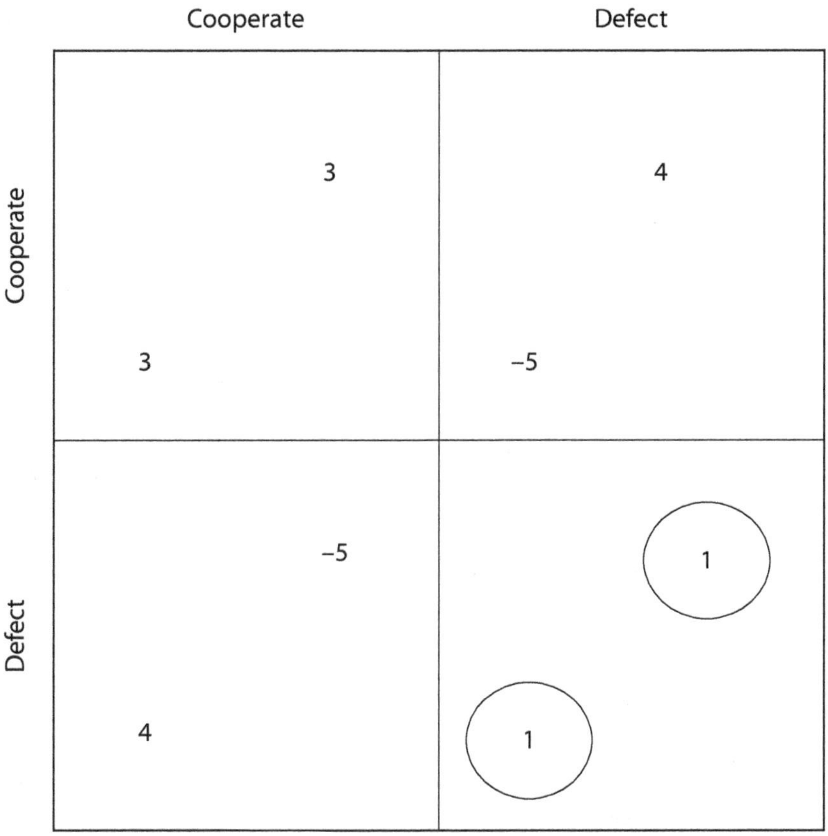
Cooperate
Defect
Cooperate
Defect
3
3
4
–5
–5
4
1
1

FIGURE 10. Revised Prisoner's Dilemma (cardinal preference weighting)

with impunity," (2) "avoid the worst," (3) "suffer injustice and be impotent to get revenge." Without a magic ring, assuming complete information, she has no way to get the best outcome—doing injustice with impunity. Meanwhile, she lives in perpetual fear of the worst—the sucker's payoff of suffering injustice without recourse. *Everyone* is assumed to be in the same position of "lack[ing] the power at once to avoid the [worst] and choose the [best]." In marked contrast to Thrasymachus on the advantage of the strong (in *Republic* book 1) and Callicles (below), Glaucon assumes equality of capability (to benefit from injustice) and liability (to suffer as a victim of injustice).

Glaucon's description of the situation maps quite well onto the PD, but not onto Chicken: According to Glaucon, each of the social contractors fears a sucker's payoff of suffering injustice and being impotent to get revenge (playing Cooperate to the other player's Defect), rather than the consequences of a catastrophe attending mutual acts of aggression (playing Straight while the other also plays Straight), or losing out (playing Swerve) due to risk aversion. The Defect, Defect equilibrium outcome of the PD does indeed land both players symmetrically "in between the best and the worst." But, as we have seen, in a PD there is another "between best and worst" outcome (Cooperate, Cooperate), which is foregone and which would be better than Defect, Defect for both players. Glaucon's description of what "they say" about the origins of social order suggests that the contractors have agreed, that is, credibly committed, to cooperate on certain rules and thereby they have gained the Pareto optimal outcome. So, if we imagine it as modeled by a PD, one way to think about the problem of social order is to ask: How did Glaucon's two craftsmen of self-interest get out of the dominant low-payoff mutual defection equilibrium to the much better (although, for each, suboptimal) situation of mutual cooperation? Of course, Plato does not put that question directly, but if we have set up the problem in the right way, his reader is entitled to pose it.

The outcome of a game (based on the choices made by the players) depends on the players' information and their motivations, that is, their moral psychology or "type." Before further considering the outcome when both players (as in the standard PD) are completely informed and motivated by narrowly egoistic self-interest, per Glaucon's specification of ideal-type hypothetical agents, we may consider the results of superficially similar games in which players are either not narrowly egoistically self-interested or asymmetrically informed. In these games, as in the revised PD of figure 10, preferences are weighted (cardinal), so payoffs are in utils rather than simple ordinal ranking.

Aristotelian Justice

Suppose, first, that the two players are equally virtuous and philosophically talented citizens of Aristotle's "polis of our prayers," the best possible practically achievable ideal community described in the *Politics,* book 7. Each chooses between a life that includes some time devoted to politics and a life devoted to full-time philosophical contemplation. We assume that in the upper-left box, each will share in doing the necessary political work of the community, ruling and being ruled over in turns (per Aristotle's specification of true citizenship in a political regime). Each will also have substantial time free for contemplation. We suppose

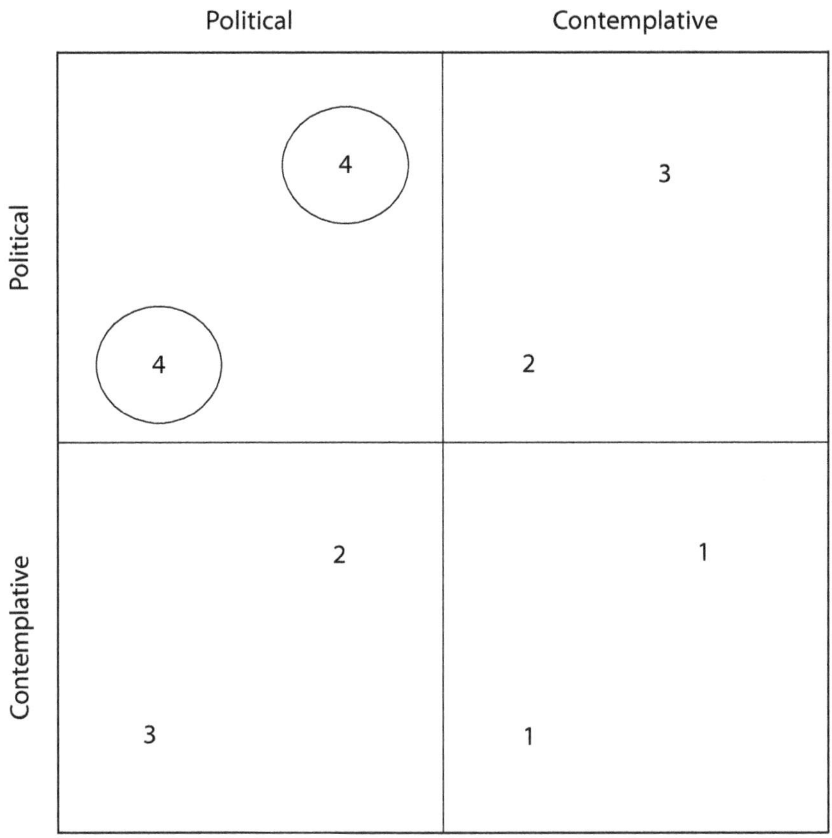

Political   Contemplative

FIGURE 11. Aristotelian Justice
NOTE: Payoffs are cardinal preference weighted.

that the Political player in the upper-right and lower-left boxes will engage in political activity full-time and will have little time for contemplation. The Contemplative player in those boxes is freed of all political duties, due to the efforts of the Political player.

Each player regards contemplation as an especially choice-worthy form of human activity, an essential part of "living well" for those capable of engaging in it (as specified in *Nicomachean Ethics* book 10 and *Politics* book 7). Having been socialized in the rules and the education of the best possible polis, each is, however, virtuous: committed to choosing and acting according to an Aristotelian conception of moderation and justice. Each will, therefore, make his choice based on Aristotle's two, compatible, definitions of justice. The first definition is based on a principle of equality: Those who are equal, in the relevant sense (here, virtue), ought to receive equal shares of whatever good is being distributed. Aristotle's second definition of justice is "the common good"—that is, the advantage of the "whole" (here, the community modeled by the two players), irrespective of the particular advantage of each of its parts (here, the individual players).[12]

Given these stipulations, each player in the Aristotelian Justice game will choose a Political life, devoting some time to the affairs of the polis, ruling and being ruled in turns. The outcome of the game will be in the upper-left box, so the payoff is 4,4. Both players cooperate in ruling and being ruled because, being equally virtuous, they choose to distribute the relevant good (the payoffs in the game) equally. The upper-right (3,2) and lower-left (2,3) boxes are unequal, distributing more to the Contemplative player, and so these outcomes are rejected as unjust. Although choosing Contemplative when the other chooses Political would enable the Contemplative player to maximize time spent in an especially desirable activity, each player prefers a just equal distribution payoff to happiness that is gained at the expense of a peer. The lower-right (1,1) box is, however, also an equal distribution. So, is the out-come of Contemplative, Contemplative equally good, from the perspec-tive of the players' motivations—and thus a second equilibrium? The answer is no, because of the second definition of justice as "the common good." The payoffs are low in the lower-right box because each knows that without political activity to guarantee security and material wel-fare, mere life will not be sustained and so living well is impossible. In this and all subsequent games in this chapter we assume cardinal prefer-ence weighting. So the sum of the quantities in each box, the aggregate social value, defines a common good. Since 8 > 2, Political, Political is the game's solution.

The game is cooperative rather than competitive because each player receives his best payoff by cooperating on Political and neither player has a better move to make in the game. So, in the terms of game theory, the Aristotelian Justice game is a variant on a coordination game with a unique equilibrium solution. The Aristotelian Justice game assumes complete information, but it violates the conditions of Glaucon's

---

12. Justice as a kind of equality, with distributive fairness, determined by relative merit: *Politics* 1318a11–b5 with Harvey 1965, and below, chapter 8.5. As the common good: *Politics* 1282b14–21; *NE* 1129b14–19, 1160a11–14. This game is not meant to decide the vexed question of whether the best life is philosophical, political, or "mixed," on which see Lockwood 2019, with literature cited.

thought experiment because the players lack the preference to benefit from injustice (an unequal distribution) if it is at the expense of an equal other.[13]

Thrasymachean Injustice

Next, let us assume that one of the players in the game has the ability always to get his best payoff at the expense of the other, per Plato's Thrasymachus' claims that the strong, unjust man always comes out ahead in his dealings with a weak, just man, to the latter's disadvantage (343c–d) and that, taken to its extreme, in a tyranny, the unjust tyrant is the happiest of men and his just subject the most miserable (344a).

We may suppose that one player is a skilled rhetorician, as Thrasymachus was reputed to be, with powers of persuasion of the sort that the Sophist Gorgias of Leontini, in Plato's dialogue named for him, asserted that he and his students possessed (Plato, *Gorgias* 452d–57c—see further, below).[14] That is, one player has sufficient persuasive power to ensure that the other player's choice will be in line with the preferences of the rhetorician. So, the story might go that the strong row player has persuaded the weak column player that the strong rule in their own advantage, but that the weak will also gain more by being ruled over by the strong than they would in any other circumstance (see further, chapter 5). Perhaps the strong player has promised to rule as a benevolent king rather than as a tyrant (see further, chapter 3). Thus, in figure 12 the strong always does better when ruling than when ruled, while the weak always does better when ruled than when ruling. If both seek to rule (upper-left), the strong does relatively better by dint of his strength; he defeats the weak in whatever contests they are engaged in. When both are ruled over the weak does better by dint of his weakness: He is not frustrated in his natural drive to rule. In the very unnatural situation of the weak ruling the strong, neither does well. So, the unique equilibrium is the upper-right: The strong player rules and does better than the weak player who is ruled, but the weak player gets what he believes is his best available payoff by being ruled and having a strong ruler over himself.

This result assumes, with Gorgias, that rhetoric actually is a power that is capable of determining others' beliefs. As we have seen, in strategic

---

13. This is a variant on a "Stag Hunt"-type assurance game, discussed in more detail below, illustrated as the Gifts of Zeus game in figure 14.

14. Ancient references to Thrasymachus and his rhetorical art: LM 35.

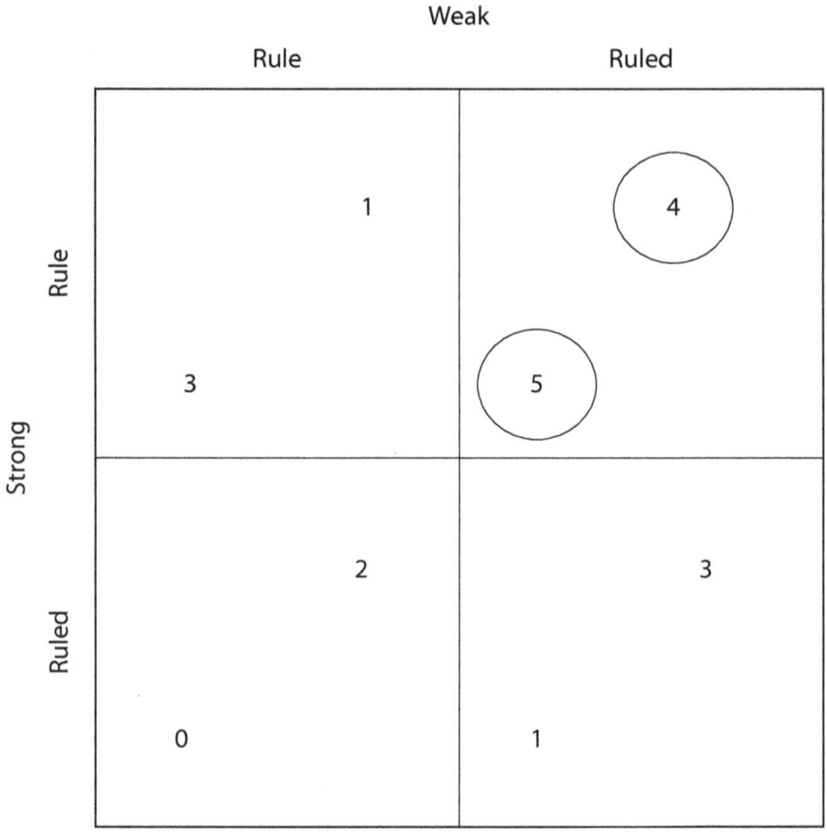

Weak

	Rule	Ruled

FIGURE 12. Thrasymachean Injustice—I (belief-based outcome)
NOTE: Payoffs are cardinal preference weighted.

game theory, a promise that is not backed up by a credible (rationally self-interested) commitment to act on it is unconvincing. As such, a promise will be discounted by a rational player, absent some means of ensuring its credibility.[15] Gorgias' account of persuasion in Plato's dialogue seeks to distinguish between the readily discounted assurance of the untrained speaker and the irresistible belief-establishing force that is exerted upon an audience by the master of rhetoric. If we assume that the strong individual is unjust in a Thrasymachean sense, the actual payoff to the weak when ruled by the strong is worse for him than any other option—per figure 13.

15. Credibility of commitments: Dixit and Skeath 1999: 308–16. Cheap talk (with special reference to legislative debate): Austen-Smith 1990.

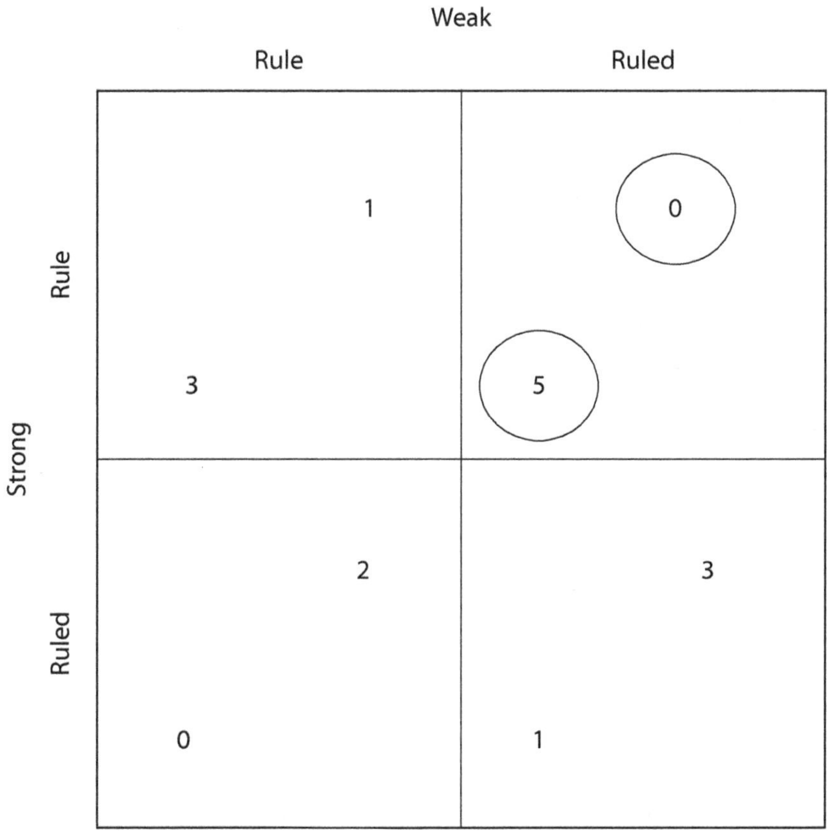

Weak

	Rule	Ruled

FIGURE 13. Thrasymachean Injustice—II (actual outcome)

NOTE: Payoffs are cardinal preference weighted. The equilibrium result violates the rules of strategic play. It is based on the false belief of Weak that the payoffs will be as per figure 12.

Assuming that row does have the power to determine column's beliefs, impelling the latter to believe that being ruled will be to their mutual benefit, the game illustrated in figure 12 has a unique equilibrium. If we extrapolate from the actual payoffs to a society, as illustrated in figure 13, we may say that the game models a highly unequal distribution of the sort advocated by Thrasymachus in *Republic* book 1 (and Callicles in Plato's *Gorgias,* below). It is a society in which the power (however achieved and maintained) of an individual or a coalition is great enough to ensure the efficient exploitation of the weak by the strong. The "social aggregate" of the Thrasymachean Injustice game of figure 13 depends entirely on the goodness to the strong of doing injustice: That is precisely the position that Socrates must invalidate if he is to answer Glaucon's challenge. The "actual payoff" version of Thrasymachean Injustice violates Glaucon's thought experiment in that one of the players is clearly not a perfect craftsman of self-interest. It likewise violates the assumption of "complete information" games in that the cooperating player is ignorant of the "type" of the other player.

2.3 REPEATED GAMES AND SOCIAL DEVELOPMENT

Having considered game variants with players motivated or informed in ways that violate both the setup of Glaucon's thought experiment and the assumptions of competitive rational choice games, we may return to what I will call "Glaucon's Dilemma"—the situation in which the players are perfect craftsmen of self-interest and playing a PD (figure 10). As we have seen, each player is predicted to defect, resulting in the unique low-payoff equilibrium of the lower-right box. This result may be described as a dilemma for at least two reasons. First, the mutual defection equilibrium gives each player his third-best (second-worst) payoff. While each avoids the worst case of the sucker's payoff, had they played Cooperate, Cooperate each player would get his second-best payoff. It is, furthermore, a dilemma because, whatever relative weights we assign, the assumed community in question gains an aggregate social value that is lower than the value that results from cooperative play.

In a one-shot game, in order to avoid the worst, each completely informed rational player will defect, so we end up at a low-payoff equilibrium. But the people in the "origins of order" story that Glaucon attributes to "them"—the Conventionalists—seem to have had repeated interactions in the course of which each has experienced *both* the advantages of doing injustice *and* the harm of suffering it: It is "when men do wrong and are wronged by one another and have experienced both," that they come to the realization of the value of the cooperative contract. So, the Conventionalist story suggests a game that is played more than once. Moreover, the ability to correct mistakes is part of Glaucon's reconfiguration of Thrasymachus' ideal-type *dēmiourgos* of self-interest (361a). So, weakening the assumption of an unerring craftsman to allow for corrigible mistakes, we may imagine that at some point each of the players had played Cooperate while the other stuck with Defect. In that case, each would have received at least one fairly large payoff (Defect, Cooperate: did wrong, and benefited substantially by it) and sustained at least one even larger loss (Cooperate, Defect: suffered wrong and was badly harmed by it). As contemporary work in game theory has established, games repeated indefinitely (without a known "last play") have multiple possible equilibria, and so it is quite possible for *us* to imagine an alternative to the low Defect, Defect payoff of the one-shot PD. The question is whether Plato could have been driving at something similar.[16]

As we have seen, Glaucon specifies that, for each individual, the *costs* of suffering wrong *exceed* the *benefits* of doing it (thus in the revised PD of figure 10: the payoff for defection if the other cooperates is 4, but the payoff for cooperating if the other defects is -5), so that each has suffered net losses as result of uncoordinated mixed play. So, we might imagine that, having each played Defect, Cooperate and Cooperate, Defect, the people in Glaucon's story would indeed have learned from experience that "the excess of evil in being wronged is greater than the excess of good in doing wrong." The implication of the passage is that having learned that hard lesson, they were in a position to act, collectively, on their knowledge: making a compact to establish rules (*nomoi*) that would enable coordinated mutual cooperation.

Learning from the experience of doing and suffering injustice apparently leads the people in Glaucon's Conventionalist folk theoretic story to make an agreement that all will renounce doing injustice, and so, in effect, consistently play Cooperate. If all stick to the agreement, this is mutually beneficial (although not optimal in any one play for anyone); everyone not only avoids the worst, but also gets his or her second-best payoff. Moreover, the society as a whole gets a relatively high payoff. And this agreement is, then, "they say," the origin of the concept of a sense of justice as some sort of fairness, one version of which is the Aristotelian definition of justice sketched above. Moreover, and essential to our question of the emergence of social order, this sort of agreement is said by "them" to be the origin of authoritative laws with the power to command each individual not to make certain self-aggrandizing choices,

16. Folk Theorem and multiple equilibria for repeated games: Dixit and Skeath 1999: 257–66; Binmore 2007: chap. 5; and below, n. 22. In an article aimed at elucidating commercial relations in classical Athens and in modern international markets, rather than the origins of social order, Halkos, Kyriazis, and Economou (2021) model the passage as a two-stage PD variant with repeated play and complete but imperfect information. In their game the payoffs for Cooperate, Defect are 5,15; for Defect, Defect 2,2; Cooperate, Cooperate pays off at 10,10. In the first stage both players defect. In the second stage, having learned from the poor result in the first stage, they both cooperate, and continue to do so in subsequent rounds. By adding sophisticated state-level inspection institutions, the article assumes considerably more than Plato provides in the passage.

not to engage in behavior that would (just so long as others were law-abiding) lead to her most-favored outcome and thereby most fully satisfy her preferences.[17]

So understood, Glaucon's account of what "they say" about the origin of social order in the choices of rational persons, resulting in a compact that creates law, is reminiscent of that of Thomas Hobbes in *Leviathan* ([1651] 1996). Like Glaucon's "them," Hobbes postulates self-interest (fear of harm to self and self-aggrandizing "glory") as the primordial motivation of individuals. And like "them," Hobbes postulates a rough equality among the persons living in prepolitical conditions; given weapons and temporary coalitions, each has the potential to threaten all others. Hobbes' solution, like "theirs," is a social contract, in which individuals agree to give up some of their pristine freedom of choice and action because they recognize that a contract is their only way out of the miserable conditions that result from mutual defection. Hobbes specifies that the contract must establish a lawless third-party enforcer, an absolute sovereign: the Leviathan.[18]

We need not leap all the way forward to seventeenth-century social contract theory to find comparisons to Glaucon's origin story. In Plato's dialogue *Gorgias,* Callicles is introduced as an aspiring politician in Athens and a student of the master rhetorician Gorgias, from whom he hopes to learn sophistic rhetorical techniques. These will, Gorgias has promised, allow Callicles to dominate others by means of persuasive speech. Thus, Callicles expects to have the opportunity to behave without concern for social constraints: In effect, rhetoric will be his magic ring. In his first extended speech in the dialogue (Plato, *Gorgias* 483a–84b), Callicles makes a point of contrasting *phusis* with *nomos,* proclaiming that, by nature, the most formidable of men, those with the power to "have more" (*pleon echein*), use their strength to take more—that is, to satisfy their preferences by maximizing payoffs to themselves at others' expense.

17. This solution is in some ways similar to that of McClennen (2001), who argues for an alternative view of rationality that dispenses with the requirement of equilibrium play in favor of Pareto optimization: McClennen's point is that truly rational individuals will prefer the highest social payoff, turning the PD into a coordination problem. He suggests that this offers a much more obvious explanation for the emergence of social order, which is the concern of the texts in this chapter.

18. The closeness of Glaucon's "origins of order" story and Hobbes' social contraction account has often been remarked on: see, for example, Irwin 1995: 185. Chung (2015) models Hobbes' state of nature (and the escape from it) as a Bayesian game in which each player has only incomplete information about the "type" of the other players; see n. 36 and section 2.6, below, on the implicit game set up in Protagoras' Great Speech.

He illustrates his point by reference to the presumably natural behavior of nonhuman animals and imperialistic Persian monarchs.[19]

In contrast to the rule-makers in the Conventionalist origins of social order story, who were equal in capacity and mutually fearful, according to Callicles, the original authors of laws that constrain the naturally strong, and thereby frustrate naturally self-aggrandizing behavior, are the weak (*astheneis*) and many (*Gorgias* 483b). They make laws forbidding anyone to "have more and more" (*pleonektein*) because they fear (*ekphobountes*) the formidable (*dunatoi*) few. Thus, the weak establish behavior-constraining laws in their own interest. The many and weak also establish norms that prescribe blaming those who do behave in blatantly self-aggrandizing ways. The many prefer that all have equal shares, because, being inferior and unable to get greater shares, equality offers them the best payoff they can hope for. In terms of the games sketched above, Callicles seems to imagine social order as a variant on the Chicken game, in which the chickens rule and have set up traffic laws to block the option of anyone aggressively driving Straight.

Callicles' argument about the origin of constraining *nomoi* recalls the Conventionalist argument of the Anonymous Iamblichi (see introduction). It is also in some ways reminiscent of Glaucon's account of the folk theory of the origins of social order. In each case, social order, exemplified in laws and norms, is established because of rational fear of the bad consequences arising from a situation in which individuals do as they please and take as much as they can get. The difference is that Glaucon identifies the motivation for lawmaking as a universal mutual fear that the cost of suffering injustice is, for each individual, greater than the benefit from the opportunity to do injustice. In Callicles' story, by contrast, the prepolitical human population is already sorted into many weak persons and a few strong ones. As in Glaucon's thought experiment, Callicles assumes that self-interest is a universal human motivation. His formidable few and weak many have identical moral psychologies; they differ in their capability and aggressiveness, but not in their motivations. The many and weak fear the few and strong, because, one-on-one, strong individuals have the will and the capability to take more for themselves. Recognizing that they will be losers if the strong are unconstrained, the individually weak many choose, as their

19. Callicles in the *Gorgias:* Irwin 1977: 28–29, 1995: 101–6; C. C. W. Taylor 2007: 8–11, 16; Kamtekar 2005 (on rhetoric and democracy); Barney 2017 (with comparison to Glaucon in *Republic* book 2).

best available outcome, to make laws, imposing an unnaturally egalitarian social order on strong and weak alike.

Callicles' distinction between the natural order, in which the individually formidable few take more, and the egalitarian legal order created by the individually weak many suggests that the existing social equilibrium is unstable. He analogizes the means by which the weak constrain the strong to a practice of capturing lions while still cubs, and enslaving them by enchantments. The enchantment consists of telling the strong that it is necessary to have equal shares, and that this is what is fair and just. He also alludes to the possibility of a transition to a new order of things, one in which nature will have reasserted itself. Callicles predicts that a real man will someday emerge, one who has a "sufficient nature" (*phusin hikanēn*). That man will rid himself of all constraints, and proceed to "trample on our documents, and magic tricks, and charms, and on all the laws that are contrary to nature. Then our slave will be revealed to be our master, and the true justice of nature will shine forth" (*Gorgias* 484a). Clearly Callicles fancies himself for the role.

2.4 COMMITMENT PROBLEMS

A central problem with Callicles' argument from nature and strength is quickly revealed when Socrates puts Callicles' conclusions to the test (488b–89b): Since the weak many were, by Callicles' account, able to constrain the superior few (recalling the Anonymous Iamblichi's superman), the many are, self-evidently, collectively more powerful than the few. The collectively powerful many do just what the individually powerful few would prefer to do: maximize their own expected payoffs.[20] Egalitarian laws are, therefore, artifacts of (collective) strength used to achieve a preferred (individual and social) outcome. Social order, in the form of *nomos*, simply is the will of the strong—that is to say, it is well aligned with Callicles' conception of *phusis*. It remains to be seen how it is that the many were capable of inaugurating and sustaining coordinated collective action at scale; that question will be taken up in later chapters. But, assuming (as Callicles does) that many self-interested individuals are in fact capable of collective action, Callicles' "advantage

---

20. This is precisely the argument of Ps-Xenophon ("The Old Oligarch"), *Ath. Pol.*, in which the anonymous author stresses that poor Athenians acted rationally (although wrongly) in their own collective interest by choosing to rule (as a *dēmos*) rather than to be enslaved by the elite (in an order he describes as *eunomia*). See below, chapter 5.2.

of the strong" argument is self-defeating. It ends in an argument that explains, if anything, majoritarian democracy: A lawless demos was one Hobbesian option for the sovereign. It was, however, Hobbes' own least favored option (after monarchy and aristocracy) and certainly not what Callicles, or Plato's Socrates, imagined as a good answer to the problem of social order.

If Callicles-type claims represent the standard sort of argument that was being made by those classical-era Greek Thrasymacheans who concerned themselves with the social and political implications of the *nomosphusis* distinction, we can see why Plato used Glaucon's thought experiment in *Republic* book 2 to set the high-bar challenge that Socrates must meet if he is to demonstrate that justice is a good in itself and the just man happier than the unjust. But Glaucon's version of the Conventionalist theory of social order, quoted above, raises fundamental questions for which, after the Gyges' ring thought experiment has been completed, it has no good answers: How is it that a cooperative social outcome determines the behavior that enables it? Why does learning from mistakes not simply drive the equilibrium back to Defect, Defect? How is it that anyone ever comes to trust another's promise to cooperate?[21]

As suggested above, the Conventionalist story implies repeated play, which allows for cooperative equilibria. But, depending on future discounting, whether the game is infinitely or finitely repeated, and punishment costs, repeated games allow for various noncooperative equilibria as well.[22] *How,* given the motivational premises of the thought experiment, does the society described by Glaucon's "them" arrive at a stable, self-enforcing Cooperate, Cooperate state, and then stick with it? There is no specification in the Conventionalist story of third-party enforcement of a cooperative agreement. So, it is not clear why, assuming that punishment is costly to the punisher, the rules are enforced at a level that ensures the cooperative outcome.

This is the point of Hobbes' social contract argument in *Leviathan.* Hobbes' prepolitical humans agree upon the original contract among themselves specifically to create a sovereign: a lawless third-party maker and enforcer of rules. That solution was indeed considered in the Greek tradition, notably in Herodotus' stories of the origins of Asian

---

21. On fallacious and nonfallacious forms of functionalism, see Barry 1978: 168–73.

22. This is the conclusion of the so-called Folk Theorem of repeated games (not to be confused with the Greek folk theory of instrumental rationality); see literature review at https://en.wikipedia.org/wiki/Folk_theorem_(game_theory), accessed November 6, 2020.

monarchies (chapter 3). But the Conventionalist theory of social order sketched by Glaucon does not take that step. The contract he alludes to seems not only to be collectively agreed-upon but also self-enforcing.

By claiming that, because a certain set of rules will be better for each and all once it is in place, it can be readily brought about and sustained, the Conventionalist story appears to run up against the conclusion of Glaucon's thought experiment: that each self-interested individual will violate rules whenever it is in her interest. The Conventionalist story related by Glaucon suggests that repeated interaction, with corrigible mistakes, allows people to learn about relative costs and benefits of defection and cooperation. But that story does not explain how learning is operationalized through credible commitments and collective action. In sum, what Conventionalists say about the origins of social order is threatened by what I have called Glaucon's Dilemma, which arises from the refined Thrasymachean rationality developed in Glaucon's Challenge.[23]

In the *Republic* Plato's Socrates ultimately disposes of both Thrasymachean and Conventionalist answers. He offers a unique solution to the problem of social order in the face of Glaucon's Dilemma: philosopher-kings rule, supported by a military coalition of Guardians and equipped with an ideological toolkit of Noble Lies. Their interests perfectly coincide with those of the ruled, resulting in stable order through social harmony. As in the Harmony game (above), each has good reason to "stay in his lane" because there are no conflicts of interest. The premise that a truly rational person would have the narrowly egoistic, materialistic preferences that the ring of Gyges thought experiment posited as universal among "real men" is refuted by introducing an objective basis for preference and a sound epistemological foundation for belief. By contrast, other, familiar forms of social order are characterized by Plato's Socrates as endemically unstable in the face of

23. Barney (2017) notes that, unlike Callicles (and Thrasymachus), Glaucon does not lean on a putative division of human society into the naturally weak and strong, and that it leaves open the question: "given the merely conventional character of justice and the constraints it places on our pleonectic nature, why should any one of us be just, whenever injustice would be to our advantage?" But she does not pursue the implications of this question for the origins of law and social contract. Chung (2016) asks a related, but different, question: How can Thrasymachus' initial argument for "the interests of the strong" be squared with Glaucon's apparent conclusion that justice is in the interest of the weak? Halkos, Kyriazis, and Economou (2021) elide the problem of credibility of commitments by reference to sophisticated Athenian institutions featuring officials with the power to investigate and punish violations.

the expected behavior of self-interested agents (*Republic* book 8: see chapter 6.2).

Other Greek thinkers offered quite different solutions to the question of how self-interested individuals might have established a self-enforcing social order, predicated on rules allowing for reasonably stable coordinated cooperation. The rest of this chapter sketches how a few Greek texts address the question of the emergence of order, focusing on the problems that order is required to solve, and assessing a mechanism by which coordinated action may be effectuated. Accounts of the prepolitical human condition have come down to us in the works of Thucydides (1.2–8), Plato (*Protagoras, Statesman, Laws* book 3), Polybius (6.5–6), Diodorus Siculus (1.8, 1.90), and a few later writers. These fragments of what was in antiquity a much fuller tradition about the primitive past were collected and skillfully analyzed by Thomas Cole (1967), who sought to make sense of the doxographic tradition (i.e., sorting out whose work influenced whose). Cole suggested that many of the surviving texts concerned with what he called "Greek anthropology" owed a debt to the mostly lost work of the fifth-century Athenian writer Democritus.

Leaving aside the fascinating, but for our purposes, tangential, puzzles of doxography, it is clear enough that the general question of the emergence of social order was raised in a wide range of classical and Hellenistic texts (section 2.5). I will argue that the specific problem I am calling Glaucon's Dilemma was taken up in Plato's *Protagoras* (section 2.6). Plato's Protagoras self-consciously amends the assumption, common to Thrasymachean versions of the folk theory, (e.g. *Gorgias* 488b), that the strong naturally exploit the weak. He invokes a moral psychology, common to most, but not all, persons, that adds to the preference ordering of rational choice-makers an inherent sense of justice (*dikē*), understood as a willingness to impose costs on rule-breakers, and of shame (*aidōs*), understood as a tendency to impose psychological costs upon oneself (internalizing others' blame) when seeking to gain benefits by acting unjustly. The PD is thereby transformed into an assurance game with two equilibria, one of which offers relatively high individual and social payoffs.

Protagoras drives his hypothesized community towards the high-payoff equilibrium by modeling human society as a repeated game with uncertainty (imperfect information) and updating (players make choices in subsequent rounds based on the outcome of previous rounds). This provides an explanation for the existence of dynamically sustainable (if not perfectly just), self-enforcing forms of productive cooperation through credible commitment to constraining social rules. It does so in the face of less-than-universal cooperation and without the metaphysics underpinning Plato's own preferred solution to the cooperation problem, as developed in the later books of the *Republic*.

2.5 FROM PRIMITIVE ANARCHY TO SOCIAL ORDER

Although the Greeks were aware of a tradition that there had been a Golden Age of ease and plenty sometime in the mythic past, the dominant Greek way of thinking about change over time was a narrative of progress.[24] That is to say, a well-educated citizen of a Greek polis, living in the age of Plato, would be likely to suppose that the technological, economic, and political level of his contemporary world was the product of prior social development. In the distant past (as, in his own time, on the fringes of what he took as civilization) people lived at a primitive level: in poverty, without advanced technology, without law or social order beyond the level of close kin. As such, they were continually exposed to existential threats.

Existential threat was a central theme in Greek accounts of early human existence: Mankind in a primitive state of development hovered at the edge of extinction. People were scattered across the landscape, living as individuals or in tiny kinship groups; there were no substantial towns or cities. Depending on the ancient source, technological primitivism might include the lack of knowledge of the use of fire, metals, and agriculture.[25] Even with basic technology to aid them, humans were endemically exposed to attacks by predatory animals.[26] But human predators were also a source of danger, both the naturally formidable individuals alluded to by Plato's Callicles and the bands of pirates and marauders who are Thucydides' concern in the "Archaeology" (1.5–8; see chapter 6.2–3).[27] It was fear of these endemic threats to vulnerable

---

24. On the concept of progress in Greek thought, see Cole 1967; Athenian embrace of progressive innovations: D'Angour 2011. Greek notions of progress do not, however, assume that all cultures progress, or that Greek progress will be sustained indefinitely, or that there is a final end towards which history is progressing.

25. Absent technology: Plato, *Protagoras* 321c–d, *Statesman* 1274b–d; *Laws* 677a–c.

26. Predatory animals: Plato, *Protagoras* 322b, *Statesman* 1274c; *Laws* 681a; Polybius 6.1.7; Diodorus Siculus 1.8.2, 1.15.5. Porphyry, *De Abstinentia* 1.10–11.

27. Powerful individuals, pirates: Thucydides 1.5–8; Plato, *Gorgias* (see discussion above); Diodorus Siculus 1.90; Porphyry, *De Abstinentia* 1.10.

individuals and small bands that motivated attempts to cooperate at greater social scale.[28]

I have suggested that Plato's *Republic* book 2 account sets up a dilemma of social development: How did rationally self-interested individuals come to cooperate well enough to move forward, from the primitive level at which they began, to the relatively flourishing societies known to classical-era Greek readers? In some other Greek texts the issue of the origin of social order is described in sociological terms as a group-level response to danger or divine fiat. Plato, in the *Laws* (3.678c–81a) says that the threat of wild animals led to the creation of communities that surrounded themselves with rough walls. Within these communities aristocratic rulers (originally heads of kinship groups) cooperated on matters of social order. In the *Statesman* (274b–d), Plato says that, after the end of a mythic "age of Kronos," during which a divine shepherd had cared for the human flock, weak and defenseless humans were preyed upon by wild animals. They were saved by the gifts of the gods: fire, technology, and agriculture, and later they came to be ruled by monarchs. Aristotle (*Politics* 1252a–b) invokes an inherent sociability that led humans through several developmental stages from the nuclear family (plus slaves) ruled naturally by the father, to villages and extended kinship groups ruled by king-like clan leaders, and eventually to the polis. We will consider Aristotle's account in more detail in chapter 4.1.

Other authors offer simple explanations that come down to individual reactions to external stimuli, specifically to fear arising from existential threats: Porphyry (*De Abstinentia* 1.10–11, with Cole 1967: 71–72), a third-century-CE philosopher, drawing on a classical-era source, says that people came together in communities motivated by fear of wild animals and men of evil intent, recognizing the advantage of mutual aid. Diodorus Siculus (1.8) goes one step further: "Since they were attacked by the wild beasts, they came to each other's aid, being instructed by expediency [*to*

---

28. Larger-scale cooperation: Plato *Gorgias* 483b–c; Plato *Laws* 680e–81b; Aristotle, *Politics* 1252b24 ff.; Diodorus Siculus 1.8. The idea that external threat is necessary, and at least potentially sufficient, for effective collective action is a recurrent motif in ancient and early modern political thought: Evrigenis 2009. Although referring to the threat from wild animals, the Epicurean account of human origins appears to be quite different. Robitzsch (2017) argues that Epicureans were distinctly "non-Hobbesian" in postulating that the social contract that brings about social order was struck only after technological advances had modified human nature to enable and require cooperation.

sumpheron], and when gathered together in this way by reason of their fear, they gradually came to recognize their mutual characteristics."

These "response-to-threat" accounts of the origins of order do not seem to assume the Thrasymachean variant of the folk theory. So, they may be modeled by some variant on one of the two coordination games (Harmony, Negotiation) discussed above. As we saw, coordination in a condition of nonrivalrous goods is facilitated by communication and by shared norms. Coordination is more difficult, however, when there is a shared desire for order and no advantage to defection, but there is no communication, no established norms, indeed no single path to follow.

Thomas Schelling ([1960] 1980) generalized and formalized the solution to the problem of coordination without communication or preset rules by reference to "focal points" (now sometimes called Schelling points). A focal point can be any commonly recognized symbol. Schelling's examples were prominent landmarks: for natives of the New York city region, for example, the information desk at Grand Central Station. Common knowledge of the focal point, among people with a reason to coordinate their actions in order to reach mutually desired result (they want to find each other for a lunch date in a big city), enables people to achieve a mutually desired cooperative outcome (they find each other), even in the absence of a prearranged plan of action (they forgot to discuss when or where they would meet). Each rationally chooses to coordinate on the focal point (shows up at the information desk at noon), so the problem is solved and all involved gain their desired end.

Diodorus Siculus (*Library of History* 1.90.1–2), in a passage that may ultimately derive from Democritus, offers something like Schelling's focal point coordination solution in a discussion of the emergence of early social organization in Egypt. Diodorus' Egyptian narrative assumes that humans had, per above, come together in groups for security against wild animals. But he then brings up the Thrasymachus/Callicles issue of the presence of strong and aggressive elements in the extended human ecology within which these groups had formed.

> When men first ceased living like the beasts and gathered into groups, at the outset they kept devouring each other and warring among themselves, the more powerful ever prevailing over the weaker; but later those who were deficient in strength, taught by expediency [*to sumpheron*], grouped together, and took for the device on their standard [*sēmeion*] one of the animals which was later made sacred; then, when those who were from time to time in fear flocked to the standard, an organized body [*sustēma*] was formed which was

not to be despised by any who attacked it. And when everybody else did the same thing, the whole people came to be divided into organized bodies [*kata sustēmata*].

Here we have a story of primeval misery (including cannibalism) that is compounded by civil strife and domination by the powerful. The response to these threats is coordination among the weak. What is distinctive in Diodorus' Egyptian narrative is the introduction of a nonverbal focal point as the mechanism facilitating coordination: A banner or plaque with a picture of an animal serves as a device that enables multiple weak individuals to assemble in response to existential threats. As in Diodorus' earlier account of primitive cooperation against wild animals (above), expediency (*to sumpheron*) is the "teacher." But it is the focal point of the animal-standard that allows many individuals to act in a coordinated manner, as an organization (*sustēma*). Notably, Diodorus says that the use of the animal-standard was widely recognized as an effective coordination mechanism: It is adopted in a cascade of adaptive imitation by the rest of the Egyptian population, which thereby comes to be organized (*kata systēmata*).

Diodorus' account, like, for example, that of Thucydides (1.3–1.6), emphasizes the high costs of noncooperation—mutual threat, strife, and self-aggrandizement by the powerful. Diodorus offers a neat mechanism, in the form of a Schelling-type focal point, which explains how coordination was effected in the face of those threats. But he does not solve our puzzle of how the advantageous new order was sustained in equilibrium. Coordinated mass action is readily explicable as a one-off event in a large body of persons (R. Hardin 1991), as it is in the costless Harmony case. But Diodorus' story concerns what becomes habitual cooperative behavior under conditions of resource scarcity (wars of aggression). That behavior is costly, both to each of the many weak individuals who must confront danger once they have rallied together and to the predatory powerful whose preference for domination is frustrated by the use of the mechanism.

How was the response-to-threat, focal-point-based social order sustained over time, such that it became well organized and dependable? Security against external threat is a public good, shared by all in a community, but dependent on willingness of individuals to act so as to sustain it. Modern choice theory has shown that public goods are liable to common pool resource and free-rider problems (G. Hardin 1968). That set of problems was recognized in the Greek tradition, notably by Aristotle who, in criticism of Plato's plan for the Guardians' communal social order in the *Republic,* points out that whatever is held in common by the greatest number has the least care bestowed upon it, and that when it comes to public goods, each individual is prone to shirk, expecting another to fulfill the need (*Politics* 1261b30–40, cf. 1263a10–15; see further chapter 7.5). In Diodorus' case, that would mean letting others take the risks involved in flocking to the standard and opposing the powerful. If we take seriously the motivational assumptions of Glaucon's Dilemma, we need an analogue to E. Ostrom's proposed solution to public goods problems (Ostrom 1990; Ostrom et al. 1999), a reason that rational individuals will forego free-riding on the cooperation of others. And we need to know why the threat of free-riding would not precipitate a cascade of defection, leading quickly to a collapse of social order.

2.6 PLATO'S PROTAGORAS ON ORDER AND MOTIVATION

A passage in Plato's *Protagoras* addresses Glaucon's Dilemma head-on, by suggesting that sustained cooperation at scale could never be achieved in a population of "Thrasymachean" narrow egoists, just by their recognition of the benefits that would accrue if the new order were in place. The dialogue features a long speech by Protagoras of Abdera (320d–28d), a famous Sophist who is visiting Athens, offering to teach fee-paying young Athenians an advanced course in the political craft (*politikē technē*), which he defines as the effective management of both households and states. Protagoras suggests that solving what we are calling Glaucon's Dilemma, and thereby explaining the fact of social order, requires modifying Thrasymachean assumptions about human psychology. Moreover, he situates choice-making agents in a repeated game with updating and communication.

As in every Platonic dialogue, it is important to keep in mind that it is Plato who provides each character with his lines. There certainly was a real Sophist named Protagoras (LM 31); a few short quotations from his works survive, but it would be wrong to think that Plato's Protagoras is true in every (or any particular) respect to the original. In what follows, when I refer to "Protagoras," I mean (as in the case of, e.g., "Glaucon" or "Callicles") Plato's character in the dialogue rather than the historical person. On the other hand, I assume that each of Plato's characters is carefully drawn to exemplify and articulate some intellectual position that Plato thought worth exploring or exposing. Plato's Protagoras presumably develops a position that Plato's original readers would have recognized as relevantly like positions being argued either by the real Protagoras or by other Sophists in the classical era. Since what we are after is a better understanding of background Greek ideas about rationality and choice, that is good enough for our purposes.[29]

Unlike Plato's Gorgias, Plato's Protagoras does not advertise his art as enabling its possessors to dominate others by special powers of persuasion. Rather, he suggests, he has developed a higher-order version of the sort of informal teaching and learning that characterizes (he argues) a reasonably well-functioning Greek polis—here exemplified by contemporary Athens. To situate his art in the democratic context sketched by Socrates in challenging Protagoras to explain how virtue can be taught, Protagoras tells a fable (muthos) of human origins. His fable seems specifically designed to address the problem I am calling Glaucon's Dilemma.

According to Protagoras' creation story, we humans were initially brought into existence by divine fiat, but the process was mishandled, leaving us without the life-preserving natural capabilities enjoyed by other animals. To secure the survival of the human race, Prometheus stole fire and technology from the gods (and was punished accordingly by Zeus). Thus provided, humans lived apart from one another. But, lacking the craft of war, which Protagoras defines as one part of the "political craft," they found themselves defenseless against wild animals. "So, they sought to band themselves together and secure their lives by founding poleis. Yet as often as they were banded together they did injustice to one another through the lack of political craft and thus they began to be scattered again and to perish" (322a–b).

What is notable here is that Protagoras has added a stage to the standard Greek origins story: As in the "response-to-threat" accounts, humans come together to preserve themselves from dangers that threaten their lives. But in Protagoras' story, they cannot sustain cooperation at scale, due to their tendency to wrong one another—to act unjustly, presumably because of their "Thrasymachean" motivations. Here, then, is Glaucon's Dilemma: The dominant strategy of defection

---

29. Farrar (1988: chap. 3) offers a thoughtful and sympathetic treatment of Protagoras, and emphasizes that Plato's Protagoras (a character she calls "Platagoras") must not be mistaken for the actual Sophist. Segvic (2009: chap. 1) analyzes the views of Plato's Protagoras, in respect to democracy, power, competence, and the good life, concluding that Protagoras' rival conception of moral learning and political and civic virtue recurs in Plato's Republic and that Aristotle's views were shaped by the dispute between Plato and the Sophists, especially Protagoras. See further, Davison 1953; Brisson 1975; Schiappa 1991; Kierstead 2018, 2021; Bonazzi 2020: 66–75; and the commentary in Hubbard and Karnofsky 1982.

makes beneficial, high-payoff cooperation impossible to sustain *even in the face of existential threats* for those with the narrowly egoistic rationality that Glaucon attributes to his hypothetical craftsmen of self-interest. Threats may be necessary for the emergence of social order, but they are, in Protagoras' tale, insufficient.

At this point in the story, divinity reenters the picture: To forestall human extinction, Zeus commands that the original (presumably Thrasymachean) human moral psychology be augmented by distributing "shame [*aidōs*] and concern for justice [*dikē*] among men, so that there would be order [*kosmoi*] within poleis and bonds [*desmoi*] of friendship [*philia*] to unite them." The new moral psychology is to be distributed generally: Zeus orders that all (*pantes*) must share in it because "poleis cannot exist if only a few people have a share, as is the case with the other crafts." But Zeus then decrees death, "as a disease of the polis" (*hōs noson poleōs*) for anyone who is incapable of sharing in shame and a sense of justice (322c–d). The fable thus acknowledges the possibility that some individuals may retain the previous, unrevised moral psychology and that their behavioral motivation could, like a contagious disease, spread through the community. Such individuals are, therefore, dangerous enough to social order to require a rule mandating their extermination. Moreover, as we will see, while the new psychology makes sustained cooperation possible, the "bonds of friendship" do not eliminate motivations of self-interest or strategic calculation.

Moving from mythology (*muthos*), to explanation (*logos*), Protagoras demonstrates the analytic value of his fable by pointing out that, now that there is social order in poleis, in an ordinary Greek community like Athens, even if a man is known to be unjust, if he publicly admits to being so, his admission would be considered evidence of madness (*mania*). And so, "everyone, they say, must claim to be just, whether he is or is not, and whoever does not make some pretension to justice is mad; since it is necessary that all without exception share in it in some way or other, or else not be of human kind" (323b–c). With this normative behavioral standard in mind, Protagoras proceeds to explain the practice of mutual instruction among the residents of the polis in terms of self-interest: "For our neighbors' justice and virtue, I take it, is profitable [*lusitelei*] for us, and consequently we all eagerly [*prothumōs*] speak out and teach one another in matters of justice and lawfulness" (327b). Part of this mutual instruction is public punishment for wrongdoing. Punishment is not, according to Protagoras, rightly understood as retrospective vengeance (an attitude he regards as suited only to beasts) but as future-oriented correction and deterrence. Those wrongdoers who do not respond to this sort of correction must be expelled from the polis or put to death (325a–b). This last proviso recalls Zeus's injunction to execute those incapable of sharing in the new moral psychology.[30]

Looking back from *logos* to *muthos,* we can recognize that Protagoras' fanciful story about divine intervention addresses the gap between rational but unproductive noncooperation (thus anarchy) and productive cooperation (thus organized community) by, in effect, running a cooperation thought experiment twice. In the first run, the premise is that humans are narrowly egoistic. Therefore, even in the face of existential threats, they fail to cooperate in ways that can bring about a stable social order: The equilibrium (reminiscent of Hobbes' state of nature) is "scatter and perish." In the second run of the experiment Protagoras assumes a prevailing moral psychology in which egoistic self-interest is moderated by a sense of shame and justice, and thus the scope of self-interest is extended from "just me" to "me and us." In the second run, as in the first, humans remain self-interested and rational, in that they have orderly preferences and act based on what they believe is most likely to gain their highest-ranked available option. But their conception of self-interest and their beliefs about what actions will promote their interests have changed in salient ways.

In describing the expected public response to an individual who admitted to being unjust, Plato's Protagoras used the same terminology of "madness" that is employed by Glaucon (*Republic* 359b) to describe what an ordinary, honest Greek would think of someone who possessed a Gyges ring and failed to use it to satisfy his preferences. In Protagoras' description of the behavior of members of a society in the "second run" of his thought experiment, with agents possessing the "shame and justice" psychology, there is no indication that individuals are doing other than what they regard as being in their own (joint and several) interest: It is because our neighbors' justice and virtue is beneficial *to us* that we choose to assume the costs of speaking out and instructing one another. One part of that instruction is punishment of violators: Protagoras conceives of the motivation for costly punishment in the economic sense of anticipated future outcomes, rather than the vendetta sense of retrospective payback.

---

30. Danielle Allen (2000: 248) discusses the Greek terms associated with punishment as rectification of past wrongs (*timoria*) and future-oriented reformative education (*kolasis*) employed by Plato's Protagoras, and emphasizes the sharp distinction between the Platonic-Protagorean and real-world Athenian approaches to punishment and its purposes.

The two runs of the thought experiment might be thought of either as describing a historical transition from the "scatter and perish" equilibrium to the "order in poleis" equilibrium, or as testing two rival accounts of human psychology. The developmental story requires a change in motivations and behavior that comes about after humans have failed in their initial attempts to organize against existential threats. In this case the myth of the Gifts of Zeus is a functionalist explanation for cooperative attitudes that arise from the experience of failure. As such, it recalls the explanation invoked by Glaucon in describing the repeated game played by those who have experienced the limited benefits and high costs of noncooperative, unjust behavior. If, alternatively, the two runs of the experiment are meant to test two rival accounts of human psychology, Plato's Protagoras may be imagined as anticipating lab experiments in behavioral psychology designed to test theories of rational choice. The results of the test are, in Protagoras' case, the observable fact that humans do cooperate willingly in organized communities. Since "scatter and perish" does not fit the empirical observations, the hypothesis that human psychology is fully explicable in terms of narrow self-interest is falsified. The alternative hypothesis, in which most humans have some share in "shame and justice," is supported, although not definitively proved.

In either case, Plato's Protagoras has developed a sophisticated version of the Conventionalist folk theories (introduction, section 0.4), which stood in opposition to Thrasymachean accounts of purely egoistical rationality. Protagoras confronts the Thrasymachean story with the observable fact of cooperative social orders, without invoking deception by rulers or gullibility on the part of the ruled. Protagoras' shame-justice psychology promotes cooperation because each person's best payoff comes with cooperating, just so long as he has reasons to believe that others will act likewise. And he has reason to believe that because cooperating does bring the best payoff to others who share his moral psychology. What this means, in the language of game theory, is that the Prisoner's Dilemma is transformed into a Stag Hunt, an assurance game in which the highest payoff for each strategic player is gained by rational cooperation, rather than by rational defection (Skyrms 2001) This is illustrated in figure 14: the Gifts of Zeus game.

The only difference between the Gifts of Zeus assurance game (figure 14) and the cardinal-preference-weighted PD (figure 10) is that the payoffs for defecting when the other player cooperates have been lowered from 4 to 2. This is in recognition of the shame-justice moral psychology: Anyone with an internalized sense of shame, as respect for social

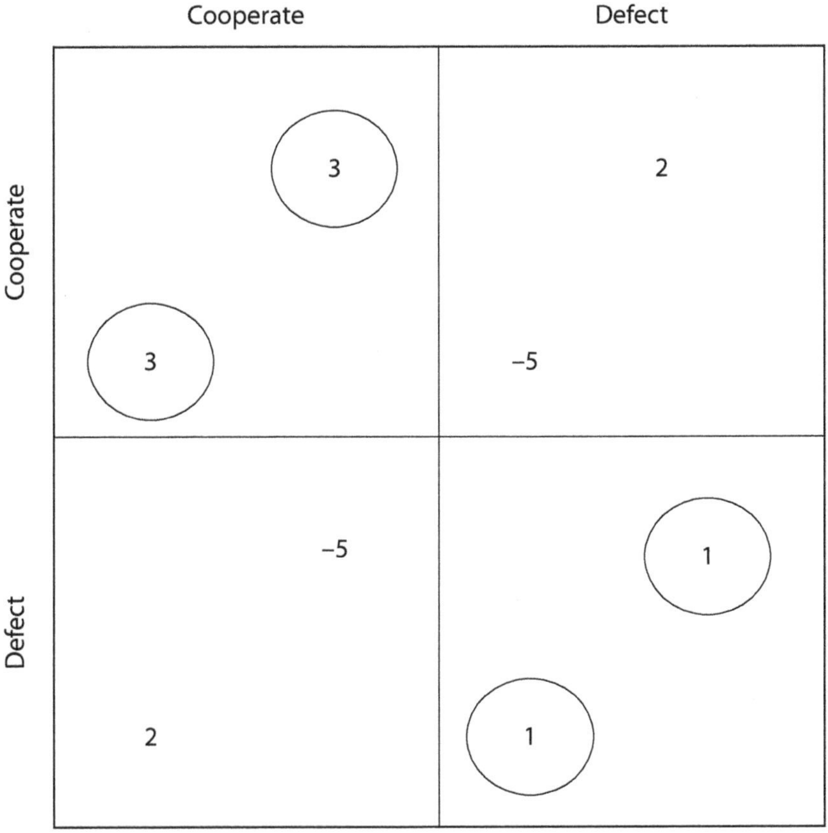

FIGURE 14. Gifts of Zeus Game

NOTE: Payoffs are cardinal preference weighted.

norms of just cooperation, bears an internal cost when she acts so as to outrage that sensibility. So, rather than the full payoff that the defecting player received in the PD, in the Gifts of Zeus game, the Defect, Cooperate player is docked part of the original payoff. While enjoying the benefits of exploiting another, she is simultaneously ashamed of herself for having done so. And so, some part of her utility is forfeit. In terms of the contents and ordering of her preferences, she may want to acquire material goods, access to sex, and power, but those preferences are now subordinated to a high-order preference to act, and to be acknowledged as acting, justly.

The adjustment to the payoffs has the effect of adding a second equilibrium outcome to the game. Defect, Defect, with its low payoff, remains an equilibrium outcome, because if either player chooses Defect, the best play for the other is Defect. If I believe that the other player is of a type to play Defect (i.e., is one of those with what is now regarded as an impaired moral psychology), I must play Defect in order to avoid the sucker's payoff. But I no longer need to suppose that every rational player will defect, because cooperation offers those with a normal psychology a higher payoff. So, assuming for the moment (1) that this is a one-shot complete information game, (2) that each player is rationally seeking his or her highest payoff, (3) that players are risk-neutral, (4) that Thrasymacheans are a small part of the population, and (5) that all this is common knowledge, it is rational to play Cooperate. Therefore, Cooperate, Cooperate (payoff 3,3) is a second equilibrium, one that not only gives each player his highest available payoff, but is also the highest social aggregate payoff. And thus, the Gifts of Zeus game models a society that has the potential of realizing increased aggregate social value, as well as individual preference satisfaction through having solved the problem of rational cooperation.[31] But that conclusion may be premature.

2.7 LEARNING, PUNISHMENT, AND POPULATION DYNAMICS

Upon reflection, in transforming the PD-like Glaucon's Dilemma into the Gifts of Zeus assurance game we might have overstated the social conditions described by Protagoras. The new moral psychology is not universal: Some agents remain rational defectors. Given that the majority regard their psychology as dangerous (indeed diseased), they have every reason to dissimulate. At least some of them may be willing to take their chances with punishment. They may reason that they will do better for themselves by exploiting the cooperative behavior of their fellows. So, in playing Cooperate with an unknown second party, each member of Protagoras' imagined community risks a sucker's payoff. Moreover, if rationality and a widely distributed shame-justice psychology were adequate, in and of themselves, to get and keep an optimal level of cooperation, there would be no need for anyone to assume the costs of the mutual instruction and corrective punishment that Protagoras

---

31. This is in some ways similar to the "constrained maximization" or "resolute choice" in the amended choice theory of David Gauthier; see the succinct account of Gauthier's theory in Morris and Ripstein 2001.

highlights. Furthermore, and seemingly fatal to Protagoras' business plan, only vicious Thrasymacheans would have reason to pay a Sophist his fee for teaching a master's course in political craft.[32]

In light of these concerns, it is important to note that in Protagoras' story the new psychology is not only nonuniversal, but also a fairly weak disposition: Protagoras' reformed humans are still rationally self-interested and Zeus's gifts of shame and justice are not imagined as doing all the work necessary to create and sustain social order. The baseline moral psychology must, therefore, be strengthened by repeated social interactions: Teaching and learning from each other, across the course of our lives, along with the deterrent function of punishment for deviation from the rules, are essential parts of Protagoras' solution to Glaucon's Dilemma.

In the myth, Zeus decrees death for those who lack a sense of shame and justice, but unless and until they are caught and expelled or killed, the community will continue to harbor some individuals whose motives for acting unjustly are undiminished. Some of these unreconstructed egoists may be "mad" and thus will be easily caught out and punished. Others, however, will choose to *pass* as cooperators—as Protagoras points out, it is insane *not* to present oneself in public as cooperative. The threat of death or expulsion may be enough to scare a risk-averse crypto-egoist into acting as a consistent cooperator. It will be the role of mutual instruction and punishment to sort out those cooperators who have fallen into the *error* of playing Defect by mistake, from the vicious egoists who are not making errors but acting on their settled preferences. And to separate egoists who can be deterred from future wrongdoing by credible threats from those who are incorrigible risk-takers and must be removed from the population by expulsion or execution. Protagoras' optimism about the cooperative society suggests that all that can be done, and at a cost that is reasonably borne by the cooperative majority.

Protagoras does not assume that humans are altruistic saints, or that the initial psychological shift would immediately or permanently eliminate the Gyges-type psychology that leads to defection. He supposes, however, that an ordered polis will be composed mostly of cooperators. In game-theoretic terms, he assumes that cooperation will emerge as the

---

32. Wiens (2012) fruitfully discusses the problem of core motivation for ideal theory: If all are fully committed to justice, there is no need for coercive institutions, and so political theory is over (solved by a shared ethical standard) before it gets going.

most common strategy through repeated play in a population in which enough share the shame-justice psychology and act accordingly. That is: the cooperative equilibrium will be achieved and sustained by ongoing social interaction leading to adequately strong norms of social coopera- tion. Like Glaucon's initial account of the emergence of law and justice in a population of individuals who have learned from experience that the costs of defection outweigh its benefits, Protagoras assumes a kind of repeated game. Moreover, Protagoras' emphasis on mutual instruc- tion over time and on punishment of deviants allows us to think of the cooperation game that sustains social order as one that is *indefinitely* repeated. The players in the repeated game are expected to learn from each round of play. And they are capable of communicating learned information to other players.

Repeated games that randomly pair a large number of players allow for agent-based modeling of populations that evolve over time: poten- tially into a stable equilibrium.[33] Depending on how agents are moti- vated (what strategy each plays), how their experience in a given round affects their play in the next round (how they learn), and what each communicates and with which others (how learning spreads), the popu- lation evolves in a process known as *replicator dynamics*.[34] Replicators are entities capable of making copies of themselves. In our case, the replicators are strategies. A strategy is successful if those who play it receive higher payoffs over the course of repeated play. Successful strat- egies multiply at the expense of unsuccessful strategies, and therefore those playing successful strategies come to dominate the population. So, by transforming the one-shot assurance game of figure 14 into an indef- initely repeated game, it is possible to predict, based on the setup of the game (motivation and learning, per above), how a population that includes both Thrasymachean egoists and conditional cooperators will evolve over time. The question is whether repeated play in a population including Thrasymacheans (some of whom learn from punishment) and conditional cooperators (willing to punish defection with defection) will result in a population that is all Thrasymacheans, all cooperators, or some mix of the two types.

33. Repeated games: Axelrod 1984, 1997; Calvert 1995; Bendor and Swistak 1997; E. Anderson 2000: 178–81.
34. This approach is adopted by game theorists concerned with explaining the evo- lution of stable strategies of cooperation, social norms, and, ultimately, morality: Bendor and Swistak 2001; Choi and Bowles 2007; Joyce 2006; Bowles and Gintis 2011; Boehm 2012 (among many others).

As Protagoras' mythic Zeus realized ("poleis cannot exist if only a few people have a share"), if there are only a few cooperators, the population is likely quickly to devolve to all-Thrasymachean and the equilibrium will be "scatter and perish." Moreover, if each round of the repeated game is played as a standard PD (as in Glaucon's Dilemma), Thrasymacheans will consistently win while cooperators consistently lose. In this case the replicator dynamics predict that the presence of even a few Thrasymacheans in the population will, over time, drive out all cooperators (Binmore 2007: 123–24 with figure 29). We will end up back at Glaucon's Dilemma. This regression to noncooperation is what Protagoras describes in the mythic stage preceding Zeus's gifts, when attempts at social order collapsed in the face of strife.[35]

Protagoras' story about the origins of order furthermore allows us to weaken the assumption of complete information. Given the incentive of Thrasymacheans to dissimulate their type, Player A must always consider the possibility that Player B is of the type that will defect. If loss in any one round is fatal (that is, the player does not survive to play in the next round and cannot inform other players of the results of the first round), then we are back at Glaucon's Dilemma. But if we assume that A can survive a loss, if play of the cooperators is based on "retaliation" (i.e., if Player B plays Defect in round 1, then Player A retaliates with Defect in a subsequent round played against B—regardless of whether A's motivation is correction or vengeance), and if punishment is meted out often enough (which will depend on payoffs and the number of Thrasymacheans in the original population), then retaliation will eliminate Thrasymacheans or lead them to change their play to cooperation. Thought of in spatial terms, repeated play with reliable retaliation creates a substantial "basin of attraction." If we start the play of repeated games within that basin (i.e., with the right number of conditional cooperators and the right payoffs), the eventual result will be an

---

35. Chung (2015) helpfully models Hobbes' *Leviathan* state of nature not as a standard Prisoner's Dilemma, but as a game in which the population includes both "modest" (nonegoistic) types and "violent" (egoistic types). Each player is uncertain about the other player's "type" (modest or violent) and highly values his own life. The payoff to cooperating against a defector is "death." Chung's conclusion that, under these conditions, "even when the vast majority . . . are peace-loving . . . universal war could still break out" is surely correct. It confirms Hobbes' requirement of a sovereign (whether sole dictator or majority tyrant) as the unique solution. But if the game with which we are concerned is, as Protagoras' appears to be, indefinitely repeated, and if the cost of losing a round is less than fatal, the emergence of a non-Hobbesian alternative of a self-enforcing equilibrium without a lawless sovereign remains available.

all-cooperator population (Binmore 2007: 136–37). Introducing communication (so that A adjusts her strategy against B in round 2, based on the experience of C playing against B in round 1) hastens evolution toward an equilibrium.

The general point is that a view of human psychology that rejects the assumption of universal narrow egoism, a view introduced in Protagoras' myth through the device of "Zeus's gifts," can produce, first, a high-order preference for cooperation because of a sense of *shame* that reduces the subjective value of the injustice payoff. Next, in repeated play a sense of *justice* leads ordinary citizens to respond to instances of unjust behavior, as punishers. They ought to do so, according to Protagoras, not out of a "beastly" vengeful impulse, but because it is in someone's interest. They may regard just punishment of noncooperators—those who act unjustly—as benefiting the corrigible and/or the society. An interest in punishment may include the satisfaction of acting out of righteous anger at acts of injustice and its perpetrators (D. Allen 2000). The point is that punishment is reliably meted out, regardless of whether the motive of the punishers is forward-looking correction or retrospective vengeance. With the behaviors associated with the shame-justice psychology driving the system toward a high-payoff, mutually cooperative equilibrium, Protagoras' "Gifts of Zeus" community can come into being despite the initial presence of a few Thrasymacheans, and it is robust to their periodic reemergence. It can retain the individual and social benefits incumbent upon a norm of conditional cooperation based on expectations: a belief that most others are likely to cooperate in turn, and that those who defect will be punished.

2.8 THE LIMITS OF EGOISTIC SELF-INTEREST

With its recognition of the endemic presence of Thrasymachean egoists in the population, Protagoras' fable has reintroduced Callicles' formidable few. But Plato's Protagoras has shown how an extensive scheme of cooperation can come about despite them and why it need not be vulnerable to them. He has answered the social development problem that (so I have claimed) is set up by Glaucon's Dilemma: How did social order first emerge in a population of rationally self-interested agents? The solution has turned out to require, first, an adjustment to the starting assumption that ordinary human motivation, in a state of nature, can be reduced to narrowly egoistic self-interest. The adjustment allows the Prisoner's Dilemma to be transformed into an assurance game. And, next, Protagoras responds to the endemic presence of cheaters by positing, in the language of game theory, repeated play with learning and updating.

Protagoras ran the "origins of social order" thought experiment a first time assuming Thrasymachean motivations. He concluded that it ends in anarchy and poverty—something akin to Hobbes' state of nature. He ran it a second time with the assumption that self-interest was supplemented by a widely distributed, if relatively weak, moral disposition to shame and justice. That disposition did not transform rascals into saints. It modified, rather than simply replacing, narrowly egoistic self-interest. It maintained rationality as expected utility via ordered preferences plus coherent beliefs. Moreover, in the face of incomplete information about the distribution of types in the community, repeated interaction, in the form of mutual instruction and corrective punishment, proved to be essential to the task of translating minimal shared moral intuitions into social order.

Protagoras' imagined "Gifts of Zeus" society is not perfectly just: The tendency of some individuals to self-seeking wrongdoing remains an issue. Some of the unjust may imitate the attitudes of the just citizen, obeying the rules for fear of punishment and a reputation of being "mad" or "not of the human kind." Severe punishment of incorrigibles, by expulsion or execution, is assumed to be necessary. Protagoras' social order is thus meant to be realistic: emergent, dynamic, and ultimately self-enforcing. As such, it is a long way from Plato's ideal of a fully just, perfectly harmonious, stable community, as sketched in the later books of the *Republic*.

Glaucon's challenge to Socrates precludes focal point and assurance game solutions by setting the problem of social cooperation as a Prisoner's Dilemma. In the course of the next eight books of the *Republic*, Socrates answers the challenge with what might be thought of as a Hobbesian solution: The authority of Callipolis' rulers is absolute and their legitimacy is guaranteed by the rational acquiescence of the ruled. Yet the solution is decidedly non-Hobbesian: It is not the result of a social contract; the rulers are perfectly just and are bound by rules established by the founders. It remains a question whether Socrates' solution is vulnerable to the kind of empirical test that (so I have argued) was implicit in Protagoras' myth of social origins: Plato's Socrates occasionally insists that Callipolis really could be, and ought to be, brought into existence in the here and now. Yet he also and famously describes the ideal city as a paradigm laid up in heaven, a model for the individual soul rather than a realistic plan for a human community.[36] In any event, it seems safe to say that Plato was not the sort of philosopher for whom experimental behavioralism would be taken as a refutation of an ideal theory.

Our selective survey of Greek thought on the origins of social order has established two main points: First, the classical tradition was fully capable of imagining a population of rational egoists and of raising questions predicated on hypothetical agents freed from ordinary social constraints: "unerring craftsmen of self-interest." The problems for social order that arise with instrumental rationality were explored by Greek writers in ways that are reminiscent of some features of contemporary game theory and their proposed solutions can be illustrated by simple games. Plato's Glaucon sets the problem of cooperation in its starkest terms, as a kind of Prisoner's Dilemma. Some other Greek political theorists supposed that societies could solve cooperation problems by an intuitive recognition of the value of coordination or by employing focal points. Plato's Protagoras took the challenge of Thrasymachean motivation very seriously and concluded that social order was inexplicable under any set of assumptions that reduced human motivation to amoral, narrowly self-interested egoism.

Since humans are manifestly capable of cooperation at scale, Protagoras concluded that the motivation of many (but not of all) humans must include at least a minimal moral sensibility, capable of taking into account the well-being of others—at least as a necessary precondition of one's own welfare. That assumption recalls the claims of Enlightenment-era moral philosophers, for example, Adam Smith in his *Theory of Moral Sentiments* and *Wealth of Nations*.[37] And, mutatis mutandis, it may recall influential work in contemporary political philosophy. John Rawls posits that the citizens of the presumptively democratic "realistic utopia" that emerges from his contractarian thought experiment have an effective "sense of justice." This means that their rational pursuit of self-interest is moderated by a "reasonable" acknowledgement of others' legitimate claims.[38] We will return to Rawls' theory of justice in

36. The question of whether Callipolis is possible: 472d–73a. The claim that it is at least possible: 499b–d, 502c, 540d; model "laid up in heaven": 592a–b.

37. A. Smith (1759) 1976, (1776) 1981. On Smith as a normative and positive theorist, whose work on moral psychology is fully compatible with his work on political economy, and readily understood in game-theoretic terms, see Liu and Weingast 2020.

38. Rawls 2001: 4, 2005: lx; with discussion in Banting and Kymlicka 2018. On the relationship between the rational and the reasonable in Rawls' political philosophy, see Basu 2020 and discussion in chapter 8.7. I am indebted to Jackie Basu for enlightening discussions of this topic.

chapter 8.7. Meanwhile, we need not suppose that the weak shame-justice disposition sketched in Protagoras' "Gifts of Zeus" story provides a thick enough moral sensibility to sustain the kind of just society envisioned by either Smith or Rawls. But the core intuition appears to be similar: Stable human social order rests on motivations that exceed narrowly egoistic self-interest, but it does not require a community of saints.

CHAPTER 3

Deioces' Ultimatum

How to Choose a Ruler

Do organized communities require rulers? If so, how are rulers identified and chosen and what (if any) limits are placed on their authority? The introduction and chapter 1 traced an ancient Greek folk theory of instrumental rationality. In common with contemporary choice theory, the folk theory regarded individuals as rational in the sense of being expected advantage maximizers whose choices are predicated on their preferences over outcomes and their beliefs about feasibility of options. Chapter 2 considered Greek theories explaining the origins and persistence of social order. Those theories answered the question of how multiple self-interested individuals could agree to make and enforce rules limiting self-aggrandizing behavior without falling victim to free-riding and commons tragedies. Each proposed solution to the social order question addressed the problem of how a mass of persons with heterogeneous interests could constitute themselves as a community, a coherent association with widely shared norms and goals. To persist over time in the face of internal and external threats, the community must have coordinated responses to threats—it must function as a purposeful organization. At this point the community has the potential not only to sustain itself, but also to grow larger and wealthier. And that in turn introduces the problems of scale, complexity, and ruling.

In this and the next three chapters we turn to the problem of cooperating at scale, in the face of interest diversity and social complexity. Problems arising from growth and increased complexity must be addressed by institutions—by formal laws and methods for making and enforcing laws, and by the extension of norms governing appropriate social behavior to larger and more diverse populations. To guide behavior, norms must become habitual; habits must be enforced by sanctions against free-riders who seek to benefit from cooperation without paying its costs. Effective institutions must anticipate the strategic behavior of agents. Rule-makers must gain the assent of subjects, who must in turn render their commitment to live by the rules credible to one another.

At the level of the state, the problem of cooperation at scale was addressed through rational processes of deliberating about, choosing, establishing, and revising a constitutional regime—a *politeia*. To speak of constitutionalism is to raise questions of authority and its limits: Who will rule over whom? What rules (if any) bind the ruler(s)? Why do those ruled choose to obey? Many writers in the Greek tradition of political thought assumed that the earliest practical answer to the question "who rules?" had been "a king." In that case, the second question was whether the king's authority was absolute or in some ways limited. Rational rulers make rules that take rational subjects into account. But who chooses the ruler? The Greek tradition addressed the rationality of ruler-choice as an aspect of social cooperation.

But is a *politeia*—in the sense of a set of formal institutions answering the question "who rules, and how?"—necessary to sustain an organized community? Plato's *Republic* seems, at first, to answer "no."

3.1 TOWARDS CONSTITUTIONALISM IN PLATO'S *REPUBLIC:* FIRST POLIS AND GUARDIANS

In the *Republic,* the question of ruling is brought to the fore in the latter part of book 2 by the familiar figure of Glaucon. Socrates, Glaucon, and Adeimantus quickly agree (*Republic* 369c) that poleis must arise from the basic fact of interdependence conjoined with self-interest: No individual is self-sufficient and so people engage in exchange, giving and receiving things from one another, "because each believes that this is better for himself." They proceed to the central project of the dialogue, constructing "a polis in words, from the beginning" (369c). Socrates proposes the social arrangement that is often called (in the *Republic* literature) the "First Polis." We will consider the economy of the First Polis in more detail in chapter 7.6. Suffice it to say here that the First Polis is based on the premises of interdependence and self-interest, and on a fundamental principle that appeared to arise naturally from those premises: Everyone must function within his or her own proper domain of endeavor, free from interference by others.

The noninterference principle initially concerns economic efficiency. By focusing uniquely on her own special task, each will do her task better, and therefore the relevant consumption goods (in the first instance, food and shelter: 369c–d) will be more plentiful and of better quality (369e–70c, with further discussion in chapter 7.4). The tasks in question concern, to begin with, production and exchange: agriculture, manufacturing, imports and exports, transport, wholesale and retail trade, and manual labor (*Republic* 369c–71e). Once Socrates has completed his preliminary list of necessary tasks, he asks, hypothetically, whether the polis is now complete. Adeimantus allows that perhaps it is (371e).

Life in this hypothetical First Polis will be healthy (372e) and relatively simple. Importantly, the population will be stable: The First Polis is not expected to continue to grow in size or complexity. Socrates describes the lifestyle of the inhabitants in lyrical terms:

> And for their nourishment they will provide meal from their barley and flour from their wheat, and kneading and cooking these they will serve noble cakes and loaves on some arrangement of reeds or clean leaves, and, reclined on rustic beds strewn with bryony and myrtle, they will feast with their children, drinking of their wine thereto, garlanded and singing hymns to the gods in pleasant fellowship, not begetting offspring beyond their means lest they fall into poverty or war. (372b–c)

At this point, Glaucon raises an objection: There seem to be no "culinary delicacies" (*opson*) in the diet of the residents of the First Polis. Socrates replies that there will be simple snacks, including roasted acorns. At that, Glaucon strengthens his objection, proclaiming that Socrates seems to be "provisioning nothing other than a city of pigs." Glaucon demands, at the very least, that there be proper couches to lie on, and tables to eat from, and the sort of appetizers and desserts to which people in his day had become accustomed (372c–d).

Surprisingly, given his evident enthusiasm for the First Polis, Socrates offers no principled objection. He agrees to enlarge the polis in light of the fact that "there are some people, it appears, who will not be content with this [simple, healthy] sort of fare or with this way of life" (373a). Socrates notes, however, that a "luxurious, feverish polis" (372e) will need to be much bigger, with the addition of many other craft and service specializations. Moreover, to accommodate its increased population, the territory of the polis will need to expand. That expansion will be at the expense of neighboring states, and so will require armed forces. Finally, the polis, now filled with valuable consumer goods, will incite the cupidity of outsiders and so will always need the means to defend itself against neighbors presumed to have similarly expansive tendencies (373a–e).

Given the prior agreement that each individual will be limited to a single, specialized task, the military imperative in turn requires the creation of a full-time, professionalized army. This is Plato's first mention of "Guardians" (*phulakes:* 374a–d). The introduction of Guardians brings up a thorny problem: The presence of a substantial force of persons with a monopoly on organized violence threatens the growing polis's stability. How, Socrates asks, "will [the Guardians] escape being savage to one another and to the other citizens?" Glaucon's sober answer is: "Not easily, by Zeus" (375b). The shadow of Thrasymachean injustice looms: Why would those who are stronger *not* use their evident advantage in strength to act unjustly, aggrandizing themselves at the expense of the weaker?

If the Guardians were to cooperate with one another they could readily employ their superior capacity for effective violence to exploit the other citizens. If they failed to cooperate with one another they would engage in destructive violence against one another. In any event, if they act fiercely towards each other or the other citizens, "they will not wait for others to destroy the polis but will do it themselves first" (375c). It is the need to forestall that undesirable outcome that leads to the requirement for authoritative rules: Educational rules will specify the upbringing for Guardians. Social rules will govern their behavior and will severely constrain their opportunity to satisfy what most Greeks considered high-order preferences for personal wealth and families. But that in turn provokes two further questions: How are the rules to be enforced? And in what sense will the Guardians be happy—or even rationally content to accept the resulting social order as the outcome of a game in which they have no better move? The difficulty of sorting out each of those issues in adequate detail provides the justification for the elaborate train of arguments that leads to the emergence of Callipolis— the "beautiful polis" that is the dialogue's eventual political product. The rulers of Callipolis will, we eventually learn, be a very small group of true experts in the art of ruling: philosopher-kings.

For our present purposes, the important point is the sharp contrast in the systems governing Callipolis and Socrates' First Polis. The setup of the First Polis had avoided the need to address any of the difficult questions about rules and rulership that arise with the introduction of Guardians. Indeed, the First Polis, while certainly a community, apparently lacks a formal political system of any kind: We are given no reason to suppose that anyone rules or that anyone is ruled over. There is a sophisticated economy, based on specialization and mutually beneficial exchanges of goods and services (see chapter 7.6). But Socrates evidently foresaw no need for political authority: The First Polis is a pacific sort of libertarian paradise. It is based on the important proviso that, in stark contrast to the fundamental premises of the background folk theory of practical reasoning, sketched in the introduction and chapter 1, none of the residents is motivated by the desire for "more and more."[1]

There is no need for rulers in the First Polis because its postulated citizens lack the self-aggrandizing psychology, predicated on *pleonexia,* that Glaucon had posited (chapter 1.2) as universal among ordinary persons, and as revealed once the veneer of social convention is stripped away. As we saw (chapter 2.1), Glaucon cited (without endorsing) the widespread belief that it was the endemic threat to each and all, arising from a self-aggrandizing psychology, that led (once people escaped the dilemma of rational mutual defection) to "the beginning of legislation and covenants between men" (359a)—that is, in the terms we have now introduced, to a *politeia.* Glaucon's Dilemma then highlighted the difficulty of getting to *politeia* without a lawless sovereign. Given the aims of the interlocutors in the dialogue—demonstrating that justice is a good in itself and that the just person is necessarily happier than the unjust person—the solution offered by Plato's Protagoras (chapter 2.6), bootstrapping a self-enforcing social order from a generalized but thin moral sensibility, is not acceptable.

Given this background, we can better understand why Socrates conceded so readily to Glaucon's demands for couches and culinary delicacies: Socrates had previously agreed to seek an answer to Glaucon's challenge, to show why the truly just man was happier than the greedy and "ostensibly just but actually completely unjust man" of the Gyges thought experiment. So, Socrates cannot then turn around and insist that the next thought experiment be a polis that rejects, *ab initio,* the major premise arising from the Gyges experiment: that is, the assumption that, absent constraints, instrumentally rational persons will seek to maximize their own expected advantage through unjust behavior. Accepting the premise that at least "there are [indeed] some people . . . who will not be contented with this sort of fare or with this way of life" (373a), Socrates

---

1. A similar concern for moderation of desires is expressed in contemporary democratic theory: Kolodny 2014; Ober 2015a: 120.

and his interlocutors must abandon the simple, healthy polis that needed no political authority, the one that seemed, to Socrates, to be the "true polis" (372e). They must become not only "founders" (*oikistai*: 379a), but also "lawgivers" (*nomothetai*: 530c).[2] They must embark upon the hard work of designing a constitution that will include a provision for ruling and being ruled—thereby justifying the traditional Greek title of the dialogue: *Politeia*.

Plato's *Republic* accepts that a self-interested desire for material goods that exceed the necessities of baseline subsistence is in fact part of ordinary human motivation. For Plato such motivations, lacking ends that are rationally chosen and objectively choice-worthy, were not truly rational. But the population of the rational state that his interlocutors construct in words includes many individuals who are instrumentally rational but not, themselves, rational in Plato's ethical sense. The advantage-maximizing motivation of those instrumentally rational agents must be taken into account and managed in order for the polis to exist. And that requires the construction of formal political order: a set of institutions specifying who is to rule and who is to be ruled over. So, even in the *Republic,* addressing the problem of instrumental rationality must precede the full specification of ethical rationality.

The initial problem of the central Callipolis thought experiment of the *Republic* is defined by the necessity of avoiding two bad outcomes: In the first, the presumptively self-interested elite warrior class of Guardians use their specialization in organized violence to exploit all others in the community, leading to institutionalized Thrasymachean injustice. In the second, the Guardians fall into an intraelite *stasis,* as each Guardian seeks to get more of a bundle of scarce resources.

The question Plato poses in the *Republic* (and, in somewhat different terms, in his later works, *Statesman* and *Laws*: Bobonich 2002) is how to specify the *politeia* capable of achieving both social stability and justice for a polis with a large and heterogeneous population—a population that included persons with both the motivation and the capacity for self-aggrandizement at others' expense. The problem of how to specify the proper relationship between polis and *politeia,* in the real phenomenal world of the city-states and in the best practically feasible polis "of our prayers," is likewise central to Aristotle's *Politics*. In *Politics* book 3, Aristotle semitautologically defines the *polis* as a community (*koinōnia*) of citizens (*politai*) organized in respect to a *politeia*

---

2. On *nomothesia* in the *Republic* see, in detail, Espeland 2020.

(1276b1–2). *Politeia* is, by definition, the primary subject of the Aristotelian *Politeia of the Athenians* (*Athenaiōn Politeia:* hereafter *Ath. Pol.*)
and, presumably, of the 157 other (lost except for fragments) *Politeiai*
of existing states assembled by Aristotle's students. The title "The
Politeia of X" was commonly used for works written in the later fifth
and fourth centuries BCE—famously by Pseudo-Xenophon, aka "the
Old Oligarch" (for Athens) and Xenophon (for Sparta). In much of the
surviving *politeia* literature from classical Greece, the establishment of
a new *politeia,* in the sense of a constitution specifying the conditions of
ruling and being ruled, is described in terms that may readily be interpreted as a game between instrumentally rational individuals or groups
acting cohesively as quasi-individuals.[3]

In the Greek tradition of political thought, constitutional order (as
opposed to tyrannical domination by force) is often imagined as the result
of a bargain. The bargaining process involves not only threats, but also
deliberation—the giving and taking of reasons in the form of arguments
in favor of (or against) choosing a course of action aimed at gaining a
particular public outcome. The parties to the bargain may reason directly
with one another through open debate in advance of the decision. Or
they may refer the decision to an arbitrator who reasons for them and
explains his reasons (if he does) only after his decision has been announced.

In either case, the outcome of rational constitution-making is far
from the perfectly just solution that might result from a set of divine
commands given from on high (think of Moses), or from an authoritative and divinely wise lawgiver (think of Solomon). While the lawgivers
imagined by the Greek tradition might be regarded as very wise indeed
(as was Solon: chapter 4), they are not ordinarily portrayed as creating
an ideally just social order. Instead, wise lawgivers were depicted as
skillfully assessing a practical situation at a given time and place and as
designing a realistically viable political order accordingly.

The upshot is that (outside thought-experimental projects like Plato's
Callipolis) *politeia* is not an ideal, but rather it is a compromise arrived
at through bargaining by self-interested parties—and thus it remains
potentially subject to further amendment if and when the parties change
their preferences, or when they update their beliefs due to a change in
the state of the world. For example, when their own state gains or loses
in relative power, or when another powerful player enters the game

3. *Politieia* literature in the late fifth and fourth centuries: Bordes 1982; O. Murray
1993; Menn 2005.

(chapter 5). Or when a change in material conditions requires adjustments to the original distribution of goods (chapter 7). But, importantly, deliberation also remains essential to the narrative. Although a bargaining game *might* be reduced to nothing other than threats, in the background there remained the common interest in social cooperation and avoiding social collapse that we surveyed in chapter 2. Arguments leveraging that baseline common interest had some chance of gaining purchase with Greek audiences, even when they were not dispositive.

In the remainder of this chapter and the next three, we turn to choices relevant to the organization and function of the state, its rules, its rulers, and its sociological parts. Taking the Greek tradition as our guide, the constitution of the state can be readily understood as a result of a "game of *politeia*," played by individuals or groups with competing interests, seeking to satisfy diverse preferences under conditions of scarcity. The game of *politeia* was played for high stakes.[4] The costs of playing that game poorly could be very high: it remained possible that some, or indeed *all* players could lose, catastrophically (through social collapse or external conquest), if they failed to come to an agreement that allowed for high-level social cooperation. This chapter concerns solutions that result in a state with a monarch as ruler; in the following chapters we turn to states in which the citizens rule themselves.

3.2 HERODOTUS ON THE REESTABLISHMENT OF TYRANNY AMONG THE MEDES

Classical Greek writers concerned with monarchy often found their material in tales about the rulers of the great western Asian kingdoms. As we have seen (chapter 1), Plato and Herodotus told stories about how Gyges (or his ancestor) became king of Lydia. Plato's Callicles (*Gorgias* 483d–e) cited the imperialistic military campaigns of Kings Darius and Xerxes of Persia as exemplifying the "law of nature": The superior rule the inferior and have a greater share of goods. Herodotus' narrative (1.95–101) of the establishment of rulership among the Medes (a western Asian people related to the Persians) presents kingship as a solution to a

---

4. There was an actual board game, called "polis," played by ancient Greeks. The rules remain unclear, but evidently (like, for example, poker or backgammon) it involved both strategy and chance. See Kurke 1999a: chap. 7; Hansen 2002. A board game of some sort, possibly "polis," usually being played by Achilles and Ajax, is illustrated on over 150 Greek vases, mostly dating from the mid-sixth to the mid-fifth century BCE: Woodford 1982.

crisis of social order. In Herodotus' story, those who ended up subjects of a king gave their obedience willingly, as part of a bargain that enabled them to escape intolerable conditions of lawlessness and injustice. To achieve that end, however, the Medes submitted to an absolute monarch who isolated himself from his subjects in order to enslave them.[5]

Herodotus introduces the story by noting that the former subjects of the ancient Assyrian Empire had freed themselves by defeating the Assyrians in battle. Herodotus then announces (1.96.1) that he will explain how these Asian peoples, all of them self-governing (*autonomoi*) after the fall of the Assyrians, "came once again to be subjected to tyranny" (*autis es turannida*). The protagonist of his story is Deioces, who is described, in language that recalls Kandaules' fatal passion for his wife (chapter 1.6), as "passionately in love with tyranny [*erastheis turannidos*]." The plot of the tale concerns how Deioces deliberately set about satisfying his desire to become an absolute monarch.

As the story begins, the Medes were living in villages. They were evidently capable of cooperating in some ways at a local level, but were, Herodotus says, suffering from endemic lawlessness (*anomia*). Already locally prominent, Deioces devoted himself ever more enthusiastically to justice (1.96.2). The residents of his village therefore chose him (*haireonto*) to be their judge. Herodotus does not specify the choice mechanism, but the choice of Deioces as judge was evidently consensual. Because Deioces wanted to rule, he was straight and just in his judgments. Deioces was praised for the excellence of his arbitrations and, as his fame spread, the Medes, who had been victimized by unfair judges (recalling Hesiod's earlier complaints of corrupt judges in *Works and Days*), became convinced that Deioces alone was a fair judge. Ultimately, they refused to have anyone but him arbitrate their disputes. The local village judge had, as his reputation grew, become a judge for the entire Median nation.[6]

At this point, however, Deioces went on strike, claiming it was unprofitable to himself (*ou gar hoi lusiteleein*: 1.97.1) to spend all his time judging others' cases while neglecting his own affairs. His retirement precipitated a return of robbery and lawlessness in the villages. So,

---

5. Herodotus' Deioces narrative: Gammie 1986: 9, 185–87, with literature cited; Dewald 2003; Thomas 2012; Karachalios 2013; Atack 2019: chap. 1.

6. Herodotus does not indicate what constituted fairness for the Medes, but Deioces' dispute resolution formula must have involved hard-to-reproduce expertise; for what that might have entailed, if we assume rational Medes, see Barry 1989: 25–29 and below, chapter 4.3.

the Medes gathered together to deliberate concerning the situation (1.97.2). Herodotus states that in his opinion, the main speakers were Deioces' friends, who argued that there must be a king. They claimed that a king would end lawlessness and allow each of the Medes to get on with his own affairs. The deliberative process, driven by Deioces' partisans, led to a consensus decision: "Saying these things, they [the Medes] persuaded themselves to be ruled by a king" (1.97.3). The next question was, who should be made king over them? Deioces was the enthusiastic, consensus choice.

Upon becoming king, Deioces hired bodyguards and ordered the Medes to embark on major building projects: a palace and royal treasury in the center of a fortified royal city (1.98.2–99.1). He then sequestered himself in the palace, ordered that he be seen by no one, and created elaborate rules of royal protocol. This was to make it appear that the king was different from all other men (1.99.1–2). With these arrangements in place, Deioces became a harsh guardian (*phulassōn chalepos*) of justice, employed a network of spies, and meted out proportionate (*kat' axiēn*) punishment for wrongdoing upon anyone he caught acting arrogantly (*hubrizonta*: 1.100.1–2). Herodotus concludes: "Deioces, then, united the Median nation and he alone ruled it" (1.101).

Herodotus describes Deioces' motives for action as straightforward from the outset: He intensely desires to be ruler and everything he does is rationally planned to achieve that ultimate goal. Deioces clearly has a conception of equitable dispute arbitration that is shared by the other Medes, but rarely manifest in their judicial practice. It is through building his reputation for straight and just judgments that he pursues his desired end. The hinge of the story is Deioces' successful attempt to become a monopoly supplier of this essential service. As shown by his temporary retirement, absent Deioces' straight judgments, lawlessness is the default condition of Median society.

Deioces' strike demonstrates to the Medes that his disinclination to act as judge for others, unless he is fully compensated for arbitrating disputes, is not a bluff. So, the Medes, imagined as gathered in a deliberative, constitutional assembly, seek to address the situation. Their choice comes down to either establishing a ruler who can be depended upon to impose order or tolerating lawlessness. The Medes are rationally averse to bearing the costs of lawlessness and seemingly incapable of self-organizing a punishment regime (à la Plato's Protagoras: chapter 2.6) that might address the problem. They are eager to attend to their private affairs and evidently either unable or unwilling to rule themselves, as a collectivity.

So, they choose to have a ruler, in essence making the same choice to be ruled as was made by the persuaded weak player in the first (belief-based) version of the Thrasymachean Injustice game (chapter 2.2, figure 12).

With reference to early modern political theorizing, Herodotus might seem to offer a version of the social contract developed in Thomas Hobbes' *Leviathan* (chapter 2.3). Legitimacy, and thus the grounds of willing obedience, are, in this story, established by a voluntary compact among rationally self-interested individuals. The contracting parties are the Medes themselves. They gather in assembly and decide that the best available solution to the problem of social order is the establishment of a single individual as their ruler. Moreover, Herodotus sketches what might be described as a satisfactory Hobbesian outcome: The monarch will be the sovereign ruler. He will ensure the formal rationality of government through his unitary will, based on his own ranking of preferences. Per Hobbes' prescription, he will be the sole source and enforcer of positive law. While not vicious, he is an absolute ruler: unconstrained by civil law but a strict enforcer of the law. The Medes thereby escaped the unhappy condition of lawlessness. But was the tradeoff of freedom as self-government for security under an absolute ruler equitable—in the eyes of the Medes in Herodotus story, or of Herodotus' Greek readers?

3.3 DEIOCES AND THE MEDES: AN ULTIMATUM GAME

Both Deioces and the Medes are depicted by Herodotus as having ordered preferences; both parties seek to maximize expected advantage by the choices they make: Deioces most prefers to rule as king. Failing that, he prefers to attend his own affairs. Judging without adequate recompense is ranked last. The Medes want to get on with their affairs without having to worry about robbery and lawlessness. They most prefer to have order at no cost to themselves, which means having Deioces act as pro bono judge. But that first-ranked preference is not available, given Deioces' credible commitment to remain in retirement if not properly compensated, that is, established as king. In proper Hobbesian fashion, the compact is made by and among those who will be subject to sovereign authority. In their assembly, the Medes "persuaded themselves" to have a king, which seems to be the best available option, given that they rank disorder last.

What the Medes do not know, *ex ante*, is what sort of king Deioces will be. Will his authority be absolute? Or will he feel constrained to share some part of his royal authority with the Medes, perhaps in the form of an advisory council chosen by them rather than by himself?[7] The Medes cannot know in advance how Deioces will behave as monarch. But they do have a choice to make *ex post,* after he has been elevated to the kingship and has revealed his type. By their revolt against the Assyrians, the Medes had demonstrated their willingness and capacity to reject unacceptable, tyrannical domination. So, presumably if, having been made king, Deioces demands what the Medes regard as an unfair share of ruling authority, they could reject him as king and return to the free but lawless status quo ante. Having been made king by a compact among the Medes, Deioces will remain king only if they accept the terms on which he rules.

Suppose that Deioces' share of rule (k), is somewhere between 100 (absolute monarchy) and 0 (having no authority at all). The Medes' share of rule (their capacity to limit the king's authority) is $100-k$. Thinking in the terms of game theory, Deioces as king and the Medes as subjects can be thought of as playing a variant of an Ultimatum game.[8] In the standard version of the Ultimatum game, the game organizer (here the decision of the Median assembly to make Deioces their king) provisionally grants Player 1 (here, imagined as Deioces) a sum of money, say $100. Player 1 chooses how much of that sum to offer to Player 2 (here, the Medes). If #2 accepts the offer, both keep their share of the money and the game ends. If #2 refuses the offer, the money is reclaimed by the game organizer; neither player gets a monetary payoff, and the game ends at the status quo ante.

In our scenario, the offer is a share of rule and refusing the offer means that the Medes revolt, rescinding the offer of kingship. In that case, Deioces is no longer king and the Medes return to the condition of lawlessness. Both end up with the equivalent of nothing. Assume for the moment that both players' preferences are defined by and limited to their "share of rule" payoff, and that both rationally prefer having something to having nothing. In this case, #1 (Deioces) should offer a minimal share of rule, say 10, keeping 90, and #2 (Medes) should accept the offer: 10 > 0. The situation is illustrated in figure 15.

7. Stasavage (2020) offers a comparative and historical analysis of "democratic" forms of government, in which the presence of an advisory council not selected by the monarch is sufficient to count as democratic rather than authoritarian.

8. Ultimatum Game variants: Thaler 1988; Nowak, Page, and Sigmund 2000; Camerer 2003: chap. 2. The Deioces game is a complex variant in that the payoff is imagined generally as "share of rule," but shares are denominated as "amount of freedom from absolutism" for the Medes and as "absolutism of kingship" for Deioces.

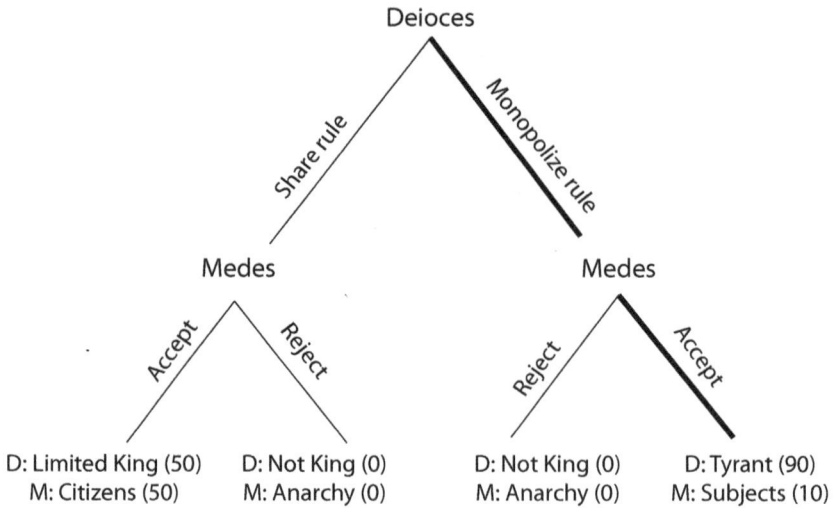

FIGURE 15. Deioces and Medes Ultimatum Game

NOTE: D = Deioces; M = Medes. "Accept" payoffs to D and M sum to 100.

In Ultimatum Game experiments, carried out by modern experimental economists and behavioral social scientists, individuals playing #2 frequently turn down low offers. That is, normative rationality, which assumes that a small payoff is preferable to nothing, does not track social behavior: what most real agents choose in an actual situation. In a standard Ultimatum game played in an experimental setting with monetary payoffs, the person playing #2 will typically reject as unfair offers that are very far below 50 percent of the original sum. That is, they prefer nothing to what is regarded as an unfair share. This result is sometimes seen as a refutation of the rationality premise of analytic game theory, insofar as the theory holds that a rational person ought to prefer something, however slight, to nothing. But game theorists respond that it is nothing of the kind. Rather, it shows that most people do not have preference orderings defined entirely in terms of money. Number 2 accepts the loss of otherwise-expected money because #2's preferences are in the order of, first: a fair share of a just distribution (whatever #2 imagines that to be); second: no money, but the satisfaction of having punished #1 for being unjust (by denying him a large monetary payoff); third: an unfair distribution.[9]

9. Meta-analysis of experimental evidence: Oosterbeek, Sloop, and van de Kulien 2004.

In our imagined Ultimatum game, Deioces, having been chosen king, is in the position of offering the Medes a share in ruling, here conceived as some measure of autonomy (freedom from the ruler's will), guaranteed by established limits on his own authority.[10] Per figure 15, if the Medes accept his offer, Deioces will gain his end of continuing to rule and the Medes will gain their end of avoiding disorder. If they refuse his offer (by deposing him), he is no longer ruler and the Medes return to lawlessness; the outcome is the status quo ante, with zero payoff to each. The questions that hover behind Herodotus' story are these: How much will Deioces, who passionately desires tyranny, offer the Medes, in term of limits on his royal authority? What will the Medes, who have a demonstrated capacity to reject a ruler they regard as tyrannical (the Assyrians), accept as a fair offer?

Herodotus' Deioces is narrowly self-interested. He judges fairly only in order to gain his end of ruling. Upon gaining the kingship, he immediately secludes himself from all others, sets himself apart by elaborate royal protocols, and judges harshly. His massive construction projects are aimed at his own security, and at ensuring his isolation and invisibility. As an invisible, authoritative sovereign who can do much as he wishes, King Deioces is in a position that is in some ways analogous to that of the possessor of Gyges' magic ring. We are not surprised that, despite his continued guardianship of justice, his authority is described as tyrannical: Herodotus' Median narrative was intended to show how the Medes, and other peoples of Asia, came "once again" to be ruled tyrannically.

Like Plato's Callicles, Herodotus' Deioces' passion for ruling leads him to seek power and he evidently views the relationship of ruler-ruled in absolutist terms. He rightly believes that the Medes value lawfulness, understood as a peaceful social order, so highly that they will sacrifice their freedom to have it. Like the player in an Ultimatum game, who supposes that utility can be reduced to a material payoff and that a rational agent must always choose something over nothing, Deioces' makes a lowball offer to the Medes. He will continue as their fair (if harsh) judge, but that is all they will get.

By their willing obedience, Herodotus' Medes accept Deioces' offer of impartial dispute resolution with no other limits on his royal authority. The Medes chose (by their obedience) to accept a *politeia* that left them in a servile condition. They did not rise up, as they had against the Assyrians. They seemingly took on substantial costs in terms of mandatory

10. Greek conceptions of freedom and "sharing in ruling": Ostwald 1996.

labor on Deioces' grand projects, and also by accepting their ruler's isolation from his subjects, his royal rules of decorum, and his pervasive system of spies, in exchange for his harsh justice. The Medes were evidently
willing to pay a very high price in terms of freedom as self-government
for the security that came with the establishment of lawfulness.[11]

When Herodotus began the story of Deioces, he emphasized that the
Medes had recently liberated themselves by their own efforts: They had
"proved good men in fighting for freedom (*peri eleutheriēs*) against the
Assyrians; casting off slavery they freed themselves" (*eleutherōthēsan*:
1.95.2). They were, Herodotus says, self-governing, unconstrained by
externally imposed law (*autonomoi*: 1.96.1). But at the same time, and
apparently as a consequence of their collective autonomy, they were
victims of lawlessness (*anomia*). They subsequently escape lawlessness
through the establishment of a king who is one of them and of their own
choosing, but at a high cost: They are no longer free men, but rather
ruled over by a tyrant. As such, they return to a condition of slavery.

Herodotus' Greek readers are, I suppose, meant to conclude that,
having "persuaded themselves" to be ruled by a king, the Medes agreed
to a higher price for lawfulness, in terms of foregone freedom and
autonomy, than Greeks regarded as equitable. And so, Glaucon's
assumption of universal "primitive" highest-end preferences that
included ruling might not apply equally well to Greeks and Asians:
Herodotus' Deioces story assumes that the Medes were instrumentally
rational, in having ordered preferences, coherent beliefs, and choosing
and acting accordingly. But the final outcome of the Median process of
choosing a *politeia* and accepting a ruler hints at deep cultural differences in the substantive content of baseline preferences, a theme that is
elaborated later in the *Histories*.[12]

The Medes' choice had revealed a preference ranking that set having
someone else taking care of the problem of social order and getting on
with their own private affairs above remaining free from despotism.
That ranking was different from the ranking of Herodotus' presumptively freedom-loving Greek readers. In terms of the Ultimatum game,
Herodotus' Medes act like model-type rational agents, accepting a small
share when the alternative was having nothing. Herodotus' Greek audi-

---

11. Dewald (2003) suggests that Herodotus offers Deioces as a model of the Asiatic
despot—the "tyrant type" of classical Greek political thought.

12. See, in general, Munson 2001, 2009. Cf. Gorgias *Defense of Palamedes* (LM
32.D25) for the claim that it is implausible that even barbarians would willingly accept a
tyrant, given that slavery is the worst thing of all.

ence was more closely aligned with the players in behavioral experiments, who forego an inadequate share, depriving themselves while punishing the proposer, when the offer is regarded as unfair. Yet Herodotus also shows his readers that the Medes, no less than the Greeks, were capable of gathering in assembly, deliberating over available options, and making a public choice among them. Could the Medes have devised a self-enforcing nontyrannical social order, something along the lines sketched by Plato's Protagoras? Herodotus' reader is left to ponder the counterfactual.[13]

The main theme of Herodotus' *Histories* is the war between a coalition of free, self-governing Greek poleis and the kings who ruled over the enslaved Asians of the Persian Empire—the successor-state to both Gyges' Lydia and Deioces' Media. The story of Deioces might lead his readers to believe that Asians identified social order with absolutism, leaving them with the stark choice of despotism or lawlessness. But that conclusion would be premature. Herodotus suggests that, at a key moment in their history, a small group of Persians with decision authority over the question of constitutional order came close to rejecting kingship in favor of a citizen-centered form of government. Moreover, Herodotus' story of the reestablishment of Persian kingship refutes the notion that royal authority in Asia must be absolute. Herodotus shows his readers that the authority of an Asian king could be limited by an agreement struck, after protracted deliberations and bargaining, among certain of those who might be king and would be subject to royal authority.

3.4 CHOOSING A CONSTITUTION FOR PERSIA

After his story of the origins of kingship among the Medes, Herodotus goes on to describe how the Persians freed themselves from the domination of the Medes. Under the royal leadership of Cyrus, the Persians became the masters, not only of the Medes, but of all western Asia. After Cyrus's death, a Median priest ("The Magus") usurped the Persian kingship. He was in turn assassinated by a cabal of Persian aristocrats. One

13. Herodotus' conception of freedom as nonslavery, and as requiring collective self-rule, is thus similar to that of a contemporary republican (Skinner 1998; Pettit 1997, 2013) or a "basic democrat" (Ober 2017a), and very different from that of Hobbes ([1651] 1996), who asserts that substantial individual freedom is compatible with absolutist government, because each subject is free just insofar as he or she is not physically constrained (in chains or prison), or Isaiah Berlin (1969), who regards freedom as noninterference, and likewise argues that autocracy could be compatible with freedom.

of the conspirators, Darius, was subsequently installed as the new King of Persia. The basic outline of Herodotus' history of Median usurpation and Persian restoration is confirmed by a Persian source: the great trilingual Behistun inscription, ordained by Darius himself (Asheri et al. 2007: 471–79). But Herodotus goes beyond the bare bones of the restoration story, offering his readers a remarkable and detailed account of what happened after the killing of the usurper: how it came about that Darius was made king and accepted certain constitutional limits on his royal authority.

The historicity of this part of Herodotus' tale is dubious at best. Happily, for our purposes historical accuracy is irrelevant. What matters is that the story told by Herodotus is perfectly designed to raise hard questions about how a constitutional regime is brought into being: the role of diverse preferences in defining the nature and scope of political authority, and the relationship of authority to the choice mechanisms by which it is formally established. In brief, we may read Herodotus' famous narrative of the "Persian Constitutional Debate" and its aftermath as a substantial theoretical contribution to a developing Greek tradition of political thought concerned with the employment of practical reasoning in establishing a constitution for a state.

Herodotus claims that, after the discovery of the Magus' usurpation, the decision to move immediately against him was made by a unanimous vote at a meeting of the Persian conspirators (3.71.1–73.3). The vote followed a series of deliberative interchanges (reason-based arguments, aimed at specific outcomes) intermixed with threats. In response to an argument for delaying the attack on the usurper in order to enlist more supporters, Darius insists that expanding the conspiracy would lead a self-interested individual to reveal the plot. He then threatens to do just that himself (3.71.4–5). Herodotus quotes the response to Darius' threat by Gobryas: "'Now, therefore, my vote [*psēphos*] is that we accede to Darius' plan, and not leave this council to do anything else but attack the Magus at once.'" Herodotus concludes: "Gobryas said this, and they all consented to it" (*pantes tautēi aineon*: (3.73.3).

On the sixth day after killing the usurper, the seven surviving conspirators gathered again to deliberate concerning "all relevant matters" (3.80.1). Three sets of questions were resolved by the small, deliberative, decision-making group.[14] First, what form will political authority

---

14. See Asheri et al. 2007: 220 on the frequency of the Greek vocabulary of deliberation (*boul-* root terms) in this passage.

take? Will the Persians be ruled by a monarch, a small coalition, or by all Persians? What, in short, will be the Persian *politeia?* Next, after a majority vote determined that the *politeia* would be monarchy, who (among the seven and the rest of the Persians) must obey the king and on what terms? What limits (if any) will there be on the king's authority? And finally, who (among the seven) will be king? How will that choice be made? Can the process be manipulation-proof?[15]

The situation obviously recalls Herodotus' earlier account of the assembly of Medes, who had gathered to deliberate upon, and to choose, evidently by vote or acclamation, first a form of rule and then a ruler. As noted above, Herodotus' Median tale traces the voluntary agreement of a people to accept an absolute sovereign over themselves, and thereby anticipates the social contract thought experiment in Hobbes' *Leviathan.* In the Persian case, the contracting parties are the seven men who might have been king. Like Hobbes in *Leviathan,* Herodotus supposes that those who make the contract do so as equals and, like Hobbes, the sovereign ruler might take the form of an individual, a junta, or a mass of citizens. Moreover, like Hobbes (Foisneau 2016: 25–47), Herodotus supposes that the preliminary decision to establish a sovereign is by a majority vote and does not require consensus. And yet, in a development that would have given both Hobbes and Deioces pause, once the decision has been made to have a king as ruler, specific (if quite narrow) limits are placed on his authority. The Persian kingship is not only established by a deliberative and rule-bounded constitution-making process, but the result is in some ways a constitutional, rule-constrained form of royal authority.

Herodotus relates three speeches that were made in advance of the vote on *politeia,* assuring the skeptical reader that these speeches really were given (3.80.1). First Otanes speaks in favor of democracy, then Megabyzus for oligarchy, and finally Darius for monarchy.[16] Otanes spends most of his speech attacking monarchy; he says nothing about oligarchy and he develops his positive argument for popular rule, described as *isonomia,* only at the very end. Megabyzes seconds the

15. Herodotus' Persian Constitutional Debate and questions of historicity are discussed in Brannan 1963 (with earlier literature cited); Evans 1981; Gammie 1986: 172–75; Pelling 2002; Dewald 2003; Sissa 2012; Cartledge 2016: 93–97; Atack 2019: chap. 1. For the context: Munson 2009.

16. The argument for rule by the many is described as *isonomia,* but was clearly understood by Herodotus to be democracy; at *Histories* 6.43.3, Herodotus alludes to Otanes' proposal that the "Persians ought to democratize" (*dēmokrateesthai*).

arguments Otanes had made against kingship; he devotes most of his speech to attacking the idea that a mob (*plēthos*) could rule. He concludes by recommending the rule of aristocrats (*hoi aristoi*). Finally, Darius says that Megabyzes was right about the badness of the rule of the *plēthos,* but wrong about the rule of the few (*oligarchia:* using the word, as Megabyzes had not). Darius propounds an iron law of monarchy: Given the competitive desire of each of the eminent to be preeminent, their tendency to violent factionalism, and the likelihood that the many will line up behind a charismatic leader, both oligarchy and democracy will eventually devolve into monarchy. In his closing argument he points out that it was under a king that the Persians won their freedom (*eleutheriē*), that is, overthrew the rule of the Medes in favor of their own superior position. He asserts that kingship was built into Persian ancestral norms (*patrioi nomoi*), norms that ought not be violated (3.80.2–82.5).

After this deliberative phase, a vote was taken: "These being the three opinions offered, four of the seven men preferred the last" (3.83.1). At this point in the narrative, Herodotus immediately turns to Otanes' offer, which we will consider below. But, given our interest in rational choice-making and decision processes, it is worth pausing to take stock. Herodotus is adamant that there really were three regime options on the table, and he makes it clear that, in stark contrast to the consensus that followed the previous debate on the timing of the coup, monarchy was not a consensus choice. Given that Herodotus reports that precisely four of the seven men preferred kingship, we must suppose that there was a vote of some kind. Herodotus does not tell us how the vote was conducted.[17] But he has presented his reader with an implicit problem in social choice, and one that, when we stop to think it through, poses some deep questions that have engaged choice theorists in the twentieth and twenty-first centuries. While there is no reason to believe that Herodotus anticipated the technical issues that are the primary concern of modern social choice theorists, his account seems designed to leave his reader with the suspicion that the vote for monarchy might have been manipulated by Darius so as to yield the outcome he desired. That

---

17. Herodotus' terminology does not suggest a secret ballot vote with tokens, but such votes were in any event rare in Greek legislative assemblies (as opposed to judicial proceedings; see chapter 6.6–7); we might imagine either a show of hands or that choices were expressed verbally.

manipulation could have been as simple as determining the order in which options were presented to the seven decision-makers.[18]

3.5 HERODOTUS' IMPLICIT SOCIAL CHOICE PROBLEM

The parameters of the choice problem are (1) there are seven voters, who must (2) choose among three options. Let us suppose, as seems reasonable from the arguments presented in the three speeches, that, at the conclusion of the deliberations, each of the seven had complete rank-ordered preferences over the three options. And let us further suppose that each option gains at least one vote (i.e., that Otanes, Megabyzus, and Darius remained unpersuaded by the others' arguments). Given these assumptions, we can arrive at the "four votes for monarchy" result by employing either one of two simple voting methods. Each of these, however, raises some potentially serious problems.

Herodotus' text permits his reader to imagine a voting procedure, along the lines of an Athenian ostracism, under which each of the seven voters chose one of the three options.[19] Assuming, per above, a minimum of one vote for each option, there are four possible outcomes. These are illustrated in table 1.

The concern that arises with this "direct voting on three options" approach is that two of the possible outcomes would be indecisive: Outcome 1 is a tie between two options. Here, if the voters for Options I and II are assumed to be committed to their choices, the outlier (Option III voter) can hold out and thereby prevent a majority result. Or he becomes the pivotal voter and is in a position to auction his vote to the highest bidder. Outcome 2 makes Option I a plurality choice, but it remains self-evidently the case that a majority of voters preferred one of the other two options. In this case, given the worries about factionalism raised by the speech of Darius, we might expect that the Option II and III voters will combine against the Option I voters, with indeterminate but potentially unsatisfactory results. Outcome 3 is the reported result: four votes

18. Social choice literature: Arrow (1951) 1963; Riker 1982; Mueller 2003. Compare Mackie 2003, for critical response. That the process was meant to be imagined as an actual vote, and that the outcome could have been unanimous, is suggested by a previous deliberation and vote among the conspirators, described above.

19. In the Athenian practice of ostracism the number of options was indefinite (potentially as many as there were Athenian citizens), and the choice (the individual ostracized) was determined by the plurality vote "winner." See Forsdyke 2005.

TABLE 1   DIRECT VOTING BY SEVEN VOTERS ON THREE OPTIONS

	Option I	Option II	Option III
Outcome 1	3	3	1
Outcome 2	3	2	2
Outcome 3	4	2	1
Outcome 4	5	1	1

NOTE: Option I, II, III can be any of Democracy, Oligarchy, Kingship.

for the chosen option (here Option I is Kingship). Given the possibility of Outcome 4, we can readily see that Kingship has gained the smallest possible majority. Assuming the vote is binding, Persia will be a Kingdom, but the result seems surprisingly fragile, given its decisive impact on subsequent Persian (and Greek) history: A single changed vote could have landed the Persians in either of the troubling Outcomes 1 or 2.

Next, let us suppose that the voting was sequential, that there were two or three rounds of polling on two options. This may well have been how Herodotus' readers would have imagined the decision procedure (presuming they gave the question any thought), since policy in Greek legislative assemblies was, it appears, typically made by a sequence of either-or, yes-no votes. Each vote in the sequence leading to the decision was on only two options.[20]

Other than the assumption that at least one of the voters most prefers each of the options, and what we might try to infer about the second choice of each speaker from the three speeches, the distribution of preferences among the seven voters is unknown. But it might, hypothetically, resemble the distribution in table 2. This distribution yields a second round, four-vote victory to Kingship, and does so without raising any troubling issues about procedure or results.

Under this first distribution of preferences, if we assume that the voting begins with Democracy versus Oligarchy, we will have as an outcome:

Round 1. Oligarchy: 4 (#4, 5, 6, 7) beats Democracy: 3 (# 1, 2, 3).

If the voting continues with Oligarchy versus Kingship, the outcome will be:

Round 2. Kingship: 4 (#1, 2, 3, 7) beats Oligarchy: 3 (#4, 5, 6).

---

20. See further, chapter 6.6, with discussion of Canevaro 2018 on voting.

TABLE 2 FIRST HYPOTHETICAL DISTRIBUTION OF PREFERENCES FOR SEVEN
PERSIAN CONSPIRATORS

	Voter 1	Voter 2	Voter 3	Voter 4	Voter 5	Voter 6	Voter 7	Total
Democracy	2	2	3	2	1	1	1	12
Oligarchy	1	1	1	3	3	3	2	14
Kingship	3	3	2	1	2	2	3	16

NOTE: Voter preferences (ordinal and cardinal): 3 = most preferred, 2 = second choice, 1 = least preferred.

TABLE 3 SECOND HYPOTHETICAL DISTRIBUTION OF PREFERENCES FOR SEVEN
PERSIAN CONSPIRATORS

	Voter 1	Voter 2	Voter 3	Voter 4	Voter 5	Voter 6	Voter 7	Total
Democracy	3	3	3	2	2	1	1	15
Oligarchy	1	1	1	3	3	3	2	14
Kingship	2	2	2	1	1	2	3	13

If the voting ends there, we have arrived at the outcome reported by Herodotus: four votes for Kingship. There was no need for a third round of voting, since that round would only confirm that Kingship beats both of its rivals. If there were a third round, the outcome would be:

Round 3. Kingship: 5 (#1, 2, 5, 6, 7) beats Democracy: 2 (#3, 4).

We can see that, with this distribution of preferences, the vote has resulted in a choice that was rational in the sense of transitivity: Democracy < Oligarchy < Kingship > Democracy. In the terminology of social choice: Kingship is the "Condorcet winner."[21] Kingship also gets the greatest aggregate of weighted preferences (the Total in the final column). And so, Kingship seems well and securely established.

But what if preferences of the seven voters were distributed somewhat differently, as in table 3?

Under this distribution the first two rounds go just as they did before.

Round 1. Oligarchy: 4 (#4, 5, 6, 7) beats Democracy: 3 (#1, 2, 3).

Round 2. Kingship: 4 (#1, 2, 3, 7) beats Oligarchy: 3 (#4, 5, 6).

21. The Condorcet winner is an option that would win a majority in sequential votes against each other available option. See discussion in Riker 1982; Ingham 2019.

But in this case, conducting a third round of voting would raise a troubling issue: Democracy beats Kingship by a vote of 5 to 2!

Round 3. Democracy: 5 (#1, 2, 3, 4, 5) beats Kingship: 2 (#6, 7).

Moreover, when we consult the aggregate of weighted preferences (Total in final column), we see that Kingship is least favored, while Democracy is most favored overall.

If voting is limited to two rounds, we get Herodotus' reported result of four votes for Kingship. But that now appears to be a bad and insecure outcome. Not only do we have the perverse result that the aggregate least-preferred option is chosen, but if there were a third round of voting, the result would be a voting cycle, in which Democracy < Oligarchy < Kingship < Democracy. That is, transitivity is violated and there is no Condorcet winner. Voting cycles violate the rules of formal rationality—the demand for complete ordinal ranking of preferences of the voting public, here imagined as a quasi-individual. The conclusion may, therefore, be that the public in question is, in a formal sense, irrational.

The possibility of voting cycles is at the core of the large social choice literature, noted above. Indeed, the *impossibility* of *preventing* cycles in the case of multiple options, under plausible procedural rules, demonstrated by Kenneth Arrow's Impossibility Theorem, is among the best-known, most robust, and most influential results in formal choice theory.[22] In the case of three options with seven voters, the theoretical likelihood of a cycle occurring, *without* manipulation, is 7.5 percent (Riker 1982: 122). Of course, it is highly implausible that Herodotus knew that, but the worry that a voting method *could* yield a result that did *not* express a coherent majority preference on the part of a choice-making public seems well within Herodotus' and his audience's grasp.

In the case of the Persian vote, we are told by Herodotus that there was a determinate outcome, with four votes settling the matter. But we may now be suspicious that the outcome could have been the result of someone strategically manipulating the process: If the distribution of preferences was as listed in table 3 (or similar), then whoever determined the sequence of votes also determined the outcome. If we have suspicions on this score they will be exacerbated when we subsequently learn, in Herodotus' narrative, that Darius strategically manipulated

22. Arrow 1963, with discussion in (among other works) Barry 1978; Riker 1982; Mackie 2003; Ingham 2019.

the mechanism that determined who among the candidates was finally chosen king.

The point of the exercise of thinking about how the Persian constitutional vote could have been conducted is *not* that there is a determinate answer to whether it was two or three rounds of votes on two options, with either a satisfactory or a seemingly perverse result; or a single vote on all options, which barely dodged the bullets of a tie or a minority-plurality choice. Rather the point is that by setting up the situation as seven voters, deciding among three options, with a nonunanimous result, Herodotus poses for his readers a neat problem in social choice. Thinking through the problem, even without mathematics, as above, reveals the complexities that can arise when choosing among multiple options by voting.

Herodotus invites the attentive reader to think about how the final vote count *might* have been arrived at, how the process *might* have gone wrong—and how it *might* have been manipulated by Darius, a man who, we are given good reason to believe, was both strategic and manipulative. The invitation is made explicit when Herodotus insists, against the expectation of his readers' skepticism, that the speeches really were given and thus that the vote really did take place. The invitation to think about choice procedures is reinforced in the subsequent narrative, when Otanes notes that the decision on the second question—who will be king?—could be decided by lottery, or by a vote of the Persian masses (*plēthos*), or "some other mechanism" (*mēchanē*: 3.83.2).

3.6 LIMITS ON ROYAL AUTHORITY

The choice of who, among the conspirators, would be king was eventually made by a deliberatively agreed-upon (3.84.3) "mechanism." The mechanism (whose horse will neigh first after dawn) was regarded as "most just" (*dikaiōtata*: 3.84.1), but it proved to be readily manipulated by Darius. Before those events, however, Otanes offered to take himself out of the running, declaring, "I desire neither to rule nor to be ruled" (3.83.2).[23] He offered a bargain that required the unanimous agreement of the other six: "Neither I nor any of my descendants shall ever be ruled by one of you" (3.83.2). Herodotus confirms that the other six did all agree to these terms (3.83.3). Their commitment proved in the event to be reliable: Herodotus concludes this part of his story by

23. Similar renunciations of the desire for tyranny: Solon F 33; Archilochus F 15.

asserting that to this very day, Otanes' family, uniquely among the Persians, remains free (*eleutherē*), and its members are ruled only in so far as they were willing to be, just so long as they do not transgress the norms (*nomoi*) of the Persians (3.83.3).

In terms of preference weighting, what has happened is this: Otanes prefers the sure thing of not being ruled in perpetuity to a one-in-seven chance of ruling. In order not to be ruled, he must gain the agreement of all potential rulers. His offer to each of them is the difference between a one-in-seven and a one-in-six chance in a kingship lottery in exchange for a specific limitation on the king's authority.[24] It is rational for each of the others to make the bargain with Otanes if a one-in-six chance at a slightly restricted kingship is preferable to a one-in-seven chance at unrestricted kingship. The weighted preferences of the six are revealed when they agree to the bargain; each did in fact value the benefit of a marginally increased chance in the kingship lottery over the cost of accepting a limit on his own authority should he be the eventual winner.

What this points to (inter alia) is that Otanes' speech in favor of democracy was not just cheap talk, and that he may have a utility function that differs from that of the other conspirators. He prefers the sure thing (assuming compliance) of perpetual freedom for his family to a one-in-seven chance at kingship. Presumably, after Otanes offered his bargain, each of the others was free to offer a similar bargain. They did not, so it may seem intuitive that the conspirators had utility functions quite different from that of Otanes: They seem to place a much higher value on kingship and a lower value on freedom. But it is worth remembering that two others had voted against kingship. Moreover, with each subsequent opt-out, a kingship lottery ticket increases in value, and so the cost of choosing freedom to anyone who sets a value on kingship also increases.[25]

We need not suppose that Herodotus' original Greek readers thought through the various issues raised by his narrative in just those terms. But the calculation is simple, and Herodotus (or his source for this story) has set up the choice situation in a way that highlights issues that arise when voters with pluralistic preferences choose among multiple options and when choices among options are understood as lotteries.

---

24. If Otanes leaves the lottery, each of the remaining six "tickets" is increased in value by .0238k (value of kingship) *minus* the limits on the king's authority represented by Otanes' freedom.

25. If f = value of perpetual freedom for one's family and k = value of kingship, then f > 0.143k for Otanes. But f > 0.167k to the second conspirator to opt out, and f > 0.2k to the third, and so on.

The passage challenges Herodotus' Greek readers' assumptions about the inevitability of Asian monarchy, about the complete absence of freedom in the Persian regime, and about the absolutism of the Persian king's authority. Based on the choices of the seven-man sample, monarchy seems not to be engrained in the Persian national character. It is not even, pace Darius, required by Persian ancestral norms: Otanes' family will obey Persian social norms, but will not be ruled over. Monarchy is adopted as a choice among possible regimes and the choice was not predetermined. Three of the conspirators preferred either democracy or oligarchy to monarchy—that is, they chose "citizen-centered" regimes over what the Greeks would regard as autocracy. Power, as rule over others, is not a universal, primitive, top-order preference. It is highly ranked by six of the conspirators, but Otanes prefers freedom to a chance to be the ruler.

The constitutional regime eventually established by the Persians resulted from a bargain among choice-makers with diverse preferences. The bargain is struck through voting and through negotiations over lotteries. The Persian regime is a monarchy, but the power of the monarch is not absolute. Otanes' freedom sets a specific (albeit slight) limit on the extent of the authority of the King. Moreover, in advance of the actual choice of the king (through the neighing horse mechanism), the conspirators agree on further limits on the powers of the king: The king is forbidden to marry outside the seven households, suggesting that the kingship has elements of a hereditary aristocracy. Furthermore, each of the seven (and presumably their descendants) will have free access to the king.

Unlike Deioces, the Persian king remains visible and accessible, at least to a select group of nobles. As we have seen, visibility and social constraint go hand in hand.[26] Moreover, the emphasis on ancestral Persian norms (in arguments by Darius and Otanes) suggests that the king's authority to make positive law may be constrained by preexisting norms that are respected, not only by the seven conspirators, but also by the Persians generally. Whether the king's power over ordinary and elite Persians (other than the family of Otanes) will be constrained in fact is a question that Herodotus' subsequent narrative addresses in detail.[27]

I have touched on only a few aspects of this extremely rich passage of Herodotus' *Histories*. The key point, for our purposes, is that Herodotus

---

26. This concern with "transparency" or at least "translucence" contrasts with the "opacity" of invisible Gyges; on the role of at least partial visibility of agents in Gauthier's theory of rational cooperation, see Morris and Ripstein 2001: 6.

27. On historical Persian kings and court ritual, see Llewellyn-Jones 2013.

sets up the problem of the refoundation of an existing state as a process of deliberating, bargaining, and strategic choices. The process is engaged by agents with diverse and (at least partially) specifiable preferences over outcomes. It is imaginable as a "game" that is played by rational players, in recognition of the choices likely to be made by others, requiring calculation, and readily described in terms of lotteries.

Herodotus' account of the foundation and refoundation of a great Asian state was not a simple, slave-versus-free, counterpoint to the Greek states familiar to his original readers: Both the Medes and the Persians established kingship through oral deliberation and voting. The Persian King's power was limited by social norms, agreements about marriage and access, and by a Persian noble's preference for freedom. Herodotus' historical narrative raises the possibility that votes on constitutional matters are subject to rhetorical and strategic manipulation. It was, in short, a sophisticated, self-conscious contribution to a tradition of political theory concerned with choice-making by rational agents.

3.7 POLYBIUS ON PRIMITIVE DESPOTISM AND MORAL SENTIMENTS

In the sixth book of his *Histories* (6.5–6), the historian Polybius, writing some three centuries after Herodotus, in the second century BCE, posed the question of the origins of monarchical government. Herodotus' narratives concerning the establishment and reestablishment of Median and Persian kingship, however fanciful, are situated in historical time. By contrast, Polybius sets his story about the foundation of monarchy in a distant past, without a geographic or ethnic referent. He posits a primeval catastrophe that reduced humankind to a few survivors. Like the "origins of social order" stories discussed in chapter 2, Polybius' postapocalyptic humans lived at a primitive level, without technology, social order, or memory of civilization. Assuming a basic, prerational, instinct for living in groups (per Aristotle, among others), Polybius supposes that humans would act like herd animals: "They would, like other animals, band together; for it is likely [*eikos*] that bodily weakness would induce them to seek those of their own kind to herd with" (6.5.7)[28]

---

28. Straumann (2020) offers an insightful game-theoretic analysis of the relevant passages of Polybius, suggesting that Polybius describes the move from a PD-type situation (before social order) to a legitimate kingship through the emergence of a cooperation game

At this point in his narrative, Polybius turns to the question of rulership. Like Plato's Callicles (*Gorgias* 483d, also citing behavior of "other animals"), Polybius finds in nature a justification for rule by the strong. Pursuing the biological logic of "herding together with their own kind," Polybius posits that, by necessity (*anangkē*), the human herd would be led and ruled by whoever among them "excelled in strength of body or boldness of spirit."[29] The limit of the leader's authority was set by his physical strength and this first constitution is called despotism (*monarchia*: 6.5.9). That the first constitution was based on domination rather than legitimacy, the condition in which subjects obey for reasons other than fear, is suggested by the next sentence in the narrative. Here Polybius postulates a change from strength-based despotism to a form of kingship predicated on higher values. It arises from acculturation via the experience of sharing and shared identity: "But since, among such organizations [*sustēmata*], after some time there are familial relations based on common meals and ethnicity, then is born kingship [*basileia*], and also for the first time there arises among men the notion of goodness and justice and their reverse" (6.5.10).[30]

Cultural Emergence of Moral Sentiments

Notably, Polybius does not leave it at that, nor does he appeal to Protagorean "gifts of Zeus" (chapter 2.6) to bootstrap this new constitutional form. Rather, he offers a probabilistic thought experiment (hedged by frequent reference to "likelihood": *eikos*). His thought experiment takes the form of an explanatory behavioral narrative of the emergence of moral norms of goodness and justice and then for the constitutional transition of domination-based despotism to legitimacy-based kingship. Polybius' account seems to offer a rational explanation for how cooperative, prosocial norms could have come into existence through an

---

in which Cooperate, Cooperate is a unique equilibrium. Loehr (2021: 161–64) discusses the same passages from the perspective of moral emotions, rightly noting (156–57) that for Polybius, as in some recent work in social science, rationality and emotion are closely connected.

29. Here, as in Herodotus' story of Gyges, *anangkē* is constraint on options: the human herd's only feasible option is "rule by the strong," the alternative being something like "scatter and perish." As we will see (next section), after Polybius' imagined human community has developed shared cultural norms, it gains another feasible option in respect to rulership.

30. On the classical Greek terminology of autocracy (*basileia, monarchia, tyrannis*), see further Barceló 1993.

incremental process of cultural evolution, through repeated social interactions, over time. In Polybius' story the outcome is benevolent, consent-based kingship.

The cultural process described by Polybius is jump-started by a universal sexual instinct that results in the birth of children. Polybius assumes that it is proper for children to show gratitude to their parents for their upbringing. Yet some one of these offspring, upon achieving maturity, may fail to show gratitude to his parents, choosing instead to harm them in word and deed. In this case, "it is clear" that others (not the parents), observing his behavior and knowing that he was appropriately nurtured by his parents, "would probably [*eikos*] be annoyed and would disapprove." Their disapproval is predicated on human capacities for observation, communication, and—most saliently—self-interest and extrapolation from current circumstances to future outcomes: "For seeing that men differ from the other animals in being the only creatures possessed of intelligence [*nous*] and calculative reason [*logismos*], it is evident that such a difference of conduct [different from the expected reciprocal norm of gratitude] is not likely to escape their observation; but that they will remark it when it occurs, and express their displeasure to bystanders, because they will *have an eye to the future, and will reason on the likelihood of something similar occurring to each of themselves*" (6.6.4–5, emphasis added).

The last, explanatory phrase makes it clear that Polybius is working within a general framework of rational, future-oriented self-interest—the third-party observers may or may not disapprove of ingratitude toward parents just on principle, but their motivation in blaming it, "express[ing] their displeasure to bystanders," according to Polybius' stipulation, is that each calculates that such behavior, if it went unremarked and unblamed, would be likely to have a negative impact on him or herself. Presumably, the idea is that other grown children may choose to imitate the ungracious, harmful behavior. The observing others are either the parents, or potential parents, of such hypothetically misbehaving offspring and thus they stand in harm's way if they do not do something to prevent it. What they do is bring the bad behavior to the attention of others, who may be presumed to be similarly self-interested and future oriented. The implication seems to be that the community will then act to blame and sanction the bad behavior, making it more costly to the malefactor and thus reducing the likelihood of its recurrence.

Likewise, in Polybius' second case, if someone is saved from danger and yet fails to show gratitude, but instead seeks to harm his savior, "it is clearly probable [*eikos*] that the rest will be displeased and offended with him, upon learning of it: sympathizing with their neighbor and imagining themselves in his case" (6.6.6).[31] Here there is an expression of direct sympathy for the victim of ingratitude, but it is conjoined to a concern for self-interest, again via imaginative projection of oneself into the role of the victim of wrongful behavior in the form of a rejection of a "good deserves good" conception of reciprocal obligation. The sense of outrage comes as each proleptically imagines himself in the position of the wronged savior. From these situations, says Polybius, there arises in each person the idea of the practice and theory of propriety (*to kathēkon*), which is the origin and end of justice (6.6.7). Here the deliberation leading to the appropriate practice appears to be internal: There is no reference to interpersonal communication.

Polybius continues this probabilistic thought experiment in the behavioral evolution of moral sentiments with a third example: the likelihood (*eikos*) that the man who stands out before others as a brave champion in times of danger, who stands firm and courageous against the attacks of the most powerful wild animals, "would meet with marks of favor and preeminence from the masses, while he who acted in a contrary way would gain their contempt and dislike." Here, we return to a situation of public response. Moreover, the praise and reward for supererogatory good behavior, only implicit in the two previous cases, is explicit, and it is paired with the negative evaluation of bad behavior, as highlighted in the previous two cases. The upshot is that there arises in the minds of the many a conception of the disgraceful (*aischron*) and the honorable (*kalon*), and the idea that the latter should be sought and imitated as advantageous (*to sumpheron*), and the former avoided (6.6.9).

Polybius' thought experiment provides a cultural-evolutionary explanation, based on a premise of practical reasoning—the expectation of future payoffs (positive and negative)—for the emergence of the moral psychology that Plato's Protagoras attributed in his fable to the "gifts of Zeus." The mechanism is the practice of marking helpful and harmful behavior, forming an opinion, and reactively according praise and reward (honors) and blame and punishment (social stigma). In describing this mechanism, Polybius employs vocabulary (terms with the *sēmeion* root) similar to Diodorus' story of the "animal standard" focal

---

31. Cf. Polybius 6.36–38, where it is clear that some people (in this case the Romans) are not only offended as an internal state of mind but will also be bent on punishment for the offense.

point that enabled coordinated response to danger among the Egyptians (chapter 2.5). For Diodorus the focal point served to coordinate mass action against external threats. In Polybius, the focal point is aberrant or exemplary behavior that serves both to stimulate and to coordinate social responses of praise and blame.

In his probabilistic thought experiment Polybius offers three very similar scenarios (schematically: Parent, Savior, Hero). In each scenario someone acts improperly and is observed and blamed. Or someone acts properly, is observed doing so and is (explicitly or implicitly) praised. Polybius focuses on incremental development of coordinated responses through repeated interactions involving deliberative evaluation of the good or bad consequences to individuals and the community. The interactions concern individual behavior and the development of appropriate behavioral responses by third-party observers. He suggests that the desirable outcome of a community whose members are (at least for the most part) committed to a commonly shared and socially valuable set of norms is a result of learning from one's own and others' evaluation of a range of behaviors and responding appropriately in the case of repeated interactions.

Polybian Tit for Tat: A Repeated Game

We can model this part of Polybius' text as a repeated game with communication and learning (see chapter 2.7); that is, a game in which a substantial number of players have reiterated pairwise interactions. They make choices, in subsequent iterations, on the basis of what has happened in previous iterations and what they have learned from others' interactions. This is illustrated in table 4.

Following the lead of some well-known computerized simulations based on repeated games, the choices made by each player at each play can be described in the simplest terms as either "Tit" (cooperate/help/reward) or "Tat" (defect/harm/punish).[32] In table 4, Tit is represented

---

32. Tit for Tat simulation of the evolution of cooperation: Axelrod 1984, 1997. Bendor and Swistak (1997) offer a detailed formal critique of Axelrod's evolutionary story, but they note that the main intuition, that Tit for Tat strategies of conditional cooperation are advantaged, is correct in the sense that such strategies stabilize under the minimal frequency and therefore are the easiest to reach and retain. Unlike simple Tit for Tat, in which an agent rewards or punishes for actions affecting itself, Polybius' story about the evolution of cooperative social norms includes social rewards and punishments for benefits and harms done to others, a situation that was formally modeled in Bendor and Swistak 2001.

TABLE 4   POLYBIAN TIT FOR TAT

Parent		Savior		Hero			Outcome of repeat play
#2	#3	#2	#3	#2	#3		
1	1	1	1	1	1	α	Full cooperation without morality
0	0	0	0	0	0	β	Full punishment: Vendetta
0	0	1	1	1	1	γ	Mostly cooperation with morality

as 1, Tat as 0. In our game, we assume that a person #1, who is not a represented as a player in the game table, has started things off by playing 1: appropriately nourishing her offspring to adulthood; saving from drowning; or standing bravely against dangers. The repeated game is played between #2 (the second generation: son or daughter of player #1; person saved from drowning; community of the brave person) and #3 (third-party observers of the behavior of #2). Player #2 can play a mixed strategy: If the previous play has been 1 (cooperate/help: per assumption), he may play either 1 (cooperate/help) or 0 (defect/harm). Player #3 always plays 1 (reward) for 1 (cooperate/help) / 0 (punish) for 0 (defect/harm). In brief, if the previous play has been cooperate, #3 rewards; if the previous play has been defect, #3 punishes.

The game table illustrates just the first three moves (Polybius' three scenarios) in what is imagined as an indefinitely repeated game. The setup allows us, however, to predict the sort of community that will eventually emerge from an indefinite period of repeated play among an indefinite number of players. The outcome options, depending on the response of player #2, are α: a fully cooperative society in which all play 1 consistently, but do so just mechanically, without developing a special social morality; β: a vendetta society based on a consistent retrospective punishment in response to consistent defection; γ: a mostly cooperative society whose members have developed the moral sensibilities discussed by Polybius.

Although, in the language of our game, Polybius describes the outcome of the game as γ, it may be instructive first to consider α and β as counterfactuals. In the Parent scenario with outcome α, #2 responds to the parent's nourishing in an appropriate way, playing 1. Since #3 plays 1 for 1, #3 responds 1: #2 is praised for helping in an appropriate way. Having received a proper return for proper behavior, #2 plays 1 in the Savior scenario, responding with appropriate gratitude to being saved from danger. Again, #3 plays 1 for 1. Likewise in the third, Hero scenario, #2 plays 1, choosing to be a brave champion and stand front-most against the threat of fierce animals. Again #3 plays 1, praising and respecting #2. We can imagine this pattern repeating indefinitely, with #1, #2, and #3 simply responding, in an unreflective way, to the stimuli of appropriate behavior and praise for having behaved appropriately. What has *not* happened is the kind of moral learning that Polybius suggests will arise when people have had not only the experience of being praised and treated with honor for right behavior, but also the experience of being blamed and treated with disapproval for wrong behavior.

Repeating the process for the β outcomes, #2 responds to the parent's nourishing with o: ingratitude and harm. Observing this behavior and recognizing that if it goes unpunished, it is likely to have bad consequences downstream for #3, #3 plays o, blaming #2. Angry at #3's play, or oblivious to blame, #2 plays o at the Savior scenario, again failing to show gratitude. Number three plays o for the same reasons as before. And likewise at the Hero scenario, #2: o is followed by #3: o and in all repeated plays. In this second counterfactual, we end up at a society defined by incessant retrospective punishment of consistently defecting others. It may be thought of as a vendetta society, in which there is relatively little chance for active cooperation, and the primary social norm is negative reciprocity.

It is the γ outcome sequence that models Polybius' thought experiment. At the Parent scenario, #2 plays o and is punished by #3, who responds with o out of concern for the negative consequences, as in β. But in the γ sequence, #2 learns from the experience of being blamed for his hurtful behavior in Parent. At Savior, #2 plays 1, expressing appropriate gratitude for being saved. #3 observes the switch in #2's behavior, and approvingly plays 1. At Hero, having experienced both blame and praise and preferring the latter, #2 plays 1, followed by #3's approving 1. In repeated play, we may suppose that #2 occasionally returns to uncooperative behavior, playing o, and is consistently punished for it, and so moves back to 1 in the next round. Over time, because of the assumed learning process, #2 defects and is punished less often.

As repeated play among multiple pairs rewards cooperators and punishes defectors, and as the players learn from reward and punishment, as in the indefinitely repeated game set up by Plato's Protagoras, the community tends to be composed of mostly cooperative members with the right sort of moral psychology. There may still be occasional outbreaks of antisocial behavior, but these are not so frequent or persistent as to threaten the community's capacity for cooperative behavior or its basic stability.

3.8 THE TRANSITION FROM DESPOTISM TO KINGSHIP

Polybius concludes his repeated-game cooperate/reward, defect/punish thought experiment by positing a transition from autocratic (strength-based) to constitutional (consent-based) rule: At some point, the leading and most powerful man (the sort who had previously used his superior strength to dominate others) consistently joins in supporting the kinds of social behavior that have now come to be regarded as proper by the majority (*to plēthos*). He gains the reputation of distributing goods to each based on merit. As a result, his subjects obey his rule not out of fear of violence but rather approving his good judgment (6.6.11). Notably—like the Anonymous Iamblichi's prediction about the law-abiding behavior of the rational "adamantine giant" (introduction, section 0.4), and unlike the prediction of Plato's Callicles (chapter 2.3) that a strong individual of "sufficient nature" will tear up the agreements that sustain cooperation in the community—the leader in Polybius' narrative has evidently learned from observation and experience, along with the many relatively weak persons making up his society. He has therefore developed a moral psychology similar to that of the many, and that psychology is exemplified in his public actions.

Both the ordinary people and the ruler are able to learn and to teach because the behavior of others is visible—their preferences are revealed: readily noticed and remarked upon. It is by observing the consistently beneficial behavior of the leader that the others revise their reasons for obedience. Rather than simple fear of the dominator (that is, expectation of loss for disobedience) they now obey in expectation of positive benefits. They stand to gain from the leadership of the moral exemplar. This in turn results in a change in their political behavior: Rather than passive subjects, they become active members of a leader's coalition.

Presumably, when the capacity to rule had been determined by strength alone, an aging ruler was quickly deposed by a stronger incumbent. But once the leader is shown to rule in accordance with commonly held social values, and when he acts fairly in respect to distribution, no matter how old (and by implication, physically weak) he is, the others support him against attacks by would-be usurpers. "In this way he becomes a king instead of a despot by imperceptible degrees, calculative reason [*logismos*], having gained supremacy over boldness and bodily strength" (6.6.12). The upshot is that visibility entails constraints on the behavior of the ruler, but those constraints may, in the long run, prove valuable to each and all—not only to the subjects but also to the ruler himself.

The reasoning Polybius attributes to his agents is once again based on interest and a calculation of risk. The subjects have now got a king whose values have been demonstrated through his repeated actions to align with their own values, which had in turn consolidated into a common standard through reiterated play, as sketched in the previous section. The incumbent king is known to use his authority to distribute goods in a fair (in this case, presumably merit-based) way. By contrast, the values and distributive principles of a would-be usurper are unknown and so his usurpation introduces uncertainty into the choice situation. Although some may benefit, others will suffer, and the new ruler's distributive principle is not known *ex ante*. Importantly, the uncertainty goes only one way: The usurper will be either as good (king) or worse (despot) than the aging ruler. The collective cost to the subjects will be high if the usurper proves to be a despot. Thus, they willingly bear substantial costs, in the form of joining the leader's coalition and fighting usurpers, to retain the current incumbent in office.

From Prisoner's Dilemma to Assurance Game

As Benjamin Straumann (2020) has convincingly demonstrated, the situation can readily be modeled as a transition away from a Prisoner's Dilemma–type game with its unique equilibrium outcome of low payoffs to both players, to a simple sequential assurance game, played by ruler and ruled, in which the people gain their highest preference. The game is illustrated in figure 16. The leader moves first, playing either King or Despot, per above. The Subjects then choose to join in a coalition with the leader in order to keep him in power, or passively stand by awaiting his replacement by an unknown other. The leader gets his highest payoff if the Subjects choose Coalition after he plays Despot. But that outcome is not available to him; if he plays Despot, they will choose Passive. So, the leader's best move is to play King, in which case the Subjects play Coalition, gaining their own highest-ranked (and the King's second-ranked) outcome. The game is based entirely on self-interest and rational choice, but Polybius' account allows us to suppose that rationality in this case is supported by a convergence of values, based on the developmental process traced in the previous section. The King and his subjects have a shared interest in an outcome in which those values are sustained over time and manifest as social norms.

The form, although not the payoffs or outcome, of the Polybian Kingship Game is identical to the Deioces and the Medes Ultimatum Game.

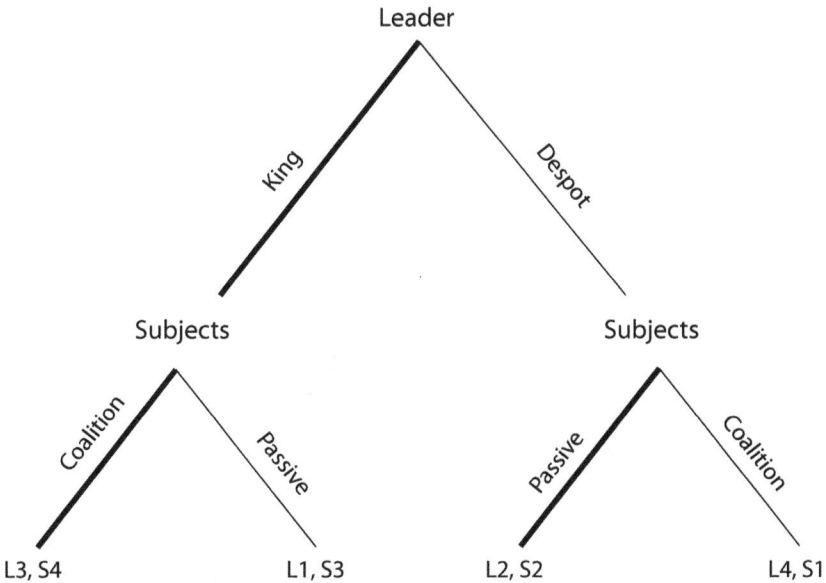

FIGURE 16. Polybian Kingship Game

NOTE: L = Leader; S = Subjects. Ordinal payoffs, 4 = high; 1 = low.

Herodotus' story of Deioces has some similarities to Polybius' account of the origins of kingship. Each is free of any hint of divine intervention or other magical features. Each is predicated on an assumed instrumental rationality on the part of both ruler and subjects. Each assumes that he who emerges as ruler will be outstanding in terms of intelligence and reasoning capacity. In both stories, ruling and justice are intertwined. In both stories the ruler, or would-be ruler, shares a conception of equity with others, and he distributes (judgments or other goods) fairly, according to merit. Both Polybius' emergent king and Deioces, once firmly established as king, expand the kingdom and engage in major construction projects, building (inter alia) great fortification walls.

But the differences are also striking, which account for the different payoffs and outcomes of the two games: Polybius' leader-king learns social norms, along with the others of his community, through a process of giving and receiving praise and blame. He emerges as king through praiseworthy action. He maintains a quotidian lifestyle: having the same food, drink, and dress as his fellows and openly sharing their pursuits. His fair distributions appear to be motivated not only by looking down the game tree and realizing that he will eventually need coalition partners to defend against a younger usurper, but also by his learned sense of justice. His construction projects are aimed at the common welfare and security of all.

Polybius' account of the emergence of widely shared moral sentiments and of justice-oriented kingship sheds even harsher light on Plato's Callicles' rival account of the emergence of order, considered above (chapter 2.3). As we saw, Callicles had no explanation for the capacity of the individually weak many to organize so as to impose rules on the formidable few. The Anonymous Iamblichi (introduction, section 0.4) had assumed a similar organizational capacity on the part of the many, but he did not explain the microfoundations of each member's costly commitment to justice. By contrast, Polybius has given his "others," the subjects of the leader, a motivation for cooperation with one another (as well as obedience to the king) in the form of expected individual and shared benefits. That expectation arose through a process of cultural evolution resulting in shared norms. The driver is the practice and experience of observing behavior, assessing costs and benefits, and blaming and praising accordingly.

Moreover, Callicles must predicate his story of the eventual victory of nature over norms on a heroic breakout from social constraint by the "man of sufficient nature." The victory is made possible by physical strength or, perhaps more plausibly, rhetorical power of the sort promised by Gorgias. Polybius explicitly takes account of the limits of individual strength and the inevitability of decline with age. He shows why the subjects of a leader would support an aged ruler long after his physical powers have passed their peak. And, finally, Polybius suggests (Hero scenario) that the leader who morphs into a king will have chosen to stand in the front lines in the fight against the most ferocious beasts. We might say, in light of Callicles' leonine metaphor, that he stands against just the sort of grown-up, demystified, bonds-breaking man-lion that Callicles aspires to be. Without positing any specific intertextual relationship, putting Polybius' culturally evolved just king into dialogue with Plato's Callicles' natural superman elucidates the close relationship between two of the existential threats to human life emphasized by the Greek "origins of order" tradition: wild animals and powerful individuals.

From Kingship to Tyranny

Polybius (6.7) completes his story of the origins of kingship with an account of how the succession process will work: The new king will be either a descendant of the first constitutional king or, should that king's descendants become degenerate, someone else chosen for his outstanding thoughtfulness (*gnōmē*) and reasoning capacity (*logismos*), not for mere strength and courage (6.7.3). Although Polybius does not say so explicitly, it appears that the choice is made by the subjects, through some method of election. Polybius concludes that these ancient kings promoted the security and welfare of their subjects "by making magnificent strongholds and surrounding them with walls and extending their frontiers" (6.7.4). They excited no jealousy because they ate and dressed much as did other men and joined readily in common pursuits (6.7.5). We may once again recall Herodotus' Deioces, who was similarly elected as ruler, expanded the state, and built strongholds. But Deioces' building projects and elaborate court rituals were designed to distinguish him from his subjects.

There is a coda to Polybius' story of kingship that points to its end in Deioces-like autocracy (6.7.6–9): Eventually, now enjoying hereditary office and increased security, kingly rulers began dressing in distinctive costumes, eating special food, and demanding increased and unconstrained access to sex; in short, they reverted to Gyges-like primitive preferences. They acted upon those preferences in spite of the potential danger of losing the support of their subjects. Perhaps these later rulers believed that their subjects had become habituated over time to subservience. Yet that assumption turns out to be invalid: The behavior of the king, who has now become a tyrant, eventually stirs up resistance against him. Polybius' narrative continues with constitutional transitions to citizen-centered regimes—the subject of the next two chapters.

As we have seen, kingship was not a foreign concept to the Greeks.[33] The Greek tradition generally held, with Polybius, that monarchy had been a first stage in the establishment of formal authority for Greek communities. But it was not the final stage, nor was it the ordinary and expected form of Greek political order in the classical era. In chapter 4 we turn to the question of the how the Greeks established, and sustained, forms of order based on self-enforcing rules rather than a monarch's fiat. Among the questions they faced was whether, without a third-party enforcer of the rules, citizens could achieve and sustain lawfulness along with individual freedom and collective autonomy.

---

33. Gammie (1986) surveys Herodotus' accounts of kings and tyrants, concluding that the historian was deeply influenced by a conventional portrait of the wicked tyrant. He notes, however, that Deioces and Darius are at least partial exceptions to the rule. On ancient Greek literature on monarchs and monarchy, see further, the essays collected in Luraghi 2013.

CHAPTER 4

Solon's Bargain

Self-Enforcing Constitutional Order

Can the citizens of a political community rule themselves in the face of pluralistic preferences and inequalities of wealth and social power? If so, how? We begin to explore those questions in this chapter. In the previous chapter we looked at how Herodotus and Polybius addressed monarchy as a distinctive form of political authority. Greek writers typically supposed that kingship was the earliest manifestation of formal public authority, and they believed that it remained the typical regime among non-Greeks—notably for the Lydians, Medes, and Persians. Greek thinkers recognized that a king might rule as an absolute monarch, free from formal constitutional constraints. The model is Deioces, king of the Medes. But Greek authors also recognized that a constitutional form of monarchy could be established such that the king was constrained by privileges retained by certain of his aristocratic peers, as well as by cultural norms. The model is the bargain struck by the seven nobles who refounded the Persian monarchy.

In either case, establishing an individual as supreme ruler solved the problem of the rationality of the state by fiat: The options chosen by the king, manifest in his legislative orders, constituted the goals of the state. The state was rational, in terms of means-ends reasoning, insofar as the king himself was rational and so long as his agents faithfully executed his commands. The orders of the king were rules for the state's subjects. Those rules, whether bluntly coercive or internalized as legitimate, limited the feasible options available to subjects. Although Herodotus suggested that royal authority in Media and Persia was established by formal agreement, Greeks tended to conceive of royal orders as exemplifying the dominion of a master. Because social order, once established, was sustained by a "third party" ruler rather than by a self-enforcing equilibrium among citizens, the Greek political tradition depicted the subjects of monarchs as slaves.

The Greeks regarded the lives of their own slaves as unhappy, and so they typically put the outcome "living as a slave" at near the bottom of their preference order—it ranked just above being dead, according to the ghost of Achilles in the *Odyssey* (11.486–492). Insofar as monarchy was equated with tyrannical rule over slaves, it was likewise low-ranked among the regime preferences of Greeks who had other options (including democracy and oligarchy) available to them. The constitutional alternative to monarchy was some sort of collective self-rule, in a bounded territory, by citizens. Since the Greeks never imagined that everyone within the relevant territory would be a participatory citizen, this also meant rule by adult male citizens, individually (within households) and as a collective, over residents who were not enfranchised citizens.[1]

Among the primary political questions facing the Greeks were these: Who among the residents of a given territory is a citizen? How can the citizens, collectively, rule both themselves and the noncitizen others who lived with them in a self-enforcing equilibrium? How can citizens manage social diversity and preference diversity among themselves, such that "we the citizens" can stand in for the individual ruler, enabling the state to choose and act rationally in seeking its ends, whatever those might be? The question of rationality in the face of preference diversity among citizens was, according to the Greek tradition of political thought, further complicated by structural social and economic inequalities. Those inequalities frequently led to conflict over social standing and political power between coalitions of ordinary and elite citizens. Conflicts could end in violent struggle over control of the state. Resolving those conflicts, and thereby attaining and sustaining a high-

1. On Greek attitudes towards slavery, see Forsdyke 2021. On the parallels between the adult male citizen as ruler in his household, and his role as a constitutive part of the demos as a collective ruler, see Campa 2019 and in progress. Here I use *citizen* in Aristotle's (*Politics* book 3) restrictive sense, as those who share in ruling, through participation in formal institutions of government (council, assembly, law court, offices). Although women were excluded from these institutions, native-born women were citizens in the broader sense of being accepted as full members of the polis community, playing essential roles in civic religion, norm enforcement, and the economy: Patterson 1987; Blok 2017.

performing and reasonably stable social order, was the fundamental problem of Greek constitutionalism.

4.1 GREEK THEORISTS OF THE STATE

From the fifth century onwards, the primary object addressed in Greek political writing was the polis—the city-state (Hansen 2006). Historically, the polis had crystallized as the organizational norm, the standard (although certainly not the unique) form taken by states within a rapidly expanding Greek world. The polis was, physically, a central conurbation and a surrounding territory. Socially, it was of a body of persons with differing and often legally specified rights and privileges: citizen and noncitizen, free and slave, native and nonnative, elite and nonelite (Kamen 2013). Compared to, for example, the Persian Kingdom, even the largest poleis (Athens, Sparta, Syracuse) were minute. Politically, a polis might be organized as a miniature kingdom, but most poleis were ruled quite differently from Deioces' Media or Darius' Persia. Greek thinkers took the similarities and distinctions among the forms of social order observable in Greek poleis, and the historical processes driving the emergence of those diverse forms, as particularly salient objects of theoretical attention. That attention, in turn, made the polis a useful object for philosophical reflection on problems of individual and collective rationality.

Plato on States and Individuals

In the *Republic,* Plato sets up the thought experiment that will result in Callipolis, an ideal-type polis established through reasoned argument, with an initially startling set of assumptions about the state and the individual as objects of analytic attention. The ostensible aim of the dialogue, as we have seen (chapter 1), is to answer the questions "what is justice and what is its value?" and ultimately to test the hypothesis that justice is a choice-worthy end in itself and a just person is necessarily happier than an unjust one. After Glaucon's challenge to this hypothesis has been set with the thought experiment that includes the Gyges story (chapters 1 and 2), Socrates suggests that the search for justice will be easier if its object is more readily apparent. He proposes, as an analogy, the relative difficulty of reading very small letters at a distance, compared to reading the same letters if they were to "exist elsewhere larger and on a larger surface" (368d). He then posits that there must be justice somewhere to be found both in an individual and in an entire state (368e). States, being larger than individuals, should have a greater quantity of justice in them. On the assumption that what is large is readily apprehended, he suggests that if "through argument we should observe the emergence of a state, we should also see the emergence of justice and injustice in it" (369a). Observations of the location and nature of justice in the state could then be imputed to the individual.[2]

In suggesting this approach Plato's Socrates establishes two premises. The first premise is *Similarity:* The individual and the state are relevantly similar objects of inquiry.[3]

Individual and state are as alike, indeed, as a text written in small letters (say on a wax tablet) is to the very same text written in large letters (say inscribed on the stone wall of a public building). The medium has changed, but the message remains the same. As the dialogue develops, Plato will be able to infer the presence of the specific psychological features of reason, spirit, and desire in the state and impute these features to the individual soul. He concludes that it is the appropriately hierarchical and harmonious relationship among those features that constitutes true rationality and justice for both state and individual.

Socrates' second premise is *Observability:* The state, along with its component features (including justice and injustice), is more easily observed, and by extension, more readily analyzed than is the individual soul. We can observe the features characteristic of both the state and the individual more easily in the state than in a single person. We can see how the relevant state-level features relate to one another, and thereby gain a better sense of what constitutes their proper organization and harmonious interaction in the individual as well. Both *Similarity* and *Observability* do a lot of work in the *Republic;* together they point to the avenues of investigation that had opened, by the early fourth century BCE, to Greek thinkers concerned with the rationality of the state.

Similarity implies that a state, like an individual, has among its constitutive features, not only justice and the other virtues, but also the psychological features, basic to instrumental rationality, of desire,

2. Ferrari (2003: chap. 2) concisely surveys scholarly opinion on the city-soul analogy, concluding that city and soul are composed of the same parts, related to one another in the same way, so that justice, for example, is the same property in each; this in turn clarifies the great gap between the happy philosopher and the miserable tyrant (Ferrari 2003: chap. 4).

3. Similarity (*homoiotēs*) of soul and regime: *Republic* 555a, 576c. The premise is repeated by later authors writing in the Platonic tradition, e.g., Plutarch, *Lycurgus* 31.

belief, and reason. Plato's developed account of rationality includes the "folk theory" elements of preferences arising from desires and beliefs about the state of the world. But, as the Callipolis thought experiment advances, Plato's reader learns that rationality, properly so understood, extends the scope of reason to correct judgments about ends. Rather than exogenously given by "primitive" desires for wealth, sex, and power (per Plato's Glaucon: chapter 1.2) or by emergent social norms (per Polybius on early kingship: chapter 3.8), right preferences are to be formed on the basis of knowledge, a precondition both for forming the right preferences and for moving from right preferences to right actions leading to good outcomes.

Knowledge is sharply distinguished from ordinary opinion-based beliefs about the state of the world and from expectation based on likelihoods. Unlike Gyges with the ring, whose goals were given by his primitive desires, Plato's just state and individual will be rational in regard to both the identification of the correct (truly best) outcome that is sought and the appropriate means to be employed in the pursuit of that goal. Rationality—as the masterful exercise of the faculty of reason in respect to subordinate desires and emotions—will be the guiding principle of the state. Rationality, so understood, will enable the attainment of justice and promote happiness through efficacious means.

The demanding principle of ethical rationality will be embodied at state level in the rulers: specially educated philosopher-kings. But the state will also include, among its ineradicable components, many persons whose preferences arise from their lower-order desires. Those quotidian desires are different from the desires of the philosopher-rulers, in that they arise from appetite or emotion and are not rationally chosen. The inhabitants of the state are necessarily diverse in their occupations (that necessity is discussed in chapter 7.6). Given the essential diversity of economic function, certain of their preferences will be not only (nonrational) desire-driven but also heterogeneous. The correct and stable ordering among preferences present in the state—as well as the specification of the bounded domains in which diverse preferences could be appropriately expressed (prominently including the domain of ruling)—is therefore a primary concern of the dialogue. For our present purposes, the key points are, first, that the state, like the individual, is assumed to be a potential locus of (at least) instrumental rationality. Next, even at the level of ideal theory, a stable social order must be predicated on the political management of diverse preferences arising from desires other than those of reason itself. These assumptions are shared by some contemporary normative and positive political theorists (see chapter 8.7).

Observability—the premise that features common to individuals and states are more readily observed in the state—is striking in that it is easy to imagine the situation as being otherwise. Psychological features of desire and reason might, on the face of it, seem to be more readily apparent by observation of individuals. The desires and reasoning processes of a state might seem to be a "black box": largely invisible and unobservable. Indeed, a ruler might take pains to make these things as cryptic as possible. Take, for example, the Median state (chapter 3.2). As king, Deioces centralized the operations of the state in his person, but deliberately hid himself and his decision processes from the sight of his subjects. The king's will was made manifest by the announcement of his commands and judgments. But he himself was invisible behind the walls of his purpose-built palace city. Many of his agents were, if visible, unobservable, insofar as they were spies.

By contrast, Plato implies that the (presumptively Greek) state is transparent. The operations of reason and desire, manifest in choices made by the state's rulers, are readily observed. Further back, the procedures by which rulers are chosen, and the processes by which those procedures were chosen, are also visible, at least to the participants in the dialogue and to Plato's readers. Ultimately, per discussion in chapter 2, the processes of social cooperation that are the preconditions for the emergence of the state as a social form were regarded as at least theoretically observable, through the activity of the political imagination.[4]

While Plato's use of *Observability* is distinctive within the Greek tradition of political thought, the premise itself is not. For Greek theorists, the state was at once complex (composed of multiple persons, psychological features, social processes) and observable. Indeed, it seems plausible to postulate that the state—in the distinctive form of the citizen-centered polis—was the most complex readily observable phenomenal object available for analysis by Greek thinkers of the classical era.[5] The state was observable because its operations were not mystified or hidden à la Deioces. Politics, as activity in and of the state, was carried out in public, "in the center" (*es meson*) of social existence (Vernant 1982).

---

4. On the political imagination, see Schwartz 2021; with special reference to Plato's *Republic*: Schwartz 2022: chap. 4.

5. Other complex objects of great concern to classical Greek thinkers that were less readily observable include the human body (the subject of Hippocratic medicine) and the cosmos (subject of Greek works on astronomy and theoretical physics).

The state was recognized as complex, inter alia, because it was at once (1) an association of diverse persons living together and sharing some things in common, (2) a purposeful organization capable of pursuing important public ends, and (3) a constitutional regime of public authority (*politeia*).

Moreover, the observable state was highly salient: It was, absent any commonly accepted natural or God-given prepolitical moral order, the ultimate source of behavioral rules. Through rules and persons empowered to interpret and enforce them, the state was the ultimate arbitrator of disputes among the state's residents. The great salience of control of the power to make and enforce rules and to arbitrate disputes made the state a potential site of conflict. In the world of the Greek poleis, answers to the vital questions of "Who rules? And in whose interests?" were not always settled in a definitive way. The state itself became a highly valued prize that might be won by the victors of violent political conflicts.[6] Those who ruled the state were in a position to entrench their own preferences over outcomes by formalizing rules. They might further or hinder the provision of public goods. They could seek rents as private goods. They could decide what associations would be permitted to exist and allowed to limit access to club goods.[7]

Aristotle on Political Ends and Factional Interests

Aristotle's *Politics* is widely and, I suppose, rightly regarded as the culmination of classical Greek analytical attention to the state. Aristotle was paradigmatically concerned with the complex problem of viewing the state as at once a community and an organization with its own constitutional order. Unlike Plato, Aristotle clearly distinguished utopian from practical approaches to political philosophy. He rejected Plato's direct individual/state analogy (as well as much else in Plato's political philosophy). Yet, like his teacher, he was deeply concerned with the rationality of the state, both as a natural end (*telos*) in itself and as a framework for the development and virtuous exercise of individual

---

6. On the frequency of violent contests for the control (or capture) of the state, see Gehrke 1985; Arcenas 2018. In modernity, struggles over primacy within an established system of government often take the place of (or, alternatively, obscure) struggles over the control of the state; see, for example, Levitsky and Ziblatt 2018.

7. On entrenchment in modern democratic governments, see Moe 2019 on the "second face of power."

rationality. It is a central tenet of Aristotle's political thought that individuals cannot achieve their highest ends except in the context of a properly ordered state. Aristotle's work on ethics (*Nicomachean* and *Eudemian Ethics*) and politics (*Politics* and *Art of Rhetoric*) are, consequently, tightly conjoined parts of the same overall project (see chapter 8.6).

Like Plato, Aristotle's ultimate concern, at the levels of the individual and the state, is with rational judgments formed by comparing the objective value of possible outcomes. But, again like Plato, his concern for the rationality of ends required answering hard problems about instrumental rationality. Aristotle recognized that rationally choosing effective means to desired ends was a prerequisite for the achievement of the ultimate human end of achieving true happiness: *eudaimonia*. In *Politics* book 7 Aristotle lays out the necessary material and institutional, as well as moral, preconditions for the best practically achievable state: the "polis of our prayers." Those essential preconditions could only be secured by the right kind of means-ends reasoning.

Instrumental rationality was recognized by Aristotle as a deep problem for the state, given the inevitability of pluralistic preferences across a socially diverse population. The problem was compounded by the possibility of strategic behavior in choice contexts. Humans are, for Aristotle, "political animals" and therefore, like ants or bees, we have a natural disposition towards sociability and the production of valuable public goods. Because nature does nothing in vain, and because humans are public-goods-producing social animals whose proper end is to live (avoid extinction) and to live well (in a condition of *eudaimonia*), the state, as the necessary condition for both living and living well, exists by nature and is an end: It is essential for human flourishing.

Yet humans are not cooperative all the way down, as are the bees of a given hive or the ants of a given nest. And so, the Aristotelian state must have a means of establishing and enforcing formal rules as laws, as well as educating citizens in appropriate behavioral norms and the habit of conforming to them. This necessity arises because, unlike social insects, we humans are capable of recognizing ourselves as individuals with diverse preferences. In order to satisfy our preferences, we can and will seek out those who share our preferences. We tend to form subassociations within the master political association that is the state. Subassociational "parts" are prone to identify their factional interests as other than those of the common good of the state as a natural whole.

Because humans are instrumentally rational, factions—especially the rich and the poor—will tend to act strategically, seeking to control the state and to compete with it.[8]

To achieve the ultimate, eudaimonic, ends of its residents, the state, as a community, must be properly organized. It must be capable of identifying and pursuing near-term and more distant goals. This requires incentives and constraints on the expected-advantage-maximizing behavior of many self-interested persons, acting individually and as members of associations. In order to function effectively as an organization, the state required rules and norms: a *politeia*.[9] The *politeia* may be either just or unjust, insofar as its rulers—one, few, or many (per Herodotus' Persian Debate)—abide by the established laws and seek, through their public actions, the common good. In Aristotle's political taxonomy, the just regimes, in which rulers were both law-abiding and common-good-seeking, were monarchy, aristocracy, and polity. Unjust regimes—democracy, oligarchy, and tyranny—were those in which the rulers did not regard themselves as bound by laws and tended to seek their own partial advantage.

So, there were many kinds of *politeia*. Some were more conducive to the ultimate end of living well. But each was more or less capable of securing the necessities of "mere life." While Aristotle's political theory is both naturalistic and teleological, the *politeia* did not come into being entirely through a teleological process: Were that the case, every polis would end up with the same *politieia,* which, once realized, would be fixed for all time. That was certainly *not* true of the political world familiar to Aristotle and his contemporaries. Aristotle's detailed empirical study of the constitutional orders of Greek (and a few non-Greek) city-states confirmed the diversity of *politeiai* and the tendency of a given state's *politeia* to be changed in favor of another.[10]

For Aristotle on the Greek polis, as for Herodotus on Asian empires, the establishment and maintenance of a *politeia* was the product of willed human choices. Those choices prominently included the activity of lawgivers. A polis constitution came about, not just by natural processes, but also through the choices of rule-makers. Aristotle states that, while there

8. On the persistence of conflict in Aristotle's polis, even in its best practically achievable form, see Yack 1985; Skultety 2019.

9. Polis as *koinōnia* of *politai* in respect to *politeia*: Aristotle, *Politics* 3.1276b1–2. On the necessity of "external goods" for the flourishing polis, and thus for human flourishing, see further, chapter 8.6.

10. O. Murray 1993, with discussion in Ober 1996: chap. 11.

is a natural impulse (*hormē*) towards communal association (*koiniōnia*) in all humans, nonetheless "he who brings a community together is the proximate cause of the greatest human goods" (*Politics* 1253a29–31). This is because, while humans have the potential to be the best of animals, in the absence of law and justice they are the worst, by dint of turning their capacities for reasoning to the attainment of the primitive ends of sex and greedy consumption (1253a32–38). Here we have an echo, albeit muted by natural sociability, of Plato's socially unconstrained Gyges and the problem of bootstrapping social order in a population of presumptively self-interested rational agents (chapters 1 and 2).

The key role played by the lawgiver in enabling the state to persist over time in the face of primitive desires and heterogeneous preferences, to act like a rational quasi-individual in pursuing its goals (just or otherwise), is a leitmotif of Aristotle's political philosophy, as it had been for Plato. In the Greek historical tradition Solon of Athens was a prominent exemplar of a lawgiver who set a stamp on the *politeia* of his polis. The ancient tradition concerning Solon emphasizes the lawgiver's virtues: his courage, moderation, justice, and especially his wisdom. But the tradition also points to a rational bargain as the basis of his achievement. The wisdom of the lawgiver, in the Greek context, involves close attention to the desires, beliefs, and expectations of value-maximizing individuals and collective agents.

4.2 THE SOLON TRADITION

The "constitution of Solon," the set of new laws established during Solon's one-year term as archon (magistrate) of Athens in 594 BCE, has been held up as a political ideal by democratic elitists since the fourth century BCE. In his *Areopagiticus* of ca. 357 BCE, for example, the political orator Isocrates describes the Solonian constitution as an ideal form of democracy in which a benevolent elite ruled with the grateful concurrence of deferential masses.[11] Isocrates' idealizing account suggests that Solon's constitution was handed down as a fait accompli by a wise and just lawgiver to a welcoming community. But the ancient tradition preserved in the Aristotelian *Athēnaiōn Politeia* (hereafter *Ath. Pol.*) and Plutarch's *Life of Solon* presents a more interesting picture: An essential component of Solon's wisdom proves to be his skill in finding a bargaining solution

---

11. Ober 1998a: 277–86. See further, Carugati 2019: 43–44, 104–7, on the importance of Solon as a model in Athenian political discourse of the fourth century BCE.

that allowed the Athenian state to move past a potentially catastrophic social crisis.

The surviving Greek tradition concerning Solon is long and complex, ranging from lyric poetry by (or at least attributed to) Solon himself, to Herodotus' *Histories,* to speeches by Athenian orators, to the philosophical projects of Aristotle and his school, to Plutarch's moralizing biography, and beyond. For our purposes the Solon tradition represented by the Aristotelian *Ath. Pol.* and Plutarch's *Life* may be treated as unitary: We are concerned here neither with debates among historians about what Solon actually did nor with the history of Greek historiography. The important thing for our purposes is that the tradition understood Solon as having served not only as a lawgiver (*nomothetēs*) but also as an arbitrator (*diallaktēs*) at a moment of crisis for the early Athenian state.[12] The crisis was precipitated by conflict between opposing Athenian factions: the wealthy and individually powerful few on the one hand, and the impoverished, individually weak many on the other. The tradition details the sources of the conflict, Solon's bargaining solution to it, and his subsequent lawmaking. It also includes Solon's own and other writers' reflections concerning what he sought to accomplish and how successful he actually was.[13]

In briefest outline, the Solon tradition followed by Plutarch and Ps-Aristotle is as follows: The crisis was precipitated by a conflict between two sociologically defined factions, call them Mass and Elite. The background to the conflict was increased indebtedness on the part of poor Athenians. Debts were secured by the persons of the debtors. When some formerly free Athenians failed to repay their loans, they were enslaved by their Athenian creditors. The impoverished Mass sought relief from their debts, freedom from slavery and the threat of enslavement, and the redistribution of landed property. The Elite sought to regain secure control of the sources of wealth they had held at the outset of the crisis and their monopoly on political authority. Accepted as arbitrator by both sides, Solon achieved a one-time cancellation of debts, abolished the practice of enslavement of Athenians by Athenians, freed Athenians who had been enslaved, and repatriated Athenians who

12. *Ath. Pol.* 5.2; Plut. *Solon:* 14.2. LSJ translates *diallaktēs* as "mediator"; the root meaning of the verb *diallassō* is "exchange": LSJ *s.v.* II. On the epigraphic evidence for the role of *diallaktai* as arbitrators/mediators in Hellenistic-era sociopolitical crises, see Simonton 2019: 195–96, with literature cited.

13. The Solon tradition is discussed in the essays collected in Blok and Lardinois 2006; see especially Noussia 2006 (Solon's rhetoric); Harris 2006 (Solon and law).

had been sold abroad. He did not institute a general redistribution of land.

Solon then restructured the constitutional offices such that access to office-holding was directly linked to income. He revised judicial procedure, so that any citizen might bring charges on behalf of a victim of a crime, and he gave the citizen assembly jurisdiction over legal cases concerning official malfeasance. He made other laws regulating various aspects of social behavior and economic activity. His laws were written and publicly displayed. The Athenians swore an oath to maintain those laws for a period of time. Following his term as archon, Solon left Athens. Some years later, there was renewed conflict, centered on control of offices; that conflict ultimately resulted in the establishment of a tyranny. The tyranny was in turn replaced by a democracy. Despite these regime changes, the Athenians retained Solon's laws as a constitutional foundation throughout the late archaic and classical periods.

The tradition clearly sees the crisis that led to Solon's appointment as a protracted, at least potentially violent conflict (*stasis*) between two parties (wealthy Elite and impoverished Mass) in which each side sought to maximize its share of valued resources: land, debt, labor (bodies of persons), and offices (authority to make and enforce rules, legal judgment). Each party had clear and opposed preference orderings over these contested resources. The ordinal preference rankings are listed, schematically, in table 5.[14] Among the core questions that the Solon tradition poses to a political theorist concerned with instrumental rationality are these: Why did the opposing parties agree to ask Solon to arbitrate their dispute? How did Solon decide on the division of the resources under dispute? Why, given that Solon could not impose his solution by fiat, did both sides accept it? By what criteria might his arbitration be judged as successful or a failure?

14. Two parties are rich versus poor: *Ath. Pol.* 5.1–2; Plut. *Solon* 13.2, 14.1–.3. The entire demos was in debt to the rich: Plut. *Solon* 13.2. Dispute was protracted and violent: *Ath. Pol.* 5.2. Dispute had reached a peak: Plut. *Solon* 13.2. Goals of the poor party: Plut. *Solon* 13.3, 14.1, 16.1. Goals of the rich party: Plut. *Solon* 14.1, 16.1. Plutarch's mention of three contending parties (Plut. *Solon* 13.1)—extreme democrats, extreme oligarchs, and those preferring a moderate and mixed government—is an outlier in the tradition and seems to play no role in his narrative of the origins of the crisis or Solon's subsequent reforms. It is unclear who Plutarch imagines the "many citizens, too, who belonged to neither party" (Plut. *Solon* 14.3) might have been.

TABLE 5 PREFERENCES OF ELITE AND MASS BEFORE SOLON'S ARBITRATION

Resource	Elite preferences (rank order)	Mass preferences (rank order)
Land	Status quo ante	Redistribution
	<u>Redistribution</u>	Status quo ante
Debt	Status quo ante	Cancelled
	Cancelled	<u>Status quo ante</u>
Labor	Status quo ante	Nonslavery
	Nonslavery	<u>Status quo</u> ante
Offices	Status quo ante	Share in rule
	Share in rule	Status quo ante

NOTE: Underlined = will use violence to stop this outcome.

4.3 A BARGAINING SOLUTION TO AN ATHENIAN SOCIAL CRISIS

I suggest that the result of Solon's arbitration should be understood as a bargaining solution of the kind that John Nash developed in one of the major breakthroughs of modern game theory. This does not, of course, imply that the Solon tradition anticipated the mathematics or the formal conditions that were the basis of Nash's (1950) celebrated solution to the bargaining problem.[15] It means only that the intuitions that enabled Solon to arrive at an acceptable answer to a seemingly intractable conflict track certain of the intuitions common to solving bargaining games. In a two-party bargaining game, one side may gain more than the other, depending on the outcome, but the game is not a zero-sum competition: one side's gain is not simply equal to the other's loss. This is because both sides expect to come out of the bargain in a position that is better than the one that they currently occupy. It is the expectation that sharing in the "surplus" (the value of making the bargain) will make each party better off that brings them to the bargaining table in the first place. In the case of the crisis confronted by Solon, the surplus was the difference between the low-payoff situation of social crisis at which the Athenians were currently stuck, and a readily imagined higher payoff situation that would result from improved social cooperation. In the Athenian case, the higher payoff sought by the Mass was a dramatic improvement of dire social conditions. For the Elite, the

15. On Nash's bargaining solution and for overviews of bargaining in game theory, see Barry 1989: 12–49; Dixit and Skeath 1999: chap. 16; Camerer 2003: 151–98; Serrano 2008.

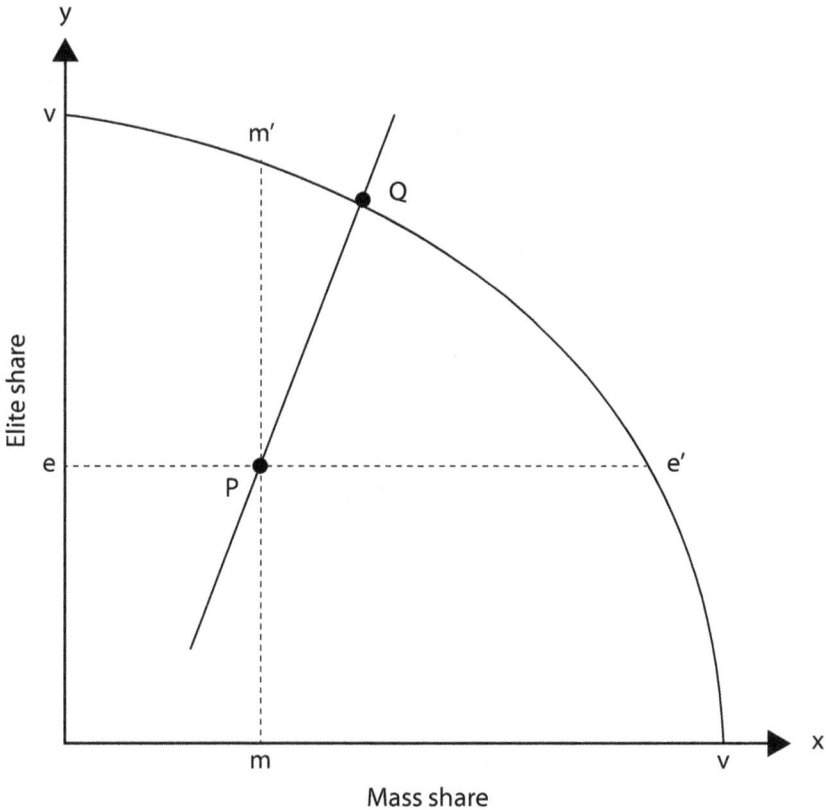

FIGURE 17. Solon's Bargaining Solution

NOTES: After Dixit and Skeath 1999: Figure 16.1, p. 525. y axis = Elite share of disputed resources; x axis = mass share of disputed resources. e, m = backstop (Best Alternative to Negotiated Agreement) positions of Elite and Mass. v = Pareto frontier. Line P-Q is the calculated ratio between elite and mass bargaining strength. Q is the equilibrium "bargaining solution"—the point on the frontier at which Elite and Mass each have as great a share of the total social surplus as they can hope for in light of their relative bargaining strengths.

higher payoff entailed alleviating the unrest pertaining during the crisis, ideally returning to the "status quo ante": the social conditions that pertained before the crisis.

The solution to a bargaining game depends on three factors, each of which can be visually illustrated by a simple XY chart. In figure 17, the horizontal x axis represents the Mass's potential share of the resources in dispute; the vertical y axis is the Elite's share. The first of the three factors involved in the solution is the "backstop" payoff to each side.

The backstop is each party's best alternative to a negotiated agreement—that is, the position it currently holds and expects to retain should negotiations fail (Pinkley, Neale, and Bennett 1994). Since each party expects to retain its backstop if the bargain fails, neither party will accept a payoff lower than its backstop position. In the Athenian case, the backstops are the shares of the aggregate of land, debt, labor, and offices that Mass and Elite held at the point that their struggle reached the deadlock that led them to accept arbitration. In our illustration, the Mass's backstop position is at point m and the Elite's is point e. P is the intersection of backstop positions: the (x,y) point at which the dashed vertical line drawn from m to m' meets the horizontal dashed line from e to e'. So, P is the starting point that the bargain must improve. In figure 17, m, e, and P may be thought of at first as simply illustrative—they have not (yet) been shown to represent an approximation of the actual backstop positions of the crisis-era Mass and Elite of Athens.

The second factor involved in the solution is the full potential value of the bargain—that is, all the improvement that could be realized if all goes as well as possible. This is represented on the illustration by the convex curve v. The section of the curve that defines the range of optimal solutions lies between m': a point on the y axis that is north of e (improving the position of Elite) and e': a point on the x axis located east of m (improving the position of Mass). Any point on this section of the curve will capture the full value of the bargain: it is "Pareto optimal" in that it adds to one party's position without subtracting from the other's position. Once again, we may take the curve v in figure 17 as merely illustrative of the bargaining situation, rather than measuring the actual full value of the Mass-Elite bargain. Although any point on the graph that is located northeast of P will represent an improvement in the starting position of both Mass and Elite, any point located southwest of curve v is "inefficient" in that it fails to capture the full potential value of the bargain. In sum: Since no player will accept a bargain with a payoff beneath his backstop, any acceptable bargain will be northeast of P and a full-value negotiated bargain will fall somewhere on curve v between m' and e'.

The third factor is the relative bargaining strength of the two parties. If either party comes to the table with a superior bargaining position (more willing to settle for its backstop and thus walk away from the table, less risk-averse, more patient), it will end up with relatively more of the surplus. The bargaining strength of Elite and Mass can be represented by a proportion (StrengthMass:StrengthElite). That proportion, when it is quantified, yields a specific slope-intercept (a line at a given angle). So long as we assume certain background conditions, an optimal (full value) and stable (acceptable to both parties) rational bargaining solution is represented by the point "Q" at which a "proportional bargaining strength line," passing through P, intersects curve v.[16] So, Q is the unique theoretical solution to the bargaining problem.

In figure 17, the hypothetical Elite party is assumed to have both a superior backstop position (e > m) and greater bargaining strength (the slope of the line passing between P and Q is greater than 45 degrees). We might regard Solon's solution to the Athenian social crisis as a (non-mathematical and intuitive) bargaining solution if the key factors in his decision included the backstop positions of Mass and Elite, their relative bargaining strengths, and a calculation of the expected total value of social cooperation that could be divided among them if a bargain were reached. As we will see, according to the tradition, Solon appears to have considered things that are at least roughly analogous to these three factors. If that is indeed the case, figure 17 may be seen as a tolerably good, if highly schematic, illustration of Solon's actual solution.

In the tradition, the bargain between the Athenian Mass and Elite was struck through the intermediation of Solon, acting as an arbitrator agreeable to both sides. Drawing on the discussion of fair bargaining in John Rawls' *Theory of Justice* (1971), Brian Barry (1989: 24–30) points out that rationally self-interested parties to a dispute will agree to turn the matter over to arbitration (rather than bargaining directly with one another) only under certain conditions. First: Neither side has reason to believe it can gain everything it hopes for (complete preference satisfaction) by fighting or by direct bargaining, that is, by prolonging the conflict through a series of offers and counteroffers, involving threats and bluffs. Next: Each side believes it will do at least as well from arbitration as it would from direct bargaining. Third: Each believes that the arbitrator is impartial, in the thin sense of not favoring either side,

16. The formal background conditions are that the outcome is invariant so long as the scale in which the payoffs are measured changes linearly; the outcome is efficient (no available gain should go unexploited); and the outcome is not affected by irrelevant alternatives: Dixit and Skeath 1999: 526–28. As Barry (1989: 16–24) points out, the last of these is not intuitive, other than to mathematicians. But the underlying condition is attention to relative bargaining strength (including tolerance of the risks associated with nonagreement) and so, "We can say simply that the parties will look for a formula that gives each of them as much as could have been expected from direct bargaining . . . and anything which produces outcomes in the general area of the Nash solution should satisfy this requirement" (quote: p. 24).

rather than in the thick, moral sense of being committed to some external decision criterion (distributive justice, however defined).[17] That is, the impartial arbitrator *does* attend to the backstops and relative bargaining strength of the parties to the dispute, but he *does not* personally favor either side. Fourth: Each side has reason to fear the results of a failure to come to any sort of agreement. Finally, we may add, given the high-stakes situation of classical Greek constitutionalism, fifth: Neither has reason to believe that the arbitrator will use his position to establish himself as a tyrant, à la Deioces.[18]

In the case of the crisis that Solon sought to resolve, each side in the dispute did have much to gain, but also had a lot to lose in the case of a failure to reach an accommodation—that is, neither had a backstop that was close to its expected position resulting from a full-value bargain.[19] The backstop for each side was low because each had a credible and not yet fully realized violence threat; for the rich, this was based on their superior wealth-power; for the poor, their superior numbers.[20] Resort to unrestrained violence could end in the collapse of social order. Meanwhile, in the background, there was an external threat: Athens was involved in a long-term conflict with neighboring Megara over control of the island of Salamis.[21] If Athens were sufficiently weakened by internal conflict, Megara would exploit the situation. Finally, there was an internal threat: the possibility of the emergence of a tyrant, who might rule in such a way as to expropriate property and labor.[22] Each of these conditions weighed especially heavily on the Elite and so tended to reduce what might otherwise have seemed to be the overwhelming Elite advantage in terms of bargaining strength.

---

17. Since, if both sides agreed on a fair distributive principle, there would be no dispute, there is disagreement over what would constitute just distribution. Arbitration based on a specific distributive principle will tend to favor one side or the other.

18. Barry 1989: 50: "Arbitration can most straightforwardly be seen as (to adapt Clausewitz) a continuation of bargaining by other means. The object of the arbitrator is to resolve a conflict on terms acceptable to both parties, when the parties consult their own interests in determining what is acceptable. This entails that the arbitrator should seek to arrive at an adjudication that will as far as possible mimic the outcome of rational bargaining."

19. *Ath. Pol.* 11.2: "The people had thought that he would institute universal communism of property, whereas the notables had thought that he would either restore the system in the same form as it was before or with slight alteration." Plut. *Solon* 14.3: "Both parties were in high hopes."

20. The rich are powerful: Plut. *Solon* 5.2. Organization of the many poor under emergent leadership: Plut. *Solon* 13.3.

21. Conflict with Megara: Plut. *Solon* 8–10.

22. Tyranny threat: Plut. *Solon* 13.2, 14.3–4.

According to the tradition as reported by Plutarch's *Life* and the *Ath. Pol.*, Solon was credible as an arbitrator in part because he had an established record of probity and concern for the community as a whole. At least as important, he was regarded as a "man of the middle" who lacked a clear affiliation with either party in the dispute.[23] He was (based on his public statements, reputation, and observable behavior) credibly committed to rejecting the option of seeking absolute power for himself.[24] The decision by both sides to accept arbitration thus fulfills Barry's conditions under which two parties will rationally choose arbitration over continued direct bargaining.

4.4 SOLON'S ARBITRATION AS A FULL-VALUE SOLUTION

The tradition regards Solon as supremely virtuous: wise (included in canonical lists of the "Seven Sages"), moderate (neither despising wealth and honors nor seeking them in excess), and courageous (willing and able to fight, but not rash). He was certainly concerned with achieving an outcome that could be widely accepted as just.[25] But his bargaining solution to the dispute was in no sense ideal in respect to an external standard of justice. In terms of understanding an arbitrator's decision as embodying a bargain that reflects the relative strength of each side (as measured by a willingness to return to their backstop, patience, and knowledge of conditions), as opposed to instantiating an ideal principle of justice (say, distributive fairness), it is imperative that the outcome aims at an equilibrium: that is, neither "player" has a better move to make in the "game." In the absence of any third-party enforcer (the arbitrator lacks coercive authority: has no way to impose the solution on a party willing to return to direct bargaining, via threats or fighting), that equilibrium must be self-enforcing.[26] And this means that, *ex post,* neither side can believe that a renewed threat of violence would improve its position. Two passages from Plutarch's *Life of Solon* are

---

23. *Ath. Pol.:* 5.3: Solon as being among the middling citizens (*mesoi*); Plut. *Solon* 14.1–2: The rich accepted him readily because he was well-to-do, and the poor because he was honest; 16.2: he was *dēmotikos* and *mesos*. Barry (1989: 76–77) cites Harsayani's super-thin "veil"—a decision-maker (arbitrator), who knows all about the differences between the two parties, but has an equal chance of being a member of either party.

24. Solon rejects tyranny: Solon F 33, 34; Plut. *Solon* 14.5.

25. Solon's virtues: *Ath. Pol.* 5.3; Plut. *Solon* 2.3, 3.2, 30.3,

26. Solon's lack of coercive authority: Plut. *Solon* 16.2, "relying as he did only on the wishes of the citizens and their confidence in him."

especially illuminating in terms of understanding Solon's arbitration and lawmaking as a successful bargaining solution, rather than an instantiation of ideal justice.

Best Available, Not Absolutely Best

In the first passage Plutarch (15.2) reports that, "when [Solon] was afterwards asked if he had enacted the best laws [*aristoi nomoi*] for the Athenians, he replied, 'The best they would receive [*prosedexanto*].'" This is a succinct statement of the outcome of the arbitration/lawgiving process as a bargaining solution: There were, by implication, "better" laws, based on some external standard of justice. But the unwillingness of the Athenians of either party to "receive" less than they believed they could gain by direct, hard bargaining imposed a strict constraint on Solon's range of options regarding the distribution of resources.

The second key passage is a story that Plutarch tells about Solon's interchange with his fellow "sage," the Scythian Anacharsis.[27]

> When [Solon] was already engaged in public affairs and compiling his laws, Anacharsis, accordingly, on learning what Solon was about, laughed at him for thinking that he could check the injustice and rapacity [*pleonexia*] of the citizens by written laws, which were just like spiders' webs; they would hold the weak and vulnerable who might be caught in their meshes, but would be torn to pieces by the rich and powerful. To this Solon is said to have answered that men keep their agreements [*sunthēkai*] with each other when for neither party is there profit [*lusitelēs*] in breaking them, and he was adapting his laws to the citizens in such a manner as to make it clear to all that the practice of justice was preferable [*beltion*] to the transgression of the laws. (Plutarch *Solon* 5.2–3)

This passage recapitulates some of the key conceptual terminology (*pleonexia, sunthēkai, lusitelēs*) and logic of "Glaucon's challenge": The practice of justice is not predicated on a moral duty but rather on the prudent obedience to the laws by self-interested agents, who, despite preferring to do injustice, fear the loss of suffering it. It is, furthermore, a clear statement of the core feature of a bargaining solution: In response to Anacharsis' challenge, Solon asserts, in the language of game theory, that neither player has anything further to gain by any other move. Each player has improved his position (advanced beyond his backstop)

---

27. On the Greek tradition of the Seven Sages as performers of wisdom, and Anacharsis the Scythian Sage, see Martin 1993, 1996.

as far as possible. Each party has got all it can reasonably hope for, in light of the moves (abandon the bargain, retreat to backstop) available to the other party. The bargaining solution has been "adapted to" the expectations of the players and therefore accepting the outcome is more advantageous to each player than is breaking the agreement.

In light of these two passages, along with other comments attributed to him and the content of his laws, it seems plausible to visualize the tradition's imagination of Solon's arbitration as a bargaining game with a solution per figure 17. He was concerned with what each party would accept (given their option of returning to threats or fighting), with the relative strength of each party's position, and with the full value of social cooperation that was being foregone by the conflict. The assumption of the game is that Solon will choose a position somewhere on the "full value" curve v.[28] Solon would not choose any point inside the line because he sought a stable outcome (neither side having a reason to think it could do better than the solution he offers) and because he wants a maximally productive social outcome. He wants that because he wishes for the best for the society as a whole: The tradition portrays Solon as a farsighted patriot who wanted Athens to be strong against its rivals and to flourish economically.

The question, then, is where, on curve v, Solon's solution (point Q in figure 17) will lie. If counterfactually, per figure 18, he had believed that the two parties were equal in their backstop position (P) and equal in their bargaining power, he would choose A (the midpoint on the curve). If counterfactually he believed the Mass (the many poor citizens) had a better backstop and greater bargaining strength, he would choose some point nearer B. If he regarded the Elite (the few rich) as advantaged in backstop and bargaining strength, he would choose some point nearer C.[29] Of course, each side will seek to convince Solon that their backstop is high and their bargaining position strong. The wisdom of the arbitrator is seeing through these ploys and finding the point Q that represents each party's true position in each case. He must, ideally, identify a solution that captures the full value of the bargain and that is in equilibrium: the one that both sides will accept because it is the best they can expect in light of their assessments of the backstop and bargaining

28. The curve represents the "Pareto frontier"—that is to say, any point that lies inside the line offers at least one of the parties a move (north or east) that will improve its own position without materially worsening the position of the other party.

29. Things get more complicated, of course, if one side has a better backstop position and the other a stronger bargaining position.

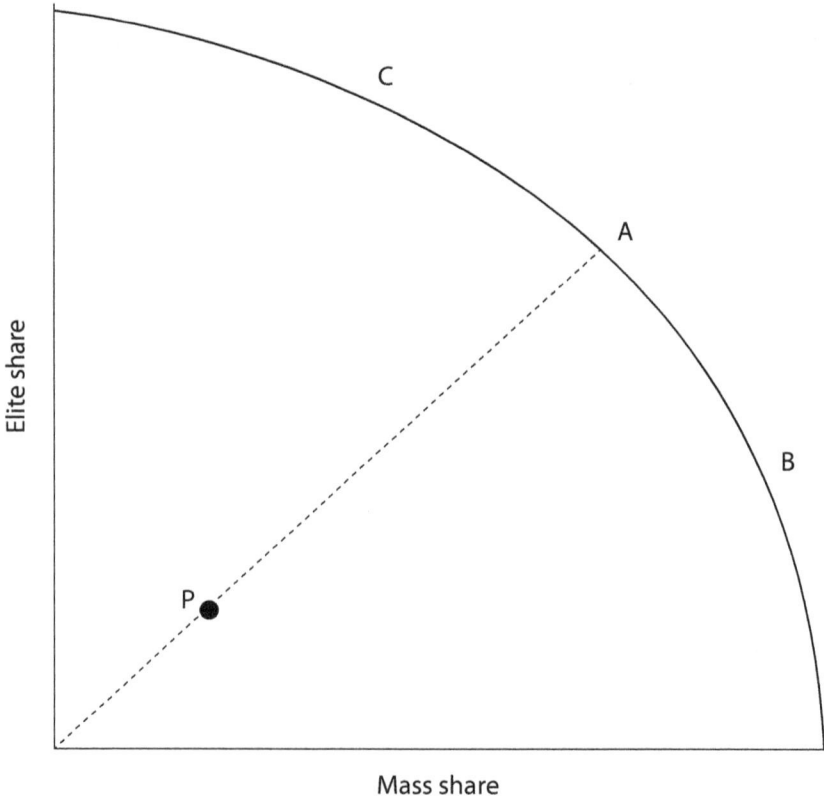

FIGURE 18. Solon's Solution Options

NOTE: Model assumes backstop positions of Elite and Mass are equal. A = equal bargaining strength of Elite and Mass; B = Elite with superior power; C = Mass with superior power.

strength of both parties. Per figure 18: the theoretical solution is the correct point on the curve.

It is important to keep in mind that the dispute between the Athenian parties concerned several resources, per table 5: land, debt, labor, and offices. The Elite prefer the status quo ante—their share before the outbreak of the conflict. If they do not believe that the conflict is likely to result in social collapse or tyranny, they have a superior backstop position: They controlled most of the agricultural land and were unwilling to give up ownership of real estate. As creditors, they were collectively owed a great deal by impoverished debtors. Debtors unable to pay back their loans were enslaved, so they had lost the option of selling their labor to the highest bidder. The Elite had so far maintained control of the system at a political level through their monopoly on the public offices, and through the immunity of office-holders to legal prosecution. The Mass, on the other hand, although having a weaker position in terms of both backstop and bargaining strength, were clearly willing to fight, perhaps even at the risk of social collapse, and might support a tyrant if the alternative was the status quo ante. They wanted agricultural land to be redistributed on a basis of equitability among Athenians. They wanted existing debts to be canceled and those Athenians who had been enslaved for debt to be freed. They wanted a greater share in public offices and more control over those who held those offices.

To solve the problem, Solon had to determine the true backstop position of each party on each of the several issues; our imagined point P is an aggregate of those points. The presence of multiple issues might seem to have made the situation not only more complicated but also less tractable. But in fact, according to bargaining theory, the opposite is true. As Dixit and Skeath (1999: 544–55) point out, "Often the enlargement of the . . . set of issues actually makes it easier to arrive at a mutually satisfactory agreement." This is because, "when two or more issues are on the bargaining table at the same time, and the two parties are willing to trade more of one against less of the other at different rates, then a mutually beneficial deal exists." In table 5, the underlined items and the nonunderlined—the things that we assume each party will and will not fight to attain—signal the possibility of tradeoffs.

Solon's solution certainly appears to have traded off the various issues at variable rates. He divided the land resource mostly in favor of the rich, in that he refused to overthrow existing claims to private property by redistributing agricultural land in elite ownership. Yet he did do something significant in regard to access to some land—he "disestablished the boundary markers [*horoi*]"—which may refer to rights of movement across the Athenian landscape or to returning publicly owned land to public (or common) uses.[30] Next, he distributed debt and labor mostly in favor of the poor many: He mandated a one-time cancellation of debts and liberated Athenians who had been sold into slavery, apparently without reimbursement to former creditors and former owners. On the other hand, we hear nothing of reparations to Athenians who had lost their land and years of their lives under the old regime.

30. *Horoi* and public lands: Ober 2006a, with literature cited.

Finally, Solon reorganized the public offices and access to legal redress. Here it is not obvious that either side had a clear backstop position (Plutarch, *Solon* 18.1–5). Nor even that "constitutional rule"—that is, the restructuring of the major offices according to income (with the highest offices reserved for the wealthiest), and formalizing the right of the many poor to attend the assembly and the power of the assembly to try cases of public malfeasance by office-holders—was within the *ex ante* preference set of either of the parties to the dispute. But the "moderate" result of the Offices category seems to point to Solon's goal of achieving an outcome that could be defended as equitable overall. Although the Solonian solution appears to have been somewhere between A and C on figure 18—and thus somewhere around Q in figure 17—he clearly advertised it as a fair bargain, one that could be described as just, and it was, in the end, accepted by both parties.

As Barry (1989: 68–76) points out, if he is to achieve a sustainable solution to the dispute, an arbitrator lacking coercive power must distribute the surplus arising from the bargain (locate the Q point on the full-value curve) according to the baseline conditions defining the disagreement (the backstop positions) and the relative bargaining strength of each side. The baseline conditions included whatever agreement there was about the legitimacy of existing claims to property or property rights.[31] Bargaining power includes the willingness of each side to follow through on a threat to walk away from the bargaining table: to accept that the negotiation has failed and return to its backstop. But, as we have seen, in Solon's Athens, both sides had strong reasons (including fear of social collapse, Megarian exploitation, and tyranny) to avoid a failed negotiation.

Moreover, unlike "Deioces' Ultimatum" (chapter 3.3), the bargaining issue was enjoined between two factions of citizens, rather than between a ruler and his subjects.[32] What this meant in practice was that the primary issue was distributing the expected value of social cooperation among two parties, rather than executive moral hazard (the risk that the ruler will violate the agreement *ex post*: Weingast 1997). Barry (1989: 107–8) notes that a bargaining solution to a distribution problem may be thought of as a prescription for the arbitrator who, for

---

31. On property rights in Greek thought and practice, see Mackil 2018.

32. On the difference: Fearon 2011. Note, however, that Fearon is focused on the question of bright lines that signal a violation requiring rebellion. Fearon's point is that in a working democracy, the failure to hold an election is such a bright line.

whatever reason (here: desire for success conjoined with lack of enforcement authority), must produce an adjudication that will simulate the outcome of direct bargaining. Barry notes further that, having reckoned as well as possible the strength of each party's preferences over outcomes, effective arbitrators will not simply announce the award *as* a bargaining solution. Rather, "they come up with some formula for relating the award to some principle, some comparison, or some precedent" (Barry 1989: 108).

In Solon's case, the "formula" was equitability and the "principle" was justice—albeit of a practical rather than ideal sort (i.e., justice as mutual advantage, not as morality: Barry 1989: 1–9). In poems alluding to his legislation, Solon repeatedly states that he distributed the relevant goods to both parties according to their desert (Solon F 5, 34, 36, 37; *Ath. Pol.* 12.1, 12.3–4; Plut. *Solon* 18.4). He represents each side as seeking to maximize its own advantage and as careless of the justice of the other side's claims (Solon F 6, 34; *Ath. Pol.* 12.2–3). And thus, initially, each side, hoping to gain more at the expense of the other side, expressed dissatisfaction at the outcome of the arbitration (*Ath. Pol.* 6.3, 11.2; Plut. *Solon* 16.1–2; 25.4). In his elegies, Solon analogizes his own position to that of a wolf beset by dogs on all sides (Solon F 36) and elsewhere to a boundary marker (*horos*), set between two hostile armies (Solon F 37). In brief, he advertised himself as having served as an impartial judge, beset by those who urged him to be partial to their side, and his solution as, overall, just because it was as fair as possible to both sides.

In the short run, at least, the solution was successful. Both the elites and the masses ultimately accepted the payoff that they were offered in the arbitration over land, debt, and labor as the best they could get in light of moves in the game available to the other side. Both sides allowed Solon to continue with his political reforms of rules governing access to offices and legal redress (Plut. *Solon* 16.3). As noted above, Solon's solution would only work if it were self-enforcing. Plutarch's Solon acknowledges this. When asked what polis was best, he replied, "That polis in which those who are not wronged, no less than those who are wronged, exert themselves to punish the wrongdoers" (Plut. *Solon* 18.5). Here we have a reference to the necessity of cooperation in punishment—the key to the emergence and persistence of social order in Protagoras' "great speech" (chapter 2.6). The Aristotelian *Ath. Pol.* (11.1) implies something similar, in explaining Solon's decision to leave Athens after his laws had been established: "He did not think it fair for him to stay and explain his laws, but for everybody to carry out their provisions for himself."

It is in connection with the necessity that the equilibrium be self-enforcing that we should understand the tradition that one of Solon's laws mandated that any citizen who held aloof when there was a violent civil conflict (*stasis*) was to be disenfranchised.[33] Solon here appears to be driving up the cost of conflict in an attempt to prevent its outbreak. Rather than allowing a matter to be violently contested only among polarized parties with very strong preferences over outcomes, and thus with much to gain or to lose, Solon pushed citizens with weaker preferences into the fray. This might incentivize those "in the middle" to intervene before the conflict was joined, especially if they were a large majority. Likewise, if many of those in the middle were to take up arms, the men who started the fight risked defeat and punishment. In either case the outcome might mean the destruction (death, exile) of those who began the fight. The result, then, was to force those with strong preferences, who were prone to fight to satisfy them, to ask themselves how certain they were of victory: Were they willing to bear the costs of a post-*stasis* reckoning if they were to lose? If the likelihood and the costs of losing were both high, the expected value of fighting would fall below the value of the status quo and *stasis* would be avoided.

Deliberation and Justification

As we have seen, the *stasis* that led to Solon's appointment as arbitrator was joined between two parties, understood in the tradition as elites and masses. Solon's bargain allowed ordinary and elite citizens to go on together within a single polity, to pursue goals (security against external rivals, economic improvement) that both sides held in common. But the bargain did not end tensions between a few who were relatively wealthy, well connected, and individually powerful and the many who were not. Nor did it end the potential of Athenian society to bifurcate into competing mass and elite factions.

33. Solon's *stasis* law: *Ath. Pol.* 8.5; Plut. *Solon* 20.1. P. E. van 't Wout (2010) argues that Solon's law on *stasis* (probably a product of fourth-century political debates) should be read as requiring citizens to play an active role in the resolution of a conflict, if necessary by use of arms, but to do so on a basis of neutrality: standing up for the community as a whole, rather than for either faction. For another skeptical view of the historicity of the law on *stasis*, see Teegarden 2014b.

As I have argued elsewhere (Ober 1989), the dynamic tension between mass and elite animated Athenian politics throughout the classical period. The Solonian bargain enabled Athens to become an exceptionally high-performing polis (Ober 2008). But for some ten generations after Solon the terms of the bargain were debated in public and private speech and periodically renegotiated through a series of major and minor institutional innovations (see chapter 6). The trend, over the late sixth through the mid-fourth century BCE, was for the masses of ordinary citizens to gain a greater share of contested goods. Meanwhile, the growth of the Athenian economy meant that there was an increasing social surplus of goods to be shared. Both masses and elites benefited from that growth (Ober 2015a, 2017b). The ongoing process of debate and renegotiation informed some of the most important works in the Greek political canon (Ober 1998a). It also provided material for thoughtful explorations of instrumental rationality.

The accounts of the Aristotelian *Ath. Pol.* and Plutarch concerning Solon's bargain confirm, and help to elaborate, the role of deliberative reason-giving in the Greek constitutional tradition. In Herodotus' stories about kingship in Media and Persia (chapter 3: *Histories* 1.95–101, 3.71–83), deliberations follow the procedural norms of democratic Athens: Deliberations over rulership took the form of open, oral arguments in favor of available options. Arguments were made, and attended to, by persons who would be bound by the decision. Following debate, the choice was determined by open voting or acclamation. In the Solon tradition, by contrast, the deliberation took place in Solon's mind, and the arguments in favor of the decision were made after the fact, in his lyric poetry.

Both *Ath. Pol.* and Plutarch make a point of quoting lines from Solon's lyric poems. A number of those poems seek to justify the bargain: Solon is presented as offering the Athenians reasons for his choices—including, as we have seen, reasons for why the constitutional order did not fully please either side in the dispute, and for why it was rightly regarded as equitable, even while it fell short of ideal standards of justice. Herodotus' Median/Persian constitutional narratives and the Solon tradition underline a general point with significance for contemporary debates between deliberative and agonistic democrats: The role of deliberation is not discounted in the Greek political tradition in favor of bargaining strength and threats. Nor, however, is deliberation elevated to an ideal that takes the place of power, threats, and strategic behavior. The Greek tradition recognized the essential role of both normative argument and strategic bargaining in the creation and persistence of a viable nontyrannical political order.[34]

Before taking leave of Solon, it is worth comparing him, briefly, with Deioces, who in Herodotus' story (chapter 3.2) was also an arbitrator of disputes, both before and after he became king. Among the key differences is that Deioces achieved his reputation by arbitrating private disputes, whereas Solon was chosen as an arbitrator by competing factions. Yet both cases invoke the language of freedom (*eleutheria*) and law (*nomos*) and raise the question of how they may be related. Herodotus' Medes, as we have seen, gave up their freedom, understood in the "positive liberty" sense of a share of rule, in order to pursue their private affairs, secure in the lawfulness that Deioces was uniquely capable of providing. In Solon's case, the *Ath. Pol.* (6.1) claims that "Solon, having become master [*kurios*] of public affairs, made the *dēmos* free [*ēleutherōse*], both at the time and for the future, by prohibiting loans secured on the person, and he laid down laws and enacted cancellations of debts both private and public."

In the passage quoted above, *dēmos* should probably be translated "the mass of poor Athenians" rather than "the body of all citizens." But the effect of Solon's legislation was both to free poor individual Athenians from actual slavery and to establish some of the preconditions that would eventually enable the *dēmos,* as the body of all citizens, to rule the state—that is, democracy. The author of the Aristotelian *Ath. Pol.* (9.1) makes this explicit when he later writes that the three "most democratic" (*dēmotikōtata*) of Solon's reforms were the prohibition of loans secured upon the person, the rule allowing any Athenian who so wished to prosecute on the behalf of another, and, most especially, the right of appeal to a jury-court: "For the *dēmos,* being master [*kurios*] of the vote [*psēphos*], becomes master of the *politeia.*" The questions of the identity of *dēmos* (the full citizenry or a social class within the citizenry), whether the relationship between lawfulness and freedom was zero-sum, and how a constitutional bargain could create a large surplus that might be fairly shared, remained major issues for the Greek tradition of political thought.

---

34. Contemporary normative literature, notably including work by Habermas (1996) and Rawls (1996), seeks to eliminate the role of unequal social power in processes of lawmaking and adjudication. Normative theories tend to regard agreements as ideally achieved through deliberation. Deliberative versus agonistic democracy debate: contrast Fishkin 1991, 2009 with Mouffe 1993, 2000.

Solon's bargain did not prevent a series of tyrannical coups; the last of these established the family of Peisistratus in power for the better part of two generations, from 546 to 510 BCE. But Solon's bargain proved enduring in that the Peisistratid tyrants publicly respected the forms of the legal order Solon had established. In the centuries after the fall of the tyrants, the Solonian bargain provided a basis for further constitutional development. Solon was enshrined in Athenian memory as *the* lawgiver; subsequent legal developments were bundled into the general category "laws of Solon."

4.5 CLEISTHENES' WAGER: RATIONAL REVOLUTION

In considering the Greek tradition concerning the next act in the Athenian constitutional drama, we retain the Aristotelian *Ath. Pol.* as a source. But we leave Plutarch behind in favor of Herodotus, whose *Histories* offer the most detailed account of the relevant events and whose text was a primary source for the later *Ath. Pol.* As we might anticipate, based on his stories of the origins of Median kingship and the reestablishment of Persian royal rule in western Asia, Herodotus' account provides the material for an analytic narrative predicated on rational choices.

Democracy, understood as collective self-government by an extensive and socially diverse citizenship (Ober 2017a), was established in Athens in 508 BCE in the aftermath of a revolutionary uprising succinctly described by Herodotus (5.66–73.1, 5.74–78), whose narrative of events is augmented at points by the *Ath. Pol.* (20–22.1)[35] Peisistratus' quasi-constitutional tyranny, established after two false starts a half-century after Solon's constitutional reforms, ended with a Spartan military intervention that deposed his surviving son in 510. In the ensuing power struggle between Athenian aristocratic coalitions, the faction led by Isagoras, who had a personal relationship with Cleomenes, one of the two Spartan kings, was initially dominant. Faced with defeat, Cleisthenes, the leader of the rival faction, tried something new. He wagered that radically enlarging his coalition by "inviting the demos to be his trusted comrade" (Herodotus 5.66.2) would give him an advantage in the power struggle. The practical means by which Cleisthenes sought to

---

35. I have discussed the events of 508–506, under the rubric "The Athenian Revolution," in detail in several papers: Ober 1996: chap. 4; Ober 1998a; and most recently in Ober 2007a (with citations of scholarly literature and discussion of sources). The debate over the origins of democracy: Raaflaub, Ober, and Wallace 2007.

enlist a mass following was constitutional reform, which would allow ordinary citizens a fuller role in the *politeia*. His wager quickly paid off: The demos accepted the invitation and Cleisthenes now dominated his rivals. Isagoras, however, responded by requesting aid from Cleomenes. Confronted by the threat of Spartan-led organized violence, Cleisthenes and many of his closest allies fled Athens. A mixed force of Spartans and mercenaries, led by Cleomenes, then occupied the city.

Isagoras and Cleomenes sought to consolidate their position by ordering the Athenian government council to dissolve. When the councilors refused the order, the rest of the Athenians rose up in arms. Confronted with this turn of events, unexpected given that Cleisthenes and his core supporters had fled Athens, Isagoras and his Spartan allies retreated to the Acropolis stronghold, where they were besieged by the Athenian demos. After three days, the besieged force surrendered under terms. Isagoras and Cleomenes were expelled from Athens; some of the mercenaries who had accompanied them were executed. Cleisthenes was recalled by the demos to the city and immediately set about implementing the reforms.

The democratic political order, like the tyranny that had preceded it, was predicated on Solon's bargain. As Herodotus' narrative emphasizes (5.74, 91), it was instituted in the face of a serious external security threat: a large-scale Spartan military response to the humiliation of their king. In 506 the Spartans and their Peloponnesian allies marched against Athens in coordination with invasions launched by the poleis of Boeotia to the north and by Euboean Chalkis to the northeast. Again unexpectedly, the Spartan-led army turned back at the Athenian border, following the defection of a key Spartan ally (Herodotus 5.75). The two other invasion forces were quickly defeated. The victorious Athenians then attacked Chalkis, seizing land and booty (Herodotus 5.77).

The dramatic Athenian victory against the Spartan coalition paved the way for a quarter-century of constitutional reforms before the great Persian invasion of 480. We do not know exactly when in the late sixth or early fifth century, or by whom, the term *dēmokratia* was first coined and employed as the name of the Athenian *politeia*.[36] But, as a practical matter, the revolutionary uprising of the Athenian demos and the reforms that followed established democracy, as collective self-governance by an extensive and socially diverse body of citizens. In the late sixth and early

---

36. Dating of the origins of the term *dēmokratia*: Hansen 1986; Lambert 2019. Its original meaning: Ober 2017: chap. 2.

fifth century, other Greek states experimented with more citizen-centered forms of government (Robinson 1997, 2007), but Athens' democratic *politeia* is by far the best documented of them.

We will consider, in chapter 6, certain of Cleisthenes' institutional innovations and later constitutional adjustments made during the fifth and fourth centuries. In terms of assessing the rationality of Athenian democracy, the prior puzzle is, however, explaining how a sequence of choices, made by individuals and groups, led ultimately to the creation of a new political order. From the standpoint of instrumental rationality, among the key questions are why Cleisthenes chose to invite the demos into his coalition, why the demos rose up against the Spartans after Cleisthenes was expelled, and why Cleisthenes carried through on the promised reforms after the Spartans had left and he was recalled.

An Athenian Democratization Game highlights the relevant counterfactuals—the choices that might have been made by various agents, but were not. Imagining a game played between Cleisthenes plus his original aristocratic faction, Isagoras in collaboration with the Spartans, and the Demos of Athens, helps to make sense of certain choices that, according to our sources, the historical actors made. Based on the accounts of Herodotus and the *Ath. Pol.*, we assign the players' preferences in the order listed in figure 19. Preferences are ordinally ranked. The game illustrated in figure 19 can be broken out into three subgames, indicated by the divisions of the heavy diagonal line into solid, dashed and dash-dot segments.[37] Bear in mind that, as in other complex games considered above, it is wildly implausible to suppose that the historical actors could have seen to the end of the game and worked out their best choices accordingly. The point of the exercise is to illuminate the role of (practically limited) strategic rationality in narratives of Herodotus' and *Ath. Pol.* It is decidedly not to suggest that history can be reduced to a mechanistic process driven by the choices of normatively rational agents.

At the root of the game, with Isagoras' faction having become dominant, Cleisthenes chooses among acquiescence to the status quo (Yield); opposing Isagoras, employing the traditional method of enlisting his aristocratic coalition (Fight), with probability of victory $p(N^1)$; and making the wager of seeking to expand his coalition (Invite Demos). Acquiescence assures his next-to-worst payoff. Fighting and winning

37. The Democratization Game is based on work in progress, co-authored with Barry Weingast.

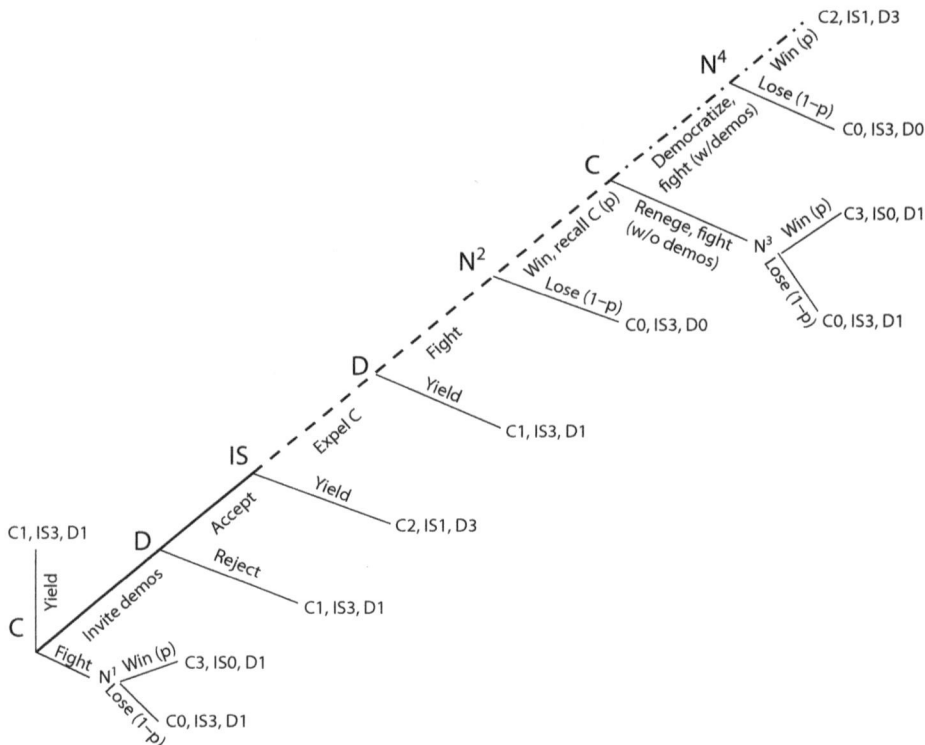

FIGURE 19. Athens Democratization Game

NOTE: C = Cleisthenes (and elite faction); IS = Isagoras (and elite faction) and Spartans; D = Demos; N = Nature lotteries over probability of winning in battles; p + (1−p) = 1. Ordinal payoffs, 3 = high; 0 = low. Probability of Win for C & D: p(N⁴) > p(N³) > p(N¹); p(N²) > p(N¹).

would give him his best payoff. But, given that Isagoras was currently dominant, had won the position of archon, and could count on the backing of Cleomenes, at node N1 the probability of victory was low and fighting and losing leads to Cleisthenes' worst outcome. This left the wager of inviting in the Demos, which, if it paid off, would give Cleisthenes his second-best payoff.

The Demos then chooses between accepting the invitation and rejecting it. Based on Herodotus' account of the events, it appears that Cleisthenes had established his credibility by proposing constitutional reforms advantageous to the demos, perhaps even passing those reforms in the citizen assembly. Accepting the invitation gives the Demos a chance of realizing its top-ranked outcome, while rejecting Cleisthenes' invitation leads to the less-preferred outcome of Isagoras' ruling. Note that the Demos is assumed to be indifferent between the rule of Isagoras or Cleisthenes *without* the Demos.

If the Demos accepts Cleisthenes' invitation, at the beginning of the second subgame Isagoras/Sparta decides whether to yield or to expel Cleisthenes. Yielding means that Isagoras/Sparta get their next-to-worst payoff; expelling gives them a chance at their best. If Cleisthenes is expelled, the Demos in turn chooses whether to acquiesce or to fight with probability $p(N^2)$ of success. Estimating that probability would not have been easy. On the one hand there was the Demos' lack of experience in acting as a collective agent, and Sparta's reputation for military effectiveness. But there were reasons to think that the Demos, if it were able to coordinate, had a reasonable chance of victory: Herodotus points out that the force led by Cleomenes was relatively small and mixed-nationality—the Demos certainly had a big advantage in numbers. A key factor, then, was the presence of a focal point (Schelling [1960] 1980; see Chapter 2.5) facilitating coordination by the members of the Demos. The Acropolis, the natural fortress in the middle of the city and the center of the state cult, provided the obvious focal point on which mass action could be (and was) coordinated, without the need for advance planning and communication. Numbers and the potential for coordination increase the probability of the Demos' victory, which in any event we can set as higher than Cleisthenes' chances against Isagoras without the support of the demos. So, $p(N^2) > p(N^1)$.

If the Demos fights and wins, at the beginning of the third subgame (actually a decision tree rather than a strategic game) Cleisthenes, recalled from exile, chooses to follow through on reforms and fight the Spartans with the support of Demos or renege on the reforms and fight Sparta without the Demos. Reneging offers a chance for Cleisthenes to gain his best outcome, ruling without the Demos, whereas democratizing gives him, at best, his second-best payoff of the Demos ruling (and himself leading). In either case, democratize or renege, we assume that the Spartans (joined by Isagoras) will attack based on their own commitment to avenging the insult to their king, so there is no third option for Cleisthenes of reneging without fighting.

If, at either of the subsequent win/lose forks, Sparta wins, Isagoras rules, getting his best payoff, while Cleisthenes gets his worst payoff. Cleisthenes' choice of democratize or renege is thus predicated on the difference between the probabilities of victory with the Demos (after democratizing) or without the Demos (having reneged). Note that the Demos has no reason to support Cleisthenes if he reneges on his promise, being in that case indifferent between the rule of Isagoras and Cleisthenes (and no doubt resentful to boot). The probability of victory against the Spartans without the Demos $(p(N^3))$ must be set as very low, certainly even lower than Cleisthenes' chance of victory against Isagoras at the root of the game $(p(N^1))$. The chance of victory with the Demos $(p(N^4))$ would have been difficult to measure, but it was certainly substantially better than without $(p(N^3))$. Even without specifying intensity of preferences or actual probabilities, the game is subgame perfect and readily solved on the path of the heavy straight line.[38]

As noted above, it is completely implausible that, in contrast to Herodotus' reader, any of the *actual* historical actors could have seen up the whole game tree; that is one reason for splitting the game into three subgames. The probabilities at various nodes (notably the likelihood that the Demos would twice be victorious over Spartan-led forces) would have been very difficult for any player to assess. The extensive form of the game illustrates the options faced by each presumptively self-interested party and highlights the role of Sparta in Athenian democratization. It shows that it is at least possible to explain the primary ancient narrative of the origins of democracy at Athens by assuming, in accordance with the folk theory, more or less rational choices by at least partially self-interested agents. That is to say, it is unnecessary to posit that Cleisthenes was either an idealistic democratic visionary or a "Thrasymachean" narrow egoist. Nor need we suppose that ancient interpreters saw Athens' path to democratization as either an inexplicable product of random contingencies or in some sense inevitable in the wake of Solon's early reforms.[39]

Sparta clearly played a key role in Herodotus' story: It is not possible to demonstrate that Isagoras' relationship with Cleomenes was a central factor in his early domination of Cleisthenes' faction (signaled by his victory in the competition for the archonship) and thus in precipitating Cleisthenes' wager. But, given that the faction fight arose in the immediate aftermath of the Spartan intervention that ended the tyranny, and in light of Herodotus' (5.70.1) claim that Isagoras had a prior

38. The probabilities of Cleisthenes' and the Demos' being victorious in the four possible fights are thus listed as $p(N^2) > p(N^1) > p(N^3)$; $p(N^4) > p(N^3)$.

39. The counterhypotheses of Cleisthenes' visionary altruism, Thrasymachean narrow egoism, mere contingency, and post-Solonian path dependency are not falsifiable; they are, I believe, considerably less plausible. See further discussion in my papers cited in note 35, above.

relationship with Cleomenes, Herodotus' account makes it entirely plausible that Sparta was a factor in Cleisthenes' fateful choice of inviting the Demos into his coalition.

Next, Sparta threatened the standing of the demos. Unlike Cleisthenes and the members of his aristocratic faction, the demos lacked the option of exit. Herodotus' narrative allows readers familiar with the Solon tradition to consider the counterfactual: Unopposed by the demos and backed by Sparta, Isagoras would have renounced the Solonian bargain, meaning that nonelite Athenians would face an Athenian analogue of helotage. Their gains from the Solon bargain would be lost. With Sparta backing a new Elite, the Athenian Mass would lack a backstop adequate to retaining its current position in any new bargain. These considerations would have made the option of fighting after Cleisthenes had been expelled more attractive in spite of the risk, thereby motivating the search on the part of the demos for a means of coordination. Finally, at the last nodes of the game, the Spartan threat emphasized by Herodotus is the factor that blocks a self-interested Cleisthenes from reneging on his bargain with the Demos.

The ancient tradition on the origins of democracy at Athens can, therefore, be explained in terms of the rational choices of the relevant players, given the particular circumstances in which their choices were made and the options available to them. Both practical reasoning and contingency (the presence of the Spartan threat, victories in battles that might have been lost) play a role in the story of Athens' democratization. Absent the instrumental rationality of the relevant parties in the face of the persistent Sparta factor, Cleisthenes would not have had a rationally self-interested motivation to make his wager or subsequently to stick to its terms. Of course, the wager might not have paid off: The uprising following Cleisthenes' expulsion might have failed; the Spartan invasion of 506 might have succeeded. Rather than taking the turn to democracy, Athens at the end of the sixth century could have been ruled by a stable elite coalition. It might have devolved into a cycle of civil conflict. As it turned out, by dint of calculation and luck, Cleisthenes won his wager. As a result, Athens democratized and flourished. Herodotus (5.78) famously links the rise of Athens to greatness in the Greek world in the era after the end of the tyranny to freedom and equality of speech that enabled each citizen to achieve something for himself. The question remains: How did those many individuals achieve great things, together?

4.6 AFTER THE REVOLUTION: RATIONAL LEADERS?

The Athenian Democratization Game described in the previous section assumes the demos as a collective agent, capable of choosing among options and acting on those choices. That capacity was tested in the decades following the Athenian Revolution of 508, when the Persian empire twice invaded Greece, specifically targeting Athens. The Greek victory in the Persian Wars (490, 480–478 BCE) was, in Herodotus' extended narrative, a result of Athenian coordination in the face of two invasions, Athens' providential choice to build a major navy, and Spartan leadership on land. The victory was followed by Sparta's decision not to join in an alliance to contain Persia. Sparta's decision inaugurated a fifty-year era in which Athens became the dominant state in the eastern Mediterranean, a history told in abbreviated fashion by Thucydides (1.89–118.2). The logic of Athenian imperialism, and its relationship to Athens' democracy will be the subject of chapter 5. In this section we introduce the question of the rationality of the democratic *politeia*: How could a demos, a mass of ordinary persons (that is, not philosophers, nor even oligarchs with a shared and consistent preference for a single end), be sufficiently rational to set goals, go for them, and achieve them often enough for Athens to become a wealthy and powerful state? One possible answer is that strong, rational leaders were the true rulers of an ostensibly democratic state.

In a famous chapter of his history of the Peloponnesian War, Thucydides (2.65) reviewed the leadership of the Athenian statesman Pericles and attributed the successful policies undertaken by the Athenian state in the years preceding the war to Pericles' dominance in public affairs. Thucydides focuses on Pericles' firm grasp of the ends that the state ought to pursue, based on a settled preference for security (exemplified in massive city walls), wealth (gained in part from levying tribute on subject states), and power (manifest in a great navy of oared warships). Thucydides associated the rationality of Athens as a state with its leaders' foresight—that is, their ability to gauge risk accurately. Foresight was not, for Thucydides, a mystical oracular power to foresee the future. Rather, it was a capacity to make sound judgments about risk and gain, based on a careful assessment of relevant facts about the world. Foresight enabled certain leaders, Pericles and Themistocles before him, to promote effective policies that maximized the expected advantage (in terms of security, welfare, and power) of the Athenian state. Accurate risk calculation was based on a careful assessment of material resources: armed forces, infrastructure, capital reserves (2.13.3–9). It was furthermore predicated on understanding the "types" of the various players in the relevant games of domestic politics and interstate relations. In Thucydides' influential characterization, the right information about resources and types enabled Athens' leaders to formulate and update reality-tracking beliefs and thus to promote state policies on the basis of the community's expected advantage.[40]

Plato offers a backhanded confirmation of the policy success of Athens' fifth-century leaders. In the *Gorgias* (518e–19c; cf. Ober 1998: 209–10) Plato's Socrates disparaged various of Athens' famous fifth-century leaders—including Themistocles and Pericles—who, "they say," had made the city great. In fact, Socrates claims, these so-called leaders were mere flatterers who turned the polis into a swollen tumor. They failed to inculcate moderation or justice in the population, instead filling the polis with just the sort of trash the demos happened to desire: harbors, city-walls, ship-sheds, and tribute.

Of course, for an ordinary Athenian, one concerned with the basic goods of welfare and security, those things were far from despicable. Having a good supply of such things was a testament to the state's strength and to its success at providing the material conditions of secure prosperity: harbors for trade, tribute for distributable state income, ship-sheds and city-walls for security against attack by sea or by land. So, the ordinary Athenian might assert that the things that the demos desired and that its leaders supplied, insofar as Plato's Socrates had accurately listed them, fell within a rational calculus.

That is precisely the point of the anonymously authored (attributed to Pseudo-Xenophon, nicknamed "The Old Oligarch") *Politeia of the Athenians,* probably written in the early 420s. The author is highly critical of democracy as the immoral rule of the "bad" many over the "good" elite, but the main point of his essay is to show his reader just how well the Athenian many manage affairs in their own interests (1.1). Their effective management includes resisting efforts of similarly self-interested members of the elite to capture the government. As the Old Oligarch bluntly notes, were the elite to rule, they would enslave the many, and the many had no interest in being slaves (1.9). The Old Oligarch has no doubts about either the instrumental rationality or the

---

40. Thucydides' positive assessment of Pericles and Themistocles as leaders, centered on their foresight and analytical capacities: Edmunds 1975; Ober 1998a: 79–81, 91. For insightful, recent assessments of Pericles as a leader, see Azoulay 2014; Perry 2018.

efficacy of the "bad" demos; indeed, the gravamen of his text is to explain to his reader the difference between rationally self-interested behavior and moral value: The intrinsic "badness" of the poor, uneducated many (1.5) did not impede their capacity to pursue their preferences for not being enslaved, living well from redistribution, sharing in public goods, and being catered to by imperial subjects. And evidently, despite their lack of education, the many had formed beliefs about the state of the world that were adequately coherent to enable their preferred outcomes to be realized through collective action—that is, through democratic institutions and policies. The Old Oligarch makes it clear that it was the demos that ultimately ruled Athens, but he allows (1.3) that the demos was content to let ambitious elites monopolize the major military offices, "which bring security or risk to the demos as a whole."[41]

The highly successful Themistoclean-Periclean imperial policy of the early and middle fifth century BCE was, in Thucydides' analysis, predicated on taking frequent, substantial, and carefully calculated risks. While some ventures failed (e.g., 1.110.4), overall the Athenian imperial ledger was positive in the decades before the Peloponnesian War (2.36.2–3, 2.41.4). In brief, Athens' policy, based on calculated risk-taking, proved effective in growing Athenian wealth and power. By contrast, Athens' rival, Sparta, in the era from the end of the Persian Wars to the outbreak of the Peloponnesian War, was relatively risk-averse. Spartan policy aimed at maintaining Sparta's prominent position as a hegemon of a major coalition. Lacking individual leaders with the capacity to calculate the benefits associated with risk, and thus tending to regard risk only as danger of loss, Sparta was not in a position to increase its power.[42]

Moreover, Thucydides' Pericles had an accurate sense of the pluralistic desires and beliefs that were prevalent, at any given moment, among Athenian citizens. His rhetorical skill enabled him to achieve his own desired ends by manipulating pluralistic desires and beliefs and thereby uniting the Athenians behind a coherent set of policy aims (2.65.8–9). That is to say, Pericles had the kind of power, through speech, that Plato's Gorgias promised his students, and that Callicles sought to gain.

41. I discuss the Old Oligarch's arguments in more detail in Ober 1998: chap. 1, with literature cited.

42. Thucydides' (1.89–118.2) account of the half-century from the end of the Persian Wars to the outbreak of the Peloponnesian War centers on Athenian dynamism and Spartan reticence; the contrast is made explicit in a speech of the Corinthians (1.68–71). See further, chapter 5.2.

The difference was that Thucydides' Pericles employed his rhetorical skills to further the interests of the Athenian state. His rhetoric enabled him to tamp down inappropriate popular enthusiasm (that is, depressing the tendency to impetuous collective action). And this meant he could limit the demos' tendency to seek desired outcomes that were unobtainable, or that entailed actions involving excessive risk. By the same token, his rhetorical expertise allowed him to counteract inappropriate risk aversion arising from excessive pessimism about the state's chances of achieving valued and available ends. In consideration of Pericles' deployment of political and rhetorical skills, Thucydides (2.65.9) declared that, whereas in principle Athens was a democracy, in fact it was ruled by its leading man.

Thucydides (2.65.7, 10–11) went on to denigrate the would-be democratic leaders who followed Pericles. None of them, he says, was of outstanding talent. Therefore, they contended with one another for popularity and in the process turned over affairs to the demos. A strong reading of Thucydides' assessment of Pericles suggests that Athens was a rational, and thereby high-performing, state *only* when it was under the firm control of an exceptionally rational, and uniquely talented individual. This strong reading is, however, undercut by Thucydides' own historical narrative of Athenian policy after Pericles' death in 429. While Thucydides highlights disputes among Athenian leaders, and the dire results of policy errors, it is clear from Thucydides' account of the war in the years immediately following the death of Pericles that Athens failed to collapse quickly into irrationality and policy incoherence.[43]

Moreover, Thucydides' own narrative also makes it clear that Pericles was not in any sense a king-like master who easily bent a pliant demos to his will. Pericles' signature defense policy of withdrawing the population behind the city walls, while resupplying the city by sea and using cavalry and stronghold garrisons to limit the effects of enemy ravaging, was, once again as Thucydides' own narrative makes clear, the result of a bargain struck between competing interests within the citizen body— some willing to abandon the countryside entirely, others demanding that extramural resources be protected.[44] Finally, Thucydides leaves little doubt that it was Athens' imperial policy in the age of Pericles that precipitated the great and ultimately catastrophic Peloponnesian War.

43. Thucydides and the "democratic advantage" before and after the death of Pericles: Ober 2010.
44. Pericles the politician and deal-maker: Ober 1996: chap. 6.

The steep rise in Athenian wealth and power in the imperial era made the Spartans sufficiently fearful about their future standing that they came to see the war as necessary (chapter 5).

Thucydides makes it clear that, in his view, Pericles' optimistic assessment of Athens' chances of ultimate victory in that war ought to have been vindicated by the course of events, in light of the resources Athens had amassed in advance of the war (2.13, 2.65.13). Yet it is also clear from Thucydides' narrative that Pericles failed to take into account the possibility (however remote it might have seemed at the time) of an outbreak of deadly disease consequent upon crowding the entire population of Attica into the fortified urban complex. In the event, beginning in the second year of the war, the plague killed roughly a quarter of the Athenians (including Pericles himself) in the space of a few years. Nor, evidently, did Thucydides' Pericles (or Thucydides himself) foresee the implications of Persia entering the conflict, breaking the frame of Athens-Sparta bipolarity.[45] We turn to the question of the rational pursuit of collective interests in interstate relations in chapter 5. We will return in chapter 6 to the question of how a democratic state could function as a rational agent without a dominating leader.

45. Contrasting views of Thucydides on the causes of the war and Periclean policy and Spartan response: Kagan 1969, 2003; De Ste. Croix 1972. Bipolarity and its limits: Lebow and Strauss 1991.

Melos' Prospect

Limits of Interstate Rationality

If a Greek polis was, under the right conditions and with the right leadership, capable of acting as a rational agent, then does rationality extend to interstate relations? Was rationality at home mirrored in the foreign policies of Greek states? Of the major powers, Athens and Sparta? Of the smaller states whose range of options was, in various ways, constrained by the prior and expected policy choices of the great powers? Is the history of interstate war and peace, alliance, hegemony, and empire illuminated by practical reason? That is the set of questions to which we turn in this chapter.

The author with whom we will be primarily concerned is Thucydides; the chapter is limited chronologically to the mid- to later fifth century BCE, the era of the Athenian empire.[1] But, as exemplified by Pseudo-Xenophon's *Politeia of the Athenians* (chapter 4.6), the questions posed here antedate Thucydides' text. They were, moreover, subsequently taken up by (among many others) Xenophon and Aeneas "the Tactician" in the fourth century BCE, Polybius in the second, and, much later, by modern theorists of international relations. The chapter's central theme, the limited rationality of interstate cooperation under

---

1. My own work on Thucydides includes Ober 1996: chap. 6, 1998a: chap. 2, 2001, 2006b, 2010; Ober and Perry 2014. Helpful collections of recent work are offered in Rengakos and Tsamakis 2006; Rusten 2009; Balot, Forsdyke, and Foster 2017. Influential recent monographs include Dewald 2005; Greenwood 2006; Hawthorn 2014. Older work is surveyed in the magisterial commentary by Hornblower (1991–2008).

conditions of asymmetrical power, can profitably be applied to developments in later Mediterranean history: to, for example, the attempts by Athens to credibly commit to self-constraint in its fourth-century naval confederation (Cargill 1981), to the development of Greek federal leagues (Mackil 2013) and to relations between city-states and Macedonian kingdoms (Ma 1999, 2003) in the late fourth through second centuries, and to the rise of Rome in the third to first centuries (Eckstein 2006).

War and interstate relations in the shadow of war were constants in the world of the classical Greek poleis. Wars between Greek states ranged from minor territorial disputes to existential struggles with high casualties and the potential for state death. The background context of interstate relations in the Greek world may be described as anarchic, insofar as there was no institution capable of setting or enforcing interstate norms or limiting conflict. While classical-era wars between Greek states tended to be fought according to certain shared cultural norms, there were no binding rules constraining the behavior of combatants. Norms could be ignored, reinterpreted, or wantonly violated. War was a primary source of uncertainty for individuals and states alike.[2]

Yet the world of the poleis was far from an endless zero-sum struggle of all against all. The game of war was played in the context of positive-sum bargaining games. These took the form of, for example, alliances, treaties, and conventions between states—bilateral or multilateral, on equal or unequal terms, with varying levels of mutual responsibility and commitment, with or without fixed terms. Interstate agreements were ubiquitous in the Greek world, as were institutionalized roles for individuals who facilitated cooperative relations between states.[3] Collaboration between states ranged from the free agreements among relative equals (for example, the Achaean federal league), to hegemony in which a strong state led a coalition of lesser states (Sparta's Peloponnesian

2. Informal rules (and absence of laws) of war: Ober 1996: chap. 5. Risk of state death: Ober 2008: 81–82. The anarchic conditions of Mediterranean states (focusing on the rise of Rome): Eckstein 2006.

3. Conflict, including most forms of war, as a bargaining game rather than zero-sum: Schelling (1960) 1980. Formal agreements between states sought to limit seizure of property or persons (asylia): Rigsby 1996. Institutionalized roles for individuals include heralds, ambassadors, arbitrators: Ager 1996; festival observers and those who received them (theoroi and theorodokoi): Rutherford 2007; local representatives of another state's interests (proxenoi): Mack 2015.

confederation), to frank domination of subject tributary states by an imperial power (Athens' empire).[4]

Meanwhile relations between states were complicated by the endemic possibility of intrastate conflict (*stasis*). *Stasis* concerned the question "who will rule the polis?"—and a change in one state's ruling body could have profound knock-on effects on interstate alliances. Like interstate wars, *staseis* ranged in intensity from brief, violent interludes with few casualties to existential crises.[5]

The conditions of war and interstate relations bring instrumental rationality into sharp focus. Motivations of self-interest and divergent preferences over outcomes sought by individuals, groups, and states stand out clearly against the background of hot and cold war—violent conflict and uneasy peace. The high stakes of Greek warfare and the complexity of factors contributing to conflicts in and beyond the city-state world meant that highly salient choices had to be made under conditions of uncertainty. The level of uncertainty might be lessened by reference to relevant information and to inferences from observable signs. If uncertainty could never be eliminated, it could, in the view of some Greek theorists and statesmen, be managed, as measurable risk.

Factors of uncertainty and risk were pressing in times of war. And that in turn meant that accurate assessment of the probability of possible outcomes became an imperative for state policy. Yet information relevant to choices about fighting or alliance was often incomplete and asymmetric. This meant that even the most expert risk assessments by the most rational decision-makers might end in choices that were catastrophic for either side (Fearon 1995). Rational choices predicated on preferences, beliefs, and expectations might be confounded by decision-making based on prospects—on hopeful reasoning that, from the point of view of expected advantage maximizers, overweighted the value of current resource endowments relative to future gains and losses (Kahneman 2011; with discussion in 5.7 below). All of this is reflected in the extensive tradition of Greek writing on interstate relations. War and the threat of war feature prominently in many genres of Greek literature.

---

4. Greek federalism: Mackil 2013; Beck 2015. Athens' empire: Ma, Papazarkadas, and Parker 2009. Discussions of Greek interstate relations, including cooperative and noncooperative (a small sample of a large literature): Karavites 1982; Lebow and Strauss 1991; Low 2007.

5. *Stasis:* Gehrke 1985; J. Price 2001; B. Gray 2015; Arcenas 2018. In Thucydides: J. Price 2001; Arcenas 2020.

Although I focus primarily on the historiography of Thucydides, as in other chapters of this book, the issues are clarified by preliminary reference to Plato's political philosophy.

5.1 WAR AND RISK IN PLATO'S *REPUBLIC*

In chapter 3.1 we surveyed the transition in Plato's *Republic* book 2 from the healthy First Polis to the "luxurious, feverish polis" that would eventually become Callipolis. The transition was required because of Glaucon's emphatic preference for a life that included luxuries. Socrates had to accommodate that preference, so I argued, because he had previously agreed that Glaucon's neo-Thrasymachean, "Gyges with the ring" account of human motivation would be the challenge he must answer in demonstrating the intrinsic value of justice and the superior happiness of the just person.

Accommodating Glaucon's taste for luxury and the psychology it assumes has the immediate effect of sharply increasing the total population of the imagined polis. This is because many occupational specializations, unnecessary in the First Polis, are needed to meet the demand for luxury goods and services. The increase in population requires, in turn, an expanded state territory, one large enough to be capable of supporting them all. Socrates assumes that the imagined polis that is to be constructed through reasoned argument will be located in a region that is already divided into states, each jealously guarding its borders: "We will have to seize some of our neighbor's land if we are to have enough pasture and farmland." Glaucon quickly accepts this necessity as inevitable (373d). The logical next step, says Socrates, must, therefore, be war (373e).

Instrumentalist Diplomacy and War-Making

Socrates pauses at this point to generalize the argument, noting that he and his interlocutors had now uncovered the origins of war in "the same desires that are most of all responsible for the bad things that happen to poleis and the individuals in them" (373e). Those desires, as we have seen, are for "more and more"—for luxuries in excess of what is necessary for life in a simple, healthy community. Thus, the origin of war between states is located in the self-interested motivations and instrumental reasoning that were described, in the introduction, as the premises of a Greek folk theory of practical reasoning. The Thrasymachean variant of the folk theory leads us to suppose that the goal of a powerful state will be to rule tyrannically, in its own interest, over weaker states.

The soldiers of the imagined state of the *Republic*—who turn out to be the military-expert Guardians, per discussion in chapter 3.1—will be employed not only to seize the territory of neighbors, but also to defend the state's now-expanded territory and possessions against invasions by neighboring states (373e–74a). The choices of those rival states in respect to war are, therefore, assumed to be motivated by precisely the sort of reasoning Socrates had just established as war's origin. The Guardians' role is providing Callipolis' military security, in the face of the endemic military threat created by the motivation, at the level of the state, to maximize "Gygean" goods, "to seek to get more and more." That motivation, conjoined with the requirement that each individual stick to his own tasks, requires the establishment of a class of Guardians with a specialization in violence provision (374e). Yet, as we have seen, Guardians are dangerous: Individuals with superior violence potential and Thrasymachean motivations would destabilize the harmonious internal order of the state. Addressing that threat, by eliminating the incentives of the Guardians to use their expertise in war against each other, or against the productive classes, is the original justification for the special education of the Guardians and for the distinctive social rules that constrain the circumstances of their lives.

In book 4 of the *Republic* Plato returns to the question of interstate relationships between poleis. Each polis is understood as a self-interested collective agent, seeking to further its own advantage. Socrates confirms that, as Callipolis develops, there must be limits to the wealth that the Guardians will allow in the polis (421e–22a). The Guardians themselves, who are both warriors and rulers, will possess no wealth. The other residents will possess only moderate wealth. The question then arises: How will Callipolis, lacking state-level capital resources, be able to compete successfully in a war against a great and wealthy rival polis, especially a polis that had gathered to itself the resources of many other poleis (422a, 422d)?[6]

Socrates' answer has three parts: First is the simple claim that the Guardians, being full-time experts at war, will be superior fighters

---

6. The question of Callipolis at war recurs in Plato, *Timaeus* 19b–c, where Socrates expresses the wish to hear a proper account of the ideal polis in action, engaged in conflict with its rivals over "those prizes that poleis typically compete for," and elucidating how it will distinguish itself "in the way it goes to war and in the way it pursues the war."

(422b–c). Next comes an argument based on rational calculation of outcomes and expectations: Callipolis will send envoys to any polis that was in the process of deciding between attacking Callipolis (perhaps in alliance with other poleis) or joining Callipolis in a military alliance against some other polis or coalition. Callipolis' envoys are in a position to make an offer that, Socrates claims, will be too good for another polis to refuse, given the assumption of state-level desire for more and more and the capacity of rational states to calculate expected advantage. Callipolis' envoys will make the following offer: "We make no use of gold and silver nor is it lawful for us to do so, but it is lawful for you. So, make war along with us and you can take the property of our opponents." Socrates then asks, "Do you suppose any [state] that heard such a proposal would choose [hairēsesthai] to fight against hard and lean hounds [Callipolis' Guardians], rather than fight with the aid of the hounds against fat and tender sheep [the residents of other poleis and their possessions]?" (422d). Here Plato's Socrates reprises Thrasymachus' (*Republic* book 1) metaphor in which the strong treat the weak as sheep, fit for consumption.

Finally, Socrates concludes, all other poleis, lacking Callipolis' fine-tuned harmonic unity, are presumptively divided against themselves, especially along class lines of rich versus poor. As such, they can be assumed to be relatively weak and liable to civil conflict (422d–23a). Once again, Callipolis will be in a position to exploit the self-interest of instrumentally rational opponents, this time by siding with one faction against another: "If you approach them [the residents of other poleis] as many [factions] and offer to give to the one [faction] the possessions, capacities, and indeed the very persons of another [faction], you will always find many allies and few enemies" (423a). Here we see a close approximation of the "primitive preferences" of wealth, power, and sex that featured as universal motivators in Glaucon's neo-Thrasymachean challenge in *Republic* book 2. In sum, in Plato's *Republic,* the conditions of interstate conflict are explicitly modeled on the instrumental rationally assumed in the folk theory. Moreover, the conventionalist's variant is off the table, because the interstate situation is assumed to lack rules or norms that could constrain the narrowly egoistic choices of the strong.

Measuring Risk on the Battlefield

One other war-related passage in the *Republic* is highly relevant to our investigation of the role of preferences and expectations in Greek conceptions of practical reasoning. In describing the education of the young male and female Guardians in book 5 (the Guardians, both auxiliary guardian warriors and true guardians who graduate from warriors to rulers, now include women), Socrates makes the point that it is always beneficial for the children of craftsmen to observe elder master craftsmen at work, even before the children are themselves able to take an active part in the craft (467a). This, he says, extends to the craft of war.

The young Guardians-in-training will better learn their craft, and thus the polis will be benefited, if the girls and boys have the chance to see firsthand what they will be expected to do as adults. Thus, it is established that Callipolis prefers that its young Guardians be exposed to war while still too young to fight. But Glaucon raises the obvious concern: Placing children on a battlefield would endanger them. That, he notes, could result in a serious public harm: If the young Guardians in training are killed while observing a battle, the future of Callipolis could be forfeit. With reference to figure 20, Glaucon seems initially to prefer outcome α: Not having been sent to battle, the children will survive. In effect, he proposes that the elder Guardians who must decide on whether or not to send the children into a battle zone as observers should ignore the rest of the decision tree. In that case, the value of having children observe a battle is foregone.

In response to Socrates' prodding, Glaucon agrees, however, that the children's exposure to war is highly desirable, because (per the premise of the value of observation to the trainee) it is advantageous to the polis. Moreover, and crucially, he acknowledges that this desired outcome is worth some risk: "[Socrates:] Do you think it makes a slight difference and is not worth some risk [*axion kindunou*] whether adults who are to be warriors do or do not observe war as children? [Glaucon:] No, it makes a great difference for the purpose of which you speak" (467c). Therefore, it cannot be the case that the potential outcome "child Guardians exposed to war" should simply be foregone in order to guarantee their safety. But at what level of risk does the danger of losing the children become so great as to justify foregoing the benefit of their early training through observing battles? To answer the question of how the rulers of Callipolis will choose between exposing the children to battle (thus benefiting the polis by giving young Guardians the right training, at the risk of endangering them) and not exposing children to battle (thus benefiting the polis by preserving their lives, at the cost of foregoing the benefit to the polis of their early training) Socrates proposes that risk can be correctly measured.

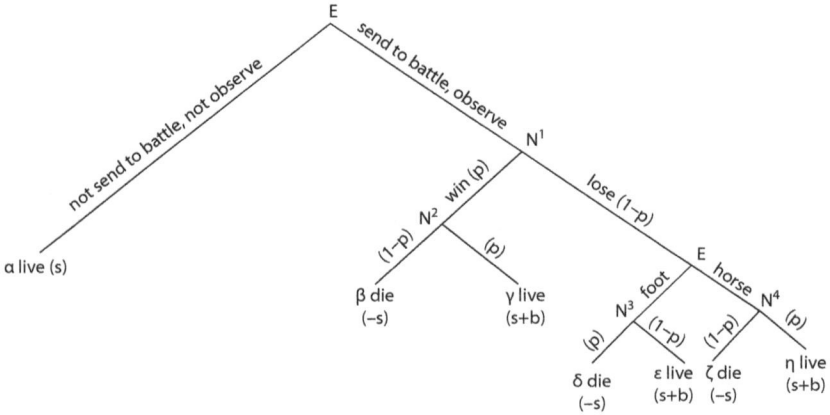

FIGURE 20. Elder Guardians' Decision Tree

NOTES: Notes: E = Elder Guardians; N = Nature lotteries over winning battles and child observer survival; p + (1–p) = 1. s = value of children's survival; b = value of children's observation of battle. At N^1 Callipolis' army wins with probability p. At N^2 child observers live with probability p. At N^3 if Callipolis' army unexpectedly loses, and child observers are on foot, they live with probability 1–p. At N^4 if Callipolis' army unexpectedly loses, and child observers are on horseback, they live with probability p. In each case, Elder Guardians calculate that p is very high, 1–p is correspondingly low.

The factor Socrates introduces to enable weighing the value of early training against the risk of early death is the relative dangerousness of a given military campaign. Socrates asserts that the Guardian (collective) parents of the child Guardians will not be ignorant (*ouk amatheis*) about which campaigns are high-risk (*epikindunoi:* i.e., relatively more likely to result in a battlefield defeat for Callipolis) and which are not (defeat is unlikely). Indeed they are said to be as expert at the relevant kind of measurement as a human being could ever be (*hosa anthrōpoi . . . gnōmonikoi:* 467c–d).[7] Here, Socrates has established a point that is highly relevant to our investigation of the processes involved in practical reasoning: He implies that risk is knowable and that experts employ

7. The term *gnōmonikos* is rare, found only this once in Plato. The closest parallel is Xenophon, *Memorabilia* 4.2.10: In discussing the kinds of knowledge relevant to various professions, Socrates refers to the architect as a *gnōmonikos anēr*. In postclassical Greek (Strabo 1.1.20) the term is used for an expert in the use of the sundial (*gnōmon*). In each case, the expertise is concerned with precise scalar measurement. Thus, it seems quite certain that in our passage Plato is also concerned with expert measurement; the object being measured is the risk associated with a coming battle.

their skill at measurement to make risk assessments that are as accurate as is humanly possible.[8]

While no quantities are assigned to possible outcomes, it is readily apparent that, with reference to figure 20, a specifiable value (*b*) is being set on the exposure of children to battle. That value must be weighed against the value (*s*) of the children's survival. In order to decide between the choices "send children to battle, enabling them to observe, but perhaps also to die" (resulting either in either a payoff of *s+b* or a payoff of *–s*) and "do not send them to battle, guaranteeing their lives but denying them the chance to observe" (payoff *s*), the probability of the children's surviving the battle observation experience must be estimated. Those responsible for making the decision are presumed to have the kind of expertise that enables them to measure the likelihood of victory or defeat in battle.[9]

The probability of the survival of children sent to observe the battle is initially assumed to be a function of the probability (p) that the battle will not be too dangerous, that is, that it will be won by the Guardian warriors. The elders "do the math" of calculating values (*s* and *b*) against probabilities (win: p vs. lose: 1–p) and thereby make a rational choice and act accordingly: If $p(s+b) > s$ then the best choice will be "expose children to battle."[10] Because the elders are presumed to have the right expertise, a clear decision can be made in every case: The upshot is: "They will take the children to some campaigns and not to others" (467d).

It is worth noting that the expertise of the elder Guardians is applied to all potential military campaigns, and that some campaigns that will be

---

8. Cf. Plato, *Protagoras* 356e–57b (with introduction, n. 43), in which Socrates expounds on the superiority of the art of measurement, understood in terms of arithmetical quantities, to mere appearance; and *Statesman* 283d–84e, in which the art of measurement is divided into the study of greater and lesser, and the part that measures in terms of "the proportionate [*metrion*], fitting [*prepon*], opportune [*kairon*], needful (*deon*), and all other standards situated in the mean between extremes." In the case of risk, the "extremes" are randomness (each available outcome is equally possible, as in lotteries for assigning individual jurors to specific Athenian courts) and certainty.

9. This issue of the *technai* that depend on measurement against some standard (in our case the value to the polis of the children's survival) is more fully explored in Plato's *Statesman* (283c–85a), where that kind of measurement distinguishes the statesman (*politikos*), the master of the political *technē*. It will be the statesman's role, for example, to decide on whether or not to go to war, whereas it is the general's role to conduct the war (*Statesman* 304e–5d).

10. For example, if, hypothetically, the value of *s* = 100, *b* = 10, and p = 0.9, then the children will not be brought along on campaign (99 < 100), but if the probability of victory is increased to 0.95 they will be (104.5 > 100).

engaged by Callipolis' warriors are estimated to have a relatively high risk factor—too high to bring along the children. Accordingly, we must reject any notion that Callipolis' rulers are infallible in their judgments about the outcome of the polis' military conflicts. The Guardians cannot be certain of winning every campaign they must fight, but they can estimate the likelihood of victory. Socrates' confidence in the factors that conduce to Callipolis' long-term military success is not based on certainty, but on the expectation that over time the polis will do well enough against rivals to sustain itself through the correct estimation of probabilities.

The military experts of Callipolis send out the children as battle observers only if there is a high probability (N^1) that the battle will be won. In that case, the Guardians can be confident in their expectation (N^2) that the children will survive, having observed the battle (expected outcome γ). The chance that the children will die (β) is correspondingly low. Yet Socrates does acknowledge that, even after expert measurement of the dangerousness of each campaign, there remains a certain level of risk to the observer-children: "but nevertheless, as we say, many things occur that are unexpected [*para doxan*]" (467d).

The elder Guardians make their judgment about sending the children to observe a given battle, and sending them on foot or on horseback, based on their assessment of risk: the likelihood that at the nodes labeled N(ature) in figure 20 something unexpected will occur. The elders will send the children out if at N^1 the probability of winning is high enough. Yet, while the probability of losing at N^1 has been calculated to be small, should the battle be lost against expectation, the children will be in grave danger. Glaucon's initial worry seems now to recur. Should the children be observing while on foot when the Guardians were unexpectedly defeated, the likelihood (N^3) that they would die (δ) would be high, whereas their living (ε) would be unlikely. Socrates therefore proposes an insurance plan: The children will observe the chosen battles only while mounted on fast and manageable horses, "so that, should it be necessary, flying off, they shall flee" (467d).

The goal of the horseback observation plan is to reduce the mortality risk to the observer-children in the event of the low-probability result of an unexpected battlefield defeat. Socrates seeks to gain the highly valued payoff *b* ("exposure of children to battle") at the lowest possible risk to the polis that they will be lost. In figure 20 the range of possible outcomes in the event of the unexpected is illustrated by outcomes δ to η: if the observer-children were (counterfactually) on foot, they would be hostage to the chance of "the unexpected" in the result of the battle.

That risk is reduced by introducing a second high probability (N^4): that flight on horseback will succeed (η). The second low probability (dying on horseback) combines with the first (Callipolis' forces are defeated) to increase the children's overall chance of survival: Combining the two low-probability outcomes substantially reduces the risk to the children.[11] The cost of the insurance is the provision of "tame and swift" horses; we must assume that, looking down the game tree, the Guardians had decided that the benefits justified the expense of raising and training the requisite number of fast horses. Given the conditions of horse-raising in Greece (Spence 1993) this cost was not negligible, but Socrates evidently regarded it as worth paying.

The horse insurance does not reduce the chance of the children's untimely demise to zero (those who flee may nonetheless be caught: outcome ζ). There remains a persistent need for accurate measurement of risks in order to calculate the expected payoffs of all possible outcomes and thus to make the right, expected-advantage-maximizing decision about sending or not sending the children out on a given campaign. That decision is not based on absolute knowledge: It does not derive from the metaphysical and epistemological premises that underpin the philosopher-rulers' certainty in domains of moral judgment. Rather, the decision is based on weighted preferences and beliefs about the state of the world. Those beliefs include expectations based on the assumption that probabilities can be accurately measured. Moreover, risk, in the form of unlikely but possible outcomes, can be limited by paying the cost of insurance. The upshot is the maximization of expected advantage. The advantage with which Socrates and his interlocutors are concerned is that of the polis. There is no hint in this section of *Republic* book 5 of a concern for the children as autonomous, rights-bearing beings who must be treated as ends in themselves. The decision process is entirely instrumental, aimed at determining the feasible option expected to be most beneficial to the polis as a community.

5.2 THUCYDIDES ON POWER, RISK, AND STATE-LEVEL RATIONALITY

Plato's comments on war in the *Republic* were written in the aftermath of the Peloponnesian War and the dialogue's dramatic date is during the

---

11. Other ancient writers also recognized that compounding low-probability results tended towards (even though it never reached) impossibility: see appendix.

war.[12] The reference to the threat to Callipolis posed by a great and wealthy polis, one that had gathered to itself the resources of many other poleis, seems transparently to refer to Athens' empire of the later fifth century BCE. The topic of Athens' imperial power—how it was acquired, sustained, and ultimately lost—is a central theme of Thucydides' history. Athens' Aegean empire is treated by Thucydides as a special case of building and preserving a coalition of states through positive-sum bargaining between parties of differing strengths. Making socially valuable bargains is, in Thucydides' analytic narrative, facilitated by an accurate calculation of potential risks and benefits. The social benefit realized by those bargains is, however, potentially threatened under the zero-sum conditions and increased uncertainty associated with existential war. Thucydides' text may, reductively, be thought of as an analysis of the interplay between zero-sum and cooperative games, and between uncertainty and risk.[13]

The extended conflict conventionally called "the Peloponnesian War" is described by Thucydides as "the war between the Athenians and Peloponnesians and the allies on either side" (2.1). The initial premise of Thucydides' analysis of the war is that the Greek world had divided into two supercoalitions with strikingly different organizational and operational characteristics: Athens' maritime empire, created and sustained by naval power, and Sparta's land-power-centered Peloponnesian League (1.1, 1.18.2).

As I have argued elsewhere, Thucydides may be understood as a political scientist, in that his historical narrative of events is aimed at empirically testing the validity of a theory of state-level power. That theory is meant to predict and to explain the behavior of great and small states in the face of power asymmetries.[14] Much of the action described in Thucydides' narrative concerns attempts by hegemonic states to preserve and expand their coalitions. The questions of under what conditions, with what motives, and with what expectations a

12. On the productive tension between dramatic date of the *Republic* and the time of its composition and circulation, see Kasimis 2016, 2021.

13. Edmunds 1975 remains fundamental on the interplay between "chance and intelligence" in Thucydides. On the long debate, inaugurated by Cornford 1907 and Cochrane 1929, over Thucydides as, alternatively, a "primitivist/tragic" or a "modernist/scientific" historian, see Hesk 2014.

14. I discussed Thucydides' as a theorist of state power in Ober 1998a: chap. 2, 2001, 2006b, 2010. See further, Reynolds 2009, for a contrast of Thucydides' optimism about his theory's capacity for determining the greatness of past and present state power, with his pessimism about predicting success in gaining outcomes, in the face of the unexpected and human irrationality.

given state would choose to join a coalition (or not to), to remain in a coalition or to defect from it, are central to Thucydides' analysis.

Thucydides' theory of power is, I suggest, built on the premise that Greek states can, under the right conditions, be understood as rational, expected-advantage-maximizing, collective actors. Such states have coherent preferences, established methods for gathering and for assessing information relevant to forming reality-tracking beliefs about the state of the world. They also have methods for correctly measuring probabilities—in something like Plato's sense (above) of estimating risk as well as is humanly possible. Although Thucydides does not reduce state-level preferences to Glaucon's primitive triad of wealth, sex, and power, or to Socrates' (*Republic* 423a: above) triad of "possessions, capacities, and persons," he does posit that states seek to ensure their own survival and the welfare of their citizens. As with individuals, the rational state predicates its choices on a strategic assessment of constraints imposed by the presumptively rational behavior of other state-level players in cooperative and noncooperative games.[15]

A centrally important factor in the run-up to the Peloponnesian War was the growth, after the end of the Persian Wars, of Athenian power. That dynamic growth was manifest in its large and effective naval forces, its immense capital resources, and the increasing size and coherence of its imperial coalition. By contrast, Spartan power is depicted in Thucydides' text as great, but relatively stable. Unlike Athenian capital-intensive sources of power, Sparta's power is predicated on the inherently limited body of fighting men that can be mustered by Sparta and its coalition partners. Thucydides famously asserts (1.23.6, cf. 1.33.3, 1.88, 1.118.2) that it was Sparta's fear of Athens' growing power that was the underlying—fundamental although unobserved by most contemporaries—cause of the war. Athens' growth in powerfulness is, in Thucydides' account, a product of policies that are closely associated with the general Pericles, but extend back to the Persian War–era leadership of Themistocles. Those policies were predicated on the integrated operational triad of a navy of warships capable of projecting state power, massive city walls and secure supply lines to ensure state security, and capital resources to pay for an immense pool of skilled human labor.[16]

15. Survey of the reception of Thucydides in the academic field of international relations and as a Realist: Keene 2014; Johnson 2014.

16. I discussed Thucydides' assessment of Athenian dynamism in contrast to Spartan conservatism, and the "triadic" bases of Athens' power in Ober 2001 and 2010.

Thucydides' narrative shows how and why the survival and welfare of weak and strong Greek states (and thus of their residents) could be advanced by rational behavior, and likewise compromised by violations of rationality. That behavior is readily modeled by positive-sum bargaining games. Under the right conditions, rational cooperation between asymmetrically powerful states was mutually (although again, asymmetrically) beneficial, enabling growth—more security, higher levels of welfare, thus larger and wealthier populations—over time. The Greek world had, as Thucydides points out (1.13), progressed dramatically in both wealth and security within historical time. That progress, Thucydides suggests, was facilitated by interstate agreements entered into by adequately well-informed, rationally self-interested parties capable of calculating expected advantage.[17] Strong states did especially well, but weak states did better than they would outside the bargains made with the strong. Athens in the age of Themistocles and Pericles was, for Thucydides, a model of the strong and successful city-state that had benefited by both rational risk-taking and cooperative bargaining.

Moreover, as Thucydides emphasized, major Greek states also sought at least to maintain, and in some cases to expand, their power at the expense of powerful rivals. When a strong, expansionist state confronted a strong rival, as in the hypothesized territorial expansion of the "feverish" city in the second book of Plato's *Republic*, there could be a zero-sum competition over limited resources. The tendency of major states to seek "more and more" wealth and power at the direct expense of rivals, through expanding coalitions and gaining control of strategic resources, is, in Thucydides' history, a primary cause of interstate instability. Athens' rising power and the threat that posed to Sparta was, for Thucydides, a notable but not unique cause of instability. The ambition of Syracuse to dominate the poleis of Sicily is another case in point.

Because of prior cooperative coalition-building, the requirements of interstate compacts, and the multiplicity of flash points, conflicts between major states led to scaled-up wars between ever-larger coalitions of states. The Peloponnesian War was, in Thucydides' view, the ultimate product of that dynamic. Under ideal conditions, rational states (or coalition hegemons) might avoid going to war, based on com-

---

17. The dramatic (by premodern standards) historical growth of the Greek economy in the era 800–300 BCE is documented in Ober 2015: chap. 4. Reynolds (2009) establishes Thucydides' grounds for his confident claim that Greek communities of the distant past were weak and impoverished compared to the relatively wealthy and powerful great poleis of his own time.

plete and symmetrical information concerning relative strengths, accurate measurement of risks, and calculation of the likely costs of conflict. But, as Thucydides recognized and James Fearon (1995) has shown for modernity, under real-world conditions of incomplete or asymmetric information, rational states will fall into costly conflicts. The size, complexity, and instability of a "world system" defined by two coalitions led by states with different "types" and different rates of growth contributed to the difficulty of estimating the relative present and future strengths of the key players in the run-up to the Peloponnesian War.

Moreover, Thucydides recognized and took account of significant deviations from state-level rationality. Given the fact of preference diversity, differential time horizons, and volatile interest-based factions within states, and in light of the range of decision-methods employed by states with different *politeiai,* it was not certain that a given state, at a given moment, would manifest the sort of instrumental rationality that Glaucon's challenge to Socrates in *Republic* book 2 claims as a universal feature of individuals.

States did not always maximize on a single material factor (e.g., power) or even on a straightforward package of factors (e.g., power plus wealth plus honor/reputation) when calculating advantage. They might instead seek to satisfice across several factors, including "moral" factors such as justice, fairness, autonomy, and ethnic, regional, or history-based loyalties. Moreover, as we will see, states might not measure probability accurately. And even if they did, they might not employ the kind of cost-benefit judgments in means-ends reasoning that were assumed in what we are calling the Greek folk theory of practical reasoning.

The sources of irrationality (behavior that is off the predicted path followed by self-interested, instrumentally rational, expected-advantage-maximizing agents), and the effects of irrational play on the possibility of correct measurement of risk and thus on actual outcomes, constitute a second major theme of Thucydides' analytic history. Once again, his point is not that the course of events is simply irrational, nor is it that probabilities are incalculable. Rather his point is that an expert decision-maker, one employing the complete tool set of practical reason, must take into account not only risk and constraints, but also the likelihood that some players in the game will deviate from the path of rational choice. Understanding the conditions that make deviation more likely is, I suggest, an overlooked aspect of the lessons Thucydides intends an astute reader to learn from a text that is explicitly didactic (Connor 1984).

5.3 ROVING AND STATIONARY BANDITS

Thucydides' review of early Greek history begins with the claim that in earliest times, before the emergence of organized states, all Greeks lived in unsettled and penurious conditions.[18] The reason for their poverty was the inability of small, unwalled communities to defend themselves against predations by mobile bandits who roved at will by land and sea (1.2). The motive of piratical strong-men in raiding unwalled settlements was personal gain (*kerdos*) and building coalitions of followers through sharing the loot (1.5.1). Walls capable of frustrating raids were not built because early communities lacked adequate capital for infrastructure improvements. The bandits, who moved freely across the Greek world, might never come back to a place they had once raided. Therefore, they had no reason to be restrained in their looting. Residents of communities exposed to piratical depredations, expecting to be stripped of all they possessed by pirates, had no incentive to amass capital. All acted rationally and the result was general poverty. The situation is precisely that described by the political scientist Mancur Olson, in defining the incentives of "roving bandits" and those who are their victims.[19] Meanwhile, such short-term concentrations of local power (*dunameis*) as might be achieved in more fertile regions of Greece were, Thucydides notes, quickly dissipated through a combination of internal strife (*staseis*) and the cupidity of outsiders (1.2).

The solution to this Panhellenic poverty trap was the providential emergence of a single hegemonic power, with a fixed base of operations, in possession of a substantial navy. The first such power known to Thucydides was Minos (1.4). Unlike the piratical roving bandits, Minos operated from a permanent base, his palace on the island of Crete. In Olson's terms, he was a stationary bandit. As such, Minos had a longer time horizon: He had an incentive to promote the growth of prosperous communities so long as they could be taxed in ways profitable to himself. So, again unlike the roving bandits, Minos did not simply loot. Rather, as Thucydides points out, he exercised hegemony over (*ekratēse*) the better part of the Aegean. He ruled (*ērxe*) and also first colonized the Cyclades, driving out non-Greek residents. Generalizing, Thucy-

18. Thucydides 1.2–19, traditionally known as "the Archaeology," has long been recognized as providing a theoretical frame for the work as a whole. Connor (1984: 26) calls it "an anatomy of power based on a view of man's nature." See further, Rood 2015, quoting Connor on p. 475.

19. Olson 1993, 2000. Cf. Skarbek 2014: 131–32.

dides states that the strongest communities, having the greatest capital resources, made smaller poleis into subjects (*hupēkooi*) (1.8.3).

Minos also had good reason to seek to suppress the roving bandits who were his rivals for resource extraction and whose looting suppressed the development of stable, taxable communities. Thucydides notes that in addition to his ruling and colonizing, "in all probability" (*hōs eikos*) Minos sought, to the extent possible, to suppress piracy. The motivation for all this activity was self-interest: Minos' "desiring that his revenues [*prosodoi*] should come to him more readily" (1.4). As Minos' navy reduced the danger of piracy to Greek communities within his zone of control, permanent settlements were established on the coasts, trade increased, and the wealth of communities grew (1.8.2–3). For their part, weaker communities recognized the value of trading the radical insecurity of the era of roving bandits for the relative security of a rationally self-interested hegemon: Thucydides notes that, motivated by new opportunities for material gain (*tōn kerdōn*), the weaker accepted domination (*douleia*) by the more powerful (1.8.3).[20]

The operative dynamic of early Greek hegemony was, according to Thucydides' analytic narrative, self-interest on the part of strong and weak alike—with the implicit proviso that the strong must have good reason (a stable base and long time horizons) to seek their profits by ruling and taxing rather than by raiding and looting. Under these conditions, there could be sustained economic growth: The growing prosperity of small communities meant that a hegemonic state could amass significant capital resources by taxing those communities at a sustainable level (Kierstead 2016).

An essential point is that, while the early Greek interstate order was built up from highly asymmetrical relationships, and while the asymmetry was expressed as domination (*douleia*), the relations between ruling states and subject states were predicated on a bargain. The motivation to enter into the bargain was, by both parties, the desire for profits unavailable outside the bargain. Realizing those profits demanded conditions of relative stability and a credible commitment on both sides to defer some rewards by making capital investments aimed at future benefits. In brief, the zero-sum game played by roving bandits and vulnerable communities, resulting in an equilibrium of poverty, was replaced

20. The choice recalls Herodotus' account of the Medes' willingness to accept an autocratic ruler as the price of ending an intolerable situation of lawlessness: chapter 3.2–3.

by a positive-sum game played between a stationary bandit and subject communities, a game that produced an equilibrium of growth.

Later imperial and colonial Greek powers followed the pattern established by Minos: emergent local naval supremacy, accompanied by suppression of piracy, hostility to non-Greek populations, domination of weaker states, and colonization. Thucydides offers first Corinth, then the Ionians, Samos, and the Phocaeans as examples of states that developed relatively powerful navies and manifested one or more of the features of what we may think of as the Minos hegemonic paradigm (1.13–14). Thucydides generalizes the point: In each case a navy was a source of strength, resulting in monetary revenues (*chrēmata*) and rule (*archē*) over other states (1.15.1). By contrast, he says, among early Greek states that lacked navies, there were neither great coalitions of states nor major wars. Violent conflicts were limited to small-scale disputes over borderlands. There were neither hegemonies of the asymmetric Minos sort nor large-scale confederations of equals (1.15.2).

Athens inherited and, under Pericles' leadership, perfected the Minos paradigm of naval power, colonization, hostility to non-Greek populations, and subjection of weaker states. By the time of the outbreak of the Peloponnesian War, most of Athens' formerly free allies had been reduced to the status of tribute-paying subjects (1.19, 1.96). Thucydides is certainly right to suppose that this was coalition-building on a scale unequaled by earlier Greek hegemonies. Based on epigraphic evidence and population estimates, at its height, Athens' empire encompassed some three hundred communities and perhaps two-and-a-half million persons—roughly a third of the total Greek-speaking population (Ober 2015a: 17–18, with table 2.3). But Thucydides had shown his reader that Athens followed a well-trodden path, and that the path was predicated on bargains based on mutual advantage.

5.4 JUSTIFYING EMPIRE

Thucydides' analytic narrative of Greek development before the Peloponnesian War seems quite clearly to be based on the Greek folk theory of instrumental rationality sketched in earlier chapters. He assumes self-interest (stable preferences for security over insecurity and wealth over poverty) as a primary human motivation, one that extends across the levels of individuals, social groups, and communities. Decisions are made on the basis of the expectation of advantage maximization, in light of the moves available to other players, great and small. While

Thucydides was, as we will see, well aware of honor-seeking as a motivation for action, he explicitly denigrated the binding force of voluntary oaths (1.9.1) in explaining the origins of the Trojan War. He ranks fear (*phobos*) above honorable reciprocity (*charis*) as the motive inducing the leaders of Greek states to join the powerful Agamemnon of Mycenae in the expedition against Troy (1.9.3).

Fear, for Thucydides, is the dark twin of desire.[21] Fear of loss of what one currently has, or of being deprived of future gains, is a powerful motivator, arising from the same kind of calculations of advantage that drove Plato's Gyges to seek "more and more." Fear is frequently cited by Thucydides' public speakers as a justification for the behavior of states. For example, in a well-known passage from book 1, unnamed Athenian speakers, who just happen to be in Sparta on unspecified business, respond to charges against Athens by Sparta's allies. In these passages, Thucydides neatly sums up the instrumental rationality of the folk theory, as it is applies to interstate relations.

> We [Athenians] did not acquire this [empire: *archē*] by force [*biasomenoi*] ... the allies [*summachoi*] came to us of their own accord and asked us to assume the leadership. It was under the constraints of circumstances [*katēnangkasthēmen*] that we were driven at first to advance our empire to its present state, influenced chiefly by fear [*hupo deous*], then by honor [*timē*] also, and lastly by material benefit [*ōphelia*] as well. After we had once incurred the hatred of most of our allies, and several of them had already revolted and then been reduced to subjection, and when you [Spartans] were no longer friendly as before but suspicious and at variance with us, it no longer seemed safe to risk [*ouk asphales ... kinduneuein*] relaxing our hold. For all defectors would have gone over to you. And no man is to be blamed for making the most of his advantages [*xumpheronta*] when it is a question of the gravest dangers. (1.75.2–5)

The Athenians reemphasize the points made in the first passage with a counterfactual, a claim about human nature, a general argument linking strength and domination, and a final assertion that the Spartans are just as calculating of their interests as are the Athenians:

> If in the Persian war you [Spartans] had held out to the end in the hegemony and had become unpopular in its exercise, as we did, you would certainly have become no less obnoxious to the allies than we are, and would have been compelled either to rule them with a strong hand, or yourselves to risk [*kinduneuein*] losing the hegemony. Thus, there is nothing remarkable or

---

21. Desmond (2006) documents the centrality of fear, including rational fear, in Thucydides' text.

inconsistent with human nature in what we also have done, just because we accepted an empire when it was offered to us, and then, yielding to the strongest motives—honor, fear, and material benefit—declined to give it up. Nor, again, are we the first who have entered upon such a course, but it has ever been an established rule that the weaker is kept down by the stronger. And at the same time, we thought we were worthy to rule, and used to be so regarded by you also, until you fell to calculating advantages [*ta xumpheronta logizomenoi*] and resorted, as you do now, to the plea of justice. (1.76.1–2)

The Athenians then go on to claim that the practice of Athens' imperial rule (i.e., the "taxation rate" in terms of forcible extraction of resources) was more moderate and the Athenians themselves more attentive to justice than required (by implicit comparison with a strict cost-benefit calculation). They offer a second counterfactual as proof of the point: Any other powerful state in Athens' place would have been less moderate, less attentive to equity (1.76.3–4). Or, we might say, another state would have acted more like a roving bandit with short time horizons, and less like a rational stationary bandit, playing a cooperation game with a long time horizon.

Thucydides' Athenians in Sparta assert that acting from the motives of fear, honor, and material benefit is a universal rule. But Thucydides in propria persona does not encourage his reader to suppose that rulers acting according to their *individual* self-interest invariably leads to the growth of a state's power or its wealth. He notes that in the past, as a Greek state grew larger and wealthier, its *politeia* often changed accordingly: Tyrannies replaced hereditary kingships in many poleis (1.13.1). According to Thucydides, from the perspective of state development, the Greek tyrants were too narrowly self-interested to amount to much in the long run: The tyrants' focus on their private affairs, their own bodily safety, and their promotion of family members to positions of authority led them to pursue security (*asphaleia*) at the expense of other policy goals (1.17). As a result, tyrant-run states were overly risk-averse and so they were noteworthy only for their lack of major accomplishments. We can contrast Thucydides' risk-averse tyrants with the risk-measuring elder Guardians of Plato's *Republic,* discussed above. While Plato's Callipolis is highly conservative in its resistance to change, its rulers, like Thucydides' Pericles (below), recognize the necessity of calculated risk-taking to state flourishing.

Thucydides' reader will soon be introduced to the risk-averse Spartans, who are accused by their allies, the Corinthians, of being excessively narrowly self-interested—in contrast to the risk-taking Athenians who consistently look to the collective interest of their state (1.68–71, with Ober 2010). Yet the tyrannies in most Greek states were eventually overthrown—by Sparta (1.18.1). With the creation of a Peloponnesus-based league of oligarchies (1.19) Sparta also finally broke the earlier trend of the absence of major, long-lasting coalitions among land-based states.

One of Thucydides' explicit motives in recounting the history of the roughly fifty-year period from the end of the Persian Wars to the outbreak of the Peloponnesian War (478–431 BCE) was to explain the origins and growth of Athens' empire (1.97.2). After establishing the voluntary nature of the original confederation of Aegean states, as an anti-Persian alliance under Athenian leadership and financial management (1.96), his focus turns to a series of defections from the alliance (1.98). Here the historical narrative confirms some central claims made by the Athenian speakers in Sparta, above.

The primary precipitating factors (*aitiai*) of defection by Athens' allies were, Thucydides asserts, failures by the subject allies to perform their duties in terms of supplying warships and funds, or their unexcused abstention from agreed-upon military operations. Defections followed from dereliction of duties because the Athenians enforced the terms of the original agreement strictly (*akribōs*); this was sometimes taken badly by communities of persons who were either unused to performing mandated services or unwilling to do so (1.99.1). Thucydides points out, however, that the conditions in which the allies were saddled with mandatory monetary contributions were the result of the allies' own preference orderings and limited time horizons. They had preferred paying money to Athens and staying home to taking on the burden of building and maintaining a navy themselves. As a result, when an allied state did choose to defect, and when Athens responded with military force, the allied state entered the conflict "without preparation and without experience" (1.99.3).

A weak state that voluntarily entered into a cooperative bargain with a stronger state, and profited accordingly, might, Thucydides suggests, find itself without the ability to exit the bargain if and when the hegemon's capacity to coerce grew as a result of investing its share of the profits in power rather than merely in wealth. The question then was whether the Athenian empire would come to be primarily based on coercion, or whether the bargain could be calibrated such that subjects would continue to recognize that they profited by their subjection.

5.5 EMPIRE-SUBJECT GAME

The passages cited above from Thucydides' book 1, when read in conjunction with the rest of Thucydides' long narrative of the war (see below), allow us to think of Thucydides' "Minos-Athens paradigm" of hegemonic coalition as a game. The game is played between a strong imperial state (E) in possession of a large navy, and a weaker state (S) that is a potential or actual subject of the strong state. The game has a positive-sum equilibrium, insofar as both E and S stand to gain from cooperation. Cooperation takes the form, first, of E providing protection to S against roving bandits and/or third-party state-level threats. Protection is offered at a cost lower than S would pay through its own capital expenditures on, for example, walls and warships. Protection in turn offers enhanced opportunity for S to invest in ways that lead to higher future profits and to gain from improved conditions for lucrative exchange with other states. Transaction costs drop as risks from pirates and third-party aggressor states are reduced, and through the coordination functions provided by E (for example, a common coinage). On the other hand, E stands to gain by taxing S at a rate that is in excess of the costs to E of providing protection. E is also a major beneficiary of the improved exchange environment. The game remains competitive, rather than being a matter of pure coordination, because E is assumed to prefer to extract maximum revenues from S, in the form of monetary taxes and required services. S prefers to pay the lowest possible tax rate while maximizing the advantages it gains from its subjection to E. The game is set out in extensive form in figure 21.

The imperial state (E) moves first, deciding at what level to set the tax for its services (protection, coordination leading to lower transaction costs). The options among which E's choice is made are schematically listed as Low (E gains little or nothing from providing protection and coordination, S's cost of subjection is therefore very low and its profits high); Medium (E's revenues substantially exceed its costs, S's costs are therefore substantial and its profit somewhat lower); or High (E extracts resources in a predatory manner, leaving S with little surplus and thus driving down the value of S's subjection of E to near or below zero).

In response to E's tax-setting move, the subject state (S), if not yet in subjection to E, decides whether to submit voluntarily to E. If S is already subject to E, its population decides whether to make substantial capital (human, social, and financial) investments, deferring short-term payoffs in expectation of long-term gains. We assume that S prefers, all

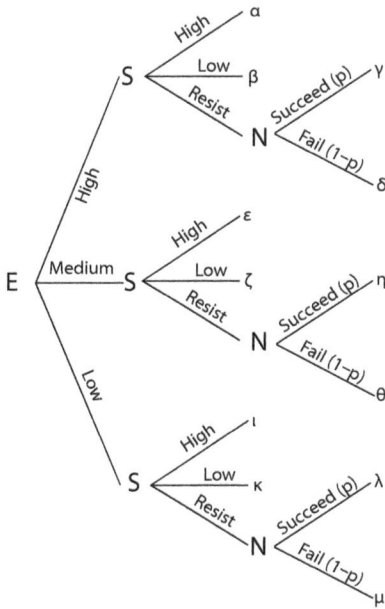

Outcome	Path	Payoff (E,S)
α	HH	5,1
β	HL	3,2
γ	HRS	low, v. high
δ	HRF	low, v. low
ε	MH	4,4
ζ	ML	2,3
η	MRS	v. low, high
θ	MRF	low, v. low
ι	LH	2,5
κ	LL	1,2
λ	LRS	v. low, medium
μ	LRF	low, v. low

FIGURE 21. Empire and Subject Game

NOTES: E = Empire (Athens); S = subject or potential subject state; N = Nature lottery over successful resistance; p + (1–p) = 1.

things considered, to invest in the future, and will do so under reasonably good conditions. In each case, S's choice is schematically characterized as High (S submits willingly if not yet subjected, makes extensive capital investments if already subject); Low (grudging subjection, limited capital investments); or Resist (fight to avoid subjection or to defect from the hegemonic system).

In the event that S chooses Resist, N(ature) decides the outcome by a lottery. With probability (p), S's resistance Succeeds (S stays out of the hegemonic system if not yet subject, or, if already subject, successfully leaves the coalition and thus is freed from the requirements of monetary taxes and service). With probability (1–p) the resistance Fails (E forcibly imposes or reestablishes domination). In the case of Fail, E coercively imposes whatever conditions or punishment on S that E deems fit, up to and including the death of S as a state and the extermination of part or all of its population.

S's decision to try the Resistance lottery is determined by the value of freedom to S and the probability of Success, set at some point between o and 1. The probability of the success of resistance depends on a variety of factors, including the resources of E and S, whether other subjects join in resistance (forcing E to divide its attention and resources), the possibility of aid from other powerful states (which may mean exchanging the existing E for some E' (e.g., Athens for Persia or Sparta). S must calculate the probability of success and the relative value of freedom and the benefits of subjection in order to decide when (if ever) Resist offers a higher payoff than either High or Low cooperation.

E's payoffs are determined by the taxes it collects from S and the advantages it gains from coordination, less the cost to E of providing protection, coordination services, and enforcement. E prefers to set the tax rate as high as possible relative to the costs of its services. E's payoffs are reduced, however, if S chooses a Low level of cooperation, because E's share of coordination benefits declines and the costs of extracting revenues and of providing protection increase with S's lack of full cooperation. E's payoff is very low in the event that S Resists and the resistance Succeeds. In this case, E pays the cost of whatever failed efforts it made to force S to submit, loses the imperial revenues generated by S, and must confront the knock-on effects of successful resistance among its other subjects. If S Resists and the resistance Fails, E's payoff is harder to determine: E must pay the costs of forcing S into (or back into) submission. E may profit by punishing S by confiscating S's resources. But if the punishment is harsh, E may lose resources due to the long-term degradation of S's economy (with potential negative effects for the economy of its hegemonic domain).

S's payoffs are conditioned, first, on the value to S of the protection and coordination services provided by E, less the cost of monetary taxes and S's service requirements. That value of protection will depend on S's assessment of threats (e.g., Persia, pirates) that are blocked by E and on the perceived value of the coordination that is specific to being within E's zone of dominion (e.g., the advantages that accrue to using a standard coinage issued by E). S's costs include monetary taxes (*phoros*), the moral effect of loss of autonomy, the possible imposition of a garrison, possible interference in local government, and the uncertainty associated with periodic imposition of new rules (e.g., the Athenian Coinage Decree). In the case of the Resist choice, the payoff to S of Fail will be determined by E's choice of punishment; if E chooses to punish severely, the payoff to S from Resist-Fail will be very low. If the Resist choice succeeds, the payoff is the value of freedom less the costs of self-protection and the loss of whatever coordination advantages accrued to S from being in E's zone of domination. Per above, S calculates the expected advantage of resistance based on the probability of its success.

If we bracket, for the moment, the Resist option, we can easily work out the predicted path and solution of the game, based on ordinal preferences (listed in figure 21) of E and S, by backwards induction. If E chooses High tax, then S prefers Low cooperation, eliminating outcome α. If E chooses Medium or Low tax, S prefers High cooperation, eliminating outcomes ζ and κ. Working back on the game tree, E now chooses between β and ε; E chooses ε with its higher payoff. So, the equilibrium solution of the game, without the Resist option, is a Medium level of taxation by E and High cooperation by S. That outcome fits Thucydides' original "Minos paradigm" in which the weak voluntarily submit to the strong, with advantages accruing to both in terms of growth in material wealth. But, as we have seen, in the case of Athens, fairly soon after the original coalition had been created on a voluntary basis, some of Athens' allies did in fact seek to leave the coalition, thus, in the terms of our game, choosing to Resist. A few states continued to try to defect from the coalition, even after Athens had proved effective in suppressing earlier defections (thus suggesting to observers that the probability of Success was relatively low) and in the face of harsh Athenian punishments (showing that the consequences of failure could be severe). On the other hand, as Thucydides' narrative demonstrates, Athens did not face a cascade of defection until late in the Peloponnesian War, after Athens had raised taxes on subjects and battlefield reverses had weakened Athens' coercive capacity.

In order to calculate the expected utility of Resist to any given S, we would need to know the probability that its resistance would be successful. That might be assumed to be fairly low, based on the historical experience recorded by Thucydides. But an accurate measurement of the probability of success for any specific S at any particular historical moment will vary with the several factors alluded to above. We would also need to measure the value of freedom to a particular S at a particular moment, which is very hard to determine. It is clear, however, that, if we hold constant the probability of Success, as E sets the tax rate higher, the expected utility of resistance to S increases. E cannot be certain that setting the tax rate at a Medium level (or even at a Low level) will ensure that rational S will submit willingly and will not Resist. But E can be quite sure that setting the tax rate High will reduce a rational S's incentive to cooperate at a High rate and will increase the likelihood that S will choose to Resist.

The game suggests that a rational E should, under ordinary circumstances, avoid the High tax rate, which will lower its payoff due to a reduction in the level of cooperation by S and will increase the likelihood of costly resistance. If we have set the payoffs to resistance in the right general range (from very low to very high), resistance by S results at best in a low payoff to E, and at worst at a very low payoff. Thus, even if E has a high probability of suppressing resistance, E should seek to avoid conditions likely to provoke resistance. Likewise, unless (1) the probability of successful resistance is substantially higher than seems to be implied by Thucydides' book 1 narrative and (2) S values its freedom from the hegemonic system very highly, S ought to avoid resistance in favor of the relatively favorable equilibrium of Medium taxes and High cooperation.

Nevertheless, as we see from Thucydides' narrative of the war years, imperial Athens did sometimes raise taxes from what we might reasonably call a Medium to a High rate. And Athens' subjects, and potential subjects, did sometimes seek to resist. So, what was happening? Clearly, the exigencies of war led to some special circumstances. Did those special circumstances change the calculus employed by hypothetically rational state actors? Or were choices concerning taxes and resistance violations of the rationality that Thucydides attributes to states in the passages of book 1 considered above? Answering those questions is among the challenges that Thucydides' text poses to a reader concerned with human motivation and practical reasoning. Here, we consider two famous test cases: the revolt of Mytilene and Athens' conquest of Melos.

5.6 MYTILENE RESISTS AND FAILS

In 428 BCE, the major polis of Mytilene, among the few states in the Athenian coalition that still provided warships rather than paying tribute, joined most of the other poleis of Lesbos in seeking to defect from the Athenian imperial coalition. Thucydides notes that the oligarchic leaders of Mytilene wished to revolt even before the outbreak of the war, but that they had failed to secure Spartan support (3.2.1). They were subsequently compelled to commence operations before they intended, because news of their preparations (ship- and wall-building, hiring mercenaries) was conveyed to Athens from multiple sources (3.2.2–3, 3.4.2). The Mytileneans eventually secured a promise of aid from Sparta, but the Peloponnesian fleet sent to support the revolt was dilatory and ineffective. Mytilenean battlefield performance was mediocre. A plan to arm the lower classes backfired. The attempted defection ended in surrender a year later, in the face of a coordinated and highly effective, although very costly, Athenian military response.[22]

With the revolt crushed, the Athenians had to decide on punishment: moderate or severe? That question was answered in the course of two meetings of the Athenian citizen assembly. At the first meeting, the decision was to execute the entire male population and to enslave the women and children. That decision was revisited at a hastily called second meeting. Thucydides presents the most starkly opposed positions at this second meeting through two speeches in the famous "Mytilenean Debate." The prominent demagogue Cleon urged that the original decision be sustained; the otherwise unknown Diodotus advocated for a substantially lighter punishment. Diodotus' proposal narrowly passed on a hand vote. In the aftermath, on Cleon's motion, something over one thousand Mytileneans, thought to be heavily implicated in planning and carrying out the revolt, were executed. The agricultural land of Mytilene and the other Lesbian poleis that had joined in the revolt was confiscated and distributed to Athenian colonists, who leased it back to the original owners. While the punishment was moderate compared to the severe punishment advocated by Cleon, Mytilene had clearly paid a high price for its failed attempt at defection.[23]

In his historical narrative of these events, and a series of speeches— by Mytilenean envoys to the Peloponnesian League meeting at Olympia and by a Peloponnesian commander, as well as by Cleon and Diodotus in the Athenian assembly—Thucydides presents his reader with a detailed account of the factors entering into the Mytlilenean decision to resist, the timing and nature of the Athenian response, the reasons for the failure of the resistance, and the arguments offered on both sides in the Athenian assembly about how to punish the Mytileneans. Thucydides' history of the Mytilenean resistance and its aftermath, along with the Melian narrative considered below, serves as a case study of empire-subject relations and as a test of the theory of power and empire that, so I have argued, is developed in Thucydides book 1.

The hypothesis that Thucydides meant to test a theory of power predicated on what we have been calling the folk theory of practical reasoning is supported by the rhetoric of the Athenians at Sparta in

22. Thucydides 3.1–18, 25–35. I have discussed the military operations, with special reference to collective action and knowledge organization in Ober 2010: 78–82.

23. 3.36–50. I discussed the Mytilenean Debate in Ober 1998a: 94–104. See, recently, Harris 2013.

book 1 (above), the Athenian assembly orators, Cleon and Diodotus, in the Mytilenean Debate, and the anonymous Athenians in the Melian Dialogue. In each case Thucydides' Athenian speakers deploy a similar vocabulary of power, similar premises about human motivations, similar claims for the priority of interests over moral considerations of justice, and a similar focus on the likelihood of salient outcomes. In each case the speakers buttress their positions with reference to counterfactual scenarios. But, contrary to the implied argument of the Athenians at Sparta, that practical reasoning mandates specific state policies, there is stark disagreement between Cleon and Diodotus about how to proceed in punishing the Mytileneans. And, as we will see, the instrumental arguments of the Athenians at Melos fail to persuade the Melians to act in a way that is consistent with expected advantage maximization. Thucydides has, it seems, offered his reader both a clear articulation of the folk theory as it applies to interstate relations *and* a demonstration of the practical limits of the applicability of that theory to real-world interstate politics.

Thucydides' account of the Mytilenean revolt and its aftermath, both in narrative passages and in the speeches, is rife with assertions that states act in accordance with instrumental rationality. While there are occasional hand-waving references to justice and right (by the Mytileneans at Olympia and by Cleon), the primary motivation of states is assumed by all parties to be their own self-interest. States and individuals (especially military commanders) receive information that results in updated beliefs about the state of the world that are in turn the basis for calculations of risk, decisions made on the basis of those calculations, and consequent actions. There are frequent allusions to individuals and states making choices (or being presumed to make choices) on the basis of their expectations, which are in turn predicated on their assessments of likelihood and their attitudes toward risk and chance.[24]

---

24. The Athenian commanders on Lesbos accept an armistice, fearing that they will not have enough forces to subdue the island (3.4.3). The Mytileneans approach the Spartans, believing there is little chance of getting favorable terms from Athens (3.4.5). The Mytilenean commanders abandon the field after a victory, doubting their chances of succeeding in staying overnight (3.5.2). The Mytilenean envoys at Olympia state that it had seemed to them unlikely (*ou . . . eikos*) that, after subjecting the other allies, Athens would, if powerful enough, leave Mytilene free (3.10.6); they posit that equal allies do not violate agreements because the chances of success are too low (3.11.2); they claim that before the war Mytilene did not expect to keep its privileged position within the Athenian coalition and so made preparations to revolt; they assert that the time is right for Sparta to aid them because it is improbable that Athens has any ships to spare. Teutiaplus of Elea

Mytileneans on Rational Defection

The Mytilenean envoys to the Peloponnesian League at Olympia seek to make a rational case for their defection. They admit that they joined the Athenian coalition voluntarily (3.10.2–4), but they claim that their attitude changed to fearfulness after the Persians were no longer an immediate threat and Athens began making its allies into subjects (3.10.4). At that point it seemed to them unlikely (*ou gar eikos*) that the Athenians would allow Mytilene to remain free, since now they had the power to do otherwise (3.10.6). The Mytileneans assert that their fears were exacerbated by the increasing power differential: Athens was "growing steadily more powerful and we more destitute" (3.11.1). They offer a generalization based on rational fear conjoined with risk aversion: The only secure basis for an alliance is a balance of fear, so each side, although desiring to violate the agreement, is deterred by expectation of failure (3.11.2). Here their argument closely maps Glaucon's description of the origins of law in *Republic* book 2 (chapter 2.1). Clearly by the time of the revolt, there was no parity between Athens' power and that of the Mytileneans. But the Peloponnesians listening to this argument (and Thucydides' reader) might well wonder, had there ever been?

The Mytileneans propose that the Athenians have thus far left them free as a signal to other potential allies that their coalition is credibly committed to growing via the voluntary choices of subject states—since Mytilene has its own warships, the choice of supporting a navy or paying tribute is, it appears, up to the new coalition member. They detail Athens' long-term strategy: lead the stronger states in military actions against the weak states first. That leaves the stronger states stripped of potential allies and less capable of resistance to the strongest (3.11.3–4). They claim that "we [Athens and Mytilene] accepted each other against

---

argues that if the Peloponnesians attempt a surprise attack they can expect to catch the Athenians off guard; the Athenians will probably be scattered after their victory (3.30.2). But Alcidas of Sparta finds Teutiaplus' plan too risky (3.31.1). Thucydides claims that had the Peloponnesians been bolder they could probably have received help from a Persian governor (3.31.1). The Ionians came out to greet what they believed to be Athenian ships, because they had no expectation that a Spartan fleet would appear off their coast. Diodotus claims that orators must have superior foresight (3.43.4); he imagines that it is probable that punishments for crimes became more severe over time as lighter punishments failed to deter wrongdoing (3.45.3); he notes that chance misleads people into overly bold actions, because the unexpected does sometimes happen (3.45.6); he notes that if the imperial power is known to be lenient, those who revolt may quickly reassess their chances and change their behavior (3.46.2).

our judgment [*para gnōmēn*]; fear made them attentive [*etherapeouon*] to us in times of war and us to them in peace" (3.12.1).

The "judgment" (*gnōmē*) alluded to by the Mytileneans is the top-ranked outcome for each state: Mytilene to be fully independent, Athens to fully subjugate. Those outcomes were blocked by the external circumstances of the Persian threat and by strategic "attentiveness" to the choices available to the other party. The Athenians rationally preferred to subject Mytilene from the start. Yet they did not do so because, as long as they were building their coalition and fighting Persia, the Athenians needed the signal of voluntary membership. They also needed Mytilene's help in subjugating the weak. And finally, they feared that Mytilene might switch its alliance to the Peloponnesian League. Later, when the Athenians had grown more powerful and most of Mytilene's potential allies were subject to Athens, the Mytileneans became more fearful that the Athenians would reduce Mytilene to the level of mere subject because the Athenians had less reason to fear the consequences of doing so. The balance of fear having become asymmetrical, Mytilene kept quiet, while secretly preparing for revolt. Asymmetrical fear among increasingly unequal allies was, by the Mytilenean calculus, inherently destabilizing of the status quo, and thus motivated the choice to resist.

The Mytileneans' stated justification for defection from the Athenian coalition is entirely based on expectations: their own anticipated loss of advantages in the face of changing relations of power and fear. They cite nothing that is particularly bad in their current situation: Mytilene remained free and nontributary. But, in a close parallel with the motivation of the Spartans at the outbreak of the war (per Thucydides' analysis at 1.23), given the steady growth of Athens' power relative to their own, the Mytileneans expect a disadvantageous outcome. Absent their preemptive action, they regard that bad outcome as certain.

All that fits neatly with the premises of the folk theory. But, upon a moment's reflection, questions arise for Thucydides' reader. Why had the Mytileneans been incapable of looking down the game tree and foreseeing the undesirable outcome of superior Athenian strength forcing them into overt subjection? Why did they agree to join in subjugating the weaker states if the game predictably ended in catastrophic Athenian superiority? The Mytileneans chose their course of action based on a calculation of expected advantage, but they were, it seems, inadequately expert at assessing the future state of the world and measuring probabilities. They claim to have updated their beliefs in light of the conditions that arose when Persia ceased to be a threat. But in choosing to resist, they evidently discounted the chance that information about their preparations would be brought to Athens and would lead to a timely Athenian response. They underestimated Athens' capacity simultaneously to mount defensive and offensive naval operations. They overestimated the value of Sparta's promises of aid. They miscalculated the likely response of the Mytilenean lower classes to being armed. The result was the failure of Mytilene's resistance—a result that, Thucydides implies, could have been foreseen by a foresighted statesman (like Pericles) with adequate information and the capacity accurately to measure relevant probabilities.

Cleon and Diodotus on Motivation, Interests, and Punishment

In making their diverging arguments for punishment, Cleon and Diodotus address the question of the Mytileneans' motives for defecting. Cleon's argument hinges on casting the Mytileneans as vicious criminals who had willfully carried out aggressive and damaging actions, had been apprehended, and now must pay for their crimes (3.38.1, 3.39.1–2, 3.40.1). He emphasizes that the offense was deliberate (3.40.1). But he also characterizes the Mytileneans as incapable of reasoning clearly about means and ends. They failed to take into account relevant information: "The fate of those of their neighbors who had previously rebelled, and had been subdued by us, was no model [*paradeigma*] to them" (3.39.3). They were incapable of correctly weighing the value of their current situation against imagined future gains: The prosperity (*eudaimonia*) they enjoyed (as a privileged member of the coalition) did not make them hesitate in attempting their rash actions. And so, "boldly confident in the future and with hopes [*elpisantes*] that exceeded their capacity [*dunamis*] but fell short of their wishes [*boulēsis*], they declared war, seeing fit to value strength over justice" (3.39.3). The Mytileneans are thus imperfectly rational agents: Even while recognizing that they cannot gain their top-ranked *wishes* (presumably, to be free without cost), their *hopes* lead to confident *beliefs* that fail to track the reality of what they can reasonably expect to achieve.

Cleon characterizes the Mytileneans, en masse, not only as imperfect calculators of their own advantage, but also as devoid of an appropriate sense of justice. They are in this sense analogs of the incurable Thrasymachean egoists alluded to in (Plato's) Protagoras' account of social development (chapter 2.6). Cleon sees the empire as the society that must be protected against the proliferation of egoistic behavior through the extermination of incorrigibles. But, unlike Protagoras, he characterizes punishment as vengeance, not education. Cleon addresses the Athenians as emotional individuals who were unfairly made to experience intense fear and anger upon learning of the Mytilenean revolt. He urges them now to maximize their own subjective happiness by exacting revenge on those who willingly caused them that emotional upset (3.38.1).

Cleon seeks to conjoin his legalistic argument about collective guilt and his emotional argument for the subjective value of vengeance with a state-interest-based argument for severe punishment: Punishing willful defectors at the same (moderate) level as those who were compelled by an enemy to defect will lead other states to choose defection, meaning Athens will repeatedly be forced to risk lives and treasure in putting down revolts. Moreover, even when the revolts fail, the subject poleis will be ruined and revenues lost (3.39.7–8). Therefore, he urges the Assembly to conjoin justice with Athenian interests by punishing the Mytileneans with death (3.40.4). He concludes that punishing the guilty as they deserve will be a salutary example (*saphes paradeigma*) to Athens' other subject states, teaching them that Athens is credibly committed to the extermination of rebels (3.40.7).

Diodotus reprimands Cleon, first for focusing on Mytilenean guilt rather than Athenian interests, as if the context were a law court rather than a policy-making legislative assembly (3.44.1, 4), and then for overestimating the deterrent effect of death penalties. He characterizes the Mytileneans' motives for defecting and their faulty instrumental reasoning as typical of a flawed (from the point of view of rational choice-making) human psychology: Buoyed by hope, people always take risks (*kinduneuousi*); no individual attempts something dangerous while believing that he will fail (3.45.1). Likewise, every subject polis that resists supposes that its own resources or its alliances will enable it to succeed (3.45.2). Of course, their calculations are faulty, but "all are by nature prone to error, both in public and private affairs" (3.45.3). Real humans are, in brief, not the perfect craftsmen of self-interest assumed in Thrasymachus' and Glaucon's versions of the folk theory.

Diodotus continues: The tendency to make errors in calculation is not a matter of specific material circumstances. Poverty encourages the boldness of necessity; plenty stimulates attitudes of arrogance (*hubris*) and greed (*pleonexia*); and every other condition of life has some corresponding passion (*orgē*) that promotes risk-taking (3.45.4). Hope (*elpis*) conspires with desire (*erōs*), "the one devising the enterprise, the other representing the chances as favorable"; and together they overpower observations of danger (3.45.5). Chance (*tuchē*) plays a role because (as Plato notes: above, 5.1) unexpected things do in fact happen. Focusing on the (however remote) possibility of the most-desired outcome induces risk-taking by those with inadequate means. This type of estimation error is especially typical of states contending for the high stakes of freedom and empire, because, when acting as part of a collectivity, each individual overestimates his own capacity (3.45.6). The result, Diodotus' audience is led to suppose, is an unrealistic assessment of collective capacity. In sum, "it is simply impossible and utterly absurd to suppose that human nature, when bent upon some favored project, can be restrained either by the strength of laws or by any other terror" (3.45.7). Neither rules nor fear can be counted on to induce willful humans to act according to a rational calculus of their material interests. Diodotus here seems to rebut popular assumptions about law's origin and function, as reported by Glaucon in *Republic* book 2, while raising doubts about the predictive power of the Empire-Subjects Game.

For all his emphasis on the irreducible role of irrationality in human affairs, Diodotus focuses insistently on Athenian interests, which, he asserts, are best served by moderating the punishment of the Mytileneans and attending to the effects that present policy will have on future choices and outcomes (3.44.1–3). He notes that punishing rebellion with death would ensure that those who do revolt (as they will, given human proclivity to err in formulating beliefs essential to means-end reasoning) have an incentive to fight to the end. Every revolt will, therefore, destroy the subject city and, with it, Athens' revenues (46.1–3). The answer to the problem of resistance is not retrospective retributive punishment. Rather it is forward-looking and careful administration (*epimeleia:* 3.46.4)—presumably this means setting the tax rate at a level that will encourage investment and discourage resistance—and watchful guarding and proactive measures aimed at preventing subjects from ever forming the idea of resistance (3.46.5–6).

Moreover, since it is not possible to prevent all revolts, Athens should (like Plato's Callipolis in conflicts with rival states: above, 5.1) exploit factional differences. Athens has an obvious way to do that by consistently supporting the lower classes against local elites. Executing the masses of Mytilene along with its elite leaders would fatally undermine Athens' current democratic advantage as "the friend of the demos" in every Greek state (3.47.2–4). In sum, it is simply impossible to conjoin justice and Athenian interests, as Cleon vainly urges (3.47.5); a future-oriented, sound, and well-reasoned policy (*eu bouleuetai*) is more effective against adversaries than senseless force (*ischuos anoiai:* 3.48.2).

Given that Thucydides is openly hostile in his characterization of Cleon, and evidently disgusted by the prospect of the mass killing, the reader is led to favor Diodotus' policy of relative leniency. But the attentive reader will not be surprised by the split Athenian vote. The instrumental rationality of the Greek folk theory is the governing premise of both speeches, and, according to Thucydides, guides the behavior of all relevant parties—Athenians, Mytileneans, and Spartans. But, by book 3, Thucydides in propria persona, along with the various speakers in his text, has acknowledged that, in practice, the folk theory does not reliably predict actual behavior of collectivities or, therefore, of states.

The problem is not that the relevant actors do not imagine that they are acting rationally: making choices based on ranked preferences, updating reality-tracking beliefs, and accurately measuring the relevant likelihoods. Rather, the problem is that people, when acting as collectivities, are often mistaken in their beliefs about the relevant state of the world and they allow hope and greed (among other passions) to bias their assessments of likelihood and risk. That being the case, it is unclear how a rational decision-maker ought to proceed—even assuming, as Thucydides does not (Ober 1998: chap. 2), that the Athenian democratic assembly, as a collective policy-maker, was capable of sustaining rationality in the absence of a Pericles-like leader. If the choices of other players in the game are unpredictable, there is no obvious way to choose rationally among available options in setting imperial policy.[25]

And yet, as we saw, Thucydides clearly expects his reader to believe that Themistocles and Pericles had been able to make rational policy in the face of these uncertainties. Stepping back from the possibility of rationality in the phenomenal world, as it is exemplified by the historical events described by Thucydides, might Thucydides' reader reasonably hope to develop a "Periclean" ability to explain and perhaps, therefore, predict the direction and level of deviations from rational behavior? That question recurs in the Melian narrative of book 5.

25. Reynolds (2009) reviews the large literature on Thucydides as alternatively a pessimist or an optimist on the question of the capacity of human agents to employ reason in guiding public affairs.

5.7 MELOS' PROSPECT

In the summer of 416 BCE Athens dispatched a large fleet against the modest-sized Aegean island-polis of Melos.[26] The goal was to force the Melians to join the Athenian coalition as a subject state. Thucydides catalogues the expedition: thirty Athenian warships, six from Chios, two from Lesbos; thirty-one hundred hoplites (sixteen hundred Athenian and fifteen hundred allied); three hundred archers and twenty mounted archers (5.84.1).[27] Athens had attacked Melos a decade before. A sixty-ship expedition (with an unknown number of hoplites and archers), led by the general Nicias, ravaged Melos' territory in summer 426 BCE (3.91.1–3). The Melians refused to submit and Nicias moved along to preplanned operations (3.91.4) against Boeotia and Locris. By contrast, the 416 attack evidently had Melos as its sole target (5.114.2).

The Athenian forces occupied Melian territory, but before they commenced ravaging the Athenians sent envoys to negotiate terms of Melian surrender (5.84.3). The envoys spoke in camera with Melos' oligarchic rulers (*hai archai kai hoi oligoi*), having been denied an audience with the Melian citizen masses (*plēthos* 5.84.3). After negotiations failed, the Athenians began a siege, building a wall around the city; the bulk of the Athenian-led forces then returned home. The Melians attacked the siege works twice in the course of the next months, inflicting some casualties. Athens responded by sending reinforcements and stepping up operations. The besieged city was betrayed from within, leading the Melians to surrender. Choosing the severe punishment option that had been narrowly rejected after the Mytilenean Debate, the Athenians executed the remaining male population of Melos and enslaved the women and children. They later sent out five hundred colonists to occupy Melos' territory (5.114–16).[28]

26. The island of Melos is ca. 150 km²; its classical era urbanized core was ca. 19 ha. (perhaps less in 416): Hansen and Nielsen 2004: 758–60. Using Hansen's (2006) calculations of ca. 150 persons per intramural ha. (for small poleis), with two-thirds of the population living in the urban area, the island's population would have been about 4,500. Even (implausibly) doubling that, it seems very unlikely that Melos' population was over 9,000. For the size range of classical Greek states, see Ober 2015a: chap. 2.

27. This amounts to a total force of ca. 10,600 effectives. Per previous note, we may assume that Melos' total population was very unlikely to be over 9,000 persons and more likely to have been half of that. Of these, less than a quarter would have been adult males. Even if most of those were available for active service (contrary to the situation in oligarchic Mytilene, for example), and even though not all the Athenian rowers would take part in land operations, it is clear that the Melians were badly outnumbered.

28. Hornblower (1991–2008: 3:216–56) offers a detailed commentary on the Athenian expedition and the Melian dialogue, with abundant bibliography.

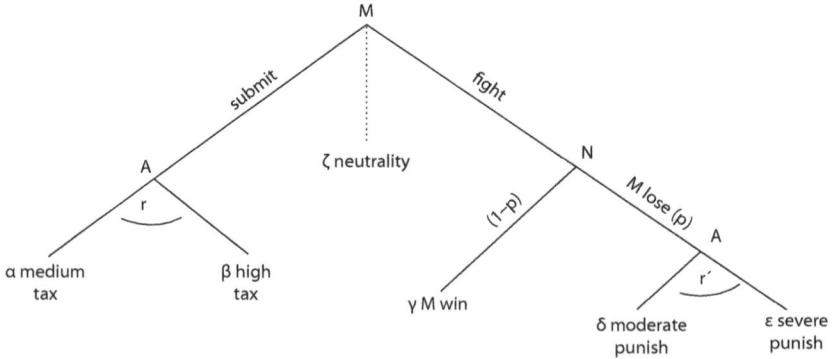

FIGURE 22. Melians and Athenians Game

NOTES: M = Melians; A = Athenians; N = Nature lottery over probability of Melians losing or winning in battle with Athenians; p + (1–p) = 1. r = range of rate of Athenian taxation on Melians if Melians submit; r′ = range of severity of Athenian punishment of Melians if Melians lose. Athenians assume that it is common knowledge that p is very high; r is moderate, r′ is very high.

Thucydides offers his readers an account of the ultimately failed negotiations between Athenian envoys and Melos' rulers in the form of a dialogue, a genre employed in extended form nowhere else in his text. As a result of nonnegotiable discursive rules set by the Athenians at the outset (5.87) the dialogue focuses insistently on state interests, reality-tracking beliefs, risk, and expectations—rather than justice, rights, and wrongs. The Athenians state explicitly that both sides must accept as the premise of the negotiations a strong (in terms developed above: Thrasymachean) version of the folk theory: The powerful, that is, the Athenians, will do just as they please. In the present case, this means ruling over others. The weak must either submit or be destroyed (5.89). The relevant question, per the Empire-Subject game (above), is what "tax rate" will be set by the dominant power. The Athenians present the Melians with the equivalent of a moderate tax rate as a reference point: They present this as a sure thing, against which the Melians would be foolish to gamble. The Melians, however, choose as their reference point their own current independent and tax-free condition and they take their chances accordingly. The failure of the two sides to agree on the reference point leads to cooperative failure and the end of the Melians.

The Athenian envoys assume that the negotiation is a positive-sum bargaining situation, in which both sides have something to gain by striking a deal. For their part, the Athenians prefer Melos' peaceful surrender to fighting because it avoids the costs of fighting and because it is in Athens' interest, just as it is in the interest of the Melians, that Melos be preserved (5.91.2). This is close to Diodotus' argument in the Mytilenean debate, to the effect that live subjects are a valuable resource. With reference to figure 22, the Athenians prefer outcomes α/β: after Melos submits, Athens chooses a tax rate between moderate (α) and heavy (β). The envoys suggest that their preference is for α: They are making an offer that will allow the Melians to retain their country while paying tribute (5.111.4). This is in line with the "Minos-Athens" model of an imperial regime of moderate taxation and high capital investment, a logic that had sustained Athens' empire to this point (above, 5.5). Here the model is summed up in an apothegm: "Those who, while refusing to submit to their equals, yet comport themselves wisely towards their superiors and are moderate towards their inferiors—these, we say, are most likely to prosper" (5.111.4–5).

The Melians ask how it can be in their interest to be enslaved. The Athenians reply that it is to the Melians' advantage to submit before they "suffer the most terrible things" (*pathein ta deinotata*), just as the Athenians will gain by "not destroying you" (*mē diaphtheirantes humas*: 5.91–93). This is the most explicit statement in the dialogue about the likely level of punishment should the Melians resist and fail. The destruction they will suffer is worse than slavery; it is presumably death. The threat is reiterated in the Athenians' summation: The Melians should reflect many times in their deliberation that it is the fate of their "one and only fatherland" (*patris*) that is at stake in their decision (5.111.5); the implication is that if they fight they will lose everything. The key point in the Athenian bargaining position is that the Melians must either take the Athenian offer or fight. Because the Melians have no realistic chance of winning that fight, their backstop position (see chapter 4.3) is zero. The Athenian backstop, destroying Melos, while it is less good than the bargain the envoys seek, is not similarly low: Subduing Melos will not be terribly costly.

The Melians' top-ranked preference is for Melos to retain neutrality and for the Athenians simply to go away (outcome ζ). That is, they seek a "third road," neither submitting nor fighting (compare chapter 1.7: Herodotus' Gyges and the queen's "two roads"). That third option is unavailable to the Melians, however, as the Athenians state explicitly, because it is Athens' least preferred outcome. The Athenians are credibly committed to fighting if Melos will not submit, because to accept Melian neutrality would be a fatal signal to the other subjects of Athens' weakness. Athens' choice to send out a large force with the announced purpose of subduing Melos was a way of binding the state to the mast of imperial expansion. It eliminated the risk that some persuasive argument (justice, pity, expedience) would blunt Athens' resolve to conquer the island polis. Backing down would reveal that Athens lacked the will and the means to gain its preferred ends (5.94–99). As such, allowing Melos to be neutral would threaten the survival of the empire.

With the top-ranked third option eliminated, the Melians must choose between submitting with a high probability of outcome α (pay moderate tax) and fighting. If they choose to fight, they will either win or lose. Winning gives them a good outcome (γ); losing means that Melos will be punished at some rate, chosen by the Athenians, between moderate and severe (δ/ε). As we have seen, the Athenian envoys represent the punishment as likely to be severe.

Assuming that the Melians take the threat of severe punishment seriously, they must accept that if they lose, they will end up with nothing but others' memory of their having fought honorably: no fatherland, property, or lives. So, if the Melians' choice is to be made in accord with the principle of expected advantage, it will be determined by the relative weight of the value they place on their current condition (independent and tax free: Current), the remainder (Current–(Tax+Honor)) left them after submitting without a fight, and the probability of losing (p) or winning (1–p) in a fight. The Athenians seek to demonstrate that (1) attaching value to Honor is foolish: it is dishonorable indeed to submit to an equal without a fight, but no disgrace attaches to submission to vastly superior power; (2) Honor aside, Current minus Tax is of very substantial value; the Melians will be prosperous under Athenian rule; and (3) the probability of Melian victory is near zero (5.111.2–5).

For their part, the Melians cling stubbornly to the idea that Honor is of high value and they propose a series of reasons to believe that they have a chance of winning. Their optimism, characterized by the Athenians as a destructively vain hope, rests on three notions: (1) the gods may favor them in light of the justice of their cause; (2) the Spartans, their kinsmen, might send them aid; and (3) the unexpected can happen: There is always a chance of things turning out favorably. The Athenians bluntly reject these hopeful thoughts as contrary to reason: The gods (if they exist) are impartial and themselves live by the rule that the strong must rule. The Spartans act in their own interest even more consistently than do other people; moreover, they are risk-averse. Sparta has no interest in challenging Athens at sea (5.104–10). The envoys are clearly exasperated by the Melians' supposition that hoping is a form of practical reasoning, and by their conflation of mere chance with calculated probability and risk assessment (5.111.1–2).

Readers interested in instrumental rationality, as Thucydides clearly believes we ought to be, are left with a puzzle. There was certainly a solution to the bargaining problem facing the Athenians and the Melians: Both sides would have benefited from striking a bargain that left Melos intact. The Melian oligarchs may resemble the wealth-hoarding oligarchs of *Republic* book 8 (chapter 6.1) in their utility function. But they do not, in Thucydides' text, seem to be Homeric in their hypervaluation of honor and subsequent memory, nor so religiously devout as to put full faith in divine salvation. Why, then, do they choose to fight? That question has often been asked and there can be no definitive answer. Perhaps the Melians held beliefs (in some aggregate of gods and Spartans) that were coherent, but failed to track reality. Perhaps they put too much weight on the recent precedent of their successful resistance to the Nicias expedition of 426 BCE and thought it likely that Athens would once again give up after a short siege. Perhaps they thought the Athenians were bluffing when they alluded to "the most terrible things."

While there is textual reason to think that each of those factors was in play, the repeated emphasis in the Melian Dialogue on the difference between hope and reason, assessable risk and mere chance, points to a somewhat different explanation: The Melians' reasoning was not modeled on the folk theory of instrumental rationality; they were operating with a different form of practical reason. They did not weigh likely gains against likely losses to choose a course of action leading to the outcome that maximized expected advantage. Rather, they based their decision on a high reference point, their current condition. The prospect of losses that left them below their chosen reference point was intolerable, leading to a conviction that there must be some way to avoid that loss. I have argued, in an article written with Tomer Perry (Ober and Perry 2014), that the Melian Dialogue can best be understood in light of the prospect theory developed by Daniel Kahneman and Amos Tversky (1979, Kahneman 2011). Here I reiterate a few of our conclusions.

In the face of the Athenian threat, the Melian oligarchs made a gamble that was ill-advised from the perspective of rationality as expected advantage maximization. Yet in so doing, they acted just as other (modern) humans predictably do when they are driven by the hope of somehow avoiding the high probability of a large loss. Overvaluing their current condition and discounting the remainder they will retain after the loss, they imagine the condition of salvation too vividly. They hope against hope, "a strange but all-too-human turn of thought" (Orwin 1994: 116), that they will be able to retain their status quo. In this case, the status quo is Melos' standing as an independent state and the oligarchs' own position of authority in that state.

As the Athenian envoys point out, there is very little chance that the Melians will win in a fight and thereby keep the status quo. The Melians do not dispute this: They seemingly acknowledge that they have slim chances of victory in the case of military confrontation. As their representatives say, "You [Athenians] may be sure that we are as well aware as you of the difficulty of contending against your power and fortune, unless the terms be equal" (5.104). But then they devise a scenario that miraculously evens the odds: Since the unexpected can happen, who is to say it won't? Rather than treating uncertainty as measurable risk, the Melians reduce it to mere chance. The dispute between the Melians and the Athenians, according to Thucydides' narrative, was not due to deep disagreement about the facts; the vast superiority of the Athenian forces can be taken as common knowledge. Moreover, we have seen, the Athenians also make it clear to the Melians that incorporation into the empire will mean only limited losses: If the Melians submit without a fight, they will be peacefully brought into what amounts to an Athenian coprosperity sphere. The current ruling oligarchs may lose their monopoly on political power. Taxes will certainly increase, since Melos will pay tribute. And, of course, Melos will lose the coveted status of independent state. But the Melians will keep their lives and property (less taxes).

From the point of view of the Athenians, employing the "Minos-Athens" variant of the folk theory as it applied to interstate relations, the Melian decision was simple. Faced with an uncertain prospect, the Melians ought to choose between the expected value assigned to different possible outcomes, based on material advantage and probability. The rational choice will be the one with the greatest expectation of material advantage, once the likelihood of each outcome has been factored in. The Melians should weigh the tiny chance of keeping everything (the status quo: their reference point) against the certainty of keeping a substantial fraction of what they currently have (the reference point offered by the Athenians). Whatever probabilities one might assign to the two possibilities, the general situation is clear enough: There is a minute chance of keeping the status quo but it is certain (presuming that the Athenians' claim that submission will not entail destruction is credible) that the Melians can keep a sizable part of what they have if they submit. That remainder is, however, evidently not counted by the Melians as a value, but as a loss relative to their chosen reference point. If that is right, their reasoning was not based on the premises of the folk theory of instrumental rationality.

The seemingly irrational choice of the Melian rulers to gamble everything on the faint hope of retaining their current position seems to take the Athenian envoys by surprise, but it would not be unexpected to anyone familiar with what Kahneman and Tversky call "loss aversion" (Kahneman 2011: 310–21). Kahneman and Tversky's experiments showed that most people are risk-seekers when they are faced with a prospective choice between (1) a small chance to avoid any loss paired with a correspondingly large chance of suffering a great loss, and (2) the certainty of losing much of their current endowment while retaining a substantial part of it. Offered the choice between a tiny chance to keep everything (avoiding all loss) and the certainty of high costs (losing a lot but far from all), most people will irrationally choose to gamble on the slight possibility of avoiding the great loss. For the outside chance to lose nothing they bet against a high likelihood of catastrophe. Kahneman sums up the circumstances and consequences of this form of reasoning:

> People who face very bad options take desperate gambles, accepting a high probability of making things worse in exchange for a small hope of avoiding a large loss. Risk taking of this kind often turns manageable failures into disasters. The thought of accepting the large sure loss is too painful, and the hope of complete relief too enticing, to make the sensible decision that it is time to cut one's losses. (Kahneman 2011: 318–19)

This somber assessment exactly describes the Melians' situation, their decision, and its outcome.

The Athenian speakers in the Melian Dialogue are exasperated because they believe that the better choice for the Melians is obvious, based on their severely constrained options and the near-certainty of the disastrous outcome should they choose to resist. Like Gyges confronted with the queen's guards in Herodotus' story, their option set reduces to live or die. Moreover, the Athenians emphasize that Athens' long-time-horizon approach to empire is, relative to the predations of a roving bandit, advantageous to its subjects (5.111.4). The Athenians could simply take everything by seizing the island by force; they do not do so because Athens plays the game of Empire aiming at maximizing returns in the long run. This is the substantive (as opposed to merely procedural) reason that the Athenians claim that the negotiation can be carried on under the banner of *epieikeia*—equitability or fairness: The envoys are in fact making an offer that is overall better than what Athens *could* demand (Orwin 1994: 97–98). Yet the Melians stubbornly refuse, acting in accord with their loss-averse prospective reasoning, turning "a manageable failure into disaster."

The point readers may take away from Thucydides' Melian narrative is that human choice-makers, when faced with very bad options, are, from the point of view of the Greek folk theory, not only irrational, but *predictably* irrational. This means that an instrumentally rational player in a bargaining situation will need to take account of the likelihood of deviation from play based on expected advantage. Any player aware of this aspect of human nature—which is to say, in the vocabulary of prospect theory, anyone who is aware of loss aversion—should anticipate a failure to employ the expectation principle when another player is confronted with dire prospects. Having paid proper attention to the arguments on both sides of the Melian Dialogue, Thucydides' careful reader will anticipate a failure of practical reason understood in the terms of expectation-based instrumental rationality. The Athenian envoys, making their arguments as if they were facing an instrumentally rational player, did not do so and the result was the failure to strike a mutually beneficial bargain. The game devolves from positive-sum to negative-sum. The Melians lose everything and the Athenians end up paying much more than they had expected to subdue the islanders.

Thucydides' Melian narrative may lead the reader to conclude that if the Athenians had a more sophisticated idea of the difference between reasoning from expectations and from prospects, they might have taken the likelihood of an "irrational" Melian choice to resist into account. But then, who are "the Athenians" in that counterfactual? There is little reason to suppose that the Athenian envoys on Melos had any room to offer different terms. The Athenian demos—off the stage of Thucydides' Melian narrative, but ever-present in the consciousness of his reader— had evidently decided, when authorizing the expedition against Melos, to stake Athens' credibility as an imperial power on subduing the island polis. That decision, in the face of the loss aversion of Melos' rulers, sealed the Melians' fate.

Moreover, the reader may conclude that by committing themselves to expanding their empire, the Athenians had abandoned the possibility of returning, in a credible way, to the status quo ante of Pericles' original nonexpansion strategy (1.144.1, 2.65.7). As Thucydides' reader will learn, in the next book of his history, Athenian commitments not to expand lacked credibility, which had serious consequences when the Athenians launched an expedition against Syracuse. The Athenians failed to recruit allies in Sicily and southern Italy when their claim to be motivated by fear and not greed was met with disbelief. In a reversal of the choice made after the Persian Wars by the Mytileneans (above, 5.6) and many other Aegean states, most Greek poleis of Sicily and southern Italy rejected Athenian offers of cooperation.[29]

The choice of the Athenian assembly to incorporate little Melos into the empire was not preceded by deliberations regarded by Thucydides as worth mentioning. Did that choice, by committing Athens to imperial expansion in the Aegean and thereby reducing the credibility of any Athenian commitment to act otherwise elsewhere, increase the likelihood that Athens would end up failing in Sicily, and then ultimately losing the Peloponnesian War? Did the Athenians fail to consider the signal that their conquest of Melos would send to potential allies? It is by his implicit challenge to his readers to confront those sorts of question that Thucydides may lay claim to making an enduring contribution to ancient and modern theories of rationality and choice.

29. At 6.83–87, the Athenian envoy, Euphemus, attempts to persuade the citizens of the Sicilian state of Camarina to ally with Athens against Syracuse, arguing that Athens seeks free allies, not subjects, and that Athens' motive for the Sicilian expedition is fear of Syracuse, not aggrandizement. Thucydides (6.88.1) states that the Camarinaeans feared Syracuse and sympathized with the Athenians, "except insofar as they might be afraid of their subjugating Sicily." They ultimately refused the Athenian offer of alliance.

CHAPTER 6

Socrates' Critique

Problems for Democratic Rationality

Can a democratic state be a rational collective agent, over time and in the absence of a leader like Thucydides' Pericles? In chapter 2 we considered a model of rational interpersonal cooperation presented by Plato's Protagoras: a democratic community, loosely based on Athens (Farrar 1988; Segvic 2009), capable of high-level cooperation through the employment of practical reasoning in establishing and maintaining socially valuable practices of mutual education. In this chapter, we continue to explore the question, introduced in chapter 4 and pursued in chapter 5, of the sense in which a democratic polis might be a "city of reason" (O. Murray 1990). The *politeia* of Athens (Ober 2008), in common with Athenian culture generally (D'Angour 2011), was open to and characterized by innovation. Indeed, it was scandalously innovative, according to some modern (Samons 2004), as well as ancient, critical assessments. Those innovations continued long after the death of Pericles, and in the absence of a similarly prominent leader.

Was innovation evidence of rationality, or its absence? Is Athenian institutional change reducible to a process of random and thoughtless flux—a cultural analogue of blind genetic/environmental evolution? Or were innovations products of coherent choices by a rational demos, manifestations of systemic robustness in the face of changing circumstances? Could practical reason identify and pursue the best available option through public deliberations and voting? If so, how? The answers to these questions potentially bear on a rapidly growing interdisciplinary literature that seeks to understand how the adaptive processes of cultural evolution relate to and differ from genetic/evolutionary evolution (Creanza, Kolodny, and Feldman 2017).

This chapter differs from the other chapters in this book, where the focus is on arguments in texts written by educated Greeks. Those arguments arose from and responded to widespread concerns in the culture, but they were written by and, for the most part, for intellectuals. This chapter responds to the critique of democracy developed by Plato's Socrates in book 8 of the *Republic* by reference to current historical research on Athenian institutional practices. I seek to show, by specifying how decisions were made in democratic institutions, that Athenian democracy was instrumentally (although not ethically) rational on Plato's own terms. That is, when acting in their political capacity, as assemblymen, jurors, and state officials, the citizens of Athens were capable of making and acting on choices predicated on ranked preferences over outcomes and coherent beliefs.

Although the evidence is open to other interpretations, it appears highly likely that important decisions were preceded by public deliberations, informed by expert testimony and debate among proponents of different options. In at least some cases, the process led to a rough consensus on the best feasible option. This chapter does not pretend to offer a full-featured historical account of rationality in classical Athens, much less in the ancient Greek world as a whole. It does not, for example, address the instrumental rationality of religious practices (e.g., the expected returns on public or private sacrifices to the gods) or the relationship between rationality and emotions in Greek social behavior and cultural practices. A full-featured treatment of such matters is a desideratum for future work, but exceeds the ambitions of this book.[1]

This chapter proceeds as follows: Section 1 considers the account given by Plato's Socrates in book 8 of the *Republic* of a degenerative cycle of regimes. With the fall of excellent Callipolis, the imagined polis devolves into timocracy, and then by stages to oligarchy, democracy, and finally tyranny. Each subsequent regime is explicitly said to be worse than the last. In section 2, we answer the question of why Plato's

---

1. Important recent work along those lines includes D. Allen 2000 on moral anger in Athenian legal practice; Johnstone 2011 on formal and informal contracts and the creation of social trust; Mackil 2013 on contractual balancing of interests via religious and economic institutions in Greek *koina*; Carawan 2013, B. Gray 2015, and Driscoll 2016 on reconciliation agreements as polis-wide social contracts, established in law and guaranteed by oaths, in Athens and other poleis.

Socrates ranked democracy below oligarchy in his narrative of the degenerative cycle. Sections 3 and 4 address the conundrum of Plato's acknowledgment of high state performance with his assertion of democratic irrationality. Section 5 turns to Plato's recognition that democracy made materially effective use of experts. Sections 6 to 8 sketch what I regard as the most plausible among competing historical reconstructions of the operations of Athenian political institutions in the fourth century BCE, the post-Peloponnesian War period for which our information is most complete and in which no Pericles-type leader dominated Athenian politics. Section 9 concludes, introducing the notion of adaptive rationality and its implications for the fate of democracy in the Greek world.

6.1 CALLIPOLIS AND ITS SUCCESSORS

Most of Plato's *Republic* is devoted to constructing, through philosophical argument, the ideally rational state that comes to be called Callipolis. The imagined state is intended, as we have seen (chapter 4), as a large-scale model of an idealized human moral psychology, with the right arrangement of the elements of reason, moral emotions, and desires. Those elements are schematically represented by the occupation-classes of rulers, warriors, and producers. When the theoretical project is complete, Callipolis is a perfectly harmonious association that functions effectively as an organization, capable of providing security and adequate resources, material and moral, for all of its residents. It is governed by a *politeia* that fully instantiates the primary virtues of moderation, justice, courage, and wisdom. It exemplifies Plato's conception of true rationality in respect to both ends and means.

Harmony among persons with dissimilar abilities, carrying out different social functions, is sustained in Callipolis by the moderation (*sophrosunē*) that is characteristic of all residents, and by the omnipresence of justice (*dikaiosunē*), understood as each resident being appropriately assigned to, and staying within, his and her own proper domain of activity. Each scrupulously avoids interference (*polupragmosunē*) in any domain beyond his or her own. Justice, so understood, defines the constraints imposed on each resident's choices, both by the rules and by the expected choices of others. Those constraints serve to limit each resident's actions in the pursuit of options lying within his or her proper domain. Justice thus enables each resident, including the vast majority whose souls are not ruled by reason itself, to act rationally in the instrumental sense of the folk theory. The "high-order rationality of ends" manifest at the level of the state facilitates the "low-order rationality of means" of even its humblest member.

Callipolis is ruled by philosophers, who are, like the model agent specified by Thrasymachus and Glaucon, unerring craftsmen of interests and outcomes. The goal that the hypothetical craftsmen-rulers of Callipolis seek and unfailingly achieve is the interest of the state, rather than merely their own self-interest. By virtue of their perfected knowledge of the right ends of human life, the philosopher-rulers of Callipolis make no errors in reasoning from preferences to outcomes. The philosopher-rulers derive their preferences, like their assessments concerning the relevant state of the world, from knowledge rather than from ordinary desires (primitive or otherwise). Consequently, they necessarily go for the best outcomes for each and all (519e). If a philosopher should, counterfactually, come to elevate his own private good (spending all of his time in the "sun" of philosophical contemplation) above the good of the whole (taking his turn in the "cave," doing the work of ruling) in his preference order, he would be corrected by the other philosophers (519d–20c): The ethically rational philosopher's preferences are corrigible through reasoned argument, unlike merely instrumentally rational residents of Callipolis, who must be persuaded in part by "noble" deceptions.

Callipolis cannot, however, last forever, even in theory. In book 8 of the *Republic*, Plato sketches a hypothetical degenerative history of regimes, beginning with the fall of Callipolis, due to a mistake concerning the algorithm governing breeding among Guardians. The result of that error is a violation of domain segregation. Because domain segregation is the principle of justice on which Callipolis is predicated, the regime collapses.

The degenerative sequence of regimes described by Plato's Socrates, which begins with the end of the rule of the knowledgeable lovers of wisdom (Callipolis), results first in the rule of the courageous lovers of honor (timocracy) and continues to the rule of the acquisitive lovers of wealth (oligarchy). This initial sequence is readily explained by reference to Socrates' hierarchy of value: knowledge > honor > material acquisition. The timocrat and the oligarch make an error, in that they subjectively overvalue ends that they falsely believe to be in their self-interest. But their preferences are ranked and stable over time, in that each aims not just at a momentary end but at a way of life. Their actions follow from their ordered preferences and consistent beliefs.

6.2 SOCRATES' CRITIQUE OF DEMOCRACY

The two final regimes described in *Republic* book 8 are, in order, democracy and tyranny. Tyranny, as a candidate for the worst regime, had been in the crosshairs since Socrates' interchange with Thrasymachus in book 1. Book 9 is largely devoted to detailing the misery of the tyrant, whose soul, rather than being governed by reason, is pushed and pulled hither and yon by powerful, chaotic, self-destructive desires. Ultimately the profound irrationality of the tyrant's soul, conjoined with his need for associates to fulfill his lusts, results in the putative absolute ruler living in an abject condition as a "slave of slaves" (577d–79e). This is the final demolition of the claims of Thrasymachus for the tyrant's happiness, and likewise the long-deferred definitive refutation of the putatively happy lives of Gyges with the ring and the "godlike" completely unjust man in Glaucon's cleaned-up version of the folk theory of instrumental reason.

But we are left with a puzzle: Why is democracy ranked below oligarchy? Based on the hierarchy of value, oligarchy and democracy might seem to be inverted. Democracy is ranked above oligarchy in Plato's later work, the *Statesman*, as it is by Aristotle in the *Politics*.[2] Plato has nothing good to say about the oligarchs and their focus on acquisition in the *Republic*. Their behavior, based on placing a preference for material goods at the top of their ranking, is obviously mistaken and blameworthy in Socratic terms (see chapter 7). Moreover, it may occur to the reader that it is odd that, in the *Republic*, Socrates and Plato's other "philosophical" characters (Glaucon, Adeimantus), like the real Socrates and Plato, choose to live their lives in a democratic state, rather than in one of the readily available oligarchic alternatives (assuming that no real-world analogue of timocracy, e.g., Sparta, would have them). Finally, and perhaps relatedly, Plato's Socrates has some evidently positive (if ironic) things to say about democracy: *Inter alia*, with its supermarket-like diversity of values and behaviors, a democratic state is the proper place for philosophers to engage in a project of ideal political theorizing (557d). That is, of course, what the participants in the dialogue, and Plato in writing the *Republic*, were doing.[3]

---

2. In Plato, *Statesman* 303a–c, followed by Aristotle, *Politics* book 6, the ranking is monarchy (lawful rule of one), aristocracy (lawful few), democracy I (lawful many for Aristotle: *politeia*), democracy II (lawless many), oligarchy (lawless few), tyranny (lawless one).

3. Marshall and Bilsborough (2010) review the debate on the ranking of regimes in the *Republic*, concluding, contra Saxonhouse 1998 and Monoson 2000, that Plato does

The answer to the apparent puzzle about Socrates' ranking of democracy and oligarchy can, I believe, be solved by assuming that Plato structured the sequence of regimes not only according to a second-order value hierarchy noted at the end of the previous section (knowledge > honor > wealth), but also according to a first-order rationality hierarchy, rationality of means aimed at rational ends (desired by reason itself: Callipolis) > rationality of means employed to nonrational ends (desired by spirit and appetite: timocracy, oligarchy) > irrationality (democracy, tyranny). In each case, Plato asks, first, what set a regime belongs to, according to a normative standard of rationality: ethical and instrumental, instrumental only, neither ethical nor instrumental. Then, within each set, the regime is ranked according to the value of its observable choices.[4]

In *Republic* book 8, the locus of democratic irrationality is manifest, in the first instance, in a failure, on the part of the democratic individual and the democratic state, to sustain over time an ordered set of preferences over outcomes, understood as goods. That lack of order is most evident (inverting the original premise of the greater visibility of justice in the big polis than in the small individual soul in book 2) in the revealed preferences of the democratic individual. Each regime in Plato's degenerative sequence is exemplified by its model citizen, whose moral psychology accurately represents the *politeia* of his state.[5] Each model citizen values certain goods. Maximizing his possession of those goods is his goal. The timocrat consistently ranks honor highest among available goods (548c, 549a, 550b). He acts according to his beliefs (valid or otherwise) to achieve outcomes (in the first instance, victory in battle, due to exemplary courage) that will maximize his honor.

---

explicitly rank democracy below timocracy and oligarchy. They also note the ambiguity that arises in light of the higher ranking for democracy in later dialogues and some of the apparently approbative comments about democracy in the *Republic*.

4. Santas (2001: 62, 67, 70) rightly emphasizes the distinction between democratic irrationality and the instrumental rationality of timocracy as honor-seeking and oligarchy as wealth-seeking. I think he is mistaken, however, to assert that the tyrant is an instrumentally rational power-seeker; at 572d–75a Socrates details the tyrant's "violent crowd of desires" (573e) for sex, wealth, and sensory pleasures. On Plato's tripartite (reason, spirit, appetite) soul and the desires arising from each part, see introduction, n. 16. On ideal standards versus feasible options, see Sen 2009; Bendor in progress.

5. Santas (2001) analyzes the isomorphism of the democratic individual of *Republic* book 8 and the democratic polis in detail. Whether the model citizen is to be thought of as a ruler (or representing the ruling coalition), as typical, or paradigmatic is a matter of scholarly debate; see Schofield 2006: 112–17, with literature cited.

Likewise, the oligarch consistently places possession of wealth at the top of his preference order. He seeks outcomes that he believes will maximize the security of his hoarded wealth (553c–55a). Each does so at the expense of his pursuit of higher goods.

By the eighth book, Plato's reader has learned that neither honor nor wealth has a valid claim to be top-ranked in the order of preferences by a truly (ends and means) rational person or state—as noted above, the timocrat and oligarch each makes a mistake about value, because his desires arise from a nonrational part of his soul. But the timocrat and the oligarch, and the regimes they exemplify, can claim to be instrumentally rational in the "cleaned-up" folk theory sense of Glaucon's thought experiment in *Republic* book 2: Each manifests a complete, ranked, transitive set of preferences. That preference set is stable, insofar as it persists over an (adult) lifetime. Based on their own orderly preferences, the timocrat and the oligarch act according to their beliefs, including their expectations, based on the revealed preferences of other "players" and calculations of risk, to maximize their own (subjective) advantage. The behavior of the democrat lacks this baseline rationality.

Democratic irrationality arises from the underlying commitment of the model democrat, and thus the democratic *politeia,* to the values of freedom and equality. Those values are closely related in Plato's view, a view that was shared by Aristotle, other critics of democracy, and indeed by the democratic Athenians themselves.[6] What is distinctive about Plato's account of democratic value is his identification of individual psychological states with state-level institutional arrangements. Moreover, unlike honor or wealth, freedom and equality are not taken by Plato's democrat to be clearly defined "ultimately most-choiceworthy" goods in themselves. Nor do they point to any specifiable or stable set of ranked outcomes. Rather, the embrace of freedom provides the democrat with a doorway onto a wide range of goods and a comparably diverse range of potentially desirable outcomes and actions aimed at securing them.[7]

Meanwhile, equality leads the model democrat to be indifferent (over time, and in the choice-theoretical sense of indifference as equally strong

6. Freedom and equality and its association with democracy in classical Greek thought generally: Raaflaub 1983, 1989; in the *Republic* books 8 and 9: Santas 2001: 61–65; Schofield 2006: 107–12.

7. Schofield (2006: 112) puts it well: "Freedom (like the modern idea of a right) is what one might call an enabling good. It is freedom *to* . . . In a society which makes freedom its good, lifestyles will be structured principally by pursuit not of freedom but of what freedom enables people to pursue: 'what a person wants.'"

preferences) to the possession of any one good or outcome, among the diverse range of possibilities that his freedom has opened to him, over any other. Each seems to him, over time, to be of equal value. As a result of the interaction of freedom with equality, each good can catch his attention momentarily, be pursued as a desired outcome with avidity, and then suddenly be dropped in favor of some other equally desirable alternative. The democrat's indifference among the diverse array thus takes the form of pursuing different ends seriatim, just as they happen to strike his fancy. Given that each is, ultimately, equally desirable, abandoning the one and taking up the next is costless in terms of his internal accounting.

In sum, for Plato's Socrates, the democrat is free, and delights in his freedom to pursue, at any moment, any of the wide variety of goods that seem to him, over time, to be equally attractive. And thus, the individual who is the model for the regime of democracy and who is rightly called democratic (561e)

> lives on, yielding day by day to the desire [*epithumia*] at hand. Sometimes he drinks heavily while listening to the flute; at other times, he drinks only water and is on a diet; sometimes he goes in for physical training; at other times he's idle and neglects everything; and sometimes he even occupies himself with what he takes to be philosophy. He often engages in politics, leaping up from his seat and saying and doing whatever comes into his mind. If he happens to admire soldiers, he's carried in that direction, if money-makers [*chrēmatistikoi*], in that one. There is neither order [*taxis*] nor constraint [*anangkē*] in his life and he calls it pleasant, free, and blessedly happy, and he follows it for as long as he lives. (561c–d)

Notably, included among the diverse ends that the model democratic man may, momentarily, pursue is the soldier's life, recalling the timocrat, and that of the money-maker, recalling the oligarch. He even may delve into what he supposes to be the domain of the philosopher. But, unlike any of those model individuals, the democrat does not take wealth, honor, or knowledge as his primary end, nor does he pursue it consistently. Plato's Socrates emphasizes the democrat's lack of *order* and *constraint*. That is, in the terms employed by contemporary theorists, his preferences are not transitively ranked and he views his option set as unlimited. As a result, his choices cycle freely, manifesting the irrationality that contemporary public choice theorists attribute to democratic voting (chapter 3.7). Even if we suppose (with Schofield 2006: 114–16) that the diversity of preferences is manifest only across the population, rather than within the typical individual, it remains hard to imagine how the pluralistic community could settle on, or systematically pursue, a long-term goal.

Along with orderly preferences, instrumental rationality requires reasonably coherent (whether or not valid) beliefs about the state of the world to guide actions aimed at securing most-favored available outcomes. Plato's Socrates does not give us reason to suppose that the democrat has beliefs that are consistently true, much less the knowledge that distinguishes the philosopher-rulers of Callipolis. Nor does the timocrat or the oligarch. But democracy, as a *politeia,* may be subject to epistemic disabilities that are peculiar to itself.

The diversity of the democratic *koinōnia* means that there is, at any given moment, a corresponding diversity not only in preferences of the moment, but in information and skills—whether genuine craft skills, whose practitioners are able to give an account of the process (*technai*), or mere "knacks" based only on experience (*empeiriai*). Because, in a democracy, all adult male natives are citizens who are free and, according to Socrates' description of the democratic man, eager to attend the legislative assembly, this diverse body of skills and information—call it generically "know-how" and "data"—is brought into the public space of collective decision-making. But how is the mass of data to be organized by those with diverse skills and momentary preferences, such that only the bits relevant to feasible options are considered and then properly weighted? How will the process yield a set of coherent beliefs that will allow the demos, as a mass of free and equal persons, to make a choice that will further its collective interests? To the extent that each of the thousands of citizens in the democratic assembly "engages in politics [by] leaping up from his seat and saying and doing whatever comes into his mind," the collective belief formation process seems likely to be as disordered as the democratic man's preferences.[8]

6.3 DEMOCRACY AND STATE PERFORMANCE

Each of Socrates' two sources of democratic irrationality—disorderly preferences and inconsistent, as well as invalid, beliefs about the state of the world—has been highlighted by contemporary critics of democracy. Joseph Schumpeter ([1950] 2008) defined the issue in his still-influential

---

8. Williams (2006: chap. 7) notes the confusion that arises due to the diversity among democratic citizens and within the soul of the individual democrat. Schofield (2006: 112–17) helpfully discusses the relevant passages in terms of democratic pluralism.

mid-century book *Democracy, Capitalism, and Socialism*. Schumpeter claimed that what he called the "classical theory of democracy"—the idea that a mass of citizens could be capable of ruling themselves—was incoherent: It grafted Rousseau's implausible conception of the general will onto Jeremy Bentham's narrowly materialistic conception of utility as pleasure. Schumpeter denied that a collective will (a rational judgment connecting coherent shared preferences over outcomes to collective action) could ever be formed by a mass of citizens, and scoffed at the notion that democratic citizens, as individuals or in the aggregate, knew, could know, or had any motivation to learn enough to govern themselves.[9]

Picking up where Schumpeter left off, William Riker (1982) zeroed in on the problem of ordering collective preferences. Rather than leaning on Plato's account of the individual democrat's irrational moral psychology, Riker appealed to Kenneth Arrow's ([1951] 1963) "impossibility theorem" of voting, which demonstrates that, under plausible conditions, a group faced with deciding by voting among three or more alternatives cannot avoid the possibility of falling into a cycle in which X is chosen over Y, Y over Z, and Z over X (see chapter 3.5). Since cycling violates transitivity, Riker pronounced democracy irrational and, in principle, fatally subject to strategic manipulation by those who understand the mechanism of cycles. Riker also sought to show that cycles were indeed prevalent in real-world democratic decision-making, an empirical conclusion that has been challenged.[10] More recently, epistemic critics of democracy and democratic realists have revived Schumpeter's concerns about the capacity and motivation of democratic citizens to know enough to vote according to their interests—even if they happened to be capable of identifying them.[11]

Modern critics who contend that democracy is beset by inherent irrationality tend to focus their worries on the negative impact of irrationality on the performance of democratic states as organizations—the capacity to deliver the goods of security and material welfare. The constitutional fixes the critics suggest (insofar as they make practical recommendations) are meant to enable democracy to perform as well as a

---

9. I discuss Schumpeter's "classical theory" and contemporary epistemic critics of democracy in Ober 2015b, 2018a.

10. Challenges to Riker: Mackie 2003; Goodin and Spiekerman 2018: 33, with literature cited.

11. Epistemic critiques of democracy include Caplan 2007; Brennan 2016; Somin 2016; Achen and Bartels 2016.

hypothetical alternative: a better-organized, more rational, meritocratic and/or autocratic regime.[12] Plato's concern was quite different.

Rather than worrying about the underperformance, in material terms, of democratic regimes relative to feasible (actual or hypothetical) nondemocratic alternatives, Plato's criticism of democracy centered on the capacity and tendency of democratic culture to corrupt individual souls. The superficially attractive diversity of the democratic ethos turned people who might otherwise pursue virtue, those with the capacity to be at least instrumentally rational and possibly even ends-and-means rational, away from objectively better ends (e.g., 492a–95a, see chapter 8.5). The dire result was denying to individuals and to their communities the possibility of achieving any part of true *eudaimonia*.

Yet the puzzle of democratic state performance remains: If democracy was a fundamentally irrational form of *politeia,* and Athens was a democracy, how is it that Athens functioned as a relatively effective organization—both in the imperial fifth century, the dramatic date of most of Plato's dialogues, and in the postimperial fourth century, when Plato was writing them? As we have seen (chapter 4.6), in the *Gorgias* (518e–19c), Plato's Socrates accused fifth-century leaders of filling the city with the "trash" of harbors, city-walls, ship-sheds, and tribute: that is, the material bases of state wealth and power. By the probable date at which the *Republic* was first circulated, say the third decade of the fourth century, the city walls and the navy of trireme warships (along with the ship-sheds to house them) had been rebuilt. The harbor at Piraeus was once again attracting a substantial trade. By the end of Plato's life, despite a severe downturn in the mid-350s, Athens was again a leading Greek city-state and a center of a thriving Mediterranean trade. By the 330s, when Aristotle was writing the *Politics* and criticizing some of Plato's arguments, Athens' state revenue and per capita income equaled or exceeded its fifth-century imperial height, even though its citizen population never regained fifth-century, imperial-era level and the empire was just a memory (Ober 2008).

At least part of the answer must be that the portrait of the democratic man in the *Republic* ought not be taken literally, at least insofar as a literal reading (in light of the "soul-state" analogy) would imply a complete failure of society-wide or state-level instrumental rationality. The model "democratic man" of *Republic* book 8 appears to be assured

---

12. On the modern history of arguments for the epistemic superiority of authoritarian regimes, see Tong 2020.

of a certain background welfare and security: Unlike the miserable creatures of Hobbes' state of nature, Plato's democratic man is not said to be threatened by material deprivation or to live in fear of threats to his security. As the *Gorgias* passage clearly indicates, Plato knew that the diverse members of the demos, in their role as citizens participating in key democratic institutions, were capable of making collective decisions that conduced, if not to *eudaimonia,* then (at least more often than not) to the ends of state-level security and material welfare.

Could those ends have been achieved by mere luck? By institutional innovations that were no more rationally chosen than are random genetic mutations? That seems implausible on the face of it. In the fourth century, as in the fifth, Athens existed in a highly competitive environment that punished states incapable of defending themselves or securing resources necessary for material welfare. An alternative hypothesis is defended below: The outcomes of security and welfare were quite consistently highly ranked, as preferences, by an authoritative majority of the many citizens who participated in the making of state policy. Beliefs held by an authoritative majority concerning the feasibility of available options were not only coherent but also tracked reality well enough to connect ranked preferences with real-world results.

6.4 QUESTIONS FOR ATHENS' *POLITEIA*

In chapter 4.6, we considered the possibility, urged by Thucydides, that democratic Athens was able to function effectively as a state in the early and middle fifth century BCE only because of rational leadership. Thucydides' claim that Athenian leaders after Pericles were incapable of directing the state was not immediately borne out in the decade after Pericles' death. But in his analysis of Periclean leadership and subsequent leadership failures, Thucydides (2.65.11) drew attention to the failed Athenian attempt to conquer Sicily—a policy that contravened Pericles' advice not to expand the empire before the war had been concluded on terms favorable to Athens. After the catastrophic failure of the Athenian invasion of Sicily in 413 BCE, the democracy was briefly replaced with a narrow oligarchy. The oligarchy of "the 400" was in turn replaced by what Thucydides (8.97.2) approvingly describes as a "mixed regime," followed by a return to democracy. Here Thucydides' text leaves off, but Xenophon (*Hellenica*, books 1–2), Diodorus Siculus (12.41–14.34), and the Aristotelian *Ath. Pol.* (29–41) provide a narrative of subsequent events: Athens finally lost the war. The victorious

Spartans imposed another oligarchy, but democracy was restored after a brief, bloody civil war. The victorious democrats defied expectations by instituting an amnesty instead of pursuing a vendetta against Athenians who had supported the oligarchy. From 403 to 322, Athens was once again a democratic state.[13]

Although Athenian democracy was long associated with the "Periclean golden age" of the fifth-century empire, our best evidence, both literary and documentary, for Athenian democracy concerns the eighty-year period following the Peloponnesian War and preceding the Macedonian takeover after the death of Alexander the Great. This period of Athenian constitutional history is the subject of the second part of the Aristotelian *Athēnaiōn Politeia* (42–69), probably written in the 320s, an incomparable contemporary descriptive and analytic source. The contemporary evidence of the Aristotelian *Ath. Pol.* is augmented by a relatively full historiography and numerous speeches by Athenian political and legal orators (Ober 1989). There is a rich dossier of legislative acts preserved in the literary record (Liddel 2019) and many documents on stone (Rhodes and Osborne 2003). A long generation of intensive work by Greek historians on those materials, and on the archaeological remains of Athens' democratic infrastructure (Camp 2001), has done much to further our understanding of the fourth-century democracy (Hansen 1999). The post–Peloponnesian War era is now widely regarded by historians, not as a period of decline, but as the mature form of the Athenian *politeia*. While democratic politicians provided essential expertise, they were in no sense dominant leaders of the kind that Thucydides claimed that Pericles had been (Rhodes 2016). The thesis that Athens was capable of functioning as a rational state only when the demos was quiescent, and when the state was in practice governed by a rational third-party ruler, cannot be sustained for the fourth century.[14]

In the next four sections, I will sketch certain features of Athenian democratic institutions. This is decidedly *not* a constitutional history, tracing the various institutional changes from the late-sixth-century Cleisthenic origins, through the Periclean imperial era of the fifth century, and over the course of the first eight decades of the fourth century.

13. Late-fifth/fourth-century Athenian history and constitutional changes: Krentz 1982; Strauss 1986; Munn 2000; Shear 2011; Carugati 2019, with literature cited.

14. I offer a brief survey of fourth-century Athenian history in Ober 2008: 64–69. Claude Mossé, who had been a leading proponent of the "decline" thesis (Mossé 1962, 1973), subsequently rejected that thesis (for example, Mossé 1994, 1995). For the wider Aegean context, see Buckler 2003.

Nor is it a complete exposition of the mature Athenian *politeia* and its functioning as an organization. Nor, finally, is it an attempt to demonstrate the reasons for fourth-century Athens' comparatively high level of state capacity and its military and economic performance. Those matters have been dealt with, in detail, in recent work, my own and that of others.[15] Rather, the goal will be to test the validity of Plato's portrait of democratic irrationality by examining the rationality (or lack thereof) of the mature democratic state. I propose to approach the question of "state rationality" at four levels.

First, to what extent did the decision-making processes of the state map onto the model of the hypothetical "unerring craftsman" in Glaucon's restatement of the folk theory of instrumental rationality? How capable was the Athenian state—which means, in practice, the Athenian demos as a collectivity—of forming ordered preferences over outcomes? Developing coherent beliefs about the state of the world at any given moment in time? Updating those beliefs over time? And ultimately serving its own self-identified interests? That is, if the Athenians were indeed collectively capable of making a rational choice by calculating the most-favored available outcome, were they also capable, as a collectivity, of acting upon that decision? Here, we must allow for preferences to diverge from Glaucon's "primitive preference triad" of sex, wealth, and power. I postulate that the relevant, alternative, state-level (that is, common interest) top-ranked preference triad was—as suggested above—individual and collective security, general welfare, and the avoidance of tyranny, understood as elite capture of the government.[16]

15. Constitutional history: Carugati 2019. Exposition of mature democracy: Hansen 1999. Explanation for Athenian performance: Ober 2008.

16. While religion was very important to individual Athenians and to the Athenian state (Parker 1996, 2006), the evidence suggests that security and welfare were primary concerns of state policy. Pritchard (2012, 2015) demonstrates that Athens spent much more annually on preparations for war than on religious festivals in the fifth and fourth centuries alike. Liddel (2019: table 1, pp. 36–37) sums up the evidence for known decrees (*psēphismata*) of the Athenian assembly from 403 to 322 BCE, preserved in epigraphic and literary sources. Totals are as follows: 381 inscribed decrees have discernible content. Of these, 306 (80%) are honorific (1 offers honors to a god, all others to mortals), 65 (17%) concern security (military affairs, foreign policy), 3 (1%) concern other domestic matters (constitutional, financial, etc.), and 9 (2%) concern religious regulations. There are 235 decrees known from the literary record that have discernible content. Of these, 80 (34%) are honorific, 96 (41%) concern security, 51 (22%) concern other domestic matters, and 10 (4%) are religious regulations. Neither the epigraphic nor the literary record offers a transparent representation of the work of the assembly. But the two sources of evidence are independent of one another. If we assume, as the texts of honorary decrees strongly indicate, that the Athenians granted honors for contributions to the state's security and/or

Next, with reference to the bargaining solutions sketched in chapter 4: To what extent did the democratic *politeia* facilitate productive (integrative, win-win, albeit unequal) bargains, and avoid costly bargaining failures, among Athenian groups, each pursuing its own pluralistic preferences? Those groups were defined in part by material interests (distributive shares) but also by identities and loyalties arising from regionalism, social status, religious belief, and other cleavages. Certain of those cleavages existed among the population of adult male citizens. Others arose among and between the broader set of persons subject to Athenian jurisdiction, including citizen women, resident foreigners, short-term visitors, and slaves. How clearly articulated and consistent over time were the preference rankings of interest and identity groups? How well known were their backstop positions and their relative bargaining power? What lines of communication were open (or closed) to them? Were groups with only partially overlapping interests able to make bargains that pushed toward the Pareto frontier of "full social value" within the existing constitutional framework?

Third, to what extent were the rules—the formal institutions, social norms, and associated habits that constituted the *politeia*—incentive compatible? Did they give individuals good reasons to act in ways that were aligned with the top-ranked preferences of the state in (*ex hypothesi*) security, welfare, and nontyranny? To what extent was cooperation by individual citizens and noncitizens willed and voluntary, rather than simply coerced? What reasons did individual citizens have to pay the relatively high costs of collective self-government, in the coin of taxes (for the wealthy), public service, political participation, and attention to the common interest? Or to join in costly punishment of those who defected from cooperative norms? We will need to take diversity of preferences into account: Athenian individuals were certainly not limited to pursuing the collective interests of the state or to the elements of Glaucon's primitive triad. Many clearly shared Plato's timocrat's high-ranking of individual honor and actively sought the esteem of their fellows. Many others, per the great speech of Plato's Protagoras, were motivated by a sense of justice, whether it was defined as helping friends and harming enemies or some other distributive or retributive norm.

---

its material welfare, then the hypothesis that security and welfare are the assembly's primary concerns is strongly supported by the available evidence. Nontyranny is prominent in Athenian laws (*nomoi*) known both epigraphically and from the literary record; see Teegarden 2014.

Finally, to what extent did the rules leave room for, or actively promote, the kinds of socially valuable competition—political, economic, for public honors and private esteem—that might tend to increase (or, when otherwise directed, degrade) the aggregate welfare of the community? When did competition become destructive? Was it only, as Thucydides asserted, when competitors were politicians and their goal was the approbation of the demos? Or was competition for wealth, honors, or other goods also potentially destructive of aggregate welfare or even of state security?

Plato's charge of democratic irrationality, as sketched above, would be refuted, within the realm of feasibility if not at the level of meeting an ideal standard, if the following conditions are met: The *politeia* of the democratic state enables the formation of orderly group preferences, coherent beliefs, and a capacity to act accordingly. It promotes productive bargains and limits the likelihood of costly bargaining failures among identity and interest groups. It provides incentives to individuals to align their public and private behavior with the goals of the community writ large. Individuals compete in ways that produce relatively more rather than fewer public and private goods. That refutation would in turn offer a response to contemporary critics who claim that democracy is inherently irrational—either in terms of the impossibility of stable collective preference formation, or in terms of the incoherence or inadequacy of individual citizens' beliefs about the state of the world.

6.5 DEMOCRACY AND EXPERTS

The possibility of shared beliefs that might allow the Athenian demos' preferred outcomes of (at least) security, welfare, and nontyranny to be realized depended on two conditions: first, the presence of true expertise in the decision-making process, and, next, the willingness of the mass audience in the citizen assembly to attend to known experts when making salient choices about diplomatic and military policy relevant to security and economic and financial policy relevant to welfare.[17] In the

---

17. I discuss the use of expertise in ancient Athenian and modern democracy in more detail in Ober 2013. See further, Kallet 1994; Lewis 1997 (both on financial experts); Pyzyk 2015 (on financial and military expertise); Ismard 2017 (on the expertise provided by state-owned slaves); Fawcett 2016 (on the expertise exemplified in taxation legislation); Massar 2020 (on the employment of skilled workers in state projects); McArthur 2021 (on expert shipbuilders and naval architects). Bowden (2005) argues that on major issues the Athenians often deferred to the religious authority of nonambiguous statements

Protagoras, Plato's Socrates, speaking from personal experience (referring to the Athenians as "we"), points out to a cosmopolitan audience that, when deliberating on salient technical matters, the "wise Athenians" were willing to attend only to those they regarded as true experts, summarily rejecting speakers who are regarded as lacking the relevant expertise:

> I say, just as do the rest of the Greeks, that the Athenians are wise [*sophoi*]. Now I observe, when we are gathered in assembly, and the polis has to deal with an affair of building, we send for builders as advisors [*sumbouloi*] on what is proposed to be built; and when it is a case of warship-construction, we send for naval architects; and so in all other matters which are considered learnable and teachable. But if anyone else, whom the people do not believe to be an expert craftsman [*dēmiourgos*], attempts to advise them, no matter how handsome and wealthy and well-born he may be, not one of these things induces them to accept him. They laugh and shout him down, until either he shuts up, having been shouted down, or else the archers [state-owned slaves, employed as bouncers] either pull him down or expel him altogether by order of the *prutaneis* [councilmen charged with managing the meeting]. That is how they proceed in matters in which they believe there is relevant expertise [*technē*]. (Plato, *Protagoras* 319b–c)

Socrates' point about the practices of the "wise Athenians" implies, of course, that the Athenians do know, collectively, *what kinds* of expertise are called for in coming to particular categories of decision (say, architects for building projects), and that they are able to identify *who* is truly expert in each field and who is not. The "collective wisdom" sorting mechanism that identifies the categories of expertise relevant to a given project, and that separates experts from nonexperts, is not specified.[18] But Plato's Socrates implies that the Athenians do get

---

made by Apollo's oracle at Delphi, rather than debating matters after hearing from "secular" experts. The evidence he cites does not support that conclusion, at least if we consider security and welfare to have been prominent among those issues (see above, n. 16). Bowden's catalogue includes twenty-eight actual (nonmythic) Athenian oracular consultations before 300 BCE. Fontenrose (1978) considers eight of these dubious or not genuine (including colonization of Amphipolis, Sicilian expedition). Eight examples in the epigraphic record concern consultations regarding explicitly religious questions, having to do with cult, sacred property, etc. Three others are predemocratic. Of the nine remaining literary attestations, the only two that explicitly concern security or material state welfare are Herodotus (7.140–44) on the decision to fight at Salamis (the oracles in question were notoriously ambiguous, generating much debate) and Aristides at the battle of Plataea (Plutarch, *Life of Aristides* 11.2). There is, therefore, no reason to suppose that, during the democratic period, the Athenians regularly deferred to unambiguous statements from Delphi when deciding matters concerning security or welfare.

18. I discuss the relevant mechanisms in Ober 2008; see further, below.

the expert input necessary for the assembly to make a choice (a vote on a specific proposal) at the end of the deliberative process in which advice is offered and the assemblymen respond vocally to those who seek to advise them.

Plato's Athenians were not, therefore, burdened with the notions that are central to the deflationary arguments of contemporary epistocratic or, alternatively, neo-Rousseauian critics of participatory and deliberative democracy: They did not suppose, on the one hand, that to be an effective participant in decision-making a democratic citizen must *himself* be expert on all matters on which (or on the basis of which) he might end up casting his vote. Nor did they suppose that the proper role of an assemblyman was to sit silently, formulating a private judgment by attending to speeches by elite speakers, until it came time to vote.[19]

Socrates' description of the Athenians as "wise" is ironic, in that he immediately points out that, when considering matters for which the Athenians suppose that there are no experts, they attend to just anyone. When the Athenian Assembly deliberates "concerning the governance [*dioikēsis*] of the polis"—presumably referring to something like a law governing choice-making procedures or the election to the generalship of a leading figure like Pericles—the Athenians willingly attend to almost anyone, whether he be "a smith, a shoemaker, a merchant, a sea-captain, a rich man, a poor man, of good family or of none." Socrates argues that they do so because they accept that general political expertise is not something that can be mastered or taught (319d). Given that there are no acknowledged experts in governance as such, everyone's opinion on matters of general governance is regarded as just as likely to be valuable as anyone else's.

For Socrates of the *Protagoras*, "governance" and the true expert in governance (the master of *politikē technnē*) must be centrally concerned with the rationality of ends, that is, the perfection of souls, and not just the material conditions of security and welfare. The Athenians reject the very idea that there could be knowledgeable experts on the vital (for Plato's Socrates) question of what they *ought* to prefer or how to go about getting it, even if, counterfactually, they knew what it was. But they were, it seems, adequately rational in the instrumental sense of (1) consistently preferring to live with security (e.g., building warships) and material welfare over any available alternatives, (2) formulating the relevant beliefs

---

19. Epistocratic arguments: nn. 11 and 12, above. Neo-Rousseauian critique of public deliberation: Cammack 2013a, 2013b, 2020, and below, n. 26.

with expert assistance, and (3) carrying through with actions that led, more or less reliably, to what they regarded as the best available outcome.

Just how did it work in practice? How was expertise integrated into democratic decision-making, so as to produce relatively high state performance? Plato's primary focus on ethical rationality meant he felt no need to offer detailed answers to that question. But it is highly salient in light of contemporary epistemic critiques of democracy. The remaining sections of this chapter shift from ancient Greek historical narrative and political theory to contemporary theoretically informed attempts to explicate Athenian institutional practice. Because "how Athenian democracy worked" is a question to which I have devoted much of my career, what follows in this chapter draws in part on my own earlier work. But recent scholarship by other historians of Greece has gone a long way towards fundamentally revising our understanding of the Athenian *politeia* and how it operated in practice. In the remaining sections of this chapter, I have highlighted some of this new work that is especially salient in addressing the question of the rationality of Greek democratic states.

6.6 LEGISLATION

Socrates of Plato's *Protagoras* takes the policy-making procedure of the Athenian assembly as exemplary of the practice of the "wise Athenians" in attending to experts in those technical areas in which they supposed true experts could be identified. Likewise, in his famous account of the possibility of the practical "wisdom of the many," Aristotle (*Politics* 3.11) seems to have in mind the legislative procedures of a democratic state—plausibly, of the one he knew best from his long residence—Athens.[20] In Athens, and other democratic Greek poleis, the citizen assembly held decision authority. That authority was not unconstrained: In fourth-century Athens, policy decisions made by the assembly as "decrees" (*psēphismata*) were legally required to conform to the established constitutional laws (*nomoi*) and were subject to judicial review. But it was the citizens themselves (represented, through synecdoche, by the part of the citizen body that attended the assembly or sat in the law court: Ober 1996: 117–20; Cammack 2021) who made the constitutional rules and reviewed the legality of decrees of the assembly when they were challenged by a concerned citizen (below, section 5.6).

20. Aristotle on the "wisdom of the many": Ober 2013; Hatzistavrou 2021; Schwartz (2022: chap. 5.2) offers a new interpretation, with updated literature review.

The fourth-century Athenian legislative process is, at this point, tolerably well understood (Canevaro 2015), and offers a case study in institutional rationality.

Preferences, Beliefs, and High Stakes

Beginning with preferences, it is vital to keep in mind that the decision-making by the democratic assembly of a Greek polis frequently concerned matters that can generally be described as "high stakes." The world of the Greek city-states was competitive, often violent, and unforgiving. While the world of the fourth-century city-states was prosperous by comparative premodern standards (chapter 7.1), ordinary Greeks lived closer to the level of subsistence than most people in modern "developed" countries. Tyranny—of an individual or a junta—was a persistent threat. Moreover, despite impressive advances in the management of state finances, the capacity of the state to borrow money or to run deficits was limited (Migeotte 2014). Therefore, despite the diversity of group-level and individual preferences represented in the Athenian population, much Athenian legislation tended to concern one or more items in the basic "security, welfare, nontyranny" triad. Decisions on relatively low-stakes questions were made by citizens who had developed habits of judgment based on a persistent need to make choices on high-stakes issues.

Matters of security (internal or external) and welfare debated in the assembly might concern all Athenians or some subset of the Athenian population. In the example cited by Socrates of the *Protagoras,* building warships, the background assumption was that the state's security required a certain number of ships to be built, within a specified time frame, and within some cost constraint.[21] The question we may suppose the expert naval architects were expected to answer was, then: How many ships of the requisite quality could be built, how quickly, for what cost? The preference ordering of the majority, if not all, citizens might be something like this: (1) high level of security at an affordable cost (minimal risk of insecurity); (2) moderate level of security at an affordable cost (higher, but still acceptable risk of insecurity); (3) high level of security, but at the cost of much lower welfare; (4) insecurity.

21. Decisions concerning building and maintenance of warships are detailed in a number of fourth-century inscriptions; see discussion in Gabrielsen 1994; O'Halloran 2019; McArthur 2021.

How the demos could know that this was indeed the preference ordering of a majority of its members remains to be seen; we return to that question, below.

Assume, for the moment, that the preferences of the assembly on the matter of shipbuilding were adequately well ordered and that the right actions were carried out following the decision. What beliefs did the assembled citizens have about (inter alia) numbers and quality of ships, time frame, and cost, that were relevant to judging the feasibility of options, assessing likelihoods of possible outcomes, and thereby choosing the highest-ranked available option (say, option 2, above, should option 1 prove infeasible)?

The standard Athenian "enactment formula" for a legislative decree was *edoxe tēi boulēi kai tōi demōi*: "It seemed right to the council and the assembly that . . ." The active verb is *edoxe*, from *dokeō*, "I expect, think, imagine." Legislation was, therefore, explicitly predicated on a claim about beliefs that were held by two collectivities: the council of five hundred citizens, chosen by lottery for a one-year term, and the assembly, that is, the six to eight thousand Athenians who attended the legislative meeting in question and voted on the final form of the enactment. The passage in Plato's *Protagoras* points to the essential role of expertise in the decision process. Socrates has confidently asserted that the Athenians were capable of recognizing and attending to experts, and thus potentially to updating their beliefs, at least on technical matters, like shipbuilding. The expert testimony by the naval architects was relevant to forming coherent, presumably more or less reality-tracking, beliefs about the relevant issues. Nonexpert incompetents were not given the opportunity to speak for long on the matter; their opinions were rejected by the collective action of the assemblymen (who shouted them down from the podium) because nonexpert opinions were regarded as irrelevant (or worse, antithetical) to the formation of the right set of beliefs on the matter at hand. Insofar as the Athenian democratic system succeeded in providing the polis with, inter alia, warships, the procedure seems to have met the basic requirements of instrumental rationality.

But how? The ability of thousands of ordinary people to decide on a complex matter like military procurement may appear mysterious— even granted a high-stakes environment conducive to preference alignment, the presence within the community of relevant expertise, and the willingness of the decision-makers to attend to them. But the mystery is solved when we consider the institutional design of council and assembly, the procedural rules that governed decision-making at each step in the process, and the behavioral habits that had emerged with experience in working the constitutional machinery.

Council of Five Hundred

The Council of Five Hundred (*boulē*), which met most days of the year in a purpose-built building (*bouleutērion*), was the product of the original, late-sixth-century Cleisthenic reforms. Its five hundred members were chosen, in an annual lottery, based on demes, thirds, and tribes. Every Athenian citizen was an ancestral member of one of 139 demes (*dēmoi:* villages and urban neighborhoods) in Athens' home territory of Attica. Each deme was assigned a quota of councilmen (*bouleutai*), based on its citizen population. A deme, and thus its council delegation, was an administrative subunit of one of thirty regional "thirds" (*trittyes*). Each third, roughly one-thirtieth of Athens' total population, consisted of several demes (occasionally just one) in one of the three (coastal, inland, and urban/suburban) primary regions of Athens' territory. Three thirds, one from each of the three regions, constituted a "tribe" (*phulē*). While each tribe was assigned an "ancestral hero" as its putative founder, the tribes were explicitly artificial: created at a specific historical moment, to answer the administrative needs of an emergent democratic state.

Each tribe consisted of a roughly equal number of citizens, a tenth of the whole citizenry, drawn from different parts of Athenian territory. Each of the ten tribes sent fifty members to the council each year. Tribes were also the basis for various forms of religious ritual and the recruitment of men for the land army. This system of artificial tribes required Athenians from different parts of Athens' extensive (by Greek standards) territory to cooperate in various domains (politics, religion, war). It facilitated the formation of substate identities that were, however, oriented toward the state-level *koinōnia,* and so served as a counterweight to traditional regional or subregional loyalties.

It is likely that in any given year the council, and the ten tribal teams of which it was composed, were roughly representative of the social composition of the demos as a whole. The limited number of citizens aged thirty and above available to serve, combined with the restriction of service to no more than two nonconsecutive terms, meant that the majority of the councilmen must have been from outside the wealthy elite. Councilmen were paid for their service, so the poor were not excluded. The design of the council thus militated against the systematic domination by any interest or identity group.[22]

The council was responsible for carrying out a variety of administrative, fiscal, juridical, and diplomatic functions, in addition to the duties that are our primary concerns here: setting the agenda for meetings of the assembly and making policy recommendations. The council's work was structured around the ten fifty-member tribe-teams. Each team held the "presidency" (as *prutaneis*) of the council for an equal (tenth of the year) period; a third of the *prutaneis* of the tribe holding the presidency (sixteen or seventeen men) were responsible for remaining on twenty-four-hour duty. During that time, they were fed at state expense in another purpose-built public building (*prutanikon*). The Councilmen were provided with a permanent secretarial staff of literate and experienced public slaves. They had ready access to the next-door public archives, which included all of the currently valid laws and decrees.[23]

The Greek term for public council (*boulē*) refers directly to a deliberative function (*bouleusis*). Although there is no preserved account of the council's deliberative process, we can readily imagine free-form discussions among the sixteen or seventeen *prutaneis* housed in the *prutanikon* (a round, one-room building) and among the members of the fifty-man tribal teams. Policy debates in the full five-hundred-member council would presumably have been more formal, modeled on the speaker-audience relationship of the assembly (below).

Given that a high percentage of all Athenians over age thirty served for a year on the council, and that virtually all Athenians would know former councilors as members of their immediate social network, an entering councilor would have begun his year's service with a good practical sense of how the institution functioned, what was expected of him, and what he might gain from his experience as a councilor. I have suggested, elsewhere (Ober 2008: chap. 4), that individual councilors would have had private incentives to use their year as a council member to establish social connections beyond their local-network deme-delegations, among other members of their tribal teams, and among the 450 other council members. Overall, the full council had a collective incentive to perform its duties well—both in light of the high stakes of polis-

22. Council of Five Hundred, its organization and duties: Rhodes 1985; Ober 2008: chap. 4. Political geography of Attica: Hansen 1999: 101–6, with literature cited.
23. Public slaves: Ismard 2017. Archives: Sickinger 1999. Public buildings: Camp 2001.

level decision-making and because the assembly would annually decide whether or not to grant the year's council special honors.

The business of the full council was carried out through attending to and responding to speeches by council members, state officials, or domain experts summoned by the council: The council-building was designed as a small "Greek theater"–style auditorium. A few surviving speeches were delivered before the full council, serving in its judicial function, and we know that the council heard expert testimony relevant to its agenda-setting and advisory functions, for example from the elected generals (see below). Council decisions were made by voting on proposals by show of raised hands (Hansen 1999: 253). Per Mirko Canevaro's reconstruction of the voting process in the full assembly (below), we may imagine that the council worked towards consensus decisions in many, perhaps most cases.

Insofar as specific interests and identities were represented among a year-class of councilors, the deliberative context and the opportunities for building trust made credible commitment, and thus productive bargains, relatively more likely. While there was ample room for strategic behavior, intimate conditions and relatively small numbers lowered the cost of collective action: exposing egoistically self-interested behavior that could have reduced opportunities for cooperative outcomes, while increasing the social incentive to join in costly punishment of norm-violators. Finally, the term limit on service (with complete turnover after each year), while setting an endpoint to whatever repeated games were played among the year's cohort of councilors, prevented the formation of a corporate identity with interests other than those of the community at large.

In sum, the conditions under which the Athenian Council of Five Hundred made decisions were conducive to both deliberation and instrumental rationality, offering adequate opportunity for the pursuit of individual and subgroup self-interest within constraints that pushed in the direction of aligning private and public interests: small- and mid-sized group deliberations; wide experience with the decision-making process; the provision of skilled secretaries; access to archives; testimony by experts; individual and group-level incentives for good performance—and all against the background of high-stakes conditions driving up the costs of failure. The small size of the tribal teams facilitated mutual monitoring, and thus pushed back against any tendency to free-ride. In sum, it is plausible to suppose that these conditions enabled the five hundred councilors to model the choice process of a rational, well-informed individual.

Citizen Assembly

In the fourth century, the citizen assembly met, usually in a purpose-built theater-like open-air space (Pnyx) forty times each year (four meetings in each thirty-five/thirty-six-day prytany). Some meetings had certain fixed agenda items; every fourth meeting was designated "principal" (*kuria*) and (at least in theory) addressed topics of special salience. The agenda of the meeting was announced, in written public notices, in advance. Any citizen in good standing could attend any meeting. Citizens who attended (at least up to a quorum) were paid for their service; the rate of pay increased over the course of the fourth century. Meetings typically lasted half a day. Although the six to eight thousand citizens present at a given assembly were never perfectly descriptively representative of the entire body of approximately thirty thousand, there is little reason to suppose that assemblies were, over time, systematically biased for or against any significant sociological subset of the broader citizen population.

The meeting was presided over by a small group of "presiders" (*proedroi*) drawn by lot from the nine tribal teams of councilors whose tribe did not hold the presidency at the time of the meeting. The *proedroi* introduced (through a herald) each item on the agenda and announced the council's recommendation (*probouleuma*), if any. At that point, the floor was opened to "any of the Athenians with advice to give." As Mogens Hansen (1999: 140, 149) has shown, given the large number of decisions that had to be made in the course of a year, in many cases the council's recommendation was accepted by the assembly without dissent and the measure passed by consensus. But in other cases, debate ensued. Expert testimony was given and attended to. The council's recommendation could be, and often was, amended or replaced by a motion from the floor.[24]

Per the passage in Plato's *Protagoras,* advice on technical matters from those regarded as uninformed was unlikely to be tolerated. In some cases, testimony was given as "point of information." But in other cases, a speaker made a legislative recommendation in the form of a written text of a decree (or an amendment to a proposed decree) that was passed to the *proedroi* for consideration by the assembly. Certain citizens, recognized as "the usual speakers," had developed reputations for having special expertise and useful sources of information on particular areas—for example, foreign policy or finance. They were likely

---

24. On the schedule, demographics, and procedures of the assembly, see Hansen 1987, summarized in Hansen 1999: 125–60.

to be recognized by the *proedroi* and attended to (at least for a while) by the assemblymen. But the usual speakers held no formal office—they were ordinary citizens, not state magistrates—and there is ample evidence for measures being proposed by citizens outside the group of well-known "active politicians" and recognized experts.[25]

Based on an exhaustive survey of evidence from Athens and other democratic poleis, Mirko Canevaro (2018, 2020a) has recently proposed a convincing, although necessarily partly speculative, reconstruction of the assembly decision-making process. Canevaro argues that in the case of multiple floor proposals, the *proedroi* played a central role by deciding which proposal would be put to a final vote. He suggests that the process they employed was broadly deliberative, in the sense that public speakers offered for reasons for policy options they proposed or supported. The process was also highly sensitive to opinions that were clearly expressed (through audience response to proposals) and widely held (as measured by the level of that response).[26] The *proedroi* accepted written proposals for amendments from the floor. They announced and allowed debate on those that they regarded as most viable, assessing the "sense of the meeting" on sequentially presented proposals. Their assessment was based on audible, via "uproar" (*thorubos*), and visible signs of approval or dissent in the mass audience. They rejected those proposals that found little audience support.

Canevaro suggests that the goal of the *proedroi,* and the collective aim of the assembly as an experienced body of citizens, was to work towards a measure that could gain wide, perhaps even universal assent. They did so by employing the process of entertaining proposals, attending to and responding to speeches, and observing public responses. The decisions of the *proedroi* were made in real time and those decisions were not subject to the formal accountability procedures characteristic of the democracy.[27] But by the same token, those decisions were made

25. On the usual speakers and participation by nonexpert speakers, see Hansen 1983, 1984; Ober 1989: chap. 3.

26. In a detailed study of the relevant Greek vocabulary, Cammack (2020) argues that the process of the assembly was not based on public deliberation. But her definition of what counts as deliberation, based on the very demanding regulative ideal employed by contemporary theorists of deliberative democracy (equal opportunity for public reason-giving by all participants, along with respectful consideration by all of every reasonable position so presented), appears to me excessively restrictive.

27. On the central role of accountability in Athenian democracy, and the contrast between accountable officials and advisers and the formally unaccountable demos, see Landauer 2019.

by a lotteried cross section of the citizenry. Decisions were transparent in that the assembly was an intervisible space, in which each citizen could observe the response of his fellows to a given proposal.

When the *proedroi* believed that a proposal had gained a high enough level of support, they put it to the vote. Most votes were by open show of hands and the yes/no result was announced by the *proedroi,* based on their estimate of the count. Only in rare cases (and through a special procedure) was the vote held by pebble-ballot and exactly counted (Hansen 1999: 147–48). Canevaro points out that, where we do have evidence of actual counted votes, largely from Hellenistic-era democratic poleis, most votes are reported as being either unanimous or nearly so. Clearly not every Athenian vote was consensual or even close to it. Thucydides (3.49.1) makes a point of the narrowness of the majority by which the Athenian assembly chose to overturn a previous decision to execute the entire male population of Mytilene in 427 (chapter 5.6). While direct Athenian evidence remains scarce, Canevaro makes a strong case for consensus or near-consensus voting as a norm in the fourth-century Athenian assembly and other democratic Greek citizen assemblies.

Assuming, *ex hypothesi,* that Canevaro is correct about the procedure (whatever the actual frequency of close votes), was a deliberative, consensus-seeking approach to large-group decision-making conducive to rational and effective choice-making? In open "show of hands" voting of the Athenian type, there can be no question of sustaining the independence of individual voter judgment, a key factor in many Condorcet-type jury theorem results. The likelihood of cascades of opinion-leader or cue following (whether positive, in respect to correctness of judgment, or otherwise) was high.[28]

Opinion-leader and cue following in the assembly might well (and no doubt sometimes did) result in a poor choice—that is, failed to select an available option that (in retrospect) would have better served the state's interests, and would have been identified and chosen by an ideal-type prudent legislator. But the process leading to the poor choice need not have been instrumentally irrational: If we assume reasonably well-aligned and orderly baseline preferences among most of those present, it may be rational for an individual to follow the lead of those he regards as better informed than himself on a given topic. If A and B agree on the high priority of security—and, therefore, that ships must be built and that cost is a factor—and A is regarded as both trustworthy and expert

28. See, for discussion, Goodin and Spiekermann 2018: chap. 4.

on naval affairs, B may rationally follow A's lead on which of several proposals is most efficacious, even if B is, as it turns out, mistaken about A's character or level of expertise.[29]

We need not, therefore, conclude that Athenian assemblies were typically irrational on the basis of, for example, Thucydides' well-known account of the cascade of voter enthusiasm that led to the catastrophic (in retrospect) quasi-consensual (in that dissenters were frightened into silence) decision by the Athenian assembly in 415 BCE to send a gigantic invasion fleet to Sicily. Consensual decisions by a democratic assembly may sometimes be, but are not necessarily, driven by strong but short-lived emotional states (in Thucydides' account of 415: *erōs*) or by beliefs based on systematically biased information (Alcibiades' claims about disorder in Sicilian poleis, the Segestans' success in tricking Athenian ambassadors concerning the resources that would be available to support the Athenian forces once they arrived in Sicily).[30]

The counterfactual fails: Were raw emotion and misinformation the primary inputs into most Athenian assembly decisions, it would be impossible to explain how democratic Athens rose to power in the Greek world, fought a long war, or recovered after that war. Moreover, we need not suppose—following, for example, Thucydides' even better-known claim (2.65.9) that, although the demos was master of state affairs in name, Pericles was the true ruler of Athens—that a demos becomes capable of acting rationally and effectively *only* when it accurately follows the lead of an exceptionally talented, rational, and charismatic leader. The Athenian assembly proved capable of making decisions that, on the whole, conduced to Athens' security and welfare, both before and after the rise to prominence of Pericles. And by the same token, during the period of Pericles' ascendency the assembly made decisions that proved, in retrospect, both good and bad in respect to gaining those ends.[31]

Nor, finally, need we accept the claim made by ancient and modern critics of participatory democracy—for example, by the "Old Oligarch," *Politeia of the Athenians* (above)—that the demos (here, understood as "the nonelite majority") was rational *only* in the sense of acting consistently as an egoistically self-interested collective tyrant. The Old Oligarch notes that some Athenians were "not by nature ordinary

---

29. I discussed this sort of rational cue following in Ober 2008: chap. 5.

30. Thucydides on the Sicilian Debate: Ober 1998a: 104–13, with literature cited.

31. A charismatic thought-leader undermines whatever wisdom of the many may arise from democratic process: cf. Goodin and Spiekermann 2018.

people," yet they were "genuinely part of the demos" (*alēthōs tou dēmou*). He attributes the choice of elites actively to support democracy to inherent wickedness and a belief that injustice would be more easily hidden in a democracy than an oligarchy. But this flies in the face of the author's own assertion that "one must forgive everyone [*panti*] for looking after his own interests" (2.19–20). Many Athenian elites did well for themselves as active participants in a high-performing polis (Ober 1989). The elite choice of loyalty, being "of the people," was not a "live or die" least-bad of the sort faced by Herodotus' Gyges (chapter 1.6). The options of exit (opt out of politics, move to another polis) and voice (object to democratic decisions, and indeed to the democratic order) remained viable for disaffected elites.[32]

The *potential* for the decision procedure of the assembly to devolve into a kind of majority tyranny was, nevertheless, a genuine concern. Arguably, the realization of that potential at certain moments in the later years of the Peloponnesian War contributed to Athens' failure in that long conflict. As Federica Carugati (2019) has argued in detail, the legal reforms of the last decade of the fifth century appear to have been aimed specifically at addressing that manifest danger. This meant building on the original Solonian bargain between mass and elite and amending the Cleisthenic constitutional order that had been established at the end of the sixth century, and subsequently modified across the course of the fifth.

6.7 LAW AND COURTS

In the last decade of the fifth century, the Athenian system of law-making and the constitutional relationship between courts and assembly were substantially revised. The stakes were especially high because they were undertaken in the context of civil war. In 411 and again in 404, the threat of violence between Athenian elites and masses, averted since the original Solonian bargain, had been realized in bloody fact. Immediately after the democratic restorations of 410 and 403, and in the years following, the potential for renewed violence remained high. As Edwin Carawan (2013) has demonstrated, the Amnesty of 403, which followed the fall of the oligarchic regime of the Thirty, took the form of a contract between the "men of the city"—the oligarchic followers of the

---

32. The options of "loyalty, exit, and voice": Hirschman 1970. Exit option for Athenian elites: Carter 1986; dissent option: Ober 1998a.

Thirty—and the "men of Piraeus," that is, the victorious democrats. Moreover, as Federica Carugati (2019) has shown, the legal reforms of the late fifth century, and therefore the Athenian legal system of the fourth century, were likewise predicated on a contractual solution, a revised constitutional bargain aimed at forestalling further conflict. The reforms left intact the Solonian foundation, the Cleisthenic institutional framework, and the established criteria for citizenship. But the new bargain enhanced the predictability of legislative outcomes and legal judgments on constitutional matters. Carugati emphasizes that, although achieved without an arbitrator, the new order was seen by the Athenians as a renewal of the Solon's bargaining solution of 594 BCE, now reimagined as an ancestral commitment to legality.[33]

Constitutionalism and Legal Procedure

In the decade following the democratic restoration of 410, for the first time since the original "laws of Solon" had been inscribed and made public, all currently valid Athenian laws were codified and archived. A fundamental rule of noncontradiction among the standing laws was reaffirmed as a central principle of Athenian law. A clear hierarchical distinction was established between a legislative decree (*psēphisma*) and constitutional law (*nomos*). All decrees must now conform to the existing laws and every new law must either conform to the existing laws or mandate the revocation of those it contradicted. The process of constitutional lawmaking, now by large panels of "lawmakers" (*nomothetai*), was distinguished from, and made substantially more cumbersome than, the ordinary process of making policy in a regular assembly.

Although there is disagreement over various procedural details, students of Athenian law have been able to reconstruct the main lines of the new system, based on the comprehensive account of courtroom procedure in the Aristotelian *Ath. Pol.* and a substantial body of preserved courtroom speeches and documents.[34] Moreover, despite an ongoing

---

33. Athens' fourth-century Rule of Law: Forsdyke 2018, with literature cited. Commitment to legality: Carugati 2019, and see below.

34. Canavero (2015, 2016, 2018b, 2020b) and Canevaro and Esu (2018) offer a new interpretation of the *nomothesia* process, in which the *nomothetai* are understood not as a body of *dikastai*, in a kind of law-making trial pitting an existing law (or laws) against a proposed alternative, but as the *ekklēsiastai* meeting in a special "lawmaking" session. They review earlier interpretations of the process. For what has long been the canonical version, see Hansen 1999: 161–77.

scholarly debate on the nature of the "rule of law" at Athens, tHere is an adequate level of scholarly consensus on the substantive jurisprudential issues of direct relevance to our question of system-level rationality (Forsdyke 2018).

Most Athenian disputes that would, in Anglo-American law, be considered civil, criminal, and constitutional cases were tried in people's courts (*dikastēria*). The ordinary procedure in most criminal cases was, in bare outline, as follows: A concerned citizen brought a charge of law-violation against an individual to the relevant magistrate. After receiving written testimony from both sides, the magistrate referred the matter to the people's court for judgment. Each case was heard by several hundred jurors (*dikastai*). Jurors were chosen in an elaborate lottery from the approximately six thousand citizens over age thirty who had taken the juror's oath at the beginning of that year and who made themselves available for duty on a given day.

The *dikastai* served, collectively, as judges; the presiding magistrate was only responsible for ensuring that procedures were correctly followed. Prosecutor and defendant each gave a timed speech outlining their positions. Speeches were of identical length, measured by a water-clock; the clock was stopped for the reading of what the litigants claimed were the relevant sections of the law code and for reading out of written testimony (provided, under seal, by the magistrate, based on his preliminary investigation). Having heard both sides, the jurors voted, by secret ballot. Unlike modern Anglo-American jury trials, there was no formal deliberation among jurors and no attempt to achieve consensus. Rather, the decision was by simple majority; the number of votes for prosecutor and defendant was publicly announced. If the defendant was judged guilty, in cases concerning various public matters, a sentencing phase followed. A second vote was held to decide between penalties suggested by prosecutor and defendant. The entire trial process was completed in a day.[35]

For our purposes, the constitutional reforms of the late fifth century and two categories of legal procedure concerning charges of constitutional violation are of special importance. First is the procedure of *graphē paranomōn* (written charge of illegality in policymaking). In this

35. What Anglo-American law would consider constitutional and criminal trials were "public" cases (*graphai*), and what we could consider civil cases were "private" (*dikai*). While procedural details varied, the basic approach in cases tried by *dikakstēria* was similar; murder trials and certain cases judged by the Areopagus were tried under a range of somewhat different procedures. See survey in Hansen 1999: 178–224, 290–94.

procedure the prosecutor (potentially any citizen in good standing) claimed that a proposal had been made or a decree (*psēphisma*) had been passed in the assembly that was contrary to the established constitutional rules (*nomoi*) or otherwise inimical to the public interest. Next is the procedure of *graphē nomon mē epitēdeion theinai* (written charge that a law was unsuitably established). In this procedure the prosecutor charged that a constitutional rule (*nomos*) had been proposed or passed that was contrary to one or more of the established laws or was otherwise inimical to the public interest. In either case, the procedure enabled any concerned citizen to serve as public prosecutor, bringing a charge of wrongdoing against another citizen, just as he would in a criminal case. The defendant was the author of the proposal, decree, or law. The prosecutor faced a penalty if he received fewer than one-fifth of the votes. In the case of a charge leveled against a proposed decree or law, the proposal was tabled until after the trial had been held. It was invalidated in the case of a guilty verdict. In the case of a decree or law that had been passed, a conviction in the trial resulted in the statute being voided.

The reforms were enacted in a context of concern that the processes of government could be captured or perverted. By the late fifth century the Athenians recognized the capacity of skilled and self-interested speakers to affect the process of public decision-making in ways that were potentially disadvantageous to the interests of the demos. Clever orators, some of them trained by sophistic rhetoricians like Gorgias and with narrowly egoistic motivations like those of Callicles, were capable of persuading the demos to take a course of action that it would not otherwise have taken. Persuasion of the sort celebrated by Gorgias in his *Defense of Helen* (LM 32.D24), and by Plato's Gorgias in the dialogue named for him, aimed at gaining the speaker's ends through the strategic manipulation of instrumental reasoning. The speaker might reorder the audience's preferences by amplifying fears or desires. The audience might come to have false beliefs regarding the availability of options or the probability of their achievement. If the demos consequently made foolish—excessively risky or overly cautious—choices, the chance for catastrophe was high.

In Plato's dialogue, Gorgias seeks to exculpate the trained orator from responsibility for harms suffered by listeners subjected to his persuasive treatment (*Gorgias* 457b). But Socrates does not let Gorgias and his students off so easily, His point is that unless the orator actually has genuine knowledge of what outcome is good for the treated "patient," he is in the position of a fake doctor peddling unwholesome snacks in the guise of healing medicine. Socrates famously did not choose to address Athenian legislative bodies and few of the Athenians who voted for the legal reforms sketched above would have had the arsenal of Socratic elenchus to bring to bear on the question of how to fix what was dysfunctional in the apparatus of public decision. But evidently a majority of them had come to the conclusion that public speakers must be held accountable for the reasonably predictable results of their persuasive speech.

The new legal procedures gave the demos an institutionalized means of holding public speakers to account and to punish those who were regarded as having misused their powers of persuasion. The man whose name was attached to the law or decree was now held legally liable for its consistency with existing law and potentially for its bad effects. Political rivals and opponents of the policy were, therefore, provided with a potent legal weapon. The rational potential proposer, looking down the game tree, would be hesitant to advocate an excessively risky policy, even if he was sure that he could stir up at least momentary popular enthusiasm for it. The new rules reduced the demos' tendency to take risks in excess of what the Athenians, in their normal, "unexcited" psychological condition, would be willing to countenance.

The legal mechanism thereby modeled one of the benefits that Thucydides (2.65.9) attributes to Pericles' employment of salutary public rhetoric: pushing back against excessive risk-taking. But what of the other side of the coin, also emphasized by Thucydides in the same passage: the importance to state flourishing of rational risk-taking and the dangers associated with excessive risk aversion? Why was the legal weapon not overused, constraining potential proposers so that valuable innovations were foregone?

Rational Agents and Constitutional Change

Building on recent scholarship on Athenian law, Carugati (2019) answers that question by revisiting the question of Athens' constitutional order in the late fifth and fourth centuries. She argues persuasively that the reforms represent a new constitutional bargain, struck in the high-stakes context of the post–civil war era, between ordinary and elite Athenians. The masses agreed not to punish elites for participation in the oligarchy and not to expropriate their property. The elite in turn agreed to participate in the democracy, inter alia by paying expensive liturgies. The bargain resulted in a stable, self-enforcing constitutional order. At the heart of the new order was a rough consensus among Athenians on the fundamental value of legality, now understood in terms of legal coherence and consistency: This meant noncontradiction among the laws, and an expectation that new decrees and laws would reflect what was reimagined as a deep, ancestral, Athenian commitment to legality.[36]

Ancestral devotion to legality was seen as having been exemplified by the original laws of Solon and by the manifest judicious wisdom of the lawgiver himself. Abiding by the bargain came to be regarded by the Athenians as a contractual obligation, and it was enforced as such. Deviation from the contract was taken as not only a violation of a strongly held norm, but also a threat to social order. The threat was real given that coordination on legality had allowed the Athenians to exit the civil war period without devolving into a downward gyre of sectarian violence. Here, in the promulgation of a legal doctrine and its associated behaviors, we see a practical instantiation of the process of mutual teaching and learning that Socrates' Protagoras postulated as the origin of a self-enforcing social order (chapter 2.6). Like Protagoras' thought experiment, the Athenian practical solution was predicated on the establishment of law, obedience to law, and reliable punishment of lawbreakers.

Carugati's account of Athens' fourth-century constitutional order emphasizes its status as a self-enforcing agreement, rather than as the result of third-party intervention by the victorious Spartans after the Peloponnesian War.[37] She conceives of the new order as an equilibrium, in a game-theoretic sense: no player had a better move in light of the moves available to others. As such, she shows why the Athenian constitutional order may be counted as rational. The new order enabled Athenians, as individuals, as interest groups, and as a community, to make, obey, and enforce decisions based on orderly preferences and coherent beliefs.[38] As Carugati demonstrates, it also allowed the Athenians to respond to new challenges, through institutional innovations.[39]

To be effective, innovations must be responsive to opportunities and demands of new situations. Yet, if a social order is to be self-enforcing,

36. Carugati 2019, drawing on, inter alia, Carawan 2013; Lanni 2006; Shear 2011.

37. This is a key distinction between Carugati's interpretation of the new constitutional order and that of Carawan (2013).

38. It is an important part of Carugati's argument that the bargain extended beyond the citizen body, to the various noncitizens whose lives were, one way or another, entangled with the lives of citizens. See further, Akrigg 2014; Claire Taylor 2015.

39. Athenian innovations: Ober 2008; D'Angour 2011.

innovations must not undermine the reasons that people have to continue to pay the costs necessary for its persistence. The dynamic rationality of the Athenian *politeia* hung on the robustness of the balance between creative destruction of institutional arrangements ill-adapted to current circumstances and the underlying stability of the shared commitment to legal order and the coherence of the institutions that reflected and sustained that commitment.

Carugati argues that the constitutional balancing act was predicated on the existence of numerous veto points. Most obviously, as we have seen, every citizen held a potential veto, in the form of a right to legally challenge any new law or policy proposal made in the legislative assembly. And yet if innovations were to be responsive to new opportunities and threats, the veto must not be overused. So, we come back to the question posed above: Why would a citizen who was in some ways disadvantaged by a new rule *not* choose to initiate a legal challenge, thereby at least delaying and potentially voiding the disfavored change? As Carugati (2019; cf. Carugati and Weingast 2018; Carugati, Calvert, and Weingast 2020) shows, through a formal model, the new procedure had implications for a decree proposer capable of working his way up and back down the game tree. Carugati's answer to the question of why the procedure did not lead to ossification is that a legal challenge to a change widely regarded as beneficial would be rejected (and the challenger in various ways punished) unless the challenger could show that his challenge aimed at preventing a violation of a core principle of legality—that is, that the proposed change was inconsistent with established norms or contradicted established laws.

Employing a variant on the well-known median voter theorem (Downs 1957), Carugati sets up a *graphē paranomōn* game, based on the following premises: In light of the consensus on legality, the "median Athenian juror" had relatively stable preferences over outcomes and had beliefs, normative and pragmatic, that were similar to those of the median assemblyman. Policy innovators (those who might propose a new rule) were capable of roughly estimating those preferences. Innovators were motivated both by concern for honor or reputation and for achieving their preferred policy outcomes. When the median juror's preferences over outcomes diverged from the outcomes expected from the status quo, a policy innovator could safely (*without* serious danger to his reputation and *with* the chance of winning honors) propose a new policy, knowing that any legal challenge would have to be in the form of defending the disfavored status quo.

So long as the proposed reform (1) offered expected outcomes that were nearer (on an imaginary line, assuming a one-dimensional policy space) to the ideal point (most-preferred policy) of the median juror than were the outcomes expected from the status quo, (2) was consistent with established norms, and (3) did not contradict the existing laws, the policy was not at risk of being overturned by a *graphē paranomōn:* If the policy was challenged in court, the challenge could be expected to fail. Assuming rational players in this game, and in light of the high costs of a failed prosecution, proposals should be carefully written to avoid legal inconsistency, should be offered only when there was a perceived gap between the status quo and the ideal point of the median juror, and should not stray too far from that ideal point.

So long as those conditions were met, innovations should be proposed whenever the existing rules were widely regarded as suboptimal, legal challenges to popular innovations should be rare, and successful challenges even rarer. Carugati's model shows that even proposers of new legislation with personal preferences for major changes were constrained to attend to the preferences of average Athenians. But it also shows that a proposer seeking change might move some way from the status quo without taking excessive personal risks. Taken together, these results suggest that the challenge procedure enabled innovations in state policy without jeopardizing the social order.

In short, the rationality of the Athenian constitutional order depended on the willingness of each citizen to obey the laws and to participate in the enforcement of them. But Athens was not subject to a strong form of path dependency and thus was able to respond adaptively to environmental challenges—if not always to answer the challenge in a definitive or fully satisfactory way. Of course, in reality, neither Athenian politicians nor Athenian jurors were ideal-type rational agents with complete information capable of flawless backwards induction; if they had been, we would expect the *graphē paranomōn* never to be employed—as of course it was.[40] The game-theoretic model predicts behavior of ideal-type rational agents. When it is tested against the evidence (Carugati 2019, chap. 4; Carugati, Calvert, and Weingast 2020) it proves to have enough predictive power to allow an important conclusion: An institution that, in effect, gives every citizen a veto over all legislation played a key role in sustaining the Athenian self-enforcing social equilibrium.

---

40. Hansen 1999: 208–12 with references.

6.8 INDIVIDUALS AND OFFICIALS, INITIATIVE AND EXECUTION

If a democratic state is to make rational choices in ways that are relevantly similar to an instrumentally rational individual, as imagined by the Greek folk theory, several conditions must be met: Public decision-making bodies (notably those considered above) must be capable of aggregating individual preferences and beliefs. Those bodies must be representative, in the sense of standing for or being taken as, the demos. Assuming that, per discussion above, those conditions are adequately met, there still must be the right relationship between collective choices and the behavior of those individuals responsible for *initiating* the process leading to the decision, and then for *executing* the demos' mandate.

With reference to their specific role in the process, the individuals in question must be capable of adequately competent performance and must be held to an acceptable standard of loyalty to the regime. The competence criterion requires that they be adequately expert in their role, or have ready access to the relevant kinds of expertise, such that they are able to carry out their duties in a reasonably competent way. The loyalty criterion requires that the public behavior of the individuals in question be adequately well aligned with the background values of the demos, as expressed in its laws and norms. They must expect to be punished if they are discovered to be treasonous or corrupt. In the case of those with executive responsibility, loyalty requires that officials act in accordance with the decisions of public bodies. They must fulfill the specific demands for action that the public decision imposes on them.

The test of the co-presence of competence and loyalty at the level of individual initiative and follow-through is whether there is a meaningful and more or less predictable causal relationship leading from initiative to decision, and from decision to execution. Of course, given that decisions are made in the face of uncertainty, the desired outcome (say, victory in war, increased volume of trade in the market) may not actually be achieved. But the collective decision-makers must be confident that the conditions mandated by their decision (say, a certain number of warships built by a certain date, the enforcement of new market regulations) will be fulfilled. An ideal-type thoughtful and well-informed individual citizen, reflecting on the process *ex post,* ought to be able to say, "The deliberative process surfaced an option capable of gaining our approval (through winning a majority or consensus vote). The public choice made by the vote accorded with our (majority or consensus) preferences in light of our beliefs about the relevant state of the world at the time. Subsequent actions by executive officials were in accord with that choice."

At each step, we must expect some slippage. Given the existence of many minds, and diverse interests, preferences, and beliefs, it would be absurd to suppose that the democratic state-level process of moving from initiative to decision, and from decision to action, could be as straightforward as a single rational individual forming the intention to do something and then doing it. Even the simplest example of joint action—as demonstrated by Michael Bratman's (2014) discussion of two persons painting a house—is far more complex than an action carried out by a rational individual. The size and complexity of the Athenian governmental machinery meant that, even assuming the highest possible levels of competence and loyalty from every individual involved, there would inevitably be slippage across the causal chain, a loss of efficiency and accuracy between the input of individual preferences and beliefs and the output of public actions. But if the slippage were so great that there was no discernible (to, say, our hypothetical ideal Athenian observer) causal relationship between public choices and outcomes, it would be absurd to claim that the democratic state manifested even minimal rationality in the instrumental sense of the folk theory. Moreover, if the process were captured by those individuals with responsibility for initiative and execution, such that the demos was a mere bystander in the process of government, it would be false to claim that the system was democratic.

In fourth-century Athens, a substantial number of individuals had responsibility, formal or informal, for initiative and execution. Both the legislative and judicial process depended on "he [the citizen in good standing] who is willing" (*ho boulomenos*). Willing, that is, to initiate the action—to propose a policy or to bring a charge of illegality resulting in a legal trial. In the legislative process, the name of the initiator was attached to the final form of the decree or the law—through the formula "so and so proposed." All valid laws and decrees were archived; at least some were inscribed on marble stelai and publicly displayed. The individual listed as the proposer gained whatever public praise, honors, and positive reputation were subsequently associated with the measure. He also took on formal legal responsibility for the measure and, as we have seen, would be the defendant in a trial if it were challenged in the courts.

Some of the known proposers of surviving (on stone) and reported (in literary sources) fifth- and fourth-century Athenian decrees and laws were famous politicians. These men were politically prominent, whether or not they held public office in a given year. They were often recognized as expert in some area of policy. They regularly made speeches before public bodies offering their advice. They engaged in high-profile litigation. Yet other recorded proposers are known to scholarship only for having proposed a single decree (Hansen 1984). These men appear *not* to have figured among the set of "familiar public orators" that Athenians referred to as "the speakers" (*hoi rhētores*) or "the politicians" (*hoi politeuomenoi*). Moreover, as Claire Taylor (2008) has demonstrated, when compared with the fifth century, in the fourth century there was a considerably weaker correlation between citizens known to be active in initiating a public action and those known to be wealthy. Taylor has also demonstrated a similar decoupling of known political activity with being known to be a member of an urban deme. Insofar as there is a discernible trend from the fifth to the fourth century, it appears to be in the direction of *weakening* the association of privilege based on wealth, residence, and fame with the likelihood of being an initiator or executor of Athenian public policy.

Given the absence in Athens of an office of state prosecutor, most legal cases arising from charges of violation of criminal or unconstitutional law were initiated by *ho boulomenos:* a concerned citizen in good standing. Some very high-profile trials, including those that gave rise to the best-known speeches in the surviving corpus of orations by the "ten Athenian orators" (those whose works were most read and recopied), were delivered by prominent politicians, as either prosecutors or defendants. Such men were invariably members of the Athenian elites of wealth and education (Ober 1989). Carugati (2019; Carugati and Weingast 2018) has, however, shown that, in light of the high number of trials held in Athens in a given year, many litigants, including prosecutors and defendants in trials arising from constitutional challenges (per above), must have been relatively obscure ordinary citizens. In sum, it is clear that many Athenian citizens, elite and nonelite, chose to take the role of legally responsible initiator of a legislative or judicial process, leading to a salient decision by a public decision-making body.

How could the demos trust that those initiating legislation or legal challenges were adequately competent and loyal? Of course, not every speaker *was* competent and loyal. But, per above, if *most* were not it becomes impossible to explain the level of performance that Athens demonstrably achieved. The answer to the "justified trust" question may be sought in a variety of formal and informal mechanisms. First, as we have seen, Plato's Socrates (in the *Protagoras*) was quite willing to admit that, on technical matters at least, the Athenians were quite capable of recognizing experts in relevant domains. He notes that the assembly refused to waste time attending to those who were not regarded as adequately expert. This suggests that reputations for expertise could be built and tested over time, and that networks of knowledge and justified trust among citizens were adequate to the task of identifying the competent and culling out the incompetent—at least on various technical matters.[41] Next, the competition among would-be proposers of legislation could be fierce. Given that proposers were seeking rewards in the relatively scarce coin of major public honors and widespread social esteem, proposers had good reason to work at building and defending their reputations, and equally good reason to seek to expose incompetent rivals.[42]

Likewise, loyalty to the background values of the demos was established by reputations that were built up over time and tested in public contests: The preserved speeches of Athenian public orators are characterized by frequent attempts of the speaker, especially in the law courts, to demonstrate his own long record of highly transparent prosocial public behavior. The lives of litigants are self-advertised as being open to the inspection of all Athenian citizens. Public speakers who failed to conform to background social norms (when, for example, there was evidence of cowardice in battle, mistreating parents, squandering one's patrimony) would be attacked by their rivals. They might potentially be charged with wrongdoing through the legal procedure of the "scrutiny of public speakers" (*dokimasia rhētorōn*). If he was convicted of having addressed a public audience after having violated the relevant norms, the citizen lost the right to address public assemblies in the future. Any hint of disloyalty to the democratic regime, whether motivated by corruption or treason, left a public speaker open to legal attack by his rivals. Conviction could, and did, end public careers (Ober 1989).

Executive responsibility for policy implementation was widely distributed. Any given Athenian citizen had a reasonably high chance of serving for a year as a responsible official of the Athenian government. Even the famously "quietist" Socrates served for a year as a councilor—albeit late in life (in 406, when he was 63) and when Athens was suffering the

41. See further, Ober 2008: chap. 4, on knowledge networks within the Athenian citizenship.
42. See further, Ober 1989: chap. 7.

demographic squeeze of the latter phases of the Peloponnesian War. In a given year of the fourth century, some seven hundred other officials served annually, either by being elected or (more commonly) chosen in a lottery. These were in addition to the five hundred councilors, chosen annually by lot. Magistrates' duties ranged from military leadership (the ten generals), to the oversight of state finance, to the various legal and ritual roles of the nine archons, to punishment of offenders (the Eleven), to the wide range of administrative duties assumed by the many boards (typically composed of ten citizens) responsible for all manner of public business. While most offices were filled by lotteries, those requiring high levels of expertise (generals, cavalry commanders, civil engineers, naval architects, later financial officials) were elective and could be iterated. Moreover, each year a certain number of wealthy citizens were assigned (or volunteered for) public liturgies: funding and organizing a chorus or taking responsibility for equipping and manning a warship.[43]

As Matthew Christ (2006, 2012) has emphasized, the Athenian citizen body was in no sense a community of saintly altruists and certainly had its share of would-be free-riders. In order to provide an annual cohort of adequately competent and loyal officials the polis, functioning as an organization, had to offer incentives adequate to recruit enough volunteers: entrants into office lotteries, candidates for election, liturgists who did not dodge their duties. It also had to have reasonably effective means of identifying incompetence and disloyalty, and of punishing those whose behavior as an official was deleterious to the well-being of the community. This is the problem that Plato's Protagoras claimed was solved through a self-enforcing equilibrium of rationally (but not narrowly) self-interested mutual education and punishment (chapter 2.6). Recruitment incentives took the form of both material and moral benefits: pay for office, legitimate peculation, public honors, and social approbation. On the other hand, sanctions for malfeasance could be severe. All elected and lotteried officials were subjected to a year-end audit (*euthuna*) in which they were required to account for all public monies that passed through their office. An initial scrutiny (*dokimasia*) of those entering office served to screen individuals who had failed in their social duties in a conspicuous manner.[44]

---

43. Officials: Hansen 1999: 225–45. Lotteries: Farrar 2010. Liturgies: Gabrielsen 1994; Lyttkens 1997; P. Wilson 2000; Domingo Gygax 2016.

44. Pay for office: Gabrielsen 1981 (pace Hansen 1999: 241–42, an argument from silence). *Dokimasia* and *euthunai*: Hansen 1999: 218–20, 222–24,

Since most officials served on collegial boards, and both responsibility and liability were to an extent collective, magistrates on a given board had a strong incentive to monitor one another's behavior and, on the other hand, to defer to those among their members with special expertise or competence. Moreover, magistrates had good reasons to make use of the expertise of the professionalized staff attached to various of the boards. Some secretarial positions were filled by free citizens. But many of those we might think of as government bureaucrats were literate, skilled state-owned slaves, who had high incentives to do their work well: They were paid salaries by the state contingent upon good performance, and, if they failed in their duties, they were subject to physical punishment. Indefensible in ethical terms (ancient or modern), the state's systematic employment of slaves promoted its own rationality.[45]

6.9 ADAPTIVE RATIONALITY

In sections 6.3 through 6.8 I responded to Plato's description in book 8 of the *Republic* of democracy—understood as the rule of a demos and modeled by the "democratic man"—as inherently irrational. The comparison was, first, to instrumentally and ethically rational Callipolis, modeled by the philosopher-king, and, next, to the instrumentally, although not ethically, rational regimes of timocracy and oligarchy. On Plato's account the demos as a collectivity, like the model democratic citizen, lacked stable, ranked preferences and consistent beliefs.

I suggested that, taken at the level of choice-making among feasible options (as opposed to ideal-type standards of ethical rationality), state-level irrationality was hard to square with the depiction of fifth-century Athens offered by Plato's Socrates in the *Gorgias*—a city filled with the "trash" of material wealth and military equipment for acquiring and protecting that wealth. That "wealth and security" outcome was surely preferred to the available alternatives by a large majority of Athenians. State-level irrationality is equally hard to square with material conditions in the eighty years after the end of the Peloponnesian War, conditions that were familiar to Plato, Aristotle, and their first readers.

Against ancient and modern charges of democratic irrationality, I suggested that the demos of Athens, represented by large and stable

45. Self-selection as basis for office lotteries: Farrar 2010. State-owned slaves and their role as experts in public administration: Ismard 2017; Forsdyke 2021: 134–41.

majorities among the five hundred lottery-chosen councilors and the several thousand citizens who gathered in the assembly, shared high-ranked preferences for security, welfare, and nontyranny. This allowed for transitive ranking of preferences over particular policy options. The alignment of preferences relevant to the triad of security, wealth, and nontyranny was facilitated by the high-stakes conditions typical of the competitive world of the city-states. Moreover, Athenians were, collectively, able to form coherent and adequately accurate beliefs about the relevant state of the world. The formal rules and informal norms for legislating allowed for deliberative processes in which beliefs were updated, based on the testimony of trusted experts. Voting on policy options often (although not always) converged to consensus or near-consensus, thereby avoiding the irrationality of voting cycles (chapter 3.5). The legal system allowed for reasonably stable, but not ossified rules. As a result, residents of Athens could make choices about future actions based on expectations rather than fanciful hopes (chapter 6.7). They could anticipate and plan for more or less rational behavior on the part of relevant others, given an adequate level of common knowledge of the background constraints faced by themselves and others.

The Athenian demos, as a collectivity, and the individual citizens who constituted it had ample reason to expect that those individuals who took on the role of initiators of decision processes, and those lottery-chosen and elected officials responsible for executing decisions made by public bodies, were sufficiently competent and loyal. Moreover, the demos had ample means, via transparency and accountability procedures, for discovering malfeasance and sanctioning those who were found wanting. The *politeia* of the Athenians lacked a formal set of rules aimed at ensuring the separation and balance of institutional powers. Athens likewise lacked the large, professionalized, Weberian bureaucracy that is typical of modern democratic states. But the Athenian democracy provided resources and incentives (in the form of rewards and punishments) that appear well designed to ensure adequately rational processes of decision and implementation.

My response to Plato's depiction of democratic irrationality was meant to show that the relatively strong performance, over time, of the democratic polis of Athens in the high-stakes environment of the Greek city-state world was not mysterious. It was, on the contrary, an outcome that was explicable, *ex post*—if not readily predictable, *ex ante*. In the Greek terminology introduced in earlier chapters, that outcome was the result of the development, ongoing refinement, and implementation of a *politeia* that enabled an extensive and socially diverse community to operate effectively as a purposeful organization.

Athens did not win all of its wars. It suffered profound setbacks in the course of its history as a democratic state. But several factors suggest that democratic rationality was effective in gaining the desired ends of relative security, welfare, and nontyranny. First, democratic Athens was, in various ways, the highest-performing of the thousand-plus city-states of the classical era. While Athens had various natural advantages, none of these is adequate to explain the difference in performance between Athens and other large and prominent Greek poleis over the whole of the classical era. Next, it is clear that Athens did better, in terms of welfare and security, as a democracy than it did in the periods when it was not democratic. Moreover, in the era 508 and following and again in 403 and following, the institution of democratic mechanisms preceded substantial growth in state performance (Ober 2008, with Carugati 2019, appendices A and B).

Finally, democratic institutions and practices first developed in classical Athens, or best attested there, were widely imitated, over time and across the ecology of Greek states. In the later fourth and third centuries, even in the face of Macedonian hegemony and the creation of new kingdoms, Greek city-states increasingly adopted Athens-like institutions and social norms. The historian John Ma (2018, in progress) has described this phenomenon as the "Great Convergence"—the Greek poleis, old and new, converged on a *politeia* that was recognizably democratic. Neither oligarchy nor tyranny disappeared in the late classical and early Hellenistic period, but in the Greek world they became relatively rare compared to democracy.

Democratic rules and norms were, for the most part, voluntarily chosen over the well-known nondemocratic alternatives. The simplest explanation for the phenomenon of the spread of democracy, long after the end of Athenian imperial power, is that, given the feasible options known to be available, it was believed to be the most effective approach to organizing a state capable of delivering outcomes that were high-ranked by many Greeks. While civic behaviors characteristic of a self-enforcing democratic equilibrium were eventually put under pressure by imperial Rome, Ma shows that at least some of those behavioral norms were sustained for a surprisingly long time—indeed that they were discernible in some Greek cities until the fourth century CE. In short, the innovations characteristic of democratic Athens proved to be adaptive for a very long time and under very different conditions: The social equilibrium characteristic of the mature Greek polis may have been an evolutionary "dead end" (Runciman 1990), but only in the very long run.

The democratic institutional rationality and cultural evolution I have traced in this chapter was, to be sure, only one contributor to the success story of Greek democracy in the centuries after the Peloponnesian War. But that story makes little sense without an acknowledgement of the capacity of Greek states, as collectivities, to form stable preferences and coherent beliefs, and to devise institutions that enabled those preferences and beliefs to be realized in decision and action. Adaptation via cultural evolution, in this case at least, seems to be predicated at least in part on practical reason.

CHAPTER 7

Cephalus' Expertise

Economic Rationality

Was the production and exchange of goods in the Greek world ever motivated by the aim of maximizing expected utility in the context of competitive markets? Did Greek economic behavior change over time, such that the Greek economy became more (or less) rational over time? The adaptive rationality of its democratic government, traced in the previous chapter, enabled Athens to regain a position as a major player in the Greek international scene after the Peloponnesian War. With the empire lost, however, Athenian prosperity—both individual welfare and the state's capacity to secure its borders and import vital supplies—depended on domestic production, commerce, and overseas trade. This chapter suggests that it was the rational choices of individuals, in the context of the rules and norms of a rational state, that enabled Athens to reestablish itself as a central node in a thriving Mediterranean/western Asian exchange network and that drove the growth of the wider Greek economy between the eighth and fourth centuries BCE. The role of instrumental rationality in the accumulation of individual and collective wealth was well understood, although frequently criticized, by classical-era Greek writers. The self-conscious rationality characteristic of classical Greek economic activity contrasts sharply with social norms of the preclassical era.[1]

---

1. Postwar Greek world and Athenian choices: Strauss 1986; Descat 1987; Shear 2012; Carugati 2019.

7.1 PROSPERITY AND ECONOMIC THOUGHT

The fourth-century Greek world in which Plato, Xenophon, and Aristotle (among others) wrote their texts was defined by violence: by external wars and internal civil conflict, by extraction of resources through exploitation of slave labor.[2] But fourth-century Greece was also defined by economic cooperation: specialized production of goods and services, sophisticated forms of mutually beneficial exchange, and, as a result, growing levels of consumption. The economic growth characteristic of previous centuries proceeded apace, facilitated by the ongoing monetization of the Greek world and by more sophisticated forms of credit and borrowing. Although exact figures are lacking, it is now clear that in the age of Plato and Aristotle the Greek-speaking world reached new highs in terms of total population and average per capita consumption. Moreover, at least in Athens, economic inequality was to some degree constrained—per capita improvement in income, and thus in the capacity to consume at higher levels, was not limited to those occupying the topmost rungs of the socioeconomic ladder. While middling Greeks lived at a level of consumption that was far below modern "developed world" standards, and others continued to live near subsistence, when compared to earlier eras in Greek history, the classical Greek world was prosperous.[3]

The era of peak prosperity on the Greek mainland, in the form of more consumer goods, infrastructure, people, and movement, coincided roughly with the increased self-consciousness about instrumental rationality that is the primary subject of this book. In previous chapters, we have traced the analytic attention paid by Greek intellectuals to rational motivations, choices, and action. Instrumental rationality was understood to be characteristic of individuals, of certain groups, and of at least some states, some of the time. Although they had no way to measure growth or to establish causal mechanisms, Greek theorists made the connection between economic growth and rational cooperation.

2. External war: Ober 1985; Buckler 2003. Civil conflict: Gehrke 1985; Arcenas 2018. Slavery: Scheidel 2008; Bradley and Cartledge 2011; Lewis 2018; Forsdyke 2021.
3. Economic growth and prosperity in classical Greece: I. Morris 2004; Bresson 2015; Ober 2015a; Harris, Lewis, and Woolmer 2015. Limits on inequality: Ober 2017c, with literature cited. Experience of poverty: Claire Taylor 2017. The vital questions remain: How does the evidence of prosperity fit with the evidence for violence—interstate warfare, *stasis*, and coerced exploitation of unfree labor? Did different forms of violence inhibit or promote growth, locally, regionally, or across the Greek world? While I offer no answer to those questions here, I believe they belong at the forefront of future research on Greek history.

In modern social theory, rationality is strongly associated with the field of economics. Rationality is associated with (if not reducible to) market-based behavior, with choices about production and exchange made by agents seeking to maximize their own material welfare. The expected utility that is presumptively maximized by rational agents is often denominated and measured in monetary terms and units. As Paul Christesen (2003), among others, has shown, the economic behaviors of Athenians in the fourth century BCE were in practice determined, at least in part, by calculations of return and risk.[4] The question remains: To what extent did Greek intellectuals understand and theorize those behaviors? It is certainly true that, in contrast to, for example, politics, rhetoric, mathematics, or medicine, there was no demarcated domain of inquiry that closely tracks the modern field of economics. The Greek term *oikonomia* usually refers to something like "household management." Nevertheless, in this chapter I will argue that classical-era writers clearly grasped the relationship between rational choices and the expected material well-being of households and states alike. They recognized that rationality and growth were to some degree correlated. They speculated that the correlation arose from a causal relationship in which rationality was a driver of growth.

In contrast with the ideal-type rational agent, the perfect craftsman of self-interest of, for example, Plato, *Republic,* book 2, the rational economic agent of Greek thought was not an ideal type, not a figure in or a product of a thought experiment. Rather, he was a real-world expert whose shrewd choices in the realm of production and exchange of goods led more or less reliably to wealth accumulation. The reference point against which the economic expert was judged was the inexpert, amateur decision-maker, a person whose self-interested choices were relatively less likely to eventuate in high levels of material welfare. The questions Greek writers posed about the expert wealth-accumulator included the extent of the domain in which his expertise operated: Was the money-maker only expert in private matters or also in affairs of the polis? And relatedly, under what circumstances did expertise in wealth-making contribute or detract from the expert's own happiness, and that of others?[5]

The Socratics diverged sharply from mainstream modern economic thought in their normative evaluation of economic growth and wealth-

---

4. See discussion in introduction, section 0.5, and appendix.

5. On ideal-type rationality versus empirical studies of expertise, and their different reference points, see Bendor 2021, with discussion in present volume, introduction, n. 7.

accumulation. For Plato, Xenophon, and Aristotle, while poverty was certainly undesirable, unconstrained growth in public or private wealth presented a threat to social order and individual human flourishing alike. Moreover, they construed behavior motivated uniquely by a self-interested focus on material welfare as a perversion, rather than a pure manifestation of human reason. Their discussions of rational economic behavior and institutions were subordinated to political and ethical concerns. That subordination, while anticipating the approach of recent scholarship on moral political economy (Carugati and Levi 2021; Bednar in progress), has led to a tendency among some modern scholars to undervalue the depth and seriousness of the Greek philosophical engagement with economic rationality. Resituating Greek intellectuals' scattered comments on production, exchange, and consumption within the broader context of Greek thinking about instrumental uses of reason by individuals and collectives, the subject of the previous chapters of this book, sets the table for a reevaluation of the history of Greek economic thought.

7.2 AT HOME WITH THE MONEY-MAKERS

The first scene of Plato's *Republic* centers on a consequential choice: Socrates relates how, accompanied by Glaucon, he was making his way back up to the city after attending a new religious festival in Piraeus, when he was accosted by his friends Polemarchus and Adeimantus. After some banter about force and persuasion, foreshadowing central themes of the dialogue, enticed by the promise of viewing novel nocturnal festival activities, Socrates abandons his initial plan of immediately returning home. He chooses instead the road that takes him back down to Piraeus, to the domicile of the wealthy metic, Cephalus.[6] When the party arrives, it is the elderly master of the house with whom Socrates begins the conversation.

---

6. Nails (2002: 84–85) and Leese (2021: 112–17) sum up what is known of the real Cephalus' life and wealth. The later fortunes of the family are related in Lysias 12 *Against Eratosthenes*. There we learn that in 404 BCE the family's wealth was expropriated, and Polemarchus was murdered, by the oligarchic Thirty. At least part of the family income derived from a slave workshop producing military shields. According to Lysias (12.19) the Thirty confiscated 700 shields and 120 slaves, along with large quantities of silver, gold, and women's clothing.

Socrates and Cephalus, the Expert Entrepreneur

The opening gambit is Socrates' expressed wish to learn from very old people. He notes that since the old have "traveled along a road, as it were, which we too perhaps will have to travel, I think we should find out from them what kind of a road it is: Is it rough and difficult, or easy and passable?" (328e). The road analogy that frames Socrates' question recalls both his own recent choice on the road to Athens and the Sophist Prodicus' well-known "choice of Heracles," in which the young hero is made to decide between the "pleasant and easy" road of a life of vice and the "long and difficult" road leading to virtue.[7]

For Cephalus the old-age road seems, if long, relatively easy. To judge by the first scenes of the dialogue, he spends his days at home, surrounded by friends and family, performing religious rituals. The question of whether it is the old man's character or his wealth that has smoothed his road leads to Cephalus' claim that wealth is merely a useful instrument, one that enables an equitable person (*epieikēs*), like himself, to be honest in all matters (329e–30a). Wealth, it would appear, allows its possessor to avoid any hard choices between individual advantage (à la Gyges) and obeying the relevant laws and norms of fair dealing.

Socrates then asks his host if he had inherited most (*ta pleiō*) of his wealth or made it himself (330a). Cephalus takes the question to be how much (*poia*) he himself had made (330b). Notably, while avoiding mention of actual figures, both Socrates and Cephalus speak easily in terms of quantities: They both assume that wealth can be measured, presumably by reference to a monetary standard (talents of silver or *drachmai*).[8] Cephalus' answer comes in the form of a capsule history of his family's fortunes: Cephalus himself is, he says, "middling" (*mesos tis*) as a *chrēmatistēs* (330b). The Greek term *chrēmatistēs* denotes expertise in wealth creation; I will hereafter translate it as "entrepreneur."[9] At one

---

7. Xenophon, *Memorabilia* 2.1.21–34. Adam and Rees (1963: 1.5) suggest that the imagery could be borrowed from Hesiod, *Works and Days* 290ff. Bakewell (2020) discusses Plato's references to roads, metaphoric and real, in the *Republic* and his route from the city to Piraeus. On the passages discussed in this section, see further, Van Berkel 2020: 216–28, with literature cited.

8. Wealth is anything whose worth is measured in money: Aristotle *NE* 1119b26–27.

9. I use the term *entrepreneur* in the simple sense of "one who organizes, manages, and assumes the risks of a business or enterprise" (www.merriam-webster.com/dictionary /entrepreneur) or, more expansively, creates more wealth through taking on risk and the productive management of capital. The term is still something of a flash point in discussions of ancient economies: Saller 2013. Thompson (1982) argued in detail for its relevance

end of the expertise spectrum is his grandfather, Cephalus I, who inherited from his own father about what Cephalus II (Socrates' interlocutor) now possesses and multiplied it many times over. At the other end is the father of Cephalus II, Lysianas, who lost all the gains made by Cephalus I and then some, passing on to his son less than Cephalus II now possessed (and thus less that Cephalus I had started with).

Cephalus concludes: "For my part I am content if I pass on to my heirs not less [mē ellatō] but a little more [brachei . . . pleiō] than I inherited" (330b). Thus, we learn two things: The family had long been wealthy and Cephalus, like his grandfather, successfully increased the family fortune. So, although Cephalus' answer does not specify what portion of his current wealth was inherited or made, the answer to Socrates' query about "made or inherited fortune" is, in general terms, "both": Cephalus had inherited a reduced fortune and increased it to its present size through his own efforts.

But "some inherited and some made" is evidently not the answer Socrates expected. Cephalus, he says, appears to him to lack the excessive passion for money typical of those who have made it themselves (330b–c). The contrast is to the psychology Socrates associates with successful entrepreneurs: "Those who have made money take it seriously, as their own creation" (hōs ergon heautōn), as well as valuing its use, "as other people do." Socrates' comparison set for those who treat their self-made money as their own creation is poets and their poems, parents and their offspring. Money-makers (as opposed to wealth inheritors) are, Socrates states, difficult to spend time with (chalepoi . . . sungenesthai) because they can praise only wealth (ploutos 330c).[10] Here Socrates seems to be a spokesman for an aristocratic attitude that regards money-making (as opposed to wealth itself) as vulgar and corrupting. Yet, it is obvious from Cephalus' short family history that each head of his family was a more or less expert as an entrepreneur. Cephalus himself, while less expert than his grandfather, had "created," not

---

to money-making in classical Athens, noting that the term is not, and ought not be, restricted to persons employing business practices typical of the nineteenth and twentieth centuries. Schofield (2006: chap. 6) provides an especially valuable study of Plato on money and the moral psychology of money-making (aimed at both use and accumulation).

10. Compare a direct citation in Aristotle, NE 1120b11–14: "Men who have inherited a fortune are reputed to be more generous than those who have made one, since they have never known what it is to want; moreover, everybody is especially fond of a thing that is his own creation: parents and poets show this." Note the particular scorn for "creation" of wealth that leads to accumulation for its own sake, rather than wealth for use; cf. the wealth-hoarding oligarchs of Republic book 8.

just inherited, at least some of his current wealth, and is quietly proud of having done so.

Socrates' scorn blocks any further discussion of the productive process of wealth creation. Rather than pursuing the question of when and how making money might or might not be correlated with a difficult, unpleasant character and crudely materialistic ethics, Cephalus answers Socrates' new query concerning the greatest benefit he had gained from the possession of wealth. He does so by returning to the issue of honesty: Possessing wealth allows one to avoid doing injustice. The wealthy man is in a position to tell the truth and to pay what he owes to other people and to the gods. The importance of being in a position to do what is right by the gods is underlined by the dramatic setting: Cephalus both enters and leaves the dialogue as a performer of religious ritual (328c, 331d). The greatest benefit Cephalus has gained from his fortune is evidently lack of fear of punishment in the afterlife for any unjust acts he might have committed while he was still alive.

All of this anticipates salient features of the Gyges story in *Republic* book 2. Adeimantus' long addendum to Glaucon's challenge emphasizes that Gyges' unjustly acquired wealth would enable him to do whatever was necessary to please the gods, thus avoiding any shadow of fear for his own afterlife (chapter 1.2). The implied comparison of putatively just Cephalus and rationally unjust Gyges, each insulated by wealth from concern about his future welfare, sets up the question of whether wealth can ever be had without some taint of injustice in its acquisition: How, we might ask, did Cephalus II's great-grandfather come by the fortune (equal to that of Cephalus II) that Cephalus I inherited and subsequently increased several times over? Was Cephalus I, the exemplary entrepreneur, also an honest man? Has Cephalus II, who inherited a reduced fortune, always been able to avoid doing injustice? If so, why is he so intensely concerned late in life with performing the right sacrifices?[11]

The Cephalus-Socrates dialogue concludes with Socrates' challenge to a contractual account of justice as "telling the truth and returning what we have received from someone" (331c). Socrates offers the hypothetical of a man who borrows a knife from another who then goes mad. Returning the knife, with which the madman will presumably harm himself or others, is, under the circumstances, wrong. At this

---

11. Irwin (1995: 170–71) notes that "Cephalus' attitude to justice is frankly instrumental, and given his conception of justice and happiness, his commitment to justice seems rather unstable."

point, Cephalus takes his leave, passing his interlocutor's role on to his son, Polemarchus.

Socrates and Polemarchus, the Inexpert Entrepreneur

As Cephalus' eldest son and "heir in all things" (331d), and as a metic in Athens descended from a long line of entrepreneurs, Polemarchus presumably is, or is expected to become, a money-maker. The question might be asked: Where on the "Cephalus I to Lysianas" entrepreneurial expertise scale does he stand? Polemarchus' name (War-leader), along with his employment of military metaphors (e.g., 335e), seems to align him with the model timocrat and honor-lover, Glaucon. It is not immediately evident from what follows in the dialogue that Polemarchus has any very deep mastery of the "creative" wealth-making that built and rebuilt his family's fortune. This has some implications for the fate of the "justice of fair contracts" premise originally proposed on behalf of the modestly self-described "middling-expert" entrepreneur, Cephalus.

As the dialogue with Polemarchus begins, Socrates presses the "madman's knife" issue by reference to lending money: "If two people are friends, and one gives back money deposited [*parakatathemenōi*] with him to the other when the exchange is going to cause harm [say, having gone mad, he intends to buy a knife], the one returning the money is not giving the other what is owed to him" (332a–b)—that is, he is repaying benefit with harm. A more expert Polemarchus might have answered this point by noting that a contract—even the implied contract in a friendly, interest-free, *eranos* loan—ought to specify the relevant terms of repayment: A complete borrowed-money contract would preclude untimely, because harmful, return.[12] This would, in turn, require that Socrates come up with some other scenario to demonstrate that fair contractual agreements are an inappropriate basis for justice. As it is, Socrates leads Polemarchus to the peculiar conclusion that justice must be, according to Polemarchus' lights, useful only when its object, in this case money, is in a condition of uselessness: "So what about justice, now? For what need, or for producing what, would you say it was useful in peacetime?" "It is useful in connection with business contracts [*sumbolaia*], Socrates." "By business contracts do you mean partner-

---

12. Millett (1991) supposed that the interest-free, *eranos* loan, a form of sharing among friends, was by far the most common and most socially important form of lending and borrowing. But see below.

ships [koinōnēmata], or something else?" "Yes, I mean partnerships" (333a–b).

Since, by reference to playing a board game, it is evidently the skilled expert, rather than the just man, who is the more valuable partner in an enterprise, Polemarchus struggles to explain when the just man is the more useful. Socrates presses the point: "So what then is the occasion for the joint use of silver or gold when the just man is a more useful partner than others?" "When it is to be put on deposit [parakatath-esthai] and kept safe, Socrates" (333c). Socrates now closes the trap: "In fact, you mean, when we have no need to use it at all, but to put it by [keisthai]?" "Exactly." "So, when money is useless, that's when justice is useful in relation to it?" (333c). Polemarchus is stumped.

But what, hypothetically, might an expert entrepreneur like Cephalus I have said at this point? Arguably, were Cephalus I the interlocutor, the dialogue would never have gotten to this point, because Cephalus I certainly did not multiply his fortune many times over by "depositing" his money in an inert account with someone else. His creative approach to money-making presumably meant that if and when he deposited money with another, he expected a return of principal plus interest (tokos: see below, 7.7). The person to whom the loan was made, in order to produce the expected interest, would also have had to put it to work.[13]

The usefulness of justice, in this hypothetical case, lay in the intention and practice of fulfilling presumptively fair contracts voluntarily entered into by expert entrepreneurs. Of course, Socrates might not have found Cephalus I a worthy interlocutor. Although he inherited a fortune, Cephalus I certainly falls into the category of a creative money-maker and so presumably, by Socratic specification, someone difficult to be with and capable of praising only wealth. In any event, the replacement of the at-least-moderately expert Cephalus II with honor-loving Polemarchus in the dialogue, along with Socrates' openly expressed scorn for those engaged in creative money-making, has had the effect of

---

13. The foolishness of hoarding (rendering wealth useless through nonuse), when loaning at interest (epi tokōi) is an alternative, is emphasized in a fragment of Antiphon: LM 37.D59 (with discussion in Pierris 2000: appendix G). Based on archaeological discoveries of coin hoards (on which see Ober 2006a: 48–52), and following Millett (1991), Meikle (1995: 159–62) inferred a Greek preference and "predilection" for hoarding over profitable investment. His argument falsely assumes the absence of productive credit. Cohen (1992), Shipton (1997), Christesen (2003), and Bresson and Bresson (2004) document the important role of banking and credit in the economy of fourth-century Athens.

foreclosing what might have seemed to be a productive approach to the topic at hand.

The foreclosure of the topic of the justice of the honest contract was, I would suggest, not accidental. It blocks the path of equating justice with *epieikeia* (equity, decency)—the cardinal virtue that, as we have seen, Cephalus claimed for himself. We cannot ask Cephalus how an equitable person would answer the puzzle of the madman's knife. But we can, speculatively, supply an answer by reference to Aristotle's discussion of *epieikeia* in the *Nicomachean Ethics* (5.10). Aristotle defines *epieikeia* is as a special kind of justice and the equitable person (*epieikēs*) as "one who by deliberate choice and in practice does what is equitable, and who is not a stickler for the letter of the law, but is content to receive a lesser share although he has the law on his side" (*NE* 1137b34–38a3). The point of *epieikeia,* for Aristotle, is to correct errors in the administration of justice that arise from the strict application of general rules—rules that, by the very nature of generality, cannot attend to particulars. Plato's Socrates took "return what is owed" as a strict general rule and used the madman's knife as a counterexample to eliminate that rule as a candidate definition of justice. *Epieikeia,* understood as a principled, situationally contingent, willingness to accept less than what was due, offers an obvious rejoinder to Socrates' dismissal.[14]

Had Cephalus continued as Socrates' interlocutor, he might perhaps have referred to the ways in which *epieikeia* was practiced in the community of those engaged in commercial exchange (below, 7.7). He might have explained that traders govern fair relations among themselves by a set of extralegal norms enforced through reputation effects.[15] An equitable person, interpreting that community's understanding of the "pay your debts" rule in light of the relevant particulars, would withhold the bor-

14. Brunschwig (1996) analyzes Aristotle's discussion of *epieikeia* in reference to law and justice. He shows that Aristotle draws on a preexisting conception of the *epieikēs* as not just a generically "good person" (pp. 119–20), but as "a man who 'cuts back on' his *own rights*, who renounces pursuit of any claim to their complete recognition . . . he decides to receive less than his share" (124–25). This understanding of the term was certainly available to Plato's Cephalus, and it exactly describes the answer I suppose he could have given to the "madman's knife" objection. Note that in his discussion of lending and borrowing, Aristotle discusses conditions in which the general rule of paying what is owed is not applicable: *NE* 1165a4–14. Irwin (1995: 171–74) proposes that "pay what is due" is not actually refuted in book 1; it comes back in refined form in book 7, in the argument for why a philosopher in Callipolis must "return to the Cave."

15. Compare, for example, Milgrom and Weingast 1990 on the *lex mercantalis* of medieval Italian traders, a self-enforcing system of rules within a community of traders, with sanctions for violations managed through reputation rather than state coercion.

rowed knife from the madman and could expect to be praised, not blamed, for having done so. The knife's owner, if also an equitable member of the same community, would, *ex ante,* accept the fairness of receiving a "lesser share" in the case of his own subsequent loss of sanity. If this speculation is on the right track, Socrates' expressed scorn for money-making, followed by Cephalus' early exit from the dialogue, has shut a window onto the economic rationality that was a background condition of the Greek world inhabited by Socrates, Plato, and Aristotle—and by the first readers of the *Republic.*

Socrates on Homeric Thieving and Perjury

Instead of a continued exploration of fair contracts, the discussion between Socrates and Polemarchus now takes a decisive turn. Beginning with Socrates' familiar military and medical analogies—the good general is expert at stealing the enemy's plans; the doctor is capable of making people ill—Socrates concludes:

> So, for whatever someone is a skillful guardian [*deinos phulax*], he will also be a skillful thief? I suppose so. If then the just person is good at guarding money, he will also be good at stealing it. That's the way the argument seems to be pointing. Then it appears that the just man is unveiled as some kind of thief, and you're likely to have learned that from Homer. For I tell you he's fond of Autolycus, Odysseus' maternal grandfather, and says that "he excelled all men in thieving and perjury." (334a–b)

Once again there is a strong foreshadowing of *Republic* book 2: the dangerous Guardians who would, were they not properly educated, seize the property of the defenseless producers (chapter 3.1); Gyges, the bodyguard who murders a king and steals his kingdom (chapter 1.2); but also, and most saliently, the ostensibly just man who is in fact motivated exactly as is the completely unjust man and, given the opportunity, will act just as he does (chapter 2.1). That foreshadowing casts the profession of lifelong honesty by moderately expert creative money-maker, Cephalus II, into doubt. It is facilitated, I have suggested, by Polemarchus' limited expertise in the productive use of money in voluntary contracts. And even if Polemarchus does know more about money-making and *epieikeia* than he lets on, Socrates' entrepreneur-shaming has precluded further discussion of such "vulgar" considerations among the company gathered in Cephalus' house.

As a result—although the setting of the dialogue is a house that active money-making built, located in Piraeus, the port town where trade and commerce were especially prevalent occupations, in the polis of Athens, the thriving center of a network of production and exchange—Socrates takes us back to the economy of theft and deceit exemplified by characters in Homeric texts. I suggest that, despite the dialogue's setting in the era of Athens' empire, this move was not predicated on a recognition of the violence-backed resource extraction of imperial domination (chapter 5.4). Nor on Plato's own aristocratic disdain for money-making—no matter how disdainful he might in fact have been. Much less is it evidence for a timeless "ancient economy" in which Homeric values and practices can be extrapolated forward to the classical era.

Rather, Socrates' retrojection away from the classical era's world of money-makers in Piraeus to the mythic past of Homeric heroes was a self-consciously authorial strategy. It was a strategic move in Plato's (and a broader Socratic) critique of economic rationality as a form of instrumental reasoning. That kind of reasoning is, by Socratic standards, morally dangerous when it is divorced from ethically rational choice-making: reason-driven preferences for genuinely valuable outcomes, along with the true beliefs and virtuous actions that connect right preferences to good outcomes. But before considering the Socratic critique of economic rationality, let us accept Plato's implicit invitation to jump back to the age of Homer, to a world where wealth-getting was, at least sometimes, unabashedly about taking what one was strong enough to seize and to hold. The values of Homer's world were familiar to classical Greeks and the Homeric texts remained influential—often perniciously so, according to Socrates' argument later in books 2, 3, and 10 of the *Republic*. But, as Thucydides' assessment in book 1 of his history demonstrates (1.3, 10–12), the communities described in those texts were thought by at least some Greek intellectuals to have been relatively small and resource starved. Relatedly, Homer's world was characterized by assumptions about the sources and uses of wealth that were quite different from those of the classical era, characterized as it was, not only by violence and coercion, but also by expertise in specialized production and commercial exchange.

A digression into Homeric epic enables me to make two points. The first point is that much of the business of exchange in the (fictive but not merely imaginary) world described by Homer, whether rational or otherwise, was explicitly predicated on violent expropriation of the goods of the weak by the strong. It was thus in line with the kind of immoralist instrumentalism advocated by Plato's Thrasymachus (introduction, section 0.4), but fundamentally different from what Cephalus describes as the ideal behavior of the successful entrepreneur who is also an *epieikēs*. Although he was a large-scale slave owner, and so deeply involved in the structural violence of labor exploitation, there is no hint that Cephalus II, or his immediate ancestors, were Homeric-style raiders, or pirates, or otherwise gained (or lost) their wealth through Homeric-type violence. Instead, Socrates' comparison cases for creative money-making, poetry and biological procreation, point to an essentially peaceful productive enterprise. Creative money-making, while it involved competition, was predicated on an assumption among practitioners of the potential for mutual benefit.[16]

The second point is that Homeric choice-making in the context of exchanges of goods acquired by violence could be instrumentally irrational, as in the case of the clueless Agamemnon depicted in *Iliad* book 1. But Homeric choices could also be imagined as rational in the sense of attending appropriately to the relevant conditions and players, as in the case of wise elders and a "counterfactual Agamemnon," who had the capacity to look up and down a simple game tree and who recognized that his own vital interests extended to the safety of his army. What is missing in the Homeric world is not the innate capacity for practical reason, but its theorization and application to creative wealthmaking.

7.3 HOMERIC ECONOMICS: AGAMEMNON'S CLUELESSNESS

Homer's *Iliad* is deeply concerned with the motivating force of human emotion, most obviously manifest in the rage (*mēnis*) of Achilles, and with the ways that human plans are overthrown by divine powers beyond any mortal's control. Yet Homeric epic is also concerned with reasoning about choices over possible outcomes and exchanges of goods. In the opening scene of book 1 of the *Iliad*, the priest of Apollo, Khryses, enters the Achaean camp. He offers a rich ransom for the return of his daughter, Khryseis, who is a captive in the possession of the expedition's paramount leader, Agamemnon. Khryses accepts without complaint the background conditions of his world: His daughter was seized by force in

16. The (in principle) mutual benefit of parents and children is self-explanatory; cf. the peaceful and seemingly mutual beneficial exchange of women with anticipation of childbirth in the weddings of *Iliad* 18.490–508: "the city at peace." In the domain of poetry, the mutual benefit might be thought of as the fame of the poets and the pleasure of their audiences.

an Achaean raid. Because the Achaeans were stronger than the defenders, they were able to take the girl Khryseis along with other booty (*Iliad* 1.8ff). Because Khryses now wants his daughter back and cannot recover her by force, he proposes to buy her back.

Khryses' offer is presented as a fair one: The Achaean army, here acting as a coherent collective, unanimously (*pantes:* 1.22) urges Agamemnon to accept the ransom (*Iliad* 1.22–23).[17] He refuses to do so, with consequences that prove to be bad for himself and worse for the many warriors who, in the course of the epic, are killed, their corpses eaten by dogs, a fate called out in the epic's grim opening lines. Those deaths are, the poet tells us, the result of Zeus's plan (*boulē: Iliad* 1.5). And yet it appears that the god's plan is not yet operative at the beginning of the action, when Khryses offers ransom.[18] Before Achilles has reason for anger, before Zeus's plan is set in motion by Thetis' successful supplication, there is an implicit counterfactual in which Agamemnon did the right thing. That is, Homer's classical-era readers may realize, the rational thing (in a cost-benefit sense): taking the rich ransom and handing back the girl. Of course, had he done so, Achilles would have had no motive for anger, and there would be no epic to be sung about it.

In the event, Agamemnon rejected Khryses' offer, sending the priest off with insults and the threat of violence (*Iliad* 1.24–32). The denouement comes quickly: Khryses prays to Apollo, reminding the god of the worthy sacrifices he has burned for him. Apollo responds accordingly, sending a plague upon the Achaean camp. The source of the plague is discovered after Achilles has promised to protect the seer Kalchas from Agamemnon's wrath. To placate Apollo, Agamemnon agrees to send Khryseis back to her father along with a large number of cattle to sacrifice for the god (*Iliad* 1.309–10). At this point in the story, Agamemnon has lost a lot, in terms of goods (the girl, the promised ransom, the cattle) and prestige. Rather than accepting the situation, he employs a threat of

17. On Agamemnon's relationship with the Achaean army as a collective, see Hammer 2002: chap. 6; and especially Elmer 2013, arguing (chap. 3) that Agamemnon's rejection of the Achaean community's clearly expressed preferences in book 1 violates Iliadic norms of consensual decision making.

18. Some Homeric scholars argue, on the basis of a fragment in the post-Homeric *Cypria*, that the plan of Zeus alludes to a scenario in which Zeus long ago decided to relieve the earth of extra population. In that case, we should view the destruction of the Achaeans in the wake of Achilles' retirement as a subplan that helps fulfill the master plan. But Kirk et al. (1985–93: 1:53) regard it as more probable that what is meant at *Iliad* 1.5 is the plan implied by Zeus' promise to Thetis at 1.524–30.

force, in the form of the numerous armed men in his personal retinue, to take Briseis, Achilles' prize-captive, as his own (*Iliad* 1.318–25).

Achilles, having suffered the loss of Briseis, and having withdrawn from the campaign, follows the pattern established by the priest Khryses: He makes an appeal to a friendly divine agent, in this case his mother, for help in rectifying the harm he has suffered. Thetis calls in a favor from Zeus, who, although supremely powerful, is tightly bound by the rules of reciprocity, as are other agents in the epic. Despite his expressed reluctance (the cost he will incur in the form of his wife's anger), Zeus agrees to turn the tide of battle against the Achaeans so as to punish Agamemnon. His plan is that the Achaeans will only regain the upper hand against the Trojans after Achilles has returned to the battle (*Iliad* 1.503–26). After much carnage, Zeus's plan leads to the expected outcome: In book 19, Agamemnon finds himself in exactly the situation he had been in with Khryses—begging a man he has wronged to accept the return of a girl he has stolen, along with lots of added booty.

It is obvious in retrospect that Agamemnon had made a very bad choice in taking Briseis by threat of force from Achilles. How to account for it? Agamemnon's own explanation is the jumping-off point of E. R. Dodds' classic work *The Greeks and the Irrational* (1951). As Dodds (1951: chap. 1) notes, Agamemnon claims, and Achilles agrees, that Agamemnon's fateful choice had been motivated, not by his own desires, but by *atē*—a sort of divine madness. According to Dodds' line of argument, building on the earlier work of Bruno Snell, Agamemnon's action was imagined by the poet and Greek readers of the *Iliad* as having been determined by a force outside of himself. Indeed, for Dodds, Snell, and their followers, neither Agamemnon nor any other Homeric hero was an integrated, deliberative, choice-making self in the first place.[19] Agamemnon's behavior, then, was strictly "irrational" in that it did not (indeed could not) arise as a result of Agamemnon's own coherent process of reasoning, choosing, and acting. And thus, in the scene of attempted reconciliation with Achilles, Agamemnon could plausibly disown his behavior as having a motivation that was in no sense his own.

As noted in the preface to this book, Dodds' work on Greek irrationality has been hugely influential, and rightly so. But his strong claims about the nonintegration of self in Homer and archaic Greek literature

---

19. See discussion in introduction, section 0.5. Gaskin (1990), in a detailed refutation of Snell's account of Homeric psychology, answers the question "do Homeric heroes make real decisions?" in the positive.

have been effectively challenged, notably by Bernard Williams (1993).[20] In light of the implied counterfactual alluded to above, in which Agamemnon, like the Achaean army, recognizes that Khryses' offer was a fair one, and that refusing it risked very bad consequences, it seems reasonable to ask whether there is another explanation for Agamemnon's apparent irrationality. As it turns out, there is an "emic" explanation, offered by Achilles in *Iliad* book 1, at the point at which he both concedes that Agamemnon's superior military force enables the king to take Briseis and vows not to help him in the future. Achilles' explanation does not directly contradict Agamemnon's book 19 ascription of his motivation to *atē*. But it does pointedly contrast Agamemnon's behavior to that of a competent decision-maker, faced with a salient choice in a high-stakes situation.

In critically describing Agamemnon's proposed plan of seizing Briseis, Achilles says this: "Truly he rages with baneful mind, and knows not at all to look both backwards and forwards in time [*hama prossō kai opissō*], so that his Achaeans might wage war in safety beside their ships" (*Iliad* 1.343–44). The phrase *hama prossō kai opissō* is a standard Homeric formula, appearing two other times in the *Iliad* and once in the *Odyssey*. It emphatically does *not* refer to an oracular or mantic capacity to see into the future. Rather, the agents who are said to have this capacity are older men, who are in a position of assessing a high-stakes situation, forming a judgment, and offering advice about the best, although not the most obvious or most popular, course of action. That advice would, in each case, avoid catastrophic outcomes—were it followed.[21] Without pressing the point too far, it would appear that the

---

20. See also Rabel 1990, with literature cited; Schofield 1999: chap. 1. Parker (2019) notes that Dodds' theory of irrationality as nonintegration of the self is no longer influential in mainstream classical studies. On the rhetoric of the Agamemnon-Achilles exchanges in books 1 and 19 (which assumes a coherent agential perspective from which to make strategic claims), see further, Martin 1989; Rabel 1990; D. Wilson 2002.

21. *Iliad* 3.109–10: "But in whatsoever an old man takes part, he looks both before and after, that the issue may be far the best for either side." *Iliad* 18.249–50: "Then among them wise Polydamas was first to speak [urging retreat before Achilles reappears on the field], the son of Panthous; for he alone looked at once before and after." *Odyssey* 24.451–53: "Then among them spoke the old lord Halitherses, son of Mastor, for he alone saw before and after: he with good intent addressed their assembly" (urging the relatives of dead Suitors against seeking revenge). The last case concludes as follows (*Odyssey* 24.463–66): "So he spoke, but they sprang up with loud cries, more than half of them, but the rest remained together in their seats; for his speech was not to their mind, but they hearkened to Eupeithes, and quickly thereafter they rushed for their arms." Here, as in the Khryses scene in *Iliad* 1, the majority fails to determine the course of action and disaster follows.

wise agents called out in the formula, those who know "how to look both backwards and forwards," are those who are capable of (1) assessing the likely behaviors of other relevant agents, based on their desires and capabilities, (2) determining the set of feasible options, and (3) thereby choosing the best option: the one least likely to be severely harmful. Finally (4) they specify the course of action leading to that best available outcome. In brief, the wise agent seems to be the one who is competent at the process of rational choice assumed in what I have been calling the Greek folk theory of practical reasoning.[22]

Achilles' point in the relevant passage is that Agamemnon, raging with baneful mind, lacks that sort of wisdom and therefore is shown up to be a poor leader: He puts his own army in danger. The danger for the army that arises from Agamemnon's rage-born folly will play out in the course of events precipitated by Achilles' withdrawal from battle, his entreaty to Thetis, and the plan of Zeus that follows. Yet, we might ask, could a counterfactually wise Agamemnon really have foreseen all that? One reason to think that the answer is "yes" is that the course of events that will follow from the taking of Briseis (provoke another's entreaty to a friendly god, suffer accordingly) and the outcome (return the girl with additional goods, after many have died unnecessarily and the expedition to Troy has been put at risk) exactly follows the scenario that has just been played out between Agamemnon, Khryses, and Apollo. What Achilles seems to be implying here is that a wiser leader, having just experienced that sequence of events, would recognize the pattern, and would not repeat it.[23]

Although it would be wildly anachronistic to claim that the *hama prossō kai opissō* formula refers to looking up and down a game tree, putting Agamemnon's choice into extensive game form clearly illustrates the similarity between the Agamemnon-Khryses and Agamemnon-Achilles scenarios. It demonstrates why a counterfactual Agamemnon, able to look backwards and forwards, would have returned

22. Dunkel (1983) considers the relationship of past and future in the formula and the issue of how it construes earlier events to be in front of later ones. Suddendorf and Corballis (2007) discuss the cognitive relationship of memory (looking backwards) to foresight and planning (looking forwards) under the rubric "mental time travel," arguing that it is a distinctive human capacity, absent in young children and in some adults.

23. As Richard Martin helpfully pointed out to me, "the poem is compressing and accelerating what, in terms of the overall saga, seems to be an ironic parallel: Helen is like Khryseis: The Trojans have rejected the ransom appeals; they suffer the consequences, via an expedition led by Agamemnon. In other words, a 'just' resolution is attained despite the injustice of the avenging force."

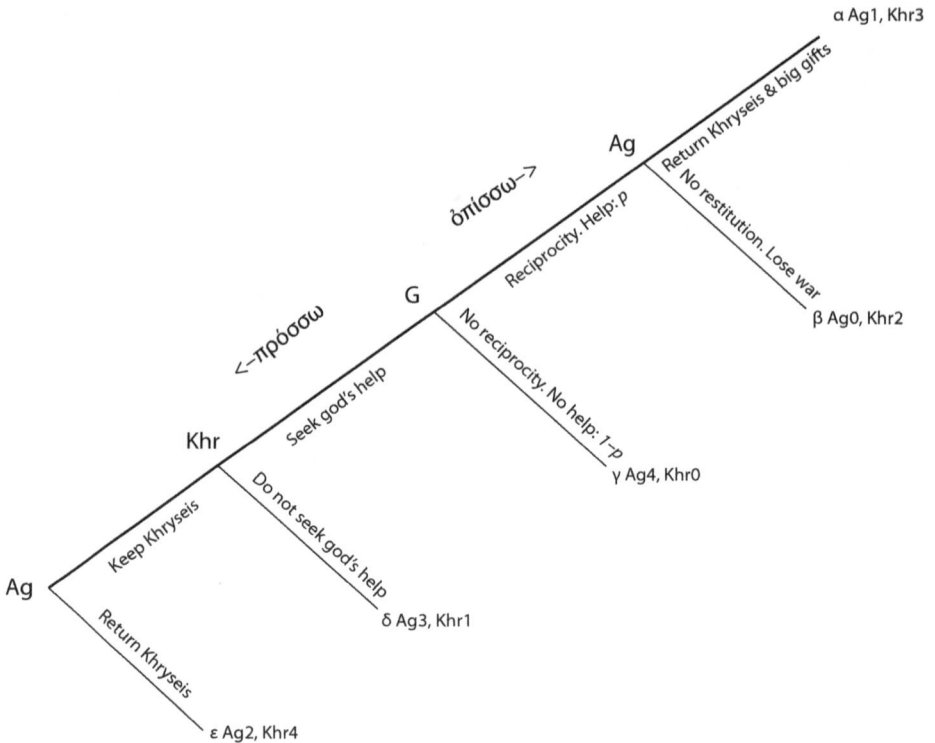

FIGURE 23. Agamemnon and Khryses Game

NOTE: Ag = Agamemnon; Khr = Khryses; G = Gods (Nature lottery); Ordinal payoffs, 4 = high; 0 = low.

Khryseis when Khryses offered full ransom, and why he would not have sought to replace the loss of Khryseis by taking Briseis from Achilles.

At the root of each of the two simple "two-players plus god" sequential games with ordinally ranked payoffs, illustrated in figures 23 and 24, Agamemnon chooses to keep/seize Khryseis/Briseis or to return/not take the girl. If he chooses return/not take, the game ends with a modest (ordinal) payoff of 2 to Agamemnon (he gets the ransom, avoids trouble); Khryses/Achilles get their most preferred outcome and thus a high payoff of 4. If Agamemnon chooses not return/take, then Khryses/Achilles chooses to seek or not to seek a god's help. If Khryses/Achilles does not seek help, Agamemnon gets a relatively high payoff of 3, while Khryses/Achilles is left with a low payoff of 1. If Khryses/Achilles chooses to seek the god's help, the god determines whether to honor the

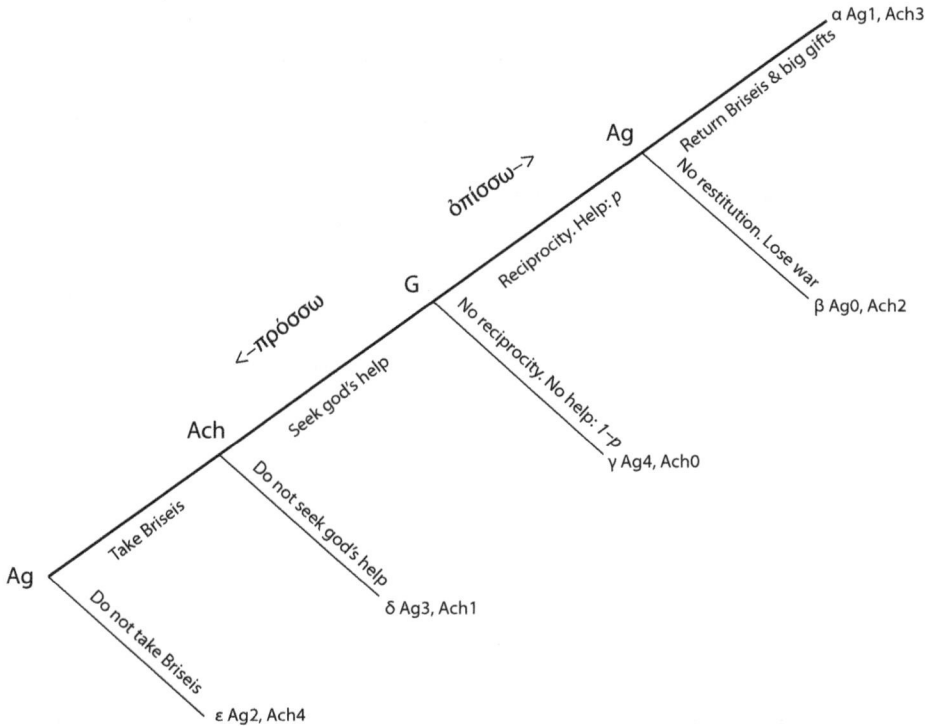

FIGURE 24. Agamemnon and Achilles Game

NOTE: Ag = Agamemnon; Ach = Achilles; G = Gods (Nature lottery); Ordinal payoffs, 4 = high; 0 = low.

prior relationship, to respect reciprocity, and thus to offer help, or to ignore the relationship and to violate reciprocity by not helping. Not helping gives Agamemnon his highest payoff of 4—he adds the humiliation of his opponent to the material advantage of keeping or taking the girl. Conversely, it gives Khryses/Achilles his lowest payoff of 0.

We do not list a payoff for the gods, putting them in the "nature" or "lottery" role of a standard game, but the assumption of this game is that the likelihood that the god will help is equivalent to certain, given the nature of the prior relationship (priest, son) and the involvement of Homeric gods in relationships of reciprocity. If the gods help, then Agamemnon chooses either to return the girl, along with other "gifts," or to not return the girl. Returning the girl and the gifts is a good outcome for Khryses/Achilles with a payoff of 3. This is second only to not having suffered the loss in the first place. It is a poor outcome for Agamemnon, with payoff of 1. Yet not returning the girl and offering gifts leads to the Achaeans losing the war, which is Agamemnon's worst outcome: payoff of 0. The payoff for Khryses/Achilles in this case is the moderate 2: The loss of the girl is to some extent made up for by the crushing defeat of their opponent, Agamemnon.

Agamemnon's choice should have been simple in the first, Khryses, game and seems painfully obvious once that game had been played and he was faced with the option to play what amounts to an identical game with Achilles. Employing the standard method of backwards induction, we can see, once the irrelevant alternatives (outcomes that will not be chosen due to low payoffs) have been pruned away from the decision tree, that Agamemnon is left with a choice between not taking the girl (payoff 2, his third-best outcome) and returning the girl along with other treasure (payoff 1, his next-to-worst outcome). The ordinal rankings used here do not express the cardinal value of each outcome, but clearly Agamemnon has lost a lot by making the wrong choice. Even granting that Agamemnon values the possession of Khyrseis/Briseis and his own honor highly, if we are correct to set the likelihood of the gods helping Khryses/Achilles at the equivalent of certain, it is, therefore, clear that had a formally rational Agamemnon done the math, as it were, he would not have kept Khryseis or taken Briseis. Agamemnon himself would have been better off and, per Achilles' comment, the army would have remained safe, or at any rate safer, by the ships.

And so, to return to the question posed above: Why did Agamemnon choose to take the path that led to the worse outcome for himself and his army? We cannot dismiss out of hand, as Achilles himself does not, the explanation that "the decision was not Agamemnon's but that of *atē*." Yet Achilles' comment about "looking backwards and forwards," when read against the three other instances of the Homeric formula, suggests that, were Agamemnon a wiser leader, he would have quieted his "raging mind" and made the better choice. And if that counterfactual is possible within the frame of the epic, then we need to revise Dodds' idea of the Homeric hero as inherently lacking in a coherent self, and thus incapable of making rational judgments. That is to say, the motivation and choice processes of at least some Homeric figures (wise elders, at least) seem potentially to fit within the frame of the folk theory of instrumental rationality discussed in the earlier chapters of this book.

In this light, Agamemnon's actual choice appears less the product of a nonintegrated self, than it is a case of cluelessness. Michael Chwe (2013), in his delightful book *Jane Austen: Game Theorist*, introduces the category of "cluelessness" for literary characters who, in contrast to other characters, are inept at strategic reasoning: They lack consistent preferences and beliefs. They are incapable of assessing other's motives. They are incapable of realistic probability estimates.[24] They are, therefore, not rational agents in the decision-theoretic sense of the term. But by the same token, the clueless choice-maker need not be supposed to lack an integrated self. Clueless people make choices that they suppose are in their own best interests. They consistently fail in that enterprise because they are bad at it. Given this context, rationality is revealed to be a kind of expertise, rather than a natural property of all agents, always.

Cluelessness, as lack of expertise in choosing among options, need not be a rare condition. Among other Homeric heroes, Achilles himself seems a prime candidate for cluelessness—had he been able to reason "backwards and forwards" he might, for example, have recognized that his withdrawal from the fight had a substantial chance of leading to a terrible outcome, for himself among others: the death of Patroclus. Examples of clueless Homeric heroes could be multiplied, and they could be contrasted with choices made by those individuals whose grasp of strategic reasoning seems much more secure—for example "wily Odysseus" and the elders who are explicitly described as knowing to look backwards and forwards.[25]

The question remains, does the prevalence of cluelessness reduce the value of strategic calculation? The chance that a clueless agent will be a player in a given game can be factored into the probability estimates of a rational player. But an unquantified-yet-high level of cluelessness in the population intuitively makes strategic calculation more difficult. I propose that one way that the world of Plato and Aristotle differed from the world of Homer was a reduced level of cluelessness in matters

24. Chwe borrows the term "clueless" from the title of the wildly successful 1995 Hollywood teen film of that title, itself loosely based on Jane Austen's 1815 novel *Emma*. He notes that standard approaches to game theory fail to account for the presence of clueless agents. He argues that "cluelessness" should be considered Austen's original contribution to game theory.

25. Schofield (1999: chap. 1, "*Euboulia* in the *Iliad*") demonstrates, against the psychological primitivism advocated by Finley (1965), that some Homeric heroes (notably Nestor, Odysseus, Diomedes, and Poulydamas) and councils (e.g., at the beginning of book 14) can, and periodically do, exhibit rationality, in the sense of seeking the best outcome through a deliberative process of reason-giving. That process sometimes (although not always: good counsel is often ignored) leads to choosing the available option determined to be most advantageous, rather than, for example, most honorable.

of exchange. And one reason for that posited reduction was an increase in self-conscious awareness of what I am calling the folk theory, an awareness associated with the teaching of the Sophists if not invented by them. The Socratic project was, in these terms, intended as a third way, enabling agents to escape from the unhappy binary of irrational cluelessness and rationality that remained incapable of identifying ethically choice-worthy ends.

7.4 SOCRATIC PHILOSOPHY, M. I. FINLEY, AND "THE ANCIENT ECONOMY"

Besides violent expropriation of goods from the weaker by the stronger, the primary mode of exchange in Homeric epic is the reciprocal giving and receiving of gifts among peers. Homeric gift exchange could be essentially rational, in that what is given and taken is understood by both parties as comparable in value. In this case the gain arising from an exchange was only secondarily the material welfare of those involved in the exchange. The primary goal was the establishment, affirmation, or enhancement of a valued social relationship.[26] But material value was not irrelevant, as shown by the Glaukos-Diomedes exchange of ordinary bronze armor for super-valuable gold armor (*Iliad* 6.234–36), a gift exchange that appears to involve an element of cluelessness, as susceptibility to rhetorical cleverness, on the part of one of the parties.[27] In any event, the "reciprocal gifts" mode of exchange, like violent expropriation by the stronger, is fundamentally different from whatever practices of money-making (whether production of goods for sale, or trade and commerce) that had allowed Cephalus I to multiply his family fortune several times over and then enabled Cephalus II to restore the family fortune after the losses incurred by Lysanias.[28]

---

26. Gift exchange: Mauss (1954) 1990; Finley (1973) 1999; cf. Millett 1991.

27. In a line reminiscent of Agamemnon's attributing his error to *atē*, the poet opines that Zeus stole away Glaukos' wits. Aristotle (*NE* 1136b10–14), by contrast, takes this as an example of a voluntary exchange of goods not predicated on their equal (monetary) value. For discussion see Traill 1989.

28. Hans van Wees (1998: 19–20) points out that, in anthropological theory, the difference between personal reciprocity-based gift exchange and market exchange is that the former is overtly based on norms of generosity, even if covertly on self-interest, while self-interest is the overt motivation in the latter. He also (29–33) discusses the intimate connection between reciprocal exchanges and social status differentiation and shows (34–41) that forms of reciprocity and markets are found in modern and premodern cultures, and that economic interests are served by both forms of exchange. Van Berkel

I suggested, above, that Plato's Socrates foreclosed further discussion of economic behavior, whether production or exchange, centered on voluntary contracts and motivated by the goal of "creatively" increasing the wealth of those involved. That foreclosure was, I believe, motivated by Plato's recognition of the prevalence of economically rational behavior among his contemporaries—that is, their habit of making choices and performing actions aimed at maximizing expected value, with value being denominated in money and the primary mechanism being the fair contract.

The economic activity that Socrates pushes off the table in the Cephalus interchange can be summed up as the practices that Aristotle, in his discussion of corrective justice in book 5 of the *Nicomachean Ethics,* lists under the rubric of voluntary (*hekousia*) transactions: selling, buying, lending, pledging, renting, depositing, and hiring out. Aristotle (*NE* 1131a1–9) contrasts those forms of voluntary transaction with involuntary transactions, involving deception or the use of force: features highlighted in Plato's Socrates' reference to Homer's Autolycus, above.[29] As we have seen, some forms of voluntary transaction were known to Homer. And Aristotle certainly recognized the persistence of deceptive and violent involuntary transactions in his own day. The difference is that, for Aristotle, involuntary transactions involved wrongdoing and required corrective justice, whereas in Homer, such transactions were a primary and descriptively legitimate basis of exchange. All of this suggests that "the world of Plato and Aristotle" was, in relevant economic particulars, quite different from "the world of Homer."

Finley and His Critics

Yet according to the still-influential work of the historian M.I. Finley, the violence and gift-exchange economy that characterized what Finley (1965) famously called "the world of Odysseus" was not meaningfully different from the economy of the classical era. For Finley, Greeks from Homer to Aristotle were driven by procedural not instrumental rationality, by a concern with status not wealth maximization. The ancient

---

(2020: chap. 1) surveys the literature on reciprocity and exchange, noting that the late classical period saw the emergence of "a new type of interpersonal relationship: the disembedded exchange; i.e. the instantaneous transaction of equivalent goods that takes place outside the norms of a durable relationship" (p. 5).

29. Deception: theft, adultery, drugging, pimping, slave-deception, murder by treachery, false witness. Force: imprisonment, murder, plunder, mutilation, slander, insult.

Greek was, in Max Weber's well-known distinction, consistently *homo politicus,* not *homo economicus.* If Finley's position were correct, it would have profound consequences for our conception of Greek economic rationality. Exchanges of goods predicated on violence and gift exchange can, per above, manifest a kind of rationality. But it is not the sort of mutual-profit-driven, "creative money-making" required to sustain a vibrant and growing market-based economy. The conclusion of Finley's argument is, in simplest terms, that because a market-based economy could not have existed in ancient Greece, given the presumed absence of the right kind of economic reasoning, it did not exist.[30]

Advocates of Finley's account of ancient economic behavior support their line of argument by reference to the sort of sentiments expressed by Plato's Socrates (above), when he queried Cephalus on the sources of the elderly metic's wealth. Since money-making was treated with scorn by spokesmen for aristocratic culture, so the argument goes, and since aristocratic culture defined the aspirations of most if not all Greeks, the conditions of Greek (and for that matter, Roman) society were inherently hostile to the emergence of the kind of economic thought and practice—prominently including instrumental rationality in matters of production and exchange—that could have produced efficient markets and long-term economic growth. This general approach sees little role in "the ancient economy" (Finley [1973] 1999) for profit-seeking, capital investment, or technological innovation. Finley's approach is variously described as "substantivism" (by its advocates) or "primitivism" (by its critics) and is contrasted by its proponents to "modernizing," "capitalistic," or "neoliberal" approaches to ancient economic history.[31]

Finley's line of argument on the ancient economy has been undermined in recent years by a substantial body of empirical scholarship. That work concludes, first, that there was in fact sustained and substantial growth in the Greek economy between the ages of Homer and of

30. On the sources from which Finley drew his understanding of modern economic theory, his sharp contrast between ancient and modern economic thought, and the importance for his argument of the lack of economic rationality, understood as the set of abstractions essential to modern economic reasoning, in antiquity, see Saller 2013. Finley's conclusions were embraced and amplified by, among many others, Millett 1991 and Meikle 1995.

31. Critical studies of Finley's work on the ancient economy and the "Finley School": Thompson 1982; Ian Morris, introduction to Finley (1973) 1999; Christesen 2003; Amemiya 2004; Scheidel, Morris, and Saller 2007: 1–12 (introduction); Jongman 2013; Harris, Lewis, and Woolmer 2015: 1–25 (introduction). I am indebted to many email exchanges with Daniel Tompkins on Finley's intellectual background and his oeuvre.

Plato and Aristotle. Next, economic growth was driven by (1) efficient methods of production, predicated on relative advantage, and aimed at increasing the quantity as well the quality of goods produced, and by (2) market exchanges based on voluntary contracts. Moreover, (3) the rational Greek state (notably, but not exclusively Athens) was increasingly cognizant—through its legislative, judicial, and administrative functions (chapter 6)—of the social (and taxable) value of providing rules and infrastructure aimed at facilitating the profitable production and exchange of goods. Those revisionist conclusions are based on detailed studies grounded in various kinds of evidence—some of it literary but much of it epigraphic, numismatic, and archaeological—for individual and state-level involvement in the production, consumption, and exchange of goods in Greek and Roman antiquity.[32]

Socratic Philosophers on the Economy: Interpretive Methods

If the "substantial growth" conclusion is correct, as I suppose it must be, it appears that in practice, at least, Greeks were quite capable of the kind of reasoning necessary to build and sustain a growing economy. That is to say, ancient Greeks, as individuals and collectives, frequently employed rationally instrumental reasoning in economic contexts. It is, nonetheless, undeniable that many passages in Greek and Roman literature manifest the moralizing attitude to wealth accumulation and money-making that was emphasized by Finley ([1973] 1999: chap. 2) and his followers. Those expressions underpin the theory of an essentially timeless and changeless ancient economy, predicated on piratical violence and gift exchange. The many surviving works of classical-era Socratics—Plato, Xenophon, and Aristotle—figure prominently in that ancient body of evidence. While scorn for those engaged in trade and commerce can certainly be found outside the philosophical corpus (Dover 1974: 172–74), absent the works of the Socratic philosophers, our sense of what "Greek literature" has to say about economic activity would be very different.

The question then arises: What is the relationship between Socratic philosophy and the thought processes and practices expressed in the visible (to historians studying classical antiquity) economic activities of the great majority of Greeks who did not leave philosophical texts to posterity? There are several possibilities.

---

32. Growth: above, note 3. Production: Acton 2014. Trade: Bresson 2015. State policy: Fawcett 2016; Carugati 2019: chap. 4.

The first possibility involves a causal argument: Philosophical literature was the primary source of everyday thought and practice on economic matters. This seems to me so unlikely as not to merit much further discussion. That rejection requires some qualifications. There is certainly no reason to believe that Greek philosophers were without social influence. Nor, *a fortiori,* is there reason to believe that they lacked any interest in influencing the societies in which they lived.[33] Indeed, I will argue, below, that Plato and Aristotle hoped to turn their readers away from what they saw as a corrupting attachment to immoralist and amoral instrumentalism. But that is very different from claiming that the Greeks organized production and exchange on the basis of philosophical recommendations.

A second possibility centers on faithful descriptive representation: The economic attitudes expressed in Socratic texts are reasonably accurate reflections of the background thought and practice of the Greek society in which those works were produced. If that were the case, comments in the relevant texts along the lines of "Socrates disapproved of money-making" would allow us to make positive claims about the relevant Greek social attitudes: "Ancient Greeks disapproved of money-making." If we were to go so far as to assume that the descriptive representation of prevalent social attitudes in surviving Greek philosophical literature was comprehensive, we would feel justified in taking the silence of our surviving literary record as reliable evidence of absence. Thus, for example, the fact that Aristotle did not produce a (genuine) work on "economics" to match his detailed treatments of, say, politics, ethics, and rhetoric would allow us to assume that there was no systematic Greek thought on economic matters. Faithful, and even "comprehensive," representation assumptions are characteristic features of arguments in support of Finley's substantivist conclusions.[34]

There is good reason to think that in some texts, for example, in the empirical parts of Aristotle's *Politics,* a classical Greek philosopher was indeed concerned with explicating the actual thought and/or practice of a reasonably broad cross section of his contemporary society: Aristotle's "endoxic" method of establishing valid premises in areas of inquiry (like political science) that cannot be advanced syllogistically draws on the opinions (*endoxa*) held by "respectable people." Nonetheless, it is invalid to assume that in most, or even many cases, an attitude expressed

33. See, for example, D. Allen 2010 on Plato's purposes in writing.
34. See, for example, Meikle 1995: 64–66, 149; Grewal 2010.

in a Greek philosophical text was, or was meant by its author to be, an accurate representation of ordinary social assumptions. The classical philosophy relevant to our inquiry is explicitly evaluative and normative rather than transparently descriptive. Evaluative texts critically examine existing states of affairs; normative texts express what their author supposes ought to be the case, rather than what is typically the case. Evaluative and normative texts thus engage with background beliefs and behaviors, but they do not represent them in any straightforward way, and do not purport to do so. The relative uselessness of philosophical texts for establishing the attitudes of ordinary Greeks has long been recognized by historians of ancient values and ideologies. Kenneth Dover's *Greek Popular Morality* (1974: 1–33), for example, abjured the use of philosophical texts in favor of, especially, comedy and oratory.[35]

My own earlier work rejected the hypothesis that philosophical texts were representational in the sense sketched above. In *Mass and Elite in Democratic Athens* (1989), which was aimed at reconstructing the popular ideologies that underpinned Athenian democratic discourse and practice, I followed Dover in focusing primarily on Athenian oratory and, to a lesser extent, comedy. In *Political Dissent in Classical Athens* (1998) I argued that much of what Plato and Aristotle (among others) had to say about democracy should be understood as evaluative criticism of democratic thought and practice, aimed, at least in part, at establishing a normative basis for more choice-worthy forms of social order. Moreover, I argued that philosophical criticism of democracy ought to be read in the context of a long and engaged debate among Athenian citizens, intellectuals, and writers of texts about the problems of democracy. And finally, I suggested that classical Greek texts critical of democracy were motivated, not by Athenian democracy's evident failure, but rather by its apparent success in securing the ends commonly sought by Greek states, when compared to other real-world forms of government known to their authors.

In a similar fashion, I now suggest a third way of relating the texts of the philosophers to the thought and practice of their contemporaries concerning economic production and exchange—to money-making and the employment of instrumental rationality in the creation and accumulation

---

35. Dillon 2004, inspired by Dover, includes illustrative philosophical anecdotes, but distinguishes them as "theory" in contrast to the "practice" illustrated by, primarily, oratory and comedy. Van Berkel (2020: 63) puts it well: "Xenophon, Plato, and Aristotle are like grammar teachers: by articulating the rules they attempt to control rather than merely reflect the norms of what counts as socially desirable behavior and what not."

of wealth. Per above, this third way assumes that the approach of the Socratic philosophers to economic rationality was fundamentally critically evaluative and normative. As with the case of democracy, philosophical criticism was motivated by the evident (and to the critics' minds, problematic) effectiveness of the relevant practices: Rational economic behavior by money-makers in the Greek world often (although certainly not always: cf. Lysianas) achieved the ends desired by and aimed at by its practitioners. Those ends were pursued though deliberation, choices based on ranked preferences over available outcomes, and actions following on the choices in pursuit of maximizing value denominated in monetary terms.

In the briefest and bluntest terms, then, I suppose that the Socratic philosophers were acute observers of the behavior of economically rational agents, operating within the rules and norms established by rational city-states, in the wider context of a quasi-rational interstate order. Of course, per the previous chapters, that blunt characterization requires very considerable qualification: Neither individual nor collective agents were analogues of the model choice-makers of formal decision and game theories. But enough Greeks (like Cephalus I and II), and enough Greek states (like Athens), were sufficiently expert at practical economic reasoning to provoke from the philosophers a profound, and historically influential critique.

Reading Socratic philosophy as a normative critique of economic rationality will be more convincing if it can be shown that Plato, Xenophon, and Aristotle understood the economic processes of a society in which rational economic choices informed the production and exchange of goods (per Christesen 2003; Bresson 2015). The framework for that demonstration has been established in the earlier chapters: Socratic philosophers (among others) sought to explain the role of instrumental rationality in contexts ranging from individual motivation, to the origins of social order, to the constitutional organization of states, to interstate relations. There is, therefore, prima facie reason to suppose that the Socratics would be attuned to economic rationality if it was a prevalent mode of thought and practice among their contemporaries.

It is certainly true that there is no sustained and systematic treatment of economic theory and practice comparable, say, to Adam Smith's *Wealth of Nations* ([1776] 1981) in the surviving literature from Greek antiquity. Yet there is, by the same token, ample evidence for sophisticated understanding of relevant economic concepts among the Socratics.[36] Here I point to a few highlights. The general point is that the scattered and compressed, but also astute and well-informed, treatments of economic behavior in our surviving philosophical texts would not have been possible if the Socratics were as blind to the motivations and practices of economic agents as is often assumed by modern scholars.

Money-Making Sophists

The backdrop to the Socratic engagement with economic activity includes not only the quotidian business of producing, exchanging, and consuming goods and services, but also involvement by the Sophists in a market for technical knowledge. Plato's Protagoras provides the most obvious example: In the dialogue named for him, the self-proclaimed Sophist proudly announces that he does charge a fee for his services. Plato's Protagoras is so confident that the value of his teaching will be recognized by his students that he offers them two payment options: Either they pay his stated fee, or they go to a temple and swear an oath to the effect that Protagoras' teaching is worth some other, presumably lesser, amount (Plato *Protagoras* 328b–c). Socrates' concern (*Protagoras* 313c–e) is that in order for the contract to be genuinely fair and honest, the seller must have true knowledge of the likely effects of his product (in this case on the soul of the buyer) and the buyer must be genuinely able to assess the true value to himself of what he has bought.

The burden of Plato's *Protagoras* is to show that Protagoras lacks the relevant knowledge and thus is not an honest retailer. Given his own imperfect understanding of his wares, and his students' ignorance of their pernicious effects, sophistic education is shown to be at best a danger, rather than a benefit, to the souls of those involved in it. Given the high epistemic bar of achieving the kind of comprehensive knowledge of true benefit Socrates alludes to, it seems implausible that any real-world retailer or purchaser of educational "soulcraft" services could meet his standard. Socrates of Plato's *Apology* (19d–20c) sharply distinguishes himself from his contemporary intellectuals concerned with justice, virtue, politics, and related matters, by his pointed refusal to accept payment from would-be students. In the Socratic philosophical tradition (although not in the comic tradition) Socrates stands

36. See especially Schofield 1999: chap. 4; Meikle 1995; Van Berkel 2020. Cf. Finley 1970; Lowry 1987; Panayotis, Kardasi, and Milios 2011; Leshem 2016.

outside the commercial relationship of exchanging expert knowledge or know-how for money.[37]

David Blank (1985: 3, cited in Tell 2011: chap. 2 n. 1) notes that "the testimonia referring to the fees, wealth, and mode of life of the Sophists are tinged with both envy and disgust. They are extremely difficult to interpret, both in specific and in their general tendency."[38] One might add that the Socratic testimonia are also characterized by their pointed refusal to detail what exactly it is that the Sophists actually taught, other than rhetoric. The knowledge that Plato's Protagoras offers for sale is summed up by the Sophist as follows: "That learning consists of good judgment [euboulia] in his own affairs [peri tōn oikeiōn], showing how best to order his own household [oikia]; and in the affairs of his polis, showing how he may be most effective [dunatōtatos] in public affairs both in speech and in action" (Plato, Protagoras 318e–19a).

We are offered no specifics about Protagoras' course in the development of deliberative judgment about private and public affairs. There is every reason to suppose that it would entail aspects of the folk theory of instrumental rationality. But there is little reason to suppose that Protagoras would have embraced the narrowly egoistic Thrasymachean version of instrumentalism, predicated on the advantage of the strong and the use of strength to satisfy the strongman's desires at the expense of the weak. It is at least plausible to suppose that Protagoras taught some of the theoretical concepts that he supposed (rightly or otherwise) stood behind the kind of effective management of family wealth that was the forte of Cephalus I and in which Cephalus II was at least moderately skilled. That need not imply a practical course in how to be an expert entrepreneur. But it might well have concerned basic principles of instrumentally rational contracting.

---

37. For detailed discussions of the classical sources on the Sophists teaching for money, see Blank 1985; Tell 2011. Tell argues, against Blank, that there is little evidence, outside the Platonic tradition and those (like Isocrates) in critical engagement with that tradition or (like Philostratus) dependent on it, for popular concern about Sophists (at least in the Platonic sense) teaching for pay.

38. Cf. Tell 2011: chap. 2 (introduction): "Why is money so important as a distinguishing trait? In this chapter I will argue that it is not a descriptive term reflecting historical realities—that the Sophists were the first to charge money for wisdom—but rather that the close association of the Sophists with money is redolent of disparagement and bias, a fact that scholars have perhaps not paid sufficient attention to."

7.5 XENOPHON ON MANAGING
HOUSEHOLDS AND STATES

Xenophon's Socrates in book 1 of the *Memorabilia* shares, indeed inten-
sifies, the scorn of Plato's Socrates for the activities of those who purport to sell wisdom:

> We call those who sell their wisdom to anyone who wants it sophists, just as
> if they were prostitutes [*pornoi:* the comparison is to a man who sells the use
> of his beautiful body]. Whereas a man who befriends and teaches all the
> good he can to someone he knows to have a good natural disposition—he is
> considered to do what befits a good and noble citizen. (*kalos kagathos
> politēs:* 1.6.13)

At *Memorabilia* 2.6, the scorn for the wisdom-seller seemingly extends
to the entire class of those overly involved in economic activities. In the
midst of a discussion of those who are valuable or lack value as friends,
Xenophon's Socrates rejects as worse even than the miser, the "one who
is skilled at money-making and desires to make money and consequently
drives a hard bargain, who likes to receive but does not wish to repay."
And likewise, "the man with such a passion for money-making that he
has no time for anything but the selfish pursuit of gain" is rejected:
"There is no profit in knowing him" (2.6.3–4). We will return to the
profitability of friendship in chapter 8.5.

In a passage that recalls the management of public and private affairs
touted by Plato's Protagoras, Xenophon's Socrates discusses generalship
with the disgruntled Athenian Nicomachides, who has lost an election
for the office of general (*stratēgos*) in favor of Antisthenes. The latter,
Nicomachides complains, has no relevant military experience and
"understands nothing but money-making" (3.4.1). When Socrates
points out that Antisthenes may well prove to be effective at logistics,
Nicomachides responds, "Large-scale merchants [*emporoi*] too are
capable of making money, but that doesn't make them fit to command
an army" (3.4.2). Socrates points out that Antisthenes has highly relevant skills: He knows how to identify and employ experts in various
domains. Moreover, "whatever a man controls, if he knows what is
needed and can provide it, he will be a good controller [*prostatēs*],
whether he controls a chorus, a household, a polis, or an army" (3.4.6).

Nicomachides is surprised to hear Socrates say that good *oikonomoi*
would make good *stratēgoi,* but Socrates quickly establishes the points
that both the *oikonomos* and the *stratēgos* are similar in that they must

make those carrying out their orders obedient and willing (i.e., loyal agents of the principal); must reward and punish appropriately (provide proper incentives); must win the good will of subordinates, and attract allies and helpers; must be good guardians of possessions, careful and hard-working, capable of outdoing enemies; and must be cognizant that victory over opponents is most profitable (*lusitelēs*), just as defeat is unprofitable (*alusitelēs*). And they must be willing to invest resources accordingly (3.4.7–11). Socrates concludes with a comment on appropriate authority relations, presumed to be common to household and state:

> Do not look down on men engaged in economic activities [*oikonomikoi andres*], Nicomachides. For the management of private concerns differs only in scale from that of public affairs. In other respects, they are much alike, and particularly in this, that neither can be carried on without people, and the people employed in private and public transactions are the same. For those who take charge of public affairs employ just the same people when they attend to their own; and those who understand how to employ them are successful directors of public and private concerns, and those who do not, fail in both. (3.4.12)

We are never told what sort of money-making activities Antisthenes engaged in. Nicomachides' comment that "merchants too" (*kai gar hoi emporoi*) are competent money-makers might be taken to imply that Antisthenes is not a merchant—so how then does he make his money? Xenophon declines to say, and the refusal is, I think, a pointed one.

When Xenophon came to write his own text on the management of a private estate, the *Oikonomikos,* he seemingly ignores commercial activities. The focus is on how to organize a gentleman's agricultural enterprise and how to train a young wife to be an effective partner in, for example, the day-to-day management of slaves. Again, the concern is appropriate relations of authority: husband to wife, master to slave. The apparent absence of "economic" reasoning in Xenophon's *Oikonomikos* has been taken as evidence of the absence of such thought in classical Greece.[39] Yet Socrates offers to introduce his interlocutor to

---

39. By, for example, Finley (1999: 19): "In Xenophon, however, there is not one sentence that expresses an economic principle or offers any economic analysis, nothing on efficiency of production, 'rational' choice, the marketing of crops." See, in more detail, Grewal 2010. Christ (2020: chap. 3), however, reads the text as teaching the aspiring elite political leader both the imperative and the strategic means of increasing (rather than just spending) private wealth. Christ notes (75 n. 15) the prevalence of the Greek verb *auxō* and its related forms. Pomeroy (1994) offers a historical commentary on the text, which seeks a balance between Xenophon as a Socratic theorist and a representative of the practices typical of an aristocratic class.

experts who could teach him how to be an "entrepreneur," capable of producing goods "more quickly, easily, and with more profit" (2.18). Moreover, as Matthew Christ (2020: 95–97) points out, the *Oikonomikos* includes an account (20.22–24) of the explicitly entrepreneurial practice of buying up uncultivated farmland, improving it, and reselling it at a large profit.

Xenophon was clearly aware of how competent men engaged in economic activities could, at least in principle, make the transition from managing their own affairs, with an aim of increasing private wealth, to managing the affairs of the polis, aiming at enhancing the security and welfare of the community. If we accept that much of Xenophon's work, like Plato's, was intended as a two-edged critical intervention, aimed at quotidian Greek economic practices on the one hand and the instrumentalist theories being propounded by the Sophists on the other, the "evidence of absence" argument loses force.

Xenophon's own grasp of the relevance of individual economic rationality for public finances is evident in the *Poroi* (*Revenues*), a work in which Xenophon advocates for various ways in which the Athenian state could raise more money.[40] His recommendations range from the use of state funds to purchase a large number of mining slaves—in a sort of wishful Athenian version of Spartan helotage—to seemingly more practical measures to encourage merchants to trade in Athenian markets rather than elsewhere (3.3–13). The goal is increasing "imports and exports, sales, rents, and customs" (Xenophon, *Poroi* 3.5). The methods he recommends include rewarding officials responsible for regulating market activity, with the aim of ensuring quick and just settlements of commercial disputes; eliminating burdensome civic duties imposed on metics; and investment in economic infrastructure: hotels, mercantile halls, houses, and shops in Piraeus and the central city. The capital for the necessary improvements could, he suggests, be raised by loans to the state by private individuals. The latter will, he confidently asserts, recognize the low-risk nature of their investment, given the state's reputation for stability.

In the *Poroi*, Xenophon demonstrates a recognition of the choices being made by a highly mobile, profit-oriented population of persons engaged in production and commercial exchange—men like Cephalus I and II. He clearly understands the kind of cost-benefit reasoning employed

---

40. Whitehead (2019) offers a full discussion of the text and its historical and intellectual contexts.

by successful, creative money-makers: traders will flock to Athens, Xenophon claims, if and only if the legal environment is favorable (that is, locals will not use the courts to cheat foreigners), if they are not saddled with citizen-like military duties that get in the way of their money-making goals, and if the publicly provided infrastructure is well suited to their needs. There is no hint here of admiration for money-makers as such, no sense that Xenophon would disagree with Plato's Socrates of *Republic* book I that such people were "difficult to spend time with." But by the same token, it is clear that he understands the motivation of the relevant population as economic rationality, rather than morally appropriate authority relations, and he understands how a rational state, concerned with its finances, ought to respond to that motivation.

7.6 PLATO THE ECONOMIST: THE FIRST POLIS OF *REPUBLIC* BOOK 2

Given Socrates' expressed disinclination to spend time with money-makers in the introductory scene of the *Republic*, we might conclude that Plato had no very deep interest in or understanding of the economic processes that had created the material conditions of the world in which he lived. But a reconsideration of the "First Polis" in *Republic* book 2 suggests otherwise. The First Polis, an imaginary community that is described by Socrates as genuine and healthy (see below), establishes an economic foundation for Callipolis. As we have seen (chapter 3.1), the First Polis lacks luxuries and thus has no need of luxury-goods industries, military-expert Guardians, or political-expert philosopher-kings. But its very existence is predicated on the basic fact of human interdependence (369b–c), which implies the practice of mutually beneficial exchange of surplus created through productive activity: "They [all humans in communities] each share things [*metadidōsi*] with each other, if there is something to share, or trade them [*metalambanei*], believing that this is better for each of them." Thus, from the beginning, the motivation for both sharing and trading is the presence of surplus and a belief that exchange is not only constitutive of the community itself, but also advantageous to each party to the transaction. Here we have a sketch of the microfoundations of an economically productive social order.[41]

---

41. Schofield (1999: chap. 4, "Plato on the Economy") and Weinstein (2009) offer detailed examinations of this section of the *Republic*. Schofield concludes that it supplies "a sort of transcendental deduction of the very existence of the market, which constitutes—

Those engaged in the relevant activities are, to begin with, a farmer, a house builder, a weaver, and a shoemaker, and "anyone else to deal with our physical needs" (369d). Each will choose to specialize in one and only one activity. The "subsistence alternative," in which each individual (or, we might suppose, each family) provides all necessities for himself, is quickly rejected as hopelessly inefficient (369e–70a). Socrates sums up:

> Indeed, as a result of this [specialization of economic functions] all these things [the necessities of life: food, housing, clothing] grow [*pleiō*] and become better [*kallion*] and easier [*rhaion*] when one man does one job according to nature, at the right time, and free from other tasks. (370c)[42]

In this succinct statement, Plato's Socrates establishes the "each to his own" doctrine that will eventually prove to be the principle of justice in Callipolis. This is a centrally important ethical result to which we will return in chapter 8.

For our present purposes, the point is that it also captures the essence of an economy of increased consumption, based on specialized production and market exchange of surplus generated by specialization. That surplus is, compared with the rejected subsistence alternative, produced with less effort. It is, consequently, greater in quantity (*pleiō*) as well as superior in quality (*kallion*).[43] This neatly captures the basic "Smithian"

I submit—the invention of the concept of an economy." Building on Schofield's chapter, Weinstein seeks to go one step further. He argues for the importance of Plato's account of the market due to its capacity to unify various aspects of the polis, and to integrate a variety of needs into a single framework, capable of satisfying those needs. Weinstein suggests that Plato's market does so via aggregated knowledge: providing "the single locus where all this disparate knowledge is integrated, converted into useful concretes, distributed, and made effective for the city as a whole" (453). Weinstein first cites Adam Smith ([1776] 1981: 1.7.8–14) as a modern example of this sort of market responsiveness, but it more readily recalls Hayek (1945) on the uses of knowledge in society: acknowledged at 454 n. 30.

42. This passage (reminiscent of Xenophon, *Oikonomikos* 2.18, cited above) is called out for special attention by Schofield (1999: 75–77), who rightly points out the central assumptions of efficiency and growth. Schofield (p. 75) also notes Finley's neglect of the passage.

43. The key term, *pleiō*, is also used by Cephalus (330b, and see above) in reference to the difference between what he inherited and what (through his own money-making acumen) he will leave to his heirs. Thus, in the context of discussions of wealth in the *Republic*, it is connected to "creative" wealth-growing processes. The term recurs in a particularly important passage in book 9 (591a) in which the "Gyges model" is definitively refuted: "In what way, then, Glaucon, and on what principle, shall we say that it profits a man to be unjust or licentious or do any shameful thing that will make him a worse man, but otherwise will bring him increased wealth [*pleiō chrēmata*] or any other power?"

idea of specialization and exchange predicated on an assumption of rationally cooperative (non-Thrasymachean), mutually beneficial self-interest (A. Smith [1776] 1981).

The possibility of an ancient Greek writer grasping Smithian economic principles was, however, bluntly rejected by M.I. Finley:

> The very few Ancient writers who mention division of labor at all do so in a context and from a point of view which are essentially different from Adam Smith's. They were interested in the quality of manufacture, not in quantity or efficiency. Indeed, the very notion of "efficiency" is one of the best examples of a modern concept which, though taken as self-evident, turns out to be missing (in such contexts) throughout Antiquity.[44]

Finley's claims here rest solidly on the assumption that Greek literature represents, in a more or less comprehensive way, the underlying social reality. Thus, (in)frequency of ancient references to division of labor is taken as indicative of its relative (un)importance. Moreover, when a conception is "missing" in ancient literature, the associated practices can safely be assumed to be absent in "Antiquity."

The key takeaway from the passages from *Republic* book 2, cited above, is that Finley's claim that quality alone, and not quantity or efficiency, is the sole concern of those ancient authors who do notice division of labor is flatly contradicted by Plato. Quality is indeed a concern for production in the First Polis (as it is in Smithian economics), but so too are quantity and efficiency. In Plato's text, the three distinct elements of economic improvement—efficiency (ease with which goods are produced), quantity (amount of goods), and quality (excellence of goods)—are tightly linked in an analytically coherent package. If we reject the representational premise as an explanation for the relationship between philosophical texts and reality, in favor of the normative/evaluative premise I have argued for above, Plato's description of the First Polis can be read as evidence both for his firm grasp of the basic economic processes operative in the classical Greek world, and for his critical stance toward those processes.[45]

As the interlocutors of *Republic* book 2 continue their construction of the First Polis, the number of productive specialists increases, such

44. Finley 1963: 29–30. The specific target is Gomme 1937, a paper critical of the conclusions of Johannes Hasebroek on the lack of Greek state involvement in trade. As Finley notes, Hasebroek was (like Finley himself) influenced by Max Weber. My thanks to Dan Tompkins for drawing my attention to this passage.

45. On actual efficiency gains in classical Athenian manufacture, see Acton 2014.

that the First Polis is no longer a tiny state (*smikra polis*: 370d–e). In addition to local manufacture, imports appear to be essential—it is "almost impossible" to establish a polis in a place that has no need of imports (370e). Given that there cannot be imports without exports, the First Polis will need to attend to the wants of those from whom it imports goods (371a). This requires local production aimed explicitly at external markets and therefore knowledge of the consumption preferences of exchange partners. The First Polis will also need to include merchants (*emporoi*) and expert sailors to convey imports and exports (371a–b). The interlocutors next return to the problem of distributing the results of production, which will, "obviously" (*dēlon*), be effected through buying and selling (371b).[46] Thus the First Polis will require a market area (*agora*), "coinage as a token of exchange value" (371b), and full-time retail traders (*kapēloi*) to organize internal trade. In case we have forgotten Socrates' scorn for money-makers, these retailers are disparagingly described as physically weak and rendered unfit for any other work by dint of sitting about the *agora*, swapping goods for money (371c–d). Finally, manual workers (*misthōtoi*), persons who sell their labor for wages, must be added to the population. These persons (unlike the *emporoi* and *kapēloi*) are pointedly described as being unworthy of full membership in the community on the basis of their low intelligence (371e).

Socrates concludes his description of the First Polis with the lyrical account of the simple lives of its inhabitants, the passage that draws Glaucon's indignant retort about a "city of pigs." Glaucon's objection, as we have seen (chapter 3.1), leads to the radical expansion of the imagined polis, due to the need for many more specialists in the domains of production and exchange of luxury goods, military security, and ruling. The First Polis was described by Socrates as "genuine" (*alithēnē*) and healthy (*hugiēs*: 372e). This is presumably because its population was both moderate and effectively self-moderating: Once the First Polis had grown, through productive specialization and exchange, to the right size, it was capable of maintaining itself at a constant level. The moderation of desire for excess consumption is signaled by the eating of simple foods rather than fancy snacks (*opsa*). That simple food is served

---

46. Weinstein (2009: 444–45) emphasizes the shift from sharing (which he describes as "communalism") to market exchange that this sentence inaugurates. Cautiously invoking modern economic terminology, he concludes (p. 446), "The market is a solution to the problem of maintaining a balance of trade under conditions of uncertainty."

on reeds or clean leaves rather than ceramic or silver plates; it is consumed reclining on straw mattresses rather than on couches. Self-moderation is further exemplified by the capacity of the residents to voluntarily restrain their own biological reproduction (372a–c).

The First Polis lacks the special and (to Plato's Greek readers) counter-intuitive features of Callipolis (equal standing of Guardian women, elimination of private property and families for Guardians, and philosopher-kings). It also lacks some of the ordinary, but to Socrates' taste, undesirable, because unnecessary, features of Athens and other Greek states. The First Polis is therefore well suited to offering Plato's readers a concise course in fundamental economic processes. The principles on which the material needs of the residents of the First Polis are met are presented as universals. The economic processes that are discussed by Socrates, Glaucon, and Adeimantus are, therefore, foundational for *any* form of organized human community (or at least any polis): whether it is the genuine and healthy First Polis itself, expanded and initially "fever-ish" Callipolis, Socrates' imperial Athens, the postwar Athens familiar to Plato's first Greek readers, or some other real-world state. As such, the First Polis is evidence for Plato's understanding of the economic drivers of material welfare and potential growth. That understanding is at the micro level of the needs and beliefs of choice-making agents seeking what they regard as their own advantage. It is also at the macro level of the processes by which those agents organize mutually beneficial and efficient means of production and distribution of goods. The result is that, in comparison to a counterfactual inefficient and impoverished subsistence regime, more and better goods are made available for consumption.

Yet, at the same time, the First Polis is a critique of the tendency of an economy based on specialized production and exchange to produce unconstrained, unregulated, and therefore unhealthy growth. The potential for that sort of growth is inherent, first, in motivation by "irrational" desires: preferences that were not consciously and reflec-tively chosen in light of true knowledge about human welfare. And, next, in the economic processes devised by instrumentally rational agents for fulfilling those desires. The First Polis is self-regulating because those imagined as its residents lack the ordinary desires for luxury goods to which Glaucon's "city of pigs" objection calls attention and they moderate their other human desires (e.g., for more children).

As we have seen, Glaucon's challenge (the thought experiments dis-cussed in chapters 1.1–5 and 2.1–4) required that Socrates take ordi-nary human desires into account in devising his ideal polis. Callipolis avoids the danger of unregulated growth through the rule of the ethically, as well as instrumentally, rational philosopher-kings. Residents of other Greek poleis lacked both the self-moderation of the First Polis and philosopher-rulers, whose rationality extended to the systematic preference for genuinely choice-worthy ends. And so, most real-world Greek individuals and all states in the age of Plato are revealed as in various ways radically imperfect. They were at once a reflection and the source of an ultimately destructive, unbounded economic rationality. That dangerous rationality was exacerbated by sophistic learning and institutionalized in state-level rules and cultural norms.[47]

7.7 ECONOMIC RATIONALITY IN ARISTOTLE'S *POLITICS*

In *Politics* books 1 and 2, Aristotle takes up the normative project of critically evaluating consumption, production, and exchange. He does so insisting on the necessity of taking humans as the partially self-interested creatures that we are (1263b1). Aristotle's project is, moreover, consistently and explicitly engaged with observed practices in Greek society. In the *Politics* (2.2–5) Aristotle criticizes Plato's account of the lives of Guardians in the *Republic* (and thus the entire project of the dialogue) as hopelessly unrealistic: The elimination of the family ignores human nature and thereby fails in its aim of creating the conditions of human happiness. Moreover, the extension of the public domain to encompass, and thereby eliminate, all private property not only makes a fundamental category error, by modeling the polis on a household, but it also invites a commons tragedy:

> That which is common to the greatest number of owners receives the least attention; people care most for their private possessions, and for what they own in common less, or only so far as it falls to their own individual share; for in addition to the other reasons, they think less of it on the ground that someone else is thinking about it, just as in household management [*oiketikais diakoniais*] a large number of slaves sometimes give worse service than a smaller number.[48]

47. See further, Schriefl 2018: 194. Schriefl argues, correctly, that "the stringent property arrangements for the philosophical rulers of the ideal state are ultimately grounded in Plato's conception of true human excellence and the associated psychological theory," rather than in Plato's putatively conventionally aristocratic attitudes.

48. *Politics* 1261b33–38; cf. 1263a11–16: if resources are commonly held, disputes arise when some free-ride on others' efforts. Commons tragedy: G. Hardin 1968. Possible solutions: Ostrom 1990. Ostrom et al. 1999 cite the passage cited above as anticipating contemporary concern with common pool resources.

As we will see, however, for all his criticism of his predecessors, Aristotle is at one with Plato and Xenophon in conjoining a mastery of Greek economic practices with criticism. Moreover, while critical of simply collapsing the role of the expert politician into that of the expert householder, he shares with Plato's Protagoras and with Xenophon the belief that at least some aspects of expert management of an *oikos* and a polis are relevantly similar, insofar as they are predicated on the same motivational microfoundations—that is, the instrumental rationality assumed in the folk theory.

Aristotle's hierarchical, naturalized ethical teleology saw "living well" (*eu zēn*), in other words *eudaimonia,* as the point of human existence. Other features of the phenomenal world (e.g., animals that could be domesticated or hunted), in common with other aspects of human existence (gaining and using the resources necessary to live), were necessary conditions for, but essentially subsidiary to ("for the sake of") that final, highest end. Living well was a demanding goal. Aristotle's works on ethics and politics seek to survey the difficult terrain and to map a road through it, one that would allow the student to arrive at the proper end.

Book 1 of the *Politics* focuses, first, on antecedent material conditions necessary for at least some humans to live well and, next, on the natural forms of authority necessary for establishing and maintaining those conditions. That is, for Aristotle, the student of ethics and politics must take proper account of "merely living" (*zēn*) as the necessary material basis for the final end of living well (*eu zēn*) in a condition of sufficiency and state-level independence (*autarkeia*). He must do so in a way that is fully cognizant of the kinds of expertise necessary for living, without losing sight of the ultimate goal of living well. The domain of expertise that is concerned with natural material conditions and forms of authority (especially master-slave) required by the end of self-sufficiency is designated *oikonomia*. But the definition of *oikonomia* and especially its relationship to entrepreneurship (*chrēmatistikē*) is, Aristotle says, contested (1256a14–16 and below).

In *Politics* book 1 Aristotle recognizes entrepreneurship as expert knowledge of a particular relationship among production, exchange, and acquisition for consumption or possession, all characteristically involving coined money. Among his goals is placing that relationship into the normatively correct place in his naturalized hierarchy of value. The critical conclusion is that entrepreneurship (or one specific type of entrepreneurship) is a subordinate part of *oikonomia*. It is not "according to nature" (*kata phusin*) but rather a craft-skill (*technē*) arising from practical experience (*empeiria*). It aims at the possession and increase of wealth, at accumulation of money, as an end. That accumulation is by its internal logic unbounded and unconstrained, insofar as wealth denominated in monetary terms has no natural limit. Entrepreneurship thus is a matter of maximizing a single resource (one thought to give access to all other resources), rather than optimizing or satisficing in respect to higher values. As such, it is at once contrary to the true end of human existence (*eudaimonia*), a prevalent approach to the management of material goods, and (at least potentially) a useful instrument for both the expert householder (*oikonomos*) and the expert politician (*politikos*). Among the delicate tasks of book 1 of the *Politics* is specifying the proper uses of this dangerous and vulgar instrument, without honoring it as a science worthy of a detailed treatment.

Much of *Politics* 1.8–11 is devoted to sorting out the contested relationship between entrepreneurship and *oikonomia*.[49] The goal is, first, to elucidate the necessary and natural form of production, exchange, and possession/consumption and, next, to distinguish that necessary and natural form from its unnecessary and unnatural doppelganger. The confusion between the two types of economic activity arises because of their practical similarity and analytic proximity. The confusion arising from similarity and proximity is a matter of intense moral concern for Aristotle: The right (necessary and natural) kind of economic rationality contributed to the achievement of *eudaimonia*. The wrong kind of economic rationality (aimed at unbounded accumulation) rendered its practitioners incapable of living well. Unfortunately, that wrong kind of

49. Meikle (1995: chaps. 3 and 5) offers a detailed analysis of these chapters, seeking to square the sophistication of Aristotle's analysis of use and exchange with then-dominant assumptions about the primitive state of the Greek economy. This ends in a "paradox" (p. 196): "If Finley's conclusion seemed inescapable that Aristotle did no economics, it seems equally inescapable that Aristotle made a contribution to economics." He seeks to resolve the paradox by assuming that *NE* 5.5 was "a metaphysical inquiry" (p. 197) and *Politics* 1.8–10 was "ethical not economic" (p. 198). The either/or becomes both/and when we situate Aristotle in his proper historical context and recognize that his discussion of economic activity was both well-informed and critical. Balot (2001: 34–43) offers a thoughtful discussion of the relevant chapters, arguing that Aristotle's primary goal was not to explain economic activity, but rather "to illuminate the psychology of human beings in their capacity as acquisitive agents and to connect these features of human nature with the household and the polis" (pp. 34–35). Again, it becomes both/and (albeit ranked: the moral psychology is primary) once we see that Aristotle was concerned with explaining the microfoundations of social behavior. Miller (2005: 128–31) discusses the chapters with reference to Aristotle's ideas on property as an external good, and its relationship to *eudaimonia*; Leese (2021: 22–26) does so in reference to profit and wealth maximization.

economic reasoning was, Aristotle recognized, not only prevalent but hegemonic in its tendency to colonize other domains of human expertise and activity. This is part of the context for Aristotle's "best achievable" polis, described in *Politics* books 7 and 8. That "polis of our prayers" is characterized by norms and rules that sustain, for the citizens, the right kind of economic rationality and push back against the disruptive intrusion of the wrong kind.

Aristotle begins his discussion of economics by rejecting the claim of those who see the expert householder as engaged in just the same activity, albeit on a smaller scale, as the expert politician (1252a11ff.). This seems to contradict the line of argument developed by Xenophon in *Memorabilia* book 3 (above, 7.5). But, like Xenophon, Aristotle emphasizes, at *Politics* 1.3 (1253b 1–11) and throughout book 1, that *oikonomia* is primarily concerned with hierarchical relations of authority within the household. He notes that some say that the greatest part of it is actually "what is called entrepreneurship" (1253b14). After (inter alia) establishing that production is subordinate to use (*chrēsis*, because making is "for the sake of" using), and an extended discussion of the natural slave-master relationship, Aristotle returns at 1.8 (1256a1) to the examination, "by our usual methods," of matters concerning all forms of possession and entrepreneurship. He rejects the notion that *oikonomia* and entrepreneurship are the same thing, by pointing out that the latter concerns supply, but the former usage, of necessary goods (1256a10–11). And yet, acquiring goods is an essential first step in using them, so some acquisitions—those arising from hunting, pastoralism, and farming—turn out to be natural and necessary. Such naturally acquired things make up "genuine wealth" (*alēthinos ploutos*: 1256b30–31). This sort of wealth is aimed at self-sufficiency and the good life; it is not limitless (contra Solon). And so "it is clear that there is a natural expertise in acquisition" (1256b38–39).

And yet there is another kind of acquisition: "that they particularly call, and correctly, entrepreneurship, on account of which there is no limit of wealth or possession" (1256b40–1257a1). It is this limitless entrepreneurship that is considered by many to be the same as *oikonomia* because of their proximity (*geitniasis*: 1257a1–2). Although Aristotle concedes that the two are indeed "not far apart," he insists the many are wrong to identify the one with the other: *Oikonomia* is natural; entrepreneurship is not. The latter arises only from experience and craft-skill (1257a4–5). This seems to me to be a key moment in Aristotle's critical/descriptive account of economic relationships: The deceptive and dangerous proximity of natural, bounded, household economy to unnatural, unbounded entrepreneurship leads to their conflation and thereby lures people off the virtuous road to living well, into the morally dangerous terrain in which accumulation of wealth was unbounded and aimed at no end beyond itself.

Aristotle reiterates the main points: Exchange itself is not against nature, but arises necessarily from the fact that human communities, beyond the level of the household, have a surplus or shortfall of certain material necessities due to the uneven distribution of natural resources (1257a14–30). Entrepreneurship arose logically (*kata logon*) from those conditions (1257a30–31). Here, Aristotle has seemingly identified a natural entrepreneurship that is closely identified with *oikonomia*. Yet as imports and exports of surplus increased (*epleonazon*), money, and then coinage, came into being in order to facilitate the necessary exchanges. Then, with the increased money supply, the "other kind" of entrepreneurship came about: retail exchange (*to kapelikon:* 1257b1–2),

> which at first no doubt went on in a simple form, but later became more highly organized [*technichōteron*] as experience discovered the sources and methods of exchange that would cause most profit [*kerdos*]. Hence arises the idea that entrepreneurship deals especially with money, and that its function is to be able to discern from what source a large supply can be procured, as this art is supposed to be creative of wealth and riches. (1257b2–5)

And thus, entrepreneurship came to be associated with money, especially coined money (*nomisma*), "and to have as its function [*ergon*] the ability to discern what will provide a quantity [*plēthos*] of riches" (*chrēmata:* 1257a5–7). Here, Aristotle has introduced the essential issue of measurement: Among the seductive attractions of this "other kind" of entrepreneurship is the ease with which utility is denominated and measured.

After noting that in certain ways coinage seems unnatural and useless, Aristotle returns to the original, natural kind of entrepreneurship, "limited" *oikonomia,* and to its difference from retail-entrepreneurship. The latter is productive of riches only through exchange (1257b22), is unlimited, and has as its end "this sort of wealth and the acquisition of riches" (1257b29–30). Thus, while in one way there is a necessary limit to wealth,

> yet looking to what actually happens, we observe that the opposite takes place; for all people engaged in wealth-getting try to increase their money to an unlimited amount. The reason of this is the close affinity [*sunengus*] of the two . . . So, some people suppose that this [increase of wealth] is the function

of *oikonomia,* and they proceed in this way believing that what is demanded is either to safeguard their property in the form of money or to increase it to an unlimited amount. (1257b32–40)

Here again, and with specific reference to the difference between his own theory and the actual conditions of his time, Aristotle raises the issue of dangerous proximity—the definitional confusion that leads people off the road to the correct end of limited acquisition and *eudaimonia* into the morally corrupting pursuit of unconstrained increase in readily quantified wealth. The root cause is the confusion of mere life with living well: Having an unlimited desire for living, "they" also desire unlimited productivity (1258a1–20).

Ominously, even those who do aim at living well seek bodily pleasures, which are available only through possessions. Thus, their concern is only with money-making, and this is how the other (unnatural) form of entrepreneurship has arisen (1258a4–6). This insight sets up a critical payoff:

> For as their enjoyment is in excess, they seek expertise productive of enjoyable excess; and if they are unable to supply it by entrepreneurship, they attempt this by some other means, employing each of the capacities [*dunameis*] in an unnatural way. For it belongs to courage not to produce wealth, but confidence; nor to generalship nor to medicine, but it belongs to the former to bring victory and to the latter to cause health. Yet these people make all these into entrepreneurship, as if this were the end, and that everything must march towards it. (1258a6–14)

Here, entrepreneurship of the wrong, unnatural sort has become totalizing. Operationalized through the driving force of human desire for more, readily measured in the form of coined money, by coming to be regarded as the final end of human activity, it colonizes and displaces other forms of worthy human endeavor—Aristotle recurs to the standard Socratic examples of medicine and generalship. What is left is the narrowly instrumental logic of unbounded growth and wealth as an end in itself. The similarity to twenty-first-century critiques of "neoliberal" economic rationality is striking.

After further rehearsing the now-familiar distinction between praiseworthy *oikonomia* and blameworthy entrepreneurship, Aristotle notes that money-lending at interest (*obolostatikē*) is most reasonably hated because what it produces is from the operation of money itself and not the exchange of other goods. Interest (*tokos*) charged on a loan, he notes, actually just creates more money. In a passage reminiscent of

Plato on the similarity of money-making to child-bearing, Aristotle claims that just as children are similar to their parents, "so too interest is money born of money." So, he concludes, this part of entrepreneurship is especially contrary to nature (1258b2–8). It is not a choiceworthy end, and it aims at no worthy end beyond itself.[50]

Having completed the part of his economic discussion concerned with knowledge, Aristotle pivots to matters concerned with practice. He notes that experience in such things is actually necessary (1258b10–11). Presumably, by extrapolation from what has gone before, it is necessary both for the material well-being of private individuals and for statesmen concerned with the conditions necessary for flourishing communities. After a discussion of livestock and farming, the "most proper" (oikeiotatē) parts of entrepreneurship, Aristotle turns to exchange, especially its major part: emporia—large-scale, overseas mercantile exchange. The relevant parts of emporia are, first, ship-provisioning, transport of goods, and marketing—these subparts, he says, differ from one another in that some are safer and others more (pleiō) remunerative (1258a23–25). Here then is a clear implication that, since greater risk is closely correlated with potentially greater profit or loss, and profit is the goal of trade, the expert practice of trade requires careful estimation of relevant probabilities. The second primary part of emporia is the related matter of money-lending at interest. As Aristotle must have known, in actual Athenian lending practices (notably loans for overseas trading enterprises), interest and risk were correlated.[51]

The third part of the topic of economic practice is wage labor. Switching from description to criticism, Aristotle notes that "detailed and exact discussion would be useful for the practical workings [ergasiai] but to spend too much time on such things is crude" (1258b34–39). Here it is clear enough that there is no meaningful attempt at what I have been calling faithful descriptive representation of social reality in the text. And yet, "it is also necessary [because the topic is, after all, economic practice] to collect the scattered accounts of methods by

50. Meikle (1995: 51–64) argues that the development of exchange is (1) the original, natural model of C-C': one commodity (C) fairly exchanged for another commodity (C'); (2) C-M-C': a commodity is purchased with money (M), which is used to purchase another commodity (C')—still acceptable, because aimed at the good end of supplying household necessities; (3) M-C-M'—perverse, because aimed at the bad end of wealth accumulation; (4) M-M'—completely reprehensible.

51. Cohen (1992) redefined the study of banks, credit, and their relationship to risk in maritime loans, in part by showing the fallacy of arguments from silence that had been employed to minimize their importance.

which certain practitioners of entrepreneurship have been successful. All these methods are beneficial for those who value entrepreneurship" (1259a3–5).

We might suppose that this last comment is meant as a scornful dismissal of money-makers, who value the wrong ends. And yet, the observation leads to the story of Thales' demonstration of philosophical acumen in business: By his expert astronomical methods, Thales predicted a bumper olive crop in the coming year. Anticipating unusually high demand for processing, Thales leased in advance all the olive presses in Miletos and Chios. He was able to do so at a low rate, due to lack of competition for the leases in the winter, long before the harvest. When the bigger-than-usual crop duly came in, his monopoly allowed him to charge whatever he wished for pressing the oil (1259a7–17). Like the philosopher-rulers' maintenance of efficient specialization in Plato's Callipolis, Thales' philosophical expertise proved directly applicable to matters of supply and demand. Thales expected, and evidently received, rational cooperation from those with whom he did business: Press-owners sold leases at low rates when demand was low; olive producers paid high rates when the demand for pressing services was high. Aristotle likewise expected his readers to grasp the economic rationale behind Thales' plan. Such matters are, to be sure, morally subordinate. But by the same token they are necessary in the sense of laying the practical foundation of material welfare, itself a precondition of living well.

Aristotle's final point is descriptive and explicitly political. It modifies, along the lines sketched above, his moral criticism of those who urge the identity of *oikonomia* and *politika:* It is useful for political experts to be familiar with these things, for many poleis need expertise in business and revenues, just as does a household, but even more so. Indeed, he notes, there are even some persons, among those concerned with politics, who are exclusively concerned with these (economic/financial) matters (1259a33–36). Here, the previous worry about the hegemonic tendency of economic instrumentalism to intrude on other domains is balanced against a recognition that financial expertise had indeed become an expected part of the organization of real-world poleis (Pyzyk 2015). Given that the polis is the natural end of human sociability and the necessary context for true human flourishing, that kind of expertise was not readily dismissed.

In book 1 of the *Politics* Aristotle offered a compressed, well-informed, and sharply critical analysis of economic activity. He isolated entrepreneurship as a prevalent part of the natural and necessary domains of *oikonomia* and *politika*. But, as a matter of philosophical understanding, wealth creation remained subsidiary to the end of "having enough" for true flourishing. When divorced from the acquisition of the material goods necessary for the well-functioning of an individual, a household, or a polis, economic activity was corrupting. As such, entrepreneurship and expertise in financial matters, although practically useful, even necessary, for householders and statesmen, given the contingent circumstances of Aristotle's world, could be subordinated as vulgar and unworthy of detailed treatment in a body of work on ethics and politics. His conclusions on this score enabled Aristotle to account for the empirical fact of what we now call economic growth, evident in increased consumption, by attributing it to the unconstrained creative production and accumulation of wealth, driven by profitable exchanges financed by loans at interest. Growth was facilitated by the invention of a standardized medium of exchange. That medium had a natural function: addressing the necessity of efficiently redistributing resources in a world of interdependent people and poleis whose natural end required a sufficiency of material goods. But the invention of money also promoted unlimited accumulation and growth for its own sake. Insofar as economic activity was pursuit of that corrupt goal, it was unworthy of closer attention within a theoretical treatment of ethics and politics.

7.8 NATURE AND NECESSITY

Among the results of Aristotle's quarantine of the variant of entrepreneurship aimed at wealth accumulation as an unnatural part of the natural whole of *oikonomia* is that those persons dedicated to money-making stand outside the natural authority relationships of household and polis. As a result, those involved in money-making need not be citizens, and indeed, need not be sharers in the polis or constituent "parts" of the polis proper. In the "polis of our prayers," all the vulgar aspects of production and exchange are evidently to be handled by metics or transient foreigners or slaves (*Politics* 1326a16–21, 1329a19–26). Trading activity is to be isolated in a commercial agora separate from the political agora; the latter is reserved for citizens (1331b1–4). Consequently, there was no need for an extended treatment of economic practices in a philosophical text centrally concerned with authority relations conducive to stable social order and human flourishing.

Most surprisingly, perhaps, entrepreneurship seems not to involve the slave-master relationship in any natural or necessary way. Aristotle emphasizes throughout *Politics* book 1 that household management is deeply concerned with expertise in ruling over slaves and directing their labor (e.g., 1255b30). Aristotle notoriously spends a great deal of space in book 1 arguing for the naturalness of slavery.[52] But insofar as entrepreneurship stands outside the natural order of *oikonomia,* it need (in theory) have nothing to do with ruling over others. As a practical matter, successful entrepreneurs, for example the family of Cephalus (Lysias 12.8, 12, 19) did employ slaves in the production of goods for sale. But it appears likely that Aristotle included the entrepreneur whose goal was accumulation in the category of the vulgar craftsman (*banausos technitēs*) who brings upon himself a special sort of enslavement through his practice (1260a41–b2). If that is so, the relationship of a money-maker master to his slave would presumably, like husband and wife in the barbarian household (1252b4–9), be lacking in any natural ruling element. Aristotle surely does not envisage money-making as a realm of freedom in a Hayekian sense (Hayek 1944). But it is a realm in which the constrained and constraining relations between free and slave lack any basis in nature.[53]

Aristotle's apparent exclusion of accumulation-entrepreneurship from natural relations of authority in some ways tracks the earlier work of Xenophon in the *Oikonomikos* and *Poroi:* Xenophon, like Aristotle, saw *oikonomia* as the realm of naturalized authority relations in respect to appropriately bounded wealth-getting activity in an *oikos.* Like Aristotle, Xenophon put a great deal of emphasis on the proper management of household slaves. Consideration of how Aristotle brackets entrepreneurship in the *Politics* may help us to make more sense of the different approaches taken in various passages of Xenophon's *Poroi:* The sections advocating the purchase by the state of a large number of slaves to work in the silver mines extends the logic of the prosperous slave-owning household to the financially strapped polis. Those sections are, therefore, based on the deployment of military forces to maintain a status-based social and economic order (*Poroi* 4.13–48). The sections advocating legal and infrastructural changes to increase the level of trading in Athenian markets (3.1–13), by contrast, concern what Aristotle called entrepreneurship. Those sections are directly concerned

52. Aristotle on natural slavery: Ober 1998a: 298–301, with literature cited; Schofield 1999: chap. 7.

53. Based on the evidence of surviving Athenian court speeches, it appears that banking families did in fact elide certain of the traditional distinctions between free and slave, notably in marriage and inheritance: Cohen 1992: chap. 4.

with the material incentives of metics and foreign money-makers who choose where and with whom to trade based on expected utility maximization. Their presence was desirable to the polis for the strictly instrumental reasons of increasing revenues. The relevant sections of the *Poroi* are, consequently, unconcerned with force or with moralized slave-master authority relationships.

Aristotle's bracketing of entrepreneurship was, moreover, realistic in that it tracked certain fourth-century-BCE Athenian legal innovations according to which slaves involved in commercial activities were, in certain carefully specified ways, treated on par with free persons, and metics and foreigners on par with citizens.[54] In Athenian banking, in the commercial activities of the agora, and in certain forms of legally binding contracts, the distinction between free and slave, foreigner and citizen, was elided in favor of economic efficiency and financial advantage.[55] On the one hand, public and private inattentiveness to the kinds of status distinctions that were highly salient in some (although not all) other domains of Greek life (Kamen 2013) surely led some Greeks to reject money-making as foreign to the circumscribed domain of the *oikos* and only contingently relevant to the material well-being of the polis. That rejection might arise either from traditionally aristocratic social attitudes or from philosophical arguments for the naturalness and/or the inherent value of authority relations. While those motivations were not mutually exclusive, it is, I believe, misleading to suppose that philosophical argument was just an alibi for aristocratic prejudice.[56]

This brings us back to the distinction between descriptive representation of social reality and critique in Greek philosophical texts. And to M.I. Finley's view of Greek society as fundamentally predicated on fixed and formalized status roles, especially the distinctions between free and slave, citizen and foreigner. For Finley and some of his followers—as for Aristotle, Xenophon, and traditional Greek aristocrats, but for very different reasons—the failure of the realm of entrepreneurship to conform to norms of status distinction rendered it essentially superfluous: Social status,

---

54. Cf. Plato's Magnesia of the *Laws*, where metics and those responsible for economic activity are to be treated within the legal framework (e.g. 8.850a–c, 12.949b–c), but not as included in the eudaimonistic regime.

55. Athenian institutional innovations promoting prosperity by encouraging trade: Carugati 2019: chap. 4.

56. Wood and Wood (1978) and Nightingale (2004) exemplify a tendency on the part of social theorists and classicists to read Greek philosophical arguments off background social attitudes.

defined by authority relations, remained foundational. Any activity that was *not* grounded in status distinctions, and in the power relations inherent in status hierarchies, was consequently regarded as unmoored, epiphenomenal, analytically irrelevant. Economic activity aimed at increasing productivity, efficiency, and consumption—in contradistinction to activities aimed at securing the status of the relevant actors—was thereby rendered more or less invisible in the resulting modern scholarship. In any event, economic activity as such was deemed unworthy of detailed study. The result was, so I suppose, both a misreading of the relevant ancient texts and a mischaracterization of the underlying social reality.

. . .

This chapter started with the assumption, supported by empirical studies, that the classical Greek world was indeed characterized by economic growth, albeit modest compared with that of modernity. It then sought to show that economic rationality, predicated on the practical reasoning about preferences, beliefs, outcomes, and actions that has been our concern throughout this book, was addressed by Greek intellectuals, prominently including Plato, Xenophon, and Aristotle. They recognized that there was a correlation between economic rationality and the wealth of households and states. And they posited a causal relationship between rationality and growth. On the other hand, their interest in economic rationality and growth was, unlike neoclassical economic thought but in common with recent work on moral political economy (Carugati and Levi 2021; Bednar in progress), occasioned by a critical evaluation. Like contemporary students of moral political economy, the Socratics were sharply critical of theories that took self-interested behavior, aimed at continuously increasing material welfare, as uniquely rational.

While recognizing the practical utility, for households and states alike, of economic rationality and the relevant forms of expertise (in production, exchange, finance) that was associated with it, the Socratic philosophers subordinated material welfare as a means to the end of moral excellence in their hierarchy of value. If and when the means became an end in itself, it was shameful rather than praiseworthy, an impediment to well-being rather than its precondition. With that in mind, we can finally turn, in the final chapter, to the larger Greek philosophical project of understanding and facilitating human flourishing. The assumed ubiquity of strategic rationality was at once an intellectual challenge, a moral threat, and a practical foundation for that project.

CHAPTER 8

Conclusions

Utility and Eudaimonia

What has practical reason to do with human flourishing? The previous chapters explored ancient Greek thinking on the relationship between motivation, means, and ends: First, how purposeful actions of rational individuals and groups follow from deliberate choices based on orderly desires and coherent beliefs. And next, how that relationship bears on individual behavior, social order, and political regimes. We saw that classical Greek writers were familiar with, and contributors to, a folk theory of instrumental rationality. That ancient theory resembles contemporary theories of rational choice in its premises concerning an ideal-type agent's motivation, and in its focus on self-interest, strategic calculation, and expectations regarding outcomes. Rational choice-making in private and public contexts was seen not only as a basic human capacity, but also as a skill, practiced and taught by experts. Ancient Greek political institutions and interstate relations were structured, in part, by expectations of strategic behavior. Tracing similarities and differences among and between ancient and modern approaches to rationality revealed both persistent and culturally contingent features of practical reason.

This concluding chapter proceeds as follows: Section 1 traces the book's theoretic and historical trajectory: from the rational individual to the cooperative community, to the state and its rulers, to relations between asymmetrically powerful states, to the rationality of democratic institutions, and back down to the psychology of individual economic behavior. Sections 2 and 3 return to the mid-fifth century BCE, when cultural intuitions about human motivation first coalesced into a theory. A reading of Aeschylus' tragedy *Eumenides,* tests three hypotheses: First, that the folk theory was already available to a dramatist and legible to his audience when Socrates was still a boy. Next, that the discovery of practical reason explains puzzling features of a famous poetic text. Third, that censorship of tragic poetry in Plato's *Republic* was necessitated by dangerously vivid depictions of viciously instrumental divinities. The validation of those hypotheses should go some way towards justifying the method of this book.

The rest of the chapter focuses on implications for ethical and political theory, ancient and modern. Sections 4 and 5 foreground the paired threats that instrumental reasoning presents to the human flourishing that is the goal of Socratic moral philosophy: First, instrumentalism may reduce to vicious egoism. Next, it can crowd out ethical attitudes and relationships. Section 6 then answers one of the book's central puzzles: Why did Socratic philosophers engage so deeply with instrumental rationality, rather than simply rejecting it as a moral error? The answer is that they recognized that self-interest and strategic reasoning are fundamental aspects of human behavior, and so, as a practical matter, *eudaimonia* must be grounded in expected utility. The upshot was Aristotle's canonical account of practical reason in the *Nicomachean Ethics.*

Section 7 concludes by reconsidering the role of practical reason in contemporary political and ethical philosophy. Although they recognized instrumentalism as a threat to social order, ancient Greek writers realized that strategic rationality is part of practical reason: a capacity whose exercise is, along with moral reasoning, constitutive of humanity. Contemporary moral philosophers have, however, often bracketed self-interested instrumentalism as an impermissible violation of an impartial utilitarian calculus or of the moral law that requires others to be treated as ends rather than means. Meanwhile empirical social scientists, while motivated by normative concerns, tend to bracket normative considerations in favor of causal explanation. Embracing the ancient insights that strategic and ethical reasoning are complementary, that ideal theory, if it is to be action-guiding, must be grounded in nonideal theory, opens the door to employing premodern thought and practice as a resource for modern social theory. It contributes to a growing scholarly literature on moral political economies and governance for flourishing. And it offers a point of departure for productive work at the intersection of positive, normative, and historical approaches to ethics and politics.[1]

8.1 RETROSPECT

After introducing the folk theory of instrumental rationality, its Conventionalist, Thrasymachean, and Socratic variants, and its relationship to contemporary theories of choice, strategic behavior, and expertise, my investigation began by specifying the motivations of the rational individual, exemplified by Gyges of Lydia. In stories told by Herodotus and Plato, Gyges' preferences and beliefs lead him to choose the available option that maximizes his expected utility, understood as subjective happiness or welfare. Herodotus' Gyges faced option sets reduced by the preferences of powerful others to "survive or die." Through the device of a magic ring, Plato eliminated social constraints on Gyges' choices, transforming the strategic problem confronted by Herodotus' severely constrained Gyges into a situation in which an ideal-type agent's actions follow directly from his top-ranked preferences. Invisible Gyges' behavior is interpreted by Plato's Glaucon as revealing primitive preferences and exposing the operation of individual-level rationality as the strategic pursuit of egoistic self-interest. The question then arises: How was social order first created and then sustained in a population of strategic, self-interested agents? How can social cooperation avoid falling victim to cascades of free-riding and commons tragedies? By positing coordination in the face of existential threats and adjustments to a purely selfish moral psychology, Greek writers addressed the problem of how a cooperative social order, capable of identifying and pursuing common goods, could emerge and persist in the face of rationality so understood.

Once the basic problem of productively cooperative collective action has been solved, and a community grows bigger and more complex, its members must answer the question: Who rules?—Who has the authority to make, interpret, and enforce the terms by which the community

---

1. For a programmatic statement concerning the value of integrating positive with normative political theory, see Knight and Johnson 2015. Barry Weingast, Federica Carugati, and I have dubbed the integrated approach "the NPPT (Normative and Positive Political Theory)" program; we have sought to exemplify that program in some of our recent scholarship—including, of course, this book. See, for example Carugati, Ober, and Weingast 2016, 2019. Moral political economies: Carugati and Levi 2021; governance for flourishing: Bednar in progress.

will be organized? The Greek answer was that in the beginning it was a monarch. Classical Greek writers found paradigms for the cooperative origins of kingship in fanciful hypotheticals about their own early history, but also, in the *Histories* of Herodotus, in the historical rulers of the great kingdoms of western Asia. Herodotus' stories about the establishment of kingship among the Medes and Persians center on motivations and choices of both would-be rulers and prospective subjects, and on the role of shared norms in determining the extent of royal authority.

In the classical period of the sixth to fourth centuries BCE, Greek city-states were typically ruled, not by kings, but rather by citizens. Civic bargaining, readily modeled as a positive-sum game, allowed coalitions of elite and nonelite citizens in early-sixth-century Athens to arrive at a relatively stable and productive, if not fully just, social equilibrium. After a late-sixth-century revolution, precipitated by the demos' collective refusal to accept domination by an elite faction, the Athenian regime developed into a democracy capable of achieving greatness. According to Thucydides, that development was made possible by the expert guidance of rational leaders capable of assessing risks and promoting public goods.

We turned next to the questions of when and how interstate relations are governed by the logic of maximizing expected advantage. In Thucydides' analytic narrative the fifth-century Athenian empire was predicated on an equilibrium: Athens, as a rational imperial hegemon, sought to maximize its own advantage in terms of security, standing, and revenue, by dominating other states while discouraging revolt by providing security and moderating the costs of submission. Athens' subjects often, but not always, acquiesced to domination because it was less bad than the other available options. Athenian attempts to expand the empire during the Peloponnesian War foundered when imperial agents, espousing Thrasymachean principles of purely self-interested rationality, and expecting responses predicated on expected utility maximization, encountered potential subjects whose choices were based instead on aversion to loss and on the vividly imagined prospect of a future in which nothing was lost.

The question of whether a democracy could be instrumentally rational, in the sense of having consistent preferences and coherent beliefs, was answered in the negative in Plato's *Republic*. But the actual historical practice of democracy, well documented for the age of Plato and Aristotle and reconstructed in detail by modern historians, shows that democratic Athens identified and pursued common interests and sustained public goods. The design of democratic legislative, judicial, and executive institutions enabled a socially diverse population of citizens to formulate orderly shared preferences and coherent beliefs. Those preferences and beliefs allowed them to identify and follow the advice of domain experts, to deliberate on the merits of feasible options, and to choose options commanding broad-based support.

Finally, we returned to the economic behavior of individuals, now assumed to be operating within an extensive system of institutions and organizations rational and stable enough to allow entrepreneurs to lay plans and calculate risks. Plato and Aristotle were well aware of the processes of specialization and relative advantage in production and exchange that had, by their time, led to demographic growth and increased levels of consumption in the Greek world. But they were, by the same token, deeply concerned that economically rational choices—motivated by the desire for profit, aimed at the accumulation of wealth, and facilitated by entrepreneurial expertise—corrupted the souls of those engaged in wealth creation and undermined the foundations of moral community.

8.2 AESCHYLUS' FURIES: FROM AUTOMATA TO RATIONAL AGENTS

The relationship between theoretical writing and real-world practice—when and how the literary expression of ideas guides action—is an enduring question for moral philosophy. Near the end of book 2 of Plato's *Republic,* having recognized the necessity of proper education for the violence-monopolizing Guardians, Socrates and his interlocutors turn to the question of the place of literature in their imagined community. They agree that allowing falsehoods about important matters to circulate in the city would be dangerous. They also assert that it cannot be true that there is conflict among the gods, or that the gods are harmful as well as beneficial to mortals, or that a god could utter a falsehood. Yet some of the literature best known to them was rife with divine strife, malice, and mendacity. To illustrate the point, Socrates cites Homer's *Iliad* and *Odyssey,* and three passages from the tragedies of Aeschylus (*Republic* 380a, 383b, 391e).[2]

Along with Homer's epics, Aeschylus' dramas are prominent among the works that will be censored by the rulers of Callipolis. While the

---

2. Aeschylus is also quoted at *Republic* 361b, 361e–62a; 550c, 563b–c.

other two great tragedians, Sophocles (329c) and Euripides (568a), are given cameo roles in the *Republic,* Aeschylus evidently tops the list of the dangerous composers of drama. Homer remains, for Plato's Socrates, the "leader of tragedy, the first and most poetic of the tragedians" (598d, 607a–c). And thus, Homer's epics are especially dangerous to the souls of poetry-lovers (607c, 608a). But among the tragedians whose works were performed in Socrates' lifetime, Aeschylus stands out.

This section and the next focus on *Eumenides,* a play by Aeschylus that, while never cited in the *Republic,* seems exemplary of Socrates' worries about the ways that tragedy portrays divinities and their relationship to mortals. I posit that Aeschylus' *Eumenides* offers a sort of prequel to this book's main narrative: a preliminary chapter in the story of the "discovery of practical reason" as a theory of instrumental rationality. Reading *Eumenides* in light of the folk theory tests a general hypothesis of this book, that attending to instrumental rationality will elucidate otherwise obscure aspects of classical Greek texts. Passing that test opens the way for further work on "the Greeks and the rational."

Reconsidering certain aspects of what is, today, a very well-known Greek play offers an opportunity to revisit the fundamentals of the folk theory. It allows us to fit the theory into a schematic developmental arc that traces the self-conscious employment of reason in the pursuit of desired ends. The arc begins with Homeric epic, in which more and less rational patterns of choice and action were closely observed and commented upon, but as yet untheorized. It concludes with the Socratics' highly influential insistence that rationality, properly so understood, requires the identification and understanding of morally choice-worthy ends, as well as the employment of reason in determining the means to those ends.

Aeschylus's play offers insight into the middle term of that arc. Aeschylus was a young man at the time of the Athenian revolution of 508 BCE and Cleisthenes' democratic reforms; he fought in the Persian Wars and witnessed the emergence and expansion of the Athenian empire. Produced in 458 BCE, Aeschylus' *Eumenides* was first performed when Socrates was twelve years old, a generation before Plato was born. The play, written late in Aeschylus' career as a dramatist, coincided with what is often assumed to be an early stage of Protagoras' career as a Sophist—and therefore, insofar as Protagoras was among the first Sophists, with an early instantiation of the folk theory in formal teaching and in (now mostly lost) texts.[3] While the origins of the folk theory remain obscure, Aeschylus' play appears to belong to an era when previously untheorized behavior was being fit into a coherent account of strategic choice and action.

The action of the play also underscores two important points. First, the discovery of practical reason ought not to be thought of in terms of transformation. It was not the case that nonrational motivations for helping and harming others were simply displaced by reasoning aimed at maximizing utility.[4] Rather, the developmental process was accumulative: A normative theory of instrumental rationality emerged from meditations on patterns of behavior originating in both means-ends reasoning and nonrational, automatic response to stimulus. And next, the discovery was immediately recognized as a mixed blessing—at once opening new possibilities for social progress and posing new threats to social order.

The plot of *Eumenides* famously turns on the fate of Orestes, who has killed his mother, Clytemnestra, in revenge for her murder of his father, Agamemnon. As the play opens, pursued by the hateful Furies—ancient deities whose raison d'être was punishment of those who shed the blood of kinfolk—Orestes has fled from his home in Argos to the sanctuary at Delphi. There he has been ritually cleansed of his crime by the god Apollo. Yet the Furies, refusing to recognize Apollo's authority to purify a mother-killer, continue their pursuit. Advised by Apollo, Orestes proceeds to Athens, where he begs for Athena's protection. The goddess in turn establishes a court of mortal men—the Areopagus council—to judge the case. Apollo arrives on the scene and helps Orestes to plead his case. With the tie vote of the jury, the verdict goes to the defendant. Grateful Orestes promises that Argos will forever be an Athenian ally.

The Furies, dishonored by their defeat, threaten revenge on Athens through famine, disease, and discord. Athena counters with an implied threat to deploy Zeus's thunderbolts against them. But Athena also promises the Furies honors and a home in Athens if they withhold their wrath. Accepting Athena's offer, they become honored resident aliens (metics) in Athens. No household will flourish without them; they will implant and sustain a wholesome fear of wrongdoing among the citizens.

3. Plato, *Meno* 91e: Protagoras practiced as a Sophist for forty years until his death at near age seventy. The death date for Protagoras is commonly assumed about 420 BCE, which would mean he was just beginning his active career in 458 BCE.

4. For discussions of nonrational motivation for helping and harming, I am indebted to Philip Petrov; see Petrov 2022.

In terms of Protagoras' great speech in Plato's dialogue (chapter 2.6), they will enforce behavior properly regulated by the "Gifts of Zeus"—the sense of shame and justice. Moreover, the solution to the cooperation dilemma in *Eumenides* closely resembles Plato's Protagoras' account of the origins of social order: Instead of the lose-lose (both parties getting their next-to-worst payoff) equilibrium of the Prisoner's Dilemma, Athena and the Furies arrive at the win-win of an assurance game.[5] With the Furies integrated into the civic and ritual order of the community, prospectively contributing to the prosperity of Athens, the play seems to end happily.

The conventional reading of the play emphasizes several elements: (1) the conflict between the angry, hate-filled, bloodstained "old gods" in the guise of the Furies and the new Olympians, Athena and Apollo; (2) the replacement of justice as vendetta, tit-for-tat vengeance, with a conception of just punishment that attends to higher principles and to contingent circumstances; and (3) the establishment of a human-centered institution for legal judgment, coincident with the retreat of divinity's direct role in the administration of justice.[6] Each of those elements is certainly important to any in-the-round reading of the play. That said, recent work has shown the limits of the conventional reading. Danielle Allen (2000) has rightly emphasized that, in contrast to contemporary norms of justice as cold, dispassionate judgment, the hot emotion of anger, the Furies' stock in trade, remained central to Athenian processes of legal judgment and punishment. Through those legal processes, righteous anger at wrongdoing was shared by the community and focalized on the guilty perpetrator. Dimitrios Iordanoglou and Johan Tralau (2022) argue convincingly that *Eumenides* breaks new ground in Greek political thought by presenting examples of logically flawed argumentation and prompting the audience to learn from them. Here, our concern is with the ways in which the play highlights the role of instrumentalism and strategic calculation in rational decision-making, without devaluing the motivating force of moral emotions.

5. "Athena and the Furies" is modeled as a Prisoner's Dilemma by setting the option pairs as Vengeance, Vengeance (both punish and suffer); Vengeance, No-Vengeance; No-Vengeance, Vengeance (one suffers, the other punishes); No-Vengeance, No-Vengeance (neither punishes or suffers). It is transformed to an assurance game by changing the final option-pair to Reward, Reward, and setting the value of Reward above that of Vengeance. Compare figures 10 and 14.

6. D. Allen (2000: 20–24, with literature cited) surveys and critiques what I am calling the conventional reading of the play. For a commentary, with review of scholarship on various disputed issues, see Sommerstein 1989.

When, in the play's first scenes, we first meet the Furies, they embody a nondeliberative, nonstrategic form of action: They do not have preferences over outcomes. They are not, in any ordinary sense, *agents,* but rather automata: They respond automatically, with murderous pursuit, to a specific signal—the shedding of the blood of blood-kin.[7] If kin blood is not shed (even if a murder takes place), the Furies do nothing. In that case they exist only as the latent possibility of action. Likewise, the Furies have no beliefs based on observed phenomena or arguments; their action is automatically triggered by the fact of the matter: Kin's blood is spilled, the switch is thrown, the Furies pursue. They make no decision; there is no possible counterfactual. They are not in any sort of game; there are no players. No institutions or norms are involved. It is the blood itself that motivates them (line 230). The Furies themselves make all this explicit in a choral passage: Self-described as the embodiment of "straight-judgments" (*euthudikaioi*), they declare that if your hands are clean (of kin blood), then, "you will go through life unscathed. But show us the guilty . . . / and up from the outraged dead we rise, / witness bound to avenge their blood / we rise in flames against him to the end" (312–15: trans. Fagles).

For the Furies of the play's early scenes, the circumstances of the act are irrelevant. It does not matter what anyone might want or plan— when the blood of kin is shed the Furies pursue, and that's the whole of it. The simple binary is illustrated in figure 25: Nature (N) determines whether kin blood has been spilled or not. If it has not, nothing happens (0). If it has, the Furies pursue (1). The dashed line is the null condition in which kin blood is shed but the Furies do not pursue. It is null because that is not (yet) a possible state of the world.

It is immediately apparent that figure 25 resembles a simplified version of figure 1 (Gyges and the Ring Decision Tree: figure 25 insert). Figure 25 lacks the not-chosen branches of the tree, modeled on Glaucon's imaginative thought experiment in Plato's *Republic* book 2. In Glaucon's story there are implicit counterfactuals in which Gyges might have made a different choice among available options, were his preferences other than those which they are revealed to be. In the counterfactual cases, he would have taken a different path and arrived at a different outcome. The counterfactuals are realistic: Most shepherds do not become messengers to the king; few messengers become kings. The point of Glaucon's imaginative story is, however, to show that, when

7. Ancient Greek conceptions of automata: Mayor 2020.

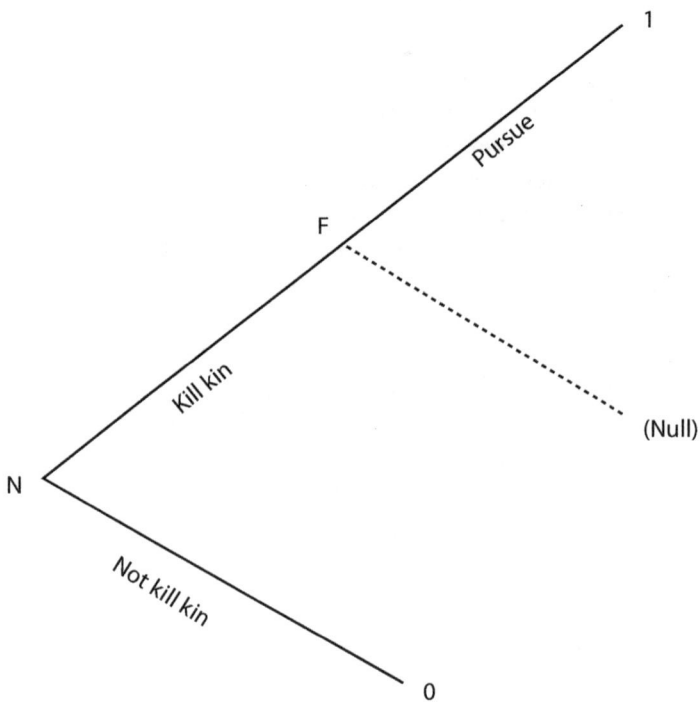

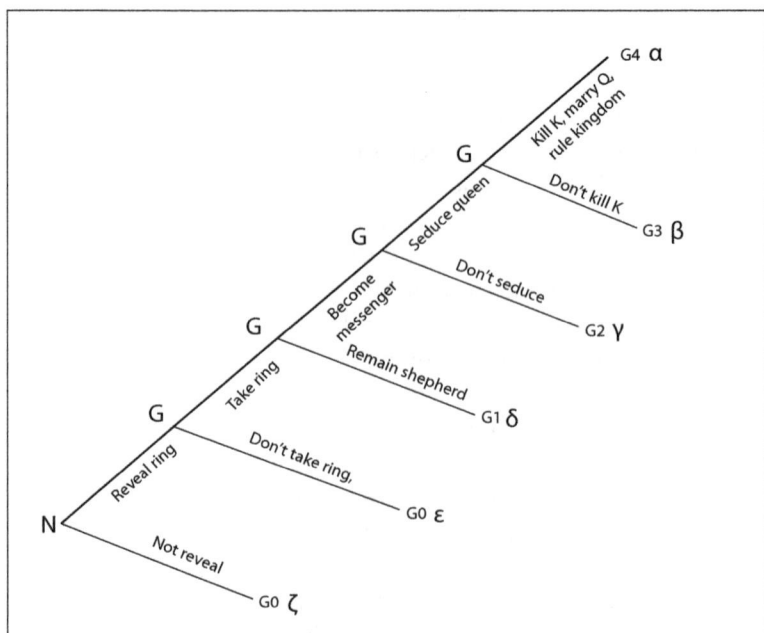

FIGURE 25. Furies Binary

Note: N = Nature. F = Furies. Insert is figure 1.1 from chapter 1.

the ordinary social constraints of rules and others' preferences are stripped away, the rational agent will act in a predictable manner. He will be motivated by the primitive preferences that are, Glaucon claims, universal, at least among "real men."

Because the counterfactuals are realistic, Plato's Gyges is depicted as a choice-making agent. But he obviously lacks what I have been calling ethical rationality, of the sort possessed by philosophers in Callipolis, that would enable him to identify and thus choose truly choice-worthy ends. He likewise lacks the knowledge that would enable him to act upon his choice without error. His behavior is driven by the part of his soul that the interlocutors of the *Republic* will eventually identify as appetitive and lacking in reason. Plato's Gyges thus responds to the signal of his desires in something resembling the unthinking, automatic way that Aeschylus' Furies respond to the signal of bloodshed among blood kin.

The contrast of Gyges-as-model-tyrant with the rational philosopher allows Plato to assimilate egoistic instrumental rationality to nonrational, signal-response-type behavior. That assimilation, in turn, reduces a triad (nonrational, instrumentally rational, ethically rational) to a dyad (nonrational, rational), and gives warrant for contemporary philosophers concerned with rationality to dismiss the history of Greek attention to instrumentalism that has been the primary focus of this book. If observed behavior motivated by strategic reasoning is indistinguishable from nonrational behavior, it makes sense to equate the discovery of practical reason with the Socratic development of ethical rationality.[8] I hope to have shown that resisting that equation, by reference to strategic reasoning in texts outside the Socratic corpus, illuminates distinctive features in Greek thought about rationality—including that of the Socratics themselves. The Socratics responded critically to instrumental rationality, and, once refined and reconfigured, it was incorporated within the Socratic philosophical tradition itself.

8.3 APOLLO DISCOVERS PRACTICAL REASON

By the end of the *Eumenides,* in stark contrast with the situation depicted in the play's first scenes, the Furies have been integrated into a civic realm. They have a defined role in a wider scheme of moral social behavior. They have a place in an institutionalized system of justice in

---

8. Frede 1996; see discussion in the preface and introduction of the present work.

which decisions on matters of justice and punishment are made by a majority vote of citizens. Far from automata that respond mechanically to a simple signal, the Furies are shown to be fully capable of deliberation and choice. They listen to, respond to, and are ultimately persuaded by Athena's threat of punishment by thunderbolt (826–29) and her offer of honors, duties, and permanent residency in Athens, as metics (804–7, 851–57, 867–69). They enter into a binding agreement that is expected to be mutually beneficial (916–27). The agreement is backed by credible commitments on both sides. In the terms we have been using in this book, the Furies have become a rational collective agent, capable of deliberating over options in light of the moves available to other players, and thereby choosing the available outcome that maximizes utility.

The revised choice situation can be modeled as a strategic three-player game, as in figure 26. The point of the exercise is that the Furies are now readily imagined as playing a game in recognition of the incentives of other players, a game with better and worse outcomes for each. At the root of the game, Athena has offered the Furies an honored place in Athens and has threatened them with thunderbolts if they harm Athens. The Furies choose whether to accept or not to accept the offer. Athena then chooses to reward or punish the Furies. If Athena rewards, the Citizens choose whether to honor or dishonor the Furies, and the Furies decide whether to bless or punish the Citizens.

The ordinal preferences listed are assigned on the basis of the following assumptions, based on the play's action: The Furies and the Citizens *most* prefer to be rewarded, honored, and blessed; they *least* prefer to be harmed and punished. Athena *most* prefers the Citizens to be blessed. The Furies and Athena gain some utility from punishing. They prefer not to reward those who refuse to accept a fair offer, or who fail to show respect for the demands of kinship, or who dishonor those who punish fairly. As usual, the ordinal preferences of each player determine the predicted path of play on the dark diagonal line. The equilibrium outcome of the game is at the upper-right end of the line.

When we compare the Furies, Athena, and Citizens Game (figure 26) to the inserted King, Gyges, and Queen Game (figure 4), we once again find some obvious similarities. Just as Herodotus' Gyges was confronted with "two roads," obeying the order of first the king and then the queen or being killed, so too, at the root of the Furies, Athena, and Citizens Game, the Furies must decide between the credible threat of punishment by thunderbolt and accepting Athena's offer. And, similarly, the Citizens face a binary choice between the certainty of famine, disease,

Upper tree labels:

F5, A5, C4
Bless C
F
Punish
F3, A0, C0
Honor F
C
Dishonor
Bless
F0, A3, C5
Reward F
F
A
Punish
F4, A2, C0
Accept
Punish
F0, A2, C2
F
Not
Reward
F5, A0, C1
A
Punish
F0, A3, C2

Lower tree labels:

K0, G1, Q3 α
Kill K, marry Q
G
Don't kill K
K3, G0, Q1 β
Kill G
Threaten G
Q
Don't kill G
K4, G1, Q0 γ
Q sees, vengeful
Kill G
K3, G0, Q2 δ
N
Q not see, not vengeful
K4, G1 ε
Obey: spy
G
Disobey
Kill G
K3, G0 ζ
Order spy
K
Forgive G
K1, G1 η
Not order spy
K2 θ

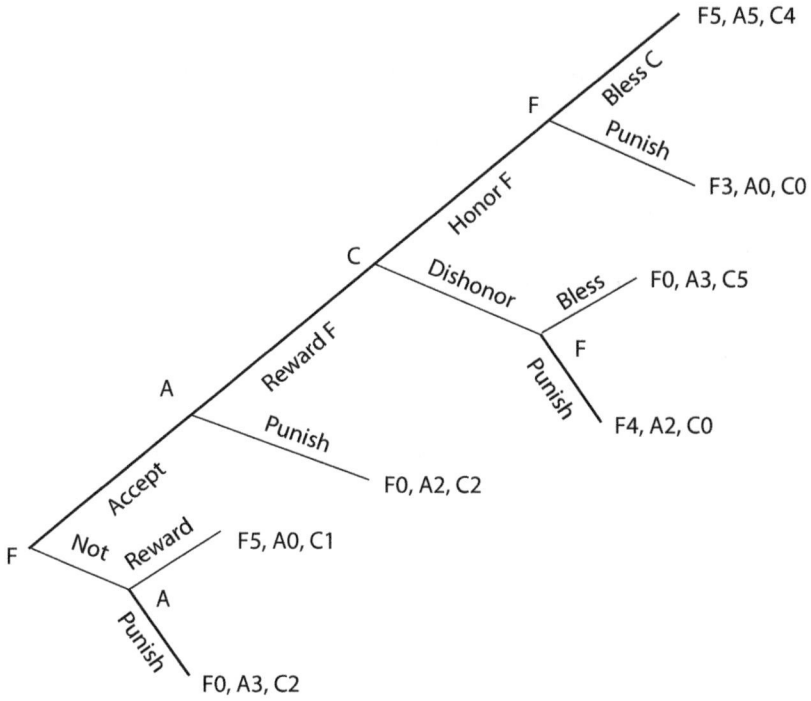

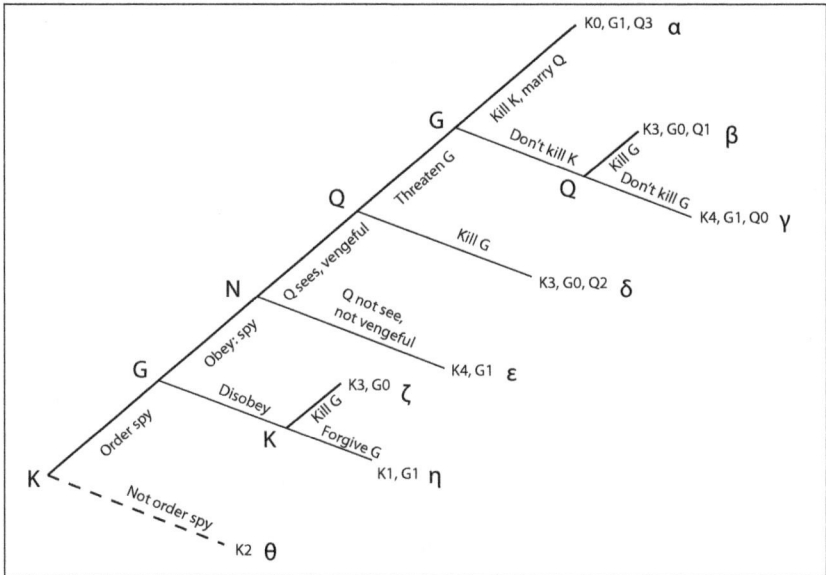

FIGURE 26. Furies, Athena, and Citizens Game

Notes: F = Furies. A = Athena. C = Citizens. Ordinal payoffs, 5 = high; 0 = low. Insert is figure 1.4 from chapter 1.

civil war, and nightmarish punishment (gruesomely described: *Eumenides* 185–90) and respecting the norms of appropriate behavior that the Furies now stand for, with the anticipated benefit of being blessed accordingly.

Turning from extensive-form illustrations to other models of rational behavior, we may say that by the end of Aeschylus' play, the Furies have entered into a positive-sum bargain, of the sort illustrated in figure 17 (Solon's arbitration between mass and elite as a bargaining solution). Before they are persuaded by Athena, the Furies can only see their situation as zero-sum: Because Orestes and Apollo won, the Furies are thrown down, their honor is lost, and their only recourse is vengeance. But Athena convinces them to envision the situation as a potential positive-sum, integrative bargain, one in which both parties improve on their prebargain baseline.

As in the Solonian bargain between the Athenian mass and elite (chapter 4.3), both the Furies and Athena/Citizens have something to gain if a solution can be found that improves the situation of each party, and if those on both sides can credibly commit to sticking by the bargain. In Aeschylus' tragedy, the credibility of commitment, on the part of the Furies and Athena, lies in the credibility of the threat each continues to wield: Athena threatens the Furies by reminding them that she is the keeper of Zeus's devastating thunderbolts. For their part, the Furies retain a credible threat of sowing civil discord (*stasis*) among the citizens and thereby destroying the basis of peaceful, productive interdependence. On the benefit side, assuming complete information, the Furies come to see that it is indeed possible to improve their baseline by being rewarded with honors and residency.

The general point is that the kind of practical reasoning assumed by Plato, Herodotus, and the Greek authors of the Solon tradition was already available to Aeschylus as a dramatic framing device, and legible to an Athenian audience, in 458 BCE. By that time, per above, Protagoras was probably already embarked on his career as a Sophist, and perhaps already teaching the ideas about instrumental rationality and the origins of social order that we reviewed in chapter 2.

The question remains: How did the Furies come by their newfound capacity for rational decision-making? The answer is that they were *persuaded,* through arguments, to understand themselves as having a capacity for deliberating over more and less desirable options, and for choosing and acting accordingly. Aeschylus deploys the terminology of persuasion (*peithō* in its various forms), recalling the centrality of the study of rhetoric to the Sophists and their students.[9] The Furies begin the process of deliberation and bargaining (892 and following) immediately upon Athena's invocation of Peitho as a personified deity (885–91).

The shift from signal-response to deliberative reasoning is foreshadowed at the beginning of the play, when Apollo, having discovered an infestation of Furies in his pristine Delphic sanctuary, urges Orestes to go to Athens. Apollo promises that, "there, having judges for these matters [dikastas tōnde], and with enchanting utterances [kai thelktērious muthous echontes], we will discover the contrivances [mēchanas eurēsomen] that will set you free from torments for all time" (81–83). The Greek term mēchanē recalls Herodotus' King Kandaules, who sought to free Gyges from the fear of retribution by assuring him that he had contrived matters so that the queen would not discover Gyges in her bedroom (egō mēchanēsomai—Herodotus 1.9.1: chapter 1.6). In Aeschylus' Eumenides, a generation before Herodotus' Histories, the assurance is of the anticipated discovery of the appropriate contrivances that will free Orestes from the threat of punishment.[10] Apollo's promised contrivances will take the form of a new institution—the "judges for these matters." But they will also involve "enchanting utterances [thelktērioi muthoi]." What can Apollo have meant by this last phrase?

Richard Martin (1989) has shown that in Homer the term muthos refers to a speech-act, indicating authority on the part of the speaker, and usually performed in public. A felicitously performed speech act (one standard example is the "I do" of a marriage ceremony) does more than describe the state of the world; it brings into existence a new social fact (J. Austin 1975; Searle 1995). With the end of the play in mind, it appears that Aeschylus' Apollo is referring to something along those lines. Athena's persuasive speech not only describes existing or anticipated features of the world, but it brings new things into existence: the Areopagus council as an authoritative law court, but also the Furies as agents now capable of rational choice-making.

On this line of thought, it is the performative power of speech-as-act to bring about a new state of the world, as if by magic, that makes the muthoi referenced by Apollo "enchanting." And that in turn brings the play closer to the realm of sophism and its later critics. Control of

9. Peitho and its derivatives in Eumenides: lines 593, 885–91, 970.

10. Note that in both cases, the mēchanē concerns the promise that a perpetrator of a crime against a queen will escape punishment; both stories center on the murder of a king by the contrivance of the queen—this is presumably a coincidence, but a striking one.

the power of speech, through the expert mastery of rhetoric as a craft, was at least one part of what the Sophists offered their students. For the Socratics, the performative power of speech, when it was not merely an illusion, was terribly dangerous. Plato's Socrates repeatedly emphasizes, in *Gorgias, Protagoras, Republic,* and other dialogues, that internalizing the methods of the Sophists, and the instrumental reasoning that stood behind them, had the potential to bring about new, and worse, conditions in the souls of its practitioners. Those practitioners lacked true understanding of the powerful effects of speech and were incapable of controlling them. Moreover, they risked corrupting the politics of communities in which their students practiced their craft. But for the Sophists themselves, and for those convinced by them, technical mastery of the performative power of speech, grounded in a theory of instrumental rationality, was a great breakthrough. Their sense of accomplishment is exemplified, for example, by Gorgias' *Encomium of Helen* (LM 32.D24) in which verbal persuasion is equated with brute force (7), enchantment (10), and the overpowering emotion of love (19).

Apollo's quasi-oracular prediction that "we will discover contrivances," may, I believe, be thought of as an announcement, in mythopoetic terms, of the "discovery of practical reason." That discovery took the form of both the creation of some of the rational democratic institutions discussed in chapter 6 and a recognition of the sort of strategically rational agents suited to devising and using those institutions. Two generations before Plato's *Republic,* at the dawn of an age characterized by empire, sophism, and a Periclean style of democratic leadership, Aeschylus' Apollo radiates a sense of confidence in the productive power of persuasive speech, harnessed to a new understanding of strategic rationality. At the same time, the play raises questions about the relationship of persuasion by interested agents and truths about the phenomenal world. Athena's persuasive speech is characterized by its sincere concern for finding a positive-sum solution, one that will be genuinely beneficial to both sides. By contrast, Apollo (barely) gains his preferred end (Orestes' acquittal) through offering bribes, flattery, and highly dubious factual claims. While the discovery of practical reason offered the potential for an expansion of human capacity, for growth and innovation, it also provoked the worry that established values and certainties were being undermined. If it announced a recent discovery, Aeschylus' tragedy was far from simply celebratory.

We certainly need not anoint 458 BCE, when *Eumenides* was first performed, as *the* moment of discovery. Nor need we imagine any specific relationship between Aeschylus and Protagoras or other Sophists.[11] Nor, equally certainly, between Aeschylus' *Eumenides* and the Gyges narratives in Herodotus' *Histories* or Plato's *Republic*.[12] But, if the reading offered here makes sense, there is reason to suppose that what I have been calling the folk theory was sufficiently well known to be prominently featured by an innovative practitioner of the maturing genre of tragedy. At the same time, the folk theory was still new, surprising, and disturbing enough to provoke the language of discovery. If that is right, the Socratic project was born and came to maturity in an intellectual milieu already defined in part by a provocative theory of practical reason.

I leave it to others to pursue the question of the prevalence of the folk theory in Greek tragedy, comedy, and the other literary genres that have been given short shrift in this book. But I hope to have shown that, at the very least, ideas from the conceptual toolbox that made the folk theory possible had been presented to Athenian audiences by the mid-fifth century. At the same time, Aeschylus' play forcefully reminds us that practical reason is a supplement to, not a replacement for, other, less deliberative and less strategic sources of motivation and action, including moral emotions, gratuitous reciprocity, and religious awe. As noted above, despite the happy ending, it also suggests that rationality was not an unmixed blessing. Worries about instrumentalism, and those who promoted it, were certainly pervasive among ordinary Athenians throughout the classical period.[13] Tracing those worries, as reflected in rhetoric and drama, would fill in an important chapter in Athenian cultural history. Here I concentrate on the Socratic response and its influential afterlife.

---

11. Such a relationship is inferred by Davison (1953), but the evidence is inconclusive. Davison's chronology would, in any event, allow for Protagoras and Aeschylus both to have been present in Athens for several years, from the late 460s to 458, when Aeschylus departed Athens for Sicily.

12. Although see Chiasson 2003: 7: "In the story of Gyges and Candaules Herodotus adapts the specifically Aeschylean motif of the decision made under duress, as a means of focusing on human rather than divine agency." *Eumenides* is cited only once in this article (p. 23), for line 426: Athena poses the question of whether Orestes killed his mother "out of necessity, or in fear of someone's wrath."

13. As evidenced by, for example, Aristophanes' *Clouds*, Isocrates' speech, *Against the Sophists* (i.e., Plato and his school) and Aeschines' (1.173) characterization of Socrates and Demosthenes, Sophists were regarded with suspicion and often with hostility; see further Poulakos 1995; Tindale 2010.

8.4 INSTRUMENTALISM AS A THREAT I: MENDACITY AND VICIOUS EGOISM

Returning to censorship in the *Republic,* although Plato's Socrates does not cite *Eumenides,* the play offers ample evidence of the kind of "falsehoods" concerning the gods that were Socrates' expressed concern in book 2: The sharp conflict between the Furies as representative of the "old gods" and Athena and Apollo, as members of a "new Olympian order," is a central theme of the play on anyone's reading. The Furies make explicit their capacity for harming mortals. The vengeance they inflict—through famine, disease, civil discord, and various vividly described forms of gruesome torture—is driven by hatred and can in no way be imagined as corrective justice. Those they punish are destroyed, not improved.

Moreover, while Apollo claims to speak only the truth (*Eumenides* 615, 657), his testimony in support of Orestes rings false: He seeks to acquit Orestes of the crime of killing kin by the startling claim that mothers are not blood relatives to their children: They are merely the vessel for the seed of the father. This must have been recognized as implausible to many in Aeschylus' audience. Seven years after the play was staged, the Athenian assembly passed, on a motion of Pericles, a law that required Athenian citizens be born, not only of an Athenian father, but also of an Athenian mother. Whatever its motivation, the law implied that mothers imparted something essential to their offspring.[14] Certainly Plato would have rejected Apollo's claim as invalid: In Callipolis the marriage lottery is rigged so that the best men (*hoi aristoi*) have frequent sex, and thus produce most offspring, with the best women (*hai aristai: Republic* 5.459d). This is mandated, on explicitly eugenic principles, based on the experience of livestock management, with the intention of breeding "gold-souled" children. If Plato and his readers thought women were mere vessels for male seed, the design of the deceptive arrangement makes no sense.[15]

14. Periclean citizenship law: Patterson 1981. Sommerstein (1989: 207–8) comments, "The audience . . . probably saw Apollo's argument as a clever and specious but fallacious piece of forensic pleading; and so apparently do half the all-male jury." Iordanoglou and Tralau (2022) offer a detailed analysis (with literature review) of Apollo's "embryology," concluding that the audience was likely to have been highly skeptical of Apollo's argument.

15. Socrates' plan is explicitly aimed at making the *poimnion* (herd or flock) as excellent as possible (459e). Notably, the use of the related term *poimnē*, with the same meaning of "human/divine herd," is characteristic of Aeschylus: LSJ s.v.

Apollo's argument against maternal kinship is supported by an appeal to Athena's origins—the goddess was nurtured, not in the womb of a mother, but in the body of her father, Zeus (657–66). This argument is immediately followed by Apollo's promise that acquitting Orestes will facilitate a military alliance with Argos (667–73). Apollo's twin arguments seem designed specifically to pander to the vanity and interests of Athena and the jurors: To achieve his desired outcome (Orestes' acquittal) he instrumentally appeals to Athenian mythology and to Athens' security situation. As such, Apollo's arguments resemble the kind of manipulative rhetoric associated with the Sophists more than they do straightforward truth-telling. If that is right, then we might suppose Socrates' disapproval of depictions of divine mendacity in tragedy was exacerbated by the portrayal of gods as employing the kind of rhetoric associated with Sophists. That kind of rhetoric was predicated on viciously egoistic varieties of instrumental rationality associated in Plato's texts with Thrasymachus and Callicles: Manipulative rhetoric aims at gaining the outcomes sought by the speaker at the expense of the listener, who is led into false belief and thereby less able to benefit himself. A rhetorical divinity thus harms mortals, a possibility firmly rejected by Plato's Socrates.

In brief, then, I suppose that the plays of Aeschylus and other tragedians were regarded by Plato as problematic, not only because they portrayed the gods as conflicted, harmful, and mendacious, but also, and relatedly, because the plays appeared to promote the wrong kind of egoistic instrumentalism. That conclusion should not be surprising. Plato saw in the public culture of Athens a variety of threats to the moral development of individual souls that is the essence of the Socratic craft of politics. Politics as soul-craft, insofar as it sets the framework for Callipolis, was intended to neutralize that threat, and thereby allow for the positive development of the capacities and welfare of each member of the community—and most especially of those few who were capable of becoming true philosophers.

In previous chapters, I have rehearsed some of the objections that Plato's Socrates raised against narrowly egoistic forms of strategic reasoning. Egoism in a broad sense is widely regarded as the basis of classical eudaimonism, which takes as its goal the happy, flourishing self (Williams 1985: chap. 3; Bobonich 2011; Annas 2017). But Conventionalist variants of the folk theory and Socratic ethics and politics alike rejected narrow egoism, in which the good of the individual self was severed from the good of anyone else. As we have seen (chapter 2.2:

Aristotelian Justice) justice, in Aristotle's polis, can be defined as the common good. Aristotle's account of friendship, in the *Nicomachean* and *Eudemian Ethics,* assumes that individual human flourishing, and every form of community, up to and including the polis, depends on friendship (e.g., *EE* 1241b35–36; Cooper 1999: chap. 15). And every form of friendship, including the most common and instrumental form of "utility friendship," is concerned in part with the good of another, rather than the exclusive good of oneself.[16]

The model vicious egoist, introduced in book 1 of the *Republic* by Thrasymachus, and the subject of Glaucon's "invisible Gyges" thought experiment in book 2, is the seemingly happy tyrant. By the end of the *Republic,* the reader has learned that the tyrant is far from happy. Indeed, stripped of the conceit of invisibility, the tyrant is revealed as the most miserable of men, doomed by his unruly, obsessive, and will-fully intensified desires to live his life as the slave of slaves. Along the way, we learned that unregulated egoism is a primary threat to social order: Viciously egoistic agents, those that see the harmful exploitation of others as a source of their own good, cannot solve the problem of creating and maintaining social order among interdependent persons without reference to a ruler who acts as a third-party enforcer.

In Callipolis—and uniquely there—the ruler ensures the best possible, overall happiest and most harmonious social order. Yet the Thrasy-machean claim, that a rational individual should selfishly seek to maximize his own happiness at the expense of the welfare of others, remains a constant, if ultimately unrealized, threat even in Callipolis. The introduction of Guardians in book 2 raised the concern that these military experts will fight one another over control of resources or, if united, use their collective monopoly on violence to exploit the producing classes (chapter 3.1). To prevent conflict and exploitation, the Guardians are deprived of their own families and the right to own private property. But this leads Adeimantus to object, at the beginning of book 4, that the Guardians are not especially blessed persons, at least according to any ordinary accounting (419a). Socrates pushes back: While it would not be surprising if it turned out that the Guardians were indeed the happi-

16. For example, *EE* 1240a23–28, 1244a2–25, with Cooper 1999: chap. 14; A. Price 1989: chap. 4. Hirji (2020) addresses how classical eudaimonism squares the dualism of the agent's self-interest with ethical demands that take into account the good of others, offering a useful survey of recent discussions of strong versus weak eudaimonism in Aristotle. See further, 8.5, below.

est of persons, the purpose of the Callipolis project was not to make any one category of persons exceptionally happy. Rather the goal was the greatest possible (*malista*) happiness of the polis as a whole (420b).[17]

That point is underlined, in similar terms, in book 7 (519d–20d) when Socrates addresses Glaucon's concern that the founders of Callipolis were harming the true Guardian by constraining him to "go back down to the Cave"—that is, to take up the burdens of ruling the polis when he would naturally prefer to remain in the blissful condition of contemplating the Forms. The possibility of disobedient philosopher-rulers, who object to doing their duty on grounds of selfish utility maximization, is raised but quickly dismissed as a counterfactual (*adunaton*). It is off-path behavior that will not occur, given that "we are ordering just things for just persons" (520e). Yet the worry that egoistic self-interest might disrupt the harmonious order of Callipolis has not been completely dispelled. That lingering threat is part of the justification for the censorship of literature, a necessity that is reiterated in book 10.

8.5 INSTRUMENTALISM AS A THREAT II: MIXING UP AND CROWDING OUT

A related threat is that a habit of choosing courses of action on the basis of calculations of maximum advantage to the agent will result in the confusion of instrumental and ethical forms of reason and will crowd out generous, helpful behavior and morally choice-worthy ends. Friendship offers a case in point. The opening scenes of Plato's *Republic* are structured by interaction among men in a network of intimate relationships. Cephalus greets Socrates as an old friend and regrets that they meet so seldom now that his age makes travel to the city more difficult. Their friendship includes the expectation of personal gain: Socrates initiates the dialogue with Cephalus with the statement that he enjoys speaking to the very old because their personal knowledge of a phase of

17. Kamtekar (2001: 202–17) shows that Plato offers an individualistic, rather than an organicist, principle of happiness (contra Popper 1963). Happiness is predicated on the distribution of the goods (notably education) produced by the operationalization of the principle of each doing his own work. The distribution is based on the capacity of each to benefit from those goods. Given vastly unequal capacities to benefit, philosophers will be much happier than all others (a point emphasized by Bobonich 2017), but each individual is made as happy as possible.

life is potentially of value to one, like himself, who has yet to experience it. So, in Aristotle's terms (below), the friendship of Cephalus and Socrates prominently includes "use" by one friend of another; the idea that each is gaining something of value to himself is an essential part of the relationship.

As we have seen (chapter 7.2), in his conversation with Cephalus, Socrates quickly raises the specter of another kind of utility-based relationship—the exchanges of material goods and services inherent to money-making—and then deftly excludes it from this part of the dialogue. Socrates characterizes those who have made their own money as having an excessive preference (*sphodra agapan*) for it. They aim at a single outcome, the increase of their wealth. They value wealth as an end in itself, as well as a means to other ends (Schofield 2006: 258–64). They find no other object to be worthy of praise. Thus, money-makers are difficult to spend time with. In essence, money-making, as an end, has crowded out the money-maker's ability to articulate thoughts interesting to a philosopher.

As a result, given Socrates' own preferences and his goals in engaging others in conversation, a full-time entrepreneur (which Cephalus evidently is not at the dramatic date of the dialogue) would be of no use to him as a friend. Socrates' goals are different from the money-maker's and they are assumed to be vastly more choice-worthy. Nevertheless, Socrates' motivation for friendship is instrumentally rational insofar as he spends time with friends in expectation of advantage to himself. His motives are self-interested, but not narrowly so, because the advantage is not expected to accrue *only* to himself. Moreover, given the no-harm principle developed in his discussion of friendship and enmity with Polemarchus, Socrates' own advantage, gained in friendly relationships, could never be at the expense of or to the detriment of others. Despite the objections of some of his interlocutors, Socrates initiated dialogue in the spirit of friendship (e.g., *Republic* 498c–d). His testing of arguments was aimed at mutual benefit; it was never a zero-sum contest. But the worry remained that some of Socrates' hangers-on would use Socrates' techniques for narrowly instrumental purposes. Being taken as friends, they would harm rather than help others (536a–b).

Aristotle on Friendship and Utility

Aristotle's two somewhat different, but largely compatible, accounts of friendship (*Nicomachean Ethics* books 8 and 9, *Eudemian Ethics* book

7) raise concerns of mixing up and crowding out.[18] Friendship is a universal human phenomenon (*NE* 1155a20–23, 1159b26, 1161b5–7), divisible into three types, based on virtue, pleasure, and utility. The highest and definitive form, virtue friendship, is rare: available only to those who are truly excellent, and then with only a few equally good others (*NE* 1156b25, 1158a11; *EE* 1237b35–36). Virtue friendship is unqualified, enduring, involves trust, and is predicated on recognized excellence on either side. Although Aristotle specifies that "each person wishes goods most of all to himself" (*NE* 1159a14), the virtue friend is nothing less than a "second self." Pleasure friendship, a relatively undeveloped category, pertains when friends enjoy one another's company for reasons that exceed mutually beneficial transactions (for example, they find one another to be witty).[19]

Utility friendship (*philia chrēsimē*), that is, friendship predicated specifically on instrumental reasoning and expected advantage, is the most common of the three species of friendship (*EE* 1236a34–35). It is, however, initially unclear whether it truly counts as friendship (*NE* 1158b6). As in all forms of friendship, the good of the other is a necessary condition of the relationship (*EE* 1240a23–28, 1244a2–25), but a utility friend wishes the good for another in order to benefit himself (*EE* 1241a6). Utility friends make agreements that are believed to be profitable (*elusitelei*) for both parties (*EE* 1243b5–6). Utility friendship is thus defined by reciprocal advantage, with the advantage measured by some agreed upon standard. Utility friends are not vicious egoists, in that they do not expect to gain from harming one another; indeed, business partnerships (*chrēmatistikai*) constitute a canonical form of friendly association premised on utility and equality (*EE* 1241b26). Utility friends may bind themselves by enforceable contracts, so the friendship

---

18. Schofield (1999: chap. 5) details the differences, concluding that the two texts had somewhat different aims and were directed at different audiences. The *Eudemian Ethics* was long regarded as earlier than, and generally inferior to, the *Nicomachean Ethics*; any apparent contradiction between the two works could therefore be finessed by assuming that Aristotle had revised his views. Recent work (notably Lee 2020) has defended the *EE* as at least as philosophically sophisticated as the *NE*. This casts doubt on the traditional chronology of the works (for which there is no independent evidence) and bears on the question of whether they offer incompatible conclusions on, or simply different approaches to, important matters.

19. On the three kinds of friendship in Aristotle, reciprocity, mutuality, and the difficult question of how egoism and altruism are conjoined; see further, A. Price 1989: chaps. 4 and 5; Cooper 1999: chaps. 14 and 15; Schofield 1999: chap. 5; Riesbeck 2016: 57–96.

may dissolve when the contract is fulfilled, or when advantage is removed, "for they were never friends of each other, but of that which was expedient for them" (*NE* 1157a15). And yet, "we must presumably also say that such people [involved in utility relations] are friends, but that there is more than one species of friendship" (*NE* 1157a30).

Given its contractual premise, utility friendship is predicated on equality of standing in respect to rules, rather than on natural hierarchies. Aristotelian equality is of two kinds: The first is an aristocratic principle of proportionality, whereby fair distribution of goods is determined by relative merit. This, however, creates the potential for disagreement about the relevant category of merit and the appropriate standard by which to measure reciprocal inputs and outputs. The second is the straightforwardly aggregative, arithmetical equality associated with democracy (*EE* 1241b33–40: a vote is a vote) and commerce (a drachma is a drachma). Arithmetical equality makes association possible among ordinary (that is, nonexcellent) persons and between rich and poor (*NE* 1159b14).[20]

Importantly, utility, along with its associated forms of equality, is the primary basis of civic friendship (*politikē philia*), that is, friendship among citizens in a polis, concerned with ruling and being ruled over in turns (*EE* 1241a31–33). Insofar as the polis is taken to be formed and maintained for the sake of advantage (*to sumpheron*), and justice is construed as advantage in common (*NE* 1160a11–14), utility friendship among citizens plays an essential role in sustaining the association that Aristotle took to be both a natural end and the necessary condition for complete human flourishing. The question remains whether utility friendship is enough for citizens, or whether the higher form of virtue friendship is somehow also involved.

In the *Eudemian Ethics*, Aristotle asserts that the relations of utility friendship among citizens are ideally predicated on rules (*nomikē philia*), modeled on diplomatic agreements between poleis or contractual agreements between buyers and sellers in a market (*EE* 1242b23–26, 33–35, 1243a7). But the model is imperfect: As John Cooper (1999: chap. 16) has emphasized, the interstate alliance and commercial exchange models fail fully to capture what civic friendship does and must entail: Citizens do share in producing and benefiting from the

---

20. Equality and hierarchy in Aristotle's account of civic friendship: Schofield 1999: 87–91. Two forms of equality: *EE* 1242b 13–21. See Harvey 1965, with discussion in Ober 2017b; Schofield 1999: chap. 6.

"external" goods (including security and material welfare) essential to living together in a state. But they also share in and identify deeply with their civic community as a moral enterprise. Indeed, it appears that for Aristotle "'civic friendship' itself is an essential human good" (Cooper 1999: 314).[21]

The extension of civic friendship beyond the narrowly instrumental domain of material interests appears to be recognized by Aristotle's ordinary (that is, not completely virtuous) civic friends. But that recognition can lead to troublesome, because divisive, outcomes. For many of their civic purposes, citizens make use of arithmetical equality. As in market exchanges, they employ a single, accepted standard for measuring and equalizing inputs and outputs: the benefit (*ton agathon*) and cost (*hē leitourgia*) of civic existence (*EE* 1242b27–31). Aristotle's example of a single, reliable, standard of measures is, as elsewhere, coined money (*EE* 1242b13–15). He seems to be thinking of something like the taxes and tax-like monetary contributions paid to the polis by the rich. And yet, because of their differences (his example is farmers and shoemakers: *EE* 1243b32) citizens in a polis must also employ some form of proportionate equality. Proportionality lacks a single standard of measurement, and thus is prone to disagreement and conflict (*EE* 1243b15–16, 23–31). Material benefits (in terms of security and welfare) gained by the inferior must be somehow equated with honors (*timai*—presumably including both public recognition and high offices) for the superior (*EE* 1242b21).

Moreover, and more troubling, civic friends not only make use of readily measured, straightforward (*kat'euthuōrian*) rule-standards, but also the moral category of mutual trust. Thus, so long as their friendship is based on contract, it remains of the properly civic and legal kind; but when they trust each other for repayment their association wishes to be (*bouletai*) friendship based on virtuous character (*ēthikē*) and

---

21. A. Price (1989: chap. 7) addresses the question of utility, virtue, and friendship with reference to the putative development of Aristotle's thought from *EE*, to *NE* and *Politics*. He concludes (pp. 197, 199) that Aristotle's mature view was that the foundation of a flourishing polis must be a kind of virtue friendship and that civic friendship may be an extended variant of full virtue-friendship. Schofield (1999: 91–94), by contrast, emphasizes the emphasis in the *EE* on the thin, contractual, commercial nature of friendship among democratic citizens. Riesbeck (2016: 69–96) likewise sharply distinguishes utility (and thus civic) friendship from virtue friendship, but he also emphasizes the non-exploitative nature of the relationship, and its association with a kind of justice. D. Allen (2004) provides a profound meditation on the essential role of something close to Cooper's conception of civic friendship in contemporary democratic communities.

comradeship (*hetairikē*). Their motivation is not mere appetite, but the "rational wish" (*boulēsis*) that arises, in Aristotle's moral psychology, from "reason's own desire."[22] The outcome of this aspiration is not, however, enhanced cooperation, but the exacerbation of disputes. The disputes arise as a result of the unhealthy mixing of two fundamentally different forms of friendship (utility and virtue). This, Aristotle asserts, is contrary to nature. Those citizens who mix things up in this way wish to have it both ways: Whereas in fact they associate because of utility, they purport that their association is ethical, "just as if they were equitable persons" (*epieikeis: EE* 1242b35–43a2). The destabilizing mixing of categories arises from the choices of those who ought to associate on the basis of utility, but who aspire to something higher and better. That domain of virtue is, by nature, inappropriate to them and, when improperly mixed with utility, becomes threatening to social order.[23]

The other side of the friendship coin proves equally troubling: virtue friendship can potentially be crowded out by considerations of utility. In Aristotle's account of virtue friendship, utility and pleasure are not simply replaced by virtue, but are carried forward into this highest form of friendship. There is nothing untoward, he says, about an unqualified, virtue friendship having not only an aspect of pleasure, but also an aspect of mutual utility (*NE* 1156b15, 1157a3, 1158b9). In the *Eudemian Ethics* (1243a32–b1) this is identified as a potential problem: Aristotle notes that civic friendship, based on utility, looks to the agreement (*homologia*) and the outcome (*to pragma*), whereas ethical friendship concerns the deliberate choice (*prohairesis*). The latter, he notes is finer, while the former is more concerned with feasibility constraints (*anangkaiotera*). And so, people sometimes begin as ethical friends, on the basis of their virtue, but then their private interests come into con-

22. On rational and nonrational desires in Aristotle, and the distinction between *boulēsis* as rational wish for what is or appears to be good and *epithumia* as appetite for pleasure, see Cooper 1999: chaps. 10 and 11, and esp. pp. 241, 266; cf. 8.6, below, on practical reason.

23. Aristotle's worry about mixing utility and virtue in civic friendship is analyzed thoughtfully by Yack (1985: 104–9). Cooper (1999: 327–30, with n. 20) and A. Price (1989: 155–57) seek to resolve the problem through a developmental account that regards the *Eudemian Ethics* as an inferior, preliminary account of friendship; but see above, n. 18. Schofield (1999: 92–93) discusses the passage as exemplifying a view of democratic political culture as thin and quasi-commercial relative to the traditional, hierarchical alternative. Van Berkel (2020: 249–50, 415–28, 456–57) proposes that Aristotelian civic friendship is a unique space of impersonal market exchange, made possible by political equality and facilitated by coined money.

flict and it becomes clear that "they were otherwise." That is, their subjective preferences are revealed in actions that expose the fragility of the virtuous premises of their previous association. Aristotle concludes that ordinary people only pursue the fine (*to kalon*) when they already have in hand a substantial material surplus.

The upshot is that virtue friendship inherits and is potentially undermined by a more narrowly self-interested instrumentalism. The inheritance helps to explain why Socrates in the *Republic* could treat his friendship with Cephalus (and others) as in some ways predicated on utility. The question arises, however: When does the instrumentalism inherent in the relations of virtue friends become corrupting? The answer would seem to be: when the pursuit of private interests crowds out virtue as the primary basis of the relationship. Socrates' comment in *Republic* book 1, to the effect that entrepreneurs can only praise wealth, implicates entrepreneurial activity, aimed at accumulation beyond the needs of the household, in just that kind of corrupting crowding out. As we have seen (chapter 7.7) Aristotle, too, saw the excessive focus on money-making as both disturbingly pervasive and as destructive of the inherent human capacity for developing virtue.

Plato on the Democratic Corruption of Souls

Political activity is another site of potential crowding out and mixing up. In *Republic* book 6, Socrates addresses the social processes by which persons with the potential to become philosophers are corrupted in a democratic polis. The point of the section is that those with greatest natural gifts, with the potential to be best, become the worst of people when miseducated and badly formed. The run-of-the-mill "private" Sophists—that is, Protagoras, Gorgias, Thrasymachus, and their like—are quickly rejected as the primary source of corruption (492a). Rather, it is "the many [*hoi polloi*], when gathered in civic assemblies or law courts or theaters or military camps," that are the "great Sophists" who educate "young and old, men and women" most completely and mold them just as they wish (*boulontai*) them to be.

The processes of educating and molding by the many operate via uproarious praise and blame in the various public venues (492b–c). Under such conditions, the "young man's" heart is moved within him; no private teaching can withstand the clamor, and in the end "he will affirm the same things that they do to be honorable and shameful and will do as they do, and be such as they are" (492c–d). Moreover, the miseducative process is backed by state-level coercion: by threats of loss of civic standing, fines, and execution (492d). Finally, the ordinary Sophists, while not the primary miseducators, serve as amplifiers: They teach nothing other than the opinions that the many opine whenever they are gathered together (493a). The Sophist, like the would-be politician or artist, must grasp the passion and pleasures of the foregathered motley masses, whether it concerns painting or music or politics. The upshot is that the options of every craftsman and politician are severely limited; each labors under constraint (*anangkē*): He must either produce that which is praised by the many or suffer dire consequences (493c–d: compare Herodotus' severely constrained Gyges: chapter 1.6–7).

This passage appears to contrast with the later depiction, in book 8 of the *Republic,* of democracy as chaotically irrational (chapter 6.2). There, Plato's Socrates denies that the democratic individual or state is rational in the instrumental sense of having ordered preferences and beliefs capable of sustaining a course of action aimed at a particular end. But here, in book 6, Plato's Socrates implies that the democratic many (in civic assembly, law court, and theater) have orderly preferences over educative outcomes, and that those preferences result in collective actions. Popular preferences are clearly expressed and reinforced by praise and blame in organized public gatherings. The many willfully and successfully educate and mold those who might otherwise form other (philosophical) preferences and beliefs, with the aim of making everyone "just as they [the many] are." Their goal is explicitly instrumental: "to make use of [the talented individual] in connection with their own affairs" (494b). They use the law courts to attack anyone who might draw him towards philosophy in order to continue to have use of him (494e). The upshot is that demotic preferences crowd out all others. Instrumental rationality under conditions of extreme social constraint buries the hope of developing ethical reason.

Meanwhile, the Sophists, self-identified in Plato's dialogues as the masters of the strategic reasoning and the rhetorical techniques useful in gaining the agent's ends, are here demoted to mere instruments of the demos' will.[24] The "political craft" taught by the Sophists is reduced to honing the skill of accurately learning and then pandering to the desires of the many. Plato's deflationary account of sophism in the *Republic* elides the possibility that the theorization of instrumental reasoning played a positive role

---

24. Compare the comic description of the pandering, servile demagogues and the ultimately masterful Demos in Aristophanes' *Knights.*

in the development of Greek political institutions. In so doing, it has contributed to obscuring the history of systematic thought on the topic of practical reasoning that has been this book's primary focus.

And yet instrumentalism remains central for Plato. As vividly illustrated in *Republic* and *Gorgias* (chapter 2.4) the Athenian many, their would-be political leaders, and the Sophists as would-be instructors of leaders are locked into a cycle of subjective preferences, opinion-based beliefs, and expected utility maximization: The leaders seek by their pandering to maximize the acclaim of the many. To become effective panderers, they pay the Sophists their high fees, thereby satisfying the Sophists' goal of maximizing their own wealth and self-importance among the elite. Meanwhile, the demos strategically employed the politicians' and Sophists' desire for power and money to maximize its control over everyone and everything in the polis. The end result, as noted above, is that strategic choices aimed at utility maximization crowd out the possibility of philosophical development. Instrumentalism thereby obviates the goal of true *eudaimonia,* at the level of the individual and the polis. This was, of course, a disaster from the perspective of Socratic moral philosophy.

What, then, is to be done?

8.6 INSTRUMENTALISM AND THE TASK OF CLASSICAL POLITICAL PHILOSOPHY

Viewed through the lens of Socratic philosophy, instrumental rationality seems, at least at first blush, to be nothing but a problem: It is associated with Thrasymachean narrow egoism. With the degraded character and practices of the tyrant. With unlimited and morally corrupting material accumulation achieved through coercive use of power by greedy states and through transactional mercantile exchange between greedy merchants and consumers. With deceptive (and self-deceptive) practices of speech and thought. With mixing up of high and low ends. With crowding out individual philosophical development and the best sorts of human relationships. With the malformation of regimes, the neglect of virtue, the withering of the best part of the soul.

Conditions for Eudaimonia

The Socratic cure for the disease of instrumental rationality, as discussed at various points in the previous chapters, is what I have been calling ethical rationality. In brief: In place of the subjective preferences over available outcomes of the pure instrumentalist, the Socratic offers objectively valuable ends. Rationality is redefined as a consistent preference for and rightful pursuit of the goods identified and desired by reason itself. *Desire for* an end is no longer, in and of itself, a *reason to* pursue it. Desires originating in the "nonrational parts of the soul"—arising from appetite (for, say, food or sex) or spirited emotion (for, say, revenge following an insult)—must be under the strict control of reason. Rational choice-making is ultimately motivated by reason's own desire for what is truly good (absolutely or for a human being), conjoined with knowledge of the good, acquired by philosophical (metaphysical and natural scientific) inquiry. Ethical reason, then, is more than a matter of ranked preferences and coherent beliefs about the state of the world. In place of opinion-based beliefs relevant to achieving the agent's goals, the Socratic offers knowledge of ends and the rightness of means. Rational choice-making is thus inextricably intertwined with metaphysics and epistemology and with the scientific grasp of natural ends. As such, it is the province of philosophy, not folk theories. Rationality, so understood, is characteristic of philosophers, not Sophists or politicians or ordinary people.[25]

That being the case, we might expect the Socratic cure to require purging the individual soul and the polis of the error of instrumental, strategic approaches to reasoning. That sort of cure might seem to be indicated by various measures proposed by Socratic philosophers: for example, the censorship of literature in the *Republic,* or the separation and isolation of the "civic agora" from the "commercial agora" in Aristotle's "polis of our prayers." Instrumentalism might have been regarded by philosophers as so dangerous that the purge must leave no trace, no beachhead from which an invasion could be launched. Given that most ordinary people were assumed to be incapable of ethical reasoning, we might suppose that an ideal Socratic polis could be predicated on a prestrategic, noninstrumental psychology in which beneficent actions were automatic responses to appropriate stimuli: Motivation would thus be "Furies-like," only helpful rather than hateful. We might expect the best polis to be simple and healthy, like the First Polis of *Republic* book 2.

25. My severely abbreviated account of "Socratic" choice-making in this paragraph generalizes from the particulars of Plato's and Aristotle's sophisticated, difficult, and in various ways controversial accounts of practical reasoning. See further, on Plato: Irwin 1995: 247–48. On Aristotle: Anscombe 1977; Wiggins 1980a, 1980b; Broadie 1991: chap. 4; Cooper 1999: chaps. 10 and 11; A. Price 2011; and below, this section.

Or based on an idealized social homogeneity, in which the preferences of individuals were indistinguishable from those of the community. Or predicated on the sort of regressive tribalism that Karl Popper (1963) accused Plato of advocating.

And yet, none of those expectations is fulfilled. As the previous chapters have, I hope, adequately demonstrated, each of the early Socratic philosophers whose texts are extensively preserved—Xenophon, Plato, Aristotle—was deeply and persistently engaged with an assumed "normal" human psychology grounded in self-interest and capable of strategic reasoning. They are, therefore, among our most important sources for the folk theory of instrumental rationality. Much philosophical discussion of instrumentalism is indeed overtly critical. Yet, as we have seen in each of the previous chapters, Plato's Callipolis and Aristotle's best achievable polis incorporate practical reasoning at every level. Indeed, these vividly imagined ideal-type poleis would be impossible without constant recourse to the strategic logic of rational choice-making.

The goal of the various Socratic ethical and political projects was *eudaimonia*—optimal happiness, flourishing, genuine well-being. Different Socratic texts offer somewhat different accounts of *eudaimonia*, but contemplation, understood as a highly refined, abstract, godlike cognitive process engaged in by wisdom-loving philosophers, is an essential part of it for Plato and Aristotle. Were human beings capable of *being* gods, contemplation could be the whole of *eudaimonia*. But since we are not gods, even the happiest human life requires a moral and material context. The moral context was the virtuous exercise of human capacities, a primary topic of Socratic moral philosophy and the subject of much contemporary work on ancient Greek ethics.[26]

Given the fact of human interdependence (chapter 2), the material context for eudaimonistic existence extended beyond the embodied individual person to the family, to extended networks of reciprocity and friendship, and ultimately to the completed human community—an autonomous state capable of sustaining itself over time. And thus, Socratic ethical and political theory were necessarily intertwined. Whether or not Socratic political philosophy aimed at the design of practically realizable states, the setting of the ideal-type communities

26. *Eudaimonia* in Plato: Vlastos (1973) 1981: chap. 5; Irwin 1999: chaps. 4 and 15. In Plato's early dialogues: Bobonich 2011. In Aristotle: Nagle 1980; Ackrill 1980; Kraut 1989: chap. 1; Broadie 1991: chap. 1; Cooper 1999: chap. 9. Compared to modern conceptions of morality: Annas 2017. Flourishing as the unimpeded exercise of natural capacities: Cooper 1999: 269; Ober 2007a; Hirji 2020: 206.

described by Plato and Aristotle is realistic, in that it assumes that the ideal state exists in a competitive world of rival states, endemic threats of civil conflict, and local resource scarcity. The population of the ideal state, moreover, will include those who are instrumentally, but not ethically, rational. The security, external and internal, and the economic welfare of imagined, optimally just and happy, Socratic communities— like the real poleis in which their authors lived—therefore required the understanding and skillful employment of instrumental reasoning.[27]

In order for a state to flourish in the Socratic sense, or for flourishing to be possible for any of its residents, three conditions must be met: (1) There must be individuals capable of complete, objective human happiness and they must be provided with the necessary resources for its potential attainment: an upbringing and education aimed at the perfection of virtue. They must be the rulers, since a nonvirtuous ruler would lead to the corruption of both individuals and the state itself. They must not engage in activities that will corrupt their virtue. (2) All residents, whose efforts are needed to sustain the state, or whose opposition could threaten it, must have reasons to act for its preservation.[28] For the rulers, this means creating the conditions in which the subjective preferences of those incapable of ethical reasoning are better served "within the bargain" than outside it. Given that constraint, the lives of those incapable of complete virtue will also be ordered so as to be as objectively good as possible, albeit inherently and substantially inferior to the lives of those excellent individuals capable of complete happiness.[29] (3) The state must be strong and prosperous enough to sustain itself in a competitive, potentially hostile environment. It must be adequately supplied with the instruments, the "suitable political equipment" essential to sustaining security and welfare, just as the individual must have an

27. Cf. Irwin 1999 on Plato's "rational eudaemonism" that "assumes that we have been given a good reason for being just if and only if we have been shown how justice promotes our happiness" (183) and must "appeal to concerns that are recognized as rational by just and non-just agents alike in order to show that the concerns of the just person are rational" (184). Irwin shows that Plato takes justice as a dominant part of happiness but rejects the thesis that justice in itself is sufficient for happiness.

28. For example, Aristotle *Pol.* 7.1329a9–11: "It is impossible that those who are capable of using and preventing the use of coercion will put up with always being ruled ... those who have authority of arms also have authority over whether the regime will last or not."

29. Bobonich (2017) surveys the assumed potential for happiness of completely and incompletely virtuous persons, arguing that the difference is profound in Plato's middle dialogues (including *Republic*), but less extreme in later Platonic dialogues and in Aristotle's ethical and political works.

adequate supply of "external goods" to realize complete happiness.[30] While (1) is the primary goal of Socratic political philosophy, because humans are not gods, that goal was unobtainable without (2) and (3).

The upshot of the three necessary conditions of *eudaimonia* is that the rulers of the ideal state must understand instrumental rationality, and they must be skilled in its employment, especially in organization of military and economic institutions and promotion of the habitual behavior for sustaining them. Those skills will include choice-making under conditions of uncertainty.[31] Rational institutions and habits were essential to securing the state against internal strife and external invasion. And they were needed in order to render the community prosperous enough to satisfy the material requirements of each of its residents. While *eudaimonia* is not predicated on the maximization of external goods, the system for supplying those goods must be efficient in that it optimizes opportunity for the contemplative activity that is essential for the happiness of excellent persons. Moreover, the external goods provide both the essential context and the means for the unimpeded virtuous exercise of human capacities: Lacking the necessary external goods, the option set among which the virtuous person may choose is shrunken, and his happiness is thereby deformed.[32]

---

30. I take the "suitable political equipment" (*summetros/politikē chorēgia*) necessary for the realization of the best possible state of *Pol.* 7.1325b33–40, 1326a5 to be the state-level analogue of the "external goods" necessary for the *eudaimonia* of the individual of *NE* 3.1 and *Pol.* 7.13. External goods (including friends, wealth, political power) defined as instruments that facilitate fine actions, and why *eudaimonia* requires them: *NE* 1099a31–b8, with Cooper 1999: chap. 13.

31. While having the external goods depends at least in part on luck (Cooper 1999: 295–304), the probability of achieving higher ends through their proper employment is a function of skill and knowledge. Cooper (1999: 308) notes that practical knowledge "would not count as knowledge at all, unless it made it likely that [the virtuous man] would succeed. It is, among other things, knowledge how the world runs, and so if it is regularly applied correctly, as of course the virtuous man does apply it, the looked-for results can be expected, anyhow a large percentage of the time."

32. Happiness deformed through the lack of external goods: *NE* 1099b2–6. Cooper (1999: 298–99) discusses how it is that the lack of external goods impedes the full exercise of virtue, citing *NE* 1178a33: the temperate person's need for *exousiai* (opportunities) for exercising moderation. Cooper (p. 299) concludes that, having external goods, the virtuous person is "in the position where the options for action that are presented to him by his circumstances allow him to exercise his virtues fully . . . [he enjoys] a normally full range of options." Hirji (2021) builds on Cooper's interpretation, while arguing that some external goods are of intrinsic value, and that Cooper attributes to Aristotle an "implausibly instrumental explanation" (p. 34) for the contribution of external goods to happiness. My interpretation emphasizes the necessary, albeit subsidiary, role played by instrumentalism in Aristotle's ethics.

In their different ways, each of the classical Socratics directly addressed the instrumental means by which political equipment and external goods could be most efficiently supplied. In the *Memorabilia* and *Cyropaedia* Xenophon discusses military strategy and logistics in detail; in the *Poroi* he proposes a program for increasing state revenues based on the incentives of metics and foreign traders. In the *Republic*, Plato sought to ensure that the incentives of the potentially dangerous auxiliary guardians and the producing classes alike were aligned with the goal of a peaceful, secure, prosperous polis. In the *Politics*, Aristotle focuses insistently on incentive compatibility in his practical advice on moderating corrupt regimes through institutional redesign. But incentive-based institutions are also essential for the perpetuation of the "polis of our prayers" outlined in books 7 and 8. Each citizen is required to own one piece of property on the state's frontier and another in the interior. "This provides equality and justice, as well as more consensus regarding wars with neighboring states" (1330a14–18). Here, the ethical conditions of equality and justice are linked to achieving consensus about response to military threats. Given that the individual property owners, the collective rulers, and the armed forces were the same persons, the fair distribution of properties on the frontier and in the interior gives each a similar incentive to respond to those threats.

The clear implication, consistent with Aristotle's point (above) that "each person wishes goods most of all to himself" (*NE* 1159a14), is that even those raised in the best way in the best possible polis, and thereby concerned for the common good, will still retain a tendency to look after their own interests first. Since that tendency risks disputes and internal conflict, the institutions of the polis must be designed accordingly, to align private interests to the extent possible. Examples could readily be multiplied, but the general point is clear: Strategic rationality was not banned or purged from the ethical-political projects of classical Socratic philosophers. To the contrary, it was built right into their foundations.

That conclusion should not be surprising. It is widely recognized that classical eudaimonism is predicated on egoism in the sense of self-interest—although decidedly not the vicious "Thrasymachean" egoism that viewed the strong as predatory, with their advantage gained by harming the weak in a zero-sum calculus of interests. "Nonvicious egoism" was the norm for classical Greek and Roman ethics, and it remained central to systematic Western ethical and political thought at least until the eighteenth century (Abizadeh 2018). That persistent notion is succinctly summed up in the "folk-theoretic" opinion offered by Xenophon's Socrates, with which this book began: "For I think that all persons choose, out of what is available to them, what they think is most advantageous to themselves, and they do this" (*Memorabilia* 3.9.4). For the Socratics, of course, most people choose poorly, because what they desire and pursue, believing it is most advantageous to themselves, is in fact bad for them as moral agents. But nonetheless, "all persons" do employ some form of instrumental rationality. And that means that political philosophers, insofar as they are concerned with relations among human beings rather than gods, cannot simply wish it away.

Political philosophy must include the management of instrumental rationality if one grants the following three premises:

1. Political philosophy concerns the ends of human existence and social order. *Eudaimonia* and the state are prominent among those ends.

2. The external goods of security and material welfare are necessary conditions for the state and *eudaimonia*. Creating and sustaining those conditions depends on cooperation across an extensive population of instrumentally rational agents.

3. Instrumental rationality, understood as self-interested expected utility maximization, if unmanaged or ill-managed, threatens cooperation, and thereby security and welfare. If properly managed, it is the means for the achievement and perpetuation of the highest ends of human existence and social order.[33]

I have argued that the classical Greek writers I have been calling "Socratics" did believe each of those premises to be true. And thus, they did suppose that an account of instrumental rationality was a necessary part of any philosophically adequate theory of ethics and politics. In practice, this meant adapting and refining what I have been calling the folk theory as a behavioral foundation for eudaimonism.

Each of the Socratics went about that task in his own way and came up with his own answers. I have focused here on Plato's approach to the task in the *Republic,* Aristotle's in the *Politics* and his two treatises on

---

33. I have not attempted to state the argument in syllogistic form, but I believe it would be possible to do so with reference to passages in the relevant works of either Plato or Aristotle, and perhaps of Xenophon as well.

ethics, and Xenophon's in the *Memorabilia*. Somewhat different approaches and answers are on offer in Plato's *Statesman* and *Laws,* Aristotle's *Rhetoric,* and Xenophon's *Cyropaedia*. But the goals of refining the folk theory of instrumentalism and finding the right place for utility in a eudaimonistic philosophical project seem to me to be fundamentally the same. In each case, instrumental reasoning is subordinated to, but also provides a basis for, an ethicized approach to reasoning. The result was the "rediscovery" of practical reason—this time as a fusion of instrumental and ethical forms of rationality.

Aristotle on Practical Reason

The rediscovery was canonized in Aristotle's discussion of practical reason (*phronēsis*) and its complex relationship to virtue, means, and ends in book 6 of the *Nicomachean Ethics*. In a key passage (*NE* 1144a7–29) Aristotle specifies that "it is virtue that makes the goal correct, and practical reason makes the things promoting the goal correct" (7–9, with Moss 2011). The *phronimos,* the excellent individual who fully manifests practical reason, has the correct ends and he employs the correct means for the right reasons. That is, he makes the right deliberate choices concerning virtuous action and consequently acts correctly.[34] Indeed, Aristotle usually denies the name *prohairesis,* "deliberate choice," to a motivated action that is not aimed at the right, virtuous kind of goal in the right, deliberative way. But after reiterating that "it is virtue that makes the deliberate choice [among available goals] correct" (20), Aristotle immediately notes that "the actions that are naturally to be done to fulfill the decision are the concern not of virtue, but of another capacity [*dunamis*] (21–22). The other capacity is "shrewdness" (*deinotēs*),

> which is such as to be able to do the actions that tend to promote whatever goal is preferred and to discover them [*tugchanein autōn*].[35] If then, the goal

34. Moss (2017: 139) offers a succinct summary: "Excellent ethical activity requires grasping the correct goal, deliberating about how to achieve it, and deciding on one's actions as means to that goal. When we act in this way we do not merely do the right things, nor do we merely do them in response to the right considerations: we do them on the basis of a full understanding of why they are to-be-done."

35. Similarly, in the *Magna Moralia*, Aristotle states that "it is characteristic of shrewdness and the shrewd man to discover the things from which [*ek tinōn*] each of the things doable in action may come about and to provide these" (1197b22–26: trans. Reeve 2013, adapted). I translate *deinotēs* as "shrewdness," rather than the usual "cleverness," in order to emphasize its practical, executive character. In translating *tugchanein* "to discover," rather than "to attain," I follow Reeve (2013).

is fine, shrewdness is praiseworthy, and if the goal is base, shrewdness is unscrupulousness [*panourgia*]. That is why both excellent and unscrupulous people [*phronimoi* and *panourgoi*] are called shrewd persons [*deinoi*]. (24–28)

He concludes that "practical reason is not shrewdness, though it requires this capacity" (28–29).[36]

Aristotle situates shrewdness, along with practical reason itself, in the calculative part of the soul, the part concerned with belief, rather than in the intellectual part concerned with abstract scientific reasoning, or the passionate part concerned with character and the locus of both natural and complete virtue (*NE* 1144b14–15, cf. *EE* 1220a10–13).[37] Shrewdness is, therefore, a distinctive cognitive capacity, with an essential, if subsidiary, and explicitly instrumental role to play in the overall process of practical reasoning and acting. It is what ensures that the goal that has been identified and chosen by practical reason is pursued efficiently. Shrewdness comes into play only after the correct end has been identified and deliberately chosen. But the process of "discovering" the sequence of actions necessary to the efficient pursuit of the goal must involve cognitive processes and subsidiary choices. I suppose that we moderns, along with many of Aristotle's contemporaries, would ordinarily describe those processes and choices in terms of deliberation over, inter alia, feasibility, likelihood, and strategy.

Aristotle's account of practical reason ethicizes deliberation over and choice among options. Under the right conditions the goal chosen by a good person will meet a high standard of excellence: It will be

36. Translation adapted from Irwin, with his notes in the Hackett 2nd ed. (1999). Anscombe (1977: 62) cites this passage to illustrate what she calls "executive choice," made as a result of "technical deliberation" about the use of means. She concludes (p. 63), "It must be admitted that Aristotle's account of deliberation often seems to fit deliberation about how to execute a decision, and in particular to fit technical deliberation, better than deliberation which is about the means here and now to 'living well in general.'" Anscombe notes that for Aristotle "there is no such thing as a choice that is *only* technical . . . there is always another 'choice' behind the technical, executive one." This, Anscombe suggests, is why Aristotle normally refuses the name *prohairesis* to the part of the choice process that is narrowly executive. A. Price (2011) and Moss (2011) discuss this passage (among others) in reference to the question of whether or not *phronēsis* is concerned with determining ends as well as means; Jiminez (2019) shows that *empeiria* (as practical experience of particulars) plays a major role in learning to assess situations and determining what means are adequate in a given situation. None of these works is, however, much concerned with the capacity of *deinotēs* as such.

37. On Aristotle's tripartite soul and the moral functions assigned to each part, see Moss 2017.

choice-worthy in itself. Under poor conditions, a choice must still be made, yet all available options lack intrinsic value. In this circumstance, the rational choice is the "least bad."[38] In any case, the essential function of efficiently organizing the actions necessary to execute a decision, to go for a preferred outcome in an effective manner, is equally available to some bad people, seeking objectively bad ends. The capacity for "shrewdness," shared by the Aristotelian *phronimos* and the unscrupulous person alike, was, I submit, a facility with strategic reasoning in public and private affairs.[39] It was manifest in (at least) the skillful employment of external goods as instruments that increase the probability, and thus the expectation, of gaining and keeping desired ends.

If this is right, Aristotle's shrewdness must be predicated on comparing feasible (as opposed to ideal) options and on a firm grasp of the motivations, including if not limited to utility maximization, and strategic behaviors of ordinary people—that is, on some version of the folk theory of instrumental rationality.[40] As such, the shrewdness characteristic of the *phronimos* resembles the skill set that the students of Sophists, as exemplified by Plato's Protagoras, paid to learn (Plato, *Protagoras* 318e–19a; see chapter 7.4). This in turn brings Aristotle (author of an important treatise on rhetoric), like Xenophon's Socrates (introduc-

---

38. Aristotle addresses mixed (voluntary but somehow compelled) choices at *NE* 3.1 and *EE* 2.8; see above, chapter 1 n. 29. Heinaman (1993) distinguishes intrinsic good from what is good for an individual in a particular situation: "Aristotle thinks . . . that an action is rational only if it aims at the greatest overall good available in the circumstances *or* aims at the smallest overall evil threatening in the circumstances" (p. 40). He connects *NE* 3.1 with *Pol.* 7.1332a7–21 and 1333a30–37, where Aristotle divides actions between those aimed at necessary (*anangkaia*) and useful (*chrēsima*) things and those aimed at noble (*kala*) things. See discussion in Hirji 2021: 36–38.

39. Reeve (2013: 249–57) offers a detailed discussion of *deinotēs* in the passages cited above in light of *EE* 1227b39–28a2 and *Magna Moralia* 1197b18–26. I think Gottlieb (1994: 289) is correct to describe *deinotēs* in Aristotle as an intellectual capacity for instrumental reasoning that enables one to act. She points out that the capacity may be held by persons who are good, bad, or "not quite good."

40. The "discoveries" of shrewdness are highly consequential. For example, in his account of the polis of our prayers in the *Politics* (7.1330b35–1331a18), Aristotle rebuts those (read Plato) who rejected city walls on moral grounds, and he offers a detailed account of situationally appropriate fortification policy. He addresses technical issues (noting recent advances in catapult artillery), and the incentives of relevant players (attackers and defenders), concluding, "For just as the attackers of a city are concerned to study the means by which they can gain the advantage, so also for the defenders some devices have already been invented and others they must discover (*zētein*) and think out (*philosophein*); for [potential aggressors] do not even start attempting to attack those who are well prepared." For discussion, see Ober and Weingast 2020: 43–46.

tion, section 0.2), closer to the Sophists than is usually allowed.[41] The difference is that the *phronimos* consistently aims at an objectively good final end. Under good circumstances (say, in the polis of our prayers), each of his highest-ranked subsidiary choices promotes that goal. Even when his choice is reduced by bad circumstances to a "least bad," within the constraints of the particular situation, he acts in accord with virtue.[42]

This book has argued that the philosophical rediscovery of practical reason, as an (unequal) alliance of low instrumental with high ethical reasoning, shrewdness with virtue, was made possible by the earlier discovery and development of what I have been calling the Greek folk theory of instrumental rationality. Among the participants in that original discovery were Sophists, like Protagoras and Gorgias, at least some of whom Aristotle would have described as unscrupulous *panourgoi*. They advertised what they taught and practiced as *dunamis* (not only capacity, but also power) and *deinotēs* (not only shrewdness, but also forceful efficacy). As we have seen, instrumental theories of human motivation and action were built into the foundations of western political thought as a result of the enduring influence of Greek literature, prominently including both Platonic and Aristotelian branches of Socratic moral philosophy. It remains, for good or ill, a fundamental feature of our global intellectual heritage.

8.7 BACK TO THE FUTURE OF CLASSICS AND POLITICAL THEORY

The classical Socratic development of eudaimonism as nonvicious egoism, grounded in ends rationally determined to be objectively good and

41. Plato *Theaetetus* 176c, 177a contrasts the ideally just man possessing true *deinotēs* with the spurious *deinotēs* of the politician or craftsman, and he emphasizes the misery of the possessor of this second, inferior sort of *deinotēs*. Among Aristotle's other near contemporaries, the term *deinotēs* was most often used in reference to a rhetorician capable of achieving his ends (good or otherwise), that is, to one who was "skilled in speech" (*deinos legein*). See for example Thucydides 3.37; Antiphon 5.5; Isocrates 1.4, 3.43; Demosthenes 18.144, 242, 276–77, 19.121; Aeschines 3.174; Isaeus 10.1 Other references in tragedy and oratory are cited in Worman 2004: 12 n. 28.

42. The assumption that, for Aristotle, shrewdness is an intellectual capacity for devising instrumental means and focused on the use of external goods is consistent with the thesis (e.g., Wiggins 1980: 221–24 and Moss 2011: 49–51) that, even assuming that Aristotle's practical reason is concerned only with deliberating on means rather than with determining ends, it includes means that themselves constitute components of a rightly valued end. An example is when a person deliberates about what kind of life he wants to live. Cf. Anscombe 1977 on technical/executive versus general deliberation (above, note 36).

the means of strategic rationality, was integrated into later Stoic and then Christian (notably Augustinian and Thomist) systems of ethics.[43] Postclassical eudaimonism remained a dominant strain in Western ethical thought for over two millennia, from the Hellenistic period to the Enlightenment. It was augmented, but not replaced, in the seventeenth century by a new conception of contractual duties in the work of Thomas Hobbes and other early-modern social theorists (Abizadeh 2018). In the eighteenth century, eudaimonistic ethical egoism was challenged by Immanuel Kant's deontological ethics, which insisted that the exercise of reason imposes on every rational agent a "categorical imperative" of treating all rational beings as ends in themselves.[44]

Meanwhile, the prudent pursuit of self-interest as, descriptively, a primary motivation for human behavior remained a central theme in the projects of (for example) David Hume in moral psychology, Adam Smith in political economy, and James Madison in constitutional theory. Nineteenth-century utilitarianism augmented ethical egoism with the moral aim of maximizing quantified aggregates of goods across populations. Just social institutions were predicated on the efficient distribution of aggregated utility, understood in consequentialist, welfarist terms as benefits to individuals less costs. Varieties of the rigorous utilitarian consequentialism canonized in Henry Sidgwick's *Methods of Ethics* (1981 [7th ed. 1907, 1st edition 1874]) subsequently dominated Anglo-American political philosophy through the mid-twentieth century.

Linking the rational pursuit of self-interest with utility maximization and quantification provided the philosophical foundation for the next, twentieth-century, rediscovery of practical reason, in the form of the decision and game theories that have featured prominently in these pages. This rediscovery self-consciously shed the trappings of ethical rationality. But it either retained (via the severely abbreviated genealogy

43. Epicureanism was a distinctive strand of ancient ethics, also predicated in the first instance on nonvicious egoism and practical reason understood as rationally choosing the course of action (and creating the kinds of compacts with others) that will maximize happiness, in this case understood as lack of pain. Konstan (2018) offers a summary and literature review.

44. Based on a study of Kant's anthropological and pedagogical works, Lenczewska (2021) excavates Kant's speculative developmental history of practical reason, from its natural (and incompletely human) origins in something that seems very much like the strategic reason of the "folk theory" to the fully moralized rationality characteristic of completely realized humans. She also argues that Kant's imaginative developmental story, which appears to me in some ways reminiscent of Protagoras' "great myth," influenced Rawls' account of the rational and the reasonable; see below.

sketched in the previous paragraphs) or discovered anew the basic insights about motivation and deliberation of the original Greek folk theory. And therefore, the methods of modern rational choice theory and the insights of classical thought are mutually illuminating. Or so I have argued. That mutual illumination highlights a pathway to new work on ancient intellectual, political, and economic history.

Rational and Reasonable in the Political Philosophy of John Rawls

The mutual illumination of formal theory and classical thought also provides resources for developing twenty-first-century theories of practical reason and human flourishing, through the integration of normative with positive political theory. That ambitious project entails a revaluation of the role of ideal theory in ethics and political philosophy and the relationship between instrumental rationality and morality canonized in the most influential body of later twentieth-century political philosophy. Happily, the work of revaluation is already well under way.

John Rawls' theory of justice as fairness (1971, 1996, 2001) transformed Anglo-American political philosophy by offering a robust alternative to utilitarian theory (Forrester 2019; Wenar 2021a). Rawls postulated that all moral agents have the capacity to utilize two "distinct and independent" (Rawls 1996: 51) modes of reasoning: In addition to "the rational" there is "the reasonable." The rational is a utility-maximizing logic, motivated by considerations of private advantage—that is, the instrumental rationality of the Greek folk theory. The reasonable is a sense of justice resulting in a desire to comply with the obligations of justice and a willingness to cooperate with cooperative others on terms mutually agreed to be fair. Thus, for Rawls, the rational motivates the pursuit of private advantage; the reasonable motivates self-moderating and other-regarding behavior.

Rawls proposed that the reasonable serves to constrain the rational, ensuring that the moral agent does not veer into narrow egoism. Unlike the external constraints of theories of strategic rationality (other agents' motives and anticipated actions), the reasonable is an internal, moral constraint. This internal constraint (in some ways reminiscent of Plato's Protagoras' "gifts of Zeus") is essential to social order because, Rawls posited, rationality alone is incapable of motivating reliably self-moderating and other-regarding (i.e., cooperative) behavior. Rational agents could not, without the aid of the reasonable, be relied upon to constrain their pursuit of private ends. In the terms developed above, they risked devolving into Thrasymachean egoists.[45]

Starting with these assumptions about human reasoning, Rawls (1971) derived rights-centered institutions, consistent with noninstrumentalist Kantian ethical deontology, from a thought experiment that he called "the original position"—a hypothetical once-and-for-all choice among a list of principles of justice that would determine the relevant rules for a society. The choice should ideally subordinate the rational to the reasonable: It is a tenet of the reasonable that citizens, as free and equal moral agents, should be symmetrically situated with respect to the establishment of shared terms of cooperation; differences among them should not influence their relative authority over the establishment of these terms and principles.[46]

To model this constraining reasonableness, Rawls invoked a "veil of ignorance." The choice-makers in his thought experiment, tasked with deciding on the principles that will forever set the fundamental institutions (Rawls' "basic structure") of their own society, are deprived of any knowledge of who they are: their social position, their moral commitments, the natural advantages or disabilities they have or lack. Within the reasonable framework imposed by the veil, Rawls models citizens as rational agents in pursuit of their private advantage; they make their choices in a rationally self-interested way in consideration of

45. "The reasonable conditions imposed on the parties in the original position constrain them in reaching a rational agreement on principles of justice as they try to advance the good of those they represent. In each case the reasonable has priority over the rational and subordinates it absolutely" (Rawls 2001: 82). "Like citizens in domestic society, liberal peoples are both reasonable and rational, and their rational conduct . . . is similarly constrained by their sense of what is reasonable" (Rawls 1999: 25). My thanks to Jacqueline Basu for alerting me to these passages, and to suggestions that have substantially improved this section.

46. "We impose on the parties certain reasonable conditions as seen in the symmetry of their situation with respect to one another and the limits of their knowledge (the veil of ignorance)" (Rawls 2001: 81). "We are concerned . . . with reasonable principles of justice for the basic structure. These are principles it would be reasonable for free and equal citizens to accept as specifying the fair terms of their social cooperation. Justice as fairness conjectures that the principles that will seem reasonable for this purpose . . . are the same principles that rational representatives of citizens, when subject to reasonable constraints, would adopt to regulate their basic institutions. What constraints, though, are reasonable? We say: those that arise from situating citizens' representatives symmetrically when they are represented solely as free and equal, and not as belonging to this or that social class, or as possessing these or those native endowments, or this or that (comprehensive) conception of the good" (Rawls 2001: 82). On Rawls' original position, see further the essays in Hinton 2015; Wenar 2021a: secs. 4.6–10, 2021b.

their general preference for their own good. But, since, behind the veil, they do not know what that is, the good they pursue cannot be narrowly "their own."

In an early, article-length statement of justice as fairness, Rawls (1958: 174) suggested that his theory was "connected with [while also differing from] a familiar way of thinking about justice which goes back at least to the Greek Sophists." He cited (1958: 174 n. 9) Glaucon's challenge in *Republic* book 2 as "perhaps the best known statement of this conception." That article lacked the veil of ignorance, and Glaucon's challenge never reappears in his later books. But Rawls' thought experiment in *A Theory of Justice* resembles the Ring of Gyges tale in Plato's *Republic* in employing a blatantly fictive device: A magic ring made Plato's Gyges invisible to others; the veil of ignorance renders Rawls' representative choice-makers invisible to themselves. In each case, the goal is to reveal the choices that would be made by model agents under conditions that stripped away ordinary considerations faced by real-world people. As we have seen, Plato's Gyges, once freed of the external constraints of others' expected response to his actions by the ring of invisibility, is, in Rawls' terms, rational but not reasonable: He is unconstrained by morality; he pursues wealth, sex, and power at the expense of others, fulfilling his top-ranked preferences by making choices expected to maximize his own utility.

Not surprisingly, Rawls' thought experiment yields a very different result. His model agents choose as the rules of justice a basic structure predicated on a robust set of equal liberties, fair equal opportunities, and a system for the distribution of the benefits of cooperation that allows for material inequality only insofar as it benefits the least-advantaged (the "difference principle"). Rawls' self-invisible choice-makers remain rational in their concern for their own good. However, under the veil's reasonableness constraint, rather than employing expected utility maximization as their decision rule, Rawls' agents use the "maximin" rule. That is, they choose a rule that will maximize each person's minimum payoff. Within the risk-minimizing logic of maximin, their choice is rational, insofar as they themselves could be among the least-well situated persons in terms of social position or natural capacities. The choice of maximin means, however, that they forego advantages that they might have enjoyed (once the veil is lifted) in favor of equal rights and a system of distribution that ensures that no one gets too little.

Rawls' original position thought experiment initiated a lively debate, engaging scholars in several fields—including utilitarians and choice theorists, who argued that the maximin decision rule would not be employed by genuinely rational, risk-neutral agents, that the difference principle is not Pareto-efficient, and that utilitarianism, rather than justice as fairness, would be chosen in the original position.[47] But, as an unintended consequence, it also contributed to widening the divide, in political philosophy, between ideal and nonideal political theory. Ideal theory in the wake of Rawls assumes (through the conceit of "hypothetical consent" to coercive public authority) strict compliance with the order chosen in the original position, "behind the veil." That is, agents are assumed to rank justice above self-interest, the right over the good. Nonideal theory considers the interests and incentives of agents, like those assumed in the Greek folk theory, whose actions are not necessarily determined by the choices of hypothetical participants in a thought experiment.[48] Within the field of political science there is a similar divide. Formal or positive political theory is based on variants of rational choice and game theory. Normative political theory (of the liberal and analytic variety) has been primarily concerned with working out the implications for individuals, families, organizations, states, and the global community, of Rawls' prioritization of the right and reasonable over the good and rational.[49]

In his later work on political liberalism, written in response to critics, Rawls (1996, 2001) replaced the veil of ignorance as the reasonableness constraint in the original position with the concept of an "overlapping consensus" among choice-makers with diverse moral commitments, especially differing religious beliefs. The consensus was, in theory, struck by deliberatively offering reasons for a preferred option that could be endorsed by agents holding different but nonetheless reasonable "conceptions of the good." Like his earlier thought experiment, this

47. See, for example, Harsanyi 1975, with discussion in Gaus and Thrasher 2015; Freeman 2019. Binmore (1994, 1998) offered a detailed critique of the Kantian premises of Rawls 1971 and developed a Humean, nonutilitarian defense of Rawls' egalitarian intuitions via a revised account of the original position as a self-enforcing equilibrium. Chung (2020 and forthcoming) offers a sustained internal critique of Rawls' difference principle, the choice of justice as fairness rather than utilitarianism, and a defense of utilitarianism against Rawls' charge that it fails to respect the distinction between persons.

48. Ideal and nonideal theory: Geuss 2008; Galston 2010; Simmons 2010; Wiens 2011; Waldron 2012; Valentini 2012; Estlund 2014; Wenar 2021a sec. 2.3.

49. Rawlsian political theory is an immense field; it has been systematically pursued, for example, in the journal, *Philosophy and Public Affairs*. Forrester (2019) discusses the original development of Rawls' theory and its subsequent impact on Anglo-American political philosophy.

new approach distinguished "the reasonable" (now a willingness to engage in deliberative reason-giving and reason-taking, as well as a sense of justice and willingness to cooperate on fair terms with others) from "the rational" (as instrumental good-seeking), taking them as distinct "moral powers." In terms of the folk theory, the Thrasymachean attitude that so deeply concerned Greek writers, and that was "connected with" justice as fairness in Rawls' 1958 article, has been taken off the table to make room for reasonable deliberation.

Normative and Positive Political Theory

Rawls contrasted his preferred reasons-based "overlapping consensus" approach to arriving at agreement on issues of common concern (laws, norms) to what he described as the merely rational "modus vivendi." A modus vivendi is a social equilibrium (that is, the solution to a bargaining problem: cf. chapter 4), based entirely on the rational choices of agents seeking their own good. Rawls argued that his overlapping consensus was superior to the modus vivendi not only on the grounds of taking proper account of the presence of a sense of justice in moral psychology and an interest in its exercise and development (again, no Thrasymacheans in sight), but also on grounds of stability: The overlapping consensus was stable, and for the right (justice-respecting) reasons. The modus vivendi was, by contrast, unstable as a result of its normative failings: Like Plato's Protagoras on the origins of social order (chapter 2.6), Rawls argued that merely rational individuals, lacking the self-moderating and other-regarding motivations given by the reasonable moral power, will not choose to engage in reliable (and costly) cooperation. And even if a rational order were to arise on the basis of a rational bargain (per chapter 4), it would be put at risk if there were any change in the distribution of power. Rational social order is seemingly doomed to quick collapse.

Rawls' conclusions have been challenged on various fronts (Forrester 2019: chap. 8). Within political theory, Realists, including Bernard Williams (1985, 2005), have rejected the assumption that politics either is (empirically), or should be (normatively), grounded in what is ultimately a Kantian conception of morality. Proceduralists, including Jeremy Waldron (2012), have called for a return to "*political* political theory" that would take into account motivations bracketed by Rawlsian ideal theory. Critics of nonaggregative social theory, including Barbara Fried (2020), have argued that deontological theories are incapable of addressing ubiquitous real-world problems that involve tradeoffs of interests under conditions of scarcity.

Most relevantly to the concerns of this book, Jacqueline Basu (2020, 2021) has directly challenged Rawls' claim that self-interest cannot motivate reliable cooperation—that is, self-moderating/other-regarding behavior—thereby undermining Rawls' arguments concerning the inherent instability of the modus vivendi. Basu demonstrates the inaptness of Rawls' analogizing the modus vivendi, a rational social order within a political community, to interstate agreements between independent polities.[50] Basu's point is not to show that a rational social order, based on strategic choice-making and centered on (nonvicious) forms of self-interest, is more choice-worthy than a moral political order, predicated on an overlapping consensus arrived at through a deliberative process of reason-giving. Rather, by reference to contemporary empirical work on self-enforcing social equilibria and by demonstrating the meaningful normative decision-making and robust cooperation that rational consensus necessarily entails, she argues for the robustness of the modus vivendi to changes in power relations. Just as in the historical case of institutionalized democratic rationality in classical Athens (chapter 6), Basu shows that a democratic modus vivendi is stable when it is founded on citizens' normatively demanding—yet still rational—choices to engage in reliable self-moderating/other-regarding cooperation.

Basu concludes that, taken on its own terms, Rawls' argument for the overlapping consensus presumes the prior existence of a modus vivendi. The liberal political order assumed by Rawls (and many others) as the setting of a just society is, therefore, ultimately based on a self-enforcing democratic equilibrium—that is, on rationality. So, it appears that the cooperation dilemmas to which the Greek writers devoted so much attention were addressed *before* any overlapping consensus could even have been attempted. Bluntly, modern ideal political theory has helped itself to a nonideal social foundation, while denying its existence. Rawls' straightforward prioritization of the right and reasonable over the good and rational is therefore open to question, which in turn reopens the question of the most promising path for future work in analytic political theory.

That question brings us back to the Socratics' core insight: Instrumental rationality was essential as a basis for a moral social order that

---

50. See above, section 8.5, for Aristotle's similar move in the *Eudemian Ethics*, analogizing civic friendship to diplomatic relations between states.

could be prosperous and secure enough to persist in a competitive world. While the Socratics were certainly not liberal democrats, they realized that a just society, if it is not to be entirely fanciful, must account for the rational choices of its self-interested members. The fundamental metaethical problem that Socrates must solve in Plato's *Republic*, "Why should I be moral?," is first motivated, not by the metaphysical and epistemological questions that are answered in the middle books of the dialogue, but rather by Glaucon's sharpening of the folk theory.[51] Plato's great dialogue is probably the best-known example of idealizing theory in Western political philosophy. Yet, as detailed in each chapter of this book, far from bracketing problems raised by Thrasymachean immoralism and the rational bases of social stability, Plato's Socrates confronts them directly. He offers thoughtful answers to hard questions about social cooperation; ruling and obedience; the psychology of individuals and groups; violence and risk in interstate relations; democratic performance; and economic behavior. He is, in sum, at once a rational choice theorist and a normative political theorist.

One direction for future work in analytic political theory is, therefore, to adapt, for contemporary purposes, the classical Socratics' solution of situating broadly normative ethical and political theorizing in an instrumentalist and (in Aristotle's *Politics* and the works of the historians) empirically tested framework.[52] That approach does not require, although nor does it preclude, a role for classical eudaimonism. It does require collaboration between normative and positive political theorists. It requires normative theorists to follow the lead of, for example, Brian Barry (1989), by mastering some of the conceptual apparatus and formal methods of positive theory and attending to relevant results of empirical social science. On the other side, choice theorists, if they are to be participants in the collaborative enterprise, must broaden their construal of the normativity of rationality, beyond merely characterizing the ideal-type rational agent.[53] If the role of ethical reasoning, the internalization of norms, and habituation in cooperative social behavior

51. For the metaphysical and epistemological problems driving modern scholarship on metaethics, see Sayre-McCord (2012), who notes (sec. 6) that "the question underlying Glaucon's concern—Why should I be moral?—has consistently been at the center of attempts to explain the connection between morality and what we have reason to do."

52. See n. 1, above.

53. Recent work in formal theory by, for example, Jonathan Bendor, Lara Buchak, Hun Chung, Sean Ingham, Barry Weingast, and David Wiens (listed in Works Cited) is exemplary in this regard. Binmore (1994, 1998) was an early, detailed, and influential entry into the field.

were frankly acknowledged in introductions to game theory, positive theorists would be less vulnerable to criticism that rational choice ignores actual human motivations while promoting vicious egoism.[54]

. . .

New work in classical history, philosophy, and literature, and in positive and normative theory, must be attentive, as the Greek writers decidedly were, to the threat to social order posed by vicious egoists. And to the threat, emphasized by Plato and Sonja Amadae (2016), that instrumental rationality, once it is systematically theorized and operationalized as a set of teachable techniques, will crowd out self-moderating, other-regarding habits of mind: *Homo economicus* can become a practical output as well as a stylized premise of rational choice theory. Reading classical texts with and against formal theory alerts us both to the dangers of rationality divorced from ethics and to the unworldliness of politics without strategic rationality. It offers us reasons for prioritizing holistic flourishing over individual wealth-getting, living well together over merely accumulating and distributing material goods. It also alerts us to the challenges and benefits of merging humanistic and social scientific inquiry without subordinating one discipline to another. It was by adopting that approach that this book traced the Greek discovery of practical reason. It is my hope that recovering a fragment of reason's ancient history will contribute to writing the next chapters in its modern rediscovery.

54. In the preface to a revised edition of their popular introduction to game theory, Dixit and Nalebuff (2008: x) write: "We started our original [1991 edition] preface with: 'Strategic thinking is the art of outdoing an adversary, knowing that the adversary is trying to do the same to you.' To this we now add: It is also the art of finding ways to cooperate, even when others are motivated by self-interest, not benevolence." In the terms employed in this book, their addition marks a shift from Thrasymachean to Conventionalist instrumentalism, and it potentially opens the way for a consideration of ethical rationality.

Epilogue

Ancient Greek writers realized that rationally self-interested individuals may choose not to cooperate with others. They saw how a market for expertise in means-to-ends reasoning exacerbated the problem of non-cooperation. What does that have to do with twenty-first-century worries about politics and society? My answer is, "a lot."

In Plato's *Republic*, the problem was framed by the tale of Gyges and his ring of invisibility. The Gyges story was designed to sharpen a challenge to Socrates' account of justice, proffered by the sophist Thrasymachus. It concludes that anyone freed from social constraint will ignore any laws or norms that stand in the way of desire fulfillment. Invisible Gyges steals, seduces, and kills. He gains a queen and a kingdom with no loss of reputation and without fear of divine retribution. Plato and other Greek theorists asked a hard question: How, given the prevalence of Gyges-type motivations, and Thrasymachus-type experts teaching others how to mimic invisibility, was cooperative social order possible? Some Greek thinkers optimistically claimed that the solution was self-evident: We must all recognize that we are better off when everyone moderates their behavior. This means foregoing doing injustice in a quest for the best personal outcome, for fear of suffering injustice and being stuck with the worst. Although there are always some inveterate rule-breakers, they are readily detected. Aren't they?

For some twenty-four hundred years after Plato, invisibility was a fiction, the stuff of horror stories and philosophical thought experiments. But in the twenty-first century it is ubiquitous: The internet has gifted each of us with Gyges rings, in ever more potent virtual variants. Thrasymachus' modern avatars offer no ethical guidance about their use. Gyges-style self-aggrandizement is omnipresent online. Law-breaking is frequent. Violation of social norms is ubiquitous and incentives are perverse: Desecration is costless, while sensationalism and extremism are rewarded with attention and influence. Meanwhile, habituation into Gyges-type behavior, gained by virtual omnipotence, bleeds into in-person social interactions: Digital blood becomes the real thing; online conspiracies threaten real-world governments. So, in some salient ways, we may now be headed towards what less optimistic Greek theorists (followed by Thomas Hobbes) imagined as the zero-point of social order: We are driven by fear and perceived self-interest, possessed by desires unchosen by reason, and schooled by experts in desire-fulfillment. We lack both the motive and means for productive cooperation. To paraphrase Plato's Protagoras, "as often as we come together, we do injustice to one another, and so we are scattered and perish."

Greek thinkers and political entrepreneurs offered solutions to the cooperation problem: Polybius' account of a "tit for tat" process, whereby the consolidation of rational responses to observed behavioral choices led to the emergence of benevolent leadership; Plato's ideal of philosophical autocrats, committed to sustaining a harmonious community in which all members stay in their lanes, and each is as happy as possible; Aristotle's assumption that innate sociability plus the right legislation could produce ethical habits enabling virtuous citizens to rule and be ruled in turns; Protagoras' fable of mutual instruction among a majority of rational, nonvicious individuals who, together, build a democratic state. In the realm of theory-to-practice is Solon's bargaining solution to civil conflict and a series of Athenian innovations conjoining self-government with rule of law.

It remains to be seen whether any ancient solution can help to address twenty-first-century cooperation dilemmas. But even if their answers are rejected, ancient theorists have posed a fundamental question for us, and they point us to where we must seek our answer. We must rediscover practical reason, uniting instrumental rationality with ethics by reimagining the task of politics as the promotion of civic dignity and human flourishing.

Appendix

It is sometimes supposed, based on background assumptions about ancient Greek worldviews, psychology, sociology, or institutions (e.g., Bernstein 1996), that the Greeks lacked anything resembling modern ideas about probability and risk. Ian Hacking ([1975] 2006: 38–42) asserted that there was no European concept of probability before the sixteenth century. Hacking's claim was challenged by Garber and Zaller (1979), who argue that conceptions of probability are evident in passages in Cicero's writing on induction in divination and sign inference. Paul Vădan (2022: 20) argues forcefully, on the basis of a substantial body of literary evidence, against "primitivist sociological" claims that the ancient Greeks in the late classical and Hellenistic periods lacked the capacity to calculate probability and risk. Vădan deploys a wealth of evidence to show that, in fact, ancient decision-makers "used abstract numbers to express odds of success about economic and military risks"; Greek writers employed a qualitative language of likelihood "to assign gradations of risk to dangerous events"; and military leaders deployed "historical precedents to present circumstances as a way to generate statistical data and shape collective expectations about the future."

The case that the Greeks lacked probability was made in an unpublished but influential paper by the classical philosopher M. Burnyeat (n.d.).[1] Burnyeat's specific goal was to disprove the notion that the Greek term *pithanon,* as used by the Skeptic Carneades and translated by Cicero into Latin as *probabile,* had the meaning of probability, in the sense of "statistical frequency." But Burnyeat's attempt to demonstrate that "Carneades was no probabilist" extended to

---

1. Available online at www.scribd.com/document/341395731/Carneades-Was-No-Probabilist.

a general claim that to suppose that the Greeks had anything like our modern concept of probability was anachronistic.

Leaving aside Carneades, there is good reason to suppose, first, that many Greeks had a working understanding of probability as relative likelihood. And, next, that calculating the likelihood of available outcomes was an ordinary part of the deliberative process of decision-making—that is, of practical reason. In a detailed response to Burnyeat, Suzanne Obdrzalek (2006: 266) concluded, as follows:

> While the Greeks certainly lacked a theory of probability, this does not preclude their having a loose, non-theoretical understanding of probability. The Greeks had games of chance, in particular dice, and employed methods of deciding by lot—that is to say, they employed both randomizers and generators of stable frequencies. Aristotle writes in *de Caelo* that to repeat the same throw of dice once or twice is easy, ten thousand times impossible (2.12, 292a29). The Athenian economy relied heavily on maritime loans with varying rates of interest, depending on the risk of the voyage. In fact, I believe that it would be very difficult for anyone to get by in life successfully without recognizing that certain events are more frequent than others and, consequently, certain outcomes more probable; this sort of 'probabilistic' thinking is indispensable to everyday practical reasoning.

Here I offer a few notes that expand on Obdrzalek's concise 2006 summary and Vădan's important 2022 article and his 2018 PhD dissertation (discussed below). First is the general point, emphasized by Diaconis and Skyrms (2017), that to suppose that choice-making agents ordinarily employ an accurate, quantified approach to measuring the relative frequency of phenomena is unrealistic for any period in human history, including our own. So, to say that most Greeks, most of the time, did not employ reasoning of that sort is just to state the obvious. Next, the existence or nonexistence of a formal theory of probability is largely irrelevant to the question of practical reasoning. The question before us is how far Greek thinkers did go in reasoning systematically about phenomena that were thought to be more and less likely, and in what domains such reasoning was employed. Greek thinking about probability and practices that depend on a coherent, if nontheoretical, understanding of relative likelihood may be roughly divided into scientific (mathematical, philosophical, and medical) reasoning; gaming; lotteries; loaning at interest; and rhetorical treatments of the plausible and likely.

Answering the question of whether any ancient Greek had a mathematical understanding of probability is complicated by the loss of almost all texts written by ancient Greek mathematicians. As Reviel Netz (2019) has shown, the likelihood of the survival of a given text from classical antiquity depends on the number of copies made and distributed in antiquity. Because technical works on mathematics circulated among a small, highly specialized intellectual network, there were never many copies of a given mathematical treatise. As Netz has shown, the fragments of Greek mathematical works that did happen to survive point to a persistent, deep, and wide exploration of various mathematical properties. But any argument from the absence of surviving evidence for mathematical thought is inherently weak.

One tantalizing bit of evidence points to the possibility that Greek mathematicians were familiar with combinatorial problems, which are in turn fundamental to determining discrete probability distributions. F. Acerbi (2003: 466) calls attention to a passage in Plutarch's *Against the Stoics* (1047c–e):

> But now he [Chrysippus: later third century BCE] says himself that the number of conjunctions produced by means of ten assertibles exceeds a million, although he had neither investigated the matter carefully by himself nor sought out the truth with the help of experts . . . . Chrysippus is refuted by all the arithmeticians, among them Hipparchus [second century BCE] himself who proves that this error in calculation is enormous if in fact affirmation gives 103049 conjoined assertibles and negation 310952.

Acerbi (446) notes, "103049 is the tenth Schröder number, 310952 is only slightly different from half the sum of the tenth and the eleventh such number."[2]

As Acerbi points out, Hipparchus' numbers could not have been arrived at by chance. Indeed, he suggests that the passage points to the use of comparatively refined techniques of calculation and requires a complete rethinking of Greek combinatorics. Acerbi notes (482) that simple combinatorial manipulations are decisive in a passage of Aristotle's *Politics* (1290b25–39) in which the possible regime variations among states are compared with the species of animals. In each case, the whole (state, animal) is composed of parts. These combine in various ways such that, "when all possible pairings of these have been taken, they will produce species of animals, and the species of animals will be precisely as many as the combinations of the necessary parts are."

Acerbi argues that Hipparchus could not have worked out the Schröder numbers without using a branching tree diagram, of a sort attested in texts on the intertwined fields of musical theory, arithmetic ratios theory, and Aristotelian syllogistic (493). He suggests that the study of combinatorics was an important facet of a more general project that arose from the interaction between Aristotelian dialectic and mathematics (497–99). He concludes (446) that "the vagaries of textual tradition have (almost) annihilated the [combinatorics] field." Reviel Netz (2009: 17–21) discusses other passages pointing to Greek interest in combinatorics. None of this disproves Burnyeat's contention that there was no ancient Greek frequentist theory of probability, but it points to theoretical interest in closely related problems.

Burnyeat (n.d. 6–7) is dismissive of the proposal of R. W. Sharples (1982) that Alexander of Aphrodisias (ca. 200 CE), "shows a more or less vague awareness of the combinatorial analysis of probabilities, and in particular of the fact that the product of two probabilities, each themselves greater than one-half, may itself be less than one-half." But a passage in Aristotle *On the Heavens* (292a28-b1) suggests something similar:

> To succeed often or in many things is difficult. For instance, to throw ten thousand Chian throws [all five astragaloi are "high": Kidd 2020: 17] would be impossible, but

---

2. The "little Schröder numbers" are used to count various related combinatorial objects, for example, to determine "the number of different ways of subdividing of a polygon with $n + 1$ sides into smaller polygons by adding diagonals of the original polygon." The first ten such numbers are: 1, 1, 3, 11, 45, 197, 903, 4279, 20793, 103049 (https://en.wikipedia.org/wiki/Schr%C3%B6der%E2%80%93Hipparchus_number).

to throw one or two is comparatively easy. In action, again, when A has to be done to get B, B to get C, and C to get D, one step or two present little difficulty, but as the series extends the difficulty grows.

Aristotle's A, B, and C are outcomes that are assumed to be less than certain, but "comparatively easy." His point is that in a sequential combination of less-than-certain conditionals, each additional step reduces the likelihood of the next outcome, and the series will eventually result in (virtual) impossibility.

Aristotle's reference to throwing astragaloi (knucklebones of sheep or goats) points to games as a possible source of examples for thinking about likelihood and combinations of possibilities. Leslie Kurke (1999a: chap. 7, 1999b) and more recently, Stephen Kidd (2017a, 2017b, 2020) have surveyed the evidence for Greek practices of gaming and gambling. Greek board games (generically *pessoi* or *petteia*) included pure strategy games (comparable to checkers) and games that mixed strategy and chance by including dice rolls (comparable to backgammon: Austin 1940; Kurke 1999b: 256–57; Kidd 2017b). Mastery of these board games was considered to require great skill (Kurke 1999b: 256), but exactly how they were played is unknown. Greek games of pure chance were also played with three six-sided dice and with five four-sided astragaloi. The Greeks correctly calculated that both sets of gaming pieces yielded exactly 56 combinations ("throws," with different likelihoods of occurrence). The method by which these calculations were done is unknown (Kidd 2017b, 2020: 18).

Kidd (2020: 6–7) cites the second-century-CE writer on unusual classical Greek words Julius Pollux (*Onomasticon,* 9.95–96) on how one of these games, "the so-called *pleistobolinda*" ("high-throw game") was played. According to Kidd's reconstruction, *pleistobolinda* did not involve individual wagering; rather, "the players decide ahead of time how much each dice pip is worth and then roll the dice. Presumably, if the dice-pip is worth a drachma, it would mean that if Player A rolls a score of eight (worth eight drachmas) and Player B rolls eleven (worth eleven drachmas), Player B would win the difference (or perhaps the whole pot)." Kidd concludes that this kind of wagering would not have been an incentive to thinking systematically about probability in the sense of frequency. Indeed, it can hardly be called gambling: Assuming repeated play and fair dice, two persons playing by Kidd's rules would eventually end up even.

Kidd (2020) seeks to explain "why mathematical probability failed to emerge from ancient gambling." But both the explicans and the explicandum are too hasty: First, as noted above, arguments from ancient mathematical silence are inherently weak. Next, Pollux described only one dicing game, not "the practice of dicing." As Kidd notes (2020: 7–8), other ancient Greek games of chance, with different (although incompletely understood) rules, are known. Third, if dice throws in *pleistobolinda* were nonsimultaneous, side-bets could be placed on whether B's throw would beat A's. In that case odds come into play.[3] The

---

3. Counterfactually assuming three six-sided dice producing perfectly random results, the chances for a given combination range from just below .05% to 12.5%. For five four-sided random-result-producing dice (a rough approximation of astragaloi), the range is about .01% to 15%.

simplistic form of wagering assumed in Kidd's reconstruction does not accord well with other evidence for Greek gambling. We know that punters gambled with dice and astragaloi at established "gaming places" (Fisher 2004), and that fortunes were won and lost (e.g., Xenophon *Hellencia* 6.3.16, with Vădan 2018: 41). Plato regarded playing games of strategy and chance as domains in which a high level of expertise was obtainable: "No one could make himself a competent expert at either board games (*petteutikos*) or chance games (*kubeutikos*) who did not practice just that from childhood but rather treated it as a pastime" (*Republic* 374c). Although nothing can be said for certain, the ancient interest in gambling and calculating combinations, along with Aristotle's use of gaming as a model for thinking about sequences of less-than-certain events, point at least to "a common-sense awareness of probability" (Kidd 2020: 18).

Greeks sought randomness in the lotteries that determined various salient political outcomes: notably (in Athens and other democracies) the composition of juries and boards of magistrates. The procedures for ensuring that each candidate in the relevant pool had an equal chance, based on random draw, and the equipment employed to make multiple random choices quickly and efficiently, were elaborate. The goals of the procedures were to ensure fairness and avoid the potential for corruption. The sophistication of the techniques employed demonstrates a clear awareness of the importance of achieving random outcomes and the presence of possible confounders.[4]

In previous chapters I have sought to show that risk was a recurrent theme in both philosophical and historical writing. Plato shows that risk management, whereby a choice among outcomes was predicated on an assessment of the likelihood of feasible outcomes, could be thought of as a matter of measurement and expertise (chapter 6.1). Elsewhere, Plato's Socrates (*Protagoras* 314a) warns a prospective student of sophism not to "risk your greatest treasure on a toss of the dice." The vocabulary and conceptualization of risk in Greek antiquity have recently been analyzed in detail in an important dissertation by Paul Vădan (2018). Vădan reviews and rebuts the "modernist sociological" (41) notion (e.g., Giddens 1990; Bernstein 1996) that risk is a uniquely modern concept, and that it is necessarily linked to the emergence of modern probability theory in the seventeenth century.

In an analysis of the term *kindunos,* Vădan (2018: chap. 1) notes that *kindunos* often refers merely to danger or military clashes. But he agrees with Daryl Grissom's (2012) claim that Thucydides' extensive use of *kindunos* reveals what Arthur Eckstein (2006) described as "profit-maximizing behavior" by rational agents who weigh costs against the rewards of their actions. Vădan shows that the linkage of deliberation to *kindunos* was not unique to Thucydides; Xenophon and other classical and postclassical Greek writers make the same connection. He concludes, on the basis of a careful assessment of a large body of literary and documentary evidence, that deliberating about the management of risk was a prevalent form of cognition from the classical through the Hellenistic period. Risk assessment was employed as the basis of decision-making and was understood as a skill (*technē*) that employed both qualitative and quantitative approaches to probability.

---

4. See Kroll 1972; Bers 2000; Tangian 2008; Farrar 2010.

Practical calculation of likelihood over outcomes was essential for real-world Greek traders and tax farmers seeking profits through the inherently risky business of obtaining and shipping large quantities of goods (notably grain) from one part of the Mediterranean/Black Sea world to another. Loans at interest, in some cases made by professional bankers, served as a kind of insurance, in that the loaning agent assumed the risk if the ship carrying the goods was lost at sea. Thanks to preserved legal cases from the fourth century BCE, we know that interest rates were calibrated to the expected risk of the enterprise—loan rates increased in times of year when storms at sea were more frequent.[5]

Meanwhile, Athenian tax farmers played a kind of futures market in grain by competitive bidding for the right to levy grain taxes from three Athenian-occupied islands in the northern Aegean. The rights were purchased in advance. After the tax grain was collected by the tax farmer (based on the harvest and at whatever level of compliance from those taxed) and transported to Athens (at the tax-farmer's expense and risk), state officials inspected the grain, and if it was determined to be of high enough quality, the state purchased it. The profit or loss to the tax farmer was clearly determined by the accuracy of the estimate of several risk factors. The institutional design of the tax farming system (detailed in a document recording the decree by which it was established) assumed, first, that there were individuals and syndicates willing and able to take on the risk and, next, that "selling risk" was in the state's best interest.[6] The assumption that ordinary Athenians could readily grasp the relevant issues is supported by recent work demonstrating the high levels of numeracy and "financial literacy" in classical Athens (Netz 2002; Cuomo 2013; Kallet 2021).

Courtroom rhetoric and theoretical writing about rhetoric offer some of the most detailed surviving Greek discussions of likelihood. Burnyeat (n.d.) was concerned with what James Franklin ([2001] 2015, 2016) calls factual or aleatory probability. Dice-throwing is a classic example "which produce[s] characteristic random or patternless sequences of outcomes" (Franklin 2016: 33). But as Franklin also points out, "logical or epistemic probability is concerned with how well-supported a conclusion is by a body of evidence . . . How probable a hypothesis is, on given evidence, determines the degree of belief it is rational to have in that hypothesis, if that is all the evidence one has that is relevant to it" (2016: 33–34). He shows that reasoning on probability before ca. 1660 (Pascal and Fermat) was for the most part not numerical or frequentist, but rather the logical/epistemic approach, which is similar in its premises (although not in its mathematical expression) to a Bayesian approach (on the distinction between frequentist and Bayesian probability, see further, Diaconis and Skyrms 2017).

In the logical/epistemic approach, to achieve the right result (whether a fact or a judgment), "they *grade* evidence by understanding that evidence can make

5. Athenian lending practices and loan rates as risk management: Cohen 1992; Christesen 2003; and especially Bresson and Bresson 2004: 7–15. Leese (2021: 40–50) emphasizes risk-taking and calculation of risk as fundamental aspects of wealth maximization by Greek entrepreneurs.

6. Tax farming mechanisms: Stroud 1998; Ober 2008: 260–63, with literature cited.

a conclusion 'almost certain,' 'more likely than not,' and so on" (Franklin [2001] 2015: xix–xx). An example of this comes from the Empiricist school of medicine. In a discussion of ancient Greek debates over the problem of why, if medical theory is correct, treatments sometimes fail, James Allen (1994: 102–3) notes that "empiricist theorems included an explicit specification of the relative frequency of the connection they report. Four levels of frequency were distinguished: always, for the most part, (roughly) half the time and rarely." Franklin suggests, wryly, that assigning precise numbers on those general levels is "not necessarily to be praised" ([2001] 2015: xx).

In rhetorical as well as historiographic contexts, a key Greek term is *eikos,* translated as likelihood, probability, or plausibility. Franklin ([2001] 2015: 109–12) considers Aristotle's *Rhetoric* "the most intrinsically important work on probability before Pascal" (quote: 109) because of its discussion of *eikos,* understood as "what happens for the most part," and for Aristotle's inferential arguments from examples, signs, and analogy. Yet Aristotle's hypothetical examples in the *Rhetoric* concern transparently deceptive techniques. The use of *eikos* claims in preserved Athenian courtroom arguments (surveyed by Gagarin 1994, 2014) provide, in some ways, a better exemplification of the practical expression of the logical/epistemic approach to likelihood.

A speech of Lysias (7. *On the Olive Stump*) is exemplary of Athenian courtroom use of arguments from likelihood and risk in the years immediately following the Peloponnesian War. The anonymous speaker defends himself against a charge of having uprooted the stump of a state-owned sacred olive tree that the prosecutor claimed was located on his property. Having denied there ever was such a stump (11), he develops an elaborate circumstantial argument that hangs on his own, presumptively rational, decision-making process: First, he claims to be the type of man who calculates benefits and costs (12), so the jurors ought to think about what benefit would have come to him from digging up the stump (13) compared to the severe punishment should he be caught (14). The profit would be minuscule, the danger perpetual (17). Had he done the crime (A) his slaves, who would know about it and could inform on him at any time, would become in effect his masters (16). Even if the slaves did not turn him in, (B) the multiple parties who rented the farm would know; to ensure they themselves were not accused of the crime, they would report the removal of the stump (17). Even if he somehow persuaded the renters to stay silent, (C) what of the passersby and his neighbors, some of whom were his enemies? (18). The whole farm was clearly visible from the road, so who would attempt such a thing? (28). In sum, was it more likely that his opponent was lying without any risk to himself? Or that the defendant dared a crime like this in the face of such danger? (38).

Conditions A, B, and C function like Aristotle's *On the Heavens* sequence of less-than-certain events: In combination, they establish the practical impossibility of doing the crime without being noticed. Were he noticed, he would expect to be severely punished. So, the expected costs of removing the stump vastly outweighed any possible benefits. And thus, no rational risk-calculator would do such a thing. Whether the jurors in this case bought the story is unknown, but the sequence of arguments would make no sense to a jury of Athenians who lacked the relevant conceptions of probability and risk.

In sum, there is a very high likelihood, arguably approaching certainty, that classical Greeks were capable of thinking and acting on the basis of (1) probability, understood in terms of relative likelihood and combinations of less-than-certain possibilities, and (2) risk, assessed by comparing the likelihood of possible outcomes, and managed by weighing expected benefits against costs. The exercise of those capacities made possible the sorts of rational calculations and choices discussed in this book.

Works Cited

Abgrall, Matthieu. 2019. "Legal Innovation in Archaic Greece: The Case of Monumental Written Laws." PhD thesis, Classics, Stanford University.

Abizadeh, Arash. 2018. *Hobbes and the Two Faces of Ethics*. Cambridge: Cambridge University Press.

Acerbi, F. 2003. "On the Shoulders of Hipparchus: A Reappraisal of Ancient Greek Combinations." *Archive for History of Exact Sciences* 57:465–503.

Achen, Christopher H., and Larry M. Bartels. 2016. *Democracy for Realists: Why Elections Do Not Produce Responsive Government*. Princeton: Princeton University Press.

Acton, Peter Hampden. 2014. *Poiesis: Manufacturing in Classical Athens*. Oxford: Oxford University Press.

Ackrill, J. L. 1980. "Aristotle on *Eudaimonia*." Pp. 15–34 in *Essays in Aristotle's Ethics*, edited by Amélie O. Rorty. Berkeley: University of California Press.

Adam, James, and D. A. Rees. 1963. *Plato, The Republic* (with critical notes and commentary). Cambridge: Cambridge University Press.

Ager, Sheila L. 1996. *Interstate Arbitrations in the Greek World, 337–90 B.C.* Berkeley: University of California Press.

Akrigg, Ben. 2015. "Metics in Athens." Pp. 155–76 in *Communities and Networks in the Ancient Greek World*, edited by Claire Taylor and Kostas Vlassopoulos. Oxford: Oxford University Press.

Allen, Danielle. 2000. *The World of Prometheus: Politics of Punishing in Democratic Athens*. Princeton: Princeton University Press.

———. 2004. *Talking to Strangers: Anxieties of Citizenship since Brown v. Board of Education*. Chicago: University of Chicago Press.

———. 2010. *Why Plato Wrote*. Malden, MA: Wiley-Blackwell.

Allen, James. 1994. "Failure and Expertise in the Ancient Conception of an Art." Pp. 81–108 in *Scientific Failure,* edited by Tamara Horowitz and Allen I. Janis. Lanham, MD: Rowman & Littlefield.

Amadae, S. M. 2003. *Rationalizing Capitalist Democracy: The Cold War Origins of Rational Choice Liberalism.* Chicago: University of Chicago Press.

———. 2016. *Prisoners of Reason: Game Theory and Neoliberal Political Economy.* Cambridge: Cambridge University Press.

Amemiya, Takeshi. 2004. "The Economic Ideas of Classical Athens." *Kyoto Economic Review* 73 (2): 57–74.

Anderson, Elizabeth. 2000. "Beyond Homo Economicus: New Developments in Theories of Social Norms." *Philosophy and Public Affairs* 29:170–200.

Anderson, Greg. 2018. *The Realness of Things Past: Ancient Greece and Ontological History.* New York: Oxford University Press.

Annas, Julia. 1981. *An Introduction to Plato's Republic.* Oxford: Clarendon Press.

———. 2017. "Ancient Eudaimonism and Modern Morality." Pp. 265–80 in *The Cambridge Companion to Ancient Ethics,* edited by Christopher Bobonich. Cambridge: Cambridge University Press.

Anscombe, G. E. M. 1977. "Thought and Action in Aristotle." Pp. 61–71 in *Articles on Aristotle 2: Ethics & Politics,* edited by Jonathan Barnes, Malcolm Schofield, and Richard Sorabji. London: Duckworth.

Arcenas, Scott Lawin. 2018. "Stasis: The Nature, Frequency, and Intensity of Political Violence in Ancient Greece." PhD thesis, Classics, Stanford University.

———. 2020. "The Silence of Thucydides." *Transactions of the American Philological Association* 150 (2): 299–332.

Arrow, Kenneth Joseph. (1951) 1963. *Social Choice and Individual Values.* New Haven: Yale University Press.

Arvanitidis, Paschilas A., and Nicholas C. Kyriazis. 2013. "Democracy and Public Choice in Classical Athens." *Peace Economics, Peace Science and Public Policy* 19 (2): 213–48.

Asheri, David, Alan B. Lloyd, Aldo Corcella, Oswyn Murray, Alfonso Moreno, and Maria Brosius. 2007. *A Commentary on Herodotus: Books I–IV.* Oxford: Oxford University Press.

Atack, Carol. 2019. *The Discourse of Kingship in Classical Greece.* New York: Routledge.

Austen-Smith, David. 1990. "Information Transmission in Debate." *American Journal of Political Science* 34:124–52.

Austin, J. L. 1975. *How to Do Things with Words.* Cambridge, MA: Harvard University Press.

Austin, R. G. 1940. "Greek Board Games." *Antiquity* 14:257–71.

Axelrod, Robert M. 1984. *The Evolution of Cooperation.* New York: Basic Books.

———. 1997. *The Complexity of Cooperation: Agent-Based Models of Competition and Collaboration.* Princeton: Princeton University Press.

Azoulay, Vincent. 2014. *Pericles of Athens.* Princeton: Princeton University Press.

Bakewell, Geoffrey. 2020. "'I Went Down to Piraeus Yesterday': Routes, Roads, and Plato's *Republic.*" *Hesperia* 89 (4): 725–55.

Balot, Ryan K. 2001. *Greed and Injustice in Classical Athens*. Princeton: Princeton University Press.

Balot, Ryan K., Sara Forsdyke, and Edith Foster, eds. 2017. *The Oxford Handbook of Thucydides*. New York: Oxford University Press.

Bannerjee, Trisha Urmi. 2018. "Austen Equilibrium." *Representations*. 143 (1): 463–90.

Banting, Keith, and Will Kymlicka. 2018. "Theories of Justice, the Strains of Commitment, and Realistic Utopias." Presentation. Conference on Political Theory in / and/ as Political Science. McGill University, Montreal. www.academia.edu/42272459.

Barceló, Pedro A. 1993. *Basileia, Monarchia, Tyrannis: Untersuchungen zu Entwicklung und Beurteilung von Alleinherrschaft im vorhellenistischen Griechenland*. Stuttgart: Franz Steiner Verlag.

Barney, Rachel. 2006. "Socrates' Refutation of Thrasymachus." Pp. 44–62 in *The Blackwell Guide to Plato's Republic,* edited by Gerasimos Santas. Oxford: Blackwell.

———. 2017. "Callicles and Thrasymachus." In *The Stanford Encyclopedia of Philosophy* (Fall 2017 ed.), edited by Edward N. Zalta. Stanford, CA: Stanford University Press.

Barry, Brian. 1978. *Sociologists, Economists, and Democracy*. Chicago: University of Chicago Press.

———. 1989. *Theories of Justice*. Berkeley: University of California Press.

Basu, Jacqueline. 2020. "Convergence Concepts. The Political Construction of Stability, Legitimacy, and Authority." PhD thesis, Political Science, Stanford University.

———. 2021. "Cooperative Capacities of the Rational: Revising Rawls's Account of Prudential Reasoning." *American Political Science Review* 115 (3): 967–81.

Bates, Robert H., Avner Greif, Margaret Levi, Jean-Laurent Rosenthal, and Barry R. Weingast. 1998. *Analytic Narratives*. Princeton: Princeton University Press.

Beck, Hans, and Peter Funke, eds. 2015. *Federalism in Greek Antiquity*. Cambridge: Cambridge University Press.

Bednar, Jenna. In progress. "Governance for Human Flourishing." Working paper.

Bendor, Jonathan. In progress. "No Computation without Representation: Standards-Based versus Comparative Evaluation and Choice." Working paper.

———. 2021. "Competence versus Rationality: Simon's Multiple Scientific Reference Points." Working paper.

Bendor, Jonathan, and Piotr Swistak. 1997. "The Evolutionary Stability of Cooperation." *American Political Science Review* 91 (2): 290–307.

———. 2001. "The Evolution of Norms." *American Journal of Sociology* 106 (6): 1493–1545.

Benedict, Ruth. 1946. *The Chrysanthemum and the Sword: Patterns of Japanese Culture*. Boston: Houghton Mifflin.

Berkowitz, Peter. 1999. *Virtue and the Making of Modern Liberalism*. Princeton: Princeton University Press.

Berlin, Isaiah. 1969. *Four Essays on Liberty*. London: Oxford University Press.

Bermudez, Jose. 2015. "Strategic vs. Parametric choice in Newcomb's Problem and the Prisoner's Dilemma: Reply to Walker." *Philosophia* 43:787–94.

Bernstein, Peter L. 1996. *Against the Gods: The Remarkable Story of Risk*. New York: John Wiley & Sons.

Bers, Victor. 2000. "Just Rituals: Why the Rigmarole of the Fourth-Century Athenian Lawcourts?" Pp. 553–59 in *Polis & Politics: Studies in Ancient Greek History*, edited by Pernille Flensted-Jensen, Thomas Heine Nielsen, and Lene Rubinstein. Copenhagen: Museum Tusculanum Press, University of Copenhagen.

Binmore, Ken G. 1994. *Game Theory and the Social Contract I: Playing Fair*. Cambridge, MA: MIT Press.

———. 1998. *Game Theory and the Social Contract II: Just Playing*. Cambridge, MA: MIT Press.

———. 2007. *Game Theory: A Very Short Introduction*. Oxford: Oxford University Press.

Blank, David. 1985. "Socratics versus Sophists on Payment for Teaching." *Classical Antiquity*. 4:1–49.

Blok, Josine. 2017. *Citizenship in Classical Athens*. Cambridge: Cambridge University Press.

Blok, Josine H., and André P. M. H. Lardinois, eds. 2006. *Solon of Athens: New Historical and Philological Perspectives*. Leiden: E. J. Brill.

Bobonich, Christopher. 2002. *Plato's Utopia Recast: His Later Ethics and Politics*. Oxford: Oxford University Press.

———. 2010. "Images of Irrationality." Pp. 149–71 in *Plato's Laws: A Critical Guide*, edited by Christopher Bobonich. Cambridge: Cambridge University Press.

———. 2011. "Socrates and *Eudaimonia*." Pp. 293–332 in *The Cambridge Companion to Socrates*, edited by Donald Morrison. Cambridge: Cambridge University Press.

———. 2017. "Elitism in Plato and Aristotle." Pp. 298–318 in *The Cambridge Companion to Ancient Ethics*, edited by Christopher Bobonich. Cambridge: Cambridge University Press.

Boehm, Christopher. 2012. *Moral Origins: Social Selection and the Evolution of Virtue, Altruism, and Shame*. New York: Basic Books.

Bonazzi, Mauro. 2020. "Ethical and Political Thought in Antiphon's Truth and Concord." Pp. 149–68 in *Early Greek Ethics*, edited by David Conan Wolfsdorf. Oxford: Oxford University Press.

———. 2021. *The Sophists*. Cambridge: Cambridge University Press.

Bordes, Jacqueline. 1982. *Politeia dans la pensée grecque jusqu'à Aristote*. Paris: Les Belles Lettres.

Bovens, Luc. 2015. "The Tragedy of the Commons as a Voting Game." Pp. 156–176 in *The Prisoner's Dilemma*, edited by Martin Peterson. Cambridge: Cambridge University Press.

Bowden, Hugh. 2005. *Classical Athens and the Delphic Oracle*. Cambridge: Cambridge University Press.

Bowles, Samuel, and Herbert Gintis. 2011. *A Cooperative Species. Human Reciprocity and Its Evolution*. Princeton: Princeton University Press.

Bradley, Keith, and Paul Cartledge, eds. 2011. *The Cambridge World History of Slavery: Volume 1, The Ancient Mediterranean World*. Cambridge: Cambridge University Press.

Brams, Steven J. (1980) 2003. *Biblical Games: Game Theory and the Hebrew Bible*. Revised ed. Cambridge, MA: MIT Press.

———. 1994. "Game Theory and Literature." *Games and Economic Behavior* 6 (1): 32–54.

———. 2011. *Game Theory and the Humanities: Bridging Two Worlds*. Cambridge, MA: MIT Press.

Brannan, Patrick T. 1963. "Herodotus and History: The Constitutional Debate Preceding Darius' Accession." *Traditio* 19:427–38.

Bratman, Michael E. 2014. *Shared Agency: A Planning Theory of Acting Together*. Oxford: Oxford University Press.

Brennan, Jason. 2016. *Against Democracy*. Princeton: Princeton University Press.

Bresson, Alain. 2015. *The Making of the Ancient Greek Economy: Institutions, Markets, and Growth in the City-States*. Princeton: Princeton University Press.

Bresson, Alain, and François Bresson. 2004. "Max Weber, la comptabilité rationnelle et l'économie du monde gréco-romain." *Les Cahiers du Centre de recherches historiques* (34).

Brett, Annabel, and James Tully, eds. 2007. *Rethinking the Foundations of Modern Political Thought*. Cambridge: Cambridge University Press.

Brisson, Luc. 1975. "Le mythe de Protagoras: Essai d'analyse structurale." *Quaderni Urbinati di Cultura Classica* 20:7–37.

Broadie, Sarah. 1991. *Ethics with Aristotle*. New York: Oxford University Press.

Broome, John. 2002. "Practical Reasoning." Pp. 85–112 in *Reason and Nature: New Essays in the Theory of Rationality,* edited by José Luis Bermúdez and Alan Millar. Oxford: Oxford University Press.

———. 2021. "Practical Reason: Rationality or Normativity but Not Both." Pp. 38–51 in *The Routledge Handbook of Practical Reason,* edited by Ruth Chang and Kurt Sylvan. New York: Routledge.

Broome, John, and Christain Piller. 2001. "Normative Practical Reasoning." *Proceedings of the Aristotelian Society, Supplementary Volumes* 75:175–216.

Brunschwig, Jacques. 1996. "Rule and Exception: On the Aristotelian Theory of Equity." Pp. 115–55 in *Rationality in Greek Thought,* edited by Michael Frede and Gisela Striker. Oxford: Clarendon Press.

Buchak, Lara Marie. 2013. *Risk and Rationality*. Oxford: Oxford University Press.

Buckler, John. 1980. *The Theban Hegemony, 371–362 BC*. Cambridge, MA: Harvard University Press.

———. 2003. *Aegean Greece in the Fourth Century BC*. Leiden: E. J. Brill.

Burnyeat, Myles. n.d. "Carneades Was No Probabilist." Unpublished ms. www.scribd.com/document/341395731/Carneades-Was-No-Probabilist.

Calvert, Randall L. 1995. "The Rational Choice Theory of Social Institutions: Cooperation, Coordination, and Communication." Pp. 216–68 in *Modern Political Economy: Old Topics, New Directions,* edited by Jeffrey S. Banks and Eric Allen Hanuschek. Cambridge: Cambridge University Press.

Camerer, Colin. 2003. *Behavioral Game Theory: Experiments in Strategic Interaction.* Princeton: Princeton University Press.

Cammack, Daniela. 2013a. "Aristotle on the Virtue of the Multitude." *Political Theory* 41 (2): 175–202.

———. 2013b. "Aristotle's Denial of Deliberation about Ends." *Polis* 30 (2): 228–50.

———. 2019. "The *Dēmos* in *Dēmokratia.*" *The Classical Quarterly* 69 (1): 42–61.

———. 2020. "Deliberation in Ancient Greek Assemblies." *Classical Philology* 115:486–522.

———. 2021. "Representation in Ancient Greek Democracy." *History of Political Thought* 42 (4): 567–601.

Camp, John M. 2001. *The Archaeology of Athens.* New Haven: Yale University Press.

Campa, Naomi T. 2019. "*Kurios, Kuria,* and the Status of Athenian Women." *Classical Journal* 114 (3): 257–79.

———. In progress. "Power and Citizenship in Athenian Democracy." Working paper.

Canevaro, Mirko. 2015. "Making and Changing Laws in Ancient Athens." in *The Oxford Handbook of Ancient Greek Law,* edited by Edward M. Harris and Mirko Canevaro. Oxford: Oxford University Press.

———. 2016. "The Procedure of Demosthenes' against Leptines: How to Repeal (and Replace) an Existing Law." *Journal of Hellenic Studies* 136:39–58.

———. 2018a. "The Authenticity of the Document at Dem. 24.20–3, the Procedures of *Nomothesia* and the So-Called ἐπιχειροτονία τῶν νόμων." *Klio* 100 (1): 70–124.

———. 2018b. "Majority Rule vs. Consensus: The Practice of Democratic Deliberation in the Greek Poleis." Pp. 101–56 in *Ancient Greek History and Contemporary Social Science,* edited by Mirko Canevaro, Andrew Erskine, Benjamin Gray, and Josiah Ober. Edinburgh: Edinburgh University Press.

———. 2020a. "La délibération démocratique à l'Assemblée athénienne: Procédures et stratégies de légitimation." *Annales. Histoire, Sciences Sociales* 74 (2): 339–81

———. 2020b. "On Dem. 24.20–23 and the So-Called ἐπιχειροτονία τῶν νόμων: Some Final Clarifications in Response to M. H. Hansen." *Klio* 102 (1): 26–35.

Canevaro, Mirko, and Alberto Esu. 2018. "Extreme Democracy and Mixed Constitution in Theory and Practice. *Nomophylakia* and Fourth-Century *Nomothesia* in the Aristotelian *Athenaion Politeia.*" Pp. 105–45 in *Athenaion Politeiai, tra Storia, Politica e Sociologia,* edited by Cinzia Bearzot and others. Milan: Quaderni di Erga-Logoi, LED.

Caplan, Bryan. 2007. *The Myth of the Rational Voter.* Princeton: Princeton University Press.

Carawan, Edwin. 2013. *The Athenian Amnesty and Reconstructing the Law.* New York: Oxford University Press.

Cargill, Jack. 1981. *The Second Athenian League: Empire or Free Alliance?* Berkeley: University of California Press.

Carter, L. B. 1986. *The Quiet Athenian.* Oxford: Oxford University Press.

Cartledge, Paul. 2016. *Democracy: A Life.* Oxford: Oxford University Press.

Carugati, Federica. 2019. *Creating a Constitution: Law, Democracy, and Growth in Classical Athens.* Princeton: Princeton University Press.

Carugati, Federica, Randall L. Calvert, and Barry Weingast. 2021. "Judicial Review by the People Themselves: Democracy and the Rule of Law in Ancient Athens." *Journal of Law, Economics, and Organization.*

Carugati, Federica, and Margaret Levi. 2021. *A Moral Political Economy.* Cambridge: Cambridge University Press.

Carugati, Federica, Josiah Ober, and Barry R. Weingast. 2016. "Development and Political Theory in Classical Athens." *Polis* 33:71–91.

———. 2019. "Is Development Uniquely Modern? Ancient Athens on the Doorstep." *Public Choice* 181 (1–2): 29–47.

Carugati, Federica, and Barry R. Weingast. 2018. "Rethinking Mass and Elite: Decision-Making in the Athenian Law-Courts." Pp. 157–83 in *Ancient Greek History and Contemporary Social Science,* edited by Mirko Canevaro, Andrew Erskine, Benjamin Gray, and Josiah Ober. Edinburgh: Edinburgh University Press.

Charron, William C. 2000. "Greeks and Games: Forerunners of Modern Game Theory." *Forum for Social Economics* 29 (2): 1–32.

Chiasson, Charles C. 2003. "Herodotus' Use of Attic Tragedy in the Lydian Logos." *Classical Antiquity* 22 (1): 5–35.

Choi, Jung-Kyoo, and Samuel Bowles. 2007. "The Coevolution of Parochial Altruism and War." *Science* 318:636–40.

Christ, Matthew R. 2006. *The Bad Citizen in Classical Athens.* Cambridge: Cambridge University Press.

———. 2012. *The Limits of Altruism in Democratic Athens.* Cambridge: Cambridge University Press.

———. 2020. *Xenophon and the Athenian Democracy: The Education of an Elite Citizenry.* Cambridge: Cambridge University Press.

Christesen, Paul. 2003. "Economic Rationalism in Fourth-Century Athens." *Greece and Rome* 50:1–26.

Chung, Hun. 2015. "Hobbes's State of Nature: A Modern Bayesian Game-Theoretic Analysis." *Journal of the American Philosophical Association* 1 (3): 485–508.

———. 2016. "A Game-Theory Solution to the Inconsistency between Thrasymachus and Glaucon in Plato's Republic." *Ethical Perspectives* 23 (3): 383–410.

———. 2020. "Rawls's Self-Defeat: A Formal Analysis." *Erkenntnis* 85 (5): 1169–97.

———. Forthcoming. "Chain-Connection, Close-Knitness, and the Difference Principle." *Journal of Politics.*

Chwe, Michael Suk-Young. 2001. *Rational Ritual: Culture, Coordination, and Common Knowledge*. Princeton: Princeton University Press.

———. 2013. *Jane Austen, Game Theorist*. Princeton: Princeton University Press.

Cochrane, Charles Norris. 1929. *Thucydides and the Science of History*. London: Oxford University Press.

Cohen, Edward E. 1992. *Athenian Economy and Society: A Banking Perspective*. Princeton: Princeton University Press.

Cole, Thomas. 1967. *Democritus and the Sources of Greek Anthropology*. Cleveland: Published for the American Philological Association by the Press of Western Reserve University.

Connor, W. Robert. 1984. *Thucydides*. Princeton: Princeton University Press.

Cooper, John M. 1999. *Reason and Emotion: Essays on Ancient Moral Psychology and Ethical Theory*. Princeton: Princeton University Press.

Cornford, Francis Macdonald. 1907. *Thucydides Mythistoricus*. London: E. Arnold.

Cox, Gary, Douglass C. North, and Barry R. Weingast. 2019. "The Violence Trap: A Political-Economic Approach to the Problems of Development." *Journal of Public Finance and Public Choice* 34 (1): 3–19.

Creanza, Nicole, Oren Kolodny, and Marcus W. Feldman. 2017. "Cultural Evolutionary Theory: How Culture Evolves and Why It Matters." *Proceedings of the National Academy of Science (PNAS)* 114 (30): 7782–89.

Cuomo, Serafina. 2013. "Accounts, Numeracy and Democracy in Classical Athens." Pp. 255–278 in *Writing Science: Medical and Mathematical Authorship in Ancient Greece*, edited by Markus Asper. Berlin and New York: De Gruyter.

dal Borgo, Manuela. 2015. "Thucydides, Father of Game Theory." PhD thesis, Classics, University College London, London, UK.

D'Angour, Armand. 2011. *The Greeks and the New: Novelty in Ancient Greek Imagination and Experience*. Cambridge: Cambridge University Press.

Danzig, Gabriel. 2008. "Rhetoric and the Ring: Herodotus and Plato on the Story of Gyges as a Politically Expedient Tale." *Greece & Rome* 55 (2): 169–92.

Davis, Morton D. 1983. *Game Theory: A Nontechnical Introduction*. New York: Basic Books.

Davison, J. A. 1953. "Protagoras, Democritus, and Anaxagoras." *The Classical Quarterly* 3 (1/2): 33–45.

de Romilly, Jacqueline. 1992. *The Great Sophists in Periclean Athens*. Oxford: Clarendon Press.

De Ste. Croix, G. E. M. 1972. *The Origins of the Peloponnesian War*. London: Duckworth.

Descat, Raymond. 1987. "L'économie d'une cité grecque au IVe s. av. J.-C.: L'exemple athénien." *Revue des Études Anciennes* 89 (3): 239–52.

Desmond, William. 2006. "Lessons of Fear: A Reading of Thucydides." *Classical Philology* 101 (4): 359–79.

Dewald, Carolyn. 2003. "Form and Content: The Question of Tyranny in Herodotus." Pp. 25–58 in *Popular Tyranny: Sovereignty and Its Discontents in Ancient Greece*, edited by Kathryn A. Morgan. Austin: University of Texas Press.

———. 2005. *Thucydides' War Narrative: A Structural Study*. Berkeley: University of California Press.

Diaconis, Persi, and Brian Skyrms. 2017. *Ten Great Ideas about Chance*. Princeton: Princeton University Press.

Dillon, John M. 2004. *Salt and Olives: Morality and Custom in Ancient Greece*. Edinburgh: Edinburgh University Press.

Dillon, John M., and Tania Gergel. 2003. *The Greek Sophists*. London: Penguin.

Dixit, Avinash K., and Barry J. Nalebuff. 2008. *The Art of Strategy: A Game Theorist's Guide to Success in Business and Life*. New York: W.W. Norton.

Dixit, Avinash K., and Susan Skeath. 1999. *Games of Strategy*. New York: W.W. Norton.

Dodds, E.R. 1951. *The Greeks and the Irrational*. Berkeley: University of California Press.

Domingo Gygax, Marc. 2016. *Benefaction and Rewards in the Ancient Greek City: The Origins of Euergetism*. Cambridge: Cambridge University Press.

Dover, Kenneth James. 1974. *Greek Popular Morality in the Time of Plato and Aristotle*. Oxford: Blackwell.

Downs, Anthony. 1957. *An Economic Theory of Democracy*. New York: Harper & Row.

Driscoll, Eric. 2016. "*Stasis* and Reconciliation: Politics and Law in Fourth-Century Greece." *Chiron* 46:119–55.

Duke, George. 2020. "The Aristotelian Legislator and Political Naturalism." *The Classical Quarterly*. 70 (2): 620–38.

Dunkel, G.F. 1983. "Próssoo kai òpíssoo." *Zeitschrift für Vergleichende Sprachforschung*. 96:66–87.

Eckstein, Arthur M. 2006. *Mediterranean Anarchy, Interstate War, and the Rise of Rome*. Berkeley: University of California Press.

Edmunds, Lowell. 1975. *Chance and Intelligence in Thucydides*. Cambridge, MA: Harvard University Press.

Elmer, David F. 2013. *The Poetics of Consent: Collective Decision Making and the Iliad*. Baltimore: Johns Hopkins University Press.

Elster, Jon. 1979. *Ulysses and the Sirens: Studies in Rationality and Irrationality*. Cambridge: Cambridge University Press.

Ericsson, K. Anders. 2006. "The Influence of Experience and Deliberate Practice on the Development of Superior Expert Performance." Pp. 683–703 in *The Cambridge Handbook of Expertise and Expert Performance*, edited by K. Anders Ericsson et al. Cambridge: Cambridge University Press.

Espeland, Amos. 2020. "Plato's Philosophy of Law." PhD thesis, Philosophy, Stanford University.

Estlund, David M. 2014. "Utopophobia." *Philosophy and Public Affairs* 42:113–34.

Evans, J.A.S. 1981. "Notes on the Debate of the Persian Grandees in Herodotus 3,80–82." *Quaderni Urbinati di Cultura Classica* 7:79–84.

Everson, Stephen. 1998. "The Incoherence of Thrasymachus." *Oxford Studies in Ancient Philosophy* 16:99–131.

Evrigenis, Ioannis D. 2009. *Fear of Enemies and Collective Action*. Cambridge: Cambridge University Press.

Farrar, Cynthia. 1988. *The Origins of Democratic Thinking: The Invention of Politics in Classical Athens*. Cambridge: Cambridge University Press.

———. 2010. "Taking Our Chances with the Ancient Athenians." Pp. 161–212 in *Démocratie athenienne, démocracie moderne: Tradition et influences; Entretiens sur l'antiquité classique 56*, edited by Mogens H. Hansen. Geneva: Fondation Hardt.

Fawcett, Peter. 2016. "'When I Squeeze You with *Eisphorai*': Taxes and Tax Policy in Classical Athens." *Hesperia* 85:153–99.

Fearon, James. 1995. "Rationalist Explanations for War." *International Organization* 49 (3): 379–414.

———. 2011. "Self-Enforcing Democracy." *Quarterly Journal of Economics* 126:1661–1708.

Ferejohn, John. 2009. "Expectations, Institutions and Rationality in Political Theory." In *Gurobaru-shakai*, edited by Masaru Kohno. Tokyo: Keiso Shobo.

Fernandez, Patricio A. 2016. "Practical Reasoning: Where the Action Is." *Ethics* 126 (4): 869–900.

Ferrari, G. R. F. 2003. *City and Soul in Plato's Republic*. Chicago: University of Chicago Press.

Finley, M. I. 1951. *Studies in Land and Credit in Ancient Athens, 500–200 B.C.: The Horos-Inscriptions*. New Brunswick: Rutgers University Press.

———. 1963. "Generalizations in Ancient History." Pp. 19–35 in *Generalizations in the Writing of History*, edited by Louis Gottschalk. Chicago: University of Chicago Press.

———. 1965. *The World of Odysseus*. New York: Viking Press.

———. 1970. "Aristotle and Economic Analysis." *Past and Present* 47:3–25.

———. (1973) 1999. *The Ancient Economy*. Berkeley: University of California Press.

Fisher, Nick. 2004. "The Perils of Pittalakos: Settings of Cock Fighting and Dicing in Classical Athens." Pp. 65–78 in *Games and Festivals in Classical Antiquity*, edited by Sinclair Bell and Glenys Davies. Oxford: Archaeopress.

Fishkin, James S. 1991. *Democracy and Deliberation: New Directions for Democratic Reform*. New Haven: Yale University Press.

———. 2009. *When the People Speak: Deliberative Democracy and Public Consultation*. Oxford: Oxford University Press.

Fleck, Robert K., and F. Andrew Hanssen. 2006. "The Origins of Democracy: A Model with Application to Ancient Greece." *Journal of Law and Economics* 49:115–46.

———. 2009. "'Rulers Ruled by Women': An Economic Analysis of the Rise and Fall of Women's Rights in Ancient Sparta." *Economics of Governance* 10:221–45.

———. 2012. "On the Benefits and Costs of Legal Expertise: Adjudication in Ancient Athens." *Review of Law and Economics* 8 (2): 367–99.

———. 2013. "The Origins of Democracy: A Model with Application to Ancient Greece." *Journal of Law and Economics* 8 (2): 115–46.

———. 2019. "Engineering the Rule of Law in Ancient Athens." *Journal of Legal Studies* 48 (2): 441–73.

Foisneau, Luc. 2016. *Hobbes: La vie inquiète*. Paris: Gallimard.

Fontenrose, Joseph E. 1978. *The Delphic Oracle: Its Responses and Operations, with a Catalogue of Responses.* Berkeley: University of California Press.

Forrester, Katrina. 2019. *In the Shadow of Justice.* Princeton: Princeton University Press.

Forsdyke, Sara. 2005. *Exile, Ostracism, and Democracy: The Politics of Expulsion in Ancient Greece.* Princeton: Princeton University Press.

———. 2018. "Ancient and Modern Conceptions of the Rule of Law." Pp. 184–212 in *Ancient Greek History and Contemporary Social Science,* edited by Mirko Canevaro, Andrew Erskine, Benjamin Gray, and Josiah Ober. Edinburgh: Edinburgh University Press.

———. 2021. *Slaves and Slavery in Ancient Greece.* Cambridge: Cambridge University Press.

Frankfort, Henri. 1948. *Kingship and the Gods, a Study of Ancient Near Eastern Religion as the Integration of Society and Nature.* Chicago: University of Chicago Press.

Franklin, James. (2001) 2015. *The Science of Conjecture: Evidence and Probability before Pascal.* Baltimore: Johns Hopkins University Press.

———. 2016. "Pre-History of Probability." Pp. 33–49 in *The Oxford Handbook of Probability and Philosophy,* edited by Alan Hájek and Christopher Hitchcock. Oxford: Oxford University Press.

Frazer, James George. (1890) 1911. *The Golden Bough: A Study in Magic and Religion.* London: Macmillan.

Frede, Michael. 1996. "Introduction." Pp. 1–28 in *Rationality in Greek Thought,* edited by Michael Frede and Gisela. Striker. Oxford: Clarendon Press.

Frede, Michael, and Gisela Striker, eds. 1996. *Rationality in Greek Thought.* Oxford: Clarendon Press.

Freeman, Samuel. 2019. "Original Position." In *The Stanford Encyclopedia of Philosophy* (Summer 2019 ed.), edited by Edward N. Zalta. Stanford, CA: Stanford University Press.

Fried, Barbara H. 2018. "Facing Up to Risk." *Journal of Legal Analysis* 10:175–98.

———. 2020. *Facing Up to Scarcity.* New York: Oxford University Press.

Fustel de Coulanges, Numa Denis. (1864) 1874. *The Ancient City: A Study on the Religion, Laws, and Institutions of Greece and Rome.* Boston: Lee and Shepard.

Gabrielsen, Vincent. 1981. *Remuneration of State Officials in Fourth Century B.C. Athens.* Odense: Odense University Press.

———. 1994. *Financing the Athenian Fleet: Public Taxation and Social Relations.* Baltimore: Johns Hopkins University Press.

Gagarin, Michael. 1986. *Early Greek Law.* Berkeley: University of California Press.

———. 1994. "Probability and Persuasion: Plato and Early Greek Rhetoric." Pp. 46–68 in *Probability and Persuasion: Plato and Early Greek Rhetoric,* edited by Ian Worthington. London: Routledge.

———. 2005. "Early Greek Law." Pp. 82–94 in *The Cambridge Companion to Ancient Greek Law,* edited by Michael Gagarin and David Cohen. Cambridge: Cambridge University Press.

————. 2014. "*Eikos* Arguments in Athenian Forensic Oratory." Pp. 15–29 in *Probabilities, Hypotheticals, and Counterfactuals in Ancient Greek Thought*, edited by Victoria Wohl. Cambridge: Cambridge University Press.

Gailmard, Sean. 2021. "Theory, History, and Political Economy." *Journal of Historical Political Economy* 1 (1): 69–104.

Galston, William. 2010. "Realism in Political Theory." *European Journal of Political Theory* 9:385–411.

Gammie, John G. 1986. "Herodotus on Kings and Tyrants: Objective Historiography or Conventional Portraiture?" *Journal of Near Eastern Studies* 45 (3): 171–95.

Garber, Daniel, and Sandy Zaller. 1979. "On the Emergence of Probability." *Archive for History of Exact Sciences* 21 (1): 33–53.

Garnsey, Peter. 1996. *Ideas of Slavery from Aristotle to Augustine*. Cambridge: Cambridge University Press.

Gaskin, Richard. 1990. "Do Homeric Heroes Make Real Decisions?" *Classical Quarterly* 40 (1): 1–15.

Gaus, Gerald, and John Thrasher. 2015. "Rational Choice and the Original Position: The (Many) Models of Rawls and Harsanyi." Pp. 39–58 in *The Original Position*, edited by Timothy Hinton. Cambridge: Cambridge University Press.

Gauthier, David P. 1969. *The Logic of Leviathan: The Moral and Political Theory of Thomas Hobbes*. Oxford: Clarendon Press.

————. 1986. "The Ring of Gyges." Pp. 306–29 in *Morals by Agreement*. Oxford: Clarendon Press.

Gehrke, Hans-Joachim. 1985. *Stasis: Untersuchungen zu den inneren Kriegen in den griechischen Staaten des 5. und 4. Jahrhunderts v. Chr.* München: Beck.

Geuss, Raymond. 2008. *Philosophy and Real Politics*. Princeton: Princeton University Press.

Giddens, Anthony. 1990. *The Consequences of Modernity*. Stanford, CA: Stanford University Press.

Gigon, Olof. 1979. *Sokrates: Sein Bild in Dichtung und Geschichte*. Bern: Francke.

Gomme, A. W. 1937. "Traders and Manufacturers in Greece." Pp. 42–66 in *Essays in Greek History and Literature*. Oxford: Basil Blackwell.

Goodin, Robert E., and Kai Spiekermann. 2018. *An Epistemic Theory of Democracy*. Oxford: Oxford University Press.

Gottlieb, Paula. 1994. "Aristotle on Dividing the Soul and Uniting the Virtues." *Phronesis* 39 (3): 275–90.

Gouldner, Alvin Ward. 1965. *Enter Plato: Classical Greece and the Origins of Social Theory*. New York: Basic Books.

Gray, Benjamin. 2015. *Stasis and Stability: Exile, the Polis, and Political Thought, c. 404–146 BC*. Oxford: Oxford University Press.

Gray, Vivienne. 1998. *The Framing of Socrates: The Literary Interpretation of Xenophon's Memorabilia*. Stuttgart: Franz Steiner Verlag.

Greenwood, Emily. 2006. *Thucydides and the Shaping of History*. London: Duckworth.

Grewal, David Singh. 2010. "The Invention of the Economy: A History of Economic Thought." PhD thesis, Political Science, Harvard University.

Grissom, Daryl. 2012. "Thucydides' Dangerous World: Dual Forms of Danger in Greek Interstate Relations." PhD thesis, Classics, University of Maryland.

Guha, Brishti. 2011. "Preferences, Prisoners and Private Information: Was Socrates Rational at His Trial?" *European Journal of Law and Economics* 31 (3): 249–64.

Guthrie, W. K. C. 1962. *A History of Greek Philosophy.* 3 vols. Cambridge: Cambridge University Press.

Habermas, Jürgen. 1996. *Between Facts and Norms: Contributions to a Discourse Theory of Law and Democracy.* Cambridge, MA: MIT Press.

Hacking, Ian. (1975) 2006. *The Emergence of Probability: A Philosophical Study of Early Ideas about Probability, Induction and Statistical Inference.* Cambridge: Cambridge University Press.

Halkos, George E., and Nicholas C. Kyriazis. 2005. "A Naval Revolution and Institutional Change: The Case of the United Provinces." *European Journal of Law and Economics* 19:41–68.

———. 2010. "The Athenian Economy in the Age of Demosthenes: Path Dependence and Change." *European Journal of Law and Economics* 29:255–77.

Halkos, George E., Nicholas C. Kyriazis, and Emmanouil M. L. Economou. 2021. "Plato as a Game Theorist towards an International Trade Policy." *Journal of Risk and Financial Management* 14 (3): no. 115.

Hallo, William W. 2009. *The World's Oldest Literature: Studies in Sumerian Belles-lettres.* Leiden: E. J. Brill.

Hammer, Dean. 2002. *The Iliad as Politics: The Performance of Political Thought.* Norman: University of Oklahoma Press.

Hampton, Jean. 1988. *Hobbes and the Social Contract Tradition.* Cambridge: Cambridge University Press.

Hansen, Mogens Herman. 1983. "*Rhetores* and *Strategoi* in Fourth-Century Athens." *Greek, Roman, and Byzantine Studies* 24:151–80.

———. 1984. "The Number of Rhetores in the Athenian Ecclesia, 355–322 B.C." *Greek, Roman, and Byzantine Studies* 24:227–38.

———. 1986. "The Origin of the Term *Demokratia.*" *Liverpool Classical Monthly* 11:35–36.

———. 1987. *The Athenian Assembly in the Age of Demosthenes.* Oxford: Blackwell.

———. 1999. *The Athenian Democracy in the Age of Demosthenes: Structure, Principles and Ideology.* Norman: University of Oklahoma Press.

———. 2002. "The Game Called *Polis.*" Pp. 9–15 in *Even More Studies in the Ancient Greek Polis: Papers from the Copenhagen Polis Centre 6,* edited by Thomas Heine Nielsen. Stuttgart: Franz Steiner Verlag.

———. 2006. *Polis: An Introduction to the Ancient Greek City-State.* Oxford: Oxford University Press.

Hansen, Mogens Herman, and Thomas Heine Nielsen. 2004. *An Inventory of Archaic and Classical Poleis.* Oxford: Oxford University Press.

Hardin, Garrett. 1968. "The Tragedy of the Commons." *Science* 162:1243–48.

Hardin, Russell. 1991. "Acting Together, Contributing Together." *Rationality and Society.* 3:365–80.

———. 1995. "Self-interest, Group Identity." Pp. 14–42 in *Nationalism and Rationality*, edited by Albert Breton. Cambridge: Cambridge University Press.

———. 2007. *David Hume: Moral and Political Theorist*. Oxford: Oxford University Press.

Harris, Edward M. 2006. "Solon and the Spirit of the Laws in Archaic and Classical Athens." Pp. 290–318 in *Solon of Athens: New Historical and Philological Perspectives*, edited by Josine H. Blok and André P. M. H. Lardinois. Leiden: E. J. Brill.

———. 2013. "How to Address the Athenian Assembly: Rhetoric and Political Tactics in the Debate about Mytilene (Thuc. 3.37–50)." *The Classical Quarterly* 63 (1): 94–109.

Harris, Edward M., David M. Lewis, and Mark Woolmer, eds. 2015. *The Ancient Greek Economy: Markets, Households and City-States*. Cambridge: Cambridge University Press.

Harrison, Jane Ellen. 1903. *Prolegomena to the Study of Greek Religion*. Cambridge: Cambridge University Press.

———. 1912. *Themis: A Study of the Social Origins of Greek Religion*. Cambridge: Cambridge University Press.

Harsanyi, John C. 1975. "Can the Maximin Principle Serve as a Basis for Morality? A Critique of John Rawls's Theory." *American Political Science Review* 69 (2): 594–606.

Harvey, F. D. 1965. "Two Kinds of Equality." *Classica et Mediaevalia* 26:101–46.

Hatzistavrou, Antony. 2021. "Aristotle on the Authority of the Many: *Politics* III 11, 1281a40–b21." *Apeiron* 54 (2): 203–32.

Hausman, Daniel M. 2018. "Philosophy of Economics." In *The Stanford Encyclopedia of Philosophy* (Fall 2018 ed.), edited by Edward N. Zalta. Stanford, CA: Stanford University Press.

Hawthorn, Geoffrey. 2014. *Thucydides on Politics: Back to the Present*. Cambridge: Cambridge University Press.

Hayek, Friedrich A. von. 1944. *The Road to Serfdom*. Chicago: University of Chicago Press.

Heap, Shaun Hargreaves. 1989. *Rationality in Economics*. New York: Blackwell.

Heinaman, Robert. 1993. "Rationality, *Eudaimonia* and *Kakodaimonia* in Aristotle." *Phronesis* 38 (1): 31–56.

Herman, Gabriel. 2006. *Morality and Behaviour in Democratic Athens: A Social History (508–322 B.C.)*. Cambridge: Cambridge University Press.

Hesk, Jon. 2014. "Thucydides in the Twentieth and Twenty-First Centuries." Pp. 218–37 in *A Handbook to the Reception of Thucydides*, edited by Christine Lee and Neville Morley. Chichester, UK: John Wiley & Sons.

Hinton, Timothy, ed. 2015. *The Original Position*. Cambridge: Cambridge University Press.

Hirji, Sukaina. 2020. "Aristotelian Eudaimonism and the Dualism of Practical Reason." Pp. 187–210 in *Kantian and Sidgwickian Ethics*, edited by Tyler Paytas and Tim Henning. New York: Routledge.

———. 2021. "External Goods and the Complete Exercise of Virtue in Aristotle's *Nicomachean Ethics*." *Archiv für Geschichte der Philosophie* 103 (1): 29–53.

Hirschman, Albert O. 1970. *Exit, Voice, and Loyalty: Responses to Decline in Firms, Organizations, and States*. Cambridge, MA: Harvard University Press.

Hobbes, Thomas. (1651) 1996. *Leviathan*. Edited by Richard Tuck. Cambridge: Cambridge University Press.

Horky, Phillip. 2020. "Anonymus Iamblichi, *On Excellence (Peri Aretēs)*: A Lost Defense of Democracy." Pp. 262–92 in *Early Greek Ethics*, edited by David Conan Wolfsdorf. Oxford: Oxford University Press.

———. 2021. "Law and Justice among the Socratics: Contexts for Plato's *Republic*." *Polis* 38:399–419.

Hornblower, Simon. 1991–2008. *A Commentary on Thucydides*. 3 vols. Oxford: Clarendon Press.

Hourani, George F. 1962. "Thrasymachus' Definition of Justice in Plato's *Republic*." *Phronesis* 7 (2): 110–20.

Hubbard, B. A. F., and E. S. Karnofsky. 1982. *Plato's Protagoras: A Socratic Commentary*. Chicago: University of Chicago Press.

Hume, David. (1739) 1978. *A Treatise of Human Nature*. Oxford: Clarendon Press.

Ingham, Sean. 2019. *Rule by Multiple Majorities: A New Theory of Popular Control*. Cambridge: Cambridge University Press.

Iordanoglou, Dimitrios, and Johan Tralau. 2022. "Murder, Logic, and Embryology: The Beginnings of Political and Moral Philosophy in Aischylos' *Oresteia*." *Classical Philology* 117 (2): 259–81.

Irwin, Terence H. 1974. Review of Leo Strauss, *Xenophon's Socrates*. *Philosophical Review* 83 (3): 409–13.

———. 1977. *Plato's Moral Theory: The Early and Middle Dialogues*. Oxford: Clarendon Press.

———. 1995. *Plato's Ethics*. New York: Oxford University Press.

———. 1999. "*Republic* II: Questions about Justice." Pp. 164–85 in *Plato 2. Ethics, Politics, Religion, and the Soul*, edited by Gil Fine. Oxford: Oxford University Press.

Ismard, Paulin. 2017. *Democracy's Slaves: A Political History of Ancient Greece*. Translated by Jane Marie Todd. Cambridge, MA: Harvard University Press.

Jimenez, Marta. 2019. "*Empeiria* and Good Habits in Aristotle's Ethics." *Journal of the History of Philosophy* 57 (3): 363–89.

Johnson, Laurie M. 2014. "Thucydides the Realist." Pp. 391–405 in *A Handbook to the Reception of Thucydides*, edited by Christine Lee and Neville Morley. Chichester, UK: John Wiley & Sons.

Johnstone, Steven. 2011. *A History of Trust in Ancient Greece*. Chicago: University of Chicago Press.

Jongman, Willem M. 2013. "Formalism-Substantivism Debate." Pp. 2715–18 in *The Encyclopedia of Ancient History*, edited by Roger S. Bagnall et al. New York: Wiley-Blackwell.

Joyce, Richard. 2006. *The Evolution of Morality*. Cambridge, MA: MIT Press.

Kagan, Donald. 1969. *The Outbreak of the Peloponnesian War*. Ithaca, NY: Cornell University Press.

———. 2003. *The Peloponnesian War.* New York: Viking.

Kahneman, Daniel. 2011. *Thinking, Fast and Slow.* New York: Farrar, Straus and Giroux.

Kahneman, Daniel, and Amos Tversky. 1979. "Prospect Theory: An Analysis of Decision under Risk." *Econometrica* 47 (2): 263–91.

Kallet, Lisa. 1994. "Money Talks: Rhetor, Demos, and Resources of the Athenian Empire." Pp. 227–52 in *Ritual, Finance, Politics: Athenian Democratic Accounts Presented to David Lewis,* edited by Robin Osborne and Simon Hornblower. Oxford: Clarendon Press.

———. 2021. "A Counting People: Valuing Numeracy in Democratic Athens." Pp. 27–57 in *Numbers and Numeracy in the Greek Polis,* edited by Robert Sing, Tazuko van Berkel, and Robin Osborne. Leiden: E. J. Brill.

Kaiser, Brooks A. 2007. "The Athenian Trierarchy: Mechanism Design for the Private Provision of Public Goods." *Journal of Economic History* 67 (2): 445–80.

Kalyvas, Andreas, and Ira Katznelson. 2008. *Liberal Beginnings: Making a Republic for the Moderns.* Cambridge: Cambridge University Press.

Kamen, Deborah. 2013. *Status in Classical Athens.* Princeton: Princeton University Press.

Kamtekar, Rachana. 2001. "Social Justice and Happiness in the Republic: Plato's Two Principles." *History of Political Thought* 22 (2): 189–91.

———. 2005. "The Profession of Friendship: Callicles, Democratic Politics, and Rhetorical Education in Plato's *Gorgias.*" *Ancient Philosophy* 25:219–339.

———. 2018. *Plato's Moral Psychology.* Oxford: Oxford University Press.

Karachalios, Foivos Spyridon. 2013. "The Politics of Judgment in Early Greece: Dispute Resolution and State Formation from the Homeric World to Solon's Athens." PhD thesis, Classics, Stanford University.

Karavites, Peter. 1982. *Capitulations and Greek Interstate Relations: The Reflection of Humanistic Ideals in Political Events.* Göttingen: Vanderhoeck & Ruprecht.

Kasimis, Demetra. 2016. "Plato's Open Secret." *Contemporary Political Theory* 15 (4): 339–57.

———. 2021. "The Play of Conspiracy in Plato's Republic and the Problem of Democratic Erosion." *American Journal of Political Science* 65 (4): 926–37.

Keene, Edward. 2014. "The Reception of Thucydides in the History of International Relations." Pp. 353–72 in *A Handbook to the Reception of Thucydides,* edited by Christine Lee and Neville Morley. Chichester, UK: John Wiley & Sons.

Kerferd, G. B. 1981. *The Sophistic Movement.* Cambridge: Cambridge University Press.

Kerferd, George. B. 1947. "The Doctrine of Thrasymachus in Plato's *Republic.*" *Durham University Journal* 9 (1): 19–27.

Kidd, Stephen E. 2017a. "Greek Dicing: Astragaloi and the 'Euripides' Throw." *Journal of Hellenic Studies* 137:112–18.

———. 2017b. "How to Gamble in Greek: The Meaning of *Kubeia.*" *Journal of Hellenic Studies* 137:119–34.

———. 2020. "Why Mathematical Probability Failed to Emerge from Ancient Gambling." *Apeiron* 53 (1): 1–25.

Kierstead, James. 2016. "The Delian and Second Athenian Leagues: The Perspective of Collective Action." Pp. 164–81 in *Circum Mare: Themes in Ancient Warfare,* edited by J. Armstrong. Leiden: E. J. Brill.

———. 2018. "Protagoras's Cooperative Know-how." Pp. 17–24 in *Democratic Moments: Reading Democratic Texts,* edited by Xavier Márquez. London: Bloomsbury Academic.

———. 2021. "Is Protagoras' Great Speech on Democracy?" *Polis* 38 (2): 199–207.

Kirk, G. S., J. B. Hainsworth, Richard Janko, Mark W. Edwards, and N. J. Richardson. 1985–93. *The Iliad, A Commentary.* 6 vols. Cambridge: Cambridge University Press.

Kirwan, Christopher. 1965. "Glaucon's Challenge." *Phronesis* 10 (2): 162–73.

Knight, Jack, and James Johnson. 2015. "On Attempts to Gerrymander 'Positive' and 'Normative' Political Theory: Six Theses." *Good Society* 24 (1): 30–48.

Kolodny, Niko. 2014. "Rule Over None I: What Justifies Democracy?" *Philosophy and Public Affairs* 42 (3): 195–229.

Kolodny, Niko, and John Brunero. 2018. "Instrumental Rationality." In *The Stanford Encyclopedia of Philosophy* (Spring 2020 ed.), edited by Edward N. Zalta. Stanford, CA: Stanford University Press.

Konstan, David. 2018. "Epicurus." In *The Stanford Encyclopedia of Philosophy* (Summer 2018 ed.), edited by Edward N. Zalta. Stanford, CA: Stanford University Press.

Kraut, Richard. 1989. *Aristotle on the Human Good.* Princeton: Princeton University Press.

Krentz, Peter. 1982. *The Thirty at Athens.* Ithaca, NY: Cornell University Press.

Kroll, John H. 1972. *Athenian Bronze Allotment Plates.* Cambridge, MA: Harvard University Press.

Kurke, Leslie. 1999a. *Coins, Bodies, Games, and Gold: The Politics of Meaning in Archaic Greece.* Princeton: Princeton University Press.

———. 1999b. "Ancient Greek Board Games and How to Play Them." *Classical Philology* 94 (3): 247–67.

Kyriazis, Nicholas. 2007. "Democracy and Institutional Change." *European Research Studies* 10 (1–2): 65–82.

———. 2009. "Financing the Athenian State: Public Choice in the Age of Demosthenes." *European Journal of Law and Economics* 27:109–27.

Kyriazis, Nicholas, and Emmanouil Marios L. Economou. 2013. "Social Contract, Public Choice, and Fiscal Repercussions in the Athenian Democracy." *Theoretical and Practical Research in Economic Fields* 4 (1): 61–76.

Kyriazis, Nicholas, and Michel S. Zouboulakis. 2004. "Democracy, Sea Power and Institutional Change: An Economic Analysis of the Athenian Naval Law." *European Journal of Law and Economics* 17:117–32.

Laird, Andrew. 2001. "Ringing the Changes on Gyges: Philosophy and the Formation of Fiction in Plato's *Republic*." *Journal of Hellenic Studies* 121:12–29.

Laks, André, and Glenn W. Most, eds. 2016. *Early Greek Philosophy VIII & IX: The Sophists.* 2 vols. Cambridge, MA: Harvard University Press.

Lambert, S.D. 2019. "Δημοκράτης the Democrat?" *Proceedings of the British Academy.* 222:153–66.

Landauer, Matthew. 2019. *Dangerous Counsel: Accountability and Advice in Ancient Greece.* Chicago: University of Chicago Press.

Lanni, Adriaan M. 2006. *Law and Justice in the Courts of Classical Athens.* Cambridge: Cambridge University Press.

Lardinois, André. 1997. "Modern Paroemiology and the Use of Gnomai in Homer's *Iliad.*" *Classical Philology* 92 (3): 213–34.

———. 2000. "Characterization through *Gnomai* in Homer's *Iliad.*" *Mnemosyne* 53 (6): 641–61.

Lebow, Richard Ned, and Barry S. Strauss, eds. 1991. *Hegemonic Rivalry: From Thucydides to the Nuclear Age.* Boulder: Westview Press.

Lee, Roy. 2020. "The Ethical Theory of Aristotle's *Eudemian Ethics.*" PhD thesis, Philosophy, Stanford University.

Leese, Michael. 2021. *Making Money in Ancient Athens.* Ann Arbor: University of Michigan Press.

Lenczewska, Olga. 2021. "Kant and Rawls on the Moral and Political Development of Persons." PhD thesis, Philosophy, Stanford University.

Leshem, Dotan. 2016. "Retrospectives: What Did the Ancient Greeks Mean by *Oikonomia?*" *Journal of Economic Perspectives* 30 (1): 225–38.

Levitsky, Steven, and Daniel Ziblatt. 2018. *How Democracies Die.* New York: Crown Publishers.

Lewis, David M. 1997. "On the Financial Offices of Eubulus and Lycurgus." Pp. 212–29 in *Selected Papers in Greek and Near Eastern History,* edited by P.J. Rhodes. Cambridge: Cambridge University Press.

———. 2018. *Greek Slave Systems in Their Eastern Mediterranean Context, c. 800–146 BC.* Oxford: Oxford University Press.

Liddel, Peter. 2019. *Decrees of Fourth-Century Athens.* Cambridge: Cambridge University Press.

Liddell, Henry George, Robert Scott, and Henry Stuart Jones. 1968. *A Greek-English Lexicon.* Oxford: Clarendon Press.

Liu, Glory, and Barry Weingast. 2020. "Deriving 'General Principles' in Adam Smith: The Ubiquity of Equilibrium and Comparative Statics Analysis Throughout His Works." *Adam Smith Review* 12:134–65.

Llewellyn-Jones, Lloyd. 2013. *King and Court in Ancient Persia 559 to 331 BCE.* Edinburgh: Edinburgh University Press.

Lockwood, Thornton C. 2019. "The Best Way of Life for a Polis (*Politics* VII.1–3)." *Polis* 36 (1): 5–22.

Loehr, Regina M. 2021. "The People's Moral Emotions in Polybius' Cycle of Constitutions." *Classical Philology* 116 (2): 155–82.

Lorenz, Hendrik. 2006. *The Brute Within: Appetitive Desire in Plato and Aristotle.* Oxford: Oxford University Press.

Low, Polly. 2007. *Interstate Relations in Classical Greece.* Cambridge: Cambridge University Press.

Lowry, S. Tod. 1987. *The Archaeology of Economic Ideas: The Classical Greek Tradition.* Durham, NC: Duke University Press.

Luraghi, Nino., ed. 2013. *The Splendors and Miseries of Ruling Alone: Encounters with Monarchy from Archaic Greece to the Hellenistic Mediterranean.* Stuttgart: Franz Steiner Verlag.

Lyttkens, Carl Hampus. 1997. "A Rational-Actor Perspective on the Origin of Liturgies in Ancient Greece." *Journal of Institutional and Theoretical Economics* 153:462–84.

———. 2006. "Reflections on the Origins of the Polis: An Economic Perspective on Institutional Change in Ancient Greece." *Constitutional Political Economy* 17:31–48.

———. 2012. *Economic Analysis of Institutional Change in Ancient Greece: Politics, Taxation and Rational Behaviour.* London: Routledge.

Lyttkens, Carl Hampus, George Tridimas, and Anna Lindgren. 2018. "Making Direct Democracy Work: A Rational-Actor Perspective on the *Graphe Paranomon* in Ancient Athens." *Constitutional Political Economy* 29 (4): 389–412.

Ma, John. 1999. *Antiochos III and the Cities of Western Asia Minor.* Oxford: Oxford University Press.

———. 2003. "Peer Polity Interaction in the Hellenistic Age." *Past and Present* 180 (1): 9–39.

———. 2018. "Whatever Happened to Athens? Perspectives on the Political History of Post-Classical Greece." Pp. 277–97 in *The Hellenistic and Early Imperial Greek Reception of Classical Athenian Democracy and Political Thought,* edited by Benjamin Gray and Mirko Canevaro. Oxford: Oxford University Press.

———. In progress. *Polis: Biography of a Political and Social Form.*

Ma, John, Nikolaos Papazarkadas, and Robert Parker, eds. 2009. *Interpreting the Athenian Empire.* London: Duckworth.

Mack, William. 2015. *Proxeny and Polis: Institutional Networks in the Ancient Greek World.* Oxford: Oxford University Press.

Mackie, Gerry. 2003. *Democracy Defended.* Cambridge: Cambridge University Press.

Mackil, Emily. 2013. *Creating a Common Polity: Religion, Economy, and Politics in the Making of the Greek Koinon.* Berkeley: University of California Press.

———. 2018. "Property Security and Its Limits in Classical Greece." Pp. 315–34 in *Ancient Greek History and Contemporary Social Science,* edited by Mirko Canevaro, Andrew Erskine, Benjamin Gray, and Josiah Ober. Edinburgh: Edinburgh University Press.

Mantzavinos, C. 2014. "Text Interpretation as a Scientific Activity." *Journal for General Philosophy of Science* 45 (1): 45–58.

Marshall, Mason, and Shane Bilsborough. 2019. "The *Republic*'s Ambiguous Democracy." *History of Philosophy Quarterly* 27 (4): 301–16.

Martin, Richard P. 1989. *The Language of Heroes: Speech and Performance in the Iliad.* Ithaca, NY: Cornell University Press.

———. 1993. "The Seven Sages as Performers of Wisdom." Pp. 108–28 in *Cultural Poetics in Archaic Greece: Cult, Performance, Politics,* edited by Carol Dougherty and Leslie Kurke. Princeton: Princeton University Press.

———. 1996. "The Scythian Accent: Anacharsis and the Cynics." Pp. 136–55 in *The Cynics: The Cynic Movement in Antiquity and Its Legacy,* edited by R. Bracht Branham and Marie-Odile Goulet-Caâze. Berkeley: University of California Press.

Massar, Natacha. 2020. "Skilled Workers in the Ancient Greek City: Public Employment, Selection Methods, and Evaluation." Pp. 68–93 in *Skilled Labour and Professionalism in Ancient Greece and Rome,* edited by Edmund Stewart, Edward M. Harris, and David M. Lewis. Cambridge: Cambridge University Press.

Mauss, Marcel. (1954) 1990. *The Gift: The Form and Reason for Exchange in Archaic Societies.* New York: W. W. Norton.

Mayor, Adrienne. 2020. *Gods and Robots.* Princeton: Princeton University Press.

McArthur, Mills. 2021. "Athenian Shipbuilders." *Hesperia* 90 (3): 479–533.

McCannon, Bryan C. 2010a. "Homicide Trials in Classical Athens." *International Review of Law and Economics* 30:46–51.

———. 2010b. "The Median Juror and the Trial of Socrates." *European Journal of Political Economy* 26:533–40.

———. 2011. "Jury Size in Classical Athens: An Application of the Condorcet Jury Theorem." *Kyklos* 64:106–21.

———. 2012. "The Origin of Democracy in Athens." *Review of Law & Economics* 8 (2): 531–62.

McClennen, Edward F. 2001. "The Strategy of Cooperation." Pp. 189–208 in *Practical Rationality and Preference: Essays for David Gauthier,* edited by Christopher W. Morris, Arthur Ripstein, and David P. Gauthier. Cambridge: Cambridge University Press.

McKirahan, Richard D. 1994. *Philosophy before Socrates: An Introduction with Texts and Commentary.* Indianapolis: Hackett.

Meikle, Scott. 1995. *Aristotle's Economic Thought.* Oxford: Clarendon Press.

Menn, Stephen. 2005. "On Plato's Πολιτεία." *Proceedings of the Boston Area Colloquium in Ancient Philosophy* 21:1–55.

Migeotte, Léopold. 2014. *Les finances des cités grecques.* Paris: Les Belles Lettres.

Milgrom, Paul, and Barry Weingast. 1990. "The Role of Institutions in the Revival of Trade: The Law Merchant, Private Judges, and the Champagne Fairs." *Economics and Politics* 21 (1): 1–23.

Miller, Fred Dycus. 2005. "Property Rights in Aristotle." Pp. 121–44 in *Aristotle's Politics: Critical Essays,* edited by Richard Kraut and Steven Skultety. Lanham, MD: Rowman & Littlefield.

Millett, Paul. 1991. *Lending and Borrowing in Ancient Athens.* Cambridge: Cambridge University Press.

Moe, Terry M. 2019. *The Politics of Institutional Reform: Katrina, Education, and the Second Face of Power.* Cambridge: Cambridge University Press.

Monoson, Susan Sara. 2000. *Plato's Democratic Entanglements: Athenian Politics and the Practice of Philosophy.* Princeton: Princeton University Press.

Moody, Peter R. 2008. "Rational Choice Analysis in Classical Chinese Political Thought: The Han Feizi." *Polity* 40 (1): 95–119.

Morris, Christopher W., and Arthur Ripstein. 2001. "Practical Reason and Preference." Pp. 1–10 in *Practical Rationality and Preference: Essays for David Gauthier,* edited by Christopher W. Morris, Arthur Ripstein, and David P. Gauthier. Cambridge: Cambridge University Press.

Morris, Ian. 2004. "Economic Growth in Ancient Greece." *Journal of Institutional and Theoretical Economics* 160 (4): 709–42.

Moss, Jessica. 2011. "'Virtue Makes the Goal Right': Virtue and Phronesis in Aristotle's Ethics." *Phronesis* 56 (3): 204–61.

———. 2014. "Right Reason in Plato and Aristotle: On the Meaning of Logos." *Phronesis* 59 (3): 181–230.

———. 2017. "Aristotle's Ethical Psychology." Pp. 124–42 in *The Cambridge Companion to Ancient Ethics,* edited by Christopher Bobonich. Cambridge: Cambridge University Press.

Mossé, Claude. 1962. *La fin de la démocratie athénienne, aspects sociaux et politiques du déclin de la cité grecque au IVe siècle avant J.-C.* Paris: Presses universitaires de France.

———. 1973. *Athens in Decline, 404–86 B.C.* London: Routledge & Kegan Paul.

———. 1994. *Démosthène, ou, Les ambiguités de la politique.* Paris: A. Colin.

———. 1995. *Politique et société en Grèce ancienne: Le "modèle" athénien.* Paris: Aubier.

Mouffe, Chantal. 1993. *The Return of the Political.* London: Verso.

———. 2000. *The Democratic Paradox.* London: Verso.

Mueller, Dennis C. 2003. *Public Choice III.* Cambridge: Cambridge University Press.

Munn, Mark Henderson. 2000. *The School of History: Athens in the Age of Socrates.* Berkeley: University of California Press.

Munson, Rosaria Vignolo. 2001. *Telling Wonders: Ethnographic and Political Discourse in the Work of Herodotus.* Ann Arbor: University of Michigan Press.

———. 2009. "Who Are Herodotus' Persians?" *Classical World* 102 (4): 457–70.

Murray, Gilbert. (1912) 1925. *Five Stages of Greek Religion.* New York: Columbia University Press.

Murray, Oswyn. 1990. "Cities of Reason." Pp. 1–25 in *The Greek City: From Homer to Alexander,* edited by Oswyn Murray and S. R. F. Price. Oxford: Oxford University Press.

———. 1993. "*Polis* and *Politeia* in Aristotle." Pp. 197–210 in *The Ancient Greek City-State,* edited by Mogens Herman Hansen. Copenhagen: Munksgaard.

Myerson, Roger B. 2009. "Learning from Schelling's *Strategy of Conflict.*" *Journal of Economic Literature* 47 (4): 1109–25.

Nagel, Thomas. 1980. "Aristotle on Eudaimonia." Pp. 7–14 in *Essays on Aristotle's Ethics,* edited by Amélie O. Rorty. Berkeley: University of California Press.

Nails, Debra. 2002. *The People of Plato: A Prosopography of Plato and Other Socratics.* Indianapolis: Hackett.

Nash, John F. 1950. "The Bargaining Problem." *Econometrica* 18 (2): 155–62.

Nawar, Tamer. 2017. "Platonic Know-How and Successful Action." *European Journal of Philosophy* 25 (4): 944–62.

———. 2018. "Thrasymachus' Unerring Skill and the Arguments of *Republic* 1." *Phronesis* 63 (4): 359–91.

Netz, Reviel. 2002. "Counter Culture: Towards a History of Greek Numeracy." *History of Science* 40 (3): 321–52.

———. 2009. *Ludic Proof: Greek Mathematics and the Alexandrian Aesthetic.* Cambridge: Cambridge University Press.

———. 2019. *Scale, Space and Canon in Ancient Literary Culture.* Cambridge: Cambridge University Press.

Nietzsche, Friedrich Wilhelm. (1872) 2000. *The Birth of Tragedy.* Oxford: Oxford University Press.

Nightingale, Andrea Wilson. 2004. *Spectacles of Truth in Classical Greek Philosophy: Theoria in Its Cultural Context.* Cambridge: Cambridge University Press.

North, Douglass Cecil, John Joseph Wallis, and Barry R. Weingast. 2009. *Violence and Social Orders. A Conceptual Framework for Interpreting Recorded Human History.* Cambridge: Cambridge University Press.

Noussia, Maria. 2006. "Strategies of Persuasion in Solon's *Elegies.*" Pp. 134–56 in *Solon of Athens: New Historical and Philological Perspectives,* edited by Josine H. Blok and André P. M. H. Lardinois. Leiden: E. J. Brill.

Nowak, Martin A., Karen M. Page, and Karl Sigmund. 2000. "Fairness versus Reason in the Ultimatum Game." *Science* 289 (5485): 1773–75.

Obdrzalek, Suzanne. 2006. "Living in Doubt: Carneades' *Pithanon* Reconsidered." *Oxford Studies in Ancient Philosophy* 31:243–80.

Ober, Josiah. 1985. *Fortress Attica: Defense of the Athenian Land Frontier, 404–322 B.C.* Leiden: E. J. Brill.

———. 1989. *Mass and Elite in Democratic Athens: Rhetoric, Ideology, and the Power of the People.* Princeton: Princeton University Press.

———. 1996. *The Athenian Revolution: Essays on Ancient Greek Democracy and Political Theory.* Princeton: Princeton University Press.

———. 1998a. *Political Dissent in Democratic Athens: Intellectual Critics of Popular Rule.* Princeton: Princeton University Press.

———. 1998b. "Revolution Matters: Democracy as Demotic Action." Pp. 67–85 in *Democracy 2500? Questions and Challenges,* edited by Kurt Raaflaub, Ian Morris. Dubuque, IA: Kendall/Hunt.

———. 2001. "Thucydides Theoretikos/Thucydides Histor: Realist Theory and the Challenge of History." Pp. 273–306 in *Democracy and War: A Comparative Study of the Korean War and the Peloponnesian War,* edited by D. R. McCann, B. S. Strauss. Armonk, NY: M. E. Sharpe.

———. 2005. *Athenian Legacies: Essays in the Politics of Going On Together.* Princeton: Princeton University Press.

———. 2006a. "Solon and the *Horoi:* Facts on the Ground in Archaic Athens." Pp. 441–56 in *Solon of Athens: New Historical and Philological Perspectives,* edited by Josine H. Blok and André P. M. H. Lardinois. Leiden: E. J. Brill.

———. 2006b. "Thucydides and the Invention of Political Science." Pp. 131–59 in *Brill's Companion to Thucydides,* edited by Antonios Rengakos and Antonis Tsakmakis. Leiden: E. J. Brill.

———. 2007a. "'I Besieged That Man': Democracy's Revolutionary Start." Pp. 83–104 in *The Origins of Democracy in Ancient Greece,* edited by Kurt Raaflaub, Josiah Ober, and Robert W. Wallace. Berkeley: University of California Press.

———. 2007b. "Natural Capacities and Democracy as a Good-in-Itself." *Philosophical Studies* 132:59–73.

———. 2008. *Democracy and Knowledge: Innovation and Learning in Classical Athens.* Princeton: Princeton University Press.

———. 2010. "Thucydides on Athens' Democratic Advantage in the Archidamian War." Pp. 65–87 in *War, Democracy and Culture in Classical Athens,* edited by David Pritchard. Cambridge: Cambridge University Press.

———. 2012. "Democracy's Dignity." *American Political Science Review* 106 (4): 827–46.

———. 2013. "Democracy's Wisdom: An Aristotelian Middle Way for Collective Judgment." *American Political Science Review* 107 (1): 104–22.

———. 2015a. *The Rise and Fall of Classical Greece.* Princeton: Princeton University Press.

———. 2015b. "Political Knowledge and Right-Sizing Government." *Critical Review* 27 (3–4): 362–74.

———. 2017a. *Demopolis: Democracy before Liberalism in Theory and Practice.* Cambridge: Cambridge University Press.

———. 2017b. "Equality, Legitimacy, Interests, and Preferences: Historical Notes on Quadratic Voting in a Political Setting." *Public Choice* 172 (1–2): 223–32.

———. 2017c. "Inequality in Late-Classical Democratic Athens: Evidence and Models." Pp. 125–46 in *Democracy and Open Economy World Order,* edited by George C. Bitros and Nicholas C. Kyriazis. New York: Springer.

———. 2018. "Joseph Schumpeter's Caesarist Democracy." *Critical Review* 29 (4): 473–91.

———. 2020. Review of Greg Anderson, *The Realness of Things Past: Ancient Greece and Ontological History. American Historical Review* 125 (4): 1360–63.

Ober, Josiah, and Tomer Perry. 2014. "Thucydides as a Prospect Theorist." *Polis* 31:206–32.

Ober, Josiah, and Barry R. Weingast. 2018. "The Sparta Game. Violence, Proportionality, Austerity, Collapse." Pp. 161–84 in *How to Do Things with History,* edited by Danielle Allen, Paul Christesen, and Paul C. Millet. Oxford: Oxford University Press.

———. 2020. "Fortifications and Democracy in the Ancient Greek World." Pp. 39–59 in *Political Theory and Architecture,* edited by Duncan Bell and Bernardo Zacka. London: Bloomsbury Academic.

O'Halloran, Barry. 2019. *The Political Economy of Classical Athens: A Naval Perspective.* Leiden: E. J. Brill.

Olson, Mancur. 1993. "Dictatorship, Democracy, and Development." *American Political Science Review* 87 (3): 567–76.

———. 2000. *Power and Prosperity: Outgrowing Communist and Capitalist Dictatorships*. New York: Basic Books.

Oosterbeek, Hessel, Randolf Sloof, and Gijs van de Kuilen. 2004. "Cultural Differences in Ultimatum Game Experiments: Evidence from a Meta-Analysis." *Experimental Economics* 7 (2): 171–88.

Orwin, Clifford. 1994. *The Humanity of Thucydides*. Princeton: Princeton University Press.

Ostrom, Elinor, ed. 1990. *Governing the Commons: The Evolution of Institutions for Collective Action*. Cambridge: Cambridge University Press.

Ostrom, Elinor, et al. 1999. "Revisiting the Commons: Local Lessons, Global Challenges." *Science* 284:278–82.

Ostwald, Martin. 1996. "Shares and Rights: 'Citizenship' Greek Style and American Style." Pp. 49–61 in *Dēmokratia,* edited by Josiah Ober and Charles W. Hedrick. Princeton: Princeton University Press.

Paillard, Elodie. 2017. *The Stage and the City*. Paris: Éditions De Boccard.

Panayotis, Michaelides, Ourania Kardasi, and John Milios. 2011. "Democritus's Economic Ideas in the Context of Classical Political Economy." *European Journal of the History of Economic Thought* 18 (1): 1–18.

Pangle, Thomas L. 2018. *The Socratic Way of Life: Xenophon's* Memorabilia. Chicago: University of Chicago Press.

Parker, Robert. 1996. *Athenian Religion: A History*. Oxford: Clarendon Press.

———. 2006. *Polytheism and Society at Athens*. Oxford: Oxford University Press.

———. 2019. "The Greeks and the Irrational." Pp. 116–27 in *Rediscovering E. R. Dodds,* edited by Christopher Stray, Christopher Pelling, and Stephen Harrison. Oxford: Oxford University Press.

Patterson, Cynthia. 1981. *Pericles' Citizenship Law of 451–50 B.C.* New York: Arno Press.

———.1987. "*Hai Attikai*: The Other Athenians." *Helios* 13 (2): 49–67.

Pelling, C. B. R. 2002. "Speech and Action: Herodotus' Debate on the Constitutions." *Proceedings of the Cambridge Philological Society* 48:123–58.

Perry, Tomer. 2018. "Pericles as a 'Man of Athens': Democratic Theory and Advantage in Thucydides." *History of Political Thought* 39 (2): 235–68.

Petrov, Philip. 2022. "Moral Cognition in Law and Policy." PhD thesis, Political Science, Stanford University.

Pettit, Philip. 1997. *Republicanism: A Theory of Freedom and Government*. Oxford: Clarendon Press.

———. 2013. *On the People's Terms: A Republican Theory and Model of Democracy*. Cambridge: Cambridge University Press.

———. 2014. *Just Freedom: A Moral Compass for a Complex World*. New York: W. W. Norton.

Pierris, Apostolos L. 2000. *Value and Knowledge: The Philosophy of Economy in Classical Antiquity*. Patras, Greece: Achaean Press.

Pinkley, Robin L., Margaret A. Neale, and Rebecca J. Bennett. 1994. "The Impact of Alternatives to Settlement in Dyadic Negotiation." *Organizational Behavior and Human Decision Processes* 57 (1): 97–116.

Poblet, Marta, Darcy W.E. Allen, Oleksii Konashevych, Aaron M. Lane, and Carlos Andres Diaz Valdivia. 2020. "From Athens to the Blockchain: Oracles for Digital Democracy." *Frontiers in Blockchain* 3 (article 575662).

Pomeroy, Sarah B. 1994. *Xenophon, Oeconomicus: A Social and Historical Commentary.* Oxford: Oxford University Press.

Popper, Karl Raimund. 1963. *The Open Society and Its Enemies.* Princeton: Princeton University Press.

Poulakos, John. 1995. *Sophistical Rhetoric in Classical Greece.* Columbia: University of South Carolina Press.

Prendergast, Christopher. 1983. "The Impact of Fustel de Coulanges' *La cité antique* on Durkheim's Theories of Social Morphology and Social Solidarity." *Humboldt Journal of Social Relations* 11 (1): 53–73.

Price, Anthony W. 1989. *Love and Friendship in Plato and Aristotle.* Oxford: Clarendon Press.

———. 2011. "Aristotle on the Ends of Deliberation." Pp. 134–58 in *Moral Psychology and Human Action in Aristotle,* edited by Michael Pakaluk and Giles Pearson. Oxford: Oxford University Press.

Price, Jonathan J. 2001. *Thucydides and Internal War.* Cambridge: Cambridge University Press.

Pritchard, David. 2012. "Costing Festivals and War: Spending Priorities of the Athenian Democracy." *Historia* 61:18–65.

———. 2015. *Public Spending and Democracy in Classical Athens.* Austin: University of Texas Press.

Pyzyk, Mark. 2015. "Economies of Expertise: Knowledge and Skill Transfer in Classical Greece." PhD thesis, Classics, Stanford University.

Quillin, James. 2002. "Achieving Amnesty: The Role of Events, Institutions, and Ideas." *Transactions of the American Philological Association* 132:71–107.

Raaflaub, Kurt. 1983. "Democracy, Oligarchy, and the Concept of the 'Free Citizen' in Late Fifth-Century Athens." *Political Theory* 11:517–44.

———. 1989. "Contemporary Perceptions of Democracy in Fifth-Century Athens." *Classica et Mediaevalia* 40:33–70.

Raaflaub, Kurt, Josiah Ober, and Robert W. Wallace. 2007. *The Origins of Democracy in Ancient Greece.* Berkeley: University of California Press.

Rabel, Robert J. 1990. "Agamemnon's *Iliad.*" *Greek, Roman, and Byzantine Studies* 32 (2): 103–17.

Rawls, John. 1958. "Justice as Fairness." *The Philosophical Review* 67 (2): 164.

———. 1971. *A Theory of Justice.* Cambridge, MA: Harvard University Press.

———. 1996. *Political Liberalism.* New York: Columbia University Press.

———. 1999. *The Law of Peoples.* Cambridge, MA: Harvard University Press.

———. 2001. *Justice as Fairness: A Restatement.* Cambridge, MA: Harvard University Press.

———. 2005. *Political Liberalism* (Expanded Edition). New York: Columbia University Press.

Reeve, C.D.C. 2008. "Glaucon's Challenge and Thrasymacheanism." *Oxford Studies in Ancient Philosophy* 34:69–103.

———. 2013. *Aristotle on Practical Wisdom: Nicomachean Ethics VI.* Cambridge, MA: Harvard University Press.

Rengakos, Antonios, and Antonis Tsakmakis, eds. 2006. *Brill's Companion to Thucydides*. Leiden: E.J. Brill.

Reynolds, Joshua J. 2009. "Proving Power: Signs and Sign-Inference in Thucydides' *Archaeology*." *Transactions of the American Philological Association* 139 (2): 325–68.

Rhodes, P.J. 1985. *The Athenian Boule*. Oxford: Clarendon Press.

———. 2016. "Demagogues and *Demos* in Athens." *Polis* 33:243–64.

Rhodes, P.J., and Robin Osborne. 2003. *Greek Historical Inscriptions: 404–323 BC*. Oxford: Oxford University Press.

Riesbeck, David J. 2016. *Aristotle on Political Community*. Cambridge: Cambridge University Press.

Rigsby, Kent J. 1996. *Asylia: Territorial Inviolability in the Hellenistic World*. Berkeley: University of California Press.

Riker, William H. 1982. *Liberalism against Populism: A Confrontation between the Theory of Democracy and the Theory of Social Choice*. San Francisco: W.H. Freeman.

Robinson, Eric W. 1997. *The First Democracies: Early Popular Government Outside Athens*. Stuttgart: Franz Steiner Verlag.

———. 2007. "The Sophists and Democracy Beyond Athens." *Rhetorica* 25 (1): 109–22.

———. 2011. *Democracy beyond Athens: Popular Government in the Greek Classical Age*. Cambridge: Cambridge University Press.

Robitzsch, Jan Maximilian. 2017. "The Epicureans on Human Nature and Its Social and Political Consequences." *Polis* 34 (1): 1–19.

Rood, Tim. 2014. "The Reception of Thucydides'." Pp. 474–92 in *A Handbook to the Reception of Thucydides*, edited by Christine Lee and Neville Morley. Chichester, UK: John Wiley & Sons.

Roy, James. 2012. "Le bérger, un personnage en marge de la société grecque classique." Pp. 221–28 in *Dipendenza ed emarginazione nel mondo antico e moderno*, edited by F.R. Marola. Rome: Aracne.

Runciman, W.G. 1990. "Doomed to Extinction: The Polis as an Evolutionary Dead-End." Pp. 348–67 in *The Greek City: From Homer to Alexander*, edited by Oswyn Murray and S.R.F. Price. Oxford: Oxford University Press.

Rusten, Jeffrey S., ed. 2009. *Thucydides*. Oxford: Oxford University Press.

Rutherford, Ian. 2007. "Network Theory and Theoric Networks." *Mediterranean Historical Review* 22 (1): 23–37.

Saller, Richard P. 2013. "The Young Moses Finley and the Discipline of Economics." Pp. 49–60 in *Moses Finley and Politics*, edited by William V. Harris. Leiden: E.J. Brill.

Samons, Loren J. 2004. *What's Wrong with Democracy? From Athenian Practice to American Worship*. Berkeley: University of California Press.

Santas, Gerasimos. 2001. "Plato's Criticism of the 'Democratic Man' in the *Republic*." *The Journal of Ethics* 5 (1): 57–71.

Saxonhouse, Arlene W. 1998. "Democracy, Equality, and *Eidē*: A Radical View from Book 8 of Plato's *Republic*." *American Political Science Review* 92 (2): 273–83.

Sayre-McCord, Geoff. 2012. "Metaethics." In *The Stanford Encyclopedia of Philosophy* (Summer 2014 ed.), edited by Edward N. Zalta. Stanford, CA: Stanford University Press.

Scheidel, Walter. 2008. "The Comparative Economies of Slavery in the Greco-Roman World." Pp. 105–26 in *Slave Systems: Ancient and Modern,* edited by Enrico Dal Lago and Constantina Katsari. Cambridge: Cambridge University Press.

Scheidel, Walter, Ian Morris, and Richard P. Saller, eds. 2007. *The Cambridge Economic History of the Greco-Roman World.* Cambridge: Cambridge University Press.

Schelling, Thomas C. (1960) 1980. *The Strategy of Conflict.* Cambridge, MA: Harvard University Press.

Schiappa, Edward. 1991. *Protagoras and Logos: A Study in Greek Philosophy and Rhetoric.* Columbia: University of South Carolina Press.

Schofield, Malcolm. 1999. *Saving the City: Philosopher-Kings and Other Classical Paradigms.* London: Routledge.

———. 2006. *Plato: Political Philosophy.* London: Oxford University Press.

Schriefl, Anna. 2018. "Plato on the Incompatibility of Wealth and Justice: The Property Arrangements in the *Republic.*" *History of Political Thought* 39 (2): 193–215.

Schumpeter, Joseph Alois. (1950) 2008. *Capitalism, Socialism, and Democracy.* New York: Harper.

Schwartz, Avshalom. 2021. "Political Imagination and Its Limits." *Synthese* 19:3325–43.

———. 2022. "Democratic *Phantasies:* Political Imagination and the Athenian Democracy." PhD thesis, Stanford University.

Schwartzberg, Melissa. 2010. "Shouts, Murmurs and Votes: Acclamation and Aggregation in Ancient Greece." *Journal of Political Philosophy* 18 (4): 448–68.

Searle, John R. 1995. *The Construction of Social Reality.* New York: Free Press.

Segvic, Heda. 2009. "Protagoras' Political Art." Pp. 3–27 in *From Protagoras to Aristotle: Essays in Ancient Moral Philosophy,* edited by Myles Burnyeat. Princeton: Princeton University Press.

Sen, Amartya. 2009. *The Idea of Justice.* Cambridge, MA: Harvard University Press.

———. 2017. *Collective Choice and Social Welfare.* Cambridge, MA: Harvard University Press.

Serrano, Roberto. 2008. "Bargaining." In *The New Palgrave Dictionary of Economics.* New York: Palgrave Macmillan.

Sharples, R. W. 1982. "Alexander of Aphrodisias on the Compounding of Probabilities." *Liverpool Classical Monthly* 7:74–75.

———. 1983. "'But Why Has My Spirit Spoken with Me Thus?': Homeric Decision-Making." *Greece & Rome* 30 (1): 1–15.

Shear, Julia L. 2011. *Polis and Revolution: Responding to Oligarchy in Classical Athens.* Cambridge: Cambridge University Press.

———. 2012. "The Politics of the Past: Remembering Revolution at Athens." Pp. 276–300 in *Greek Notions of the Past in the Archaic and Classical Eras:*

History without Historians, edited by John Marincola, Lloyd Llewellyn-Jones, and Calum Maciver. Edinburgh: Edinburgh University Press.

Shields, Christopher. 2006. "Plato's Challenge: The Case against Justice in *Republic* II." Pp. 63–83 in *The Blackwell Guide to Plato's Republic,* edited by Gerasimos Xenophon Santas. Malden, MA: Blackwell.

Shipton, Kirsty. 1997. "The Private Banks in Fourth-Century B.C. Athens: A Reappraisal." *Classical Quarterly.* 47:396–422.

Sickinger, James P. 1999. *Public Records and Archives in Classical Athens.* Chapel Hill: University of North Carolina Press.

Sidgwick, Henry. (1907) 1981. *The Methods of Ethics.* 7th ed. Indianapolis: Hackett.

Simmons, John. 2010. "Ideal and Non-Ideal Theory." *Philosophy and Public Affairs* 38 (1): 5–36.

Simon, Herbert Alexander. 1955. "A Behavioral Model of Rational Choice." *Quarterly Journal of Economics* 65:99–118.

Simonton, Matthew. 2017. *Classical Greek Oligarchy: A Political History.* Princeton: Princeton University Press.

———. 2019. "The Telos Reconciliation Dossier (IG XII.4.132): Democracy, Demagogues and Stasis in an Early Hellenistic Polis." *Journal of Hellenic Studies* 139:187–209.

Sinhababu, Neil. 2017. *Humean Nature.* Oxford: Oxford University Press.

Sissa, Giulia. 2012. "Democracy: A Persian Invention?" *Metis* 10:227–61.

Skarbek, David. 2014. *The Social Order of the Underworld: How Prison Gangs Govern the American Penal System.* Oxford: Oxford University Press.

Skinner, Quentin. 1998. *Liberty before Liberalism.* Cambridge: Cambridge University Press.

Skultety, Steven C. 2019. *Conflict in Aristotle's Political Philosophy.* Albany: State University of New York Press.

Skyrms, Brian. 2001. "The Stag Hunt." *Proceedings and Addresses of the American Philosophical Association* 75 (2): 31–41.

———. 2004. *The Stag Hunt and the Evolution of Social Structure.* Cambridge: Cambridge University Press.

Smith, Adam. (1759) 1976. *The Theory of Moral Sentiments.* Oxford: Clarendon Press.

———. (1776) 1981. *An Inquiry into the Nature and Causes of the Wealth of Nations.* Indianapolis: Liberty Fund.

Smith, Kirby Flower. 1920. "The Literary Tradition of Gyges and Candaules." *American Journal of Philology* 41 (1): 1–37.

Snell, Bruno. (1948) 1953. *The Discovery of the Mind: The Greek Origins of European Thought.* Oxford: Blackwell.

Solmsen, Friedrich. 1975. *Intellectual Experiments of the Greek Enlightenment.* Princeton: Princeton University Press.

Somin, Ilya. 2016. *Democracy and Political Ignorance: Why Smaller Government Is Smarter.* 2nd ed. Stanford, CA: Stanford University Press.

Sommerstein, Alan H., ed. 1989. *Aeschylus: Eumenides.* Cambridge: Cambridge University Press.

Sørensen, Anders Dahl. 2021. "On the Political Outlook of the 'Anonymus Iamblichi' (Diels–Kranz 89)." *The Classical Quarterly* 71 (1): 95–107.

Spence, I. G. 1993. *The Cavalry of Classical Greece: A Social and Military History with Particular Reference to Athens.* Oxford: Clarendon Press.

Stasavage, David. 2020. *The Decline and Rise of Democracy: A Global History from Antiquity to Today.* Princeton: Princeton University Press.

Stone, Peter. 2004. Review of S. M. Amadae, *Rationalizing Capitalist Democracy. Perspectives on Politics* 2 (2): 347–48.

———. 2015. "Hobbes' Problem." *Good Society.* 24 (1): 1–14.

Straumann, Benjamin. 2020. "Leaving the State of Nature: Polybius on Resentment and the Conditions of Cooperation." *Polis* 37:9–43.

Strauss, Barry S. 1986. *Athens after the Peloponnesian War: Class, Faction and Policy, 403–386 BC.* London: Croom Helm.

Stroud, Ronald S. 1998. *The Athenian Grain-Tax Law of 374/3 B.C.* Princeton: American School of Classical Studies at Athens.

Suddendorf, T., and M. C. Corballis. 2007. "The Evolution of Foresight: What Is Mental Time Travel, and Is It Unique to Humans?" *Behavioral & Brain Sciences* 30 (3): 299–313.

Tangian, Andranik. 2008. "A Mathematical Model of Athenian Democracy." *Social Choice and Welfare* 31 (4): 537–72.

Taylor, C. C. W. 2007. "*Nomos* and *Phusis* in Democritus and Plato." *Social Philosophy & Policy* 24:1–20.

Taylor, Claire. 2008. "A New Political World." Pp. 72–90 in *Debating the Athenian Cultural Revolution: Art, Literature, Philosophy, and Politics 430–380 BC,* edited by Robin Osborne. Cambridge: Cambridge University Press.

———. 2015. "Social Networks and Social Mobility in Fourth-Century Athens." Pp. 35–53 in *Communities and Networks in the Ancient Greek World,* edited by Claire Taylor and Kostas Vlassopoulos. Oxford: Oxford University Press.

———. 2017. *Poverty, Wealth, and Well-Being: Experiencing* Penia *in Democratic Athens.* Oxford: Oxford University Press.

Teegarden, David. 2014a. *Death to Tyrants! Ancient Greek Democracy and the Struggle against Tyranny.* Princeton: Princeton University Press.

———. 2014b. "The Inauthenticity of Solon's Law against Neutrality." *Buffalo Law Review* 61 (1): 157–75.

Tell, Håkan. 2011. *Counterfeit Sophists.* Washington, DC: Center for Hellenic Studies.

Thaler, Richard H. 1988. "Anomalies: The Ultimatum Game." *Journal of Economic Perspectives* 2 (4): 195–206.

Thomas, Rosalind. 2012. "Herodotus and Eastern Myths and Logoi: Deioces the Mede and Pythius the Lydian." Pp. 233–54 in *Myth, Truth, and Narrative in Herodotus,* edited by Emily Baragwanath and Mathieu de Bakker. Oxford: Oxford University Press.

Thompson, Wesley E. 1982. "The Athenian Entrepreneur." *L'Antiquité Classique* 51:53–85.

Tindale, Christopher W. 2010. *Reason's Dark Champions: Constructive Strategies of Sophistic Argument.* Columbia: University of South Carolina Press.

Tong, Zhichao. 2020. "Political Realism and Epistemic Democracy: An International Perspective." *European Journal of Political Theory* 19 (2): 184–205.

Traill, David A. 1989. "Gold Armor for Bronze and Homer's Use of Compensatory TIMH." *Classical Philology* 84 (4): 301–5.

Trautmann, Thomas. 2012. *Arthashastra: The Science of Wealth.* Gurgaon: Penguin.

Tridimas, George. 2011. "A Political Economy Perspective of Direct Democracy in Ancient Athens." *Constitutional Political Economy* 22 (1): 58–82.

———. 2012. "Constitutional Choice in Ancient Athens: The Rationality of Selection to Office by Lot." *Constitutional Political Economy* 23 (1): 1–22.

———. 2013. "*Homo Oeconomicus* in Ancient Athens: Silver Bonanza and the Choice to Build a Navy." *Homo Oeconomicus* 30 (4): 435–58.

———. 2015. "War, Disenfranchisement and the Fall of the Ancient Athenian Democracy." *European Journal of Political Economy Economics* 38:102–17.

———. 2016. "Conflict, Democracy and Voter Choice: A Public Choice Analysis of the Athenian Ostracism." *Public Choice* 169 (1–2): 137–59.

———. 2017. "Constitutional Choice in Ancient Athens: The Evolution of the Frequency of Decision Making." *Constitutional Political Economy* 28 (3): 209–230.

Tvedt, Oda E. W. 2021. "Plato's Republic on Democracy Freedom, Fear and Tyrants Everywhere." PhD thesis, Philosophy, Uppsala University, Uppsala, Sweden.

Vădan, Paul. 2018. "Crisis Management and Socio-Political Risk in the Hellenistic Age." PhD thesis, Classics, University of Chicago.

———. 2022. "Foreseeing the Past: Probability and Ancient Greek Decision-Making." *Classica et Mediaevalia* 70:17–58.

Valentini, Laura. 2012. "Ideal vs. Non-Ideal Theory: A Conceptual Map." *Philosophy Compass* 7/9:654–64.

Van Berkel, Tazuko Angela. 2020. *The Economics of Friendship.* Leiden and Boston: E. J. Brill.

van 't Wout, P. E. 2010. "Solon's Law on Stasis: Promoting Active Neutrality." *The Classical Quarterly* 60 (2): 289–301.

Van Wees, Hans. 1998. "The Law of Gratitude: Reciprocity in Anthropological Theory." Pp. 13–49 in *Reciprocity in Ancient Greece,* edited by Christopher Gill, Norman Postlethwaite, and Richard Seaford. Oxford: Oxford University Press.

Vernant, Jean Pierre. 1982. *The Origins of Greek Thought.* Ithaca, NY: Cornell University Press.

Vlastos, Gregory. (1973) 1981. *Platonic Studies.* Princeton. Princeton University Press.

Von Neumann, John, and Oskar Morgenstern. 1944. *Theory of Games and Economic Behavior.* Princeton: Princeton University Press.

Waldron, Jeremy. 2012. "*Political* Political Theory: An Inaugural Lecture." *Journal of Political Philosophy* 21 (1): 1–23.

Wedgwood, Ralph. 2017a. "The Coherence of Thrasymachus." *Oxford Studies in Ancient Philosophy* 53:33–63.

———. 2017b. *The Normativity of Rationality*. Oxford: Oxford University Press.

Weingast, Barry R. 1997. "The Political Foundations of Democracy and the Rule of Law." *American Political Science Review* 91:245–63.

Weinstein, Joshua I. 2009. "The Market in Plato's *Republic*." *Classical Philology* 104 (4): 439–58.

Weiss, Roslyn. 1989. "The Hedonic Calculus in the Protagoras and the Phaedo." *Journal of the History of Philosophy* 27 (4): 511–29.

———. 2007. "Wise Guys and Smart Alecks in *Republic* 1 and 2." Pp. 90–115 in *The Cambridge Companion to Plato's* Republic, edited by G. R. F. Ferrari. Cambridge: Cambridge University Press.

Wenar, Leif. 2021a. "John Rawls." In *The Stanford Encyclopedia of Philosophy* (Summer 2021 ed.), edited by Edward N. Zalta. Stanford, CA: Stanford University Press.

———. 2021b. "A Society of Self-Respect." Working paper.

Whitehead, David. 2019. *Xenophon: Poroi (Revenue-Sources)*. Oxford: Oxford University Press.

Wiens, David. 2012 "Prescribing Institutions without Ideal Theory." *Journal of Political Philosophy* 20 (1): 45–70.

Wiggins, David. 1980a. "Deliberation and Practical Reason." Pp. 221–40 in *Essays on Aristotle's Ethics*, edited by Amélie O. Rorty. Berkeley: University of California Press.

———. 1980b "Weakness of Will Commensurability, and the Objects of Deliberation and Desire." Pp. 240–66 in *Essays on Aristotle's Ethics*, edited by Amélie O. Rorty. Berkeley: University of California Press.

Williams, Bernard. 1985. *Ethics and the Limits of Philosophy*. Cambridge, MA: Harvard University Press.

———. 1993. *Shame and Necessity*. Berkeley: University of California Press.

———. 2005. *In the Beginning Was the Deed: Realism and Moralism in Political Argument*. Princeton: Princeton University Press.

———. 2006. *The Sense of the Past: Essays in the History of Philosophy*. Princeton: Princeton University Press.

Wilson, Donna F. 2002. *Ransom, Revenge, and Heroic Identity in the Iliad*. Cambridge: Cambridge University Press.

Wilson, Peter. 2000. *The Athenian Institution of the* Khoregia: *The Chorus, the City, and the Stage*. Cambridge: Cambridge University Press.

Wood, Ellen Meiksins, and Neal Wood. 1978. *Class Ideology and Ancient Political Theory: Socrates, Plato, and Aristotle in Social Context*. New York: Oxford University Press.

Woodford, Susan. 1982. "Ajax and Achilles Playing a Game on an Olpe in Oxford." *Journal of Hellenic Studies* 102:173–85.

Woodruff, Paul. 2006. "Socrates among the Sophists." Pp. 36–47 in *A Companion to Socrates,* edited by Sara Ahbel-Rappe and Rachana Kamtekar. Oxford: Blackwell Publishing Ltd.

———. 2010. "Socrates and the New Learning." Pp. 91–110 in *The Cambridge Companion to Socrates,* edited by D. Morrison. Cambridge: Cambridge University Press.

Worman, Nancy. 2004. "Insult and Oral Excess in the Disputes between Aeschines and Demosthenes." *American Journal of Philology* 125 (1): 1–25.

Yack, Bernard. 1985. "Community and Conflict in Aristotle's Political Philosophy." *Review of Politics* 47 (1): 92–112.

Yates, J. Frank, and Michael D. Tschirhart. 2006. "Decision-Making Expertise." Pp. 421–38 in *The Cambridge Handbook of Expertise and Expert Performance,* edited by K. Anders Ericsson et al. Cambridge: Cambridge University Press.

Zhmud, Leonid. 2006. *The Origin of the History of Science in Classical Antiquity*. Berlin: Walter de Gruyter.

Index

References in boldface indicate page(s) on which terms are defined. References to figures and tables are indicated in italics after the page number.

Founded in 1893,
UNIVERSITY OF CALIFORNIA PRESS
publishes bold, progressive books and journals
on topics in the arts, humanities, social sciences,
and natural sciences—with a focus on social
justice issues—that inspire thought and action
among readers worldwide.

The UC PRESS FOUNDATION
raises funds to uphold the press's vital role
as an independent, nonprofit publisher, and
receives philanthropic support from a wide
range of individuals and institutions—and from
committed readers like you. To learn more, visit
ucpress.edu/supportus.